CW00430964

THOUGHTS ON THE VASTNESS OF KARMA

An Antidote to Suffering

Ulrike Muller

May All Beings Have Happiness and the Cause of
Happiness
May All Be Free From Suffering and the Cause of Suffering
May All Never Part From the Happiness of No Suffering
May All Remain in Equanimity, Free From Partiality,
Attachment and Aversion

THOUGHTS ON THE VASTNESS
OF KARMA
© Ulrike Muller 2020
All rights reserved.

ULRIKE MULLER

Foreword

GESHE LAMA AHBAY RINPOCHE
(JIGME THUPTEN TENDER)

Date ___21 June 2019___

Foreword by Geshe Lama Ahbay Rinpoche

I am very happy that Uli la has been able to write and compile the *"Thoughts on Karma"* book making it possible for people to benefit from the Buddhas's teachings.

As Uli la's friend and Dharma teacher, I feel confident that her deep commitment to Buddhist practice shines through the words she expresses in her published work.

I trust that the knowledge contained in this book will be of great value to anyone who reads and practices it, in this way serving the greater good of humanity.

My wish is that all those who read and practice the Dharma expressed in this book attain wisdom, compassion and enlightenment.

Geshe Lama Ahbay Rinpoche, Ph.D.

Gajang Hardong Khangtsen L. C. No. 1, P.O. Tibetan Colony – 581 411 Mundgod
Distt. Karwar (N.K.) Karanataka State, INDIA Ph: 91 – 08301 – 245640 Mobile : 91-098456-24682
E-mail : tulkujigmethuptentender@yahoo.com E-mail : ahbaytulku@yahoo.com

Prologue

When I was given the inspiration to start writing a book about Karma more than 10 years ago, I became a little self-conscious, by default. Who was I, to speak on such an important subject? I feared if my book was ever published, I imagined my work to be exposed and scrutinised by the finest critics and scholars on the matter, only to be found lacking in true knowledge and finesse. After all, such an all-encompassing subject has to be dealt with appropriately so as to pay homage to it, as well as the revered teachers on the topic.

What spurred me on in the end was the fact that each and every one of us is a valuable and irreplaceable component of the ultimate essence of Karma. I felt that we all deserve to have the true principles explained to us in an uncomplicated way that all of us can benefit from. I believe that a book such as this might be useful to help us optimise our individual life experiences on a Karmic level, in order to be truly able to own our Karma with awareness of the value of inner wisdom.

Whilst writing, I became aware of my own incomplete journey and realised I could therefore not ever claim to be an authority on Karma. However, I admit I thoroughly enjoyed pondering the subject and debating aspects of it. I revelled in reconnecting with thoughts and catching glimpses of the wisdom of a greater consciousness, by whatever name we know it. I loved indulging in the energy of being encapsulated with the unconditional infinite, and I tried to find the common denominator underlying many of our externalised thoughts, language and behaviour. By asking many questions on the subject throughout, I tried to find the root of the expressions of our individual energy experiences. I also tried to give Karma a voice, echoing between the lines like the first sound of the universe; the frequencies of Karma that we all have in common and which has brought us here. I feel this book will be important as a reminder of who we really are, in times when it has become habitual instead in our modern society to feel separated and stressed, isolated and unwell. I wanted to share the hope, the empowering sensation of knowing and remembering that we belong; that our Karmic energy system has created us as temporary individuals who are nonetheless very tangibly, visibly and intricately intertwined. I wanted to emphasise that there is logic in this madness, and not just the obvious conflicts that present themselves.

I also wanted to give an explanation of what I believe to be a link between a commonly assumed, superficial interpretation of Karma and the deep and meaningful esoteric Eastern philosophy, in order to merge the differences between the two. My motivation was that if only one person read even just one sentence and gleaned insights from it, I would be happy in the knowledge that talking to an invisible audience in my musings has not been completely futile.

I am new to this experience of writing to an imaginary group of friends, about a subject I meditated on and studied, and yet one that remains so elusive that not many humans make it their life mission to truly understand and master it. The masters I have met would probably smile at my modest efforts and remind me in one short sentence that it is more important to simply be kind to all. I can only be honest about attempting to describe my findings and sharing my own experiences as part of my studies during the past 20 years, by sharing my insights and inspirations which transpired throughout this time. Almost all the insights I wished to convey in this book appear as if they were passed on from a much greater mind into the flawed interpretative channel I must necessarily be in human form; a humble vessel filled with spiritual concepts, writing in a language not always well equipped to convey the full experience of energy flowing freely in an infinite experience of being a part of the state of eternal bliss. As a result of turning it into a 3-dimensional event, it is logical that must necessarily enter duality, to which most will have been conditioned to react by either resonating with it, or not; and we will also have learned to determine that either we will like the resonance, or we won't. Ancient calligraphists used beautiful energy symbols to describe the elusiveness of life's principles in a much more beautiful and meaningful way, filling their symbols with pure energies and observing the deeper meaning of the universal energy flow swiftly in just a few precise brush strokes. Most of us have not been trained to comprehend these symbols, and the art is becoming lost. Instead, we use endless information streams nowadays fragmenting Truth into infinitely small bytes of information, trying to interpret an infinite energy source and getting caught up in the process itself. Artists attempt to express it by painting, sculpting, being musical or dancing using their body to feel a part of this beautiful life energy, whilst writers use complicated words. Poets encrypt it, encapsulating universal energy flow in their own personal language nuances. But absolutely everyone on this Earth lives and breathes it every moment of the day.

I wanted to write about something so complex and complicated in as simple a language as possible and convey it to you, so that it would be accessible at all times. I wanted to make these ancient concepts simpler for the Western mind to understand, for everyone to be able to harmoniously integrate them into their lives. And yes, I ended up using thousands of words for the single phenomenon of oneness, just like so many other writers. The essence of the experience that we feel within, however, stays the same. It still is surprisingly simple, once we know what we are looking for.

I have a knack for philosophical pondering, I think I inherited it from my granddad. My brain is full of thoughts, with me trying to catch their drift, as they blow past like clouds over a vast ocean. I don't think that I can write about Karma as if it were a dogma, a pre-formed path, where everything is set in stone. It has been done before, much better than I would ever be able to do it. I named this book 'GOOD Karma - Thoughts on the Vastness of Being', because it is exactly that: if we want to create good Karma, we will want to know how. Our inner process of thoughts, questions, insights and ideas on experiencing the infinite energies within is as good a start as any, given that our daily ability to be alive in an endless and vast ocean of phenomena is often overlooked these days. I thought it might be quite nice to be reminded of how this is actually possible. I try my best to stay open to other ideas, questions and input, too. Thoughts are thought-provoking, and I invite that. Our thoughts can also be limited, and incomplete. I invite readers to make up their own minds about what they want to believe.

I am aware that some readers would be expecting a full referencing system, a fancy publisher, an introduction by someone famous and a neat shiny enticing cover. In this day and age of internet availability, downloads and sharing information, there are myriads of thought processes put out there every second of the day, and the usefulness of the format of a paper copy of a book has changed. This is not an 'Oxford Publication on the Principles of Karma', at least not yet. We can't prove with scientific findings and fancy footnotes that this is the way that Karma exists, and neither would anyone want to. I do not wish to prove anything with this book. I am inviting you to make use of the concept of what might be if we dare to peel away layers of make-believe from our lives, if you can invite the free-style surfing of my own wave of insights into your stream of consciousness. It depends whether you enjoy analytical thought processes and pondering reality as much as being open to channelled information, and are able to merge these rather than see them as mutually exclusive. If so, you may possibly enjoy reading this book and I encourage you to use it to spark off your own ideas on the subject.

"The fact that you create your own reality is so powerful, that you can use it to prove that it is not true".- Lazaris

✽ ✽ ✽

5

'Upon ignorance depend the Karmic formations,

Upon the Karmic formations depends consciousness,
Upon consciousness depend name and form,
Upon name and form depend the sense organs,
Upon the sense organs depends contact,
Upon contact depends sensation,
Upon sensation depends desire,
Upon desire depends attachment,
Upon attachment depends becoming,
Upon becoming depends birth,
Upon birth depend old age and death,
In this way, the aggregates of suffering
arise one from the other.'
(Interdependent Origination)

© White Tara with Consort; Image Credit: Himalayan Art Resources

'Under the power of ignorance, we perceive the luminous creativity of the mind as 'external' and 'foreign' to ourselves. 'Others' includes all external phenomena, to which we attribute real and independent existence. We form three sorts of relationship with these others: attraction or desire for those phenomena that are judged as pleasant; revulsion or anger for unpleasant phenomena; and indifference or neutrality toward phenomena regarded as being of no interest. From these three reactions are born the five passions: ignorance, anger, desire/attachment, pride and jealousy. When these passions dominate the mind, they are translated into thoughts, concepts, and finally concrete actions. These are known as Karma. In accordance with their tone, whether negative or positive, our actions provide the causes for the later experience of effects of the same nature. We ceaselessly experience the fruits of past Karma, and at the same time we continue to create new Karma.'

Tibetan Astrology, Phillippe Cornu

Preface

I have always felt that, as soon as we make use of language to describe and discuss philosophical concepts, we not only have a solution, but also a considerable problem. This may sound like a contradiction in terms - after all, language is a very useful and necessary tool to express our thoughts, ideas and feelings in order to convey them to others, is it not? My question is, what prompted us, why did we develop the desire to use language in the evolution of human history in the first place? Why could we not simply continue to sit quietly in our caves and grunt, all those aeons ago? Could we not trust that our fellow beings understood us, simply by using body or sign language, or by simply being and living by example? At what point was this not enough; where did it threaten our survival so much that we felt we needed to change? Did we evolve to believe that language was going to be the perfect solution, our hope that finally, we would understand each other better, not bash each other's heads in and live in abundant peace and harmony forever more? Was that our true motivation, and is that our motivation still now, thousands of lifetimes later?

The reason for my line of questioning is this: I realise that as soon as I write down my ideas, opinions and insights, my guess is that you, dear reader, are immediately forced to interpret every word. I think, therefore I am...not. I must put a disclaimer here. The disclaimer is this: 'I am not the Messiah!' - to quote a famous line in one of my favourite British films, starring the inimitable Monty Python Crew. What I mean is that I am just as subject to my own ignorance of my Karmic connections as the next person. I am not even 100% sure whether this book is actually going to help people or not. Perhaps my musings are annoying and will therefore be largely ignored. Perhaps they will go under in the vast information and sensory overload that is the 21st century. Perhaps it will cause controversy, and people arguing about religious concepts will be outraged and accuse me of being a heretic. I, of course, really have no influence over that, and fair enough if it does happen. However, let me repeat, just in case there is even only one person who actually sees a little of themselves reflected in what I am trying to say and convey - just in case that it might be true - I thought I would write it all down anyway, motivated by this simple thought, and the impatience that comes with having started this book all those years ago. All I can say in my defence is that this is my motivation, simple but true.

This whole book is, of course, also subject to Karmic law. It will have created a certain outcome unknown to me by my applying focus and attention to it, investing time and effort and then setting it free to become whatever it needs to be. If my focus has brought me nearer to an ultimate Truth that might exist out there and if I have been able to share this with you, Dear Reader, with the right motivation, then it may possibly have a good outcome. A good outcome is not necessarily that it will be successful, but one where, more importantly, it may be of benefit to some. Writing this has also created its own timeline dynamic. Many ancient scriptures went missing for a long time until found by those who were meant to find them. Just as many were destroyed, never to be found again, by those who did not want the masses to be knowledgable and the material they contained was considered blasphemous. Many books have been read by millions, others disappear in the back shelves never to be read. What the outcome is here, I cannot see. That's because I am not enlightened.

One thing I have found to be true thinking about Karma, is that there is nothing like honesty with ourselves and others in order to find out who we truly are, warts and all. I shall be the first to admit that I am a very ordinary human being, with ideas and questions just like everyone else, and I may not even have a single answer to offer you. Hopefully though, one or two people will find something in this book to relate to. Maybe it will even strike a note within us, reminiscent of ancient knowledge, mystery and transcendence but most of all, the vast resources of Karmic energy we were previously unaware of in ourselves. Maybe it will stimulate our enthusiasm enough to explore and tap into all of it again, as we might have done before we knew language.

I dedicate this book to all my family - Mama, Papa, Elena, Eva, Rain Zom, Uschi, Jörg, Biggi & Phi, to whom I am eternally bound in love and gratitude for their existence, love and support in my life, allowing me to grow into the proud mother and grandmother I now am. I live in gratitude also of all my ancestors, especially my grandfather, 'Opi' Ranff, whose great philosophical spirit was there for me to observe during my childhood. I loved simply being in his presence, and he still seems to speak to me often. Special thanks also to my beautiful friend Ben for all this help and assistance, and Tom Barrett for the beautiful cover image. My eternal gratitude goes out to present day masters, too many to mention, but namely those two who most inspired me to write this book, His Holiness Dalai Lama and His Holiness Sakya Trizin; and the third great master who made it possible for me to finish it, the wonderful Geshe Tulku Lama Ahbay Rinpoche, who so kindly wrote a beautiful foreword for this book.

* * *

Chapters:

1. First questions about Karma

2. The Effects of Karma

3. Karma Ripening

4. Who Are We, Really?

5. What is the 'Karmic Energy Mind'?

6. What is 'Mind'?

7. A Brief Digression into Darwin's Evolution Theory

8. An Even Shorter Digression into Quantum Mechanics

9. Inside the Karmic Mind

10. Our Energy Body and the Creation of Karma

11. Karmic Recordings and Energy Auras

12. Karma is Energy Completing Itself

13. Taking Responsibility for our own Karma

14. Explaining the Phenomenon of Energy Imprints,

'Breaches' or 'Chinks' in Our System

15. A Hypothesis About Our Personal Karmic History

16. Repairing Our Karmic Energy System

17. Letting Our Karma In

18. Karma and Dystopia

19. Global Kundalini Rising

20. Karma and Our Karmic Energy Body, Illness and Death

21. The Undistracted Mind

22. The Karma of Conflict

23. The Karma of Finding Out Who We Really Are

24. Karmic Energy and the Omnipresence

25. Finding Our Karmic Truth

❄ ❄ ❄

Introduction

Karma is a funny old word. We all use the term by now at some point, but few if any of us really know what it means. We use it in every day language nowadays, in fleeting remarks made about others, mostly in hope that there must be some fateful consequence when we deem the behaviour of others not to be quite up to scratch. The true meaning of the word 'Karma', however, is so complex and complicated, that it probably cannot be comprehended with our 'normal' mindsets in relation to our every-day lives. In order to tune into the laws of Karma we must transcend our everyday logic. Karma is enigmatic, elusive, changeable and different according to each situation and individual. The fact that we use the term so easily everyday, may perhaps show a certain reverence and respect we might have for it, but perhaps a puzzlement, too, because the workings of Karma have eluded us so far. Perhaps we already have our finger on the pulse, or there is something nagging us in the back of our heads, trying to draw our attention to it. I believe it would help mankind to lift the myth a little by learning more about Karma; to learn methods so we can trust in it more, lest we may want to steer our lives more consciously in the direction of our Karma bringing increased benefit to our lives.

No matter which religion or beliefs you were brought up with – Karma exists without us being aware or believing in it, regardless of which country we grew up in or background we were raised with. Each single living being, every single one of us is subject to it. Karma exists as the great dance of interaction between ourselves, all sentient beings and our environment, powered by the energy of life pulsing through us, mimicking on Earth the immensity of the dimensions of the universe and beyond. It is such a vast and mysterious subject that most of us can only scratch the surface of in our lifetimes whilst we are here on this planet, only to realise that despite how important we think we are, our tiny brains in our tiny bodies are only great when we are in unison and living within the context of a greater consciousness. Our cognition of the concepts of the great clockwork of creation, including the phases of pre- and post-creation, is usually limited by the nature of our experience of physical existence.

Of course, we can remember and learn again to become incredibly powerful and ever more knowledgeable; but if this is our sole aim, we will be easily led by the many distractions that promise us invincibility, immortality and power for a price. This is not what we want to aim for, as the results can only be fleeting or misleading. You are already immortal anyway. One of the jobs of this book is to remind us how we can become more aware again of who we truly are and how one of the most important and logical things to aim for in life, are wisdom and compassion for ourselves and others. We can be wise, as well as knowledgeable. We can be insightful, as well as intelligent. We have the ultimate ability to channel all available universal energy into our everyday existence.

The existence of every-day turbulences we are all submitted to is proof enough that many things in our lives are currently out of balance, but we can exercise ways to get ourselves back into balance.

However, I don't think I know many of us who are mindful enough to be able to be alive and well without applying methods and receiving assistance. Can we make fire without tools, manifest water or food out of thin air? Would we survive without? How would we even be here had it not been for the fact that we all have parents who gave us life? Someone already sustained our lives for years when we were too young to do so, so that we are here, right now, reading this. Is the fact we sometimes feel so small and incomplete the reason for us wanting to be so big and invincible? How many people do we know who are superhuman, who can stretch their bodies beyond their usual physical limitations, survive hostile conditions such as freezing cold or scorching heat, or overcome the physical limitations of time and space? As much as we want to be out there again in limitless existence, right now we are not time-travelling superheroes. We have vulnerable little physical bodies which need the right balance of sustenance and circumstances every second of the day to assist us to survive - but we also don't like to be reminded of the fact. Is that because we subconsciously see it as a weakness to be in a really quite small, fragile, separate body, that we feel it puts us at as a disadvantage? What we do not see and mostly take for granted is the miracle of our good Karma; that we must have, at some point already accumulated the very attributes, abilities and circumstances we currently enjoy to exist, through the good Karma we created. Granted, this also means that our status quo right now is by no means a given, as we have probably already noticed by the endless amount of suffering on this, 'our' planet.

Yet, it makes us uncomfortable to be reminded of our shortcomings. Are we insecure about not knowing everything about ourselves, not helped by the fact that we have apparently been kept in the dark about the full extent of our true ability, despite the vast educational resources available in modern times? The positive that has come from the sensations of powerlessness we often experience through not being able to surpass our limitations, has made us at least be inventive and develop many a substitute for this elusive something that we are not fully aware we are missing out on. Some of our inventions of how to pass time in the golden cage are obviously better than others. Some of us are very adept at endlessly inventing a stream of expensive and sometimes devastating distractions driven by a thirst for power, for control. If our thirst for power is driven by our unawareness of Truth, then it is not power at all that we will create. Some of us feel the need to be in charge of situations, of others, even whole countries. For the true megalomaniac, only world domination will do. Our human diversity ranges from good people simply craving a sense of belonging to individuals who seek the extremes of blind dictatorship. These opposites might not have anything in common, other than one underlying denominator: We are all missing something. And that something is to feel reconnected with the principles of Good Karma.

Whilst most of us are not that dysfunctional, we are nevertheless functioning on a limited understanding and capacity of what we are capable of. We have always been afraid, and probably had plenty of reasons to be, no matter what era we were born in. In the light of our fear of survival in modern society we have - on a much smaller but currently very popular mainstream scale - found a niche by hiding behind electronic avatars and invented escapism into fantasy realms of super-human super-heroes. Underlying this might be our old friend fear, feeding off our as yet unfulfilled need to reconnect to our true Karmic nature. We want to experience again what it was like to have boundless energy, weightless universal energy bodies, feel blissfully happy and unconditionally loved, as well as having an ability to do and create anything we want. Our sense of disempowerment for being unable to truly do so or remember how to, has created a deep desire in our childhood as well as grown-up fantasies to expand and surpass our own mortal boundaries. The goal? To feel more in control of our own destiny. Often, our cravings for a super-human reality are expressed in a slight-second, slightly misguided if ingenuous mini-memory, allowing us only glimpses of escaping our mundane reality and the Earthly laws that accompany it. But the cravings do not seem to go away, there is still something missing, something elusive that remains outside of ourselves which we continuously try to grasp. And just like in real life, an inner madness befalls the baddies in our fantasy world, just like the power-hungry of this real world, where a desire for control gets mistaken for greatness, takes over and becomes so misguided and destructive that single human beings are capable of initiating the destruction of whole countries and millions of lives in their quest to further themselves.

The devastating consequences are all around us. If only we could see how simple the solution is to our grasping, to our craving, to resolving our fears. There is everything right with acknowledging that we feel this way, trying to find what it is that will help us get back to our true Self. It's certainly not boring, it's a journey that we have been longing to take. We just forgot how and where to start. To reach the heights of our inner Karmic memory bank will reconnect us to our own greatness. We just need to remember how to get to it.

Even looking very briefly at the history of those who excelled at surpassing human boundaries and remembering infinite existence, we find, amongst many, the blossoming of magnificent minds such as the great philosophers, artists, mathematicians and so on. Take, for example, Leonardo Da Vinci: His avant-garde concepts of flying machines and his vision of our spiritual geometrical truth underlying the creation of the human body in the middle ages are great examples of an accomplished mind, able to experience reality far beyond a linear time-line. Even more so, great masters in the East were already fully aware of the concepts of rebirth and reincarnation and predicted the outcome of Earth's destiny thousands of years ago, wisely dedicating their every moment hence to easing suffering for all living beings.

Since then, matters have followed a different path. Religion became prevalent, organised by those who wanted to own, and thus we were segregated from believing in our own natural inherent greatness, and we gradually forgot that it was up to us to find the complete methodology of how to connect within us. We were made to feel lesser than others, and became property rather than free beings. People started to forget who they were, separate from a true, sustaining, all-encompassing inner practice in their every day lives. It was replaced by formal attendance at places outside of ourselves where others preached and taught. Thus was born the externalisation of religion, education, work and so on. Our lives became compartmentalised and taken over by external organisations, gradually increasing in wealth and power and announcing themselves as the new norm. According to how much we could be persuaded to part with our inner being, related to how much we lived in fear of our lives, we felt more and more that we had no choice but to be suppressed and disenfranchised. But we forgot, too, how it once was to be truly free.

These days we base our freedom on the amount we earn, on what we can afford to buy, on being allowed a weekend here and there to do things we enjoy. We cram into our timeline everything we are told to do and do not even realise it has little to do with our true Self. Trying to escape from the inevitable outcome of stress and by then disillusioned by the rigid dogma of institutions of religion, we invented a different form by which to express externally our inner need for a reminder of that elusive substance which surpasses human ability. From the early 20th century onwards and with the invention of radio and TV, fiction started to be more mainstream accessible expressions of those superpowers we missed in our human form. With an effervescent colour explosion of energy imagery in the mid 20th century, TV sets in ever increasing numbers of households depicted our fantasies of extending, expanding and escaping reality and exploring life beyond Earth. Fantasy creations were the trends where fiction started to outdo facts in our preference of pastime. The arrival of motion pictures eventually developed into our modern versions of individual PCs, consoles and of course, multifunctional mobile phones which facilitated and escalated the fantasy of being more than human in a myriad of personal productions. Whilst there seems to be no direct relation between religious icons and that of cinematic artistic license, the underlying reason for their creation appears to be the same: We are trying to express our belief and rediscover our place in this external medium that seems much greater than our little human existence. Lately, worldwide internet accessibility for almost everyone almost everywhere has seen an explosion of popularity and online presence, promising a revolution of the age-old interpretation of what we thought it means to be a super-human avatar and able to exist beyond what appears to be humanly possible, beyond space and time. Our online representations even seem to reflect that we want to look more like supernatural beings endorsed with superhuman features. And yet, that is all they are – a step into the external again, snippets of truncated information this time in byte-size pieces, yet still not big enough to comprehend the vastness. Perhaps an external representation of infinite vastness can only be as big as this particular age on Earth allows, according to the frequency that Earth is currently passing through. And in that, it is what it is. Most importantly, we all have the ability to recognise the vastness in its parts, however small – pars pro toto as the Romans said. Will we try to do it, though? Will the external manifestations help or hinder us? Will they distract us so much that we forget to search inwards, or will they help us feel it more and more easily? Will we get side-tracked and forget what we are looking for, forget what we are here to believe in again and re-create? Or is that indeed what the next generation is already doing? Will we still need the ancient methods of reconnecting with our true nature, or will there not be any distinction between external and internal, wise or not, clever, creative and connected or not, in a foreseeable future? The struggle to remember what it was like to be part of the infinitely wise and compassionate omnipresence has at least become a more internationally connected, if not yet united effort, a phenomenon that could potentially occur for many more humans simultaneously in not so many words. After all, we don't need words to connect to source, only to communicate our intention to do so with each other, to help each other remember. Even though it may not be recognised as such, it is in this era perhaps more than the world had ever experienced on a global scale. The quest is not an individual one any longer, but one where that particular desire to be more than human has shaped our intention accordingly, to try and save an aching planet and all living beings on it is actually started to spin a fine frequency web across the world. With the result being that even more people than ever have access to resources to spur their intentions to manifest the impossible, live the dream of true freedom to be who they are meant to be.

In the meantime, on the screens of make-believe before us, the fact we are still so wobbly on our new legs of uncertainty, feeling defensive of our new discovery in ourselves reflecting in our external creations. More and more unusual-looking superheroes who don't quite act like it, with many still struggling with their more human attributes and being drawn into online brawls despite looking the part. Becoming more than human is becoming a mainstream strife, accessible to almost anyone anywhere, simultaneously, as it has never been before. We don't realise we already are. There is no struggle in that. It's enough. Do we recognise the power of this, even? Do we, in our every day display of behaviour, realise that it doesn't take super-hero looks to be. We don't question why we are still asking when we will be connected to greatness. We are still asking for something we already are. However, do we feel we are truly connected to our higher selves? Perhaps not yet. Our latest shift might be yet another leap from unattainable superhero status to everyday human being with hidden superpowers, but because we externalise this, we will probably continue to manifest our desire for being special somehow by designing gadgets that are becoming ever more transparent, with ever more futuristic ideas on the horizon. All the time whilst you read this, your consciousness is being expanded beyond the usual experience of time and space. Will this mean we are getting ever closer to understanding about Karma, the union of the body and spirit, and the mysteries of who we are, and why we are alive?

One thing is certain, the desire for superhuman status itself has Karmic implications – as every action does. I will go into explaining this later in the book. In my humble opinion, what is happening to us on Earth is that universal laws are becoming more apparent and visible, according to what stage we are at both individually and as a whole Earth community on our Karmic journey within and beyond the prescripts of our manifest universe. This process is something we often remain unaware of, simply because our perception is still limited to our belief that we only have our five senses to rely on; all we tend to do is look no further than the end of our working week in the context of our freedom in our day-to-day lives and thought processes. We sometimes positively enjoy being blinkered and remain easily hoodwinked by our own programming limitations, fully distracted by what presents itself as real.

As of late though, more and more people are going through an awakening process. It is something that was always destined to happen and can be explained by the extended logic and insight into consciousness in connection with universal developments, that is, if we choose to 'see' beyond our usual brain functions and sensory perceptions.

Einstein famously said: 'I have never had a single idea just by applying logic'.

More and more people are developing their 'sixth senses', discovering universal truths, tapping into sacred geometrical patterning during their theta-wave stages, experiencing insights, seeing through falseness, untruths, destructive man-made structures, systems, beliefs and more.

We are meant to become awake like this, we were always meant to find out more. Most of us just did not remember it prior to this moment in Earth's timeline, because we could not believe it yet, as we hadn't (re-)experienced it yet; which is a bit of a conundrum and a Karmic vicious circle, if you so will, that has most likely been repeating itself for aeons of time, and may continue to do so for us as long as we still believe in time and space.

What we needed in order to manifest was to be reminded of the greater Truth, of who we are. What we need to manifest next are good conditions, to be reminded over and over again.

We had to catch at least some glimpses of the whole Truth with a capital T, in order to be reminded that we are more than what presents itself to us. Maybe glimpses are fine at first, because to see the whole truth at once might drive us mad.

The law of Karma which is creating the universe and us within it, underlies everything that we do, say and think. Without truly understanding it, we will be forever trapped in limited perception, unable to truly live to our true potential.

There are, of course, many sentient beings on this planet who don't want to do this, and are not ready to see or face the whole Truth. Maybe it is a scary concept, or people are worried about the consequences. At the same time, it is not up to us to decide who is and who isn't. Whatever fear exists, is there because of deep-rooted reasons that stop us doing many good things, and maybe that applies to all of us. Secretly, we are often just not ready to move on and be what we proclaim to deeply long to become. Paradoxically, it might be this very fear of the great unknown that stops us being at one and at peace with ourselves. After all, the majority of us have not yet learned or remembered how to move inwards in order to move onwards and upwards, so we have not even seen yet that we evolve in spiral motion rather than following an imaginary linear time line.

Karma is there independently of our belief system, itself bound and attached to the cyclic existence of living beings according to the dimension and frequency they reside in, waiting patiently for all to come on board, seemingly saying to us all: 'When you are ready'. Karma does not judge. Karma is simply a universal law of moving energy forces. Everyone underlies Karmic principles, as a law of nature. Even the timing of our individual awakening is Karmic. Whether you believe in it or not, whether you know or instinctively feel it or not, it still exists and functions all the same. Our 'ordinary' thinking mind still likes to have proof in order to feel justified in what we are trying to do, which is probably exactly what we need in order to keep searching for the Truth.

To sum up first introduction, I really do hope you enjoy finding out more in this book, not least because I would like to think a future is possible where we see ourselves not just based on interacting by competing, judging, condemning, defaming and disagreeing all the time. I would love to see what our future might be like when it is simply based on being the best we can be.

I have inserted essential 'thoughts on Karma' in large, bold italics through-out this book, for all those who enjoy flying through a book to grasp its general gist, and for those times when you just want to open a page to find inspiration.

I have also refrained in writing everything in absolutely chronological order because I know everyone reads a book differently. Some like to start at the end, some in the middle. Some just want to read a random page that they open, and I have therefore decided to place chapters so that you can start reading at title that you might be drawn to. I have also made a point of repeating some important information at intervals throughout the book. I love all of these methods, we can't hear about them often enough to really 'get it', and I do hope you will find snippets of wisdom on every page you open.

There are also lots of hints, tips and methods of how to begin working on our inner Karmic Self, at the end of this book. Of course, the list is quite endless by now as to how many ways exist to find out more about any esoteric subject, so I have limited it to those that I have personal experience with and know work well.

✳ ✳ ✳

1. First Questions About Karma

Knowing that the law of Karmic action and reaction is incredibly and infinitely complex, this was my dilemma: having written a whole book about it, I have to admit right from the beginning that I do not understand all of it - and possibly never will; possibly I am not meant to - and possibly none of us except the few true accomplished Masters - ever will be. Having said that, I will, of course, try to outline much of what we know of the basics so that you can benefit from having fun trying out the principles for yourself. This was one of my aims, that the subject would be handled in a manner that it would be accessible to all, in simple terms and as easy to understand as possible. After all, many of us have an interest in esoterica these days and have heard of cosmic ordering, the Course of Miracles, the teachings of Abraham etc. Many of us are curious about the subject of Karma, which serves like an umbrella to cover many esoteric subjects and more.

I first started writing because I had so many unanswered questions about Karma that I felt I wanted to get my thoughts straight. I then realised that those questions are exactly what is needed in order to find answers, and that the skill lies in asking the right questions in order to get the right result.

What I did learn about Karma that was definitely worth sharing right from the beginning was something that, in hindsight I learned many times over, the hard way: It is virtually impossible to judge somebody else's Karma and we would be altogether better off not to attempt it. As much as we would like to think we can, we usually judge with those parts of our mind that cannot grasp the concept of understanding another at all. What most of us do instead is to use our flawed inner judging system almost unconsciously in our daily lives in almost every situation, because something within us wants to still believe that when we tap into this inner judge that everything will become clearer and better as a result. It very often doesn't though, because we are only trained to try and understand by intellectualising, reasoning and rationalising. I am not writing this to blame or shame, after all, this is what we picked up and copied at some point in our lives, and this is what we habitually continue to do as a result. Doesn't everyone get absolutely outraged with those who are behaving wrongly, especially when they have wronged us? We want reassurance and confirmation somehow that they will not get away with it, that they will not be allowed to hurt us again and that we will be safe forever after. Who can blame us? How can we feel calm and empowered when someone is not being kind or playing nice? As a small example, we might all have experienced that someone who cuts everyone up on the motorway, speeding away on the motorway leaving people upset and angry - and then we see their car stuck at a traffic light right in front half an hour later. They did not get anywhere faster by cutting corners and upsetting others. Many might laugh – instant Karma, we think, and might even say it out loud with some satisfaction.

But Karma is not that simple. Karma teaches us to remember much more complex rules, and Karma does not so often work instantly, either. What Karma is doing is that it poses a question, first and foremost to us and us alone. We need to bring it back to ourselves and know that a situation is about us and not anyone else; also that it is not meant as punishment but much more often can work in our favour. Karma can bring back our focus on our energy within ourselves, our thoughts, our actions, our reactions. It can allow us a moment in time to internalise and check in with ourselves. As a symptom of checking in with ourselves, there can be unanswered questions like: is a situation trying to warn us to slow down? Is the other person in need of something we are not aware of that we might be able to assist with? Even if we never find out what is truly going on, is it not better for our health and peace of mind to take the opportunity to think and act in a way that will benefit us, and as a result, others, too?

First of all, we would do well to learn that it is always preferable if our real focus is on our own Karmic energy, instead of 'the other', since we are hardly likely to ever know the full Truth of what goes on for another being. Opposite to what we might believe, we are not being Selfish by doing so, we are taking responsibility for improving our own Karma. In this case, it certainly is all about us - and is that not what we are missing? It is what we want, is it not, to be given some care, some attention, some time to reflect? If we allow our energy to be so easily taken away from us in any external situation, the depletion then makes us feel worse, to the point where we become prone to a downward cycle of wrong interpretations of the causality of our own reality. Looking around at where the world is at, I would say we see proof of that everywhere we look. Would we not rather want to know how it works to not let that energy escape in the first place and use it for maximum benefit instead? Do we not deserve to have our Karmic energy work for us and be full of energy?

Do we not want to know how to be serenely 'power-full' in the true sense of the word and not some watered-down version? Do we not deserve how to live our lives to the max and find out what that actually really means?

What we tend to churlishly fob ourselves off with instead, is what I have termed a simplistic 'Western concept' of our understanding of how our Karma is generated. First of all, we tend to water the concept of Karma down. We treat ourselves like children to be seen and not heard, and are not owning what it means to be adult to the full extent we are due. We focus inadvertently on the inner child and what we are missing out on, whilst being powerless without any insight into the motivation of those who we perceive don't want us to have the Best. That way we feel we are constantly missing out, we want to see justice because we see life as being unfair. Whilst that may be so, we are looking to the external to do something for us which it may never provide, whilst we simultaneously have no method of how to bring balance and peace into our own mind. You can easily see how hard it is to live our lives fully conscious and enjoy our 'selves' and others truly as long as we think that way. We put ourselves in the weakest position, trying to point the finger to find balance but losing our energy in the process of analysing someone else's life actions. We are too concerned with the concept of the 'other, which becomes a formidable autonomous authoritative force outside ourselves.

One of the first principles of Karma and one of the ways of how we can teach ourselves to see through it, is to understand that we can truly only be 'a law unto ourselves', in the nicest sense of the term. We cannot be the judge of another, their lives and choices, by our own subjective perceptions.

Put another way, we cannot simply judge others by our own personal 'filing system' of what is right and wrong. Generally, we are very quick to judge by very limited standards. There are of course, situations and exceptions where we might clearly be correct and where we will hardly need to find proof, and yet our mind, having gone through any traumatic situation, tends to bunch together a whole lot of events ever thereafter, based on a relatively short section of our lifespan. if that is really what is happening to us internally, we need to understand that our mind does this automatically, without us realising. We need to also understand how it does this and learn to see that

Our Karmic 'bodies' are much more than just physical presence.

We cannot often be absolutely certain that all facts are as they present themselves. Please understand that I am not talking about really clear-cut situations, such as one person wilfully harming or god forbid, killing another. There are, of course, certain Karmic laws that are to be observed by everyone with devastating consequences if we do not. We have just learned that one of them is that interference with another's Karma in a detrimental way has potentially hugely negative consequences. We all know this and most of us have the ability to feel it. It is not hard for most of us to understand the Karmic logic that the more the interference escalates, the more severe the consequences for everyone involved, with the termination of another being's existence having the biggest impact. Even then, there are complicated nuances around the circumstances to do with mental states of mind, motivation, intention and remorse and so on. With any trauma, an intricate and invisible web is woven around all involved and each case has its own Karmic energy dynamic. It might be invisible but it is certainly tangible and detectable.

The consequences and sequential events following any wrong-doing draw to them a complex web of Karmic interactions that may last for lifetimes if they are severe and remain unresolved. Having said that, have you noticed the good news underlying all the darkness we are just now touching on?

We can do something to repair our Karmic energy.

I will let that sink in for a moment, because it is a very important statement that most of us no longer believe to be true. All of it will have

26

to be taken carefully into consideration in order to be understood and cleared up. The longer we leave it, the more complicated it will become to untangle and it often becomes a painstaking and a very long-term process to recreate at a later stage. The reason I am mentioning this so early on is because it is so important to learn that once we realise the full repercussions, it could have the benefit of allowing us more time to think and be less hasty in losing our precious energy to anything or anyone external. The result being the induction of a learning process that involves us getting to know our inner Self better without having it reflected back at us by others in a bad way. It does not mean we cannot defend ourselves. It does not mean 'do nothing' when your house is on fire. More details on this subject and how to deal with difficult scenarios later on in this book.

Karmic law is an invisible fact of life, which is very hard for most of us to comprehend fully.
But before we talk more about complicated concepts such as consciousness and reincarnation, let's ask a few more simple questions first.
We may already feel that we have our own examples of Karma at work in our lives and have immediate and pressing questions on the subject, such as one of the biggest global ones we all want to know: why are some people living in poor circumstances and not others? A straightforward answer can be very difficult to find and once again, the power of the question lies between the lines. Until we become more aware of the full extent of Karmic laws, I will try to give inspiration to find answers by asking even more questions which already exist within ourselves. For example, do beings exist who somehow deliberately incarnate into poverty? Can some beings choose their future life in order to serve a community, for example? Would they be able to consciously steer their energies in a direction so that we can overcome our concepts and judgements of others? Would they be able to make others understand suffering and what it takes to survive in a different light, perhaps even spur us on into more compassionate actions?
At the very least, we have a deeply thought-provoking question lest we become complacent. How do we know who we will become in our next life? If we assume that we have some influence over the decision-making process, would we not want to have everything we need to ensure a great next life? What makes us so terrified of the idea that we will be coming back again, and again? Is it because we fear that the person begging us for a meal today might be us, in another lifetime? Are we running from our own fears or would that very thought not be enough for us to want to truly understand how precious our lives and Karmic actions are if they play a role in determining our future? Right now that is a scary thought, I know, but it might also be a good reminder to remain alert and not to become too complacent. I see a lot of people trying to

manifest huge amounts of money utilising the laws of cosmic ordering at the moment, under whichever name it is presented. Funnily enough, not everyone succeeds, and I might add that there is a good reason for that which I will go into in Chapter 37.

There are other groups of people who believe in, for example, thinking only 'positive' thoughts, following the belief that only positive thinking will prevent something bad happening to them. It is perhaps one stage of our inner development, but it does not necessarily follow that thinking happy thoughts will mean we will only have good Karma or that we are making good use of Karmic laws. We may still be motivated by fear manifesting itself in a type of superstition, but there is also good merit in repeating our good intentions to remind ourselves to attract the best outcomes, respect universal principles of manifestations and not to use up good Karmic resources for a lesser purpose. All stages of our inner development are natural and valid, of course, and we often require validation and reassurance that we are on the right track.

What about our law systems, I hear you say. And what if someone commits a crime and is not convicted? Should we just stand by and lament? This is a prime –and most tricky - example of how we can feel utterly disheartened and discouraged when we have seemingly no longer any power over a situation, and where matters appear out of our hands. This is the moment where - if we really understood how Karma works - we would take courage and solace in the fact that Karma is part of a process that will take place to sort matters out, regardless of whether the justice system has failed or helped. All of us will have witnessed situations in which crimes have gone seemingly unpunished or those committing crimes have done so again after a sentence. All of which indicates to a certain extent that we could certainly do with believing in and supporting an alternative where we can become actively involved in the healing process for victims of crime.

Our Western belief system has oftentimes in our history been based on this air of superiority that it already knows everything, that it is shameful to admit that there are things we do not know. We are all geared up at school into thinking we are learning all that we are made to believe we have to know in order to adult, that we should cram knowledge into our brains and retain facts so we are worthy of a future salary; that without knowing about everything or at least specialise on subjects we know everything about, we are less worthy. That mindset has made us prone to thinking we must know what is best for one and all and even if we don't, we must keep up the pretence. At what cost, should we not have asked? We no longer trust each other, we are losing our ability to be kind and our health is suffering. Neither are we familiar with a whole ethos of trusting the laws of Karma, because we do not know what it is or how it works; because for most of us, it did not appear in a school book.

Most of us in the West still only believe in one lifetime and it is almost dangerous to voice the view that this might not be the only thing we have been missing out on. This underlying idea of a You-Only-Live-Once approach to life has brought on many of the issues we face in today's society where we have a white supremacy that feels entitled over all else and who let everyone else feel the consequences of their actions. We have countries with boundaries and separate currencies, we live by handing over authority to a few we abhor and argue their sincerity, we wage war against all whose countries we can invade and resources we may plunder as if it's still the dark ages. We have a need for money exchange and a system that judges, a system that condemns, a system that imprisons and often favours perpetrators over victims. It should be no surprise then that we all complain that it does not work, that it is unfair, flawed, not immediate enough; that it ignores the victims suffering and lets murderers get away with, well, murder. Is this how it is, simply based on the collective Karma we have accrued?

Unfortunately we may, as a society, have as yet to realise that we might have paradoxically - Karmically even - contributed to this situation by not fully understanding Karma. Underlying this is the fact that we do not know how Karma is present every second of our lives and exists within everything that is living. And yet, we do not fully know what it is and we do not fully know who we are. We do not understand it or know it well enough yet to be able to fully benefit from it. We do not believe in it, we do not remember it, we have not been taught it or been shown how to utilise it. But how can we even begin to understand it, or ask the right questions, if we cannot even remember that we have lived before? Most of us do not even remember what we dreamed the previous night. How can we say for sure that we have never lived before? And how would knowing more about Karma fit in with or improve our lives anyway?

A fundamental truth underlying the laws of Karma is this:

Whatever actions, thoughts or words have been created in any sentient individual's life will leave an imprint on their Karmic energy body.

In order to understand Karma, we must first get an idea of how it affects us.

Simply explained, this particular aspect of Karma appears a bit like imprints in the sand: they may stay there for a very long time – even lifetimes - until such time when the tide swells high enough; then, the pattern of the imprint may be erased slowly and gradually, or perhaps quickly and violently from its sandy surface, making it one again with its surroundings. I hope you like the metaphor – because in a way, that is exactly what Karma does. We all have these 'imprints', only we are not usually aware of them. They may be ripples in the sand or deep crevices in our energy river, be washed away in an instant or remain for lifetimes. It all depends on circumstances being one way or another and circumstances themselves again depend on Karma.

A Karmic imprint will be automatically be sorted into 'positive' or 'negative' or 'neutral' into each individuals' energy system. Our conscious Self will not always have any influence over the sorting process at that time. In order to resolve again in future, each imprint will create its Karmic match, in an appropriate Karmic setting according to exact Karmic timing. At those points it will either remain, reduce or be neutralised back into emptiness.

Seemingly, once an action has been taken, we do not always appear to have conscious control over how these positive, negative or neutral imprints will be integrated by our internal energy system. This complex process happens inevitably and whether we like it or not; we may have little choice but accept the idea that we can learn how to cope with it to help us resolve any negative Karma that has already been created as soon as possible. Liken it to a see-saw – in the centre hub of a see-saw there is little movement, the centre stays still, but on the extensions left and right, there is much more movement, a 'see-saw' effect that we often experience in life, too. It can go up, or down, seemingly at random. It can be fun one moment but not the next, and if we don't enjoy the ride, there does not seem to be a way to get away from its up and down motion. However, the analogy is not so far-fetched, because all we have to remember to do, is to centre ourselves again, to work our way to the middle of our inner being, to feel calm again.

The process of resolving Karma internally is itself subject to its own laws. Only very few may be predictable to some realised individuals to a certain extent. They may be able to decipher as to why a certain Karmic situation arose and when the effects of those imprints may surface again in each individuals' set up of existence, but most of us will not realise exactly how or when. Of course, that does not usually stop us from guessing or trying to predict when anyone who has wronged us might be met with their comeuppance. We have to remember again that we will do well to influence our own courses of action and the resulting Karma first, which is complex enough as it is. Also, even if we did know when our Karma ripens, we have not always learned methods to properly resolve our internal Karmic imprints. Of course, knowing such methods and how to apply them is also down to when we are Karmically accomplished enough in order to realise them. If we already know as much as that it gets complicated, it should be a no-brainer to start as soon as we can to unravel the knot. We do have the choice to start any time to actively pursue the knowing and learning process of such methods, it is never too late. The way Karma works for any of us, is to steer us in the right direction in order to gain more insight into ourselves.

Hopefully this knowledge serves to lessen the shock a little that, once an action has been taken, your conscious Self is often pretty powerless in the determination of how your actions will imprint your Karmic body and what their Karmic re-actions will be. How so? A good analogy is perhaps a sudden event, perhaps an injury. Did we consciously choose to get injured? No. Did we have a say in it? Maybe on some level, but our conscious Self would not have been fast enough to prevent the injury anyway. We usually ask ourselves the natural question of how we could let this happen? To which the answer is as above: once Karma has accumulated in our energy body, we have little or no conscious choice as to when it will ripen. Luckily, this goes for both good and negative actions, which means that if you have been accumulating good Karma, you may also be in for some nice surprises and lucky escapes. But is there a way can we gain more insight into why and how events happen in our lives?

More good news for a start is, of course, that you are alive, living and breathing in the here and now, which, believe me, is an advantage over many other outcomes, even if it doesn't always seem that way. I am by no means belittling the lives of those of us who are truly suffering and in pain, where it does not seem to make sense to rejoice in being alive.

What I am saying is that you can choose to steer any future actions in the direction of good Karma, right here and now, whether you are in good physical or mental shape or not. Even if it will be harder for some than others, there are infinite good actions to choose from for most of us. Depending on our individual situation, we can choose how to act and react - let's say, for example, we can choose in certain situations to assist someone who needs help, make amends, apologise even. We can start to take any situation more seriously when seen from the angle that it matters. It matters very much so whether you choose to make a positive move, and it does not matter if nobody is watching. in fact it is better if nobody is watching so no energy leaks away from the situation. A genuine act of kindness when nobody else wants to help, an apology when you know you have done wrong, as soon as possible, works perfectly when it is given wholeheartedly. Add to that the act of making a vow to yourself and anyone else involved not to repeat any wrongdoing and to increase on doing acts of kindness, first and foremost before yourself and then any other involved party, can change the course of Karma for yourself and those near you quite tangibly and sometimes dramatically..

Despite what we might think or feel, the here and now is the best shape, time & place we will ever be in to have a conscious influence over our Karma as it presents itself in this moment. By making the right choices at each stage of our lives, we will change the outcome of future situations in our lives.

❋ ❋ ❋

2. The Effects of Karma

Karma is most often described as the law of cause and effect – a highly scientific and esoteric law that no-one on this planet can escape, based on the laws of the universe, as sure as gravity is pulling us towards Earth and quantum mechanics taught us about the co-existence of two or more events simultaneously. If you observe a falling ball, you will notice the ball will fall towards the Earth every time without fail. This is the outcome we have expected since birth without question, and we are co-creators of this outcome. However, in another time/space continuum, this may not be the same. Similarly,

Certain actions, thoughts and words we do, think and say will have a specific effect according to the situation in relation to us and others at that specific moment in time, affecting the outcome of our and others' lives accordingly.

I will try to keep it simple in order to introduce the subject with as much simplicity as is possible for something so complex. Generally speaking, we have 'positive' imprints, 'negative' imprints and 'neutral' imprints following certain events along a time line which we generally call our 'life'. We interact with others and our environment, and this exchange can encompass thoughts, speech and deeds. ANY individual sentient being is subject to Karmic laws, but it is considered the most effective to be human in order to make progress on Earth in order to evolve, like it or not. We have already imprinted ourselves into a Karmic time line by entering a 3-dimensional world, meaning we will have taken actions prior to this lifetime which resulted in our incarnation into this life. Our choice determined by our Karma has made all humans incarnate into a 3-dimensional, individual shape, a 'timeline' perception and a 3-dimensional physical experience.

You may be wondering why I point out the obvious. This is because my logical deductions in the past have made me consider that If it is true that there are infinite options for any being to react in infinite situations with infinite different outcomes, this of course would imply that there could be infinite amounts of other outcomes of Karmic actions that may not necessarily always end in a 3-dimensional time line.

If the above has left you puzzled, let's see if this makes sense. An example of a *'neutral action'* could be, perhaps, walking, sleeping or sitting, but only without affecting anyone else in our vicinity. 'Neutral' actions do not usually affect our future selves and lives in any positive or negative way. Although, of course, it depends where we walk and with what purpose and intention, what we do whilst we sleep or sit – and that is where it can become unexpectedly complicated again! If we sit still somewhere and have in mind to save the planet, then it must be a positive action. If we walk somewhere with the intention of breaking into a place, then this is obviously not a neutral act The fact that things are so varied and complex is certainly reflected in the great complexity of life itself, where we can observe infinite different outcomes of actions we tend to group together for the purpose of simplifying. I have given simplistic examples to give you an idea. The best we can probably do – which is something our poor brain habitually does all the time - is to group some actions together according to their similarities and likely outcomes.

Meanwhile, an example of a definite and genuine 'positive' action would be, for example, offering unconditional help and assistance to someone else to do something they cannot do on their own, I.e. looking after the sick or elderly, giving something of value to help someone, somewhere survive or stay healthy...you get the picture. It is not about the action alone, the Karmic outcome also depends very much on how fully present we are when we do this, with what motivation, intention, and how much energy we expend in doing this. The more Selfless and direct an action the better, in terms of what positive Karmic effect it will result in. As you can probably already guess, any action will be worth doing wholeheartedly. If we do something good but are distracted by other energies, we cannot fully engage in the current action. If we attach expectations to our actions and therefore expect the full benefits from this action to occur at a specific time in our future, we may be disappointed because that is not how it works. If we do something simple but with the right intention, it will bear fruits more than a good action does if we get paid a lot to do it and are distracted by the money. If we do something with the wrong intention such as giving something unwillingly, we may end up repeating this as a lesson over and over until it's time to evolve, but we may not be in control or even conscious that life is trying to get us to move along into happier outcomes. Now that you are beginning to be aware of these principles, do you recognise where we are going with this? Good.

The last group is 'negative' actions – a wrongful action that attracts a negative reaction, which for any individual's existence and evolution is the least desirable. Actions that fall into this category are quite Self-explanatory: those born from Selfishness, greed, hatred, anger, ignorance and even fear. There are sadly infinite possibilities and combinations, as we are already painfully aware on this planet, so I don't think I have to point them out individually. What they mostly have in common is that our mind is not 100% focused on a good outcome to say the least. We might be distracted and of split mind, focused on the wrong intent and unaware of the Karmic consequences.

All of this may sound like some menacing cosmic being frowning at us from some elated place, judging and watching our every move. However, Karmic law has better things to do and leaves us to do the finger-pointing if we feel we have to. Karmic law has more to do with the completion of the inner puzzle of our own consciousness and our inner selves rather than any external authority. The authority we may still believe exists is a fiction of our minds, established in moments of our own past where others dominated and governed our every move. It left a Karmic imprint in us and it has been repeating like a broken record since, until such time when we rid ourselves of the vision. It seems perfectly logical then that when we are still ignorant of this fact, we may make 'negative' choices in what we do, say and think, without realising the consequences.

This is the downside to the relative invisibility and time-lapse of Karma: most of us do not realise that there ARE consequences.

I do believe, however, that we are slowly waking up to the fact. Whether as a group consciousness, in fact or fiction, the subject of Karma is spoken about more often these days and it appears to make people curious, which is a good thing.

If we are seriously considering learning more about Karma, we need to be aware that we are all in it together. We cannot continue to act out as if there is no tomorrow, and even this has finally started to sink into mass consciousness The way we think right now, leaving the planet for the next generation to worry about, initiating and propagating wars and so on, will have just as much consequence for our future selves as it will for those we leave behind when we are gone. If we chose not consider the consequences, at the very least we would have to repeat the time spiral over and over again until we 'got it'. It does not matter whether we are young or old. Remember the film Groundhog Day? In it, the hapless and bad-tempered protagonist has to repeat the same day in his life until he is 100% focused on the sequence of all events he influences, just so he can make things happen the 'right' way and move on to another day. It teaches him to not be out for , but to create a good outcome for others he should care about around him. It pretty much sums it up - except Karma is not a punishment. It is, however, very often just the same as in the movie: a waiting game that seemingly goes on the same forever and ever and literally has us spinning round in energy circles instead of our designated upward Karmic spiral. We will be going over the same scenario again and again (and it will feel that way, too) until we find the right way and the right actions to take in order to improve our Karma and therefore our lives by helping others.

Here is a Karma tip:

If you are ever bored with life, ask yourself if this is due to your Karma trying to change you - and for you to learn how to change your life. You might be absolutely right by being bored, when there is your true calling to discover and the heights of your capabilities to achieve. Who knows, you might never look back.

If you find you have things in life that you resent doing – change. Change what you do or change how you do it. There is little gain in doing good but resenting that you have to do it. You can, of course, find yourself in a situation where you absolutely have no choice, and where you are already making huge unconditionally on behalf of another. It is not easy to not at times feel disheartened and in those moments, offset your feelings with knowing that you are still doing the right thing, regardless even of whether this is appreciated. If this does not help you, you can also ask how to change it, that's ok. Just ask the question into the space before you, you will be shown. You will be assisted, you will know if it's time to change. In addition, we can learn to make a dedication that helps shift our energy pattern, which I will talk about more as we go along and also give an example of in chapter 51 at the end of this book.

Having said all of the above, it is always better to do a positive action even if we do have resistance to it, rather than doing a negative one that you rebel against. I guess it also happens sometimes that we start off doing something with resistance at first and eventually get over it and learn to master and see sense in it? Life is complex, after all.

Good actions create a positively charged energy field around us.

Sometimes, this simply means that you create good conditions for yourself in the future. It is such a simple sentence to write, but the true meaning of it is priceless and much underrated. It is never often enough that, when we are asked what we really want, we should be asking for good conditions for ourselves and others. Who needs jewellery? Can't take it with you.

It is said that as a human being with the potential for rational thought combined with our capability for love and compassion, we have the ideal soil for creating our own amazing future. So how come we have forgotten this? How come we do not do this? How come so many people get so despondent about human life, they say that in the next life, they would rather be an animal rather than human? In fact, plenty of people already wish they were an animal right now.

Perhaps it all sounds a bit vague, and a bit religious, a bit old-fashioned, but I believe one of the reasons is because

We do not always see, feel or understand the results of our actions straight away.

It might take days, weeks, months, years, decades – or even centuries, i.e. lifetimes, for any action's result to come into fruition. Frustratingly, it could also be cancelled out altogether against a previous one – without us even knowing! And there we are, slaving away. Not even getting a penny or words of encouragement for it. No rewards! How can we stay motivated and believe that there is light at the end of a long tunnel? How can we believe that our time is precious when nobody around us believes the same, when there seems to be no hope and everyone is on a downward spiral? No wonder we feel like giving up and don't see the point: we have been led to believe that a lot of our actions are reward-oriented, but we don't see that there is anything to show for our efforts. Remember being a child and being told that only if you eat up your dinner, you get a sweet? Well, our brains still want to work that way. It's the Pavlovian Reflex which we have to overcome here, after the famous experiment. We want to see results, preferably instantly, for our efforts! We want to press a button and instantly be gratified. If you don't believe me, look at how this desire is so strong that we have built a whole industry on it. Retail is almost entirely built on this concept that often we feel so unappreciated that we just cannot wait to treat ourselves. An exam, a positive action at work we perceive to have done well and deserve a reward for – especially when it's a whole week's hard labour, or something similar that we invested ourselves in, equals a crazy weekend to let our hair down. We even educate our own children that way, bribing them to do what we tell them to do – chores against the reward of gold stars which equal an ice-cream or similar. Added to this conditioned thinking, we learn during most of our lives that if we do not do as we are told by our parents, teachers, bosses and ongoing authority figures, we are punished and taught that we lose our right to be respected or loved. I don't have to point out that this is the only way we are conditioned that has huge implications on our environment, often to the detriment of all living beings and the planet itself.

No wonder then, when our ideas are so preconceived that when we do look at the Truth, it is hard to take in that the 'real' world does not work that way.

Instead, if we could only see, it works in an even nicer way, just slightly more invisible and unpredictable. We don't need to escape reality, we need to see through what presents itself to see its full potential. But first, we have to learn to trust and want find out more about how things really work. We also need to learn how to 'be', unconditionally, meaning that there are no strings attached to our good deeds, words and thoughts that we choose to create. For a good future outcome, we learn to do good stuff without any outcome attachment. Why would we not invest time into the best hobby there could possibly be? If the outcome is the greatest future Self that we can be, would we do it? Or continue to go to the gym for eternal youth? Would we spend a fortune on surgery to look great? Amass a fortune in wealth and possessions? No need to answer those questions I think, but does it not seem slightly insane?

At this point, I want to add that I have absolutely not got it in for anyone who lives their life the way they want to, even though I am drawing comparisons here to make a point. Perhaps this was not always so, I certainly remember a time when I got very despondent the way things are on Earth. At some point, i looked at nature though, which I regard as one of the highest teachings we have on this planet to help us see how things are. I observed an oak tree, and next to it, a beautiful silver birch. i looked at how different they are, and it suddenly dawned on me. At no point does the oak mind the birch standing next to it. They are not mutually exclusive, they both co-exist, in the same environment, thriving next to each other. They are both trees but they could not be more different. It helped me to see that this is how Earth is - it allows everything. It allows things to occur, phenomena, beings to coexist. From then on, it felt easier to observe some of the great injustices done, because I could see that we are all at different stages on our Karmic journey, and even though we look similar, our Karmic energy is on a unique individual path that nobody else has in quite the same way. Not any of us have arrived here the same way, not any of us will have had the same past, and none of us will have exactly the same future. When seen with this logic, it becomes understandable why there are so many different opinions, paths and outcomes to each of our journeys, and none of them are better than another. I believe each of them have their validity, and from the depths of darkness in someone's journey there can be a moment of awakening at any time that will last forever after.

If we give something, we don't need to ask anything in return. At first, we can practice doing this here and there, until at some later stage, we do it habitually all the time. It can gets hard at times, it is not always easy. Most of the time in the beginning, we still want to see a reward. Money. Compliments. Friends. A house. A car. We see ourselves valued in an hourly wage because we base our worth in the physical realm that can be perceived with our 5 senses. i do ask myself though: Why do we not see ourselves valued in a happy and amazingly fortunate future? Is this because nobody talks about it, nobody has told and taught us how to do this? Is it that we simply do not trust what we cannot see? Perhaps it's time we tried something new and shifted our focus. It's entirely in the two hands of one being only. You.

3. Karma Ripening

Before we get impatient, we should tackle the question of who or what decides as to when your Karma ripens. First of all, it is a hard question to answer as we will not be able to perceive it with our five senses, our expectations and perception of time. Everyone's path is absolutely different, so different things happen at different times to different people which is easy to see as that is what presents itself on Earth. We can be certain that there will be uncertainty and we are not trained to be comfortable with this idea that we do not have direct control like walking into a supermarket and buying a packet of good Karma. That's why it is hard to understand that when you work hard at being nice and kind, and it looks like you get nothing but bad luck whilst the next door neighbour who is a scoundrel has an amazing house with a swimming pool and five cars. What we have learned so far and can absolutely trust, luckily, is that our Karma does and will ripen. It bears fruit. And we know it ripens in the future. We also know that it takes good actions, thoughts and words, great even, to bring great Karmic results - not that we are comparing ourselves or keeping score. Doing that brings delays as it diverts our energy away from what's important, and so does our resistance to all that is good and pure and well. Our anger and angst about it is very understandable but it may bring repetition. Our resentments put on the reverse gear. But just when we want to give up for being short of ideas of how to overcome these hurdles, and when conditions are just right, it is your turn: you finally receive abundance, sometimes even as if all your Karmic bundles were bunched together and released all at once. Keep going! Great results spur us on to continue, don't stop when it has started to work for you and for those you care about. When less desirable things happen in your life – great! They spur us on to look into and understand our involvement in it, so we can change what needs changing in order to get a different outcome. It is always a good result if we are prompted to take right action, as laid out in the Buddhist principles of the 8-fold path and the six parameters which we will pick up on a bit later on. When bad stuff happens, we end up thinking that we would never, ever want to repeat this, or for it to happen to another. Then we have an opportunity to live by our promise! We make sure we take care of ourselves and others around us. Isn't it that simple? We have a friend whom we cherish and would do anything for, and they would do the same for us. What if we had 20 friends the same? What if we can expand and send out our compassion to 200? Or 2000? The whole world? Our ability to share our inner love and compassion is endless, and it replenishes all the time like a Holy Grail. Love and compassion do not deplete, they do not run out. They are feelings we all have within that we can exercise like muscles, and we have lifetimes before us to make friends. Does it not make sense to see the world full of friends to help, and who help us, so that we, too, are a part of this huge circle, so that we, too, are taken care of, now and in the future? Is this not our greatest human asset, to love, and be loved? Is it not the greatest gift we have to give, and also the greatest gift to give away? We can be convinced otherwise, it happens so easily that we get deeply hurt and end up hating people, hating the world. And the world may will appear as such – a menacing place, full of hatred and fear. We may feel so low at times that we only see what is wrong, and stay within our own thoughts and lack of good actions. i have also felt like this, at times. And again, an answer came from nature, another tree, in fact. A tree that loses a branch, does it stop growing? No, it will grow more. It has energy within it, a life force, that is a smaller amount of life force that we have within us. If this life force is stuck within, it will make us feel terrible. We may feel depressed, hopeless, lethargic. All of these words are expressions of what we feel inside: that our energy is stuck, and not flowing. We can use many methods to make it flow again, and at the end of this book there are some ideas to learn how to do this. Karma does not say that you deserve to feel like this because you are bad, have done something bad, or are doing something bad. Karma is saying, here is an opportunity of how you can feel better again, and it opens its arms wide, just for you.

If things are not shifting in our lives, there is only one reason for that – our Karma is not ready for us just yet. It will happen, it will ripen, it is a work in progress. Never mind the rich neighbour – they very likely did something positive some (life-)time ago, but what they are likely doing is cashing in on their past Karma possibly without realising that once it's gone, it's gone, and they will have to start to accumulate good Karma again. This is not a new idea, it is also something laid out in Buddhist teachings, which, like so many others, relate very much to real life situation. A parallel to the above can very much be found in the ancient principles of the Wheel of Dharma, in particular the description of the Demi-god realm. The best thing we can do is, be happy for them, but also make this about our reaction to this. If we can see through the Karmic attachment and not get drawn in with envy or resentment, it will be beneficial for us as well as for them. Remember if our focus is on winning something, on gaining or competing, if we are jealous or envious, it will slow our energy down. You will first need to learn about this 'non-attachment', so that your Karma finds that path of least resistance, does not deplete and remains intact. Anything in the way, will delay! Think nothing of it. Do everything for the sake of it. If it's not perfect, see it as practice. There is no goal to achieve, focus fully on the moment. Seeing someone in need, is no coincidence, it's an opportunity to help. Seeing something good and beautiful, multiply it by a million so everyone else gets a share in it. Feel hatred, find the right method to help yourself reduce it.

For most of us on Earth, there is a time factor involved in Karma ripening. How do we get out of 'human doing' time? That's the million-dollar question we all share. Can you see it already? We are all here to do exactly that, get out of being humans doing time. We all want to be truly happy, and being truly happy means we live without outcome attachment and have enough insight so that we an idea, an inkling of the greater picture of Truth. The first step is always to ask. If you want to know how to do something, ask; not just anybody – ask into the wide-open space before you so that everyone in the universe can hear you. If you like working with that imagery, make it your own: find a space out in nature where you can take some time to ask the right questions for you at that very moment in time. Give it context and also ask for the best outcome for all involved. Ask for the most fabulous fast track method so help you. Ask for yourself and for every being that has ever lived. Ask quietly, ask out loud, ask however you want. You will get the answer you need the clearer you become about the questions you need to ask. And the answer always contains: This Moment. Right now. You. You are making the best of this very moment. And then it gets better, and even better after that. You will see more. Understand more. Expand more. But I digress. Back to you. Ask. You will receive, as you give.

Does the example above make sense to you? Does it make you feel less envious of others' success? It might possibly give us more incentive to do good things, even though the rewards are not always material or, for that matter, instant.
But look, for example, at something we tend to completely overlook and undervalue.

The greatest reward you received in this life-time is that you ARE.

Really. Even if you cannot see any reason to appreciate it and think it has all been a waste of time. Consider this.

You have the chance, now, to make a difference, mostly to your future Self. It does not matter who that is or where that is. What matters is only now. It might be painful right now, and you might not know a way out. But that does not mean there isn't one. It does not mean a life without pain is not possible. Again, and I say this with all possible respect, we do not always see it that way. I am aware that some of you reading this might not feel well, right now. I am talking to you. And I see you, and hear you. Everyone does, and everyone wishes frantically for you to feel better. But how? When everything seems lost and nothing left, when all there is is pain, and darkness. Can you believe me when I say, it's only a part of it? The whole thing that contains darkness, it's not separate from that which is light? That there is still something else we haven't seen yet? Is it not logical, when you see around you, that there is some force that eludes us, that makes stuff happen. That makes flowers grow through concrete. Perhaps you have no strength left right now, and feel all alone. I am not here simply to give you 'hope'. I was once there, too, and a voice in my head said, give it up, this thinking about this and that. Give up thinking, go on, sink, but sink within, into yourself. Don't act on it, don't do anything silly, just sit there, and let it sink. Where does 'it' go? Where do 'I' go, where do 'you' go? Where do thoughts go? If thoughts just...go, and then go on without us thinking...are they even real? Do they tell us about something that is there, outside of us, that we might just be quiet listeners to the aches of the universe? If we let them... go, are they still there? And if they are, can other, different thoughts, be there, too, that we do not always hear? Are those the happier voices of an intact universe full of sparkles and light and exploding rainbows? Who are we, without thought, if the thoughts don't belong to us?

You will find something, I believe, sinking into your deeper layers beyond thought. Let the thoughts be. It might take a little time, but thought is replaced, by something bigger. But that's all I am going to give away, for now. Take your time. And know that we are all still learning skills we were not taught, often deliberately, to keep us in thought. We are taking baby steps learning about our true Self. Check in with yourself, maybe it's time to come out of the prison of ongoing thought processes and follow new methods of replacing them with something that you deserve. You deserve happiness.

I must add something important here – I am not telling you to take any illness lightly. I am not telling you to carry on feeling bad, or blaming yourself and beating yourself up, put up with others' bad behaviour, or that everything is your fault; quite the opposite. I just want to pre-empt that, before anyone thinks I'm some hypnotic guru that turns your life around by autonomic suggestion. Far from it. I am saying, examine things, ask questions, ask to be shown. Where do our beliefs come from? Where do yours come from? How did you get here? Who contributed?

Some of us really do have an intensely bad life, through absolutely no fault of their own and nothing to do with previous negative actions. How do I know? Simple. We all had to get here, somehow, didn't we? So where did we all start? We all had to push through, and in a million gazillion past lives, guess what – we died; so now we are terrified we will die again. One way or another, we are all scared out of our wits, and it shows with some of us more than others. We are learning, growing – and showing growing pains, although we are all the same underneath the fancy clothes. Some of us have certain talents, and some of us have certain tendencies. Some of us will find it easier to 'get' life, and others will work hard at not losing the plot, for a lot of their lifetime.

If we start to get depressed, for example, it is indication that our inner Karmic energy system is suppressed and not working well. A bit like a smart phone that has no space left for new programs because it's overloaded with data. it might even malfunction, as can we. We tend to think thoughts like 'what a rubbish life I have – I lost this and that, I haven't got this or that..I feel anxious/worthless etc.'. Understandably, the train of thought is easy to get stuck in, and depression is one of the major mental illnesses of the present time in the West. Around a third of the population in the UK is suffering from some form of mental illness, including depression. Many people have very valid reasons for feeling awful, and terrible things have happened to them, at the hands of others. Is there not fundamentally something wrong with how we are taught to think, so that our perception and evaluation of life itself does not help us recover any longer? When did our society forget to look out for each individual component? We are all sentient, sensitive beings. Have our minds become compromised? Are we all so stressed and over-worked that we have forgotten what it is we are here to be? Have we forgotten what it feels like to feel precious, and valued, and taken care of by life itself? There is definitely something amiss. We need to learn the Truth. We need to learn how to feel the miracle of the nature of life again without becoming entangled in the dark side. We need to learn to trust again in the highest source. It seems all of these things have been kept away from us, safely locked away in the hands of a few who wish for us to be compromised. It is not our fault. We have been kept isolated, separate and in fear. We have been kept in a mental melt-down, clamped down by an authoritative belief system that does not have our best interest at heart, giving us part-truths, conditional terms and limited contracts for being happy. Maybe it will help us to reflect on this:

You Karmically EARNED your right to be on this beautiful Earth as a sentient being by

your good actions from a previous lifetime.

If you are not well at the time you are reading this, I send you my love. You may be angry with me now for saying all this. 'How can this be?' You ask. 'I don't even want to be here, get me out!' But please read on.

In the greater picture of everything that exists, it is notoriously difficult to come to Earth as a human being, knowing that there are billions and billions of life forms on this planet alone, have been since beginningless time and you could have become any one of them, including an amoeba. You might be sarcastic and say that an amoeba is preferable to your life form, but believe me, it isn't. Animals don't have it easy. There is no voice, no developed body or brain to execute a decision-making process. An animal has much less chance of survival than a human, but even more importantly, it has less chance of a Karmic evolution on a huge scale such as in a human life. Humans in their physical bodies are capable of such greatness – if they are also connected to the great wisdom stream available to them. Combined with our ability to feel and create life, it is quite rare, even in the vast realms of the universe where other life forms certainly exist. We have so many miracles to be thankful for, and our suffering is not in vain. Our pain and our emotions make us able to determine what is right from wrong. Our ability to do good is escalated compared to billions of other life forms. All we have to do is not be Selfish, or do anything we will later regret when we find out there was always a price to pay. Everything within us strives for something greater, yearns for the great connection to the ultimate remembering of a beautiful heaven-like state. Is that not what we are remembering when we are down, that we have something greater to compare our state of limited existence to, that we have an inner knowing that suffering is not the point of it, that there is somewhere beautiful we came from and are supposed to be again? You are already en route, and let me tell you, that serene state of mind is not far away. You have already incarnated as a human body, by hook or by crook – you already ARE! Your Karmic energy body first had to be complete enough to make you your entire physical body. It is a complete miracle, but because of a flaw in the limited perception we have of ourselves and the world around us we get bored with miracles - and also slightly scared of them. What happened to us? At what point did we get so distracted? We have lost our trust in being here to be a part of the big Truth, we forgot how to be reconnected with it.

In the meantime, everything seems to be going wrong. All we can see is what we do not like our lives, our jobs, our spouses, where we live, the money we do not have, the shape of our bottoms, the length of our noses, colour of our skin and so on…Seriously, what are we like? We find ourselves completely justified in pursuing our moaning and as of late, we even have a live audience for it, all around the world, at our finger-tips; and guess what: we have built yet another industry on this con-dition - and it is thriving. Cosmetic surgery, botox injections, slimming pills, implants, tanning booths, hair salons, nail extensions…this is what the industry & media will have us believe is important and will make you feel better. Is it? Does it? Of course not. When you come closer to the Truth, you realise to what extent the world that we have created in the name of advancement is fake.

The world we live in is fast becoming a result of our desires of wanting to be better, bigger, thinner, faster, richer. The Karmic result of these dis-astrous short-sighted wishes is a distraction and a diversion from that which is our inner Truth, proof being that we are still not happy with what we have when we get it, simply because it has not contributed to our completing our consciousness of who we truly are and where we belong. Instead, it has distracted us from the real goal of achieving happiness within ourselves. We have been hoodwinked into being anx-ious and over-thinking, thinking that material things matter more than anything and acquiring them will make us happier. They do not. Our po-tential for happiness is already there, it is inherently ours, waiting for us to find it and reactivate it - only we have been keeping too busy looking in the wrong direction: externalising instead of looking inwards. Time to go home. It's never too late.

✽ ✽ ✽

4. Who Are We, Really?

This is about You. Everything else follows. Our perception of others and our surroundings are a reflection of our state of mind. This is never meant as a punishment. Life is meant to be on your side, so that you can focus on what is real and worth pursuing.

You have 'Karmically' inherited and, at the same time, co-created your state of mind, too, not just your physical existence. Everything is as you perceive it and everything becomes according to your input. The way you see the world, the way you were brought up, liking or disliking family, introvert, extrovert, enjoying your life, hating it – down to the tiniest thought, the tiniest perception – you have earned it – and you have created it. But who – is 'you'?
When we examine our 'Self' –

Our physical bodies, our lives, our names, families, possessions, our jobs and concepts of who we think we are and what we believe we own are just a very tiny, minute part of our Karmic Self, which can be subject to great changes in this life. Any shift in our circumstances, for better or worse, is subject to our Karma and may serve a purpose of helping us see who we really are and what we are truly capable of.

If you give this some deeper thought, the above 'phenomena' – the physical attributes, surroundings and possessions in our lives – can only ever be just a tiny part of who we really are. Because these are all things subject to change, we cannot expect to gain any lasting value from them. Compared to how we perceive ourselves usually, we probably need reminding that this is not to our detriment. Since our Karmic Self is a continuation from past into present, present into future, we would gain so much more stability, joy and comfort from our inner knowing that we will gain the feelings of security we crave by exercising focus on our true Self, the true nature of Self that is not dependent on external things. It does not mean we cannot have anything, it simply means that a focus on your Karmic Self is more likely to provide us with the balance and stability we crave in order to cope with the many changes that life throws at us. You were a child once (as any growing children will remind you even if you cannot remember!) and you will at some point become old again. All of these aspects are you, but none in themselves constitute the whole you. The life that you lead right this moment is yours, but it can just as easily change from one day to the next. The possessions you have, are yours, too, at this moment in time – or they could be taken away from you in the next. Our next question in the light of this must surely be this: is there nothing reliable to tell us who we truly are? What about our name? Our ancestors? Our DNA? Even though we may not understand the full details and impact thereof, and even though our physical existence is temporary and subject to change, there is, of course, a connection between your Karmic Self and your physical attributes. We can even go as far as saying that your Karmic Self has had a direct say in all that you are now - the circumstances before and around your birth, your naming, your early childhood, your ancestry and your DNA, the way you look and the choices your make. Your Karmic Self, your Karmic energy body, has made you 'You'. The question is…who are 'You'…really?

You will have chosen your DNA, your name your body, date of birth…and your family. But you might still not know who you are.

48

Are you sure you know your 'Self' well?

According to Karmic law, your Karmic energy body chooses automatically the unique incarnation which matches your energy imprints. This will include your 'mission' to complete your path towards full consciousness. All this happens totally without your conscious input. How is this possible? Let me try to explain.

We are not always conscious and aware, even though we pride ourselves so much on our intellect and base most of our identifying attributes to our brain and its capabilities to steer us through life. However, whilst our brain is active almost all of the time when we are awake, it depends on many factors as to how our brain is processing the world around us. Environmental influences, our IQ, our health, even our childhood experiences and what food we eat influence our braincells. Of the things that are happening to us every day or going on around us, we do not know how or why they happen, how they come about – or how to have an influence over them or indeed have an influence over what happens to us in our lives. So who or what is it that decides? There must be something that runs the show, within and around us, and it must be true for each of us who share this planet. What if we have to come to the conclusion that there is something bigger that we don't know about within and around us, some mechanism that decides for us and, much to our constant annoyance, overrides our precious 'conscious' ego bodies? We probably have some resistance to that concept straight away. How dare there be someone tell us what to do? Are we like puppets in the hands of some gigantic Grecian God? The rebel against authority within us raises alarm bells. The fear that there might be someone somewhere steering our destiny sets off the fight or flight reflex in us, or it might do the opposite where we feel we must abide and surrender our lives to this great being like a rabbit in the headlights. Our conscious 'ego'-Self has its fists raised, guarded against any potential intrusion against our will; and yet we appear to be helpless in the face of Karma which rules our every move regardless of whether we feel we chose it or not. Is this where we started to try to ignore the true power of Karma, because we felt we had no control or free will? Or did we play ignorant and ignored it for centuries to see if it would just go away, hoping it could not hurt us any longer?

Enter stage left all the pent-up resentment created by our fear of not knowing where we came from and what's next. If we did choose to ignore Karma for so long, how can we expect to learn more about it? If we chose arrogance and entitlement to override our fears instead so that we continue to grab what we could of what we feel must be rightfully ours, how can we make peace again with the concept that we are simply not that much in charge? This is the perfect time to start to understand how we can best influence our own path, our own Karma, by trying to learn and understand how we gain control again over our destiny, rather than carry on destroying everything around us with our fears and passions. Are we a people on Earth who are really happy within our ego minds? What is it within us that chooses all these circumstances for us, and how can we choose for the better?

Our brain can process data input from our bodies and surroundings. It uses a binary code system to help keep us safe and functioning. It can judge, discern, analyse, criticise – but it cannot easily perceive cause and effect over a period of lifetimes.

In order to understand what it is that 'chooses' all these Karmic connections for us, we need to bypass the brain for a while, even though it's helping you to read what I am being helped by my brain to write. No offence and nothing against our poor little overworked miracle brains, they are not a bad thing really. The same as the word 'ego', it is not bad to have 'ego' or a brain, although some people use the term 'ego' like a dirty word in their frustration of seeing themselves and others stuck in a limited frame of perception. Whilst some of the functions are very limited, its mechanism is still miraculous in keeping us alive after all. However, despite what we think and how proud we are of our brain function, it is not always this part of our Self that comes up with the great answers to life. There is instead something else which is a part of us that can. It is even a permanent part of us. It might even be more 'us' than our physical body components are. It is there for us, always and forever. You could say it is our forever body. And yet we are not even aware it is there, because our brain cannot compute it. This is because whilst it there to keep us from harm, it also has a mind of its own: its decision-making process is designed to only rely on our five senses and the experiences it has accumulated and stored from those senses over a period of time. It has such a strong autonomous power over all our bodily functions spurred on by our will to survive that it often tends to take over a bit, especially when it is overworked. Under any stress, our brain goes into fight or flight mode. It sends out adrenalin, and is ready to run the show in case we are under attack. When our brain is in tress mode it is set to control our reactions, thoughts, language, actions and needs but it also seems to leave us with a deficit and chemical imbalances that make us have illusions, such as a feeling that we are anxious and in need of something to rebalance, such as permanent reassurance or attention, or to be rewarded, or need to run from danger constantly. Needless to say that all these attributes are useful in case of emergencies, however, in our stressful lives our poor little brains are taking a constant beating, tend to be highly strung and take over almost all the time. It is an automatic process that occurs under stress which makes us be very vulnerable to deception. There are a host of different states of mind that we can start to suffer from which affect our mental health, as paradoxically, our brains are capable of urging us to press the Self-destruct button, at which point the miracle of our brain malfunctions and causes us more harm than good. We can either recognise this is occurring to most of us at some point to some degree or remain unaware. Looking around, at times it seems we like we have all been mass-hypnotised and made to feel scared on a large scale which would probably not be far from the truth. Once we see that this happens to all of us and is not our fault, we can decide what to truly do about it. We have help! The very part within us that overrides brain function when it's all gone wrong is there to assist us. Whilst we still have precious choice, we can try to keep healthy or submit to sabotage., it must Whichever we decide, it might become clear to see how we can easily be putting ourselves into a precarious position if we trust what our brain perception alone would have us believe. So – who is the boss and who is the slave? Who...are you?

The 'something' we are searching for within us, the 'other' mind, the wise one that knows better, is something I will call the 'greater mind' for now. Its function is even more mysterious than those of our brain and body. It is the free spirit that resides within us and gives us our identity, ideas, and dreams. It is weightless and formless and nonetheless accessible, tangible and visible. This greater mind that is within us is a part of the same expansive consciousness that also transcends our physical body and surrounds us in all directions. It is the same Karmic energy that created everything. The same that merges with the greater energy that humans have tried to describe since beginning of time, with as many words. It goes by names such as God, Allah, Yahveh, Buddha, Shiva and many other names in so many religions and has been described, loved, denied, fought over and killed for in as many different ways. It is the ultimate stuff we are made of – and also the stuff that 'is' not. It is the energy that incarnates into life, and also the energy body that remains after death. There is no word for it really, there cannot be a word. It cannot be perceived, it is not simply a human concept, it is beyond words. Not everyone believes it is there through its very essence. It is always our choice what we believe, of course. Although we tend to believe with our brains, based on our five senses only, and if we feel threatened by something, our brain might not be so open to anything new. After all, do we not believe in electricity and yet we cannot see it? Do we not know about gases although they are invisible? We connect up to the internet lifting us out of our physical surroundings into a different, virtual reality which we would feel lost without and yet, do we really know how it works, this formless, odourless, weightless realm? All we know is how we feel when it doesn't work! The analogy I am making is quite apt; only, the virtual reality we are hooked up into is still connected to very 3-d concepts and components to make it work. it is also designed, run and used by humans who still run on 3-d concepts and components and it is therefore fallible. In future, I predict we will work without electricity - or the need for electronics. Perhaps we might even by then not get angry any longer if it doesn't work.

I would quite like to continue with the modern and topical analogy of virtual reality. Since we know how much information can be stored in a tiny manufactured computer chip these days, we might be able to work with this metaphor to express how much more powerful our own Karmic energy minds are. When looking at the Karmic mind, we are trying to perceive and convey the most incredibly complex and far-reaching 'computer' ever made, much more complex than a brain. It has an endless memory, logs absolutely every single action ever made, every sensation and experience we ever had, every thought, emotion; every move we ever made, in every second of our lives and endless lifetimes before this, constantly connects us up to higher realms and finer vibrations as we become ready for an upgrade...and it sure as heck is nothing like Windows10.The mathematical concept of infinity is hard for us lay people to understand, and yet, infinity underlies all principles of the endless universe. A part of us really does already understand it, because we are a part of it. It's not that hard to start to get into. Even my daughter can enter the space when she asks me how much I love her and I always say 'infinity' and she replies, 'I love you 'infinity plus 1". We giggle then about our little insider joke. You might think that understanding and connecting to the highest energies is an impossible task, but it is not really. You will remember. You will remember because that is where you came from, and that is what you are made of. It is who you are. You already are infinite potential.

Your Karmic energy body utilises and is created via sacred geometrical patterns based on infinitely available energy so that it has an endless hard drive to create and store all of your Karmic imprints. It does not sound believable when we think of how limited all our physical gadgets' memory is and how much we struggle with the limited capacity of electrics and electronics. But our Karmic memory is based on universal energy, of which electric energy is only a minute part. Added to that, the greater mind is based on the same energy exchange, so it can automatically merge with our system, as it does with everything else in physical dimensional existence. It's the best Bluetooth ever you can tether to and the signal strength is set maximum. I will in a little while further down explain how we don't always pick up those signals with our bodies and brains, just like our electronic counterparts. We are selective about what we believe we are here to perceive and deal with. Our systems can be in lock-down and shutdown mode, but we can also learn to become aware of and maximise the particular physical imprint we have chosen for this lifetime. Unlike any electronic computer system though, our aliveness is infinitely more magical. In times where we are supposed to forget our great advantage of being alive, it will serve us well to be reminded that our Karmic energy body is all-knowing...and that it should not be underestimated.

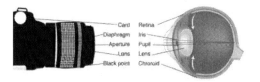

The Internal creates the External, examples
image credit: © optilase.com;

	Brain	Computer
Processing Elements	10^{11} neurons	10^9 transistors
Element Size	10^{-6} m	10^{-6} m
Energy Use	30 W	30 W (CPU)
Processing Speed	10^2 Hz	10^{10} Hz
Style Of Computation	Parallel, Distributed	Serial, Centralized
Energetic Efficiency	10^{-16} joules/opn/sec	10^{-6} joules/opn/sec
Fault Tolerant	Yes	No
Learns	Yes	A little

The Brain vs A Computer

Image Credit © DR. Y. M. PURI MOHSIN DALVI

Can our creations ultimately be more powerful than we are?

What I haven't reminded you of yet is one very important matter. One that makes you immensely valuable. The most valuable thing on Earth, to be exact. A commodity in the eyes of commerce and the money lenders. Do you know what it is? It is so easy to take for granted, yet so complex that no human has yet been able to replicate it, although many have certainly tried. It happens naturally and without us feeling the miracle every moment of the day, although we should:

We are all alive, actually.

Did that bowl you over? Did it make you buzz, remembering? Or are you just sitting there thinking 'yeah…so?' If that happened, fear not. We are all just a little brainwashed into thinking it's normal, nothing to write home about, it comes with strings attached, it's painful etc. etc. but – we are…ALIVE. What is that, exactly? Have we ever truly thought about what that means, other than a lot of pain and bother? Is it because we have forgotten where we came from? Yes. Yes, that's why.

Recently, an artificial intelligence, i.e. a computer, designed to look human, a female in fact, received not only a name and much publicity for being so clever. No – this AI also received citizenship in Saudi Arabia. Nothing wrong with that, you mean? Interestingly enough, we have been so desensitised that we don't think it's strange that this has occurred and it's not causing a proper stir in us, as it should. In comparison, children are being sold, abused, harvested and killed, and if they are from backgrounds our society files under 'not important', we hardly blink an eyelid any longer as it has become normalised news that a child dies every few seconds. Since when has it become mainstream that we believe human life is not precious any longer? When we awaken to our own miracle, we see what's wrong with the picture, and it hurts, deeply. Until we awaken to the miracle within, there will always be suffering and it will be obvious on a daily basis. It is painful to observe, and most of us can only take so much pain before we become numb to it.

Until everyone awakens, we may not have a planet that supports all life, human or otherwise. Are we bothered? Can that even become a reality? Yes, we are, and yes, we can. I hope so, at least. Certainly once we are realigning ourselves to create a good outcome for everyone involved and ditch the brainwashing that has gone on for aeons of time. Who are we? We are ecstatic beings, capable of so much more happiness than we choose to be having, held back by our very real past Karmic links of fear. What we do with this information, is also down to Karmic rules, although we can't use that as an excuse because that would be a catch22, trying to justify doing nothing by saying my Karmic Self has not wanted me to do anything about it. if we can do something, let's You could simply make a start by reading on to find out more.

We are alive; and most of us are functioning, subject to a bit of food, water and TLC – unlike computers which have to run on electricity, be switched on and are dependent on a human being's input. Have you ever thought that despite all our technical advances and scientific discoveries we have actually never yet managed to create something 'alive'? It is not for want of trying – you ask science! It seems it cannot be done. Even when we invented cloning, and skin grafts, and organ transplants, and viruses, we always needed a base of ingredients that were already alive. When we create something electronic like computers, components, vehicles, aircraft, drones, cameras, artificial intelligence and so on, we create them by copying what we see to be alive. We do not have the secret, the mystery ingredient, and in my humble opinion we never will, although we will bankrupt the planet trying to do it. Even the smallest leaf on a tree, the tiniest virus bridging life/non-life status is more alive than anything that man has ever created.

Despite our not inconsiderable god-complex we will probably have issues acknowledging this, especially when confronted with our shortcomings. We do not like having the obvious pointed out to us, it makes us feel small and vulnerable - just like that tiny live, pesky fly seemingly has it in for us and we just want to finish it off, as if its life didn't matter. We don't believe we matter and it causes us endless aggravation continuing to act as if we have something to prove. This is likely to be down to our frustration and inability to really understand what makes life tick; but instead of having found answers as to how, we have focused on wanting to own it, rule it, kill it - and then recreate it in metal and plastic. We forget how precious being alive is, and how to have a sensitive regard and healthy respect for the amazing and miraculous process that is needed to make something come to life. We have some strange fascination as old as life itself with killing live beings, as much as we have an attachment to trying to make things come to life, in a Frankenstein sort of way. We want something we can't have. Perhaps it is because this is possibly the first and last prerogative that has been denied man: to play god and be the creator of a new life-form. The closest we may ever get should also remain to be the focus of all our attention in that respect: to co-create and co-parent a precious human life by the mystery of witnessing, giving birth and nurturing a new being on Earth. This may be the closest we get to experiencing the feeling of being involved in the creation process - and even then we manage to make quite a hash of it. By now I know i sound like a constant judge Judy to all that we are doing on Earth, but I still feel it needs to be pointed out what is going wrong as opposed to what we are able to create if we are given back the blueprint. It is not meant to be a judgement, as we all live here to make our own choices based on the best way we know how to.

In terms of taking care of the next generation, we are all equally responsible for what we are giving our children as a start-up pack. If we connect the dots and become aware that with our infinite Karmic energy having created infinite lifetimes before this and after, this would mean we must all have been men, women and quite likely mothers and fathers, too! Would it not be fascinating to think that all the phenomena which present themselves right now, all the possibilities of men choosing to be stay-at-home-dads, mums being offered the choice of whether they are able to take care of their babies or allow them to be parented by others who they feel are more able to, same-sex parenting, fostering, adoption and all the myriad of different parenting styles all around the world are possible because we are governed by experiences before this lifetime which play a part in the decision-making process of how we want to shape our and our children's lives. Our Karmic consciousness is so much bigger than we think, constantly influencing our every-day decision-making without us even being aware of it. If it was left to us to give our body the right commands, I have a feeling we would not live longer than a minute. Think about it – if we were in charge of our bodily functions we would not even really know how to breathe regularly, let alone keeping a heart beating or any other organ for that matter. Does it come as a surprise that we are not in charge at all, and we don't know anything about how we work usually? What a mess we would be in if 'we' were in charge of everything! And yet, we tend to blank this big stumbling block out, seem to be happy to let the autopilot take complete charge, whilst continuing to think that we are the centre of the universe, top of the creation process and know it all. Perhaps it is exactly this fact that we know so little about ourselves that makes us we feel we have to externalise and overcompensate so much. However, instead of finding out how amazingly powerful and vast our Karmic minds truly are and how to utilise it properly, we prefer to find distractions in all sorts of petty and useless ways. There is proof all around us how crazy it can get. We prove our worthiness to exist to ourselves by exploring unnecessary, costly projects on many levels in our every day actions. We have externalised power to governments creating projects costing billions of $s so we can beat our chests and prove to ourselves that we really are a race worthy of attention and a forces to be reckoned with. If we were being observed elsewhere in the universe, would we not look a little stupid? Don't we look like the emperor with no clothes, having not even noticed our greatest vulnerabilities? And who capitalised on our vulnerability to sell us all these ideas? Outside our front door, there is whole world caught up in politics and hell-bent on distraction and destruction. Should we start sweeping around our own front door before we start sweeping around others? If only we could take a good look into ourselves, we might realise how much easier, healthier and cheaper life would be - and we would perhaps also find what we are looking for is already there.

Well - we can.

The inner astronaut is the role you may have been looking for all your life since you were a child with dreams and an imagination: the inner explorer that finds out what makes you tick, finds answers for you, finds out who you truly are, makes you and the ones around you happy and will come up with hours of endless entertainment. Rome was not built in a day though, and even the Buddha took a few days to become enlightened, but I believe it is this journey you have always yearned to take. You are promised a journey with an irresistible mixture of excitement, suspense, intrigue, love, passion, romance and more. Sit back, relax, and enjoy the show! We are used to having the approach that it will somehow happen externally, come from somewhere outside ourselves, like a prompt to take us by the hand and lead us to salvation. I believe this is possibly a hangover of the dependency we experienced for many years where we had to wait for the prompt or even permission from our parents. Perhaps we never thought about taking that responsibility back now that we are grown up and might still be waiting and expect someone outside our selves to supply and cater for our every need. Unless we have good reason to be dependent on another, this is not how it works once we are supposed to be adulting. There is great power in centring our focus again in our inner Karmic world, and we can become aware again of our aliveness by learning what it means to say 'I AM' and feel it. The alternative is apparent everywhere around us. Our unfulfilled yearning for the external satisfaction of our inner needs, and the dissatisfaction that settles in our unfulfilled lives if we do not have the courage to take this journey into ourselves, will prevail if we do not learn, adapt to and utilise new methods to go inwards. Our frustration and anger with our environment and almost everyone in it is age-old. Ancient cultures suffered the same and already came up with solutions, but we need to re-connect to what our ancestors are screaming for us to do from their graves. The angst is only there because on some level we *know* we have lived it all before, are getting frustrated that we cannot recall how to get back to sanity and serenity and that we are desperate to find a way to plug ourselves back in as quickly as possible. To try and find it, we are forever engaged, always in motion, busy in the pursuit of adding new excitement in lack of wisdom of where we came from. Of course, 'know thyself' – i.e. our own Karma – is something many people are really frightened of, as well as intrigued by. It is this very fear of suffering again and again that makes us do anything but find out who we really are.

There is no one else to blame.

What if there were no-one else to blame? No governments, no author-ities, no partners, parents, siblings, friends, family or foes responsible for our choices in life – other than our 'Self'? Who is this 'Self', anyway? We need to know so we can grab and shake him/her for all the stupid mistakes (s)he has made; or making our lives so difficult, for distracting us when we needed to focus and for waylaying us when we were on the right track!

Looking at Western history and our attempts at trying to define Self, we have amongst others, of course, no other than Sigmund Freud, the Doc-tor of Neurology and founder of psychoanalysis, and Carl Jung, founder of analytical psychology and their combined vision of human psych-ology, trying to explain. Both appeared to have some understanding already in the early part of the 20th century. Freud came up with the thesis that to him, there seemed to be a distinct divide between the id, or animalistic, instinctual mind, on one end; and the super-ego with the moralising tasks of a higher consciousness on the other, with the con-scious mind, or 'ego' mind stuck somewhere in the middle, which has the job of making rational and organised, realistic decisions, with the aim of getting the best outcome for us every second of the day.

Despite their differences, we still use some of the concepts both Freud and Jung came up with today to explain a part of our Western under-standing of humankind. We can also fuse this knowledge with the ex-plorations about Karma. The internal decision-making process, which often has to happen in split-seconds, depends evidently on each indi-vidual's own personal vault of experience. How lucid and aware we are in the moment and whether we make a good decision or not depends on our Karma and what is already manifest within us as a result. Because our ordinary 'ego' mind tends to be so wrapped up in our base interests, decisions based on them and the 'id' are naturally not always the best outcome for ourselves, never mind everyone else concerned. It appears that we need to have reconnected with our own ability for altruism and consideration of others' welfare as well as our environment, in order to put Selfless actions for the greater good before our own immediate Self-gratification; otherwise, chances are the ego mind makes decisions like a drunk in a brawl at closing time outside a pub; or whatever analogy works for you to catch my drift. If our 'super-ego' is meant to be an ana-logy for our Karmic Self and if it has not been connected yet to our 'ego', it may not have made us aware of how, for example, based on our own

Karma, we are not just governing our internal world, but we are also co-creating the environment outside ourselves. If we are unaware of how our own Karma is affecting our every move, thought and communication, then we cannot expect that our decision-making process is consciously based on anything other than the ego-mind's Self-interest for survival. The ordinary every-day mind is bound almost entirely by internalised rules according to sensory perception combined with past experience and predictions based on avoiding harm and the varying levels of fear this creates. It is no surprise therefore, that our 'ego' mind is often misguided and limited in its perception, making decisions and acting out on the basis of an overly personal, subjective, faulty mind 'map' of right and wrong. This is becoming ever more apparent in one situation amongst many when we look at, for example, the insanity involved on the stage of world politics. We hand over authority to what we believe to be a greater collective mind, with the hope that we can continue to pursue our ordinary mind's quest for peace of mind on a small individual, Self-absorbed scale. Without realising, we have disconnected ourselves from governing our own inner world, and this expresses itself in our environment, too. Instead of rectifying the situation because we do not know how to, we start to blame those we elected on our behalf. In order to feel complete, we must find out again how to feel complete within whilst being connected to all the greatness possible in this universe.

We cannot expect or rely on the ordinary 'ego' mind alone to make reliable decisions for the benefit of the greater good.

By now, we only have to look around at what happens when human decisions are made purely on the level of the ego-mind. We also have countless historic examples of how humans could easily and finally have finished off the whole planet. We have experienced it in Governments, Religion, individuals vying for world leadership, cultural revolutions which brought on genocides under the name of progress. Every century, every decade even, has sported its own wars, for as long as we can think, somewhere on the planet. For the fact that we all want peace, we have certainly blown up a lot of places and killed endlessly to warrant the imagined result.

And yet, even though we have already lived lifetimes in constant fear of these unimaginable threats, those appear to be the same threats we still face today. Has any of our warmongering solved any issues which started the wars in the first place? Do we live with less fear, do we feel safer? It does not seem that way to me. Did we look in the wrong direction to find peace in the first place? Is it not a situation that repeats itself over and over under slightly different pretences? Which part of our mind decides to accept all of this an inevitable and unavoidable reality, based on how it was sold to us? Did you, or I, set out to kill hundreds of thousands of men, women and children? You decide.

Our ordinary ego-minds alone will not be able to reach the 'right' decision for everyone. Without using the wisdom and compassion of the greater mind, it will always be a decision that has pro's and con's as a result. Based on what we know about how the ego-mind works, it would be a logical conclusion that most of its actions, thoughts and decisions will by its very nature be incomplete and subjective. It is a fascinating fact, if we look at it without trying to be for or against it; the results of this conclusion happen to be all around us. If our ego mind alone makes a decision based on keeping us safe, it will choose the nearest option of keeping us alive, faced with an external force or event that makes us believe we are unsafe.

It is an internal mechanism that is hard to override or rewire. Often we find it hard to even include thinking about the safety and well-being of our nearest and dearest. We have to draw the conclusion that this is one of our biggest vulnerabilities: we are easily drawn into feeling unsafe and as a result, our nervous system starts to activate the fight or flight reflex.

Now, if someone came along who knew about this and put it to us that we are in urgent danger of being annihilated, and we were being shown images to accept as proof, would we have enough thinking space within to examine the validity of the claim, or the integrity and motives of those making the claim? Would we feel we have time, considering the urgency of the matter? In an emergency, the reflex we experience within is even more limited to saving ourselves. If we do not have an opportunity to verify the urgency of the matter, never mind connecting to a higher source to find solutions outside us saving our own skin, this can have devastating consequences on those around us and our environment.

Whilst we have faced many such situations on Earth over aeons of time, individually or as a community, our ego minds have not changed that much in terms of the choices we have in our inner repertoire to react to them. It seems that modern technology has not stopped disasters from occurring and people perishing, perhaps quite the opposite. Are we really entirely at the mercy of our inner functioning as to our survival? Faced with this fact, what is it within us that could make a difference?

What is the point of us being here, if our physical body will pass, again and again, every single time - and our beautiful planet along with it? If we found a way so that we could override our ego-mind and react differently when we are faced with danger, if we had a moment to connect to our higher source, the universal mind, or the super-ego, as Freud called it, would this not make a difference when every second counts?

There is another consideration that we may not have thought of. If we do not have the resources to validate any claims that threaten our survival, is it possible that there are humans with ego minds on our planet that have used their fears of dying against us? In the fight for survival, are there those who historically wanted there to be guarantees that they would not be threatened by others, so that their ego minds turned them into killers and megalomaniacs?

Is the urgency card of the game being played against us? Has the fight or flight within us been activated for so long that we are more or less all agitated, turning against each other? Who started it? Is anyone acting behind the curtain and creating this 'Wizard of Oz syndrome', creating scenarios that make us live in fear and continuously triggering us into Self-preservation, taking away our freedom of choice and ability to connect long enough to our highest source to find a better solution? Is humankind not constantly living in a state of stress, making us rise against each other, and is this state of stress real or is it the creation of some who will profit from us being slaves to our fear?

There is an answer to all of the above. Whilst we have been continuously living in fear, we have forgotten our own true power: the power that makes us alive, and the aliveness that is our gift to connect fully to our highest Karmic potential. Whilst we feel small and insignificant in our fearful ego-bodies, we can only think to survive, from one terrifying moment to the next. We have given our power away already, and it seems that we don't even have to answer the question whether this is by design or not, because the power lies with us to turn it around, no matter who is out there after us. When we are aware of the inner energy flow, we are connecting to our source, our Karmic Self, our 'super-ego', if you will. We will remember who we truly are more easily, and with practice will less easily be taken in by anyone trying to instil fear. This is where we can make a difference to the world and its inhabitants, by becoming who we truly are, being real and living wisely and in tune, teaching others by example how to live true to our ability to our given right to be alive without fear.

Before we allow the conundrum of how to do this at five to midnight to turn us into quivering wrecks, we can, with added wisdom and our inherent and accessible awareness of the bigger picture, already - right here and right now - request to reset our Karmic minds to making conscientious choices by activating our higher selves. We are all learning to 'hook ourselves up' and link in to the higher realms of wisdom consciousness. The first step is to want to do it, to recognise that this is the most direct way of bringing peace, starting with our 'Self'. Most of us need to ask to be shown how to do it, and we can simply start doing this by repeatedly asking into the space before us. You could call it praying, and it might be a form of prayer, but the analogy far surpasses any religious connotation because there is no religion where your request is going. Your request to be shown the Truth and how to live Truth instead of fear will go out into the formless vastness of endless potential, no less. All you need is to want to be shown, for your motivation to be present, as well as your intention to live it. It's simple, it's yours, it does not cost millions and you do not have to sign up to some secret society or give anything up. Anyone can do it.

This is where the Truth comes out in the wash and where anything that is less than truth will be exposed and no longer have validity for those who have seen past it. When we make decisions based on Truth rather than fear, it will in turn influence our Karma positively for our future and create good conditions, not just for ourselves but for others, too. Overcoming fear will start to expose automatically all that is not Truth. If we accept that the ego mind is always going to be fallible, then we can work with it, instead of overusing it, rejecting it or trying to mould it into a stupefied subconscious state, where it festers and can come out sideways in limitless ignorant ways. Just look around if you don't know what I mean.

We can then become aware of the whole process of how to make an appropriate choice in most situations, based on more than just the ego mind.

We can transcend our ego minds and start living, looking up to a different outcome. We can truly become who we are meant to be.

Every action will meet with its Karmic re-action.

Of course there is something much bigger than our physical existence out there, otherwise there would not be so many philosophies, religions, spiritual orientations, sciences, and searchers in general trying to give it a name, form, find out what it is and how it works.

in terms of universal justice, people who seemingly 'get away with it', and in case we still believe there is a get-out clause, the fact that there is not always a visible result or immediate repercussions to our actions might explain this, and the fact that many people we know of are seemingly allowed to continue causing havoc all around us. There may also be other interferences which we have no insight into. As we know, we can never be the judge another's Karma. Understandably, this is very frustrating for those who have been wronged. At our level of perception, most of us will never really understand that the way Karma works is infinitely wise. A Karmic action always has a reaction. Any negative Karmic action of any being will still strive by its very nature to be balanced at a different point in their lifetimes, based on Karmic law and timing. It's an amazing process that the intrinsic nature of existence has provided, and it is fascinating to see it is trying to be understood more in those parts of the world that have stepped away from teaching it in the past. People are finding more esoteric solutions to living their lives more consciously and are actively choosing to incorporate it into our every day lives. Even our very limited understanding of using the principle as well as misunderstanding how Karma works is a step in the right direction. The nature of universal principles is to be inclusive and to allow to exist. By our very existence and aliveness we can choose to avert any of our actions, thoughts and words that do not support it. There is no judgement or target there, it simply 'is'; it does not cease to exist and neither do we. This simply expressed complexity can be taken the wrong way, but we may also be lucky enough to observe some highly evolved beings averting bad Karma by shifting energies away from their and others' Karmic energy bodies through some incredibly miraculous practices. Such esoteric practices are usually based on sacred teachings, and they can and do work. It's always so much more satisfying to see something transcendent at work rather than something destructive.

To conclude, a reaction can indeed be turned around, depending on the type of action and considering the right circumstances and recognition. As indicated, we don't get away with wrong action as easily as we might think, as our own Karmic energy bodies patiently make a log of what has happened, and our inner Karmic timer automatically makes sure that we will all get an opportunity to sort it out when the time has come; this may not always occur under ideal conditions, which we often forget to consider beforehand. Bad Karma may also deprive someone of stepping up into an expanded experience of happiness. A short-circuit 'memory' in the Karmic energy body will have been created that will rise up time and time again, until such time that it is recognised and neutralised. It isn't simply a case of holding up our hands and saying 'I repent' and hope for the best; we need to accurately address the inner memory imprint, just like you would with a malfunction in your computer software. We also cannot at all rely blindly on our Good Karma, believing that this will make any negative Karmic imprint simply vanish. What we also often choose to do is to procrastinate, believing that we are able to redeem ourselves in a future situation. Whilst we have been ignoring those facts and they have been accumulating like a feeling of dread within, many believe in a kind of 'judgement day' where we will all be faced with the consequences of our actions. Whether this is true, whether this is figuratively speaking or an actual phenomenon the same for all mankind where we are all supposed to face some threat of punishment or chance of redemption the same for all at the same time, remains to be seen. Just an observation, but it doesn't have to get cryptic or complicated. I believe that we are constantly facing the result of our actions on a daily basis, with a chance to make it right, right now; no need to wait anxiously for the future.

As I said before, there is no 'finger in the sky' who will point at anyone. It's all an inside job.
It is within ourselves that the effects of our Karmic actions take place, and because we carry their imprint, they will reflect outwards into our external surroundings and dealings with others, too . It is also possible that we become embroiled in another's Karmic actions, and will have to become ourselves aware exactly what our Karmic purpose is in these actions. Often this is also a process that is ongoing, and we will only find out its purpose in hindsight. Sometimes, reasons cannot be identified in their entirety.

We will all be presented with choices and opportunities again not to make the same 'mistakes'.

(I will not define the word 'mistake' here, I will leave that up to you, but if you prefer, we can substitute 'mistake' with ''unskilful action')
Every day we will be given the chance to think about expanding our conscience. Every so often, we might catch glimpses of our own inner mind map which makes us act in certain ways including taking any unskilful action. We can decide if we would like to continue down this road - or change. It is down to our Karma how we learn that these situations come about and how they continue to pan out. We may have awareness, we may not. Others may not, either, in which case we exercise caution and compassion. Compassion in its true sense means that we truly wish other beings enlightenment. We may feel remorse, in which case our actions may have an opportunity of being revised. We may receive help, we may not. We may see changing our actions as a good thing, or we may

have resistance, feeling that we have no choice but to continue on our cyclic vicious circle of action somewhat longer; in which case we can start simply by asking for the right help and the circumstances to support us. Again, according to our Karma, we will either be aware enough to recognise what could be 'nudges with a sledge hammer' and act accordingly - or we will not.

It is not granted that circumstances may always be as favourable for us as they are now, next time around. They are at their most favourable at this very moment for that which we have to learn, even if they are not perfect.

* * *

5. What is the 'Karmic Energy Mind'?

I will be using this term all throughout the book to describe our Karma which we have accumulated so far, that has co-created our current existence, resides within us as frequency recordings, continues to record and adjust internal events and will determine our future existence accordingly.

There are unlimited examples in our every-day world for all kinds of Karmic actions and re-actions, in all walks of life. How easy it is to get caught up in our beliefs about right and wrong! Is there ever an end? Does our suffering ever end? Is the human story always about survival, and how are we so different from any other species struggling to compete for the best outcome and easiest way to get what we need? Could there not be an easier way? Is there not an alternative or is this our lot? Are we taken for a ride by our merry-go-round life keeping us in the slavery of our own beliefs, and how we see our environment in the limited Karmic vision we have?

Until we have cleared our inner 'wardrobe' enough of all the outmoded clutter that is stopping us from seeing the bigger picture, we will not be able to become the observer to how our ego-mind appears to be running the show. In fact, we will not even want to get rid of it! Because we have become so comfortable with it, it keeps us in our 'box', in our comfort zone – where everything on the outside of it feels hostile. Our constantly re-appearing dread is based on the fear of being harmed by outside influences. But is there more to it? Are we not instead afraid of our own Karma and what it might have in store for us?

Ideally, we will at some point reach a stage where we see through everything straight away, make a choice based on the best possible outcome for everyone involved and create good conditions for our future so that we are supported in making cultivated choices more and more often. There are people on Earth who already live by these principles, very much able to be in control of outcomes and with the clarity gained, also able to see through another being and their Karmic path. Many of them have learned it is wise to stick to one of the basic rules of Karma – even though they might be all-seeing, it is better to allow each being to learn to see theirs for themselves. Often, it is not ultimate wisdom to be telling another what to do or make a decision for them. However, we can ask as many questions if we want. Even if we do not direct our questions at any particular person, answers and advice can always be obtained, even if they do sometimes come in many different forms and even cryptic clues, riddles, insight and foresight. Help is there if we care to ask.

Karma is actually there to help us do this all the time, and it gets better and better the more we follow the principles of Karmic action and re-action. Since most of us do not yet live the fully blissful state of the continuously peaceful, eternally happy state of a pure Karmic mind, which comes from making all the right choices, having realised and annulled all wrong-doing of the past, in addition to taking actions with good outcomes only - even if we are only able to catch glimpses now and then we can guess that it must be possible, amazing and blissful for us to be in this state all the time. Karma is on our side – it wants us to have the best outcome. But if we want the best outcome, we do have to follow some of the rules. Here is a mini guide to Karmic bliss:

- *Nobody is responsible for our thoughts, words, actions and re-actions, other than ourselves*
- *Others around us can sometimes reflect our inner Karmic 'map' of where we are at in terms of completing our energy field, what we believe in, our generosity, awareness, compassion and what we have created for ourselves and others so far*
- *Past and present Karmic actions create and affect future outcomes in form of a time-line; even if we cannot always trace or pin point to any specific moment with certainty, accepting the fact that this process exists will nevertheless help us to put our actions and thoughts on the right track and our lives into perspective*
- *Karmic timing is beyond our ordinary perception of time and can span life-times*
- *Good actions have good outcomes. Unskilful decisions are followed by less fruitful or less desirable conditions; according to circumstances, the individual involved and/or their actions, the outcomes can hint at parts of the wisdom mind that still have to be activated*
- *Any condition that presents on Earth and everywhere else in existence can serve to make us aware of Karmic laws and aid our decisions from moment to moment to act well*
- *There is already a complete blueprint of all of our Karmic actions from previous times that travels with us on our physical journey in and around our body, temporarily presenting in the 3rd dimension. As it has also created our physical body, some of it is visible, yet other parts are so subtle they are not visible or tangible to most of us until they surface. Unless they are altered by a higher form of insight, all of them do, over a stretched-out timeline itself created by their ripening*

- *Our moment-to-moment actions, thoughts and speech, accumulated over life-times, are the deciding factors in determining our future selves*

- *It is therefore predictable to an extent, 'who' we are going to be, based on what we decide to do, say and think, from moment to moment; certainly when we are willing to include accepting the responsibility for any negative Karma from our past, even though we may not consciously find out what this was in detail*

- *By default, the ordinary 'ego'-mind has flaws and works with a limited belief-system. Because of this, it cannot fully understand the bigger picture. It can only create a partial and subjective picture of our world as we perceive it based on our senses and brain function. If we work with the ego-mindset only, it can create separation and incompleteness in our separate bodies in this 3-dimensional world, due to ignorance of the whole Truth of who we are; if anger and greed add to the creation of external phenomena of a world of suffering, it can draw us back to not feeling alive or even allowing ourselves to be pulled into a less-than 3-dimensional world where we are not able to use the functions we have when being alive*

- *We can and will have help, any time when we are ready to want to learn how to create it. Paradoxically, as soon as we know how to constructively ask for help and also commit to taking responsibility for our own actions, we have created help.*

- *Help comes in many forms, sometimes even the opposite of what we asked for. We are here to learn to see through what presents itself to understand the full extent of the principles of creation behind it*

- *The actions, thoughts and words we thought we could get away with but do not without harming ourselves and others, form part of these Karmic laws:*

- *We must not harm another being in any way by thought, intention, speech or action. If we chose to not see the consequence or ignore it, and use our bodies, brains and/ or energy minds to perform actions to harm ourselves & others sentient beings, including the smallest forms of life and our environment, it will create certain Karmic outcomes for each such action according to its Karmic energy imprint. We must not use our thoughts to harm the above in any way, causing distress and unhelpful conditions by confusing, alarming, upsetting, slandering, manipulating, harshness and such like. We must not use our energy minds to harm or influence others in a negative way*

- *There are groups of 'negative' Karmic actions that always meet with a negative future re-action. These are: Negative bodily actions such as killing, stealing or sexual misconduct; negative actions by speech: lying, slander, abusive language or idle gossip; negative thoughts such as coveting, ill will or wrong view.*

Of course, even the way we perceive all this information, our reaction to it, is governed by our understanding of the bigger picture so far. It may trigger some inner memory and may even sound familiar, and not all of us who are reading this will have the same reaction of joy and hope. Where might we have heard this stuff before? It may immediately resonate with the reactionary within us, so we feel angry and say 'don't tell me what I can and what I can't do, say and think'.

If this is what is happening to you as you are reading, please allow me to remind you again that this is no finger-wagging by some scolding god or beckoning by an evil-minded creature, meaning that we do not have to defend ourselves by nursing a religion-induced persecution complex any longer either. We are here to talk from the experience of Truth we are gaining. This is a guide-book to inner peace: the more we understand what it is really trying to say, the more we will understand about ourselves and others. I repeat quite happily that I believe the entity I have called 'Karmic energy mind' likely lives on after death and is the very thing that transcends our physical life form. It also determines how we transcend, where we will be drawn to in the next life, and the one after that. It is easy for me to see and grasp the concept; it is logical to me as a conclusion of observations of all that we can see around us. I will probably also go so far as to state it is not simply a hypothesis or a belief system, to me it is a fact that will at some point in the future be proven to be true, once Science catches up. Nobody said this stuff was easy, as life shows us every day. We have infinite crazy outcomes to our actions, is that not visible? We have people shouting, screaming, beating each other up, wondering when they are going to get what they wanted. It's gone a bit awol, hasn't it. Incredibly, even that was foreseen, thousands of years ago; but how do we make sense of all this mess, we ask? Good question. Let's continue with another good question.

6. What is 'Mind'?

We are not usually aware of what our 'mind' really is, how it works and just how sensitive our minds are; how easily influenced, how easily manipulated into thinking and behaving in certain ways. We confuse our brain with our mind and use the terms interchangeably. When we speak of 'mind' we usually point to our heads, indicating that our mind lives somewhere in our brain. But do we ever question what is actually meant by 'mind'? Where is our 'mind'? Where does it live in our body, and how can we sometimes lose it if it is not a physical thing?

In this book, the term 'mind' is given a different definition than our usual colloquial one, or even the one in the Oxford Dictionary. It is not because of personal choice, but rather one of the most tangible differences in Western and Eastern philosophy. In the West, the term is used more for describing our individual intellect and brain activity, but in the Eastern philosophies' definition, mind means so much more. It refers to the intangible Karmic energy field that lives within, around and beyond us. It is not synonymous with or limited to a physical brain or our intellect alone. Mind is infinitely more complex, so much so that many definitions fail to really give an interpretation of what it is and what it is capable of, with the result that we have probably not even given it much thought up until now.

In the context of talking about Karma particularly, the term 'mind' includes its connection to our 'Karmic energy mind'. Both terms are therefore used in this book to describe the same phenomenon. If we haven't ever before thought about the connection of our mind to our Karmic presence, then we are not alone. However, it would serve us well to find out more, because there are repercussions to the fact that we do not really know what the nature of mind truly is, what it is capable of and how to use it properly to help ourselves and others. If we are unaware of its power, it is also easier for us to be manipulated and taken advantage of.

If we think that this does not apply to us or it's not something we are concerned about, here are some examples of where the nature of our mind is used in order to manipulate a certain outcome. Observe how, on a daily basis, we unwittingly follow others without questioning - in our routine behaviour, our work environment, our belief systems, in the way we interpret occurrences around us. Similarly, we have certain die-hard habits that do not change as long as we are following a rigid mindset, and at times we even find we take on what others may want us to believe at any point in our lives. Whether this is through friends or family, or remotely and subconsciously by people we have never met, who set up systems which do not work for us. How can it be that we are so easily manipulated into a certain way of thinking and acting?

Let's try to find an answer to that question by firstly posing another, maybe slightly odd question: Have you ever had the opportunity to observe Mentalists performing tricks of the mind, especially when they are working with random people chosen from the audience? Perhaps you have, on TV or even live. Even if we do know the tricks behind the 'Magic', our brains cannot easily perceive or process the procedure and we therefore cannot resist the deception. The trick relies on the fact that we end up believing only the messages our senses send to our brains, and because of this, we are easily taken in, even if we are aware that we have just observed something that is not true. Added to that, we develop a sort of Stockholm syndrome reaction: we react by positively loving being fooled! Our brain just needs it simple and wants to rely on our senses, it is limited to processing what we see, hear and feel. How astonishing it is then to find out that things are not as they seem, but rather than applying logic to find out more information, we often paradoxically prefer to get stuck in the illusion of how things did not at all turn out the way we were led to believe. As we have all had this experience of not knowing better since childhood, the thought of being 'wrong' can also run deeply connected with less enjoyable emotions such as shame, inadequacy, embarrassment, fear and resentment. Yet again, our brain decides that we want to avoid feeling like that if we can at all help it, in case we start off on a downward spiral that could be dangerous for us. It tries to keep us safe. However, this is something others may capitalise on and if you look around, I am sure you already know that you will find lots of external enterprises that try to make fools of us. The tricks are not limited to illusionists. Just as an example, observe what politicians do when it's voting time. We hope there will be a change and we believe the promises every single time, however, we do secretly know that whoever gets voted, we will be the ones at the rough end of the stick and things will be the same again after the show. It is designed that way, and it works every time. It relies on us not making a different choice based on logic and actively wanting to see through the illusions. It also relies on us not wanting to leave our habitual thinking, but most of all, on us not noticing that we are handing over a part of our precious mind for someone else to handle on our behalf. When we then become the weakest link, and are chastised and scolded for it, too, the illusion becomes watertight. Added to the fact that when you keep pressure on so that people feel stressed, then our inner fun emoticon quickly turns into that expressing a much more sobering state of anxiety. We are much less likely to have the strength to fight back at this stage. It's easy to see how the whole scenario is already in place all over the world, which becomes a matter of life and death for many when a whole society chooses to not look behind the deception en masse. Our brain's reaction at this late stage is that we start to pass the buck amongst each other, because even then, we believe that one of us must be at fault when we are told that's just how we wanted things to be. And lo and behold, that someone at fault is usually the weakest link in the chain, refugees maybe, from some country with a language or religion we don't understand. Someone so different from us that it is all too transparent we are trying to blame our siblings for breaking a toy.

On hearing a loud, distracting noise outside my house whilst writing this, I thought I would use this as an example of how our brains work together with our bodies, to explain why we think we are when we are not. I heard the noise – which means that my sense of hearing picked it up. Another time, it may have been one of my other five senses. The impulse of the sound vibration is passed on to three small bones in my ear, and on to the inner ear where nerve cells carry the sound signal to my brain as electrical impulses. My brain then compares the vibration without delay, to a kind of filing system it keeps on pretty much everything it has experienced so far, including similar sound vibrations to the one it just picked up. It may be successful in finding the sound signal in its filing system that match the vibration, or it may not. It quickly narrows down, assesses, compares, and tries to identify what the sound could be, all in a split second. It can only ever identify the sound it has had an experience of before. In my case, my brain told me it must be a car alarm. If my brain never had an experience of a car alarm before, it will not know what it is and it will not know how to interpret it. It will give me an impression of what it sounds like, but not exactly know what it is, a bit like the Myth of the Invisible Ships. My brain might even go so far as to prompt me to get up and investigate, to make sure I am safe.

A brain is able to sense and identify an electric impulse such as sound, so that the 'I' can then make a decision on what to do with that information. Whilst this can be a life-saving trigger-based chain reaction, it is also where it can often go horribly wrong – all because the 'I' has a choice as to what to do about it. The 'I' can choose to ignore it and allow to let it affect 'me' if it sees no threat or harm in it. This is an ingenious system that we rely on for our every decision. But there is a downfall. It can easily be compromised if someone sets out to do so.

Coming back to my own example, as my brain has just interpreted the sound to be most likely a car alarm, I then also try to 'see' the car in my mind's eye, and even make up a whole story about why it is sounding off, whose car it may be, where it is located, what the car looks like, colour, make etc., whether I know it, how long the alarm might continue etc. In short, without even noticing, I have fully reacted to the sound, got majorly distracted from my task and spent minutes speculating, perhaps even getting agitated as a result of the continuing sound. By now, you are probably with me on this, imagining it, too, as it's such an annoying sound, is it not? But whilst my brain has merely interpreted it and given me information, 'I' have chosen to react. And then, one thing leading to another, I will react some more, now that I have decided that I know exactly what is going on. Even though I can still only hear the alarm, and I have no further information about what is going on, it is all happening in my very own mind – it's all an 'inside job', so to speak, as a very dear teacher of mine once said. But it does not stop there. I also get secondary reactions, based on interpreting that the sound is probably going to last quite a while, and I react to this speculation of my own speculation with annoyance, distraction, discontent. I grumble, I get up, I am disturbed from my work, I cannot concentrate, I may even go as far as unlock the front door and look out down the road to see what is going on and be off on a complete tangent. I have let my mind become disturbed by my brain and I am marginally out of control. My next choice is to now blame the car alarm, an inanimate object, for everything that I have just chosen to do, say and think. By now, I even have a clear picture of the person who set it off, I know exactly what I would say to them – and on and on it goes in my head.

Does it ring a bell, literally? This is just a simple example of what happens within us, all the time. Can you count how many times this might happen in a day? Does it drive you mad just thinking about it? Not once does it occur to me that the flaw might be within the short circuit in my brain; that we might even be able to change our brainwaves in order to cope with situations in a different way that keeps us slightly more sane. We can only wonder why we have created so many disturbances to our peace of mind in the first place, but of course, with so many distractions we have become insensitive to our own selves and the functions within our bodies. We have identified with our surroundings so much by now and not least with the immediate interpretations of our bodies and brains, too. We have become less adept at looking after our mental health, not realising how badly we can be affected, how easily distracted, and how sensitive our system really is. We seem to allow it to be abused on a daily basis and are overreacting to the overstimulation we subject ourselves to. Another thing that has happened without us noticing is that, when the 'I' reacts, and we had a split second to delay the reaction to wonder if we can exercise our choice not to, we did not realise that others are well ahead of us and have already examined this repercussion on all that we do. In a world that is full of triggers by now, we end up mighty confused as to who we thing we are, what we believe we need, and the discrepancy between this and how our lives actually turn out. Do we really want to be like this, at the mercy of others who take advantage?

Or do we want to protect our Self more than ever against increasingly zany input from an ever-more insane, 'modernised', technological world? I know we think we do, give me more you say, Netflix and all. But that's not the real 'Self', far from it. The real 'Self' is far, far more fascinating than anything on a flat screen.

The solution - if we are even ready to contemplate it - can only be that we need exercises and environments to support our bodies & brains becoming strong and healthy again, able to keep the 'I' independent so that it has the all-important choice of governing the decision-making process, so it cannot so easily be compromised. Perhaps I am clutching at straws, though. Perhaps we will not be able to snatch back our sovereignty quite so easily. AI is so far advanced already that by hooking up specialised computers to brain synopses can move machinery on our behalf. That's useful in medicine, but it can also be a terrifying prospect in the wrong hands.

There is a much simpler solution. Quietening our thoughts again, so that we can come back to our pure Karmic energy minds to make us happy again, rather than just binging on one consumer choice click after another. This does not happen easily within the world we have chosen to live in, that much is clear. It cannot happen in many of the situations we are already deeply embroiled in either. This world we co-created could literally be killing us – as it is already killing so many species we seem to have no power to conserve. Subtle radiation is disturbing our energy fields, pollution, electronic gadgets and gismos cause adverse frequencies, toxic materials, housing and work places are all slowly destroying our ability to use our ability to determine what is good for us, never mind who we truly are without it. By now, we have withdrawal symptoms when we are not triggered into a reaction of some shiny object in front of us. Our brains are more confused than ever, our bodies are becoming sick, and signals are unclear and getting lost in translation in the perma-stress of survival mode. In addition, there is an incessant noise level that we even CHOOSE to surround ourselves with, because we are afraid of finding out how afraid we are when it is silent. However, our mind is not just our brain. We have more than that within us to stop all this illusionary nonsense. Our mind is where the real miracle is, and miracles happen every moment of the day. Your mind is so much more complex and intricate than we could ever perceive with just our five senses. How can we understand what our Karmic energy mind is, or how miraculous life is, if we weren't even taught how to understand our minds! We talk about being 'out of our minds' when we simply mean to say we have lost our instruction manual for connecting to our higher purpose.

In order to understand the difference between the processes of the brain and the mind better, observe the likes if you will, of any mentalist or illusionist and their choice of words, when they manage to hypnotise a whole audience - including the TV audience at home - into believing something they portray as real, leaving the observer without even having a conscious memory of being led into believing it. I saw many a trick of the mind on TV shows, including broadcasts not even designed to be for the purpose of leisure, where the audience is dumbfounded in having been duped, and often unable to tell what the trick is. I am quite sure we spend many of our waking days in some sort of hypnotic state by now, being submitted to manipulations of the mind wherever we go. But we don't have to talk about Magic tricks any longer: the Truth with a capital T is much more exciting and awe-inspiring than that.

Our mind is a fascinating and complex construction largely uncharted by science, physics, philosophies, mathematics and so on. Although some are on to unveiling parts of the mystery, whatever is discovered can end up in the wrong hands. I wonder why we are not being taught anything useful by the MSM these days, aren't you? We don't have to look far to observe the many who suffered and even died for their inventions and ability to see through the mysteries. I am also sure that anyone who ever entered the quest of finding out more about the elusive life force, is onto trying to figure out the connection between the power of our minds and our ability to manifest. This is the essence of the quest: how to be alive, and create the best outcome not just for ourselves, but for all living beings. It is a very simple, short sentence, but it holds all the power of initiating the quest within. It also withholds that power if anyone enters in order to manipulate it for their own gain or for any lesser motive for that matter. It is reflected in many a fictitious character, the nobility, purity and truth-finding quality that endows the hero, but we can all see that this is simply an aspect within all of us. We are all ultimately on the same quest. The universe provides for all those scenarios naturally, through the means of our Karmic energy mind.

Chances are that in some of us, an aspect of human nature arises, so that predictably, a percentage of those who come across some knowledge of the mysteries, wish to keep it to themselves, or sell it to profit from it. After all, we are limited in our three-dimensional perceptions, and really quite simple-minded in lots of ways. It's nothing new and part of the pattern of cyclic existence and suffering; everyone who is trying to uncover life's mysteries and finds some nugget of truth, seems hell-bent on doing something with it that you cannot succeed in doing in the grand scheme of life; or if we do, it doesn't make us happy. Or if it does, it makes a whole lot of other people unhappy. Do we really want to be an eternal part of that? Wait, don't answer that. I'll answer for you. No you don't, not any longer; trust me.

If we do want to see through the deceptions, surprisingly, we do not even seem to know exactly where to start, what our mind is or even where it is. Where do you locate it in your body? It is not your brain – we have already established that. But what is 'mind'? What substance is it made of? How does it work? We have to assume that there is indeed something that does not just contain our sense-based memory banks such as the brain, which regulates our physical functions and perceptions. Although it seems that, whatever it is, our physical sensations are linked to it, our thoughts can relate to it and our emotions may be governed by it. But what sets the mind apart from the brain and its functions? Is mind what carries all of the information that makes us call ourselves 'I'? The 'I' we are talking about here is that which we perceive to be a physical experience where our ego-mind combines with the glimpses we catch of our higher consciousness. Is our mind, this Karmic energy mind, much bigger than the two combined? Is it possible that our 'I' experience is just a small and temporary part of something that we inherently are? Something that is much more complex than we are currently perceiving, that we might not be conscious of the fact that it survives the aforementioned?

I have been hinting at the fact that we are usually not making full use of our mind when we simply stay in our 'ego' mind. I propose that

In an ideal and complete state of mind, where all the components of our mind are balanced and working well, even our individual 'I' has the inherent potential and ability to connect to the wisdom mind and remember everything. Universal wisdom, and the understanding of its indescribable and infinite vastness which many of us can already feel and try to explain and interpret in different ways, is where real miracles happen.

How does this work? How can we make it work? In the context of Karma, it's important to start understanding how our mind energy is inextricably linked with our Karma. Of course, I can only give you my words and analogies to try and explain one of the biggest mysteries of life, and please forgive me if my simple terminology is entirely inadequate in the light of such enormous consequences for all of us. However, I feel I must at least try to convey my take on the subject, which is that the mind is perhaps much like an infinite memory storage system similar to that of a modern computer, only much, much more complex; in fact, as I say, it is infinite. When we try to cram more and more electronic memory into the tiniest physical space, it will not work to get it to be infinite. Since the mathematical potential of anything is infinite when it is beyond physical mass, the mind is also infinite in its potential. It must also follow logically that it is weightless. I even believe that

The tiniest bit of information within the mind is stored as a type of energy vibration. It has the capacity of storing all memory of any of our experiences in every second and even pico-second in all of our lives, for endless lifetimes, past, present and future.

I believe that this endless vault of individual information results in certain thoughts and beliefs within our physical realm that is created for us as a result of our previous experience. It carries our talents as well as our shortfalls forward along a timeline created by its own merit from day to day, year to year, lifetime to lifetime, evolving as we carry on existing. It also has the ability to 'change its mind' in an instant when a new impulse arises, adding different nuances to our Karmic energy frequencies as we learn through experiences on our journey.

You see, I think we have just not been thinking big enough; endless enough. Our individual, relatively short time-lines, which look understandably very linear from our perspective of limited brain space, are really just the tiniest, tiniest sections of an infinite and curved experience of a vortex, the spiral motion of existence. This interpretation really has fascinating implications, and the potential of bringing ancient philosophies, individual experiences and modern science all together. That's because we all have something in common: we, by default, all work with the same phenomenon that underlies our physical existence: the infinite mind.

I believe that our Karmic energy mind within, between and around the myriad of atoms that form our physical bodies, is perfectly able to be one with the amorphous energy field of the infinite universe. I believe that it understands it perfectly because it can be one and the same. We can all tune into this ultimate memory frequency if we learn and know how to. Why, atoms themselves are nothing but vibrating energy, particles and wavelengths are the same, and any outcome is possible as we already know according to Heisenberg's discovery in the 1920, and the Newtonian idea of a solid nucleus is so 1900's. Only now are we starting to incorporate these principles into modern technology, but wait - if we already ARE this, do we need to buy it? We already have the ability to 'download' memory, some from our own timeline, some from ancestors, and some from Karmic energy fields far, far away. It might be a much more important quest to find out who we are and where we belong on our timeline, rather than spending time buying the latest gadget we will get fed up with sooner or later. The funny thing is, if we knew how to transmit energy between us and had practised the technique enough, I would not have to write this on a computer for you to download and read it. The universe really does have a sense of humour, and i also predict that we will be doing this in the not so distant future.

The experience of tuning into the vast energy field and its Truth, whilst bringing much knowledge to us which can then be further interpreted, is, by nature, truly blissful and transcends any physical limitation. It plays a role in many healing processes that cannot otherwise be explained by the science of physics and allopathic medicine. We are all keepers of the mysteries by default, because we are an inextricable element of it. We are not separate and never were.

❋ ❋ ❋

7. A Brief Digression into Darwin's Evolution Theory...

I personally also believe that the electromagnetic vibrational memory storage system that we have called 'Karmic energy mind' so far, links in with every part of our cellular structure and our DNA. In fact, I believe it has created it, it continues to feed into it, and it can change its structure again at any time according to the circumstances we find ourselves in and the choices we make. It has created the 'I' throughout our own personal timeline over lifetimes, as well as being reflected in the great evolution of all life forms in this universe and others. I always thought that Darwin had a point with his revolutionary evolution theory of natural selection. Although many religions disagree, I believe that he saw a part of the greater principle of how life is formed, in progress. Perhaps the reason his theories were not acceptable to some, is because of what people have done with their interpretations of them, in lack of seeing the bigger picture. I have had my own ideas when studying his writings and artwork. I feel that he stopped short of publishing one but crucial step, and that is the introduction of the concept of reincarnation and the process that occurs when an individual life form leaves its physical body and merges again with the greater Karmic energy field. We have already learned about the survival of the individual energy memory past physical existence, by what we have already called here to be 'mind' or 'Karmic energy mind'.

I wonder if Darwin was influenced heavily by the limited beliefs of his time, the immense influence of the churches and the hold they had, on the people of his time, on his research, on his personal status? Could it be that he found a connection, but that there was a reason why he did not indicate such a connection? Could it be that in his time, it would not have been possible to publish a theorem on a higher instance than the churches of the time would allow, since it would question those in power and their interpretation of a God who created all? Could he have gotten away with talking about Karma, a formless entity within and beyond ourselves, rather than the interpretation that ruled - and still rules - some of this world now? The figurative incarnation of a bearded white man who performed miracles and also came back to life after three days? I am in no way being blasphemous or trying to ridicule any existing religious orientation. I am asking the question whether It is possible that this is why science had no choice but to omit certain theories, and still does to this day. It seems a shame in this day and age where everything can potentially co-exist, we still fall for the illusion that religions need to fight each other. All religions speak truth, and all arise from the same Truth.

I am fully aware that this very book could be interpreted to be heretic by some. After all, I am talking about a nameless energy and its reunion with the vast potential of the universal mind after physical death. It seems perfectly logical to me, but it might be an insult to some, although it is certainly not meant that way. Will people like me have disappeared because of their beliefs, because us mere mortals - men, women and children, could become elevated creatures with the potential to be at one with the greatest energy that we are capable of being at any stage? Will we still be persecuted and decimated because we will not please the 'powers that be', when they will no longer be able to profit from our aliveness once we are able to comprehend who we are, what we are capable of and finally all learn to tune into this, our Truth? Will the principles described in this very book become hidden and remain a secret, will they be ridiculed or benefit only a fringe few who can afford to read it? Or will it fall short in many ways, because the ideas I am expressing aren't even revolutionary or scientific or practical or believable enough, for some? We have all the resources in the world we need right now to make this planet great again. Why is there not equal distribution of at least basic resources to everyone on Earth, in this age where we can have everything? It's meant as a sincere question, not as an accusation. I really want to know: Is it because we have not quite truly understood what we are all capable of doing and stepped into our own power to manifest? Is this phenomenon itself connected to our evolutionary Karma? Or is there a force working against us, trying to hold us back? Poor old Darwin, getting all the bad press. The world is full of those who are profiting from marketing the real secret and keeping it elite, and here we are, giving the game away.

Going back to Darwin and his theories, which I have fond memories being taught in A-level Biology at school, he explained by the term 'mutation' how vast the power and creativity of the infinite mind was, although that might be just my interpretation. I am not sure he deliberately chose to put it that way. My further investigations into the workings of Karma lead me to believe that 'mutations', rather than random genetic occurrences, could have come about because a life-form was inherently capable of bringing about a further, improved or 'adapted' potential life-form through its Karmic energy mind that reincarnated into the next life-form. The theory of mutation, however, is based on chance; that it only occurs as a random one-in-a-million genetic difference which has no intention or purpose. It just happens as a natural occurring change in our genetic coding and it so happens that, as a result, a percentage of mutated beings would have a better chance at survival because of it.

My suggestion is that if it is true that an infinitely vast omnipresence exists which holds all information ever recorded in all life forms, it would automatically have the capability to assist an individual's Karmic energy body to incarnate into a new physical existence according to each beings' Karma, as they are made of the same energy. Not only this, it may well be the unmanifest presence of existence itself that creates all that is. It may not be random a selection at all, as Darwin suggested. However, could this not indeed fit in quite easily with Darwin's theory? In any individual being's state of perceiving infinite wisdom post-death but prior to their next reincarnation whilst still connected to the greater mind, could this infinite 'energy mind' combined with the Karmic memory of an individual being actually *influence* its new body to some extent, and bring with it a slightly different, slightly improved, slightly advantageous one that might excel others' bodies? Would this theory not make 'mutations' totally credible as a natural part of the history of evolution, and somehow much less questionable or surprising? The fact that it does not happen very often does not count against the theory. It could be explained by reasons that only a fraction of alive beings are aware of and aligned enough to consciously bring about a new outcome by raising their Karmic vibration whilst on Earth. Perhaps this is less so if beings are in non-human form due, although many people believe that animals have their own Karma and create along a timeline just as we do. Who are we to say that animals are not better, quicker and more efficient at incarnating in higher life-forms than we are, but it is said that they suffer more because they cannot communicate or do things that humans can. Neither, I believe, do they create half as much bad Karma as humans do, so we best not jump to conclusions. It may well explain the immense time span that it can take for a new species to arise, but it would be fascinating to think that because we are able to take our Karmic awareness beyond physical existence, there is a possibility that this awareness can potentially also bring the necessary changes we need in order to survive in the next life.

We have touched on how little time we are spending on practising the real art of creating miracles by transmuting our energy mind in life, never mind the afterlife. Interesting though the subject matter is to speculate, I would probably have to write another book on how Karma and reincarnation may be influencing each and every one of our individual steps of evolution specifically, as well as that of life on Earth in general. My intention here though, is simply to nudge our over-worked thinking brains into a different direction, perhaps even breaking out and start living outside the box. I am doing this with confidence because as you probably realised, I am not the first to do so. There are already much finer minds who have done this before, and many sacred scriptures exist, depicting quite clearly the existence of a greater mind as described above, including all concepts of rebirth and reincarnation. It's not that new, it's ancient news written and painted on papyrus and vellum, walls and rock faces. What I am trying to do here is to bring this knowledge into a new context, easier to understand for our modern ways of life, and to make a difference to our lives of limited perception. What awaits is an amazing outcome capable of experiencing peace, fulfilment and love on a much grander scale.

✳ ✳ ✳

8. An Even Shorter Digression into Quantum Mechanics

Our cells resonate and vibrate on certain frequency levels. To simplify, cells are a magically orderly accumulation of large amounts of vibrating atoms consisting of a charged nucleus made up of protons and neutrons surrounded by spinning electrons. Cells within an organism have developed certain interdependent and co-operating functions developed over aeons of time, following laws and universal principles. Whilst it is certainly impressive how enormous an organism can grow simply from an accumulation of cells, looking at life from a sub-atomic angle, we can hardly even talk about physical matter. There is no solid nucleus, for example. There is an electromagnetic relationship between vibrating particles, some form of electromagnetic tension that allows the nucleus to interact with the electrons spinning or oscillating around it, with lots of empty space in between. Even this 'tension' is subject to fluctuating laws that make us feel out of our depth, as we cannot really grasp this concept with our intellect. The Heisenberg principle we already briefly touched on above explains just such a concept, by which the components of an atom react differently when being observed and have different outcomes in different surroundings. To add to the confusion, we now also know that on this unimaginably minute level, particles can be in two places at once. Fancy the path of atomic particles or wavelengths changing as soon as they are being observed, and several reality outcomes existing at once. Science has had to introduce new laws and equations to explain the phenomena they observed, and new theories arise all the time, such as quantum physics, string theory, quantum mechanics and quantum field theory to explain phenomena we could previously not perceive.

What we can stipulate is that it is this very same energy, subject to universal laws, that we have been talking about which is making these particles spin and vibrate; this is what gives it life, although many different molecules have to co-ordinate their vibrations in certain patterns to be able to form life. Basically, that is how elements are formed, and from the elements arise various chemicals and compounds that continue to adhere together and start to spin in a certain pattern close to or around each other. The vibrating frequencies that eventually form cells and living structures carry on doing this until the energy subsides at some point, according to laws of physics but also laws of Karma, a sort of pre-determined disposition if you like. Physical manifestations of energy within the cellular structure of a living being, from what we know on this planet at least, appear to be subject to a shelf-life, a time-line which can and does expire; a process which is observed by us as individual life-spans, and for certain phases of which we have names like 'ageing' and 'death'. What we cannot easily see is that at one of the most confusing but profound points, the moment of death, the energy that had just moments before been tied up in all parts of the physical body, is set free. In that instant, it changes to another state of existence beyond the phys-ical. Because it happens to every part of the body in turn, this may well be what we perceive to be present as a 'spirit' or 'soul' or 'essence'. Some people are sensitive to energies and can feel it, but most of us are not trained to 'see' this transformation easily, if at all. This transformational process of the energy leaving the cells can take several weeks to com-plete. But as we cannot easily see it and very often, the moment where this process is initiated is in a clinical environment, a result, in the West we treat it very differently to some cultures in the East. We almost al-ways entirely focus on the physical form left behind. Would it not be much more comforting to learn that the energy that once occupied the physical form is actually still there? Perhaps some of the pain we feel is not completely understanding that something of the being we once knew very much lives on. The Karmic energy body is set free from the confines of the physical again, to find its way to whatever is next. It is a hugely important process, one that is even celebrated in some cultures. After all, we all work hard in our physical lives, so that we may at some point be free from suffering. Would we not wish for any being to be re-leased from their limited existence, to allow them to be set free so that they may rise to the best they can possibly become? In my mind, it is a more painful process to ignore it or simply come to the conclusion that it does not exist and that this is the end of a life, forever. Whilst it cer-tainly is an end of this physical incarnation for this particular form of being which will never, ever be the same again, and for that we are very much entitled to have extremely mixed and confusing feelings, on a sub-atomic level, without us being aware, things carry on being very much alive and kicking, though. Perhaps having learned a little about quantum mechanics, we might get an idea that it is at least possible, even if it is still beyond our full comprehension. Our 'standard' physical laws of gravity of course do not apply on a sub-atomic level and ergo, nothing physical survives the moment of death. However, even those theories are, according to scientist's own observations, missing an im-portant link. They do not explain where we go. What happens to us, really? What happens to life, where is it before and after death? Who is to say we know everything, simply using our brain and five senses only? I will elaborate on these questions a bit later on. Stay tuned.

Meanwhile, until the time of its expiration, an atom will carry on doing what it does best. It will evolve to form molecules, re-inventing itself and developing further according to universal geometrical laws which again, takes some doing for us to have any insight into. Atoms will have been pulled together by electromagnetic forces subject to principles of physics & chemistry in the physical realm whilst also being governed by invisible electromagnetic blueprints based on the laws of attraction, focus and intention. Interdimensional energy patterns like, fractals, toruses, flowers of life and other sacred principles weave energy strands into beautifully intricate bodies in infinite varieties of life forms, with an apparently formless and inexplicable force driving it, simply governed by 'wanting to know itself'. Where energy strands converge from all directions and overlap myriads of times, energy points are created that shine brightly with the pure force of creative energy, forming important physical manifestations, singularities that become the corner stones for a new physical existence, a body ready to incarnate. In front of our very eyes creation, for aeons of time, has given birth to infinite physical life-forms according to Karmic law. By the focus of combining energy manifestation and intention, universal forces have merged form, matter and energy from the stages of formlessness into unlimited varieties of life across the many stages of multiple universes. Is our time here as Earthlings pre-destined and by design? Do we have unfinished business here? Or is it purely the great dance of the endless universes, re-inventing itself, life and form randomly from thin air, oscillating eternally between existence and non-existence?

If i were to try and find an answer to these questions, I would search for it in my firm belief in the energies of Karma, which means that physical manifestation arises from the focus of our Karmic energy mind. Our individual Karmic energy mind that has survived physical existence after every incarnation and carries on evolving in the after-life, becomes the driving force behind each new life-form, shaping its intrinsic converging energy patterns into dense matter again to ultimately form the miracle of a living physical body. The process can take lifetimes, or an instant. The intention, focus and power to manifest that arises from the part of any living being which we have called 'Karmic energy mind' so far, is destined to play the part of the 'drive' and consciousness behind forming energy into matter, which we may even interpret to be encompassing the 'I' (including all its higher and lower forms and experiences of 'Self'). Is it not something to consider, something that feels somehow strangely familiar? And if it is really true that this is how it works, would it not make sense that we look after our energy mind at least as well as we look after our physical bodies, to have the most auspicious outcome for our Karmic energy mind, so that it can create what we need to best exist in future? Or are we happy with our lot?

Whilst we are in physical form, this 'mind' stays more or less invisible to us, which makes it so much harder to believe it is there. All the same, it is very tangible and present, it can certainly be picked up by technology that measures electromagnetic frequencies. It is not just a gimmick; what i am saying is that this without the frequencies created by our Karmic energy mind, our physical body would not have become manifest, and we would not exist. The Karmic energy blueprint for each individual, the intention for the evolutionary process for each sentient being is so immensely complex that it is not only difficult to describe and comprehend for us, it will most likely remain a mystery to most of us. It would be a very difficult code to crack for any earthly being, since its energy patterns and components are only barely detectable by certain phenomena or, alternatively, by looking at certain outcomes over a lifetime. How could we possibly ever learn to interpret them and the 'choices' presented to us as a result, physical body and the eternal changes it undergoes included? For what reason would we want to analyse and dissect it again with our limited intellect, only to get a lesser result than its intended blissful state of mind. Perhaps you can see what i am implying - I have a feeling that some will be enthusiastic to try, but that this is not at all the point. The point is, once we know that this is how it works, we need to practice how to optimise it, and none of us need to be rocket scientists to do so. All of us can have a beautiful Karmic energy mind, because all that is needed is good Karma arising from good actions, thoughts and speech. Other than improving our Karmic energy mind by understanding the influence our actions have on our inner frequency levels, it could easily become a diversion away from learning how to create good Karma, to ask too many questions about the intricacies of creation. Some things may always continue to elude us, and being faced with this limitless terrain of trying to quantify 'infinite' I have a feeling that we may have met our master and it may simply not be ours to reason why.

Assuming then that our Karmic energy minds are detectable and defined through the outcomes they create, such as thoughts, perceptions, emotions, beliefs, physical scenarios and phenomena, perhaps our next question might be this: 'Is my Karmic energy mind really invisible?' We humans as a whole have an existential fear of having no control over our lives, or the next moment, or any outcome really. If we were given some sort of clue, would this not change everything? Would it also then not be worth looking for clues, and to not just leave it in the hands of a few, but for all of us to realise we are equally important, and equally qualified in being alive to bring our concepts to the table, constructively? As you might guess, I am hinting at something again and I am not talking major arguments on social media. Let's have a closer look at what presents itself as potential candidates of Karmic phenomena in our lives. To our untrained eye, as I already said, perhaps it is largely invisible, this 'Karmic mind'. In science, in quantum physics, it might just about exist in mathematical equations and abstract formulae. In religion, people express their faith that it exists in a variety of different terms like soul, spirit, god, or any name given to this unfathomable life force energy that we keep arguing over so Self-righteously. This abstract, incomprehensible entity is virtually impossible for our physical brains to grasp and it is no wonder that it has hence been the object of much argument and speculation by the limited capacity of our over-stretched ego-minds, which can only create duality, a 'for or against' separatist conclusion for us as a result in all walks of life. It's such a tragedy that lives are still lost as a result of us not seeing the miracles behind creation in every second of our lives, and we are too easily led by our ego minds instead to argue over each of individual validity of perception of something so vast and beautiful.

So what happened here that has made us ignore the facts of such breathtaking beauty? Why is science and so many still fruitlessly hunting for the missing link of how to connect us to being able to create life ourselves? it is my firm belief that we cannot, and will not be able to. Life creates itself. What we cannot comprehend is the infinity element of it. When faced with the seemingly incomprehensible symbol ∞ representing infinity, our brain cannot compute it. As i said before, we usually believe what our brain tells us based on sense perception, and if it cannot perceive or sense the concept of infinity, how can we believe what we are seeing? However, it is exactly that which we cannot see which is giving us the answer all the time: the ultimate Truth underlying everything in life is based on the Truth that existence is ad infinitum. Based on our ego mind perception only, we tend to automatically choose a dual system for everything, causing not just a split between spirituality and science in our society, but rather a split within anything and anyone, really. It should be a matter of interest for us, enough to want to contemplate why we think in a dual way only. Why did we choose for this, our universe, to be based on duality? Do we even have to continue believing that there is any division, or can we simply put it down to limited perception that we see everything in existence as opposites? Are there not logically infinite possibilities, endless outcomes and therefore, infinite physical places and existence, too? Is it the vastness of these concepts that we have a problem perceiving, and do we simply just need to be taught a method to perceive to feel our oneness with everything again and not our separation?

For all the beauty of the unfathomable vastness and potential of experiencing the endlessness of existence, there has also existed its opposite in our split perception of all that is limited in physical existence. Whilst co-creating our existence in the physical limitations of a binary uni-verse, we have unwittingly fallen prey to its limitations. Limited beliefs that took root in our minds developed into anxiety, poverty, fear, sick-ness and a host of physical and mental health conditions. In our despair, we tried to find answers and turned to those who we thought could be our teachers, our salvation, our ticket out of misery. Have we found them? Have they assisted us well? Or have we been led astray, or even forced to have to trust in those we trusted were our representatives and teachers? Looking at humanity's historic evolution, there are many examples of how humans have triumphed, but also had to endure tor-ture and separation, and in the many forms of external historic events we are still subjected to this day, this separation seemed to have been reinforced over centuries; the repetitiveness of these are obvious across the board, when we look at it from a bird's eye perspective; the separ-ation between ordinary life and its spiritual components through influ-ences based on Karmic consequential events became the unquestioned norm over centuries; once wars were created out of fear, and religious persecution by ways of power and control, this became a part of our lives we were in no position to question; it continues in politics, harvesting power and knowledge in elite societies to enable select individuals to amass wealth and power, ruling the belief systems of our world's society to this day. When we look at this separation beyond the guise of calling it a democracy, it is horrendous to witness that it still results in the genocide of whole cultures on every single continent, with a devastat-ing Karmic effect of new generations of humankind continuously being born into situations of fear and loss, into a chain of creating more fear and loss as a result.

Nevertheless, as was prophesied thousands of years ago, some philoso-phies thankfully managed to stay intact up to now, despite the prosecu-tion of so many people, their cultures and tribes over centuries. We have not given up hope that there is more to life than just the greed that pre-sents itself. Many of the secret teachings that were hidden are becom-ing more openly available to those who are ready to search with their eyes wide open. Teachings exist which incorporate the examination of the vast potential of our mind in order to find a way of understanding the meaning of life and apply those methods in practical ways to form the basis for a happier lifestyle. A separation of mind and body did not occur in all parts of the world or to everyone, despite infiltrations by a variety of aggressors throughout many centuries; although this is surprisingly still very much in danger of happening on an even larger scale. As the planet is becoming more knowledgeable through world-wide communication, information can still be sent with the intent to save lives, or the opposite. By the same ways that we try to form com-munities and hope for peace, there are still those whose Karmic path is one of instilling fear, a misguided few trying to gain power and control over many others. This is, however, once again a subject for yet another book and I am deliberately choosing not to go into the subject too much further here. Suffice to say that, having experienced this historic separation, we must become aware of these flaws we inevitably inherited, and try to overcome their potentially devastating consequences on our minds. We must find the space within where we are whole and find our path of unity again on this Earth. We would not do well to carry on choosing the notion of being separate that is not ours inherently, as it would mean continuing a downward spiral of control that others chose for us, leading to destruction of ourselves and our surroundings faster than we think. Those who are awakening are choosing to remember our destiny and true nature, and they are trying to reclaim the miracle of our true minds; we are all together on an inner quest to find it again and reconnect to our spirits, our ancestors, fellow humans, the universe, its wisdom, compassion and endless vastness of potential.

In pockets around the world where holistically orientated environments and communities practice and learn, people have been actively involved in reconnecting with their Karmic mind as an important part to consider within ourselves, as it was in ancient times. The Karmic energy mind, as I have called it here throughout this book, has taken on many different words, but it describes the energy that exist throughout all of our lifetimes, as I have said before. The process by which it is channelled into our physical body is through an electromagnetic energy network flowing within hundreds of thousands of minuscule meridian channels in and around our cellular structure, linking up with our vital physical organs, enabling their existence and functions. The energy charging through these electromagnetic chains in turn links together a real and tangible energy field within and around every sentient being. This energy field is often described as an aura, but I would say it 'has' an aura. I am aware that this definition is not to everyone's liking, and it is often dismissed as humbug without scientific backing, but please humour me.

If we examine what we have learned so far, do not most of the above, most scientific theories, holistic angles and religions, too, have something in common? A belief that something like an inner memory-bank other than our brain must exist beyond our physical existence? An inter-connected, all-knowing mind, perhaps even? Maybe it's just that we have interpreted and compartmentalised this knowing mind into smaller sections to suit our own individual ways, because the whole Truth is just so vast that it is incomprehensible for almost all of us? Maybe we have just used different 'filing systems' in our brains to explain the same phenomenon. Is it worth fighting wars over? Why do we not look for the common denominator? We all seem to know deep within that something is out there – or to be more precise – in here, within us.

I believe it may be that this is our individual 'Karmic energy mind' that survives death, and stores within it the information that is usually contained inside and around a physical being. At this point, most of us have our own beliefs and theories as to what happens next, based on our individual Karmic experiences, which is perfectly ok. I don't intend to change this at all or contest it. I am simply stating my own opinion: It is my theorem that this mind then becomes a determining factor for another incarnation, which, when the time is right and subject to all the stored memory of that 'mind' and its levels of realisation and completion, will become a physical experience once more. Various religions obviously disagree, others describe very similar beliefs and just call 'mind' by a different name. In my mind, if you pardon the pun, we are all talking about the same thing, and I am very at peace knowing that everyone is entitled to their own interpretation of the same phenomenon. I will admit that I have added to the confusion a little bit by bringing in my own creative terms for the Karmic energy that prevails, simply because I felt that, because Karma applies to all situations in our aliveness, it will also have its own energy as it filters down into these different sections in our lives. You will therefore find several different combinations of the term 'Karmic', and by this is simply implied its appearance in all aspects of our existence.

I also feel very at ease with the opposite of filtering down into tiny individual increments and components in our lives. My next proposition is that the electromagnetic vibrational energy we have discovered to be present within atoms that make us 'us', is the very same vibrational energy that ultimately creates everything else in this universe, too. It seems logical to me that its nature is identical. It has the same potential to create and become, according to certain interdependent circumstances. It is only due to our separate individual experience in our own Karmic history, our own Karmic evolution stored in our minds, that this energy has formed itself with the help - or should I say, sometimes hindrance - of the direction our bodiless 'floating' Karmic memory minds have taken into the separate beings we are right now, into this specific, individual lifetime. We have been before, albeit in a different way, and we will be again, different once more. Our Karmic memory is the pioneer of this great mind, and it has determined that we shall be in a separate body once more, for better or for worse. It does not mean that this has to be a bad thing. It is inherently full of potential. And it is down to our Karmic memory what will become of us, in our Karmic body hulls, in this one lifetime in this one body – one, of many.

We are so much more than we think. 'I think, therefore I am', deducted French Philosopher Descartes. My ironic remake of the famous quote inevitably is:' I think, therefore I am not'. The reason being that, whilst we are on Earth, our perception of who we are really is limited by our blinkered belief system. We think too much and we forget who we really are. Our Karmic body chose for us to be Earth-bound, become subject to the laws of gravity, and limited to one individual body, despite the vast amount of life forms possible here on Earth. Most of us have to limit ourselves to a physical body to be here to 'fit' the relatively low vibration and density of 3-dimensional existence here on Earth. Every physical life-form on Earth has to conform to the laws of physics whether we like it or not; that is, to the 3-dimensional star-tetrahedron geometrical shape that underlies the atomic structure of every being on this planet. Our 'higher' minds know this, but our ordinary ego mind can hardly ever remember being anything else, once we have become a human body. We, or rather, the ego mind we identify with, have largely forgotten our origins, and how to access the memory of our Karmic energy bodies. Our 'higher' minds will try to remind many of us every so often that there is more to us than merely a physical body, at certain times of our lives where we are more perceptive than others. It will depend on our Karmic beliefs to see if our ego-minds pay any attention or not, or whether we can finally incorporate the wisdom of who we truly are into our life's mission.

Of course, for aeons of time we have been evolving, getting closer and closer to the Truth, sometimes in very convoluted ways.

9. Inside the Karmic Mind

One question that is surely on all our minds by now is how the Karmic mind stores something infinitely complex as to the complete memories of all events that have ever taken place in every one of our lifetimes.

As mentioned before, I am sure that some of the answers lie in the complexity of the electromagnetic impulses not only running through, around and beyond every atom of our body, but surviving and evolving even after our physical demise. All the information that we have gathered as a being remains as an encoded energy 'cloud', even if the physical body ceases to exist. It would already have existed as part of our personal evolvement for an indefinite time before our current existence, and will continue to exist and evolve indefinitely beyond this current lifetime. When we are in physical form, the amorphous energy cloud that incarnates as 'you' and 'I' converges to apply these impulses to enable us to become a physical being. The infinitesimally small components of energy information is transmitted by means of the frequency coding they have adapted at every moment in time, creating not only the life-form itself, but also infusing it again with the fully intact memory of each of our personal timeline. Even if we do not know how to access all the information, it is there to assist us indefinitely and even obtain conscious clarity from, once we are knowledgeable enough. This is, as I also mentioned before, understandably a nigh impossible concept for us to perceive, simply because we do not have a brain competent enough to compute the information of it. All the same, the question we must ask should not be, 'how does it store everything', but rather, 'how does it store so little for each of us in such a separate, individual way that we barely ever have insight into who we are and where we came from'. Since it has such a vast memory potential as to hold the creation of the universes and all that is, forever more, why are we having an experience of our own individual timeline only? The answer is simple and yet impossibly complex, partly because we are dealing with the vast, unfathomable, endless power of creation that simply 'is'. So why are we apart from it, and how come are we a part of it?

We are currently visibly and definably human, so we all have something in common, other than all wanting to be happy: Does it not seem strange that we are all experiencing a separateness in individual bodies, all at the same time? If we all have this Karmic truth in common, a

belief on some deep level that has made us become temporarily disconnected from the 'all that is' and become a living, breathing 3-d individual, is that good or bad? Or is it all simply Truth in whatever form it is
experiencing itself, at any moment of time? What is our purpose? How
did this happen?

The Karmic mind is likely to be some sort of 'code' that occurs naturally in the electromagnetic frequencies present within the body. The
frequencies transmute into the Karmic energy body which survives
physical experience after 'death'. Since these frequencies and how they
might rearrange and evolve during their existence in the afterlife determine what our next experience is, we are by nature a process that
is in flux from moment to moment. If at some point we have awoken
to the fact that we are not separate from anything that is the stuff of
existence, this will influence our future being. If we are fearful of the
fact, and fear having to solve yet another puzzle piece of the Karmic
energy system, it will remain there and influence our future experience
until we have solved the riddle of fear. Only when we are in neutral gear
about all experience here and beyond, things change. It does not mean
that we do not care, and it will by no means turn us into robots; far from
it and quite the opposite. It will simply allow us to transcend our current and often heavy beliefs about how things must be in 3-d, and once
we have mastered the skill, our Karmic timeline can move forward
accordingly. It's like we are currently encountering so many inner road
blocks, that we cannot yet see the clear road ahead or rather, the clear
pathways within.
Human beings have been inspired to invent so many words, written so
many books, created art about the space that is simply 'being', the place
beyond words, pure existence, the realm of emptiness where there are
no phenomena, but the extent of what this is escapes most of us in every
way in every day life. We might catch glimpses, and accomplished ones
incorporate the bliss in those moments into their existence on Earth. So
what we can do is to return from those moments of vision, not escape
from life but to learn to nourish it, cherish it, and most importantly,
realise that we are here to make a vow to help others experience the
bliss of knowing, too, from that moment on.

You may have noticed I am stating my own theories here, my own
findings and musings about the mysteries of life and its connections
to our sub-atomic structure as I go along. The fact that scientific investigations based on knowledge and brain power are also trying to solve
the mysteries of life and its underlying connectivity encourages me to
make up my own mind based on intuition, experiences within myself,
gathering information from ancestral wisdom, ancient scriptures and
within spiritual networks as well as through meditation, and I encour-

age everyone to find facts and do their own more intricate research. Question everything.

We are slowly gaining more understanding the importance of knowing that energy flows through our body and some or all of it is of electromagnetic nature. Each atom vibrates at certain rates determined by an incredibly complex yet immediately transferable coding, which in turn is created by our Karmic memory based on external Karmic incidences as well as experiences within the body and mind. Each of these resulting constant changes to our sub-atomic memory structures have an effect on our Karmic energy body and change its frequency, sometimes locally and subtly, sometimes affecting whole areas at once or even our whole energy body in turn.

This is one of the reasons why I feel it is important to form a bridge between all-encompassing general philosophising and active actual advice to aid our intricate personal interpretation. The process I just described above is no different to what occurs when we are creating Karma for and within ourselves. When our energy levels are disturbed, our frequency will alter. When we are able to increase our energy frequency, this will have a positive effect. If it stays the same, it means that no effect has been made on our current situation. Whether no change is good or bad depends on how much time we think we have, and how many times we want to repeat the same scenario. We might be missing our on our own personal growth evolving. Our Karmic energy vibration is the blueprint for what happens next. Whatever complexity it has taken into itself, will become a part of its future manifestation. The vibration that each nucleus, each cluster of energy at the centre of an atom creates, allows a spinning motion of particles to surround it in such a way that a unique tension and bond is formed. This in turn means that groups of atoms can attract or repel each other, build molecules to form elements, and groups of molecules to form living compounds and structures. Elements vibrate and fuse and become the building blocks of everything on Earth and in this universe; and in between vibration is vast space.

It should naturally follow that it could all be up to us. Everything that is continually created within us, based on what we already chose to do, say and think, however long ago, either helps us connect up all the dots within our Karmic reconciliation, or is still blocking us; of course, some of what happened to us in some cases was probably not very nice, so it makes it hard to differentiate what was chosen for us, whether we benefited or not, what conclusions to draw from it, and how to recover from it, to put it mildly. We may never find the answer, but it is still in our power to choose what we do about it right now, how to find ways and methods to neutralise any suffering and its influence on what will be. Is it better to know what happened than not, so that we find ways to recover and methods to not repeat unhelpful patterns? The good, the bad and the ugly timeline that is created in this way only exists because our Karmic energy has altered according to past influences that have created it, consciously or not. The timeline we have as a result becomes our perception of 'us' and our life around us; we believe in it, identify with it, treat it as if it were unchangeable as we inherently own it and were stuck with it. In reality, it is based on interdependent origination and constantly changing elements. It was created by our Karmic energy, and it can change again, once we know how to handle our Karmic energy. Whatever it is that we call our individual accumulation of Karmic energy history has created it, and we are completely enabled to change it if we do not like it, subject to the laws of Karma.

The conclusion we could draw from this is monumental: we can change our own Karmic energy, which in turn makes peace with our historic timeline, and creates a different outcome in our future. Isn't that what we are all looking for, to be released from suffering? If this is true, then we would all be able to lead better lives, and we would all be better off. In order to find methods of changing the outcome, it might be really useful to start by having a sense of awe and respect for the process, for ourselves and others, and to look after ourselves and others, in order to find ways of unravelling the knot. I am not sure what we are waiting for.

* * *

10. Our Energy Body and the Creation of Karma

Isn't it strange that we only seem to have a relatively small number of elements on Earth? As it stands, there are currently 118 listed elements so far found on Earth, at the time of writing this book. Molecules created by fusion of these elements forms the basis for physical life on Earth. Does this mean that there were only a limited variety of different energy vibrations physically available in the first place to form a limited amount of these atoms? Is this limited amount of atoms somehow related to the limited visible spectrum of electromagnetic radiation measurable in hertz, manifestations of which apparently only exist in a physical world? And if this is true, could there be other places/universes/dimensions based on a much larger spectrum or other atomic or non-atomic structures? Are we not perceiving other elements because we lack in our ability to perceive beyond our spectrum perception, and does this become a vicious cycle? As long as we are in our physical realm, we cannot see them, and because we cannot see them, we believe they are not there? If we assume that our physical world is limited in such a way, then logically it must follow that elsewhere, possibilities of other varieties and combinations could be potentially unlimited and infinitely large; they may not present themselves in physical, never mind visible, form. It is almost like we speak one language limited to one country only, one example of many perhaps, in terms of what we have created and keep defending with our molecular structure based on 3-dimensional concepts only. Within our ordinary minds' structure, we are often struggling to admit that other countries and their inhabitants are also a part of and of consequence to our lives, are we not? Are our brains, our ego-minds, able to understand, much less accept that there might be life elsewhere, even that other universes may exist? As our planet becomes more and more pressed to stay balanced in our presence, can we afford not to learn more about who we are, and what goes on with our Karmic mind?

As we learned, in order to keep a being alive, the energy that was formed within every vital atom must be continuously channelled and fed through the indispensable cellular structures and vital organs within any living thing, every second of the day. (Remember that it does this inherently, without our conscious prompting) In order for this enormous enterprise to happen, energy flows through a living body within a unique phenomenon still largely ignored in Western understanding of life. Resembling an enormously complex system of channels, orbs, pools, clouds, lines and vortexes entering and leaving every single body every second of its living, breathing, complex life-form, it's hard to comprehend that aeons ago, we were all born from a singularity.

Without these vibrational charged fields, particles and channels, energy could not be exchanged, renewed and passed on, and our body would simply collapse and no longer function. Similar to the fact that most of us would die without water, our bodies would also simply cease to function – as a body often does – without energy flowing through it.

Why are we not paying more attention to this, I wonder? Whatever this channelled energy is, whatever name it has been given since, it has been recorded since ancient times, as part of the sacred teachings of medicine practised thousands of years ago. These teachings have only relatively recently entered our Western understanding which we now often refer to as the well-being of body, mind and spirit. Interesting how it only slowly influenced the history of Western medicine to this day. Western medicine is historically based on treating all three aspects separately. We think it the norm that it is necessary to open and dissect a body in order to heal it, often treating it with little respect. Not having the awareness, we subject ourselves to degenerating practices which hinder and sometimes entirely stall the energy flow through their tiny invisible energy channels, leading to more pronounced illness which can develop as a result. It might be good for us to balance out our view, and remember that the successes of modern medicine are based on trial and error throughout centuries of rather gruesome sacrifices in the name of science; which, more recently has been funded increasingly by pharmaceutical companies making them some of the most influential but not necessary best option on the planet. Whilst undoubtedly it has saved many lives, both ways of looking to sustain a healthy body and mind must inevitably work together to help make us complete.

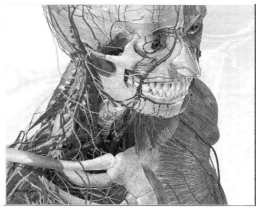

Image of nervous/muscular/skeletal system as we are familiar with in Western Medicine

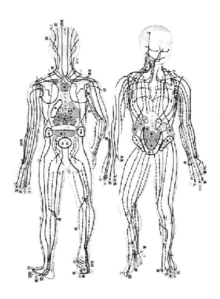

Image of Meridian Energy Channels, the basis of many treatments in Eastern Medicine, but not typically acknowledged in traditional Western Medicine

The basis of Eastern medicine is the holistic treatment of mind, body and spirit as the whole entity it always is, with each 'part' intricately interconnected with one another. Fortunately these days there is more awareness than ever amongst most practitioners of either orientation, who are open-minded enough to integrate holistic therapy with the teachings of Western medicine. Each should certainly not have to work without the other, I for one strongly believe that both practices might always have been meant to work together and be allowed to do so, and that they do not have to mutually exclude one another.

So – to repeat once again, the energy created by the vibrating frequency within every cell of our body plays an important role in keeping us alive. Without it having been created by our Karmic energy mind in the first place as well as it constantly maintaining energy vortexes to circulate energy flowing through every part of our body, we would not be. Quite a busy enterprise inside each of us, which we are obviously not that aware of, otherwise we would be more careful with it. But are we careful with any other, more visible processes within? Have we not created toxins for consumption, for example, and happily, even joyfully, ingest that which is poison to our body? It's plain to see that we treat our bodies like an experiment, but is this perhaps because we feel that we are at the mercy of the unfathomable nature of Karma? Not so long ago in this country, people fed alcohol to babies in order to quieten them and thought that was a great idea. I am not trying to say people are stupid. What I am trying to say is this:

Just because we cannot see something does not mean it does not exist.

The brain does, once again, not always compute what really goes on within the trillion cells that make up our body and we can often remain blissfully – or rather stubbornly - unaware of facts that are right under our noses despite the evidence.

Can you try to imagine every single cell of your body and every atom within those cells vibrating, oscillating and creating energy, constantly, 24 hours a day? You can't? Neither can I. Heck, we can't even count them! It is quite impossible for the brain to fathom how vast our inner world really is. Perhaps that is the reason why we have long since given up, ignore the process altogether and switch to autopilot. It is just too much, and it all seems overwhelming and also quite scary. It makes us feel out of control. We are too incredible within, too much of a miracle to accept and apprehend. Trillions of cells, without our conscious input (that we are aware of) are creating energy for us to be alive, every second of the day. We do not even know today - not even approximately - how many cells there are in the human body. And yet, here they are, all working together to keep us alive. But believe it or not, they do even more than that: they are registering our every move, change, simply everything that we live through with an ingenious but simple system based on a binary code of electromagnetic signals translating into vibrational memory. A little magic show on quantum physics level that's going on every second of the day, and we are completely unaware of it. That's how much we are in charge. Are we trying so hard to be in control on a conscious ego level, because we simply are not? Luckily, our Karmic energy mind is, and it is a benevolent force on our (in-)side. All we have to do is to forget a lot of what we think we know and are, and learn to tune in.

Each cell within living beings will adapt its frequency according to certain physical laws and conditions.

An energy body with different frequencies to our own, positioned near our cellular structure, will influence our system. This was found in the experiment I mentioned before, called the Heisenberg principle. It states that the position and the velocity of an object cannot both be measured exactly, at the same time, even in theory. *(https://www.britannica.com/science/uncertainty-principle)*

Basically, it means that a watched atom – an atom that is being influenced by another entity close to it, i.e. an observer - may change its behaviour, simply because it is being in close proximity of another entity or energy being.
This was, of course, quite something of Mr Heisenberg to observe. It makes perfect sense here to mention it because of its importance in relation to what we perceive Karma to be, because the conclusion we can draw from the above theorem is this:

Our Karmic energy body is influenced by what we do every moment of the day.

To give an extreme example, if we place a powerful radioactive material near a living being, it will change their frequency irreversibly, causes their molecular structure to change and the being will die within days of radiation poisoning. Sadly, this has been proven in all too many extreme situations around the planet, such as nuclear wars, weapons fired, power stations and experiments gone wrong and the aftermath of their fallout, usually to the effect that not only beings, but the whole environment ends up poisoned. Living tissue experiences disruption on a cellular level at an accelerated rate and cannot survive.

Fact is, everything around us can and will influence us more or less strongly, not always as extreme as the examples above obviously, and fortunately not always in a negative way either. We could go to the other extreme and talk about very subtle and barely noticeable influences, such as the magnetic influence of nature, for example the moon and planets around us. It is possible that we can be influenced by the waxing and waning of the moon cycle, knowledge that is even upheld by police and hospitals reporting a measurably higher percentage of incidents around a full moon. It should not be surprising when we remember that the cellular structure of our bodies is based on electromagnetism and our bodies consist of around 70% water, being highly conductive to magnetic energy.

We could go a step further still and mention how the energy which another person sends out to us has an influence on how we feel, think or react. I would hazard a guess that perhaps the feeling between people and what they think of and intuit about each other is to a large extent based on this automatic interaction between their energy systems. Consider how we all see each other completely differently, that we have issues with some people but are in love with others, whereas our friends might see the same people in a completely different light again. We probably don't even realise how literally this is meant. Again, it seems very logical to me that we are all reacting to each others' 'light' - our Karmic energy. Sometimes our vibrating energy fields just simply clash, when with others, or even just on a different day, we might be getting on just fine. And it is not unusual for people who are very close, such as families, to know what is going on for one another even though they might be thousands of miles apart.

Would it not be a great idea for us to become aware of this energy interaction and learn how to integrate it wisely into our relationships, before we are about to react to it, before we create negative Karma? Do we not perhaps have our own energy system to become aware of first? Could it be that every interaction might be giving us clues as to what is happening within us first? What is it that we are still learning, what is our Karmic energy mind subconsciously drawing us to?

Please don't think that any of what we are talking about here is a guilt trip or telling off for any of our ways of figuring out what we need to do in life. It is my intention to touch on this fascinating subject so everyone can elaborate and explore to their own heart's content. I am trying to be fair to all, in a way that I feel best assists in empowering us. Some of this empowerment can happen by triggering key memories. Life has a habit of doing this anyway, and it can be a sore spot to touch when we are reminded of times that we were unhappy in the past. In terms of making us as aware as possible, there are quite a few different methods on offer that do not entail a traumatic memory recall in order to heal. I feel that this is important to mention, because there really are some miraculous healing methods by now that heal our Karmic energy field, so we do not have to suffer any longer.

The reason for us getting upset about memories can be down to various things outside of our usual understanding of ourselves and our consciousness. There are ways this book can help leave a vicious cycle we feel stuck in once and for all. If there is a timeline of events, situations and people that our Karmic energy memory has made a negatively charged memory of, may be the reason for our energy system being a bit skittish. Every time we are reminded of such past events, it triggers our inner energy memory and will remind us it still needs attention to heal. It isn't always easy to see past what presents itself when it's painful, especially because our instinct is set to avoiding any more pain; we live in stressful times and perhaps always have. Life can mean suffering on many levels.

Later on in the book, we will explore explanations of what can be wrong within us and why, before we then also look at solutions.

In addition to our inner work, I am going to focus for a moment on the external environment we have created to live and work in, the modern 'civilised' world, as they call it. Even before the climate emergency was something we finally took seriously, what comes to mind when looking back over the past few decades is built-up cities, man-made buildings, dwellings, their structure, materials used, layout and even lighting; deteriorating green spaces; power stations, traffic; electric pylons, microwaves, mobile phones, radiation, computers, deforestation, GMOs, toxins, smart metres, viri and bacteria thriving on a deteriorating Petri dish of waste, rolling out G5 and whatever figure comes after that for even faster electric radiation that disturbs our own frequencies – the list goes on and on. These are all every-day man-made structures and in(ter)ventions, designed to make our lives easier, safer and more productive or enjoyable. But did we not forget to consider one important thing – one important question we should have asked before entering into the contract of modernising our world forever? The question nobody asked in time is: how do all these phenomena affect us, our physical bodies, our energy system and therefore our overall health and well-being, as well as that of all our fellow furry friends? I am particularly talking about us humans and our human functions here. Needless to say we all know the consequences for flora and fauna on this planet were devastating and we didn't stop at those to think long enough whether it was going to be sustainable, either. So I am going to start with pondering mostly on the effects of what has happened to us humans, because we started it and have somehow been hypnotised into allowing all this to happen. There must be a way to find out why and try to backtrack a little to find ourselves again in order to remedy the damage we have done, and observed being done without questioning.

Some people are so sensitive to energies that they literally collapse under the influence of certain frequencies. Others can blow up electrical and electronic gadgets just by touching them. Some are sensitive to certain substances, which can be much to their detriment in terms of getting sick, but it can and always has had advantages, because we were meant to be sensitive to our environment. It was crucial for our survival to have skills that meant, for example, that we can dowse for bodies of water with our own individual energy frequencies. Our own connection to water is so important, some people have spent their lives finding out more about it, people like Victor Schauberger and Dr Masaru Emoto. Others are so sensitive to UV light that their skin has to be permanently protected from it, and yet we cannot survive without it. There are lots of toxins we are inadvertently inhaling and consuming on a daily basis, and people are reporting more sickness as a result. Yet others seem resilient as well as oblivious to the presence of the changing energies around them, and are often more sceptical of their subtle presence as a result. Either way, there is one thing we are constantly taking for granted without which we would not even exist; we are all of us, everyone included, constantly connected to our environment's electromagnetic charge.

We report being more stressed and suffer from ill health more than ever. Many feel that the world seems to have been speeding up, that we have less time than ever, less quality of life, feel unwell, sleep less well. We have more money than ever and yet get less out of life; meanwhile, the quality of our air, food and water deteriorates as we change the frequency of our environment. In turn, everything external that is stressful to our energy body has a weakening effect on us, similar to a disagreement with another leaves our energy frequency feeling lowered. We have reached a point where many of us have become aware that it is high time these 'imprints' are ironed out. When we continuously spend time influencing our system in a negative way, it will have an accumulative effect. Whatever is happening to us on the inside is intricately connected to our environment. None of us really want this to happen, so why does it and what can we do about it?

I once had a poignant example of environmental poisoning that really made me think, and there are lots of cases all around the world, many of which are being brushed under the carpet for the sake of commerce. I was asked to help a really lovely man with terminal lung cancer who had been working with asbestos for a long time. Nobody could change the fact that he was dying at this stage, but I was asked to do as much as I could. Sadly, his time on Earth was shortened by the accumulation of toxins in his body, but he had asked to learn methods to manage his illness. We spent a few sessions doing gentle healing, which I was hoping would open up his energy system and at least allow him to see beyond his physical suffering. His wife came to me after he passed, as she wanted me to know just how much it had helped him. She said that his very last word to his family was 'meditate'. I was very affected by this, and have never forgotten it. He seemed to know there was a connection for him beyond physical existence and found how to access it. I knew and trusted in the practice of meditation and healing in order to help the energy system repair itself. Although it came too late in this lifetime to have an effect on his physical condition, I like to think he assimilated this knowledge within him in his Karmic energy body, and that his incredible ability to remain aware at the point of his transition, helped him as much as possible. I was also very moved by the message he carried to his family that he wanted them to benefit from the huge amount of care and love he felt he had received through the practice.

Even though we have all of us experienced sad and sometimes traumatic scenarios, there are, of course, also countless examples of how our environment and all beings around us affect us in a positive way, tirelessly trying to balance out the negative impact of ill effects. We often choose these subconsciously, because our body often knows what's best for us and automatically tries to counteract a deficit on the deepest level. Simply having enough rest, time spent outside breathing clean air, detoxing our body with the right food and water, eliminating poisons within and avoiding autoimmune system reactions, adjusting our stress levels and prioritise our health and well-being, even spending time laughing or processing, meditating, healing, being in love with partners/friends/family/pets/parents/plants/hobbies et al, can give us what we need to recuperate and offset some of the deep Karmic lessons we endure. More and more people are turning to a gentler lifestyle by default, learning to meditate, try Yoga, Chi Gung, Tai Chi and similar mindful therapeutic movement, have a spiritual practice and/or learn more about energy therapies. We do know in our heart of hearts that drinking, smoking, taking drugs, being stressed or working too hard do us more harm than good.

On the other hand, we can sometimes put ourselves through a lot of stress in order to achieve the highest outcome for all involved. Noble causes call for noble and Selfless actions, and if we are able to fully apply ourselves to the cause with the right intent, effort and motivation, we can become part of a stream of consciousness that has the outcome of a healing process for many sentient beings including ourselves. These actions can draw a Self-healing process to us and others, so our bodies can actually start to heal almost overnight, even from deep trauma. What seems like a miracle healing to the sceptical ego mind, is second nature on the higher vibrational levels beyond the sheer physical endurance of our 3-d bodies. How much more would we be doing for ourselves and others, if we were actually able to see and perceive our energy bodies and what they are capable of? If we could understand that we can complete our Karmic energy field with good actions, and that it would become diminished through harmful actions, would we more readily live by those very straightforward principles?

The big mystery we remain mostly unaware of in our every day struggles and strives is the Universal energy being the underlying source of the processes I have tried to describe above. Even though the enormity of the concept is in itself virtually impossible to grasp, we are seeing examples of the effects of the vastness of creation all around us. It flows through our planet in general and every living thing in particular. I call it Universal energy simply to describe its vastness, but also because I wonder if it needs to be associated with any particular religious belief, philosophical concept or scientific definition. The energy that is present is weightless, formless and limitless, indicating that it is all-encompassing and prevalent even beyond our concept of this one universe. Having said that, I do believe that any belief system, philosophy as well as scientific findings have good reason to exist as a result, because they, too, are part and proof of the inherent existence of the pure unnamed endless Universal force that just 'is'. I also believe that this very same 'Universal' energy exists not only well beyond our own good old universe, but that it has created others with different paradigms to ours (such as non-physical realms) and will continue to do so, too, long after we are gone...but first things first.

This very same Universal energy that creates all is the basic premise for the underlying structure of our own existence, too. It flows through us, determines our mental, physical, spiritual and emotional health on a second-to-second basis and as such also serves as our 'early warning system' for any illness and perhaps even incidents, sometimes before we even realise we are falling ill.
In principle, if there are changes in the flow of our energy field first, this is likely to be felt on a physical level next. As we are often unaware of what to look out for when it is still at a seemingly invisible stage, we may miss the symptoms of anything that is awry on our inner energy levels

and only become aware of an issue once our physical body is affected. An illness might announce itself in our energy field as a disturbance first, long before a physical symptom is diagnosed. If it is true that the Universal energy which creates our Karmic energy flow through us, and the energy flow determines the well-being of our physical body, then the lack of function in parts where there is a diminished energy flow would, certainly after a period of time of a disturbance within our energy system, logically affect our physical body accordingly. This is something that can potentially be capitalised on if we find early detection devices to determine whether energy is flowing through our system efficiently. Could we not be saving any Health System huge amounts of money and effort, if such devices existed? If we could detect and demonstrate energy being restricted in its flow in certain parts of our bodies, would we not be more inspired to look after ourselves? Since whatever we feed and do to our body will have an effect on the energy flowing through it, we could see with our own eyes the effect it has on the recordings within our body's energy system. Some of us have a pretty good idea about this already and can intuit what is going on within, without any regulatory testing. We can sometimes sense and feel what is going on, our body gives us hints and even if we cannot see into our body, we can actually become very sensitive to its functions and also become versed at visualising any arising issues. We can also transfer this intuitive process onto all other phenomena around us, people, situations, scenarios, world problems. It is a great way to describe that it might be very necessary for us to become more sensitive to ourselves and the world around us, rather than going in guns blazing. If we can become mindful about these and other issues and execute good actions, these effects will have a positive and healing effect; if we are careless, the effect of any positive action may be temporary at best. If we are not yet aware enough to know how to give ourselves and others appropriate attention and are doing actual harm in addition, this can stay in our Karmic energy system for lifetimes when left undetected and/or untreated. All along, we are talking about actions that we actively choose to engage in, actions we take part in without being conscious of, and those we become involved in as a part of a group, community or society, sometimes even in a passive way. They are all actions, and we can probably at least appreciate if we have the privilege of becoming aware of the part we play in them.

If we take a current example from the list above of how we are passively and sometimes unwittingly partaking in affecting our environment, we will have a valuable opportunity of playing a more conscious part of creating a less harmful environment for ourselves and others. We can also see what happens if we choose not decide to play that part, how it becomes more and more difficult to see how we are involved without having the insight into what to look for, never mind knowing how to counteract its effect. Perhaps it is time right now, at least for those of us who are ready and able, to ask for our good Karma to kick into action and take some much needed steps towards helping our world regain balance. By raising these issues and putting them into context, we are taking an important step in becoming aware of each of our global impact, but also our inner power of finding solutions for cleaning up our internal and external act before its too late.

We have already touched on the subject of how our actions have already affected our environment, whether we are actively or passively involved. The drastic effect the energy of toxic materials has on our 3-d body; even subtle energies from toxic items we are surrounded by on a daily basis can have an accumulative effect. When our energy field is constantly lowered due to exposure to energy frequencies such as radio-activity; even electric energy hubs such as pylons near residential areas, computers, microwaves, mobile phones, X-Rays, certain chemicals, materials, food stuffs, pharmaceuticals etc., this can all be harmful for our energy and ultimately physical bodies if it is a constant influence over a prolonged period of time, potentially resulting in immune system illness and even terminal illness. We have become so used to seeing and handling technology all around us that we no longer see the harm they may cause. It appears, however, that the longer we are exposed, the more we might find we become prone to illnesses caused by these influences on our energy bodies, resulting in our bodies becoming more prone to immune system malfunctions. Some say that some of the objects in the above list may be causes of an increased risk of cancers within the body. I am sure at least some of us would think this to be a logical conclusion, especially when we discover that important findings and knowledge about their effects on us are not shared or researched further and officially declared to be important factors to consider in our quest for good health. It seems that what presents itself is that we are catching the aftermath of our choices to insist to exist the way we have been in recent decades. Overstretched health systems that can only assist us to a certain extent and treat illness only with limited resources, often under great duress, shocking responsibilities that many don't take for their own well-being, means that pressured staff and personnel have no choice but to try and put right what society as a whole is passively endorsing and doing wrong.

Whatever the reasons are as to how and why we let it get so far, we can choose from the influx of information and take from it what we need in order to become wise again, in order to further our state of mind, body, emotional and spiritual health. We are learning again the skills that are inherently ours, so we can complete our inner energy and what it means to feel truly awakened. As part of this, we can find out how we can regain trust in our intuition and find out what is really going on internally, including behind the scenes where nobody usually cares to look any more. I will leave the conclusions of this train of thought to you, Dear Reader. I encourage you to start your own research and take heed as well as personal notes on whatever you might want to follow up on.

Let's focus again on the other end of the scale; if we are surrounded by pure energy, clean air, light, nourishment and the right energy balance within our Karmic mind in its space & time experience - in short, if our Karmic energy flows freely through us to express itself fully, then we ARE that energy stream, we again become this very same energy consciousness. We are not just 'in tune', we are – 'it' and are able to become one with 'it'. When we have been able to BE in the flow again, any form of unwellness that might arise would be caught at the earliest stages. It can mean our energy field has a chance to fully recover – something that some of us have known for centuries. It may not be too late – there are enough documented cases of people recovering unexpectedly even from terminal illness, tumours, immune system illness etc.
Knowing and experiencing being in this energy consciousness stream is intensely blissful, like almost nothing on Earth except perhaps the most breathtaking natural energy points that might hint at the enormous energy force creating and flowing through it all, including us. We become one with all around, and all dual existence falls away in those moments that stretch beyond time and space. Should we not be more intent on creating this energy flow for ourselves more often, caring deeply as a result about what happens to our energy bodies so that we can prevent sickness, as well as learn more about why and how this happens in the first place? Should we not look at the causes, the mysteries of existence behind them and follow the red thread throughout, about how well-being is established and illness prevented, and make this knowledge known on a large scale so that everyone can benefit? Should that not be what mankind is here to do, rather than bash each others' heads in?

When we are truly seeking to find out more about our Karmic energy body and how it sustains and feeds our bodies by its subtle but constant energy flow, we will find the connection lies in our Karmic energy body being able to conduct energy from the unlimited Universal energy flow existent in our surrounding environment and beyond. This energy is freely available to anyone without restriction and exists in abundance all around us, being absorbed by our bodies on invisible wavelengths. We are able to absorb energy on many levels, some consciously, some in more subtle ways. Especially when we are talking about pure forms of energy being absorbed through energy centres and certain points within and along our body, we usually struggle to perceive the work that our body puts in if we cannot see it occurring. We are not always versed in the knowledge that has been widely acknowledged in Eastern ways of looking at health for thousands of years, where knowledge about spiral-shaped vortexes and certain energy points of measurably lower frequencies all along our torsos take in energy into our own energy stream. Every cell in our body needs to have energy flowing through it to survive, every second of the day. We know somewhat about the physicality of our inner organs, and even if we are not medical staff we usually know for example that our heart pumps blood, but we don't usually know very much about how these functions actually come about. How is a heart formed, how does it work continuously? We would have to turn to a doctor if anything went wrong, and very often a surgeon would need to use emergency procedures involving additional electric energy in order to remedy any malfunction.

We have to come to the conclusion that most of the time, we do not know how to truly support our bodies in their functioning and even end up hindering the process instead. It comes as no surprise then, that we are not giving any time to being shown how to look after an invisible Karmic energy body. Why, we are not even convinced it is there. And because we don't know about it, we can end up Self-sabotaging one of the most precious resources we have in this life. If only we were taught about the Universal energies that helped us come alive, because it would show us how this affects our Karmic energy body inside and out, as we co-create our Karmic lives including our bodies and minds by everything we do, say and think. As important as this profound energy intake - without which none of us would exist - is, there is also an equally important process of 'exhaling' energy from our bodies that has expired and needs replenishing. This seems to be an automatic process we do not have to be conscious of to work, which is very much connected to our breathing; it might even help initially for us to picture this energy flow to be a little like our whole energy body consciously breathing in pure universal energy like the purest air on Earth. If we can imagine this miraculous process like an in-breath and out-breath of pure energy, the deeper meaning of how our energy field is charged with universal energy may even start to reveal itself to us during in the process of practising conscious breathing. Our whole system is designed to exchange energy with our environment and be a living part of the universal energy flow. Perhaps we can also liken it to a form of osmosis, except we are still talking in terms of weightless energy streams and a subtle energy flow that is really not easy to perceive or believe in; except we would be able to feel it, intuit it; and we do, however, we are so used to the process we forget it happens, just like we forget we automatically breathe or blink or have a heart that beats without us having to think about it. This is why it's hard to explain and prove, to those who simply do not believe it exists. I am not here to prove anything though. You are perfectly allowed to believe whatever you like. I am talking about something I inherently know to be true as we all have the ability to consciously experience it, and I simply try to form my thoughts based on my continued experience of its existence over many decades. All the same, my thoughts and words are inconsequential in this process, and I certainly hope they are not getting in the way of any awakening process that is happening within whoever is reading what I have written. Sometimes words are difficult as they do not express the full inner experience we are capable of, but we can read between the lines and often sense a truth about what is being said, whatever our belief system, status or religion. We may not be able to fully learn and make our own experiences simply by listening to someone else's words, but they can point us in the right direction.

As Picasso once said, 'a process of creation is also a process of destruction'.

Fritjof Capra sums up the essence of the Dancing Shiva in The Tao of Physics:
'The dancing Shiva is the dancing universe, the ceaseless flow of energy going through an infinite variety of patterns that melt into one another'. (ref to his book)

The dance of Shiva, the great flux of Universal force, releases us at regular intervals from the illusion that we can continue to play God to try to manipulate the greater concepts of the cosmos so we only get to experience what we want. We cannot deny that our 3-d body will deteriorate and at some point end, we cannot change that fact no matter what technology we come up with. I don't know why we even spend billions trying, if we get to have a new body anyway and take all our energy with us into a next life! Yet again a good reason to spend time achieving a good Karmic energy body instead. If we focus on the physical body only, and on ourselves only never mind everybody else, we will not get it. We will not have understood the principles of interconnectedness that have brought us here to see through the illusion of a singular physical existence. The struggle to achieve only positive outcomes such as perfecting our creature comforts at all cost and earning masses of money in one lifetime is futile, even if we do pass it on to our families afterwards. The more important task in life is to enhance a process of allowing the flow, to remove our obstacles to give the inner process space, and allow it to happen for us and everyone else accordingly, subject to where we are all at in our own inner Karmic dance. We will gradually learn to remove our fears of everything that is limited within us, until we are fully aware of being in the process of all Karmic energy that arises. The only thing that is unlimited is this very Karmic force that arises and persists within us. To sustain it is not a simple task, but it is a noble and worthy one. As a result, we will be able to start to be more conscious of the true nature of all things alive, the simple intake and exhalation of energy which forms the foundation underlying every physical process within. If we are in conscious agreement with it, we will gain awareness, not least of the repercussions of our acceptance to contract with life and the appreciation and awe our realisation of its greatness brings. I say 'if we are', because when we make a conscious decision at some point based on what we are learning to believe, we will then also be prompted to apply this in our lives and be living according the results of the process. This is no theoretical knowledge that stays outside of ourselves in a certificate or passed exam. This is a life-changing experience which we are better off choosing to be a part of, as it is not even entirely up to our ego mind if we do or not. We are already alive, but are we conscious? Nobody can make that decision for us, and nobody can force us to do so, but as they say, the universe has a way.

As each individual enters their own inner realm with their own motivation, intention and personal consent, there is no outer entity as such responsible for what we learn, despite the universe and our own Karma probably nudging us nicely along the way. No school, no work place, no boss, no parent, no authority, no government, no church, no university - nothing external governs what we internally have to learn, and nobody gets to tell us what to do or give us grades or certificates of how we are doing. There are nuggets of truth in all instances which we can take from according to what we feel we need to know, but each generation trying to find itself by rebelling against authority is probably about this one statement - that nobody will be able to truly tell who we are and what we need to learn according to our inner Karmic breaches. All we probably inherently crave is to be shown is the greatest mystery: the way to unlock our inner Truth. We can't just sit there and complain, that would be wasting our precious lives. Time to look inward and find out how we can be our own best teacher.

The greatest asset we have in our lives is also life's greatest mystery. What we do know is that it is absolutely free and available to all.

Whilst insights will be formed within each of us according to each individual's Karmic learning curve, universal energy around us will also converge and align to give us signs and hints. These can appear in many forms such as asynchronicities, inner realisations as well as physical manifestations. It could also be that we start to see things differently, and assess accordingly what we have been looking at but not seeing all along: we already ARE. What we are able to improve on is that we may learn to be able to truly appreciate what this means, and how our environment and the beings who live in it can be seen for the miracle that they each are. We can accelerate and maximise this process of energy enrichment, when we learn how to become still. In this stillness, we are part of the universal energy stream for prolonged time spans. The acceleration is not the same as revving a sports car on a motorway. The stream itself is always there, endlessly existing without a timeline. It is how quickly, easily, calmly and frequently we will be able to access it with practice that changes. In this constant stream of Karmic consciousness, each of our cells forming our body parts can become engaged in the process of maximising its functionality. We are entering a process of inner healing on all levels. Logically it follows that we could attain the potential to make ourselves well, sometimes much faster than we think. How this happens depends only on our individual Karmic records held encoded in our Karmic energy mind, including our understanding and abilities bound by our physical aggregates in this lifetime. It will be futile to think, for example, to think we would be able to grow another leg if we lost one in this lifetime, however it's very possible that in our next lifetime we will not carry over the same physical limitations again. Once more, the underlying principle is simply that: when we alight the memory of how our inner energy exchange flows and functions properly, it helps to remind us to learn to co-create, sustain and maintain a healthy body and mind. As we are all aware when we do not, universal energy does not flow well through our bodies, and/or is not absorbed properly, and/or it can 'leak' out again, all with the same result: it leads to us feeling and being unwell. The physical body is created, sustained and affected by the flowing chi or pranic energy flow which we need to learn to support, not hinder. When there is a lack of energy flow, this will make us unwell. We need to also learn how to maintain this energy flow one Karmic level so that we learn to live well, act well, speak well, think well.

This process of gaining inner wisdom by aligning with the universal consciousness stream is open to anyone. It can accelerate and be more effective the more accomplished a being becomes, but we can all learn to utilise our own energy to start healing our cellular structure on this supra-conscious level. It is important to remember that healing is not limited to physical processes, but also means we can heal past situations, such as our own Karmic past choices. We can make peace within with things that did not go according to plan, situations where we feel we did not act with care and attention for ourselves and others. We can heal past suffering to avoid future discord. This also very much includes emotional and mental healing, and/or the recognition process of insight into what is needed to aid a healing process along. What also helps is dedicating our energy exchange to include and help others too, whenever possible. Dedicating simply means that we can start including others in our inner practice, by simply wanting them to experience happiness and awareness, too, as part of our own process of realisation that we are not separate from each other.

Perhaps we already know what this process feels like, as we are all potentially able to do this at least to some degree, each according to our awareness and skill. We are not that different from each other at all. We are all born from the very same Karmic energy stream.

We are still trying to explain the greatest mystery of all, because it is one of the hardest to comprehend: By we I don't just mean you and I, I mean everyone on this planet, past and present. If we gain insight into this mystery, it might serve as a golden key to unlocking what occurs within and around us, and our understanding might be a key to taking a step closer to our and our planets survival, so I thought it would be well worth publishing the news. During this incredibly beautiful and complex process that ensues, the energy flow created within us becomes a personal record of our present state of health and mind in its own right. Somehow some of the apparent formless energy that surrounded us before becomes a part of 'us'. It absorbs, mimics our energy patterns and becomes personalised. Every cell in our body puts its memory stamp on it, its own electromagnetic finger print. This becomes our Karmic memory mind, flowing, morphing from moment to moment. Of course, it is not bound to a timeline at all, but it will seem like it if we observed it from our perspective. As we change, so does our Karmic energy memory. As our frequencies alter through all that we experience, do, say and think, so does our Karmic memory mind. As long as we are alive, it is within and around us, in our every cell, forming a memory bank for a future cosmic library of everything we have ever been that will exist even when our physical body we currently occupy is long gone. Behold just for one moment what this actually means: this is an example of Karma at its most complex, creating an imprint of itself every split second of the day, every moment in our lives, right under our noses. We create our own inner universe right here right now, within ourselves! We are the observers to our own universe, we are witnesses to the sacred process of life. We have a choice of what we co-create, every second, every moment of our day! If we are even a tiny bit aware enough of the principles behind it, we can begin to free ourselves from any stagnant energy stuck in the form of old inner belief systems right away. When we start working on our inner energy whichever way we choose, it is only a matter of time before we learn how our very own timeline was created by the energy imprints based on events in all our lives.

The Karmic imprints made by our experiences in all our lifetimes are left within our Karmic energy body until we find methods to neutralise them.

Fear not! Many of the methods we can utilise are mentioned at the end of this book for you to choose and use. We might not know it yet but any negatively charged particle residue created by any of the memories made within our Karmic energy body can be calmed by certain methods and techniques. We do not necessarily have to continue to be held back by anything that has happened to us at, and it will help us to realise our healing process without messing with our brains or manipulating who we are. We are not talking about losing a memory, it is about defusing the effect of any of its residual 'negative' charge that it is still emitting. There are already very gentle methods by which we can become more conscious of how our energy is set free to do more important things than get stuck in fear. Would it not be wonderful for everyone to know how this inner peace and freedom from fear can manifest in our bodies. It is something we would all be able to enjoy without exception.

The greatest obstacle we need to overcome in life in order to experience bliss and conquer anger, hatred, greed and ignorance is - fear.

Our Karmic energy mind, which is the result of this constant energy exchange between the universal energy flow and our selves, is intricately involved in and constantly connected to this elusive energy process. It is like an information exchange that constantly shifts and changes in a vast variety of energy memory patterns, taking in renewed universal information on sub-cellular levels and expelling any obsolete energy to be transformed and recycled. To think that, on an ultimate level, our individual Karmic energy mind has the ability through this process to eventually become identical with the vast energy field that created it, no longer seems a far-fetched fantasy. I will go even further to say that, if our Karmic energy mind develops gradually during each of our individual lifetimes including the ones we lived before we were born into this very life now; and if our Karmic energy body is a complete recording of everything we are and that this initiates our reincarnations, then it seems a logical conclusion that our Karmic energy which remembers everything about us, will also have chosen every detail of each of our next physical identities to enter into, once it was ready and complete enough to do so. It is a fascinating and extremely complex hypothesis which probably takes some time and re-reading to fully grasp, but it is a belief system that many millions of people already follow.

Over lifetimes, our Karmic energy would have gone in and out of individual bodies to temporarily exist in the confines of the 3-dimensional world, each time experiencing more and more of the complete Truth that is. Of course, many believe by now that there are other worlds that exist, other planets, other universes where we may have already had lives, and this cannot be ruled out. It is in keeping with the infinite magnitude of existence. It is also conceivable that, as stated above, eventually individual Karmic mind and universal energy will merge and have the potential to become one and the same. There is a stage beyond death where our Karmic mind will certainly merged and be compared again with the infinite greatness of all that is. At this stage, at the very least, both our and the universal mind overlap and both remain interconnected, perhaps like clouds do in an endless sky, conforming to certain universal laws according to the nature and consistency of our individual Karmic energy mind. To me, once again, the unfathomable feels logical and true, almost imaginable. Either way, this Karmic energy field created us, was created by us and continues to exist within and around us, all the while keeping our universal connection alive. It also appears to colour our experiences in an individual way with thoughts and feelings, so that what we call the 'I' – our physical, thinking and feeling body and brain, our 'ego-mind', as we have called it – is heavily influenced by what goes on in our energy body. Sometimes it feels as if the universe has a pallet of infinite energy shades and hues at its disposal, with a daily dose of diverse frequencies filtered by various factors, and we are simply the canvas. The energy paints itself within and around us in the form of a unique art work, and it changes continually like a happening rather than a rigid sculpture. We will never be a blank canvas, though, not with all the Karmic hues that we bring into each lifetime from the ones before. We have learned that we carry our blueprint from previous existences. Everything that we have transformed from lifetimes before -after a certain amount of recalibrating in the after-life - has brought us here, including that which has agreed to limit us again to an individual experience in this duality system, together with all our physical attributes, earned assets and talents, as well as any Karmic energy baggage we have not been able to resolve so far. Apart from the memory encoded in our Karmic energy mind, we have also brought our own laptop with a limited hard-drive into our physical existence: our brain. Whilst it is undoubtedly a miracle that we have such an immensely capable index of information to keep us safe and hopefully sane, it is unfortunately also flawed, as we are now aware.

We now smile at early computers that ran with a few kilobytes to bring up black and white lines on special stencilled coding cards. However, we still use the same system today, a binary coding system, to do all of our computing. Do we smile at our brains often enough? If you can smile at your brain, that means you are not your brain. There – you have just broken it. Sure, it's easier to remember all this when we can tell that it's not functioning properly. Although not everyone can see that it this flawed, we almost always rely on it blindly for all our decision-making. Some of us even identify wholly with our brain and what it comes up with. On the other hand, we ignore our energy body because we can't see it or name it, questioning and dismissing its credibility. We do not know how to perceive it, understand it, operate it, maintain or enhance it. We might admit we have 'hunches', 'intuition' or act on 'impulse' or even 'gut instinct', but what are those? They are probably all expressions of us tuning in to our true wisdom energy. Even then it's not common practice to rely on this as much as we emphasise the importance of our intellect and knowledge. We have forgotten that

Our Karmic energy memory is capable of carrying our complete blueprint; it travels with us, records all that we are and remembers all that is, as well as being able to merge with the universal energy mind.

It adapts to who we are and the experiences we make by being constantly in flux; forming, disassembling and re-shaping in a continuous flow. It is sentient but not of itself, it exists as energy memory shaped by our own lifetimes' experiences. Needless to say, just like a trusted pet, it even forgives us for not remembering that it's there, or how to find the user manual. The energy potential that it holds is infinite, but once it · has assimilated within and around our physical body, it is subject to events in our lives shaping our Karmic learning experiences as to what becomes of it. We can deny all knowledge of its existence and block its energy flow, like a beaver blocks a river by building a dam with tree trunks. A beaver might only know instinctively that a dam is useful for it means more fish will gather in one place; but we are able to put inner blockages up without noticing that we are acting against our own good. We are capable of Self-sabotage. Maybe we call this 'free will' nowadays, especially when we do nonsensical things that don't just affect us personally, but also so many around us. We might have reasons why we do this, but all those have one underlying common denominator: fear. All the clues we need to find to unravel our fears lie embedded in our own individual Karmic energy minds. Just like a virus spoils a good computer programme, even the whole system, one trojan horse, one chain of fear, can disable our whole energy system. Although these clues are often not easy to find, once we do, our Karmic energy has the ability to right itself so we can heal, and start to also right the wrongs we commit; but it does not do so if we don't know how to allow it to work for us. None of this is necessarily our fault, it is how we have been programmed and educated. It is like we have been kept in the dark by design. But whose design is it, if our Karmic energy mind is set to giving us best case scenario at all times? Is our brain to blame, or the limited perception we have in our physical body? Our body and brain are designed to protect us by shutting our systems down when we are in fear, preserving the status quo for safety reasons by keeping us on a low flame. It seems we are not ready on a level that we are not even conscious of, so how would we know it's there, never mind fix it? Even if we did, we have so far not learned how to use it wisely. And yet, these are exactly the questions we must ask to find answers; this is the time some of the mysteries of life can be solved, when our Karmic energy body is dropping us hints so we can try and reconnect. When we tune into who we truly are, we start feeling, thinking and acting differently, more or less according to the state of reconnection to the energy flow within. When we become aware of our Karmic energy potential, we are then no longer just functioning robots following orders from our brain synopses for reasons of Self-preservation. Now that we realise we have so much potential, how do we tap into it all? Why does it stop and start, why can we connect sometimes and at certain moments, but not constantly? How do we act wisely all the time? Will we ever know how to find the key to our Karmic wisdom and learn to use it? What happens if we, accidentally on purpose, block our true Self? Have we actually put up barricades already, maybe throughout all our lives, without ever being aware of them?

If this is so, and if we really have put up blockages within our ego-minds that have affected our Karmic energy system, we could draw the conclusion that we might not feel completely present or well. Although blockages like these start off being existent on an electromagnetic level, when we observe the diminished potential of our individual energy levels we have created with these blockages, we probably know already that these can act like a stop sign in our lives. Blockages like these do exactly what we have asked them to do: they stop us in our tracks and halt our Karmic energy flow. it would logically follow that this will also have an effect on our physical body, how we think and feel. In other words, if there are ' frequency blockages' recorded within our energy body of a nature that is detrimental to our energy levels and flow, then we may also suffer as a result on an emotional, mental and/or physical level. What do we do when we discover that there are not just a few of those blockages, but a whole load? What are we to do?

I know it sounds bizarre, but in our panic in looking inward at some of the chaos, it is common that we very often inadvertently make it worse. For some inexplicable reason we also believe we must punish ourselves for having only limited energy accumulated over the course of our laborious lifetimes. This is difficult to process! Our Karmic energy mind is checking in with where we are at, and as a result, we employ our brain to take stock. We are used to using our brains to judge what is going on and make an executive decision. Having determined at some point that we are to feel bad about our limited levels of ability, rather than go easy on ourselves with kindness, we make an inner label for ourselves saying 'must try harder'. Common conditioning through education only partially points us in the direction of where the actual problem lies, and we often get lost down the cul-de-sacs of life to try and solve the inner puzzle. Since there is little help and understanding, we get disillusioned at some point and instead try to distract ourselves by everything external we can think of, to try to make us feel better. Does that sound about right? This is exactly what we need no longer do. We probably don't like being reminded, either, and have resistance to seeing it how it is, without having a new solution. However, in that, we are all in the same boat. As always, it certainly helps to simplify matters, if we wish to have a more reliable outcome for ourselves and a reasonable amount of good mental, physical and emotional health. We no longer need to create a paradox within our think tank. We don't need to 'do' or 'think' anything. We just need to be kind to ourselves, and realise that this is the process that is occurring within, without judging. Just being aware that we are the observer is enough for a start.

We can also gradually re-set our ego-mind to being gentle with ourselves and constructively ask the universe for help. We can learn to work out how to top up our Karmic energy levels again, through practices that are helpful to our energy mind. This in turn should gradually have the desired positive effect on our mental, emotional and physical health: when we know how to exercise not just our physical body, but our Karmic memory body, too, we will be on the path to feeling well again, slowly but surely. We will all sooner or later on this inner path come across a sign. There is a point in all of our lives that makes us realise there is a task at hand which we have come to tackle and resolve in this lifetime: We are being asked to choose to commit to mending our Karmic armour, with lasting effects.

Many questions will arise as a result of becoming well enough to reason, which is a good sign. Questions such as: how come we do not feel enough good results from our efforts to simply breathe properly, sleep well, eat well, and take time off? Why can't we be happy, healthy and carefree just by becoming very rich? How come it is so difficult to be eternally happy in our every-day dealings with our fellow human beings and animal friends? How is it that when we do everything right, look after ourselves and others and have a healthy lifestyle without too much stress, we can still fall ill? Why are there so many nice people we know, who have something happen to them that is not nice at all? It should be as simple as that: look after ourselves and our loved ones well. But how is it that even when we know we followed the above, we are still not entirely happy, healthy and wise? Looking around, as a human race we are clearly not, are we? What important information are we missing? We are all noticing the symptoms, is it logical to conclude we are definitely missing something? Have we not ever thought as to why we are not as happy, healthy and wise as we could be, and at least given some thought as to what might be the answer?

Perhaps the answer could be the fact that we have disregarded just one little thing in our calculations so far; that one tiny catch, the small-print in our contract. The missing link could be that many of us are forgetting the effects of one deciding factor in our experience of true happiness: our good old friend Karma, you know, the thing we are probably fed up going on about in this book. Our elusive friend Karma, the unfathomable phenomenon that is annoyingly visible everywhere in its effects, so tangible in and around us that we try to avoid it altogether and despite which, it creates itself over and over again within us like some form of curse, taking charge of our next shape based on our past actions. Why wouldn't we rebel against it? It's so easy isn't it. We can't see it, so it can't fight back. We can't even remember it, so how can it still be relevant. And if nobody else knows about it, why should we own up. We have made one little mistake, however. Karma is not a separate force from us. Karma is a part of us. it is our Karma, it IS us. Only we have tried to distance ourselves from it, not knowing that the price for this is prolonging our misery and making things worse than they would be if we were just brave enough to listen.

You can't blame Karma, it does what it does best. It's an energy principle within us that makes us who we are. We each of us share the same responsibility for our own fate, rich or poor, old or young. Everyone who ever lived has their own Karma to deal with. We can only win if we become wise to how it creates, and how it is created by us. Once we are less triggered by its existence, we can then choose to make an active effort to create best case scenario and the best outcome for all involved. Even then we are allowed to start small and exercise the idea in our heads first before embracing it more fully in all parts of our lives. It's really up to us, there is nobody out there to scold us, remember? We will probably realise soon enough that in this case, resistance really is futile, as futile as it is to argue against breathing, or be cross that we have to drink water or need to relieve ourselves. We need to befriend our Karma again, we need to remember that it is pretty amazing, actually. It helps to remind ourselves that our Karmic energy body has been in existence for aeons of time and has made our very own special energy recording of everything we have ever been, done, said and thought during all this time. It should sound a bit less suspicious than that, certainly less than any of our electronic gadgets with their ability to record what we say and do that we so willingly allow near us. We have created our Karma and our Karma has created each of us, with our own help and assistance. I think it deserves a better look.

As mentioned, our Karmic energy mind has created energy recordings that go back a long, long way, maybe even lifetimes. Heck, let's not stop there; once merged with the Universal energy mind, its recordings can be infinite. Sometimes, though, as a result of what happens to us in our lives, in our perceived timelines, these recordings contain energy 'breaches', tiny disruptions to our inner energy flow, like chinks in our energy armour. When we have no idea that they exist, we may only find out about them through a next incident or moment in time where they seem to play a role in what is occurring. Whether we realise that they play a role in something that happens to us or not is another matter. It would be so easy to say that something occurred because we did something else a while ago, but matters are often a bit more complex than a direct causality. Events, it seems, just 'happen' to us, as do illness and misfortune. We try not to think about it and carry on as if there is no connection at all. It would be wrong though, I believe, to just dismiss a connection between what we do, say and think, and something that happens later down the line. Although our Karmic time-line appears seemingly from nowhere, it does not mean there is no causality at all. Just because we did not know it was not there, does not mean it cannot exist. But if we have not looked for evidence or reasons for their existence or even known how to, and we did not know they were there, how do we deserve for them to materialise? How can we be guilty of co-creating a bad scenario without knowing? Nevertheless, these 'breaches' in our Karmic energy system have been within us all along, and often we only become aware of them when we are confronted by an illness, or a situation or person outside of ourselves. Could they even be the reason why, despite looking after ourselves really well, we suddenly succumb to an illness? Are they part of the secret of ageing, and the reason why we eventually die? I believe it is a question we should definitely ask ourselves, especially when we try to find an answer as to why it is that any young being who we perceive to be perfectly healthy can develop an illness and die before their time? Are the 'breaches' in our human energy system responsible?

After looking into the matter for years, I firmly believe that we all have these breaches in our energy fields. We must be born with them and have brought them with us, otherwise why would we all not be perfectly healthy and live eternally? I will make a bold statement and say it's hard to see how it can be any other way. It seems they are a part of our experience in a human body; so could they, too, not have been formed as a result of our previous lifetimes' of Karma we accumulated? They are a part of our human body blueprint that has been formed by our 'Karmic energy computer', which has carried over the Karmic memory for everything that we are, our appearance, our talents, our memories. Perhaps we can even learn through the reflection from our external symptoms. Our Karmic energy mind (to say computer is so limited an analogy, i don't want to be misleading) also has the ability to determine to a large degree how we will likely react in our environment, for many of us from the moment of conception. Our personality traits and character are additionally shaped and formed as a result of our growing experiences in our new life. As we learn over time, as much as we might try, we can never quite achieve perfection within our human life. It is is a fact of life that many try to deny and flee from in fear. Ageing, illness, flawed appearance, death are all things that people are more scared of than they realise, and many will spend vast amounts of money to halt the ageing process. In their frustration, millions are turning to having the perfect physical appearance, the perfect job, the perfect family, the perfect life. It is no use at all. Not many I am aware of have lived eternally in the same body, which makes me state the same statement again. As long as we are human beings, we will continue to have these Karmic energy flaws and they are what eventually make our bodies perish. Unfortunately, such is the human condition and we cannot escape the fact, although as we can see, many have tried. We all start off young and we all cannot escape the fact that at a certain age, our energy tends to decrease from then on. The question is, why are we spending so much money on perfecting our physical appearance but have never given a thought to why we are all deteriorating in the first place? Science has found the physical reasons why we cannot live forever, so that must be our lot, is it not? Cryogenics promises to keep our flawed bodies alive, but our Karmic energy body will have long detached itself, so all that is left is what we are desperately trying to cling on to, our physical body. What if we attached just as much energy, time and attention to detail to our

Karmic energy body? Could it become a fad now that I have mentioned it? I am sure cults already exist, relieving unsuspecting victims of all their possessions promising to reveal a big secret to do with eternal life in return for personal favours. Excuse my cynicism. There is no big secret. The secret is not a secret. Even if there was something we didn't know, it isn't hard to find out, and it doesn't cost anything either. It's very simple: it's up to you and what you do how your Karma turns out for you in the future - how YOU turn out in the future. And here is a promise: despite us not being able to take our physical body with us, there is a lot more future to think about than we realise, and I would give as much advice as this: if we can be a bit more thoughtful about what we do with every moment that we have right now, then it could turn out to be pretty useful for us and everyone involved in future, and the future starts as soon as the next moment.

It also follows that if any of this is true, then we could find a method to decrease our energy chinks and keep them to a minimum, and that this could very well increase our life span. Some individuals alive today manage to seemingly defy physical laws and look a lot younger than they actually are. Others, for example, live a lifespan of more than, say,120 years, especially in some regions where there is little toxicity, a steady lifestyle and a simple, staple diet. Even then, these admirable elders are still the exception and they, too, must eventually give up their current physical existence. We do not like to be reminded of this fact so very often, but would we not want to know why some people live longer than others? Do some people live longer because they have fewer problems within their Karmic energy system? Are genetics, the basis for so many deductions about human life in the Western mind, governed by Karmic circumstance just as much as any physical phenomenon we are subject to in our bodies, in life?

There are obviously examples of people who have thought about the answers to questions about Karma before, and have followed their own inner path of wisdom to make the most of their existence. Perhaps the practice that makes humans stay alive beyond a certain age or even that of staying alive without taking in any nourishment other than prana is actually proof that there truly is a way out of this samsaric existence. It is just simply a fact that most of us mere mortals can't escape illness, or death, or suffering as a human being. Is it not all the more reason to try and do our utmost in this short time to uncover life's greatest mystery? In Buddhism, the whole train of thought of summing up all physical existence is contained in four statements called noble truths. Four simple but powerful sentences that describe a way of understanding the science of everything that underlies our being here on Earth. The last Noble Truth is: There is a way out of suffering. Hurray! Once we have aligned with the Truth, the rest really isn't quite so depressing! There is a way out of suffering, it says, and we'll come to that a little later in this book.

To reiterate, each and every one of us has our own inner 'log' of everything that has ever happened to us, encoded within our energy field,
created by the vibration of every cell in our bodies, which in turn is fed
by the universal energy around us. Knowing how complex this system
is, and however many gazillion cells are involved, we can imagine that
there must be some scope for the incredible recordings we are not at
all aware of and which scientists are only just finding out about, trying
to describe something that our brains are ill-equipped to comprehend.
We might have been missing something altogether, considering that we
cannot even see with the naked eye most of what is going on right in
front of us.

Interestingly, despite this, most people can actually sense what is going
on, at least to some extent, and a percentage of us have at least some
awareness of the energies in question. Actually, we do all have the
ability to intuit this energy field naturally, for example, when we have
affinities with some people and aversions to others. We literally 'attract'
or 'repel' one another – or can feel completely neutral towards someone
else. Perhaps we feel fine with another one day, but not the next. And
are appalled by someone at first, but get to like them as we learn to know
them better. We are usually so quick to judge another based on this initial assessment of energy attraction or rejection, that we are mostly not
even aware we are doing it. If only we actually saw the energy exchange
in action at those crucial moments, we would have proof of what is
underlying the sensations we are getting, and it would be easier for us
to see why and how we react to another, and how to understand each
other better. By saying this, I don't mean to say, go out and trust everyone in the streets. What I am saying is that there is a reason for why we
are reacting to events and people in our environment in a certain way;
we can become more conscious of it and could base our decision-making process on a more comprehensive picture of what is going on with
another person and the interaction we have with them, which could
possibly help us understand a lot more of what is going on behind the
scenes on a daily basis.

There seems to be some hope. Quite a few people claim they can actually sense, see, feel or hear what is going on, and you might have experienced this yourself when you can actually sense someone's energy field
when they are in the same room. It's not so far-fetched – after all, the
animal kingdom has most of these instincts intact and works with
them naturally to stay alive. But as humans, we don't like to think that
we base a lot of our reactions on animal instincts, it seems a bit beneath
us. Those who can see auras, read minds, dowse for water and other
elements, see beyond the physical into peoples future, view remotely or
can diagnose and heal illness without surgery for example, are just not

taken seriously by an evidence-based society that wants to see hard physical facts. Humans all have the ability to become aware of 'invisible' energy fields and how to interpret them to a certain degree. Auditory, kinaesthetic and visual factors play a part of this ability. An aura is nothing other than a visual sighting of the energy frequency field that surrounds a being, human or animal. We have been talking about our Karmic energy mind and its frequencies so far, creating our individual energy frequency tapestry within us by our uniquely arranged vibrating atoms. Our unique atom formation builds our DNA incorporating certain frequencies of our parents, too, which means our DNA molecules have their own particular frequency energy that at the same time relate to our parents DNA, too. To a certain extent, this energy is visible as it emits an imprint of some of our energy onto a visible spectrum. Scientific research has much advanced in learning about DNA and complex processes exist by which it is possible to make DNA visible and sequencing possible. Minds divide whether it is actually possible to record the Karmic energy field itself and make it visible to the human eye, but I don't think it is far-fetched an idea at least to some extent, as indicated by thermal photography and imaging, as well as measuring equipment for kinaesthetic energy. It's certainly in its infancy, but how incredible would it be if we could read each others minds, eventually. As usual, I guess we would have to start first by deciphering ours before we can let ourselves be distracted by others, but it might be helpful in our interactions with others to understand each other better. Even in its various forms, imagery based on visible frequencies might at first by nature be a much diluted and reduced version of the vast complexity of our Karmic energy mind, much as images from the Hubble telescope have to be interpreted in colours as the rays emitted by space objects are way beyond our visual spectrum. I wonder if our Karmic energy clouds would look equally as fascinating as those colour-adjusted ones from the Hubble Space Telescope, although we must remember we would not be taking images of actual elements around us but rather the Universal energy transformed into individual Karmic energy that drives any of the elements within us.

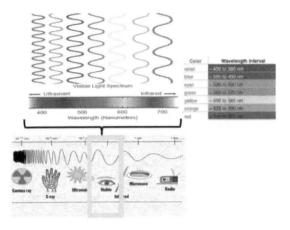

image credit: ©flamecolourwordpress.com

Just like a pixelated image will not give us a full complexity of reality, a thermal image is only able to show a few different coloured clouds and spots of heat radiation within and surrounding your energy body, as fascinating as it is. Incidentally, thermal imagery has been known to detect some illnesses where organs and tumours in the body may show up a different colour, as they radiate at a different frequency where blood flow and therefore heat emission is restricted. Whilst an instrument able to measure our kinesiology frequency in Hz would give you a graph of the flow of electromagnetic energy within a body, any technology would only show energy blockages or flow within the physical body to some extent, but none would be able to form a picture of the whole entity that is our complete Karmic energy body. It looks like it's a catch22, because we are limited to physical media invented and interpreted by physical beings using their physical senses only to report on non-physical phenomena, we are not able to think or see outside the box. We know already how this phenomenon has influenced historic events, where we just did not acknowledge Truth until we could see it, and even then it was not taken as fact until we could interpret it with our brain. There was a classic example of this, in the 'ships not seen' or 'glass walls' phenomenon, where items cannot be perceived by an individual or even groups of individuals if they do not have a concept already of what they are looking at, as in Columbus' ships that apparently could not be perceived to be approaching the natives who had never before seen ships.

Since we cannot do either with our brain, it seems we are fighting against our inner judgement all the time. The most striking example would have to be Einstein discovering the very same relativity theory, his thought experiment of 'running along side a light beam', discovering mass-energy equivalence. We are talking about the very same phenomenon; our brains think this way: 'If i cannot see it, it is not there'. We think that we are our brain, so we do not question what our brains come up with. If we are not able to integrate the facts and findings of evidence because we cannot 'see' or 'feel' it, ie compute and understand it through our brains, how will we be able to gain any benefits from the existence of these concepts in the first place? How can we tap into their potential? How are we even alive? Luckily, by asking questions, we are getting closer to the Truth, all the time. You are reading this, and we are all the same - all able to channel energy through our physical bodies all the time that keeps us magically alive, without even knowing consciously how it's done. This is part of the Truth, that we are connected to concepts that are way beyond us, much bigger than us, but we are a part of it, and an important part at that. Despite us not being able to truly grasp these concepts, even small pieces of the jigsaw can gradually help us form a bigger picture and bring us closer to the truth. Luckily, miracles work beyond our comprehension, on principles that are not based on brain work. The fact that we are alive, and everyone around us is alive and has the right to be alive, speaks volumes of the magnanimity of the vastness of Truth underlying it. Universal energy does not judge, it creates, and it 'uncreates' itself - and so do we.

If we are able to grasp the above concepts, it is plain to see how we understandably still remain unaware of how complex, intricate and complicated the various vibrations are that form the basis for our inner energy being, created by a myriad of different converging and coinciding energy strands to begin forming life on subcellular levels. This creates an energy source with myriads of energy points connected by hundreds of thousands of energy channels flowing through us like a circuit board, which is able to draw from its universal energy source constantly and thus keeping us alive. Our energy circuit constantly creates energy which is able to invisibly interact with the space around us, too, according to how strongly and on what frequency it manages to hold in order for every atoms vibrate. At this point, you can probably picture that a complex system like this internal energy show it pulls off every second for us to survive, will be subject to fallibility on occasions. Easy to imagine that faults can occur on an energy level at any time, with effect on our physical body as a result, but are they random or is there a pattern, or both? And what if the very existence of our energy current converged to form us, in this lifetime, as a result of its own programming, not just random energy strands having a party? Of course, it makes logical sense that there must be a pattern to form a complex life form, otherwise there would just be infinite types of conglomerates of energy clusters that do not make anything other than pretty patterns; which of course there certainly must be as well, according to laws of probability. Perhaps you already realise where I am going with this - I am referring to the Karmic energy pattern that we, all of us, will have left somewhere in outer space, when we last left our physical body behind. Are these our very same Karmic energy patterns that will recreate a new life form, ready to become physical form again after a span in the Universe repair workshop? is this 'us', floating in outer space, ready to become a new being whenever the energy converges and it's time to 'incarnate', to gather enough - what - strength? Momentum? to immerse into physical existence again? If so - and i have a feeling that this is exactly what happens, if never quite expressed like this - we could have reason to feel pretty awesome and special, because this does not happen so very often in infinite space.

The energy waves and vibration that life is created on occur on a variety of different frequencies measured in Hertz, including the visible and audible spectrum of light and sound respectively, which eventually our brains would be able to try to then compute. Since our brain can compute information based on the tiny visible and audible spectrum only, its interpretation skills will be limited. Just like when we are learning a second language, we will know some of the words but will never be a native. Our brains are quite amazing, being able to form concepts and make a log of quite a few million visible and auditory portents it is able to perceive, their frequencies having physically manifested on this planet. tangible to most humans as either different coloured light, sound or kinaesthetic frequencies. We do not usually give the process much thought, either, as our brain does not fully comprehend what had to come together first in order to form all physical manifestation over a vast time span; proof of which is our nonchalant ability to thoughtlessly squander all our resources in a minute section of said time span.

If we have such relatively little brain capacity that we are able to destroy ourselves so easily, should it also be no surprise that our Karmic energy field contains frequencies from beyond this world, which our brains are not letting us perceive until such time when we have learned to perceive beyond its capacity? After all, as we speculated above, these frequencies might well be what created our Earth bodies in the first place and helped us incarnate. It seems logical that they would also contain universal elements and frequencies. Perhaps they could also be made detectable, especially by those who dedicate time and effort to follow a more intricate path into exploring the subject. We do not have to leave it to others to make it their mission to gather more insights into the whole phenomenon - that would be once again letting our brain decide what's good for us. We are much more than our brains. It would be more than good for us to learn techniques on the subject ourselves; it would change our Karmic energy resonance for the better as we get more aligned and assure a better future outcome for our own existence. Truth is that nobody else can do it for us.

We do not have to act out of fear, or because it's the right thing to do. We do not have to follow what someone else says or does because that's what we have always done. We are currently in a climate where we are carving out evolutionary new ways to exist, and we would do well to do so sooner rather than later. Creating ways of improving our Karma is the way forward.

If we are motivated enough to sit calmly and meditate, that is one of the best ways to make a start, paradoxically. Meditation is a way of bypassing brain function. We are basically winding down all physical function by simply sitting still. There is no movement to interpret, and our eyes are perfectly still, fixed to one point only without distraction. Already, we are thinking again with our brains: how can I sit still? How can I just look at one point? We are so used to thinking that we are doing it constantly without thinking. In order to override the process, we give the brain permission to do very little, for a change. As a result of this unusual practice, our brains will try to think more, so it will take time for us to get past that, but it is very possible and it will happen eventually. Just keep practising. Meditation is the method, not the result. Meditation helps to get beyond our physical processes within our body. There is something that will happen for each of us as a result that is very beneficial. We will eventually, when the time is right, see beyond what presents itself. Already our brain starts piping up: when will that be? When is it going to happen for me? Can I go to the shops and buy it instead? The answer is, allow your brain to chatter on if it has to, but stop buying into everything it says. Just remain still, keep breathing calmly, allow thoughts to arise, think what you will, but then allow them to ebb away again. When another thought arises, and another after that, do the same. Again and again, do the same. There is nothing else to do. You are not even waiting. You just...are. And you will...become. Until then, rinse, repeat.

✽ ✽ ✽

11. Karmic Recordings and Energy Auras

In the meantime, whilst we are reading, we can do something by contemplating the fact that there might be more to our existence than meets the eye, if you pardon the pun. If our experience on Earth is a vibrational one on an atomic level, which can be recorded within our own Karmic energy system and which is not limited to a physical existence alone, does this not automatically mean that we most certainly would have had previous incarnations, perhaps here on Earth, but perhaps even on other planets and planetary systems, in other experiences of being within a 'body', by another name? Is this experience also not limited to just a few of us, but infinite life forms in unlimited 'timeline' experiences? If there is life beyond the perception of a physical body or time line, does this not mean there are other parallel universes, other beings without physical experiences, right now? There might be life, but not as we know it! If the universal energies exist beyond time and space, beyond a timeline, it must mean pretty much most of us have lived before, perhaps even met before, but not all in a human body all the time, or at the same time. It could, on the other hand, mean that if we are able to exist as awareness in a Karmic energy mind beyond this life, we would be weightless and therefore have the opportunity to be omnipresent as well as 'one' with all that is in existence. I conclude that we are all aliens! Should this surprise us? Not when we are open to learning that we are already able to perceive much more than our five or even sixth senses allow us to be aware, and are willing to practice the art of an inward-looking and -listening procedure carefully.

Even without much practice, we should already be able to perceive the energy around some people at least some of the time. Do we not talk about the 'red mist' coming down, or being green with envy? Having 'yellow belly' or feeling blue? We have many of these sayings, and they all have a grain of truth in them. We are describing energy frequencies created by the vibration of these highly emotive and tangible reactions. It helps to become aware of how these energy frequencies affect us, because on their low levels, they can make us feel unwell, uneasy, and agitated. Have you ever observed people being angry with another? Low frequency energy often prompts us instinctively to interact with the energy created by another. The low frequency we are receiving is actually triggering a very human auto-response: needing to raise the energy vibration again to a higher, safer level. Perhaps this was set in early human evolution when it was crucial for our survival to be safe from attack by others. It also seems to be relevant today, and we still see this response everywhere around us when the energy level of one or more beings drops: we try to help, we try to assist, we try to deflect the outcome of a potentially dangerous situation. As low frequency levels send out an emergency message to us, we need to quickly respond and assess the situation. Internally, our adrenaline levels go on overdrive: Are we safe? Are others around us safe? Do we need to fight, or do we take flight? If we can safely 'talk someone down', then we do not need to expend extra energy to fight or flight, and if we can still think, then that might be an option that runs through our mind. If we can lower their adrenaline level and raise their vibration with positive affirmations of acknowledgement and showing that they are safe and understood, then this might in some situation mean that everyone survives. There are good reasons why police adapt to this method in the first instance, unless it's already too late and someone's vital energy frequency levels might be so low or suppressed that their adrenaline has kicked in sky high, in which case anything can happen with disastrous consequences, and it does not matter if it were the good guy or the bad guy, if energy levels are dangerously low, it is a situation where anyone can end up attacking anyone else to try feel safe again. It should make us more aware and perhaps also question whether situations that feel 'safe' could be a set up, or at least something we should think about carefully before entering without being conscious of our inner energy status. For example, we could be sitting in front of our computers in our own safe environment, ending up in low frequency situations with others we have never met, and when we do not feel safe, rather than shutting down our computer we end up arguing and failing to raise others and our own energy mode...I wonder who dreamt up this neat little idea to keep us feeling small and scared, because it certainly seems to be working. When we are in company of someone unwell, it's easy to see how this 'spark' can be contagious at times. These energy breaches, or holes, inclusions, in-completions in our energy field can spread like wildfire, like a stampede or a mass panic is created by a small element in the crowd. If we don't have the tools to be discerning, if we don't see just how easily someone's energy field passes itself on to us, then we quickly become taken over by their energy and take it into our own inner sanctum. It can be a great healing tool by which we can help another very quickly and skilfully, however, it is just as easy to take on an energy which is not helpful and become manipulated by it.

In fact, the energy breaches we talked about earlier have the ability to cause breaches of low energy around them, if we allow them to continue. We must become aware of where they originated from in order to contain them, otherwise the energy can spread really quickly and not actually heal or be resolved. If we recognise that we have the ability to right the situation with the appropriate words and actions, we are able to bring up the energy levels again accordingly. In slightly less precarious examples, how many times have we personally picked up on someone's energy and asked 'what's wrong?', even if they have not said a single word. We can feel their energy within us, and in turn could make them feel worse and pick on them, if we did not recognise that we have simply taken on their energy level in order to actually help heal them! Our greatest human ability of feeling empathy could quickly turn on us, and them. If we are sensing their energy lows, or breaches as we called them earlier, then we should also know that we are there for a reason, and the reason might be that we are just the right person to help them overcome what they need to overcome at that moment.

They themselves might be influenced by energy breaches from their past, which were caused by previous energy breaches elsewhere and so on. The whole low energy thing can snowball really quickly and it can badly influence energies in future just as easily. We would do well to acknowledge this as a human condition that we could turn around if we were aware of the skills we need in certain situations to recognise and reconcile all our energy levels in order to bring back equilibrium. Otherwise it is what it is: the perpetuum mobile that appears in life as a never-ending struggle, it carries on carrying on until it has burned off all its energy invested in it, or someone actively puts a stop to it. We can diffuse it, with our empathy and some learned skills. I am not saying it would be easy, not at this stage of waging world wars, no. It would be good all the same for us to create empathy with each other rather than fall for the stress that something outside ourselves has tried to load onto us. Look around for examples of how this happens all around the world every day, and how fast communication channels become carriers to perpetuate mass hatred and hysteria. If we are able to remain alert to these energy breaches around us, then we do not have to internalise them and can assist better in alleviating them. This in itself is such an incredible vision and insight into how, as a population on Earth, we could overcome the influence of energy 'chinks' in the ethereal make-up around us, which have probably been trying to govern us for aeons of time. Are we not all subject to these, and some of us more than others? Are we not all in the same boat, even those who are obviously subjected to their energy defects more than others? Can we help those whose energy breaches have led them on a downward spiral right their internal low frequencies again? I do believe that is one of the greatest aims that humanity ever could achieve, the understanding of our internal processes and how to master them. Perhaps one of the reasons why we aim so high in trying to send rockets into space is because we really can't seem to be able to get to grips with our inner world and it's bugging us more than we would like to admit. Little do people know that we have all been adversely affected by the past, otherwise we would not be in 3-d on a timeline right now. We all need help, each others' help. The way we are going we think we can keep this show up for a few million more years, but I don't think our planet will hold out that much longer. It would probably have to throw us off the roundabout a lot sooner by some Self-fulfilling prophecy of an impending disaster we co-created so that it can finally rid itself of the virus that is the human energy chink. What I will say, though, is that it gives us the ability to separate out the good in all beings, from their inner demons they are trying to conquer. It isn't that anybody is bad, it is that we have not fully understood how it works that low energy frequencies have created situations to all our detriment within us all.

Perhaps it's for the Best that we do all individually have a choice how to find out more. As we should be aware by now, flaws in our inner energy flow do not just go away. If anything has lowered our frequency, it will stay there until remedied. What we should also be aware of that each time it creates an external situation we deal badly with, we may create more negative Karma for us and others. If we have been consciously involved in lowering our Karmic frequency ourselves by committing negative actions, we need to face up to the reality that this has left a residue within us which needs tending to. The process of recognising this is not always easy and probably entails we have to first experience it for ourselves in order to become aware of it. It is one of the most important tasks for us to learn to free ourselves from it at some point in our own evolution. Is there ever any point in blaming anything outside ourselves, if we already know that we need to look within to fix everything? Which does not mean that we should sit still when the Earth is burning, or stay in our house when a dam has burst. We need to be awake to take the right action and not be so docile that we just fall over and crumble like protagonists in a sci-fi film. When that happens, we can then make others aware of our own experience, give hope perhaps, share methods, find solutions together. Will others take it on board? It's up to them to find out in their own way, not for us to decide where they are in their own Karmic evolution process and how they experience their individual energy breaches. If we have gained something from recognising our Karma and how it affects all of us, if we are working through it ourselves bit by bit, our job is to be present and share our knowledge, perhaps even become a helper and assist, as long as it's not in a condescending way trying to convert the world to our point of view. That's already been done before, people misunderstand and it does not end well. We are not better than others, and it would not serve anyone well to act out by becoming preachers and suddenly think we are enlightened messiahs. Our experiences of an individual, separate physical body may already be the result of misaligned misunderstandings, creating watered down energies which formed an experience of 'Self' torn loose from the ultimate experience of being whole. How truly happy the experience makes me feel – even fleetingly - of the inner sensation that I am whole, and that you and I are connected even though we have never met. We all are.

As already mentioned, an intensely emotive reaction within us may be caused by the vibration of another being, which is of a nature that it can be sensed by others in a room. It is determined by an intuitive recognition of a certain individual frequency by our individual Karmic energy minds, or rather, a complex combination of frequencies. They may be more consciously sensed by those who know what they are looking out for, similar to a coloured 'fog' that can be seen, felt or - by some of us - even heard, tasted, smelled even. But all of us have it in our nature to be able to intuit the Karmic energy field around others. What's important then, is to become conscious of it enough so that we remain in charge of our own reactions to it.

If we only had the right video equipment to film us in action with all our colourful energy emissions visible, I don't think anything would prepare us for the real light show of trillions of cells vibrating to create the kaleidoscope of our real, incomprehensibly dense energy cocoon within and around us, each atom dutifully vibrating its response to our life experiences and thus registering our Karmic

energy history on a moment-to-moment basis. Would we all be much more in awe of each other, have more respect and understanding of who we are, if we could read each others past suffering, our current struggles like a book? Would we make each other feel less bad for misunderstanding, for not being able to 'read' each other better?

Having given an example of how this so very delicately balanced, invisible-to-the-naked-eye Karmic energy dance can be manipulated, on the other end of the spectrum it must be awe-inspiring to be in the presence of those beings who are accomplished masters of the potential vastness of their inner universes. In fact, in a way we already know this to be true. If we observe how amazing we feel in the presence of some people, how well they make us feel. Some people have a true ability to shine, and they seem to have this effect on many people around them. It's awe inspiring to see how some people on Earth have accomplished much in terms of sorting out their own Karma, and their energy fields are pure and clear. They have special healing talents and abilities that are almost superhuman, on many levels. Of course they are. This is also a fact that should be unsurprising, if we consider that Karmic connections know no boundaries, that many of us have incarnated from various higher planes of vibrational existence, and have brought energy with them that is often much more refined than normal. We can be in their presence, take on some of their energy vibrations and immediately experience healing transmissions, no other words or interaction needed. At the same time, these abilities come with great responsibility, and in order to be accomplished, it also means we learn to be humble not boastful, to have compassion with everyone not just a select few, to have wisdom we must also at some point have learned first-hand what it means to suffer so that we do not look the other way when someone needs our help. When in the presence of greatness, we will never hear someone say they are great and they know stuff. There is no blog and no vlog, no YouTube tutorial on how to put on the face of greatness. There is no payment for it and very often no thanks either. These beings walk amongst us unseen, it is what goes on in their Karmic energy system that is so awe-inspiring, and that, of course, remains invisible to most of us. Whatever positive and healing changes greatness brings about, happens below the surface of what presents itself. We might walk past anyone and not realise who they truly are underneath. Would it not be great if we treated everyone as if they had something important and amazing to teach us?

Some theories say that our Karmic energy body emits vibrations up to 55ft around us. I reckon with some accomplished beings who have mastered their inner understanding of oneness it must be nearing levels of infiniteness, whilst some of us mere mortals probably choose to keep our energies very close to our hearts. Is that being Selfish, or scared, or both? Perhaps it's time we allowed ourselves to expand, even if it is just a little at a time.

Our Karmic energy system is continuously recording our own personal history.

❋ ❋ ❋

12. Karma is Energy Completing itself

This is where we can come back to Karma itself. If Karma really does exist, there can be no other place for its record than within the energy fields created by our very own vibrating atoms. After our physical bodies perish, I believe that some of this energy vibration we talked about persists and continues to exist, in the matrix of the universe, if you like. Where exactly and on what level, depends, I believe, on the quality of our energy 'emissions'. We have literally left an energy imprint of our selves and our life recordings behind, a sort of vibrating energy 'cloud' that used to be bound to a physical body, but now returns to its own weightless experience of Self, according to all that has gone previously and all that has been recorded within its confines. Equally important I find is - as much as it's a controversial view point - that we take the 'we' with it, meaning that the energy cloud that survives is itself inherently who we are, not the temporary experience of our physical body as we most commonly believe. It is therefore very possible, even probable, that 'we' carry on existing indefinitely, and that 'we' are able to incarnate again when conditions converge to indicate that it will be so.

I also wonder if all the ethereal phenomena that people see and are so fascinated by, are to do with these, our Karmic energy emissions: Is this why people perceive ghosts? Or have a sense they are visited by deceased relatives and friends after they have passed over? Is this why fiction is fascinated with ghosts and the afterlife? Are the phantoms of our imagination – and sometimes our nightmares - real after all?

Examples exist of spooky - but very real - accounts of highly accomplished yogis passing to their next lives, leaving their bodies in a semi-state of existence at first, sometimes even for years. They master the art of completely transforming their bodies into pure energy, and often leave almost nothing behind after their passing. The achievement is called a 'rainbow death' and is considered extremely auspicious, meaning fortunate, in terms of how accomplished a being has become, so that on their passing, where a being's transformation into pure vibrating energy is achieved, it is accompanied by rainbow light forming above the place where the being has passed. It takes a very special being to be able to transform like this, needless to say. It seems viable to me that it must actually be possible to do so, and the phenomenon has been observed and documented many times since, being a firm part of some Eastern cultures' rituals and beliefs.

As certain as there are some very wholesome energy bodies at one end of the scale in the realm of physical existence on this planet, there may also be those energy bodies that are weaker and in need of completion on many levels, be that during their time on Earth as well as in the stages before and after physical existence. If we think about it, this is, I feel, a good indication why phenomena such as ghosts may also exist. However, more important than a discussion as to whether they do or do not exist, might be the fact that this is also the very same reason we are here right now: to complete our journey, to complete our energy field, for our Karmic energy body to become as whole as possible, on all levels, at all times – with all that it pertains in turn for the rest of all beings everywhere.

How far we must we have been removed from that aim, if we were not even aware of it! What a shame we do not even realise how precious this very lifetime is that our Karmic energy was drawn to incarnating into in order to complete itself. Checking a dictionary and you will hardly even find a definition for the term as a Western verb that describes the process of incarnation. I am using it here in this book frequently for a reason, so that we get more used to the idea that it happens. We are not just energy incarnate, we have actively incarnated into this lifetime, and some very precise and perfect processes had to conspire to make it happen. If we truly realised it in ourselves in our ego-minds and ego-bodies, then perhaps we would feel more secure in ourselves and our existence. Instead, we find ourselves in generation after generation being unaware of the thaumaturgy of the process, unaware of what we can do to feel better about who we are in this great wheel of existence. If we really felt how precious it is to be here instead of fear, would we damage ourselves and each other, our children, animals and our environment less? We would perhaps feel no need to abuse ourselves, or one another. We are here to learn who we are, and how we got here, and how to overcome our fear which underlies all suffering. Maybe once we had more of an idea, we would realise that there must be more to life than that –and there certainly is. To me, it figures logically, that

There are other lives. There have been other lives before – and there always will be. They are all precious existence.

With this heightened awareness, even if it's tentative at first, can grow a sense within us of losing our resistance to becoming more responsible for ourselves. A curiosity arises as to how we can sustain our well-being, as well as a recognition of and respect for the interconnectedness of all life on Earth. The centred feeling that comes from being aware we are being nurtured by our inner Karmic energy core and the lightness that we can tune into within as a result, might make us aware of many more possibilities on Earth, maybe even other planets, too, maybe even other universes. Let's not forget that

The language of Karma is universal. It exists every-where, at once. It has created this universe and per-haps many others, too, on the basis of similar but at the same time a variety of unknown principles which we are not aware of just yet.

If we follow this thought in terms of a logical deduction, this must mean that we are not the only ones out there. Science has shown for a while that there are particles out there, faster than the speed of light, which was once the standard for the fastest moving physical force; but we can think beyond light, because what if there simply were other fre-quencies out there that move much faster than light, which we just have not witnessed yet? Why does something not exist, simply because we have not witnessed it? I'll give you an example right here by which you will notice how something works faster than light, and it is right under our noses: at this very moment, we do not even have to rely on the speed of light to connect us all. it is our mind energy that is already faster than light. It can be here one moment and at the end of the uni-verse the next, if we train it well. Of course, the weightlessness of our Karmic minds can exist here, and be at the end of the universe in the next instant, or even simultaneously bi-locating. We will experience this any time when we are travelling in our minds to other places and focus on beings we are connected to around the world. It might be new to us, but this is a strength we have that can move mountains. Would this not be the greatest 'online' game we can actually all already play, for free? If only we could train our minds and focus them enough! Of course, people would want to turn it into profitable nonsense if we could manifest on order, but this is not what it's about, at all. Our main reason for honing our Karmic energy minds is to earn peace, and the highest aim we must keep in mind is to not slip back into the pain of a lower rebirth. Experimenting is fine, if the idea is that we are learning to use our skills wisely. Skills like how to heal ourselves and each other, how to transmit energy to an important project or being to help it along and ascertain its fruition. When we eventually can see beyond the limitations of time and space, we would see that some things are not worth pursuing. Perhaps we are already feeling this, on this planet, right now. If our energy emissions are of a particularly pure and unspoilt vibration, it must be more likely that they can then merge with the greater mind, the universal energy, the 'whole' we talked about before, not just the experience of 'Self'. Ultimately, this may be the 'goal' to achieve, should there ever be one: to refine our energy vibration in such a way that it is possible to merge with the greater mind, the universal mind. We can do this in physical form, by recognising what needs to be done to bring about a healing outcome. The more we clear our energy, we will also realise that there is no 'goal' at the end of a time-line. At some point, too, we may feel that another process kicks in; there is a feeling that there is no turning back: when we are at a certain point, we realise we can't leave everyone else behind, feeling separate - because there is no separateness. Whilst not all of us will ever 'get it' at the same time on this Earth, and dark will co-exist with light, what we all have in common is the pure wish exists for everyone to be happy and to feel their complete energy within, even if we are in an incomplete physical existence. It comes highly recommended to feel our complete energy field within, even if our physical body is incomplete. This is something that is very possible to do, and for everyone to feel. The spiral of life, our cyclic existence, means that we are re-inventing ourselves every moment, becoming more aware over and over again, until such time when time has ceased to exist and our minds have merged with the greater mind, alongside many others.

It is important to remind us again that when we talk about 'mind' in this context, we are not talking about the word 'mind' that we use in every day language, such as 'having things on our mind' or 'losing our minds' or any such phrases referring to the activities we associate mainly with our brains and thought processes. This is not the 'mind' we are exploring or referring to – those are processes I consider are part of the 'ego-mind', a phrase I will continue to use throughout this book in order to describe ordinary functions of the body in order to keep us alive, including 'rational' thought, physical and subconscious processes, brain functions and those automated and attributed to physical body,

thoughts and emotions. These processes are described in so many different ways, such as the 'lesser' mind or 'ordinary' mind, which does not
mean they are bad. They are also important as part of our existence on
Earth. We are supposed to be some of the best equipped beings to attain
insight into the higher processes present in the spirals of life within the
multiverses. All our functions can benefit us, are all good and well and
necessary to assist us in our quest, even miraculous in their own right,
but still they give us the illusion of a separate experience being removed
from the 'greater' mind, which is what I am trying to draw attention to.
The confusion might arise from the fact that they are both connected,
one influences the other and vice versa. As our Karmic energy field incarnates, bringing converging energy strands together in a much more
dense, overlaid way rather than the ethereal weightless coding that has
survived from our previous lifetimes, the slowly forming physical form
is also created of the same energy substance, which changes into dense
matter as energy strands keep converging forming linear and geometrical shapes in certain set directions according to our Karmic blueprint
first, then condensing and solidifying as cell matter is formed. if on
different frequencies.

More good news is that, if this is indeed the case, it means it is also to
our great advantage. Both our Karmic energy mind and our 'ego' mind
are both energy 'bodies', so to speak. We keep the potential choice every
second of the day whether to act from our 'lesser' mind or access the
'greater' mind. The 'lesser' or ego-mind has to be, by nature, more dense
as it manifests in the physical, so its frequency is lowered as it enters
the 3rd dimension by condensing energy into matter. As miraculous
and inimitable the process is, it also means we get more easily confused
the more complex and invisible these processes are. We are often riddled with controversial thoughts, patterns and convolutions that keep
us firmly wedged in our physical bodies, in separate lives and individual
comfort zones. We can choose to stay there indefinitely by our selective
programming and not see through it, indefinitely. In the background,
the 'greater' mind remains faithfully and eternally as true potential; it
surrounds us at all times, accompanies us, connects us everywhere and
is present not just in us, but in every living thing in the universe, regardless of whether it has consciousness or not. If we do choose to tune
in, even to a small extent, the greater mind creates synergy instantly;
it merges our Karmic energy field according to its vibrational blueprint with matching forms of existence; situations of synchronicity and
serendipity are symptoms of higher vibrations. IT is the vastness, the
emptiness, the full potential of everything that exists, and doesn't exist,
however much of a contradiction this seems to be. This is the 'mind'
that we may find it really useful to focus our attention on, find and tune
in to, as part of our journey as inner astronauts. It is part of our inherent
nature of non-separate beings, and the news will become less and less

difficult to understand the more we focus on purifying its energy frequency by clearing our Karmic 'debris'.

We have the ability to connect with all that is, in an instant.

Remember I said at the beginning that I am not here to prove anything? It just is that it is so: The greater, universal, eternal mind is weightless, telepathic, all-being - a higher-than-earthly impulse frequency created by forces of a magnitude beyond our comprehension. When we attune our Karmic focus and intention through higher practice, we can perceive its nature, that it is everywhere at once. Even if we find this quite an impossible thought, it will, all the same, ultimately lead us to where we want to be, nevertheless: true happiness; not just the one dependent on circumstances around us. Increasing our awareness - raising our vibration - will make our minds healthy. It is not just something for the few who study hard, it is achievable for everyone, and we can start any time we want, with as little as a few minutes to spare. Our realisation will be proof that we are and always were connected; that we do not have to suffer alone from angst, stress, illness or worry any more without hope or help, but can learn to understand and trust the universal processes to support us. Will we want to carry on choosing ignorance, torment and suffering? It can be a long journey finding out how things work, until we can achieve this on all levels, at all times. It can be a bit of a hike; and yet, all that is needed in order to start realising this journey is to dare take a short precious hop into ourselves. There is no other destination and not really any time to lose. There is no other road to follow externally, no time-line – only the 'BE-ing' within. This is where we find all the space we need to breathe, to relax and immerse in answers to the questions we have of the existence of living beyond ourselves, observe closely but without effort, as the answers will come. We will find methods to help us on our internal quest and become a student of how to truly grasp the meaning of our connectedness.

ULRIKE MULLER

* * *

13. Taking Responsibility for our own Karma

Karma and how it has come to be recorded within us, is crucial in our understanding the processes that have lead us here, to our individual existence, in this very body reading this text, right now.

External energies and events can and do have an influence on our inner Karmic energy mind, including when we react to them by neglecting to process the fact that they have affected us. Some of the time, we are able to wander through life unaffected by many events that don't have to concern or trigger us. Those are the 'neutral gear' Karmic events that do not leave an imprint. However, all of us are subject to many more events at various points that we have an aversion or attachment to. It can get quite convoluted and as complicated as life itself. Let's try to explain it like this: our internal physical reactions to external events - the expressions of our thoughts, emotions, our words and actions we decide on, as part of our journey as a being on Earth - will determine the Karmic energy recording that will be set within us accordingly and in turn alter our future existence. To say it bluntly: stuff happens - we react - we get stuck with the energy imprint afterwards, at least until such time when there is a new influence and we can either deal with it and heal it, or get further distracted and it becomes more complicated. To add to the confusion, both external and internal events can be interlinked and interconnected on a Karmic level – one can set off the other and the other way 'round, like a vicious circle. In fact, that is a good expression to use, as that is exactly what happens within: whilst our Karmic energy body is affected and not yet repaired, it will seem like we keep repeating past events, mistakes even. We might need reminding that our reactions themselves to situations might be influenced by our Karmic experiences so far, even from lifetimes before. Would it not help us to deflect some inner irateness when we realise it's just a glitch in our system? Inner processes such as feelings, thoughts, preferences and aversions can easily develop a 'mind of their own'. They can cause us to have physical reactions and lead us to taking the wrong actions leading to creating more suffering, strong enough to influence our Karma, others' lives and future conditions. As a simple example, let's say you are walking along a road, minding your own business. People come and go along this road, without you interacting, a bit like life itself. You hardly notice them. At some point, someone catches your eye, you don't know why, but you are drawn to interact. This could be one of many combinations

– you might look at them, you might smile at them, you might frown at them. You might say something to them, and at that moment, an interaction and an exchange of energy has been taken further than just an initial assessment on whether to interact, one that you may or may not be aware of or decide to act upon, even if 'instinctively'. How this energy exchange that happens in split seconds is then taken further depends entirely not just on your Karma, but that of the other, plus circumstances in that moment, too. You can imagine the endless possibilities and chain reaction, can't you...it's happened many times before, and it will probably happen again. There is no default setting - we cannot simply decide never to interact, or to interact the same way every time. We are prompted to, at times, think on our feet and learn to rely on our senses and intuition as well as our inner Karma to guide us. I am sure we all have lots of examples of how life will give us many opportunities to learn to do just that. Just bumping into someone in the road we might find a life-long friend, or someone we have met before and did not recognise. We might get chatting and realise the other person needs something we can offer, or that they have just the information we need to know. We might find we have mutual friends, or have been visiting the same places before. We might be in a strange place and this person is a familiar face, in a world that suddenly seems small. We might also be in a situation that's not pleasant where we feel alone and threatened, and need to say and do the right thing to get out of it. All our actions and words can and will influence any situation. There are countless situations every second of the day, and how we react to each one is how we get to come face to face with our inner Karma. Any situation in life can help us find out who we are, where we are at, what we are all about and where our inner calling is; how to learn to do the right thing, with the right tools, actions and words, with any combination of other beings around us, in the right circumstances is often like a VR game where we either get to level up - or not. Situations can be opportunities, as some of us who believe that there are no coincidences will already believe. We are learning all the time to fine-tune our reactions, and we can choose for any interactions to serve for us to learn to be of the highest help in order to assist others. If we are able to set our baseline to be of the greatest assistance to others, we have kind of got the right idea.

As they say, the Truth will set us free. If this is the case, and we are starting to see the chain reactions we are a part of in life and have been for aeons in time, then we can draw conclusions that our reactions, thoughts and feelings themselves may have been created by our Karmic interactions in the past. It would also follows that, as soon as we have the strength and methods to recognise when any of these interlinked events have gone AWOL, they can also be unravelled and put right again if necessary, in an instant of recognition. This must be immensely helpful to those who feel years of remorse burdening them, not knowing how to lessen the impact of those pangs of guilt where they feel they did wrong and now want to right that wrong. Whilst it may not always all happen in an instant, there are very good methods known today to help us make sense of it all, some of which are covered later on in this book. It is essential to first want to do what's right, that it comes from an inner process of wisely recognising where we might have been wrong. This is a necessary first step, and You can then use some of the techniques at the end of this book to learn to undo unhelpful Karmic tangles before they continue to create more convolutions in your life. Even though Karma is undoubtedly, infinitely and intricately intertwined and goes on endlessly, this should not be overwhelmingly bad news. Think about it - this is excellent news! It means we all have the chance to liberate ourselves from the shackles of our present suffering, if we choose to give ourselves permission to do so. We have the inner power to break a chain of recurring events, and because this is sometimes easier said than done, find out excellent and often free & easy to learn methods and tips on how to do this later on in this book.

It might be worth me pre-empting a couple of questions, which come up time and time again in the quest for good Karma: what if someone has done something very bad, such as harming another being? Will their bad actions cause bad Karma and unravel them straight away, just like that? The answer is: it's complicated. For a being to be so removed from their compassion so as to be able to harm another, you would imagine that there would have been a succession of many negative Karmic events leading up to their losing the human ability to have enough empathy, thinking time and foresight to prevent themselves from doing harm in that crucial moment. Bad Karma does not always just unravel us instantly, as we like to think. It's not necessarily instant, like the guy who kills the bear cub gets eaten by its Mum in the next instant. We wish it to be so, often, so that we can see justice in action, because we don't trust it to happen over a longer term. We have an inherent need to witness Karma in action, so that we can believe and trust in it again. Our trust in Karma must be so run down, so low. Not a day goes by without some bad news, and it does not seem to be getting better either. It does not help to learn that not everyone who commits a crime gets caught straight away, and not everyone caught gets convicted. Historically, there also seem to be a host of people in high places even getting away with genocide, the world over. Did they get away with it? It might look like it, on the surface. At those times, we would probably prefer to believe in Karmic justice - who would not like to think that Karma gets to them all in the end. But we need to take it a step further still: we should not have to just hope that Karma works, we deserve to trust it so much that we can rest assured that Karma works. Why should life be so cruel as to have any victim of an injustice suffer, feeling that they actively have to make justice happen, having to continue their own suffering in their own thoughts? We don't even have to spend any of our precious energy wishing anyone who wronged us the worst, because they have already brought it upon themselves. I would love everyone to get to that level of understanding that they know that Karma will sort any situation out, according to the particulars, down to the smallest detail of each and everyone involved. It is already more than enough to grieve for any suffering and loss that has occurred. If we are already amazingly conscious, we would manifest that any ill-will, any torture, any injustice, any violence be reversed, that it won't repeat itself, that people will become conscious of their precious existence sooner rather than later. It sounds paradoxical, but this is where our true power is, our power of being able to turn events around with our greatest assets: our wisdom, and our compassion. And may everyone who is suffering be reminded of their strength and be guided back to the true nature of their existence. Because Karma is a hugely complex process, we have no choice but to have lost sight of how and when it works, especially when we observe an injustice and feel a perpetrator is getting away with it. I do believe sincerely that it's not up to us, although there is a Karmic energy exchange that occurs when people meet, even when the exchange is not pleasant. Just because we can't see what is happening beneath the surface though, does not mean it does not happen; behind the scenes and not always visible to us, the cogs have been set in motion, by any action, thought or speech. That is a given. Not understanding the true effects of our actions is not an excuse to do harm and it will not annul the Karmic processes set in motion in order to alleviate ignorance. Just because we think we know that we can undo bad actions again, does not mean it happens as we think it does. Karma itself is not vicious, it is proportionate to the action that has been implemented, and the circumstances of Karmic entanglement it has created as a result. If someone intends to be violent, the violence is not released by a violent action. it is further complicated by the results of violence and the energy that is caught up in those acts, meaning that all those who have been hurt and affected directly and indirectly can become involved with the aggressors energy. Energy strands sent out by victims will remain in an aggressors Karmic energy field until appropriate actions resolve and release the victims; energies. It is not that easy, and it can take lifetimes. This is what so many people misunderstand about the concept of Karma, the simple action-reaction relationship becomes so much more complex in the third dimensional world of timelines and hidden energies. As is often the case, not knowing enough about it, the majority of people would obviously think they are off the hook if they did not visibly get convicted by an external judging force, and this is exactly why it's such a shame some really believe there is no harm that comes from hurting someone. If any of us think that, we are using excuses, not being aware at all of the consequences.

There is no big guy in the sky that strikes us down for our actions. Rather, it all happens within our own Karmic energy system. Added to this is the role those play whose lives have been affected by our actions; how we are harming ourselves first, then others, then our whole future, by denying ourselves and others access to the magic that can be good Karma by creating good conditions and connectedness to others. Doing the 'wrong' thing doesn't always mean someone is going to come and take us away, as we have already noticed. However, doing the 'wrong' thing means we deny ourselves; it creates a psychological defect caused by the passive-aggressive choice we make, caused by us pushing away complete responsibility for our own actions, therefore losing energy from our Karmic system. By wrong-doing, we are creating our own chinks in our energy armour that most likely we would regret at a later stage, except by then it's probably unlikely we will make the connection between cause and result. In this manner, a whole unresolved chain-reaction can result from our own Karmic wrong-doing in the past, if we never recognise the power play we are instigating - including the power we are draining away, sometimes for a very long time. We can probably already imagine the rest, since it presents itself in real life in infinite ways of discontent, demonstrating to us every day how a leaking Karmic energy system could easily mean a continuation of suffering. Taking a mediocre life at best for granted, we might have settled for not seeing the miracle, trading the easy way out, as we thought, for being a slave to how our ego mind controls us without actually being able to see a way out. If we choose to just carry on like this, we choose to continue to have no influence over when we get the chance to unravel our Karmic threads, if at all. Life becomes a tangled mess of who said what, who attacked whom and who did it first, who retaliated, who is involved and out to get us, so that nothing can be resolved in the aftermath. We are lost in the 'you started it' attitude of the blaming stage of our planet, already on the defence to react to anything and anyone threatening us, to the point where we can't say any longer that we were harmed first, because we don't remember any more, and if we ourselves stop harming, we feel vulnerable to being attacked. Does this feel like war to you? It does to me. The inner war we fight with ourselves as a result of unresolved Karmic actions is not much different to the external state of affairs. It might even have played a part in creating it. We have forgotten our skills to create with our inner miracle because we do not feel it any longer. And yet, we may not always have conditions such as we have right now, to complete our energy system. Do we still have a roof over our heads and a warm place to sleep? Food to eat? Clean water to drink? If we do, we are amongst the luckiest on Earth, and are so easily manipulated that we may prefer to squander our good lives in blissful oblivion rather than think about complicated stuff. Oh - wait a minute - isn't that what most of us decide to do? We may be stuck wandering blindly throughout lifetimes, without the magnificent insights hinted at in lucid split-seconds. We may be angry when someone points out to us that we have the chance to take charge of our own lives and their outcome. We may not want to see, we may want to keep traipsing around in the dark. We all have to make that crucial choice. When we are defensively lost in ignorance, we may not remember how to choose to want to see the light. Maybe we fear that feeling love will not come around for us for a long time, or that it will be really hard work. We need to also remember that each of us can only make the choice of for ourselves, not for another. We can only sincerely wish that they see the light, see the connections, see the error of their ways, and hope that they will awaken sooner rather than later.

Do we know our Karma enough to draw analogies to our own situations? How can we tell if we are giving away our own healthy control over our actions, words, feelings, thought, lives? Do we know what we are sacrificing, and why? How can we become aware of our own Karmic past? Are there exceptions to when it might be useful, appropriate and even beneficial to swap our own lives and happiness for others, and offer the willingness to do so, unconditionally? Few of us know how to do this well and not come to any harm. Does that mean we need to learn how to do this well enough so nobody comes to any harm and everyone will win? We may not know why another being chooses a tough existence, what they need to experience and overcome in order to learn more about themselves and others. Nobody should have the right to have a say or have influence over you in your life without your consent. Even in writing this sentence I may not be able to convey the full impact and importance of it. Pointing it out may not help either, but it is as we all know, a part of our human rights act. How can we enforce it when it is being breached? What about those of us who are trying to make sense of others behaviour on a daily basis? Do we know the Karma that we are each enduring? Do we ever really know each other enough? At what stage does our Karma end, and another's begin? There will be much resistance in human evolution, diversions and distractions, for sure. All I am hoping, in a non-attachment sort of way, is that this book will help someone recognise the principles of Karma be and glean some insights about our life, anyone's life, and how it can help to include the healing that is ours inherently as beings of the universe and beyond.

I know the above example will ring true for many people who have suffered similar, whilst to others who can't relate it might seem far fetched. All I can say is that if this hypothetical example rings true for you or someone you know, and they or you are on the brink of giving up or waking up or both: it's never too late, and it's not impossible to change things for the better. We may have simply not yet found the right method to put things in order. Please see the end of this book, for ways and methods to help change our reality for the better. I really do hope it will work for many and wish for everyone to feel peace.

If we were to go a step further in terms of what it means to learn more about our own Karma, we would have to talk about what it means to have our Karmic energy body with us at all times. Our Karmic energy body is intertwined with our physical body when we are incarnate, in fact, our physical body would not exist without our Karmic energy body. Even as a new-born baby, we already have our Karmic energy field with us, and it can be with us right from the start of our incarnation into the womb. Our Karmic energy body creates the circumstances for 'us' in order to experience a physical incarnation in this very life-form as a human being. It seems callous to suggest that even as new-born babies with our pure innocent energy we have these energy imprints or even breaches and chinks in our armour; but does it not figure somehow, since we can see how so many beautiful babies on Earth find themselves in such a diversity of situations, including being born with great difficulty into a life full of struggle? Is this not one of the biggest questions humans ask themselves: how can it happen that we are not all born perfect and have a new fresh and equal start to life? Science cannot yet give us an answer, so many have turned to religion to ask for reasons why but often gain no clear answer. If I believed there was a God who is punishing us, it could create guilt and shame which did not feel right. If we dismiss the differences we all have in life as pure coincidence, it seems to create a competitive 'better than you' attitude that does not help anyone. Personally, I wanted more - I wanted to find the missing link to some inner memory reflected in a chain of logical thought that would give justification and an inner sense of proof that there is indeed a good reason to believe a pattern to all of life. Perhaps it would also help others more to find their own inner sense of a solution if we only allowed ourselves to have an open mind. If we can consider even for a moment that there might be more to life than just this single one, would it not offer a different perspective to consider, perhaps even an answer as to why there are so many suffering? I don't believe there is anyone punishing as such, instead it makes more sense to me that there is our more or less complete energy system to consider which creates us according to its blueprint and what we learned and earned last time round, which we bring along with us every time. Each lifetime we learn more and more how we can complete our 'selves', which includes improving our Karmic light body. All of it is progressive learning and growing, no stage is a lesser stage as we will all have been through similar events in order to learn Truth along a myriad of different choices and paths to get to the same insights. There can logically only be a succession of lifetimes in which we learned before, and we will hopefully learn more each time how important and precious it is to be able to do so. We would have to repeat the process so many times over and over in order to grow, in fact it is said that the growing has no beginning and no end which is hard for us to fathom since we are clinging so tightly to our perception of just one timeline in just one lifetime. One lifetime is far too short to make the experiences and talents that are necessary to form the miracle of an alive being, considering how our physical body grows according to our inner insights and connections. We are developing all the time and have been for aeons of time, which in itself must demonstrate that we would do well to make it a positively charged experience. It takes many, many goes and we need to let ourselves and each other off the hook a bit. Nobody is responsible outside of our own Karmic timeline for what happens to us. We might be tempted to think that Karma does not work because we cannot see it in action – but we are living proof that it does. The Karmic energy you have that makes you alive, is what brought you here, through millions of previous attempts at life. There is no blame, this is your learning time-line that was created within you by your own previous lives, actions, thoughts and words, and all of it serves to make you even more alive and aware. We should be concerned more with finding out about our own path and that we stay on the right track. We don't need to concern ourselves with others' Karma simply because those who are still learning that they have miscalculated their own strength and misused their power as a result, will have their own demons to reckon with.

It's up to us to sort out our own lives, our Karma, our timeline, in order to clear up and become wise. As part of the wisdom and compassionate journey we take, we will certainly meet with many opportunities to help others which we would be wise to take on as unconditionally as possible, since they are valuable chances to allow our Karmic energy to increase and connect. Even if it does at times seem we are clearing up others' mess and wrongdoing, it is still about what we are learning from it: we are slowly but surely turning any energy lack around into a positive scenario, allowing energy to increase for ourselves and others. We do have often have a choice, of course, of what we take on, but even when we think we know what is happening, we are still learning from it, too. If we cannot remember anything, how can we say with certainty that we, too, have not once been just as ignorant as those we are being prompted to help? We are still pupils in this whole process of finding out who we are, so maybe we were once not so different from those who we sometimes condemn or despise. Perhaps any precarious situation shows us that we would never want to live in ignorance ever again, and that has got to be a good thing to be reassured of, and prove to ourselves over and over that we will not take a step backwards. We have choices on a daily basis whether to do right or wrong, and if we know the definition of what that means and are not tempted to do wrong, then we are on the right path. When we see others acting in ignorance, it might evoke feelings within us of pain and upset. It is not easy to do, but it is more useful to show humility and gratitude of the process of being shown what to do with our wisdom than to give in to lesser energies. This sounds like 'turning the other cheek', and maybe there is truth in that, but it does not say forget your precious energies and let yourself be hurt and die, far from it. It shows us how to learn to use our amazing Karmic energy resource under sometimes very adverse conditions. Yes, it will seem unfair at times, because it's not often visible to us why someone is behaving badly towards us and others, and at times horrendously. Perhaps others have attacked us, hurt us, even killed us in many, many lifetimes. Most of us must have had experiences of being victims, and attackers, too, by default. If there are infinite possibilities, most of us will have led benign lives, brutal lives and also brilliant ones. Some of us could be relatively new to this game of a human existence and some have been thousands of times before. Sometimes some of us have acted wisely, sometimes less so. All of us will be given the opportunity for redemption. All of us will learn from experience how to have feelings of remorse and regret as well as joy and bliss. If we have not experienced pain and loss, we will find it hard to feel empathy for others Likewise if we have suffered too much, it's hard to think about anyone else outside our own healing process for a time. This must be the explanation: we, as precious people, have precious potential, and

Our Karmic energy minds right now are a gift from our past selves, and our good actions, thoughts and words form the totality of our future Karmic minds once reborn. We ourselves decide what we gift our future Self.

Our ego mind is not our God. We have had and always will have choices, although they will not always be the obvious right ones or present themselves at every opportune moment. The choices that are offered and those that we make are subject to Karmic conditions ripening. We may not always recognise them as important or appreciate them for what they are, and we won't always be fully aware either of what they mean in that instant. Karmic reasons why things happen to any of us and how well we understand those reasons for our experiences can be down to many different possible causes, which we cannot often be certain of or speculate on straight away. Knowing that we cannot easily be sure what each situation means for us until some time has passed, it must be almost impossible for anyone else to know what each of us is going through; it can also potentially be damaging for us and others to make assumptions unless we truly come from a compassionate aspect with the intention to try and understand each other better.

An important thing to remember is that the principle of Karmic imprints applies to all living beings. Equally important is for each of us to have our own realisation that there exists a Karmic imprint for all of us in the first place. Karma applies to us all, and it can connect us all and intertwine, but unless we all realise the importance of it, we may not be able to appreciate it, grow together and make use of the fact. Most of all, without realisation, we will not be conscious of how to increase good Karmic energy. Our Karma and us may just be like strangers walking past each other in a street. This is where we are all quite similar to each other, all of us can become more aware of how we can actively improve our internal and ergo our external world, too. When we are lucky enough to have become at least somewhat aware, we might gain an understanding as to the meaning of some of our Karmic imprints and how they arise at certain points of our lives. If they are good imprints, we can learn to express gratitude and allow more good to come from them by building on the fruits of our good Karma. If they are less desirable imprints, then we may have good Karmic connectivity within us to at least be able to recognise them. If we do, then can also search for and discover good methods of how to counteract any damage that has been caused as a result of these imprints, as well as the negative imprints themselves to prevent it happening again. If we can do this within our physical, mental and emotional bodies, then we can consider ourselves extremely fortunate, because we get to see through a number of causes of our damaged Karmic energy tissue and have an opportunity to repair them in this very lifetime.

The concept of there being a sort of 'damaged' part within our Karmic energy body that is affecting our every day lives, but which we cannot even see with our own eyes, may be difficult to accept at first, let alone repair. This is where it gets very interesting. The damage caused to the Karmic energy body can be fixed, if we can apply the correct method(s). Just as our body can heal a wound when it is bandaged, our Karmic energy body can also hold 'wounds' that can be repaired. However, since these are on an energy level, we need to not use a physical bandage, but an energy method that accesses the tear in the energy fabric. Maybe I will politely ask you to sit with the analogy and humour me a little while longer before we get to collect more insight; but if you can't wait and want to go to some of the exercises at the end of the book straight away to get some ideas and try it for yourself, please feel free to go to the last chapters in this book.

As far as I am concerned, the proof is always 'in the pudding', as the British like to say. I cannot prove it to you, and the best methods are those where you get to try it for yourself and see proof before your very own eyes. And that is something I wish for you, for all of you – that it does work for everyone. Even if we are at first scared, sceptical, tentative, terrified as to what we might uncover and/or at our wits end - when we are ready, we get to experience that this very feeling that was stopping us from finding out more is just another tear in our Karmic energy fabric that can also be dealt with, just the same as any other Karmic residue from the past. It can be done, or undone, if need be. We are all learning to trust, and also to trust our own existence.

14. Explaining the Phenomenon of Energy Imprints, 'Breaches' or 'Chinks' in Our System

I've been talking about energy breaches, chinks, imprints, tears or flaws before, to describe that most of us are here on Earth with what could be described as an incomplete Karmic energy system. Our Karmic energy system is not static within us. It flows, swirls, forms patterns, shapes and disperses; it goes convex or concave, and sometimes even shows imprints like a physical body would on an X-Ray or MRI when it has been hurt. Our Karmic energy mantle already brings with it into this life lower frequency spots where it's been weakened before as if from a previous injury, much like a healed fracture in a limb still shows up as a thin line on an X-ray; except that it is much harder to detect these 'breaks' when they appear purely as an energy frequency, and pretty much the only time we will know we have them is when we come across situations where they begin to show up as our internal reaction to a situation. It can be experienced on a physical, emotional, mental or physical energy level. If an energy 'break' exists somewhere in the body, it will have its own electromagnetic resonance 'identity'. As has the Karmic energy system itself which is an entirely unique, alive pattern for each individual living being. Usually, the resonance of an energy 'gap', hole or tear is different from its surrounding areas, and different from what it would be if it were fully functioning. Often, these breaks are infinitesimally small, but can increase in size if they are not taken care of. Just like a battery that does not connect with its terminal, a tiny gap between the both means that energy will not flow. An electric gadget will not work if it's not connected with an energy source, and even if it's plugged in it needs to be switched on so an energy circuit can be established. Similarly, the Karmic energy field that creates connectivity within our physical 'ego' body transmits and transforms its energy blueprint into cellular structures accordingly. Where we are born with or have had transmitted to us energy breaks or tears or malfunctions in our Karmic energy field, energy might not flow, or not as well, and since our physical body needs this energy to flow as unhindered as possible to be healthy, it should make sense that physical, mental or emotional conditions and illness may follow as a result of inner energy breaks.

This must be fascinating to learn for the first time if we were not aware.

How does the energy actually flow through our body, how does it work? What happens to us if it doesn't flow in places, and how does it affect us accordingly? Would our physical DNA be formed as a result of our Karmic energy field or does the Karmic energy field adapt the frequency of our DNA into its own nature? We know so little about how DNA functions, but we are finding out more and more that it is based on energy frequency coding.*

*(Article by H Patel and Lawrence A Loeb: DNA polymerase active site is highly mutable: Evolutionary consequences (https://www.pnas.org/content/97/10/5095)

However fixed we see our physical body, its nature is that it is mutable and adaptable, meaning that, just like its components like DNA, it it is composed of energy frequencies which can shift and change. Again we find that on subatomic levels, the rules we take for granted in our physically slow and dense existence do not apply. I drew the conclusion a long time ago that in order to cure any energy dissonance within our bodies and avoid further damage on emotional, mental and physical levels, it is possible up to a certain point to realign the frequencies of our Karmic energy body. There are limits - i.e. it is definitely preferable that the dissonance is recognised as early as possible before it is 'set' in physical form. Also, we are working towards optimising our Karmic energy blueprint, so there might be limits to our physical appearance as well, although we also know how much this can shift already through processes of ageing, illness etc. Our bodies can be a little like slowly moving sand dunes in the desert, you hardly know that it's happening as all looks the same on the surface, but by measuring we find that everything actually moves relatively swiftly, at least for something in physical form. If we are not well physically, it would also greatly help our physical body if the affected energy area were treated accordingly and healed as fully as possible as well. The causality seems to be that often there is an energy dissonance first which announces physical consequences at a secondary stage when left untreated. We could ask ourselves then, whether our Karmic energy also has the power to determine certain occurrences in our lives, and we might be wondering if some things that happen to us are entirely pre-destined? Do these events become predictable therefore, and does this mean that hypothetically speaking, all of them are predictable or just some?

Whilst we may only know questions and not straight answers to so many phenomena in life so far, what we do know is that there is an advantage to working with Karmic energy worth pursuing as it can pre-empt physical illness, much as if you would exercise or eat healthily to prevent feeling unwell. Also, it is non-invasive, not painful and there are many techniques available which can readjust and boost our Karmic energy system in order to benefit frequencies already. Another advantage is that it doesn't have to be rocket science to boost our Karmic immune system - everyone can do it, just like it doesn't take a degree to be alive. A lot of frequency work is based on working with intuition and theta levels of consciousness frequencies, rather than ego-body intellect. In order to become the right vibrational resonance again and sync with its surrounding field, we luckily do not have to know what the exact resonance is or needs to be, in order to be able to cure it. We will instinctively know and will learn more and more to trust and use our valuable input from our inner energy frequency body. All we have to do to start off with is to become aware of which area of our physical body, thought process or emotions might have been affected. Even then we don't have to be a scientist to work it out, and we can use our own words to tune into our inner Self. I shall give you an example. In my practice working with PTSD (Post traumatic Stress Disorder) sufferers, I have come across many people who were involved in accident, often as a driver or passenger in a vehicle. What they and many others experience after the event is grouped under the term PTSD - Post traumatic Stress Disorder. It affects many millions of people over time, and many more probably go undiagnosed as they are not familiar with the term or symptoms. For us energy therapists, it is logical that an event would leave an imprint in our Karmic energy mind, not just our physical body, that needs treating just as urgently. The symptoms of PTSD include thoughts that are repeating the incident in our brains like a short circuit many times over, especially when confronted with similar conditions as in the accident. This can include thoughts and even internal compulsive visualisations such as an inner revisiting the site where it happened, re-running the whole event despite not wanting to consciously, even feeling phantom pains in their bodies linked to similar body positions that they were in when the event occurred, such as feeling as if they are still sitting in the same seat in that vehicle and being restricted by their surroundings. Even smells, sounds and body sensations are linked to the unfortunate incident, and they can still be as intense as the event itself even years later. When we observe this in so many different cases, It is evident that our energy body records everything that has happened to everyone in an incident in incredible detail and it will replay the incident over and over, sometimes for a lifetime, until something resolves the issue. This often never happens, as we remain unaware of the solution, resulting in many different symptoms such as panic attacks, agoraphobia, claustrophobia, sleep disturbance, mental health issues etc. This is often then treated with medication, having an ongoing detrimental effect on their physical body and in turn, our energy body some more. However, we can avoid or at least soften the impact of this whole lengthy and painful process by addressing the energy frequency imprint any incident has left on our energy body.

In the example of the person involved in the accident, we treat their energy imprint by simply asking their individual recall of the event whilst using techniques to access the energy body via certain energy points along the physical body, much like an acupuncturist would do, except this method is more psychological and does not use needles. The result is often instant and stunning. Most people describe an instant and very noticeable relief from symptoms, which indicates that the traumatic incident no longer has an imprint on their energy body or that it least has lessened to a manageable degree. Eventually, it can happen that the person involved will no longer experience any symptoms at all, with the result that they can recall the accident and details of it, but this is no longer connected to feeling any symptoms of pain or PTSD.

Whilst this is an incredible discovery by itself, it makes complete sense that it should work knowing what we do, and I have had many thousands of success stories in energy therapy which to me confirm the idea to be worthy of consideration: our physical, mental and emotional processes displaying certain individual symptoms and memories are representatives of an energy 'breach' in our Karmic energy body that

has sometimes occurred through a traumatic event but does not have to stay there and affect us indefinitely. Once the majority of symptoms are addressed appropriately, this will have the effect of full or at least partial recovery from our ailments.

imagine what this discovery that has only been applied in this way over the past 40 or so years, would be able to do for everyone on this planet who has suffered trauma at some stage. In the context of my work and my increasing focus on Karmic energy patterns since I started to work with energy therapies in 1998, I have also been working with more and more people who are happy to fully acknowledge that their Karmic energy patterns have unwittingly affected them in this lifetime, and we have found that techniques like the one described above work just as well on those Karmic energy body patterns as any other. As I said before, universal energy does not discriminate, and all energy work can be accessed by anyone equally successfully.

At this point, I do feel it's worth mentioning that I have quite a zany sense of humour which helps at appropriate times, as I do feel humour can be a great healer. I am often reminded of a sketch by a famous comedian, where he is waxing lyrical about his wife's profession as an alternative therapist, and ends up in a hilarious anecdote about how you would not be asking for aromatherapy when you've had a serious accident. Apologies if this feels insensitive since it lacks the whole context of the comedian on stage which is no other than the great Billy Connolly, it is certainly not meant in an offensive way against anyone. It does however always reminds us to be careful about touching a sensitive subject, because he is absolutely right, you wouldn't ask for aromatherapy in an emergency situation, would you, so he's just pointing out the obvious. There are times when alternative therapies are incredibly useful and times when they are not the main option to go for. He makes a point we would all do well to take more seriously, because by the time there is a dramatic event manifesting itself in our physical body, it's far too late to look at anything that might be wrong within the world of our subtle energy channels and how to treat them gently before it's too late. And so, I always thought he proves a point, in inimitable style. Having said that, I did go through surgery recently which i was very grateful to receive from some amazing experts in their field, and managed to get by entirely without painkillers after just one day post operation, and halving my recovery time much to the amazement of Doctors and nurses who were very interested in how I was managing it. I explained about energy therapy and the greatest result is always when both allopathic and alternative remedies actively respect each other and come together to work as one.

As already said, depending on what method of energy treatment is used, we often do not even have to know or be able to diagnose exactly where the affected area is. That is how miraculous these therapies can be, but if we think about it, ALL of our body functions without us being fully in the know of how it works. Although these techniques may be against the analytical paradigm of everything we have been schooled to believe in, our scepticism does not affect their effectiveness. They still work no matter how sceptical we want to remain. It is a realm we cannot usually fathom anyway and it might be the exact reason we so often doubt it, as well as we doubt our own strength to recover. I also, over time, have experienced the techniques successfully on myself and others tens of thousands of times, and often liken the healing process to polarised charged particles attracting each other, aligning and thus allowing the healing energy current to repair and flow again, similar to the way that a molecule can form when atoms attract, or synapses pass on electric impulses along nerve pathways in the body. In a more crude way, imagine a lock and key system where both fit neatly together, or even batteries in an appliance where a gadget won't work unless all batteries are the right way round. Even the analogy of an electrical current running from a socket to an appliance will work, because if there is no current, nothing will happen. You need to switch on the current first, and if a fuse has blown, it needs repairing, much like our body works by a transmission of energy which formed our physical body in the first place, cell by cell, and which continues to allow life and new cellular structures to form, affecting our DNA, cellular structure and as a result, all our well-being on all levels. Sometimes it is nothing short of a miracle how an energy dissonance often rights itself so that our body, once treatment is complete, is able to align again. Like a musical instrument being fine-tuned, it allows energy to flow freely and at the right frequency through the body's energy channels again, thus making a live being feel noticeably well again. Ancient as well as new therapies that work on this basis have been deemed useful, rejuvenating and successful, especially recently with the addition of even more finely tuned and adjusted versions, sometimes with the result of managing to completely avoid the need for invasive surgery or medication.

In many recorded cases, a healing process occurs regardless of knowing either location or even the type of resonance discrepancy within. It seems that our body inherently 'knows' this information already and, as usual, will do the work for us. It does this quite naturally with the choice of a variety of different methods available to suit everyone, and it is definitely worth looking into it as early as possible to prevent our energy flow deteriorating before any damage is done. If you are interested to learn and would like to find out more about the therapies that deal with our energy 'breaches', please see more about this at end of book.

Some even specialise in resolving Karmic energy residue, focusing bravely and intensely on finding the interconnectedness between their Karma and how this might affect their body, mind and spirit experiencing illness and its many symptoms in life. I also see there being a connection not just between Karmic energy patters within us and our physical manifestations, but also between our physical experiences on Earth and our beyond in the in-between. Our Karmic links might give us clues as to who we are, where we came from and why we exist right now, right here, in these, our bodies in the first place. Whilst we could be accused of navel-gazing, this is valuable theoretical research into why humans behave the way we do. Finding inner proof would perhaps give people reason to not act out and think differently about how we progress through life. Perhaps it is true that some people would never be convinced, but this is also not something that we need to set out to do. It is up to each of us to decide, hence this book exploring the existence of these links and my thoughts on the subject. If we were able to find out more about our own personal timeline and how we got to be in this particular incarnation by actively making a decision to go within and find out what we are made of warts and all, then logically we would at some point understand ourselves better, especially if we have the tools we need in order to solve the puzzle of our 'Self' having evolved into the way it is at this very moment. If we want to learn about the nature of cause and effect, we can search for and gather information simply by looking at what presents itself, the way we act, look, think, behave, our symptoms, the events that occur in our lives, recurring patters and so on. They all indicate who we are now, and point at who we might have been before. We could simply say that we are very lucky to be alive, which is very true, but I would also like this to include all of us who don't feel that way, not just the few who appear fortunate to feel it. Also, would we not want to know what the reason for the difference might be, between those who live a good life and those who apparently don't? Would we not be interested in having a choice where we can examine all the evidence, and then apply the remedy for anything we find lacking? Would it not encourage us if we could find conclusions to promote methods for a better existence when we know it will have the right result? We will never be all the same, at the same time, and thank Mother Nature for that.; but at whichever level we can do this, in that combined effort, we would stand united rather than dispersed and disillusioned. The approaches of finding solutions that each of us are already displaying are not dissimilar in that we all feel lost without our inherent wisdom, and the result that each of us would feel in this inner search might be even more similar: we would come to the conclusion that in order to feel peace and create a good outcome, we have to know what is going on within us, so that we can feel well enough and have the right conditions to improve matters for ourselves and others. This is such a huge statement with massive implications. Most of us are never shown how to know and apply methods to properly make ourselves feel well internally without a lot of external stuff necessarily going our way. A lot of us are losing our ability to feel naturally happy, which is great reason for concern because we don't want to become prey to those who take advantage of that. If you do get at least some of the idea of the connection between your Karma and your present state of mind, you may have had enough fortunate Karmic experience to already possess that thought pattern. If you don't quite get it yet, at least you are sitting here reading this book wanting to find out more. We can and should at any point reach out to those who are not fortunate enough to be blessed with good health, and the answer must always be that we do as much as we can to help, with the intention of and our full attention turned towards wanting to assist in improving their health which will, in turn, include having a positive affect on ours. Altruism works both ways, but we can't use it Selfishly. In the end, none of us are separate existence anyway, we are the temporary result of phenomena created by our own Karmic beliefs. in this lifetime, it includes a separate – and fallible - 3-dimensional physical body for each of us, according to what we have created so far. I wonder what it's like in other dimensions. Star Wars has nothing on my brain.

The analytic approach we are taking here of looking at Karmic connections and finding answers is not the only one of course, and you might argue we could just become more healthy and well by exercising and eating well. But do we really? Does exercise stop us from suffering injury or distress? Are athletes not just as prone to becoming ill and dying as we all are? Do those rich, gorgeous and famous people we admire so much live forever? And anyway, does a that lifestyle come cheap and easy, and does it stop us from succumbing to illness or experience heart ache? Or does it encourage us to mask our problems with temporary fixes and spend a fortune on filling the breaches in our lives like the wrinkles eased by a Botox injection? As always, you decide.

* * *

15. A Hypothesis About Our Personal Karmic History

I will be doing a little detour a little later in this chapter, in order to explain these energy 'breaches' further, and give a personal example in form of my own history of Karmic recalls. As well as giving others' accounts and theories of the concept of Karma, it might help us contextualise our own ideas of how we might find out how our Karma arises. This has probably never been done before in this format but I am hoping that in its relative simplicity it can give an example of how we can think differently about how our individual historic timeline arises. The danger in this is always that it simplifies too much to the sceptic so that it may sound unconvincing unless we ourselves have made similar experiences. We started the process in the chapter above, making a link between own Karmic history and our current state of being, however, I have kept it vague so far as to what this actually means. We can each draw our own necessary conclusion from it so that we can follow suit with our own interest in research. The more of us there are making connections with our past, the merrier - not that we should start making things up or spend our whole life wondering, because it is after all more important that we draw the right conclusion from it in order to live happier, more meaningful lives. Life is about our Karmic choice of behaviour in the here and now that we should focus on, as - together with our Karmic choices in the past - it determines our future Karma. Many people including many youngsters have recollection of past life events which have been recorded before, and there are so many recorded cases by now in several studies that even science cannot remain sceptical about these stories especially when they check out. What is unusual about this open approach is that I am trying to link it directly to how Karma works, to give ideas of how our own personal lives may have evolved over aeons of time, as well as examples to encourage anyone to find out that all their previous recordings of their choices, too, are still intact within their Karmic energy minds, affecting the way they think, feel and act on an every-day basis.

To me, these experiences remain as real as if they happened yesterday, and I say this so as to try not to put off anyone who might decide that finding out about their own Karma is not for them. I find that the power behind them hopefully does not come across as ridiculous or off-putting, but rather becomes all the more grounds for acting well, since it obviously affects us in our long-term future. I do not see any external force that punishes us - far from it - and the examples below will give a plausible explanation of causality that speaks for my belief. It seems that our inner records are so exact and incredibly detailed that I have no doubt they created everything on the basis of what happened to us before. There is no 'guilt trip' involved, only an inner process that results in our choice of assessing our Karmic responsibility. At no point in the many recollections I now have of my past events from before this life-time did I feel any judgement from another entity, only the enhanced recognition of our own liability at any stage of our lives, now and in retrospect.

I do believe it might help us understand the ideas behind why things are happening in our lives - the situations we find to be out of our control, that seem too difficult, painful, unfair or unjust to cope with. There is a chance in my mind that learning we can shine some light onto our past Karma gives us an opportunity to understand how it may have been created in the past as well as the ways it may be affecting us right now, and that this might make the process of accepting our status quo a little easier. Knowing about our Karmic past is not there to serve as an excuse for wrong action in the present, but it may instead support an easier and wiser decision-making process for us all.

If we find out and resolve some of the mysteries concerning our present and connect with our true Self more deeply, are we not finding the solution to why we are craving so many external distractions and so much validation from others? As much as the process of turning inwards scares us perhaps, are the alternatives not even more worrying? ? If we are more at peace within, are we not more likely to live more peaceful lives as a result? Let's begin with a few simple, calming reminders before we panic and dismiss the idea before we have even tried it.

Firstly, have you ever asked your 'Self' who you really are? You are a human being, a highly complex and evolved being on this planet – if a little misguided at times. You had to come through many hundreds of thousands of different stages to get here, and your chosen life-form is very, very rare indeed. It is said in the Buddha's teachings, for example, that it is more likely for a turtle swimming in the vast oceans of the Earth to surface through a small ring floating randomly somewhere on those endless waters, than to be present and alive here on Earth as a human being. On this basis, we could make ourselves aware again of the miracle of our own birth, painful thought it may have been, and the fact that we even have a body (however wrong we perceive it to be), including a more or less functioning brain with which to assess, think, deliberate and make decisions. Even if we hate being here and some of us do have good reason to, we have undoubtedly been given a way of connecting to other sentient beings on this planet, and even more encouragingly, we all have the inherent ability to connect to the abundant universal energy that surrounds and permeates all of us. Even if we did despise mankind, we are made of space dust and remain connected to all things on and beyond Earth at all times through the universal Karmic energy bond we carry with us and which has brought us here, again. Many of us also have the benefit of our five senses: sight, touch, hearing, smell & taste. Even if we do not have all of those in this lifetime, it still means we are capable of expressing ourselves, experiencing phenomena in this world, communicating with others and relating these stimuli to the Karmic memory banks in our internal world. Some but not all of us have access to nourishment, water, shelter and knowledge to sustain our prolonged existence. The fact that some of us may not, does not necessarily mean that we cannot survive or adapt, or that the reason for this is because we did something bad in the past. Remember, there is no judge, or guilt trip. What it should tell us if we have much, is that we are more privileged than we sometimes feel. But something that all living beings have in common is that we have the ability and opportunities to create good Karma for ourselves, others and our future - every second of the day.

The fact that we have certain attributes in this lifetime is due to our Karmic history.

Does this come as a bit of a shock? If it does, perhaps we need to remember that barely anybody knows their full history yet, including you and me. How these aggregates develop is very difficult to assess for us lay people, but it's not impossible. So all we can deduct from this is that we logically must do away with preconceptions or judgements of punishment or reward, for ourselves or anyone on the planet. They are often based on limited or even false information and over-zealous bias.

The place, day and time we are born, amongst many attributes are also decided by our Karma, the sum of our previous accumulated energy. All other circumstances we have chosen to be born

into, arise as a result of our Karmic attributes combined with opportunities converging for us to make choices to enhance our Karmic Energy Mind along every instant of our spiral life time-line experience of our existence.

Our incarnation is determined for our conscious 'ego' Self by our Karmic energy mind. This survives our physical body and 'chooses' to be attracted to another life by the laws of Karmic energy convergence.

This, amongst other complex others, is an instantaneously induced process via electromagnetic attraction which we have touched on before. As this is a virtually automatic process governed by the attraction of our Karmic energy field to our physical surroundings and situations, we probably have little intellectual and conscious insight into it on a moment-to-moment basis. Virtually all our Karmic information appears to be stored in the form of polarised frequencies on this planet at least, so this means that we will not usually have a conscious recollection in our ego-bodies as to why or how we have chosen to be here - unless our Karmic memory is extraordinarily good and/or we can make sense of situations in hindsight. is being alive is not somewhat like waking up with amnesia? Although, as universal beings, we may well have come from all corners of the universe, most of us consciously recollect very little - if any - detail of what happened before we were born. The fact that most of us do not remember being born or being a child either hints at the reality that past lives and Karma could exist - we have simply stored the memory of them somewhere we we can least remember how to locate it. Many people I have asked do not remember anything about their childhood, as if it never existed, buried in a deeper part of consciousness. There are fascinating exceptions of course, such as young children who remember their previous existence who can even be taken to the home of their previous lives which they remember very clearly. They often recollect a past life in great detail such as their name and those of their family members, even attributes of the family, meals they had, pets, the way their home looked, where it was located and the way they passed on in that lifetime. This only gives even more incentive that it would be worth starting to put the pieces together by finding methods that help us locate our lost Karmic memory banks. Many memory flashbacks of imagery and events that occur in our subconscious mind and our dream state which we might normally ignore can serve as indicators for a previous Karmic existence and might help point us in the right direction.

If we were able to perceive the Karmic energy that permeates and surrounds us every second of the day (which, incidentally, some processes, practices and people lucid enough to see and interpret them could help us do) we would have such an advantage to start off with. Since we mostly do not, and additionally also do not generally believe in Karma in the West, we are at a disadvantage. As already stated, our energy field is too complex to be grasped in its entirety by our brain, but if we are at all open to exploring the subject on levels which go beyond the brain itself, we could start to receive a more complete idea of why we are the way we are, why we have certain issues, feelings, attributes and behaviour patterns to deal with in this lifetime, why we had an incredible ability to play the piano at five years old or could recite poetry at age two. We may find information stored in our Karmic energy system within us that really is significant and crucial to our existence, development and perhaps survival, too, right now at what seems like a point of no return in Earth's time. Or we might simply come across some mundane information that does not make sense just yet – which is certainly also possible as an outcome and thus becomes equally acceptable as a result.

Whatever method you choose in order to do this, there are very valid ways to find out more about ourselves and our existence. We can start quite simply by looking at what presents itself - our character traits, our talents, our good and bad sides. Odd as it may seem to our Western thinking, our full astrology birth charts would be a very good idea (as opposed to single repetitive tabloid lines giving the process a bad name), because they function like a map to our inner world and can give much information about us as well as indicators to our past, present and future; all of these constituting important parts of who we are now as the results of our previous Karma, they may hint at the formation and development of components of our physical presence, thoughts and emotions based on our Karmic energy field that created our physical existence in the first place. We could also focus on writing down our dreams and repetitive dream sequences as a way of accessing our subconscious, our preferences in terms of what we are most passionate about, our likes and dislikes as well as everything that we strive for or avoid at all cost. We can look at our memory and try to recall important events in our lives and how we reacted to them; what conclusions we drew from events we seemed to have had no power over; or how our conscious decisions in the past have influenced our lives since. There are many techniques and therapies that encourage healing, understanding and closure on a number of events in our lives that we have struggled with. The memory-finding techniques which I have tried and tested myself and still like to advocate as coming from pure Truth are the ones I found to be most suited to my high standards and preferences: to be certain that the process remained as accurate a recollection from my past lives, any process had to be entirely substance-free so that any result I would retain from my research would remain pure, free from mind-altering processes induced by potential nerve enhancers or even toxins would be eliminated. It had to be cost-free or virtually free, to avoid any processes falsely advertised as being effective, my personal take on it being that any true form of spiritual knowledge that comes from highest source is always freely given. I also honoured that these techniques prompting inner snippets of wisdom would be offered as and when they came along, and weren't forcefully induced by any form of Self-flagellation. Of course, above all my intuition had to be drawn to the technique in the convolutions of all that there is out there to experiment with, so my internal radar was set to the highest and best outcome, purpose and benefit for all sentient beings. I was also convinced it could on each individual inner Karmic 'knot' as quickly as possible, sometimes in an instant; even if that meant working through a host of issues that took my whole lifetime which, as it turns out, is quite quick in terms of universal timing. I will comment on why those attributes set the high standard of importance: because they all fit in with what I concluded is the very thing we have been exploring all along. Underlying these requirements is the fact that I found them to be true requisites for finding our inner Truth.

The universe provides free help, at all times. All we have to do is learn how to ask, and then ask. Ask wholeheartedly. Ask wisely. Know how to ask for what it is you need, at any given moment.

Our Karmic energy minds work best for us when we are fully aware and awake. Any process that is artificially induced or sped up by any substance outside of our Karmic mind, is deemed counterproductive to the process and has the potential of falsifying results. For example, the 60's and 70's I grew up in, were all about taking mind-altering stuff, but I didn't feel drawn to its energy and never took part in it; simply because

I thought if I wanted to see pink elephants, I would find them within me quite easily without needing external intervention, but it would not have been anything to do with my search for my true Karmic path. I remained convinced that if something did not contribute to finding the pure way, I would have struggled to stay on the path of remaining on a pure, altruistic path afterwards. I was entirely convinced that the answers were already present and needed no prompting; they would come when they were ready to present themselves, so I didn't have to go searching for them or go out of my mind to find them.

I also knew that things could happen in an instant when the timing was right, and I knew I was not alone, having read a bit about it when I was 14. Whilst reading some of the material, I had an epiphany: that everything we needed to know, was already existent within. I stopped reading there and then. It took a little while longer to free my brain from too much external stimulus, and learn the art of going inward to find the Truth. Even though i was doing fine in many subjects including Art, Maths, Physics, Languages etc. and became a Life Artist for a large part of my life, going inwards and learning not just how to manifest is the only art-form I found I wanted to continuously practise, pursue and perfect, as it was all i needed to learn to create good conditions and keep a balance of healing and well-being for my family and all those who included in that circle. Combined with some application of not shying away from hard physical work from a young age to help bring energy down to Earth, it found me everything I needed to know - and a lot more besides that i hadn't thought of.

Everything already exists, we just need to learn how to tune in to find it.

We also need to learn how to manifest it, value it, harvest it mindfully, and share it.

In my teens, I met with fishermen in Sri Lanka, who taught we in an instant what it was that I had been missing. Caught up in a civil war, these families got by on the equivalent of 10 pence a day and yet, they beamed happiness and generosity, treating me like one of their own sharing their simple meal. It was such a contrast to Europe in the throws of Yuppie-ism in the 80s, the 'bigger/better/faster go-getter generation trying to outdo each other in amassing more fortune and out to outdo each other no matter what. Education was all about first come, first served, best marks got the best jobs got the most money. Did it create eternal happiness? No. I found more happiness amongst those people I met in that month spent in Asia and it made me long for the simplicity of inner happiness in my life in Europe. Besides having a very active life observing the external, I became a bit of a hermit after my determined path. It can be a bit lonely being a purist despite being in a massive crowd, but I wanted nothing else more than to persevere to see what i would find. Art helped me go inwards, and a continuous and sometimes restless pursuit of the inner world ensued. I was so drawn to Eastern philosophies that were not at all represented in Western education where I grew up, and we did not have subjects at school, internet or even books to teach us. Again, i found all I needed within, in many meditative hours spent in rural peace and quiet. The peace I had made it easier for me to understand my inner voice, which helped me find the solution to all external longing and reduce it down to the two simplest and most profound answers that I have ever come across in any doctrine, religion, inner path since: the concept of truly understanding what is meant by applying the combination of the two terms of compassion and wisdom in every day life. It seems that everything was different after that, at age 19, and yet there was still so much to unravel to live that Truth.

Later on in life, once I learned how to meditate, I found more quickly what truly worked for me in terms of learning to undo our inner Karmic damaged pathways, having come across a therapy called EFT™ in the late 1990's which had a profound effect on how I perceived we could all change and iron out our Karmic energy creases. I am still so eternally grateful for all those who facilitated my learning, and gratitude still accompanies me when I realised that it meant we automatically create more positive outcomes when we are unconditionally grateful for the ones we already receive.

I had many, many thousands of individual experiences of energy shifts, some of which I describe below. All of them examples of how these are available free, or virtually free, accessible to all, portable, useable at any time or stage of life, with no contraindications and no substances necessary ever to artificially induce an altered state of mind. I loved the process, all of it, still do, even the deep parts, especially the deep parts. It started by taking away my fear and I realised that this was such a necessary process for us to feel secure enough to trust the process of life again. I went through the motions, but i know I was very fortunate as I never had to shed endless tears of hopelessness. A reduced intensity and time for any pain felt during healing is a part of the process. How opposite to everything else i found in life that was overwhelming, painful, emotional and fear-inducing! I found many answers, and some of them I would even go as far as to say they were THE answers I had been looking for. Many of them were right in front of my nose and kept recurring, dancing around me until I got the message. I learned how to ask into the clear space before me of what I needed and know that I was heard, and I learned how it was fine to give, give and give some more as well as receive once in a while. I found help everywhere I looked, and everywhere there were signs of serendipity, synergy and synchronicity.

Over 20 years ago, Meditation, my Buddhist practice and EFT™ became my daily practice. Of course, there are plenty more therapies, mind training, courses, retreats, meditation groups and help centres up for grabs these days; we are still very fortunate despite these troubled times on our poorly planet, because we are privileged to be able to make a difference to ourselves and others; and you have a vast choice of methods that may help you specifically find your path.

As we already said, as part of your inner practice you have a choice to go back on your timeline in order to repair what you feel did not serve you and put it right. Some people will not notice this as a conscious process or effort, but just find it is a part of their daily deep meditation. Others make it a much more ceremonial, creative and conscious event. Find your way, and learn to be comfortable with the process. By going back for a short while, or regressing, we can become aware of more details of our personal history and make amends. Of course, your physical body will still remain in the same room, but it will feel like a part of you is going back along your own personal timeline. What you are really doing is checking in with your Karma, and allowing your Karmic energy repair you psychological state of mind, your emotions, your Karmic time line, your ancestry, your family, your life and yes, probably also your DNA. This is a process that is incredibly important but it also should be done, at least at first, in a safe environment with someone you trust and who knows what they are doing so that you do not feel any fear or concern. This practice is of course something that has been done for aeons of time on Earth, In all original cultures there exists a ceremonial practice or initiation where we learn to be alone with ourselves and our inner world. Some people swear of the benefits they achieve by doing this, many of them famous. Almost all report that they have taken many a comforting vision from these procedures into their perception of themselves and their lives as they are now, helping them cope better and come to terms more with their reality within their present lives. Many books are available on the subject and many other techniques, equally valid. Even if you are sceptical, you need not make up your mind at all whether this is right for you. The prospect of finding out more about yourself can be daunting as well as exciting. if you find resistance and/ or find it all too scary and far-fetched, just carry on reading; the process of slowly discovering happens by reading about it, too. Keep your scepticism, be discerning, examine everything you come across, to see if it suits you and feels right. Even this very process of you reading this text is Karmic! I suggest you just sit with it for a while without judging, before making up your mind whether it all makes sense to you personally at this point in your life. Needless to say there are plenty of techniques that release the fears we might have, safely and gently.

At this stage, it's finally time to explain and to let you in on one of my own personal experiences that initiated me into finding out more about my own Karmic history. You may not find this helpful at all, especially if it doesn't fit your own paradigm for your life experiences right now. That's ok. I am not saying that you suddenly need to believe in anything you do not want to, in order to benefit from some of the theories and thoughts laid out here. Everything is an experiment so we can see what we individually discover, and the following just happened to be a part of my journey.

We are trying to understand processes in the mind and Karmic energy body which are still largely uncharted. I have come across many methods in my quest for finding out how they work, and have chosen the ones below because I feel they demonstrate well what I am trying to convey. My aim is to show you what it taught me, how it encouraged me to find out about the links between my personal experiences within my lifetimes, to realising the reasons why they are there in the first place. I found out so much and it helped me find answers as well as solutions. For me, these techniques worked perfectly and did everything I hoped for; and therefore I thought them worthy of sharing with you. You must reserve your own judgement until you have tried your own way, of course. It makes no difference to the fact that I feel more complete, alert and aware knowing what I know now, and I am certainly happier and more content because of it.

I first came across a process called Emotional Freedom Technique™, or EFT™ for short, in 1998. it was my first experience of regression – although I did not set out with an intention to experience it. The group of Meridian Techniques that EFT™ belongs to allow us to become more insightful, and they link in very well with ancient methods of Meditation and other similar techniques to access our inner information to bring about transformation. I had heard of EFT™ first in the mid 90's and it was very new in the UK then, but it sounded positive and I was willing to give it a try. In my first session, it just took me into an inner zone of calm by chance, naturally and with ease. I had decided on the spot to work on my fear of swimming in deep water, because I could not think of anything else that was really bothering me. It certainly was seemingly unrelated to any form of regression that then automatically occurred in this session. I later found out that a regression does not necessarily happen as part of an EFT™ session and is also not necessary for it to work. However, something called an 'abreaction' occurred, where we disassociate from the present and our mind goes into other memories as if they were happening right in that moment. My fear of water did not seem like a huge issue to me; it simply annoyed me and I wanted to be free of it, because it was stopping me enjoying swimming in open water. I now know that many people share this fear and that it is very common and for good reason.

Nowadays, EFT™ and many other Meridian Techniques are widely used and acknowledged. In my first session back then, I also mentioned - again seemingly unrelated - an intense and inexplicable dislike of the colour pale blue. I used to have this irrational thought that if a man dressed in a pale blue shirt they were not to be trusted. It seemed an odd thing to come up and also not very relevant, even mentioning it made me feel slightly embarrassed as I knew it was irrational thought. However, I was interested in getting to the bottom of why I even had these thought patterns and fears. Despite feeling a little embarrassed and exposed, I knew it was useful not to dismiss these recurring thoughts, emotions, even nightmares and flashbacks, as I wanted to know where these peculiar hints from the past would take me. Without realising, I had just found a very exciting tool in helping to unravel the individual knots of our Karmic experiences. Little did I know then that this amazing technique for treating the energy 'breaches' I mentioned before, was to be my future of 20 years discovering, writing and teaching about how we can quite easily release any apparent fear, thought- and behaviour patterns permanently without side-effects or damage to ourselves, all the while learning more about who we really are as we go along.

Throughout the session, I was reminded of an experience in this lifetime when I was 9 years old and felt I nearly drowned. I had blanked the incident from my memory right up until that day, but I started to see how it was connected to my current fears. But that was not all. My memory flash backs seemed to be rolling back even further than that of their own accord, so i went with it with my wonderful therapist's help. It was as if a film had started to roll backwards. Even though I was not prompted to, I suddenly and quickly felt taken back even further in time into my early childhood, then further back still, until I was able to feel within my present own adult body what it was like to breathe amniotic fluid in the womb. It was an amazing - if entirely unexpected - experience. There was no part of me who was assessing at that time, I was just fully engaged in re-living the experience. Still fully immersed in the process of rolling time backwards somehow, I had a sensation I instinctively knew to be prior to being in the womb. It was like being pulled upwards through a tunnel of light i sensed had been to my left, taking me back up to what I can only describe as existing before this lifetime. It felt like a different plane of existence, like a level I had entered via the tunnel, upwards and out, onto a plane of a misty white expanse of light. I was no longer in a body, but I was me, and i was filled with joy and had never until that moment remembered such an immense longing to be back in this place of light and peace. It was very emotional, as I felt the presence of beautiful light beings around, reassuring me. They appeared to be made of pure light, an upright oblong shape of pure bright vibration, emanating and radiating love and they welcomed me into their circle. i felt so at one within this circle of beings that the experience has stayed with me to this day, and I managed later to turn the intense longing for this external experience into another session, which simply and again, unexpectedly, allowed me to bring it back into my own body so that it is with me now again at all times, as it should be.

Later and in hindsight, when my deliberating thought process kicked in again, I realised I could not have reckoned with such an intense and unexpected outcome like this at all! I was overjoyed and felt very present again and alive, in the moment. The session was not hypnotic, in that no words were spoken or any visual journey suggested. The process was not premeditated, it just happened. It all felt completely natural, and I was helped only by the EFT™ process of tapping with my fingers on Meridian acupressure points on my face and upper torso all throughout my session to facilitate my experience, to take away any potential pain, fear or discomfort I might have felt. All memories flashed by in a matter of minutes, although it seemed like light-years had passed. Memories kept coming even after that, and i realised I was not quite done yet with regards to my fear of deep water. i kept using EFT™ tapping on the Meridian points as before and the next thing that happened felt again, beyond my conscious control. The whole event that followed I felt like it was happening to me in real time, like it was happening there and then and that I was more of a powerless observer, subject to my own fate that had already been determined. Another tunnel appeared in an instant, again on the left side of my body, this time pleasantly warm drawing me up into it with a pulling sensation. It took my mind even further back and inexplicably upwards into a very real, bright and detailed scenario. It felt like I had landed in the experience of sitting in a small plain wooden fishing boat. As soon as I was aware of the situation I had an ominous feeling of recognition about it, a sort of calm before the storm. I was almost overcome and sick by a restless, inevitable, fateful feeling, although the scenery was stunningly beautiful, calm and should have felt very safe. Even though it sounds like it could have been a dream-like state of mind, it was much more than that. I felt completely within the body of a little boy of about 8 or 9. This was 'me', I was that boy. I had no choice of having thoughts outside of that experience to oversee events, I was just in that experience of this boy, in that situation, feeling what he felt and doing what he did. I could determine his every sense of his inner mind, his thoughts, feelings, experiences and knowledge. I could feel his sense of belonging, knew his words. I obviously knew his age, too, and I saw myself from the inside as he knew he was, with curly red hair and freckles, and in the boat with me were my older brother and father. The water around us was a tropical turquoise and the weather calm and very warm. It did not feel like any dream I had ever had, it felt real. I could not be the observer, that kicked in afterwards when it all made sense. In those minutes, I knew that the boy was me, there was no question about it, it didn't even occur to me to doubt it. I know about the curly hair and freckles because that was who I was, inside his body, with his level of understanding about what he looked like. I am, to this day, not sure where I was, which country, or which century, but I believe now that this was in keeping with a young boy's perception, who would probably not yet have a great understanding of this sort of information anyway. I - he - didn't seem to know yet where he belonged on a world map. I guessed, after my session was over, that it would have been somewhere in the Atlantic, off the Central American coastline.

Then, all of a sudden and for no apparent reason whatsoever because I cannot recall any motion or even having moved around, I (as the little boy in the boat) find myself toppling backwards out of the boat. Maybe I nodded off, maybe I was thinking of getting up – I do not remember, but then maybe I wouldn't have any recollection, because otherwise I might have anticipated me bringing on an accident. It all came as a complete surprise. The reason why I consciously keep saying 'I' is because I am living through this whole experience in the session: I am not a bystander, watching; I am the little boy, and I feel how he feels in his body - terrified. Immediately as I fall, I know I am lost. I fall below the waterline quite quickly - and I cannot swim. I cannot swim, I cannot bring my body upwards. My feelings are those of utter panic as I flail and unexpectedly, an overwhelming sense of guilt and responsibility for seeing, as I fall, the shapes that I leave behind of my bereft father and brother looking over the edge of the boat. I feel like I fall quite quickly and I am helpless as I see them with my eyes that feel wide from panic from below, frantically trying to save me, soundlessly crying, shouting in disbelief and panic at what has just happened, total fear etched on their faces. A helpless sensation of falling backwards follows, water pressing against my body, my ears only hearing that weird muffled under-water sound under increasing pressure. i am scrambling for a halt but being dragged down by the weight of the body of water, compressing my body as I so quickly sink deeper and deeper down, the water compressing me and dragging at my useless limbs trying to struggle free. All the words I am using here describe the sensations I felt for what seems like ages. Then at some point, there is no more struggle, just slowly sinking, not being able to hold my breath any longer, wanting to breathe, all my body intent on wanting to draw another breath, sheer, helpless panic, but having to hold my breath – until...when? 'What happens next? Who helps me?' seem to be my last thoughts, unanswered. It really feels like in this part of the session I live through every split second of what drowning feels like. I would have had to let go at some point, and breathe in water, but I have no memory of this. Then moments of utter stillness and inner recognition, as the inevitable feeling of looming death takes over. I am going – forever, I know what the finality means then. My feelings of fear and the last vision of my family, trying to cry out, the intense guilt and responsibility I feel for their anguish, are taken over by an overwhelming realisation of not ever being able to breathe again, of not being allowed to draw the next breath, of the sensation of futile fighting, of physically needing to, so urgently and violently.

Even during the session I literally cannot breathe for a while, I am holding my breath because I truly believe at that precise moment that I cannot breathe. I go hot and cold. It is a moment I will never forget. I am still the little boy and I am lost. All I can see from where I am in the water is the pale blue sky. It dawns on me much later: Of course – not the turquoise sea I am used to and still love so much and yearn for, in this lifetime now! Only the pale blue sky I could see then, looking up from below the water, twinned with the feeling of dying. Pale blue becomes the colour of having to die! Only later will this make sense to me. But for now, as I am dying in that lifetime, feeling an intolerable pressure that will soon squash me and burst my lungs, my ears and my every cell in my body, it feels like it is getting darker and colder. A kind of uncertain, dark, lonely nothingness has taken over from the panic. A last conscious impression but at some point very soon after, I would have had to have surrendered and died, because the next feeling I remember is an unusual peace and acceptance after the panic, which is a pleasant and unexpected surprise. I did not know this would happen, that there would be something else to feel, least of all something pleasant. Suddenly it feels as if I can breathe again, normally and easily. I am still the boy, but this is how the session ends, with me experiencing the last part of that lifetime feeling at peace.

After the session, I realise this is something that has even recurred in my dreams in this, my own lifetime, where in my sleep I have had a similar sense of being able to breathe again, after a period of not being able to breathe as if under water. I am certain I was even holding my breath in my sleep. In my actual dreams, the next thing that almost always happened was that I reached the bottom of the sea and found an amazing city there at the bottom of the ocean, almost as if life was telling me that I will live on even after experiencing death.

Coming back to the past life experience as the little boy, I cannot recall what happens to me after drowning and then feeling peace and 'breathing' again, because once I feel I am conscious again, the vision stops. I assume therefore, up to this day, that the real 'me' left the body of the little boy behind. I feel I must have left that life at that moment and moved to another plane of existence, which would be the in-between phase before being reborn into another life. Years later, I have an idea what these phases look like as well, but that is for another time to speak about.

You can imagine that it was a dramatic and fairly exhausting experience; and even though it only lasted about 30 minutes, it took me some time to process everything. All throughout the session, though, I remained sitting upright and fully conscious, just 'seeing' and intensely feeling what I just related here as if it was happening in real time. My therapist kept using EFT™ on me throughout parts of the experience, and despite feeling everything the boy could feel, and it being a vivid and intense half hour, I can't say that the whole process was too overwhelming. It was an eye-opening and life-changing experience that i totally welcomed into my life.

Afterwards, I naturally felt tired and a little in disbelief, but mostly incredibly elated and free. After this 'aha' experience I could relate many more issues than I had previously thought to this episode of my past life. I am sure I run risk sounding ridiculous to some and that as such, they will be sceptical of what i tried to convey happened to me, but in my mind everything felt completely real and especially in hindsight, all of it made utter sense.

I would like to add here that I, like many people, had before that day forgotten many visual and kinaesthetic impacts from my childhood. Once I had started the process, there seemed to be many more of them awaiting my attention. What is clear to me is that the whole process changed my life for the better and made connections clearer, and that is invaluable to me. I also would like to state again, that I do not subscribe to any form of recreational drugs or drink alcohol, i do not suffer from any illness nor do i take prescribed medication. I am of sound mental and physical health and do not partake in any other methods of therapy other than EFT™ and meditation. I also do not subscribe to different therapy sessions as a form of entertainment. I am quite down to Earth and logical, and when I come across something that works for me I will share it with many others, because I do believe that I have a duty to make the most of the opportunity of being alive wholeheartedly.

And the outcome, you might ask? Unsurprisingly, as a result of re-living this experience, several changes occurred in my life quite naturally and effortlessly, without ever having to re-visit the experience:

- I started to enjoy swimming in deep water without any fear whatsoever and even had the opportunity to take up sailing for a few years, even diving off the end of a boat into murky, deep, cold UK water as well as going on many a snorkelling expeditions abroad, in waters unknown to me. One other aspect that arose after my session was the thought that whatever was beneath me in the water was 'out to get me', as if there were beings with a special radar homed in only on me. Anyone with a similar thought pattern will know what I mean and obviously it's not so far-fetched knowing that plenty of fish in the sea can actually sense a lot more than we humans can and may also be looking for their next meal. All the same, when I did another round of EFT™ on this particular thought pattern, it also disappeared...I now can swim in the sea without an ominous panicky feeling, but with my healthy instincts intact. It has not turned me into a daredevil but rather someone who thinks of the oceans and their inhabitants with deep respect and awe.

- In case you wondered, I stopped having my deep disregard for the colour pale blue, started to notice it more vividly and in a happier context - even bought clothes in that colour for the first time in my life, without realising that this is the colour I was suddenly drawn to wearing with a new-found confidence

- I used to be fiercely independent and yet, unable to speak up about my needs and for my causes because I feared there would be nobody coming to help, so I had given up before I even started. Nowadays I am fiercely independent WITH lots of help from loving friends!

- I stopped feeling so guilty and responsible for others' feelings, although I admit I am still working on that one.Perhaps it means there might be more than one past life connected to that, and I look forward to unravelling more mysteries and becoming clearer in my thoughts and actions still.

Of course, this was a very dramatic example of what can happen when we tune in. I can't promise that it's always going to be quite this dramatic for everyone, and more than likely most issues will be more mundane and easily dealt with. At the same time, I also don't want to make it sound too easy, because I know that it is not always that simple for most of us to make time or a decision to make a difference. However, we need to perhaps ask ourselves if we have a choice? Do we ever have that much time to spare in our busy lives, or is it the other way 'round: are our lives so crazy busy because we don't take enough time to sort things out on a Karmic energy level? Is a lifetime really too short to at least make a start and deal with some of it? This is such an incredible chance that we have, to find our way out of the maze that is our life, or even lifetimes. We have massive shortcuts nowadays compared to previous generations to get our lives straight, and the opportunity is there for us every day to go inward and start the most important tidying -up process of our life. Let's at least start somewhere! We are all faced with such finality at this time on our planet - can we afford to keep distracting ourselves, ignore what's going on and wish that it will just go away, or that others will sort it out for us? We really do need to awaken and there really might be no gentler way to return to our true strengths, which are, simply - feeling our true inner compassion again for ourselves and others, and unearthing our wisdom to know how to apply it.

After this experience and quite a few other spontaneous and just as unexpected regressions I have had since, it makes more sense to me than ever that any of the 'chinks' in our Karmic energy field – and there must be plenty of them for most of us – are the result of many lessons we have taken on board over many Karmic life-times. We have accumulated many dents in our Karmic armour, and they keep reminding us they still need sorting out by expressing themselves in memories, likes and dislikes, recurring dreams, visions, flashbacks, hunches, insights, intuitions, deja vu and jamais vu, preferences, avoidances, and yes, even our own perceptions of Self, including emotions, thoughts and what we habitually do and talk about. There are quite a few more oddities within our personalities than we probably bargained for, and it sure makes life very interesting. It also seems logical to me assume that this is the reason why we have come back into yet another lifetime once again, in order to sort them out - perhaps once and for all; and if we are lucky enough, we are incarnated as human beings. This may seem like an oxymoron, but it really is the best incarnation to have on Earth, as it gives us the potential to discern, to make educated choices, and to move around physically and mentally in order to shift our Karmic actions on to the next level. We have the potential for instant Karmic action to take place, so that we can help all those around us. I know we could all become despondent and cynical about who we are choosing to be as man(un)kind, but think about it - if this is how it works, if Karmic action really has a reaction, and all Karmic action is caused by a previous Karmic choice that can be undone with the help of a simple therapy and some quiet meditation time, then we really need not look any further to make a difference to our lives, and others. Even if we feel life has been unjust, even if we know there is plenty of adversity in those who don't yet see the harm they are doing, we need to focus on our simple strengths. If we take matters into our own hands again, it certainly means we are stronger in case of external forces against us, and it is the best action to take in these trying times. It rules out that someone 'out there' is pointing the finger at us and has got it in for us, because if they are, we need to withdraw our energy from those forces so that they can no longer function with our consent.

We Are in Charge of Our Own Karma.

It is simply a rule that we have ignored or misunderstood so far in our understanding of how our existence fits within the laws of the universe. We are here to complete our energies, make ourselves feel well, whole and healthy. We have the benevolent universe here to assist us with this process. If what we have found above is true for all of us, our lives may be complicated, but are also simply a continuation of all our previous existences, chosen by us according to Karmic laws of energy attraction; what we have chosen, we can also undo again. Much like a flame continues burning, sustained by the available energy molecules feeding it. The flame looks deceptively similar all the time, but it is never the same flame twice in any subsequent split-second. How we are sustained in this lifetime and how brightly we shine is based on the choices we made already before now...If we are like the flame, it is a baffling statement, I know, because simply put, it is a level of reality that would potentially make us all stop blaming others for our predicaments. Imagine the consequences if we could all live in peace – IF we all understood it simultaneously. Alas, it is a fact of nature on this planet, universe even, that we don't, not in the physical realm. Any statement like the one above can cause three reactions, as we have learned: some will like it. Some will be indifferent to it. And some will hate it. As long as we still react, especially with hatred, anger, aversion and fear, all based on our invisible previous Karmic convolutions, we will continue to create new suffering. We might, as a whole community on Earth, not be ready. At least, not yet.

As it stands, I will say that it all makes sense to me. We all co-exist. We are all allowed to be here, learn here, grow here. Some of us may be more conscious than others, and if it's true consciousness, that would mean we help each other even more the best way we are able to. We appear, though, to have incomplete energies, all of us, and some poor souls apparently have more than others. Some of these incomplete energies make us trip up at times and fall headlong into situations to show us that it's time to address them. I would even go so far as to say that the very same patterns created in the energy system within and around us, can arise as a correspondent mirror-like blueprint in our physical lives. This involuntary Karmic attraction to disastrous circumstances is not often that funny, it can cause even more hurt feelings until we are able to pick apart the reasons why and find a permanent solution to resolve things once and for all. This is no easy thing to come across and be able to do, so one of the reasons I am writing all this is to show that there might be solutions out there for all those situations we resign to and feel we just have to put up with. Once we are healing from something adverse that has occurred for us, we can see how it relates to parts of our past if we recognise it in ourselves. When we observe it in others, it should make us feel strong emotions of deep compassion for those beings. Does it though? Do we not separate out all the time who we feel sympathy for and who we don't? Have we not displayed just as much cold-heartedness, detachment and Schadenfreude when others are in misery? We have free will to consciously refuse to recognise and accept our responsibility for sorting out our Karmic energies, however, this comes at the cost of recognising others suffering and not being able to find and share solutions that will help others, too. All around us there are reminders of how others suffer, every day. Not knowing how to ease their condition, we feel we must try to justify our inaction, so it becomes inevitable that we turn a blind eye, we become judgemental of others, separate ourselves from them and believe ourselves when we say they somehow must have deserved what they got. We usually remain unaware of the danger of these behavioural patterns. They are affecting us just as much since we are not asking for being shown ways to help those we come across. If we don't ask to be shown, our thinking pattern is then compromised into lesser forms, which can then so easily be taken advantage of and take us nowhere but onto a path of our own duality and dependence on circumstances in lower frequencies ourselves. We have a chance to recognise everything in the right way, right now! We can choose not to, but our Karmic thought patterns are likely to remain and repeat on us again and again in more and more incarnations in cyclic existence. If, on the other hand, we can try not to be hard nuts, we will do well to assist others in their plight of trying to recognise their own Karma, which is often easier said than done. It can be a minefield. We can't become missionaries and say we are better than others and everyone must follow what we do. We can't come across belittling or give unsolicited advice. We can't pretend that we can walk in someone else's shoes and know what they are going through unless we have been there ourselves. We can, however, truly help on many levels if we ask to be shown how to act with sincerity and integrity, and we can learn to be discerning as to which one is best according to each individual situation. Sometimes it's better to lend an ear and make a cup of tea than to stand on a pedestal waxing lyrical about anything, including Karma. We need to decide what's appropriate, and I m putting myself out on a limb here writing about this stuff so that it can be used to help others, but it does not mean it's not important for you to recognise for yourself what is right for you and what is not. It is up to you. Needless to say, if this is not for you, no need to read on - unless you want to find out more about why there is resistance within all of us to doing what would be really good for us. in this case, do read on. I have a few more tricks up my sleeve.

* * *

16. Repairing Our Karmic Energy System

Whilst it could be a potentially depressing thought that perhaps not all of us will be enlightened all at the same time or even in this lifetime, who am I to pre-empt the future and say it is not possible? Perhaps there really is such a thing as divine intervention, and mass enlightenment will manifest through some great and immediate manifestation or apparition of a medium-to-large size miracle. At the present status quo it might be a nice notion to hope for. Is it useful to await an external miracle? Or will we dismiss and nail it to a cross? It might still be the better option for each of us individually to look at the miracles we already have and work out what's amiss, even more so if it gives us the opportunity to get and stay healthy and well. We have miracles every day when we look at nature and how it just makes everything grow all the time without making a fuss of it. If our ability to see the beauty of life is affected by our denial and refusal to sort out the state of our Karmic energy system, is it any wonder really, that this is what should be making us fall ill at some point? If we need a miracle to believe in miracles, but cannot see the miracles around us to remember how to create our own, why is it that we do not think it is worth exploring the possibility that we could be a miracle ourselves? Is it still because we find the concept hard to believe, trying to get our heads around the staggeringly complex system of different levels of our Karmic energy storing system? We can bring in, with continuous practice, a joyful cosmic energy of blissful formations, auspicious symbols, patterns and rays, amazing vibrations of higher meaning, sacred geometry, abstract light forms and shapes. Mostly though, in our relative ignorance to the whole abundance that is, we settle for an energy system consisting of patches, clusters, layers, breaks, kinks, daggers, cracks, arrows, tears, holes and more, all affecting out physical existence and potentially denoting different leanings towards a variety of illnesses. But even if we do this on a daily basis and want to get out of it badly but can't, we are still worthy of a solution, because nature is like that. Nature is there to help us grow. Fear not - there is a reason why we can sometimes be wired like that, and there is a great way already designed to overcome the psychology of set-backs within our Karmic energy. There is even a relatively simple solution.

If this is so and we do have a solution that everyone can learn indiscriminately, does this mean there are no 'better' people than others? No other human being greater than another? Is it simply a difference in the level of understanding and mastery of our own energy systems, simply a difference in the accumulation of amounts of light and purity of frequencies in our Karmic energy minds? Does it mean that everyone is made of the same stuff, and has the same potential to achieve this? Do our energy systems simply react to each other, trying to see where we are each at, in our great quests? Does this make judging another obsolete, if we are all the same and just at different levels of the game? One thing is for sure, it is not a theoretical exercise. Although this book of pondering the subject of Karma is getting longer, we still have to go inwards and rummage around to find our own truths. It's no good following others' orders, or keeping on about how others are getting it entirely wrong. We are in our own sphere, and nobody can find for us what we must find for ourselves within.

Fundamentally, the more light energy flows through us and the brighter and lighter our Karmic energy field, the more complete, healthy, flowing and radiant the energy system sustaining our physical well-being will be and therefore the illness in our lives may become less, on all conceivable levels. Also, it could follow that

The more completely we are connected to the all-existent energy, the more easily we are able to heal ourselves.

We could be really cynical and dismissive about all of this. However, the more we find ourselves rejecting, sceptical, angry, frustrated, full of blame, shame, insecurities, guilt, hatred and fear, the more we can actually diagnose that we are simply still stuck in a cycle of internal negativity of reversed energy flow, which is the single reason behind why we feel this negative in the first place. We could choose to remain stuck there, but why continue to do that if we don't have to? The diagnosis of the psychological reversal of our inner energy flow is simply genius. Being stuck in a vicious cycle solves very little, and although of course people are entitled to feel whatever they want to feel, I do wonder why we would want to do this, when it does not make us feel well or happy? Instead, we can allow ourselves at any moment to increase our happiness by realising that we do not have to be stuck in the doldrums. There seems to be something within us though, that makes us feel that sometimes it's really necessary or even fun to be stuck for a while and drop out of all the expectations we set ourselves to excel, and sometimes we feel a need to really revel in it like a pig in muck, and it's all part of being human. Even then, whilst rolling in the muck, we can make a commitment to ourselves to free our minds from the ties of any burden once and for all. We can simply ask the universe from the bottom of the well. Usually, though,

When we are feeling low it is the darkest place to try and read the manual of how to get out.

We all tend to do the same: we identify with the energy stuck in our bodies and we do not realise that we are doing it. Many a time when we feel stuck in the lower frequencies, when really it is simply a matter of identification. 'We' are not stuck, our energy is. We are simply diagnosing that our energy is stuck and we are feeling it; quite likely we can also feel it in a particular area of our energy bodies; this is affecting us, our thinking and feelings. We are already a step closer to getting out of our being stuck if we realise we are diagnosing as observers to our own inner energy universe, and the symptoms are what is showing up in our behaviour. Now all we need is the remedy and we will get to it asap, via a short digression into learning how energy flows in an ideal scenario through our bodies and finding our how we can repair it if it doesn't.

Let me use the energy frequency of the base chakra as an example. Also called the 'Earth' or 'Root' chakra, it vibrates at a frequency of 4×10^{14} Hz at the lower end of the spectrum of rainbow light, which is detectable with the right equipment. But we do not need to measure it, because we can often feel it or even see it, too, because our eyes can see the vibration as the colour red. This chakra or energy vortex in our bodies corresponds to creating survival energy and life itself through conception. It is situated at the base of our spine pointing downwards, connecting us to grounding Earth energies and all that is physically manifest in the form of 3-dimensional matter. It vibrates at the lowest frequency of all other vortexes in our body and helps funnel energy for the physical manifestation of the cell structure in the developing fetus in the womb. The energy that is drawn into the cell mass in the womb is funnelled in an ongoing spiral motion helping cells move along into an elongated shape, with one part pulling into the bottom half with the region near the anus forming the lower part of the torso, and the other end funnelling energy towards the crown of the forming body. It easily shows that lower frequency does not mean bad, it means a lower frequency wavelength that has different task to the others. Since all chakras function like two-way funnels, it also works by emitting energy from our bodies as well as taking in energy from the environment around us. The chakra then sends energy up into the rest of our body via thousands of energy channels circulating and spiralling upwards and outwards through our whole body to feed it with vital life-force energy. Without this vital energy, we would not be alive. It is this energy that has been fascinating humankind for centuries...how can we make something alive? We simply cannot, because the Karmic Life-force energy is an omnipresent energy that prevails long after this planet, even this solar system, even this universe has gone. We are simply not able to fathom its presence and the magnitude of it, and those who want to make it work for them and who have tried for hundreds of years to create something alive for all the wrong reasons, are probably really miffed they cannot harness this energy for some sort of monetary gain.

How quickly and efficiently this magnificent energy flow happens within us depends on our health, in turn determined by our individual Karmic energy blueprint at any given moment, which is ever-changing and forms the invisible pattern for all that happens to us and within us. Kundalini energy which is the vital life-force energy that constantly pushes like a current through the whole energy system within us and keeps us alive, can sometimes pool in any part of the energy channels and vortexes on its journey circulating around the body. Sometimes this 'pooling' is a fleeting process, sometimes it happens for longer periods of time, only then to rise again, spiralling along the spine and upwards again, moving out of the top of our heads through an important point at our crown at the top of our skull. When it moves up above us, it can circulate well away from our physical body, refresh and collect vital information that renews our energies when it returns back through the crown. If we do yoga or even simply meditate, we connect to higher sources of energy outside ourselves. The process can renew our energy and refresh our memory, especially during gentle, conducive forms of respectful connection, such as sleep and meditation. Both these can leave us fully refreshed, feeling happy, calm and able to function again. Forcing an energy connection in any way means we can take in energy not conducive to our functioning. It can bring about any combination of symptoms as complex as our vast catalogue of illness symptoms we can summon. If we are unable to replenish our energy in the correct way, our hormone centres within the energy vortexes along our bodies will not work. We will at first feel out of sorts and usually our body quickly deteriorates thereafter. Perhaps we can now understand why people crave the feeling so much and try induce it artificially by using recreational drugs; this is not the way to replenish our energies, in fact it will do the opposite and deplete us as we lose influence over what our energy does, how it connects, what frequency level it runs at, what information it collects or whether our energy is even able to return into our bodies. There are so many things that can go wrong, it is a very delicate balance between many symbiotic processes within us and our environment that have to remain in balance. Sometimes our energy does not leave long enough to replenish, sometimes it cannot at all. Sometimes it leaves and cannot return back into our body. All of those phenomena will have consequences and affect how we feel and think. Sometimes when we feel 'out of it', that is because some of our energy literally has left our body and needs to come back in. I often wonder if that is what happens when people are in a coma, or if we have an out of body experience, or as some people do, go journeying or 'astral travelling' perusing natural or artificial substances to induce the process. It is when we hand over the reigns of our precious well-being to chance that we lose power over our body's natural ability to balance the process, and even if only meant to be temporary, there are plenty of energy trips when people don't make it back.

When the energy settles in the base chakra, it needs effort to rise again, a sensation often associated with a restlessness, feeling stuck or even in pain, resulting in a need for arising passion, anger, over-assertiveness or frustration; or we could realise what's going on and save ourselves a lot of hassle by simply doing some physical exercise to help the stuck energy move along. If our Kundalini energy doesn't easily rise, we will feel lethargic and low, unable to get going. Sometimes, we subconsciously repress our energy and suffer illness associated with base chakra problems, such as lower back ache, suppressed anger, depression, shame, sexual repression or trouble with reproductive organs. Whilst the rising Kundalini energy is regretfully often confused with sexual energy, perhaps because of the sensation it gives us as it rises past the sexual organs, the two are not the same. Sadly, in the West we are quite confused about what goes on with our bodies; rather than truly enjoying what it means to have a mindful exchange between two people and how beautifully serene and respectful it can be when the Kundalini energy dances between two people simply conscious of the invisible bond between them, we have created a blunt industry exploiting a short-lived stimulus of brush-past sensations that is shamefully exploited, keeps people in the dark about their true powers (as usual) and totally overrated if you ask my opinion. But where were we. Kundalini energy is the term for the whole energy cycling through every part of our body all the time, rising and falling through each level of our body and giving us the all-familiar sensations of our whole existence as a result; pulsing through each chakra in turn, exiting through each vortex if we allow it to 'breathe', letting it out and letting it in again, one after the other, each deep pranic breath of life-giving energy freely given by our universe to sustain our physical, mental, emotional and spiritual well-being governed by the hormonal centres at the core of each energy vortex, operating all our every-day functions. Passion, anger, frustration, enthusiasm and all the thousands of different feelings and thought patterns we have even in one single day, are all labels given to the sensations that are really caused by our energy rising up from the lowest point in the body and then interpreted in various ways as it makes it way upwards through our chakra system. Our life-force is an incredibly strong yet also vulnerable and delicate energy keeping us alive, much like the blood circulating through our veins, and if we learn to appreciate its miraculous ability and take care of it well, it is capable of amazingly positive and often simply breathtaking creations as a result. We need only look at the abundant variety in nature and its ability to give birth to new life in order to get a glimpse of what Kundalini energy is capable of.

Its ability to create life has sadly also by its very nature been subject to being abused by people using it for their own gain, power and control. It seems that when we try desperately to understand how life works, our ego-brains cannot make logical sense of the beautiful, constant, all-giving and never-ending flow of eternity that pulses through us and the very veins of our Earth. We feel we need to dissect and dismember to make it smaller so our limited intellect can comprehend, feel proud that we can hold a piece of it in our hands to say 'we can be the master of this' and for once feel good enough to do it. Perhaps we just felt inadequate in the light of the infinite wisdom of all that we were provided with, naturally. It seems a shame that our beautiful 'Earth light' has been misunderstood and maltreated so many aeons in time repeatedly by so many. Maybe one of the reasons for this is because as humans, we all have to start at the root chakra in order to incarnate on Earth, and our early life experiences connect to many fears and issues around survival. Cyclic existence will have it that we repeat the pattern over and over until such time when we can transcend the process. By transcending is meant that we don't have futile ambitions to change the process itself, but instead feel empowered by how 'we' are able to interpret it, express and integrate our 'selves' within it. We can overcome feeling threatened by it, by learning that there is no intention of it trying to overpower us. We can overcome any hurdle as a result and turn it into our experience, a necessary learning phase of maintaining equilibrium whilst finding out who we are and why we are here.

Alas, it is the way it is and it is down to each individual to choose. Many generations of humankind over aeons of time have evolved only slowly and laboriously through it. Our Karmic Kundalini energy has to evolve and spiral upwards through each chakra, through each higher frequency to learn how to connect and transform stagnant energy. If it stays stuck in our base chakra or on any other energy level for that matter and we don't nudge it to budge, we become set in our ways and stubborn; our energy stagnates and we display symptomatic illnesses as well as behaviour patterns, clinging on to the past, hanging on to material things and not learning to let go and let some fresh energy in, move on up and surrender to change. Sometimes, looking at the situation on Earth today, it may seem that we are no closer to finding a global solution to these same stuck ideas that we display internally. I do connect this strongly to issues related to the base chakra on an individual as well as a global level. We are not letting anything breathe or grow, and strangle the life out of every species for fear that we may not survive ourselves. We are not allowing new life to survive and the code for survival of the fittest still applies in our Neanderthal minds.

If we find the right practices to set our Kundalini energy free to do as it is meant to, it will spiral upwards and outwards of our body freely and unhindered to connect with other energies of like mind. En route, it will also replenish and enrich itself again, as well as collect valuable information from above and beyond ourselves, this planet even, on much higher and finer frequencies; only to then curve back into our bodies to re-enter through the crown and continue on its spiral path downwards again, feeding energy to each organ, branching out into every cell in our body as it goes along, finding points where stagnant energy needs to be stirred, replaced and refreshed. It will continue to keep doing this spiral motion, again and again, all throughout our lifetime. It gathers and renews energy on its journey, and it can vary in speed according to our level of accomplishment, health and age. When we are aware, Kundalini energy manifests very quickly and brings with it a multitude of benevolent energies to assist us. This is what we need to concentrate on practising, this is what we need to learn, this is what is worth knowing. It may well be so secret a teaching that we have never heard of because it has been withheld from many of us over centuries; maybe for good reason so that it would not fall into the wrong hands, maybe because those who wish to be in power over others live in fear that we may also become well and powerful. Despite our access to the inner realm of potential, despite so many achievements, as a whole, mankind is ailing. How can this be? Is it to do with us having forgotten how to take care of ourselves, our inner Magick? If we really are alive and well, there is no need to be on a power trip, ever. We will feel how big our hearts really are, how truly incredible creation is, and how Magick life can really be. And if it truly isn't that Magick for us right now, if we have experienced loss and nothing is going our way, then to find our inner strength is the absolute antidote.

On a positive note, many people have by now got some idea that fear, greed and aggression have never been our greatest options within the potential of all the light frequency energy waves available to us. Even though it still seems such a popular choice for a bunch of humans to create and sustain wars, famine, corruption and manipulation, there literally seems to be light at the end of the tunnel. It can't come too soon. The instant we realise that all of the above issues are created with the imprints of limiting beliefs within our ego-mind, the mind that has not yet 'seen' beyond its own limitations, we can also start to visualise beyond it. We can more and more easily see now that in its fearful, limited perception, the Karmic energy stuck in our bodies has created outward structures resembling prisons within our beautiful natural world, reproducing externally the faulty energy patterns we are held prisoner by within us. Stuck energy has been manifesting a fake world on the outside, mimicking our stagnant internal thought patterns and stunted belief systems. it is recreating an unhappy world, because we are not happy within and we crave more and more external stimuli whilst our true and beautiful inner energy potential is drying up inside like deserts. We can work with this realisation to create a different reality for ourselves any time, if we so wish, and there has never been a better time. Right now, we even have access to some fantastic methods to work on the sabotaging thought virus stopping us from doing so.

We have the capability to create freedom, and the freedom to create our own reality with the power of our Karmic energy system every moment of the day. Once we fully realise and embrace this inherent reality, we hold the potential of becoming wise, compassionate and happy.

❊ ❊ ❊

17. Letting Our Karma In

The first thing that will likely happen if we suggest a change to our ego mind, its internal computer will start to check through our filing system to see what information we have on the subject of 'change'. As a result, our brain, true to its nature, will want to be clever and it will upload within split seconds every file it can recall on every situation where we have ever encountered change. It will most likely give us reminders of those times first where it all went pear-shaped, because that's how our brain rolls - it's there to protect us from harm and consider all the pro's and con's, especially when it thinks we are in danger of putting ourselves in danger. Perhaps last time we tried to change, something did go terribly wrong. Perhaps we changed our car and we had an accident. Perhaps we changed our job and that was a disaster. Perhaps we were forced to change something drastic, challenging our basic needs for survival = change home, change town, change country even. Perhaps it made us feel exposed, like we were unworthy, perhaps we lost something, someone. Almost all of us would have such experiences at some time, so you can imagine what happens internally: our ego brain has already decided that change is a no go - it thinks is not safe or wise to make any more changes and that's that - we avoid change from now on. But what if we continue to feel ourselves to be far from being wise or happy with how things are? What if our controversial split ego mind, our inner schizophrenic dialogue with a stubborn inner filing cabinet full of fear will never go away and is exactly what is stopping us every time we want to be a better, happier being? Is that, perhaps, the only reason why we can't change, why we find even change for the better so difficult to integrate? Are the flaws from the past in our inner filing cabinet still keeping us prisoner? How can we get past our inner barriers to bringing about a positive outcome, for all involved?

Believe it or not, if you got this far in your reading, this is the point where we need a drum roll. There is actually a very simple solution, and it's brilliant. However, not enough people know about it yet; probably because everything simple is dismissed in our over-complicated world. It seems like we are no longer allowed to (or perhaps we no longer believe we can) have, cheaply and easily accessible, presented to us on a plate, a method that works so easily and perfectly that it will bring about a much needed change for all of us: a change for the better. Perhaps we need to be shown advertising for it, perhaps we need some flashy re-branding, perhaps we are waiting to see it on telly over and over before it will sink in. There isn't any, because perhaps it's just up to each of us to say it's worth a try, because we get to a point where things are no longer going our way. I will give you a brief outline for these techniques so that you get an idea of what we have in our hands that is worth its weight in gold. I hope you will find it as useful and incredible as I did when I first came across it.

Oh, and just a little heads-up - the chapter after this one is slightly less fun and serves as a reminder of what has been going on in our minds and what will continue to happen as a result, in a world where we are choosing to remain unaware, seeing no choice but to let our fears run amok and continue to not seek help, but instead carry on letting others take over the show. This world as it is now, and many thereafter, since we are creating our future Karma with the choices we make right now.

A very clever group of people - well, one guy at first, actually, an American Psychologist called Dr Roger Callahan - came across a very important discovery in the 1980's. I agree with the enthusiasm he showed for finding out about this phenomenon and refining it into an easy-to-use form of Self-help therapy. I find it's important because virtually everyone I have come across in the last 20 years who has tried it has made progress using it, and for many, the benefits have been life-changing. You may wonder why you have not heard of it. I feel this is because it does not easily fit into a 'system' that works like a template for our society based on analytical intellectualism, so that when something comes along that really does work for people, is freely available and can bring about positive change for the better, it is portrayed as 'non-scientific'. I suspect that exactly for the reason that it works so well, it actually counts against it, and our inner paradigms by now that need to be reset, which is something that these techniques definitely help us do by losing the fear. I have used them for over 20 years now and I can only say: it works. Suffice to say that modern science has slowly been acknowledging and including the very same principles that these therapies are based on for the past decades.

As usual, all we need to do to start off with, is ask ourselves a few good questions: What would happen if many of us no longer felt as fearful as we did before? How would it feel if we were slowly coming back to life, to a state of extended awareness even? What if we re-discovered not only insight, but also our compassion of how we loved our neighbour and wanted to save the world after all? What would we do if we then gradually regained our inner strength that we had been missing, and found the peace and time again to see the validity of repairing our inner connections and family dynamics? What if we then had time and energy to actually make a start on fixing our environment? We may have thoughts that it sounds utterly Utopic and idealistic and it would never happen because we are far too stressed and it's too late anyway. There is no pressure for us to 'think' any differently. Allow it to continue. All that will happen is that we might find an inner answer to why our ego brain comes up with all this fear and all those questions in the first place, and for that to happen, read on and simply humour me for a while longer.

The techniques I am talking about all have something in common: they acknowledge a phenomenon that occurs within us which Roger Callaghan called 'psychological reversal'. Whatever name the various Meridian Therapies use, it all points at the same process and principle within us: our health is very much dependent on energy flowing through our body, as we described in the chapters above. If for some reason something happens to us so that we end up feeling out of sorts, not quite 'with it', ill or unwell, these techniques have found that what has happened within us is that our energy is literally switched around in a part or parts of our body and/or brain, and sometimes our energy is even switched off completely, in parts of our body and/or brain. The most disconcerting part of this phenomenon is that we are not even aware that it happens; it happens without us noticing or registering it, thus often denying us a process of repairing an issue when it has just occurred. It's like having a leak in a pipe somewhere in our home, and it's either just a small leak or leaks slowly dripping, or a burst pipe somewhere in the system. But rather than being aware of it, we do not know how to interpret the signs and symptoms and carry on thinking that we are fine, when we are not.

Imagine you find yourself in an area where you have been exposed to radiation, or a toxic substance. Would you know that you were in danger, if nobody warned you of its invisible peril? Probably not, or not until much later when you start to display symptoms. This 'switching' of our inner energy is very similar, it happens somewhere within us, outside of our conscious control and we remain unaware. Symptoms can be very subtle or remain undetected, sometimes even until it's too late to do anything about it.

This news may not be something so new or seem too alien to some of you - perhaps you will have come across it already. Perhaps you already know that it happens naturally every moment of the day, in a small way, in every part of our body. Usually, when it happens, the body tries to repair the damage, and if it can, then great. If it can't, it starts to override it.

The more our body tries to override these energy glitches in parts of our body, the more complicated it can become, especially because we are exposed to external situations on a daily basis that add to our energy being switched little by little, more and more. Still, you are still functioning and you seem alright, so you believe it doesn't affect you and carry on as normal.

This can go on for quite some time, and bit by bit, our internal energy system is switching – in some cases even switching off - in tiny places at first, then gradually larger areas. There are many ways our energy can get switched like that, and if you have ever had a health crisis of some sort, then you will probably know what it feels like if your energy gets switched off for some time until it has hopefully been repaired again. But often we recover and don't even give the process any thought, are able to shrug it off, no big deal, we are ok. Except, it gradually adds up - despite our bodies' resilience and finding ways to function, after a while what can happen is that we don't seem to feel quite so fit any more. We start to feel physical symptoms, get more aches and pains, feel tired more easily, suffer from sleep problems, get brain fog and so on. Or perhaps the issues are more on a mental level - you are showing symptoms of stress or anxiety, your body isn't any longer able to cope with stressful situations at work or at home and you are gradually feeling more and more anxious. You are trying to wind down, but even this is hard. For most, the answer is to simply turn to taking tablets, or drink alcohol, or smoke or find some other distraction to try to de-stress. Of course, most of these just mask the symptoms and don't make it better, in fact many make the issue of managing our inner energy flow even worse and you are at a loss as to why. Questions arise, such as - Why am I feeling so rough? Why do I get aches and pains, can no longer tolerate noise or light like i used to and get information overload? Why am I not sleeping well, why does my stomach ache all the time? Why do I feel depressed and anxious for no reason, why do I have pains everywhere and just feel so tired all the time, and even when I lie down, I am so restless and everything seems to hurt?

The techniques we talk about above try to counteract the one very good reason why we find ourselves in a downward spiral of ill-health: our body reacts to our external world by an internal electromagnetic sequence of events. Simply put, if the input into our bodies is conducive, the energy system within us will be nourished. If there are things put into our body that our body deems toxic, it has no choice but to react to it by shutting down parts of itself, resulting in gradually worsening ill-health.

It all sounds ominous but perhaps also inevitable, probably because we recognise that is exactly what is happening with all of us, at some point. Short of a solution and putting it all down to old age, we try to ignore it as much as we can, because we have not found what works for us. However, there is some really great news: we can catch these processes and our body's reaction to external and internal detrimental input and address them by simply re-establishing the energy flow within us. It is such amazing news with such widespread consequences that I can't stress enough how important these discoveries are. Our body can fix quite a few situations if our energy is flowing well. it can rid itself of some toxins, aches and pains, and even fix some more severe illness. We have seen proof of this, time and time again, working with these techniques. But the most important 'switch' these techniques can assist with, is when we are seemingly wired for sabotage. When there are thousands of reasons of why we simply cannot seem to get better, there is an answer in the way that these techniques can help find the 'leaking pipes' within. And it is not always as complicated as it sounds.

What we have seen over decades is that as a result, people experience more health, establish more awareness of what goes on within them and then have better understanding how to remedy their illness and ailments, especially when given some skilful assistance from a professional. All any of us need to do is donate to ourselves a little focused time and effort simply sitting in a comfortable seat and tapping on various acupressure points whilst focusing on the issue, which isn't hard to do, even when the issues at hand can be quite complex.

For most of us, we would all be able to alleviate thought and behavioural patterns that often stop us from getting well again, which weaken our energy system and have repercussions on our physical, mental, emotional and Karmic well-being. I am making a deliberate link here to our Karmic health, because these techniques tie in automatically with how our Karmic energy body relates to our physical energy body. Every time we spend improving our physical, or ego mind, we are also positively impacting our Karmic energy body that will eventually survive our physical presence. We are crossing the limitations of existence by focusing on energy work within us, because it is this very energy body that writes the script for our Karma and our future existence. If we manage to make more sense of the energy paradoxes within us, it can have a lasting effect on us, improve our decision-making and the actions we choose to take. As a result, we create good Karma, with less inner baggage that might have been holding us back from making good choices. It will therefore bide well for our future existence - even if we can only see and pay attention to the tricky health situations we find ourselves in right now, this is exactly all that is needed in order to make a difference. It is worth doing wholeheartedly, on every level, however small we start!

There is no catch if you need to know - or perhaps, the only one is the same reason why we cannot always 'do' life: it gets complicated, especially when it's been left untouched and the lovely flowers we wanted to have in our lives sometimes turn out to be quite stubborn, Self-seeding weeds. Our issues are intricate and complex, but as you can imagine, even weeds are beautiful - and alive. The process of discovery of who we are inside, with all the help we need offered when we feel we cannot cope, is a gift that is ours, whenever we want it. Absolutely no disrespect to anyone who is not feeling well, in any way. There is a way. And despite so many people feeling like they want to give up, even understandably, there are methods designed for each of us individually which are there to make it easier. The only reason I have ever seen people not stick with the techniques is because they hadn't realised just how complex our inner world is, and how long it might take them to make sense of it, find all the missing pieces, dust them off, and put them back together again. There is hope. For all of us.

Maybe you are a step ahead of me and are thinking 'what if we can avoid the vicious circle that allows illness to become established in our bodies and minds in the first place?' And yes, you are absolutely right. Whatever technique you end up feeling drawn to, to get the most from it, make it a regular event in your life. Make it your daily practice, and if you can't do it daily, make it weekly, and if you can't make it weekly, make it monthly. If you can see already how vast the benefits will be, know how blessed you already are; then don't make it your daily practice: make it hourly; make it a practice every minute of your life, every second. Make your life your practice. If you cannot see the benefits yet, read on, because we can start at any place you are at, any time.

The techniques work on the principle of adjusting this inner reversal of parts of our energy flow, and they are so easy to use that everyone can try them out and feel the benefit. It does take a little perseverance, and also some skilfulness in terms of putting a few sentences together that try to pinpoint where the problem seems to be. But this is not hard to do, as it usually is no different to us trying to explain to another being what we feel is wrong with us, in a conversation. In the conversation that we might have with a Meridian therapist, or even just ourselves if we are trying it out alone, we also use an additional move that allows the energy flow within us to be directly affected - and it is this very combination of an open dialogue about our symptoms and the process of actively 'tapping' on and into our energy flow points that seems to do the Magick. it appears to alleviate symptoms, whether they be physical such as pains and aches, or emotional such as anxiety and fears, or psychological, such as mental health issues. Everything we have a freedom of choice to address individually, is connected through our inner energy flow to all other parts within our body, so no matter how we address it, there is mutual benefit between all categories of issues including our inner symptoms. Meaning that, addressing an emotional issue can also help a physical symptom and vice versa. This is because underlying all these issues is the same stuck inner energy flow that is causing the problem in the first place, and when it is adjusted by using a simple technique, it will gradually flow more and more efficiently again through our bodies. It takes a bit of learning how to do it well, but really everyone can try it out, without ill-effect or side symptoms.

Once we find ourselves becoming more focused on what goes on for us by using these techniques regularly, we probably feel more encouraged to have a really good tidy-up within. After all, it does make us think more clearly when we don't have to suffer from constant pain and are not anxious every second of the day - and if the techniques help us feel less pain and think more clearly, what else can we achieve with them? We could become able to feel more at ease again, be aware of and take comfort in the universal flow of energy that is meant to be there for us. We might start to feel well enough again to realise we have matters in our hands as to the outcomes we want to create. At times when it's hard, we have a simple but profound tool by our side that helps us to see things through, taking the edge of any emotional turmoil we are going through, for example. What's not to like? If we choose to take it into our lives as a constant practice to feel better within, we are on the right tracks to being capable of not just help ourselves, but may even have time and space left over in our busy lives to still include others. The more love we feel within, the more it radiates out from us. It's not supposed to sound like a cheap commercial, really it's not. I am trying to convey that it helps in so many situations, and that there are some very straightforward reasons underlying our feeling unwell most of the times. Granted that if we have not felt well for a long time, we might not be so optimistic as to how it can help us, but it's definitely worth a try. Sometimes the results are instantly visible and tangible, and sometimes they take more time. As a side-effect, you may find yourself being more alert and aware, that you see through some of the conundrums that life poses us, and that you are able to make clearer decisions to help you in the long run.

If, at first, you have no idea where to start, this is what I would advocate to try these techniques on: use it on something you fear or are concerned about. We all have fears, and none of us know how to tackle them, really, other than trying to ignore them or override them with medication. As humans, we are wired to run from our fears or bury them deep inside, rather than find a solution to get rid of them. It is crucial that we recognise this in order to get better, before these fears get the better of us. This is exactly it, this is why I sound so insistent - it really is possible to get rid of fears, otherwise I would never bother writing about it here. It's the reason why it's such an exciting finding, maybe even why we are meeting over these pages here, to find out how our lives would change if we allowed ourselves to be naturally without fear. And don't worry, you won't throw yourself off a mountain, it's not that kind of fearlessness. It's an absence of electromagnetic disturbances that have caused numerous short circuits within us that we will feel, and that simply makes us feel happier, less stressed, more able to cope and feel at peace. As a society, we need to feel this again, desperately.

Our world needs us to feel it again, our children, our loved ones - and our Karma. Our Karma is intricately connected to our inner electromagnetic resonances. The myriad of various vibrations we feel within and label as feelings and symptoms are the ones that are creating our present moment, and therefore our future outcome - here is the biggest helping hand we could ever imagine reaching out to us, and it is coming from ourselves, from within. Our own Karmic energy body wants to remind us that we have everything we need within, to help ourselves. We just need reminding, and we need encouraging - and we need to overcome our fears. If we are living infinite lifetimes, it is logically never too late to make our lives useful, to make them count. There is work to do, and we can do it.

This is perhaps the single most important thing that we all can learn to do, to help ourselves, and with that knock-on effect, help those around us, which will hopefully lead us to connecting up more and more in order to make this world great again, no puns intended.

18. Karma and Dystopia

I hope it doesn't sound like I am forcing you. Perhaps I sound like a happy clapper, trying to motivate you into doing something you don't want to do? Does it make the sacred life-principle of Karma sound like some weird cult-like religion based on blind belief? Do I sound like a clever politician promising the Earth, full of myself but never delivering, out for myself only? I really hope not, but of course everyone can make of it what they want. I am convinced though, that we are closer than we think to answers to do with our Karmic path by looking within and yes, perhaps even external solutions to some major issues. Instead of taking immediate action and trying out a remedy for some very simple changes, we can do the usual and start a discussion for or against until we all fall out with each other and are no step further. I have already done a bit of homework in my head and pre-empted it - probably because i don't think we have much more time on Earth stalling with more discussions without taking the necessary action required to make some urgently needed changes. In order to bring about changes, I think this is the point where we can acknowledge that most of us fear searching for the truth, and combined with fearing changes in our lives, we are more comfortable staying as we are. In order to acknowledge and alleviate any inner anguish, we can ask ourselves some honest questions to find our truth, like the examples below:

What happens when we gradually awaken from ignorance, the 'state-of-not-knowing'?

What if Karma opens our eyes and we won't like what we see?

What if what we have done so far in our lives dawns on us in its full intensity?

What happens if we want to bring about change at 5 to midnight?

When we ask questions that are to do with bringing out Truth, we often get some truthful answers that are not always comfortable, so we don't always want to hear them either. We stop asking questions because it usually makes us feel uncomfortable and guilty like the children we once were, being told off for doing stuff that children do. And just like children, we end up trying to brush anything that might have repercussions under the carpet, including the truth. The main reason we still do this as adults is that we still do not have any viable solutions to solve lifetimes worth of issues, which understandably makes us feel uncomfortable and hopeless. It's too much to bear to have this all loaded on top of our already stretched capacity in light of impossible workloads for so many of us. It feels like the last straw that broke the camel's back when we realise that something needs to change, and many of us are no longer open to the suggestion of change. It doesn't feel safe for us to be open, even if it were for the better.

Imagine what would happen then, if we lost some of the anxiety that is keeping us small, feeling powerless and insignificant. I am talking about the same anxiety that is allowing us to lose the battle of defending ourselves against anyone with more power and authority, every time. If those in power had anticipated decades or, God beware, centuries ago that at some point in future we would be able to lose our fears, could there not have been developing equally strong powers to try to actively keep us in fear? Are there people who see through all this and are utilising the principle of fear-mongering for their own benefit? Would they not have acted out of their own fears of losing their privileges if they lost their power over us? If that was the case, would it not be a good question to ask if they also attempted to ascertain and increase their power by increasing the amounts and intensity of scenarios for us to be fearful of? Such as, perhaps, battles and wars, unrest and abject poverty; disease and famine - all iced with a reigning layer of delegates in place to make others feel lowly and less worthy, whilst brutalising the poor into slavery and distributing their loot only amongst themselves? What if they did not get much resistance, and merrily carried on with their harrowing schemes of world domination? Has it changed that much in modern times, times where a worldwide focus by nations exists, of creating weapons capable of mass destruction many times over and yet nobody seems to think it odd, being told we have to be afraid of enemies, that this is all in our defence? As you can tell, it is easy to get drawn into discussions about factual issues and our own perceptions, however, this is not where we have to go with this line of questioning at this point. It is meant as an example of what has been created over centuries of humans trying to catch their own tails in the name of greed. It causes dissonance, it causes more pain, more fear. We need different ways to cope with our inner conundrums that have kept us in massive amounts of fear, so much so that it has been making us sick. In lieu of not having any method at all to help us cope, we have also been an easy target for any potential evermore complex and intricately designed system of control. If someone with ill-intent came along and created areas with hidden agendas overtly exerting their power, what would we be able to do about it? Our media, ethics, health systems, food manufacture – any physical manifestation of our need for resources presents a paradox in itself. If we have to rely on others to provide for us and we have lost track of who does what, then we will be vulnerable to deception. We are constantly told to externalise and outsource our own inner energies, and the underlying structure of any politics are only telling us which external authority can best rule over us and make our decisions for us.

I am fortunate to have come across so many beautiful, trusting beings in this lifetime who would not hurt a fly. And yet, this well-earned gentleness that has prevailed over time since we existed on Earth has met with those who wanted to exploit it, cleverly creating false impressions by simply messing with our minds. We are allowed to be more discerning than that, and we are allowed to look behind some of the wrong-doing that presents itself. It would be futile to brush it under the carpet. In the ancient scriptures I lean on with many of my musings, there are protective elements we call on within us, who are depicted in quite frightful grimaces, squashing all those principles that are of no use to us. And however many present themselves to us in our lives, they can all be grouped together into stemming from three different inner Karmic origins: greed, anger and ignorance. If we add that it has created us so much fear, we must wonder why anyone would ever want to reside in those realms. And yet, that is precisely what we are doing.

These three core defilements – anger, greed and ignorance – are created by fear and they in turn continue to create fear. Everything that comes from those realms is limited and restricted. Staying in fear promotes a limiting of many areas, which could be summed up as our Karmic freedom. We are presented with the duality of 'choices', keeping the masses unassuming, confused, overwhelmed, poor, sick, addicted and believing in the false gods of external authorities who they might still believe to be their saviour. And since it got that way without us noticing, we need to add the guilt it has created in all of us as well, because the shifting of blame on to us meant we were all led to believe it was all our fault. It affects our ability to stay connected to highest source when energies get shifted on to us by others, and if we haven't learned how to transform the arrows into flowers, if we have never been taught, how are we to know what our power really is? Would those who still take our energy and create privileged lifestyles with it, after centuries of history repeating the same convenient pattern over and over, willingly give up their pole position their rich ancestors had already prepared for them to have? We can only wonder of the consequences for them and those they affect, by choosing to hold on to their authoritative make-believe stories

and sustain more suffering, thus creating more Karmic terror. Where does it end, other than with us opting out in our Karmic minds, because who would want to be in this Catch-22 for any length of time? We can only use our own inner power to create a better outcome, to make deep and sincere wishes for these situations to be disclosed and for them stop. We do this repeatedly for and within ourselves, making a commitment to ourselves to remain in balance and in alignment with compassion and wisdom. The more people do, the more impact it will have. We do not have to be a part of keeping fear levels high amongst world population by actions such as actively promoting new fraction groups to cause continuous terror in vulnerable parts of the world, spreading a horror show of random and unpredictable attacks on civilians. The depths of negative Karma have been blurring the lines between attack and defence for too long already; we are confused with an ambush of information and yet, if we remember who we are, if we find our infinite inner strength, we know we can each of us peacefully make a difference. All the while, it may continue that power-owned media are making sure that our energy lessens, observing news and images of casualties and distraught civilians we fully identify with. These reports are seen by new generations of confused observers who might find it even harder to see through the forests of doom. It's understandable that the next fear then creates increased justification for a need of more aggressive sanctions. Is it any wonder then, that people have started to believe in warfare, taken it into their household screen time even and thus normalising it, so that when the time comes for recruiting troops for the next invasions to prevent more wars, those who subscribe to it feel they are doing the right thing, but end up with trauma, Depression, PTSD and suicidal tendencies, having observed the injustice, the futility of losing precious lives sent out in their thousands, driving even the meek into madness. It is never a good thing to kill. With an unprecedented ongoing amount of sorrow, loss and suffering and millions of casualties on every continent for generations worldwide, an ecosystem destroyed to the point of no return, what will be the actual outcome for mankind? We need to go there for a moment, to realise the history we have been subject to on Earth and comprehend that it has led us to being rationed into some state of emergency existence. It almost seems that some force does not want us to live in peace and comfort. By an artificially induced emphasis on commerce and productivity only instead of the promotion of the preservation of preciousness of all life, nothing has been achieved but an acute likelihood of natural disasters and world famine by engineering nature, crops and wildlife – and now human beings, too. As much as we don't like to be reminded, as much as we worship our right to freedom, by the introduction of an ever-escalating system based on borrowing off the energy of every living, seeing life as nothing but a production line based on each individual's worth in terms of their ability to be productive and able to labour for decades of their precious existence, the 'powers that be' promoted - directly or indirectly - an increase in sacrificing lives. sickness, crime and violence especially against minorities and the vulnerable, creating political instability and inertia and yes, even melting ice caps, exploding volcanoes, causing Earthquakes and a resulting climate emergency. Everywhere around us are beings that suffer, be it human or animal, not because they want to, but because they believe they have no choice, because they are told it is demanded of them - and we still wonder why we are suffering from anxiety.

Whether by design or not, it seems that beings have all suffered at one time or another, been mistreated and misused to be kept in an overload of fear. It is difficult to think that people would do this to each other, seemingly with the result that nobody wins, as we would crumble eventually under the pressure when our overloaded Karmic energy gets to a point of no return. Fear causes greed, ignorance anger, turns into hatred, and hatred creates death. How convenient, don't you think, if we didn't know that this is really what is being used against us, when we have also had the antidote withheld to the suffering that presents itself? People would not even notice it wasn't their fault that their delicate energy systems were compromised, leading from bad to worse - and who could prove such a thing and find tangible evidence anyway. It's the perfect crime: no suspect, no evidence. It appears that only when all of us have shared examples of our suffering with each other that we might really take any of this seriously, draw the right conclusions and apply solutions, rather than doing the animal instinct thing of just turning against each other.

We need to find out the cause of our suffering and then use methods to alleviate it, in order to break the cycle. There is a method, and there is an end to suffering.

As it stands right now, when we are not 'productive' enough, we are given little white pills, and in the case of animals, turned into food. Does that not sound utterly ridiculous? We are so detached from our true nature, our true ability, our true compassion, our true wisdom, that we are not able to see straight at the moment. Generation after generation has passed on the fear gene, unable to truly resolve the trauma that each individual has suffered at the hands of others. When looking at the destruction, we wonder what happened to innocence; and what have some of those who have no morals left, done? They have turned our children into their victims, seeing them as commodities, thinking they can gain something from taking their gentleness in a mad rage of lunacy. Without an infallible, uncompromised justice system that is able to adequately deal with crimes against the innocent, there is no time to lose to find what works in order for any of the victims to recover.

I am truly sorry that we have had to briefly go through any of this in detail, in order to make sense of the entire situation of how our suffering comes about, and why it continues to do so. I truly hope it helps us understand, rather than create more suffering. It only sounds hopeless because it's impossible to make it right, the way we have been going about it. However, knowing what we now know, I think it makes perfect sense how neglecting the principles of Karma may have something to do with why we are in such global demise. Perhaps we see our thoughts reflected in what we suspect has occurred and find hope in sharing ideas. This time on Earth is meant for us to increase our awareness and share our wisdom and compassion. If any of this sounds familiar and makes sense to you, our new-found wisdom would only work if we used it to make our own lives better and used our excess happiness to allow others to share the benefit of our wisdom, too.

To draw a final conclusion from this chapter, it would be that nothing physical works in our bodies without vital life-force energy running through it. if anything blocks this energy, most, if not all, poor Earthlings would suffer extreme adrenal fatigue, along with immune system illnesses and toxic overload, either quickly or gradually leading up to organ failure so that there would be no chance of living to a wise old age. What happens if our energy flow is so gradually reduced, so that we don't notice for a while what is happening? With all that is going on in the world, toxicity and anxiety rising with more extreme climates as indicated above, what if we might lose our physical well-being over time without our ability to discern and diagnose, never mind fight back against any dis-ease? And what if the medication we were given - even unbeknownst to those trying to help us - contained their own time bomb of toxins working against the energy flowing through our physical bodies? Last, but not least, if all of this degeneration begins with any new generation at a younger age than ever, the perpetrators who have it in for the majority of population, who didn't want them to be fighting authority and just needed their work power without any trouble from themselves, could get clean away with it. Based on a common belief in the West that 'we don't remember anything that happens before age 3', if the next generations were being conditioned, they could be brought up to believe in the authority of adults, the dystopia that made families dependent, feeling forced to 'give away' their young at an early age if they were put under enough stress and fear. Putting parents under pressure to give up their children at an extremely young age that used to be quite unnecessary and unheard of, could be manipulated to be seen as normal. Issues that parents are increasingly faced with, such as being nuclear or even single-parent families, with the stigma of low chances of regular income, constant pressures arising on issues such as weaning and vaccination, early external child care from as young as 3-month young, forced adoptions and increased reports of child abuse etc., it means that it is becoming normalised in a society that a complete stranger takes care of your offspring. We often do not have the insight from elders around us telling stories of how things used to be, to give balance to our decision-making process. People are played off against each other and the good that can be passed on in peace and with good-will, is degenerating as quickly as the good bacteria in our antiseptic society.

These are degenerate times for many, it would be callous of me to pretend that it is fine to always answer with 'everything is one, everyone is at peace', when our Karmic energy remains so affected by unresolved issues that we are more likely to be compromised more easily and react differently as a result. We sometimes feel no choice but to defend ourselves against any external circumstance against us, but as a part of our compromised system that sees an external situation as a threat, we end up creating a reality that is based strongly on an authority-driven defensive system as a result...As our energy minds have become compromised and imprinted over time with others' lower mindsets, we may subconsciously recreate this ourselves without realising. Until it becomes visible enough to us, we hopefully start to see through that this is what is happening for us, that it is a temporary reality and may even be the glitch that made us reincarnate on Earth, in a binary code setting where everything is black or white, left or right, we have two strands of DNA and all of us simultaneously have the experience of a separate body without a full memory of what it was like before we got here. Until we gain the ability to overcome and heal all these Karmic imprints we carry with us, a time-line is created by which we are apparently forced to delay our instant happiness until we recognise where our unhappiness stems from. That conundrum takes some recognising - it must do, because we don't often see through the simplicity of it but instead keep creating ever more complicated diversions and distractions. The time-line we created, started to exist outside ourselves when our Karmic energy was violated and therefore some of our energy became separated from us, presenting itself so vividly that we have had no choice but to suffer it until help came along to remind us who we were and where we were at. Because we have now been 'out of our minds' long-term, the effect it has had on our inner energy stream is that it may repeatedly show signs of blockage and stagnation. This is what is presenting itself to us, right now: we show symptoms of a malaise, we are presented with the cause herewith, and we are now looking for a remedy. Our Karmic energy system is trying to show us every moment of our lives where the damage has been caused. However, it can become so convoluted within that it becomes difficult to see the wood for the trees. What was first – the blockage or the people and the circumstances who put it there? Did our inner Karmic blockages create the external situations which are confirming the blockages to us in a multitude of offences against us, or did people do harm to us first and thus caused the blockages within us? Are we dealing with the aftermath of violations from people outside of our control, or a situation where we ourselves were at fault in a previous existence we cannot recall - or both? It is confusing, and we can easily drive ourselves even more mad and spend extortionate amounts of money and time trying to find out. We might find out, we might not, and for the most part the pursuit of trying to find out everything that ever happened to us in past lives can become a distraction we could easily prevent. For this reason that we might never find out what it is, here is the answer to save you time, money and aggravation: in order to heal and move on, we have to understand something and it is always the same:

we have no influence over the outcome of others' Karma, only our own inner channels which we can learn to be kind to, in order for them to repair. This should be a healthy focus in our lives - to realise that our Karmic minds need repairing and to find methods that allow us to do so. In order to try and make sense of everything and be open again to one another and the rest of humankind, we need to focus on finding solutions for healing our own energy and convoluted conundrums – and we need to know how important it is and that we deserve it. If we spend too much time trying to fix others and give them a piece of our mind, if we continue to worry about external matters, we may be ignoring our inner convolutions and losing power over our own inner processes, thus in some way continuing the violations done to us. Once we have some idea of what it is like to heal within, then we will be more open and helpful to others automatically. The process of wanting to help others has more effect then. Those two principles of advancing our inner energies and helping others to do so, too, are, for example, laid out in the great vehicles of Mahayana and Hinayana Buddhism. The path of Hinayana is to achieve enlightenment for oneself, which, as I said above, is important so we gain an understanding of what we are dealing with within ourselves and how to resolve our inner conundrums. Mahayana speaks of the stage of awareness that sets in when we realise we are never alone, we are always a part of everything surrounding us, and thus we need to connect and heal the other, external, too. Both methods are equally valid in my opinion, but can easily be misconstrued if we do not see them as equally important. Both can be applied to any scenario simultaneously and they do not have to be completed one before the other. They can be applied alternately, I feel. We need to be discerning in each situation whether we instinctively use one or the other. If we see another being suffering, are we going to turn away and say 'I need to sort out my own suffering first'? It is really where the world is at, because most of the time, we do exactly that, faced with the conundrum of so much suffering in this world. We have not yet seen the benefit of what it's like to have been kind enough to ourselves. Perhaps we really have not had enough time and opportunity to find ways to go inward to help ourselves. If we had, we would feel that we have much more room for compassion for others. We might need some time and effort to be able to take a moment to ask ourselves: Are our actions justified, are they adequate to create best case scenario for us and everyone else involved? Are we able to help and assist others despite having been hurt so deeply, so many times, and having had so much taken from us? This has nothing to do with 'turning the other cheek'. These are profound questions that take us on an inward journey of discovery, often with profound results.

It all sounds dystopian and unreal, but unfortunately it is really what happens to many people on Earth already these days, with most of us at a loss as to what to do about it.

As an example, what we appear to have created with our governments and finance systems is an externalisation of our inner fears. The fears themselves may well have not been ours in the first place, but may have been created by violations against us, going back centuries and still prevailing to this day and age. Even if we are not at fault, the fears created over long periods of time - and therefore the breaches in our Karmic energy - stay with us as long as we have not healed. The result is always the same: the externalised systems created based on the reflection of our inner fears start to have a life of their own. Institutions outside ourselves gradually establish the right to hold the reigns, holding an image of 'the masses' and their productivity and liability rather than a value of the individual's ability and right to life, controlling by creating punitive legal systems, governing our 'selves', our property - including our family and children. Understandably, we then have very real reasons for a continuation of our fears. When externalised manifestations have in turn become radicalised by the greed of individuals hiding behind systems that are taking advantage of alive beings, we are subject to forms of slavery in modern society without complaint. The cycle of fear is complete when those who took away land and labour and used it for their own advancement then created 'money', meaning nothing more than a piece of paper with the promise of giving something in the future in return for the hard labour and time spent by workers. The labour, time, physical, mental and emotional effort of each alive individual and their property including families were turned into a small piece of paper. It's a very clever concept, because in energy terms this meant that each individual's alive energy was diverted into something external and dead of no intrinsic value, and yet the whole world fell for it and still has not found the answer to the question of how it got this far. By now, we have even stepped away from a paper exchange to a virtual money exchange, as the illusion has become so manifest in people's minds that nobody is seeing through the Magick trick.

We have 'companies' who we have no idea what they are or who they are, 'charging' us for using our money in investments that do not belong to us or serve us or humanity as a whole, and yet they appear to hold some of our externalised power and use it to watch our every move as if we were children or worse, slaves. If we do not oblige by their terms, we are in real danger of forfeiting our property. How did we let it get this far, that our land, our life force, got sold out to those who have no regard for our individual plight? We have been cleverly distanced from our own and our ownership of our 'Self' and our inner energy source, and those who hide in the system justify being there by living their own lives in fear. 'We' and 'them' was created, and the two might never meet, might never find out who each of us really are. The distance grew bigger and bigger, our fear for our and our loved ones' lives grew so that we were easy prey to the concept of heavy defence systems, increasing in a power struggle to this day where everywhere we look there are now military systems in place that battle with each other for fear that the other might be first to attack us. Our internal fears and insecurities inevitably created the horror of wars and famine, seemingly holding our lives in its hands. Perhaps we have Stockholm syndrome which makes most of us feel that this malaise has always been that way and we cannot live differently. Some of us even live in a golden cage with the door wide open but cannot find a way out. We have not asked for, found or utilised the methods that exist in order for us to alleviate our fears. We do not even know that we have to ask for it, and we don't know what 'it' is. Instead, mankind does not seem to mind being manhandled. We enjoy complaining, but still go along with this ridiculous show that has been put on for us, without anyone who we appear to have put 'in charge' offering to find and show us how to use the tools for seeing through the illusions and find solutions instead. Instead, we are appeased and apparently happy to accept that we are being lied to, as we started to expect to be lied to a long time ago. We are being promised the Earth whilst the Earth is being destroyed in our name. We have not been shown how to find and use solutions, because those who have been put 'in charge' do not know them.

The solution is within us, it lies dormant in our Karmic strength. When we activate it, we will gain the ability to make better choices to bring about positive outcomes.

It is up to us to decide as to when we stop trying to find solutions where they cannot be found. We carry on sustaining the creation of our sub-conscious beliefs and mindsets and therefore the illusion of there being a benefit in blaming 'them', denoting someone, something, any entity outside ourselves. We have learned to procrastinate out of fear, and we need to hand ourselves the UNO-reverse card - meaning, we will only find the answer if we come back to ourselves. Our Ego minds forgot that we have created this way of expressing ourselves entirely within our own Karmic energy system, and this is where our true power is hidden. As long as we carry on acting based on belief sets we were told, possibly even force-fed by others who had their own best interests at heart, as long as we still have aggressors and their ways of manipulating us, we are sitting in a glasshouse and should be careful enough who we allow to continue to throw stones at us. Without knowing our true selves, our true power, we become vulnerable and our aliveness can be exploited by anyone who we become a visible target for. We would do well to go back to grass-roots level and allow ourselves some changes within, in order to effect external peace.

When we are finally ready to wake up and accept what it takes to find out more about who we are, how we got here and how to put things right again, we might become aware how we have created these systems with and within our powerful Karmic minds. We deserve the greatest care whilst we take this path as it can be a tricky process to apply those concepts in our already formed reality, which may heavily oppose an awakening process at this compromised and divided stage in Earth time. Sometimes it's obvious we cannot be certain that we get support, but this is also not the first time that Earth has gone through this pro-cess. It may have done so before, and might again on its own path of cyclic existence. Cultures come and go, and whilst much is expected of those who are given much, those who are given insight and wisdom, who freely share what they have learned have historically been ridiculed, os-tracised and persecuted. Often, we only realise in hindsight when the seers of our tribes have been right all along. We can all of us become inner ninjas, all of us have the power to think on our feet, all of us have the potential to recognise our true nature and learn to juggle our inner selves; we need to understand our precious inner energy, the way it works on our external situations, its convolutions and belief systems; we need to become our own inner superheroes and be back in charge of our external creations; never in human history have we had connectivity all across the globe like we have now, and we have the potential to increase our inner light so much more quickly and easily. Our children are asking us to, as they still recall much more easily the light that they came from before they were born here. Our Earth goes through cycles, and we are all at different stages - not all of us have the opportunity to do this all at once. If you are reading this, you are one of the very special ones who has - we can be beacons of light and love without becoming dictators. We can, simply and unconditionally reach out to others who do not have the same privilege. If we aim for autonomy over our fears within our own ego-minds, we can learn to be free and well, and create health and wellness for ourselves and others on all levels.

We can become forgiving and learn to see others for who they are, thus setting ourselves free to literally change minds as well as set our Karmic minds free in the process.

What seems to become more apparent all the time is that we do not have as much freedom in our human form within the paradigms we created as we have led ourselves to believe we have. Are we not puppets hanging off the knotted ball of string of our Karmic energy history? Have we sold our souls, and slowly slipped into slavery? As the Earth is increasing its own vibration all the time whilst it moves through its own chakra system along its own timeline, it appears we are destined to move along with it like tumble-weed in the desert, whether we like it or not. Whilst we might even subconsciously agree to this unseen contract, we are also regularly reminded to bring our vibration to a higher level in all our circumstances by working through our mind blockages and deal with our negative Karma, hopefully even once and for all. Rather than being swept under with the swift energy shifts that are occurring along our earthly journey, we can learn to be on top of things again if we have the know-how. If we don't see the connections between Earth's evolutionary process and acknowledge the prompts to further our own Karmic development and grasp the opportunities of precious growth phases we are being given right now; if we fearfully and stubbornly remain on only the lower rungs of our energy ladder, we may continue to attract the negative flip-side of the Karmic coin over and over again until it is too late. We absolutely do have a choice of whether to stay stuck in issues of basic survival, war, famine, problems with finances, aggression & sexual violation, stress, defence mechanisms, materialism, pain, aggression and problems manifesting in our physical bodies repetitively – because they are all issues associated with stagnation and a reduction of electromagnetic frequency at certain break points in our body that can be adjusted again to ascertain the correct flow. We can make a conscious choice to move along in all our individual ways of our inner Kundalini energy rising. We can start shining, ready to explore other levels of experiencing our inner energy vibration in meaningful ways rather than exploit them like there's no tomorrow, and instead learn methods of wisdom to utilise them for the benefit of all living beings..

Perhaps just reading this will help trigger a little action to find our own truth. Sometimes, to start to feel well and happy, we only need to read or listen to a few chapters as a positive reminder. After all, your healing process may take its time - or it can be immediate and instant, since your Karmic energy mind already inherently knows how to be well and can pass this on to your physical 'Self'. You do not necessarily need to throw large sums of money at being healed or be a rocket scientist to be happy.

Becoming aware of our priceless Karmic energy which flows through our body continuously, can become the holy grail it is meant to be at any key moment in time and which we have searched for aeons in time, as have many beings before us. It may happen for just a short glimpse of time at first that we become conscious of its full power charging through us, or we may be subject to experiencing a prolonged period in our lives when our energy feels like it is inducing in us a process of heightened state of existence. It may be a bit of both and all in between, like a roller-coaster ride. Everyone's experience is different and it is probably best to try not to have too many expectations or preconceptions to distract from our practice of the calm state of awareness that is mindful meditation. If we compare ourselves or become frustrated waiting for it to happen, it means we are losing energy from our inner system which does not bring the right result. The key is to try and not think, or leave thinking in the background, surrender to the energy of every moment and relax into it. It will take time to untrain our brains to not constantly analyse everything. If it's not happening, we can ask to be shown what to do, no matter what. We can also use the process of setting our energy free at the end of each meditation, or poignant inner exercise that we take. Setting energy free is called a dedication in the practice that I am used to, in Buddhist terms. A dedication at the end of everything good that you have noticed or created is considered essential. It means you are allowing your energy to connect with the universal energy out there, by wishing others to experience the goodness of what you have just witnessed. There is an example of a dedication you can use at the end of this book. Giving ourselves regular bursts of time to 'check in' with our inner selves, recognise where we are at by creating expansive moments of stillness, allowing the level our body and Karmic energy mind are vibrating at to be main priority regularly and preferably every day is key to feeling more at ease with what's happening to us and finding a remedy for when it does feel out of sorts. It's a learning process and often easier said than done, but a lot of practice in short spans at first goes a long way towards achieving more peace of of mind in the long run. Slowly we will have less outcome attachment, less of a target practice where something external needs to show itself as a result or a reward for what we are doing. All of these expectations from ourselves and the external will slowly but surely ebb away, since they were never real in the first place, and something else will again take their place, something much more valuable. if we could see it and feel it right now, we would be practising all the time if we knew that this was the result.

Eventually, free from negative Karma, we will become what we were always meant to be: the manifest result of the pure fountain of Kundalini energy flowing through us, bringing with it health and vitality, enthusiasm for aliveness and creation. Especially when we manage to experience this Karmic energy dance of life time and time again, we learn to let it wash through each chakra without obstacles more easily each time, learn to remain present evermore, even in more complex external situations. Eventually, our core energy will be able to move freely in its spiral formation; unhindered up- and downward along our spine entirely without obstacles, constantly scooping up vital universal source energy freely available in the clear space outside of ourselves. This dance of life - incidentally depicted in the symbolic image of the caduceus often unwittingly used in images representing Western Medicine - is the very same dance of Shiva, the creator of the universe and his snake denoting the surpassing of energy and time, its three coils representing past, present and future in Hinduism. It is also reflected in many practices in Buddhism, such as the purification practice of Vajrasattva & Consort. The intertwining of the yin and yang Taoist symbolise meridians in the black and white swirling parts of a whole circle which contain a small part of each other within; the male and female energy components of our spiral energy DNA, connecting us via our crown chakra to the source of ever-existing energy.

❈ ❈ ❈

Yin Yang Symbol

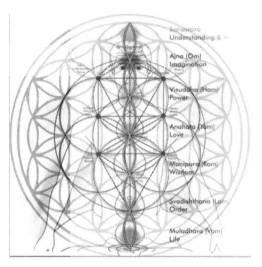

Energy Lines Converging Into Sacred Geometry Patters in order to form and sustain Life I
Image credit: © https://www.pinterest.co.uk/pin/55591376623827695/

Caduceus – Medicine Staff depicting two energy lines swirling around the central spine, with connection to higher energy source above
Image Credit: © http://clipart-library.com/clipart/1940483.htm

No matter what philosophy, science or religious orientation, the fact of the matter stays the same: it is the eternal energy source allowing universal energy to flow through our physical bodies, collecting vital life-force frequency from source which we need in order to constantly replenish our energy body. The higher and finer the vibrations are that we can access with our own energy merging with it, the clearer our connection will be with the Divine energy that heals us, bringing wisdom particles of vitality and eternity back into our body when looping back into our crown chakra again, in order to spiral and swirl downwards along our spine once more. Moving all the way down to just below the base of our physical body it thus connects us with the divine Earth energies, too, making our body a pure channel and completing the circuit for spiralling healing energy within. Our body is a conduit for cosmic energy – who knew! When this concept is manifest within us and safely practised over and over again, blockages can become less and less likely, illness rarer and recovery from illness quicker. As a result our lives are prolonged and our thoughts turn to promoting and prolonging our and others' inner health, too. The more often this is practised, the more Self-healing the body becomes, at a noticeably faster rate than what we are used to when subjected to our often stagnant inner energy alone.

As I understand it, a body, mind & spirit that is unwell occurs when this beautiful and powerful energy flow has become blocked in one or typically several parts of our energy channels and points. Usually, we only notice this once it is manifest in emotional, mental or physical form particularly. We are still fighting the stigma of mental and emotional illness, but physical symptoms such as aches, pains and injuries through accidents are deemed more acceptable and 'real' to physicians as well as the general public in the West, although ironically the stage of physical illness is often the last and tends to manifest when we have not acknowledged other warning signs in our bodies in the form of subtle energy deficiencies first. Faults in our energy system are intrinsically connected to faults in our physical body, but since most of us are not able to 'see', perceive or interpret blockages in our energy channels or listen carefully to our body for its many subtle hints and messages, we only tend to notice and acknowledge an energy fault as an illness when it has finally manifested as a physical ailment.

Many people are still sceptic and cynical when they first learn about the ancient knowledge of our Karmic energy system holding the energy blueprint for all our potential illness which is then passed down to physical level. However, I feel that the cynicism and scepticism we display at times are energy blockages in their own way, perhaps reactions based on fear that can potentially distort our 360-degree view, making us dismissive and rejecting anything new we perceive as threatening at first. Luckily, these symptoms, too, can be balanced out with certain practices and exercises. We have the opportunity to be well on any level, even in this very Karmic lifetime right now, and we get to trust our ability to heal the more we use techniques and ways of life which support us in our quest.

19. Global Kundalini Rising

Some examples of Earth energies shifting dramatically all the time are most memorable because of the effect they have on us, seeing as we live here as a part of her population. Global events that stick in our memories are often of a nature that is destructive, and whilst I am not sure why that is, they are sometimes even named by us to pay attention to, and some that have had devastating consequences for our Earth's population stick in our memories for generations, such as hurricanes and tornados. Volcanic eruptions, seismic shifts, tsunamis, meteors, earth quakes and wildfires are also events that often everyone remembers the dates of. Such big signs that nature sends us seem to be accepted as stark reminders of who is in charge. Events such as this, including for example the Boxing Day Tsunami in Indonesia in 2004, as well as more man-made shifts such as deforestation or the creation of continuous war zones throughout the Middle East, with many millions of living beings dying or displaced, are all events that we remember because of the negative effects they had on mankind in our times. Historically, each generation of mankind on Earth had its own disasters, natural or man-made, and I am sure you can add dozens of your own examples without having to search for very long. In a consecutive cyclic yet hidden pattern, the Earth periodically gives us a chance throughout those periods to work through the 'red' frequency of its own chakra system, the Kali energy of the destroyer of the physical realm. Should we become aware that our Earth is going through its own pattern of cyclic existence? Is the Earth moving through its own vibrational shifts, bringing different situations for us to deal with at various poignant Earth times? Does Earth have its own Chakra points and its own Karmic Energy veins? Does its energy flow through it as if it had its own physical body? There are people on Earth who already believe this to be true, and the image below show the Earth energy flowing through and around it continuously in the shape of a torus.

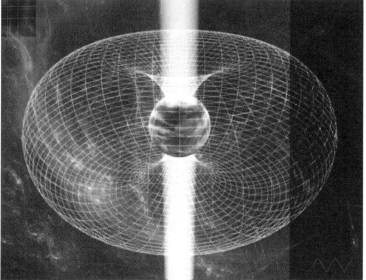

Torus Energy pattern surrounding Earth and each Sentient Being on it.
Image Credit: © The Golden Light Channel

It is possible to imagine that this could well be true. The Earth may well have its own universal energy core similar to us individuals, as we are all subject to the principles of 3-dimensional manifestation. It may well have its own energy points. too, where energy flows in upward and downward motion spiralling along its core, branching out in a pattern of subterranean energy networks much like our circulatory systems. Some of those energy veins may well surface at certain points on the Earth's crust and coincide with energy points recognised by those sensitive enough to feel them, including many who have declared such points to be sacred places on Earth. Maybe veins coincide with physical activities on Earth's surface to an extent that they run parallel causing chasms, ruptures and cracks, and energy points may result in erupting volcanoes. From this angle, it would be interesting to measure whether the energy pattern that Earth resembles is perhaps a little like our own bodies, with a central nervous and vascular system that branches out from our spine, but is also subject to the external forces that affect it, i.e. what occurs on the surface of Earth and in Earth's atmosphere.

In any case, I believe that it would mean we are all ourselves subject to the effects of each Earth chakra shift, as we go along with Earth's vibrational frequency patterns. Our Karmic energy may well 'choose' for us and incarnate at certain Earth times to live through this evolutionary process within ourselves as well as within our environment. If this seems an alien concept, we need to remind ourselves that we have come far away from being able to determine and interpret the signs of these shifts and patterns. The sensitivity some of us inherently have to Earth's multidimensional shifts and patterns has been denounced in favour of computerised graphs based on man-made technological measuring devices. Despite our age of technology and virtual reality - which incidentally is also meant to be and could itself be foreseen as a particular vibrational interpretation of universal energy flowing through Earth - any shifts in subterranean patterns still mostly come to us as a complete surprise, and still result in many casualties even when technology was able to predict certain events. The Earth has been going through cyclic shifts since the beginning of its existence and it will continue to go through its own shifts and weave energy patterns until the end of its existence. Sun still follows after a storm, at least for now. Whilst we can still see blue sky without having obscured it with so many chemicals that it has become a symbol of how blurred mankind's vision is, we would do well to be like our ancestors and learn more about how to read and respect the beautiful and equally fragile power of nature, and refrain from abusing it any further.

As we have learned, Kundalini is an everlasting energy flow, moving through to the highest chakras above even our physical bodies to connect with universal energy and download highest wisdom, only to then start being drawn downward again through the top of our head chakra from where it starts the spiral cycle through all over once more. There are beautiful and wise ancient descriptions of how this process can be envisaged, through thousand petalled lotus flowers and sacred symbols and protective Masters envisaged on our crown, protecting us from harmful energies and allowing only the highest and purest energy flow into our bodies. The imagery is a reminder for us not to compromise as to what we allow into our physical presence, and to be careful and discerning so as not to disturb this delicate process. Periodically, we are prompted to allow this energy flow to be given the chance of activating our base chakra. The whole process is asking us to relinquish our forcing it, meaning we have to choose whether we allow it to occur naturally and only aid the process with our own abiding by its natural laws. If we cannot give up our urge for power and control and relinquish our fears that drive our identification with money and status no matter the consequences, then it will make it harder to let go of the ego roles that we assume and gently replace them with a healthier perspective and understanding of who we truly are. Sadly, many of us have not been shown how to do this, our education fails to see the bigger picture and instead increase our cravings and desires for materialistic thinking focused on external gratification. Those who, sooner or later, lose their grasp on the finite experiences of the external such as money, status and belongings, often cannot cope without identifying with these and fall into depression without ever having learned their infinite value within which was given them by simply being born. A culture based on striving to achieve something in the external by losing our own life force energy cannot give us a manual of how to do life on life's terms. It has instead increased the numbers of those who feel no choice but to end their lives rather than feeling that they were shown how to live knowing who they inherently are, able to survive without what they believed to be them and theirs.

Whilst we cannot be the judge of what each of us go through at any point in time, that certainly has not stopped people from doing so. However, there might be a better alternative to remaining lost in our limiting belief systems of who we are and what we have, and it does not have to be menacing or spiteful. It can be so much more fulfilling to learn again how we can be in tune with existence and all that is. We are meant to learn how to live in tune with the Universal energies not against them, but since we have come such a long way away from living Truth, the fear of 'losing' anything has taken over our existence and we live in the limbo of duality instead, subject to 3-dimensions in which we are never quite rich enough, never quite well enough, never quite knowing enough, so that it feels like we are in survival mode all the time. Earth and all other inhabitants are suffering separately, and we don't know how we cannot turn back the clock to who we once were. Perhaps we don't know everything, but there might be any need to, because as we have already heard, we live in a false impression of time-line based thinking processes. This was introduced to us to indoctrinate and make us more productive, not to make us happier or feel better. A linear timeline is just a small section of the whole spiral of existence. When we look at the comparatively short timeline of one lifetime only, from our perspective it might seem linear, like a short section of road will seem straight; but looking at it from a higher perspective, it is neither straight, nor does it lead anywhere – it curves around. It is not too late, it cannot be, because we live in a spiral existence where it is never too late. We can learn to recognise our inner energy flow temporarily climbing up and down our inner energy ladder, and when this is calling us to clear out all old stuck energy from our lives and belief systems, we can make room for the pure stream of energy flowing freely through us as is meant to be. We can learn to step up a rung or 12 on the inner journey of our spiralling Kundalini energy, letting our consciousness rise upwards along the spinal cords. Rather than a linear external time line of 'bigger, faster, better, stronger' competitive thinking-based existence, we will be able to raise our vibration, find what we are looking for with our inner practice and learn to be at peace, a true representation of our inherently content selves. We are subject to all these shifts continually, and are influencing our world around us every day as we go about our lives in deed, thought and word.

We are all the fortunate ones who can benefit from recognising all-encompassing energies that created our Earth and its global shifts. This planet has been trying to teach us all for aeons to help us be in tune with the already existing abundance.

Since we still need help to understand this, how do we go about tapping into omnipresent abundance? Again, I bring practical answers to our own healing path at the end of this book, if you prefer to have a sneak preview.

For each blockage we experience in our lives, there is, lo and behold, a Karmic reason: an accumulation of mindsets, body barriers and emotions which have caused and were caused by disruptions to our Karmic energy flow. They can be traced back to fearful beliefs, based on our perception of our pasts and our minds running on limiting 'programming'. As an example, an inner energy blockage can be based on a fear that has grown over time due to certain incidents, and has created in turn created its own energy convolutions, giving us limiting thoughts such as 'life does not support me' or 'I cannot have a healthy physical/mental/emotional existence' or 'I have to work hard and fight for my life'. These are actually examples that are archetypical for mankind, as they appear again and again in each generation. The mindsets and beliefs that arise from fears causing blockages within our energy make our lives move away from the simple and healthy constant energy flow within, into an external whirlwind of trying to catch up in an effort to make things happen. We will always do well to look inwards to find reasons why we are not well. We can look at other thought patterns, other emotions as well as physical symptoms to find out their connection to our well-being or feeling ill. Each main chakra or energy centre within us is working together with a hormone-producing gland in the body, so when energy is not taken in or released properly, it can have a detrimental effect on our health, especially over a prolonged period of time.

Energy centres along our spine are often called 'chakras', here in relation to hormone glands

For example, a blocked third eye may cause an inability to 'see the bigger picture' and underlying beliefs such as 'I cannot see for myself' or 'it is dangerous to trust my intuition'. You may argue that this is too simplistic. However, we have to take into consideration that any combination of phrases, thoughts and actions that have ever existed in our heads and which are at the core of a limiting belief, can be at work here. This, of course, does make it extremely comprehensive, so that each individual human being has a multitude of combinations of apparently separate beliefs. As this reflects the fabric of life itself in its kaleidoscopic diversity and with our fears propelling us into the sensation of external experiences outside ourselves, we have opened up to the Pandora's Box effect: endless manifestations of manifold life-forms and limitless, inexplicable and barely foreseeable possibilities co-exist alongside each other; endless outcomes have burst from a singularity, just as the universe and life itself once created itself in an instant. Something that is so vast is difficult to grasp, but at least it seems logical that it must be vast in order to have created the diversity we face in this universe. Just look at all the possible life forms on Earth alone and take comfort in the fact that our very own individual Karmic energy minds have performed the miracle of creating our very own human existence on Earth.

But we are subject to another force in action, based on another blockage within our energy systems that in these times we all seem to have in common: our existentialist fears of existence, and the conundrum of the coinciding fear of non-existence. Those two fears are very real archetypical opposites within us that are influencing the decision-making process of all mankind. It seems that a paradoxical part of us is actively stopping all this diversity of life on our planet, and doesn't want a paradise on Earth. It seems strange to think that a part of us does not want an abundant paradise, but it is an undeniable truth we cannot turn away from: we are trying to protect ourselves from unseen forces we perceive to be against us by building neat little blocks of square sterile concrete for homes with no wildlife allowed in a square sterile manicured garden we can pest control instead. We don't want children who run around free, we want them sitting still and listening to what we tell them. We don't want friends or relationships and all their myriad requests on our attention, we are so stressed out we would rather sit in front of a screen projecting our inner world and preferences day after day after day, than to communicate with a real being standing in front of us. We segregate our society into sections in terms of what wages we earn, Some of our beliefs are so based on fear, so contradictory and short-sighted, they are able to successfully trap us in this, our cycle of existence for any length of time. Not only that, but as we now know, our fears and limited beliefs have killed billions of animals, caused whole ecosystems to collapse and are causing the whole surface of the planet to slowly cave in on itself. We need to separate our fears from our true selves before they kill us. Whilst we cannot blame our fears for everything, untreated fear keeps us on a one-level existence in a one-track mind and will not allow us to see through it enough to progress. We cannot see the wood for the trees - which is the case for most of us living in a 'civilised' world on a daily basis. Perhaps it does not seem so far-fetched and simplistic now, talking about a blockage in our third eye chakra.

If we carry on not acknowledging where our behaviour patterns come from and what our internal beliefs look like, if we do not recognise the origin of our mindsets, we will continue to subjugate ourselves, our families, everyone and everything around us to leading separate lives with separated identities. We will continue to follow the anxious individual paths we have trodden again and again and carry on feeling that we are not getting anywhere. More and more individuals don't get on with our own families and communities, often with tragic consequences. For those of us who cannot see through the reasons for our own undoing, it will be very difficult to progress into awareness, as we may carry on forever sabotaging ourselves and others.

They say ignorance is bliss... but I believe that true bliss lies in undoing our ignorance, looking at the holistic view behind our separateness, learning how to find peace again within, knowing and feeling connected to the simple singularity of the universal Truth: that

we are one.

There are many such archetypal energy blockages that hold true for almost all of humankind, such as blockages in the abdomen area, connected to the vital adrenal glands producing hormones such as cortisol which are linked to stress symptoms when not functioning properly. Giving us 'butterflies' at the very least, there are more severe symptoms of the production of adrenaline and cortisone, which occurs when our fear is realised for example in the 'fight or flight' reflex, a handy thing our body can come up with to ascertain our survival in times when we have to muster all our energy to run for our lives. Prolonged states of stress, however, exhaust our body's ability to produce hormones and neurotransmitters such as adrenaline, noradrenaline, dopamine, serotonin, epinephrine, GABA, cortisone or histamine amongst others, with the result that we are no longer able to respond well to stressful situations. We end up suffering from acute anxiety disorders. The knock-on effect is that we start to function differently and feel fear more often, even unreasonable amounts in normal situations as a result, as PTSD sufferers will well attest. These have severe symptoms and consequences until the balance is restored by replenishing the energy needed to bring our functions back to normal.

Blockages in the heart chakra, as another example, hold beliefs about our emotions and connection to others around us. Again, limiting thought patterns tend to correspond to the energy blockage, or the two may even be identical; by which I mean that, as long as a limiting belief pattern exists, it continues to sustain a blockage within the Karmic energy system, and in turn the blockage carries on feeding the limiting belief. It sounds like a vicious cycle, like cyclic existence itself, and it may be just that - but there is a way out. These energy blockages, once addressed with the appropriate method, become neutralised and tend to remove their corresponding belief patterns and fears in the process too, which is uncanny but makes sense; plus it's very handy when you think about it.

I formed the theorem some years ago that an inner energy blockage and a limiting belief or negative feeling are not just related, they can be one and the same. As I learned more about Karma and energy therapies over the years, especially EFT™, I learned about the symbiosis between an energy blockage and a corresponding negative belief or anxiety; that neutralising the energy blockage can also remove a long-standing negative belief and vice versa. It is very fortunate when we can recognise our limiting beliefs as early as possible, even before they manifest in our physical existence. Once they are established in actual physical form, in the shape of acute or chronic pain, accidents, addictions, nutritional disorders, unmanageable behaviour, emotions or thoughts for example, we may have an arduous task of backtracking through lifetimes of Karmic blockages. Fortunately - miraculously even - the resulting blockage often stands synonymous for many situations that have contributed to it, and by treating it, the Karmic time-line that created it also starts to dissolve. I have treated many people with PTSD over the years, and when we address the symptoms such as a phobia, we are often treating the event that contributed to it, often naturally leading to a totally different and calmer perception of events, i.e. feeling that one is more of an observer to the event rather than still being at the mercy of it.

It's such a shame we don't get taught any of this at school, and I wonder why not? Since we don't have our tribe around us any longer, and have to find out almost everything for ourselves individually, this is something that most of us are forced to do at this stage of the Earth's and our own personal development, in order to keep up with our speedy and stressful lifestyles and ever-changing challenges and roles. But do we really? Or do we not see through how we have been kept apart, get distracted en route and bypass the journey inwards altogether? Despite methods that become easier to use all the time, more freely available and more sophisticated with ever faster results, it is often still a tricky and time-consuming task to make the connection between our limited perceptions and Karmic energy flow. Many of us despair and give up their search for the answers within the Karmic energy system in favour of the 'oh look – a squirrel!' syndrome nicely presented in a little square meme; we make light of having to give up sometimes, and even though I do have a sense of humour and love a good distraction myself once in a while - and I do hope it shows all throughout this book - I also hope we never lose our wisdom of where our humour comes from: a healthy naval and solar plexus chakra which allow us to help us manage even in deep and meaningful tasks and the more tricky situations in life. I have always striven to assist others see light on their journey of making more sense of what is happening to them, and I will do my best to not tire of it. The tools and therapies available nowadays are making it easier all the time to see right through the illusion of illness and may even make illness obsolete in future which would be something so very useful at any Karmic stage of our global and personal development.

✳ ✳ ✳

20. Karma and Our Karmic Energy Body, Illness and Death

So what to do when we get ill? This chapter is about gaining insights into situations that face all of us, sooner or later. I wish talking about Karmic energy and how we can easily apply methods to alleviate fear could become a thing. Until that happens, we can learn to work on our own. It's got to be scouts' advice: it's always best to be prepared! It might help us to recognise that any bodily illness has been building up within us for quite some time and that we have just not 'seen' it; especially if it had previously only existed in our almost invisible energy body. As many of us do not even believe that these layers of energy exist or are of any consequence to our well-being, we resist looking into ourselves to check in with our energy body once in a while and see what is really going on. An 'Energy MOT' is what's needed, on a regular basis; but we have a tendency to get complacent. When everything seems ok and we feel reasonably alright, we have an inclination to abuse our systems with all sorts of unbalanced behaviour: working too hard, living too hard - recreational drugs, bad foods, drinking, smoking, staying up all night, doing things to excess. These are the more extreme examples, but even on a more subtle level, we are often not aware of how we are abusing ourselves: ignoring our need for proper rest and a peaceful environment, straining our brains and bodies with unsympathetic work structures; perusing the wrong mental and physical exercises, i.e. trying to be competitive in actions and thoughts; being unkind and insensitive to ourselves and others emotionally; not having any spiritual grounding and not knowing how to nurture ourselves and be gentle yet agile, Self-contained but not insular, still but alert, peaceful but awake within. We do not even know how to breathe properly! In the name of personal choice and free will, the signs of the level of Self-harm which our bodies openly demonstrate are often guiltily ignored, even though they are obvious symptoms of our Self-abuse and could easily become positive pointers to a more wholesome lifestyle. Our physical bodies are far from our temples, they are seen as machines which must be thrashed. it is interesting that there are many sports that demand of those who take part that they are trained to demonstrate a physical fitness which is untenable over prolonged period of times. Enhanced through daily regimes of strain, these often lead to life-long physical problems in order to keep up. And yet, this is hailed in our society, with astronomical sums of money spent on promoting sporting events every year. The world of competition is keeping us locked in a world of faster, better, stronger, and our work ethics and competitive thinking are not far behind; making us believe that we must be someone else, someone younger, thinner, more muscular, handsome or beautiful. All these are aggregates of the physical realm. Everything appears to be goal-orientated. Does the winner really take it all? I am even sure my pointing this out is going to cause an uproar, as we don't even see anything wrong with this. I don't have anything against athletes, or anyone being who they are and doing what they do - please don't get me wrong. I am merely giving an example of how our understanding of health appears to be heavily biased on physical perception and visual stimulation in our current society. That much is undeniable.

Our physical bodies and our over-worked minds are crying out to be cured, except in these modern days we are subject to a baffling Self-sabotaging paradox: we commonly say, without even being aware of it, that we mean to get better, when our subconscious in fact finds as many reasons why it cannot actually allow us to do so. Consciously, we may decide that we absolutely want to and need to stop bad habits such as, for example, smoking. As soon as we have made the decision to quit, our subtle, anxious, ego mind whispers things like, 'no way will I allow you to give up, look at how afraid you are! Smoking is the only thing that has helped you so far to mask all the anxiety that comes up in quiet times; what else is there to replace smoking? Nothing else helps, you have tried many times before to give up. You can't do it! Remember last time, it was awful! The withdrawal symptoms...and you ate so much food instead and became really depressed, last time! Smoking is not so bad...people get old despite smoking...what makes you think you're strong enough to give up anyway? Everyone smokes these days! Let me carry on helping you ignore the bad thoughts'...and so on. Do you recognise any of the Self-talk symptoms? Our gentle, subconscious energy system has been corrupted by our fears, stress and ongoing Self-harm that it has now got a bit of a chip on its shoulder. There is a chink in the armour and it's that flaw in our energy system which is giving us the scared Self-talk, wanting us to know that it's there; it seemingly has a 'mind of its own' that is a strong contender for running the show instead of us, if we don't know where the inner small talk comes from and give in to it. Thing is, the small talk isn't going away unless we address it. It gathers momentum instead. If we gave it some thought, we would perhaps admit to being a certain percentage convinced the small talk is right. In fact, if anything over 50% of our energy system is being taken in by the energy of fear, this has the effect of so dramatically lowering our resolve, that we are very likely to cave in and give up. It's because the energy that is running our physical body - our brain, nervous system, musculoskeletal system, vital organs and so on - all rely on energy flowing through them. The moment we have allowed our subtle energy mind to collect enough negative charge, our physical body will not function properly. in fact, it can be opposed in its electromagnetic charge to permitting us to get better, it has enough negative charge to not allow us to proceed and succeed. It's a physical process similar to electric current flowing through gadgets - no power, no function. You don't have to take my word for it. The medical world has lots of proof.

This principle of our energy system having become compromised is applicable to all sorts of situations, not just giving up addictions. Whenever possible, we would do well to find ways to become sensitive and conscious of this reversed energy process within us. It does not matter how long our inner Karmic energy has been compromised, how or when it started or whose fault it was and how emotional we feel about it. This can all be addressed by utilising one of the methods which work specifically by recognising what is going on within our own energy body. For example, if we ask ourselves how much we want to do something to improve things, consciously we might say 100%. However, we can simply measure the resonance of our inner energy truth quite well, by applying methods of kinesiology. Our physical body will give us its own reading of what state it is in, and those answers may not be the same as our conscious thoughts. Importantly, it can show us where our body truth differs from our conscious truth. All we then need to do is to know how to use the right method to read the signs correctly, interpret the answers, and not forget to apply the remedy of releasing the fear energy that is stuck in our body and mind. If it sounds complicated, it really isn't, and you can quite easily find out online how to do it. it's a bit like learning to do DIY, only in this case, it is vital for our health and wellbeing, so what's not to like! It doesn't all have to be doom and gloom. It can be exciting and sometimes even funny when we can find out our real inner truth of why we are not succeeding in giving up bad stuff, not getting that job, not getting healthier, not changing our behaviour etc. All of that is good news and I wonder how long it will be before someone will turn it into a new online craze. Giving ourselves an inner make-over is much more rewarding than spending thousands on external products that will only last a short while. We need to want to awaken at least to some extent and we could carry on asking for more input to become conscious, even when most of the world seems hell-bent on remaining unconscious. What if we suddenly woke up and don't need half of the stuff we are addicted to any longer? If we are subconsciously sabotaging and stopping ourselves from becoming conscious, that is also something we can easily work on, it's all within our own energy field after all. The problem is that remaining unconscious is so prevalent right now, with almost everyone relating to suffering anxiety, stress and a lack of energy which makes it harder to actively make a decision to bring in something new. Even more a reason to find an answer, especially if we don't have to put a lot of effort into it. Most of these techniques are armchair efforts - we can choose to do something in our own homes without having to move much, and still get results. Thing is, if we don't, remaining unconscious comes at a cost, even if you feel it may be blissful at the time. It is so common in my experience to observe that most of us only want to listen when we actually get to the stage when it is almost too late. The stage I am talking about is of course, irreversible illness and death. You may hate me for reminding you and getting all serious. Sorry. Most people in the West think it is some kind of peaceful release to a trying life, or at last a kind of credit for a more or less successful life, a final 'thank you very much, good night'. Again, we are thinking of a time line and a reward system. That is not quite the way Karma works, though. At least, it's not as simple as getting a pat on the head for doing what somebody has asked us to do. We need to be doing this conscious compassion thing for the benefit of ourselves and others as well as realise what that actually means to maximise its potential. Fortunately, there are many clues, and the inner journey connects and guides us, it doesn't all happen in a day, usually. Might be good if we try not to do it thinking of what there is in it for us, but even if we do, Karma doesn't judge. It just helps us put things right.

Luckily, there are more and more people nowadays who are willing to give a thought to what really happens, and how we can achieve a healthy mind in a healthy body. The reward is that we get well, even if there is no telling how exactly and how quickly. Our Karmic energy system definitely wants us to be well, whilst our body energy system can be lagging a little. Our Karmic energy system knows exactly how to achieve this state of being well, if we only listen with our ego minds and eventually also learn how to fine-tune our methods of interpreting the sometimes not so obvious clues. There are quite a few people by now who don't mind thinking about the afterlife. We know that at the point of death, our conscious control over a physical 'Self' ceases and the Karmic energy body, our energy recording of all that we are and have ever been, activates and takes over from our ego minds. The same energy body that has been with us all along for aeons of time is now in the driving seat! It is all-knowing, and all the information contained in our Karmic energy field now determines what happens next. It is this what makes us feel the 'I'. All this time, it wasn't our body that we so identify with, it is a weightless consciousness, we finally realise - again. We have been here before, we are taking everything we have experienced and become, with us - and we might even have a chance to be remembering the whole event at this crucial point where a crossover process of our temporary perception occurs, and fading timelines of an ego-mind are being integrated again into the omnipresence we are all an ultimate part of. Is it suddenly dawning on us why it's so important to pay attention to our Karma in this lifetime? Why we haven't been wasting our time reading all this? Death does not mean we just go to sleep and disappear. Death is a transformation, one that we want to prepare for, in this lifetime. We are going , to be quite busy after death. Our ego-mind has no choice but to relinquish control over our physical functions at the point of our death. The physical functions including those of our brain are no longer present, and guess what? You are still there! You still exist, but the physical aspect of 'You' is ebbing away and it can no longer be accessed in that form, except for maybe those times when we are only 'dead' for a short time and are being resuscitated. In those moments after death, many who come back into their physical body recall a process of seeing that there is more on the other side, most report leaving their physical Self behind and a weightless floating experience follows, being drawn to something that feels very loving and light. This is just the first phase of the after-life, but if you have been conscious of the fact that it might exist, then all the better. It would be such a useful practice to be more prepared as to how to navigate in those phases shortly after physical death, because there is little you can consciously decide to do for yourself after this point any longer. Consciousness as we know it, connected to our brains and physical body, will not remain the same. Not that people who remember dying and then return to life, come back saying they didn't like it. Most report that they didn't want to come back into their physical body, that it was much nicer on the other side. After physical death is determined, 'You' would be reunited with your true being, which is much more expansive than a physical 'Self' and carries all the Karmic memory experience of all physical experiences that have gone before, as well as all the stages of existences in-between. This is the stage where any form of regret, remorse and subsequent assessment and potentially repair might set in, when you get to experience the instant recall of everything that has happened so far. The 'You' becomes the observer of the life that has just passed and the life we have left becomes fully visible in all its aspects, including the Karmic influences any moment our lives will have had - good, bad or neutral. Depending on circumstances, we will have a window during which we become witness to the lightning process unfolding that automatically assesses what happens next as a result, but cannot further influence it after the fact. All physical form, each molecule and the space between now merges with the Universal energy that is omnipresent. The unique translation of our physical energy into formlessness, including the pattern that emerges in the spaces where it either completely merges or cannot completely merge due to a more dense energy residue we have left behind as a result of our physical experiences and choices, creates a pattern that determines the new, un-manifest 'You'. There are infinite possibilities and numbers of such patterns, i.e. un-manifest life forms, no two are the same. I believe though that for a short time after passing - and certainly we would be able to all throughout our physical existence - we can react to it, and our 'reaction' is still crucial in determining who we become next. If we had not so far ever been conscious and aware of all the facts that magnificently converge to mean we survive physical existence, how elaborate and precious they are, this is a moment where we have our chance to see the whole breathtaking beauty of it. If we see our unwitting mistakes in the light of such delicate symphony orchestrating life and react in that instant with awe for the construct of reality, able to add regret and remorse for those times where we acted unconscious of it, then our Karmic energy can still register this accordingly. In this tiny window of opportunity, and our very yearning to be complete becomes a part of the blueprint for another future in physical form. In the power of this moment of recognition and reconciliation we can and will actively have a last influence over adjusting our Karmic energy body for our future lives.

It is an important stage in our development, but we cannot rely on it and simply say 'I do what I want whilst I am still alive because I will still have time to put it right when i die' and think it will all be ok. After all, the moment of our passing is the summary of all our previous actions, thoughts and communication which determine our future outcome. If our presence is infantile and Self-serving, we will be presented with situations out of our control to give us opportunities for inner growth. You will probably be already aware that those can be, but are not always pleasant. If they are pleasant, we might get the hint gently and learn gratitude for every moment of our existence, learn to cherish the miracle of it and every living cell in our body. If they are unpleasant, it's so much harder to make that connection. All the more reason to be grateful and try to fully embrace the moments where aspects of our lives are going well, starting with the tiniest things. We can introduce offerings to make those tiny things grow, like watering seedlings in the hope that we may have more in future. This is how to increase awareness slowly but surely, in the right direction, by nurturing all that is alive, flora, fauna, our families, our selves. The universe is not against us. We are, and we may be sabotaging ourselves without being aware of it, and repeat patterns and learned behaviour that we were taught by the madness of others who also did not know better. It takes huge amounts of effort to be kind, to be gentle, to be nurturing, to have compassion - and yet, it is the greatest wisdom alive.

Once our Karmic energy mind has 'uploaded' every bit of information from our lifetime, it will separate from our body and ego mind completely. How long this process takes is interpreted differently in various cultures, but it can take up to 49 days according to some Eastern philosophies. What a Magick, happy moment this must be for the individual, if not for those they leave behind – the realisation of a survival, the vastness of our existence, the love that we feel from all and everything around us. The regret must be simply that we did not do this sooner, learned how to feel like this when we were still alive, lived to experience this more fully, and shared it with everyone we saw! Even if we weren't always present on Earth, we are still very much able to beam beautiful Karmic energy at those who we still connect to, and we will be able to continue to do this according to the fabric of our prevailing ineffable Karmic energy cloud.

After death, our future direction is subject to determination by our Karmic energy according to how it has evolved up to that point.

Some people say the moment you pass is supposed to be like watching your life pass before you, in great detail. I believe that in some ways, it can be described to be so, since we are in the process of reconciling our physical experiences, transmuting again into our everlasting Karmic energy body. For those lucky enough to have reached Karmic completion to such extent due to their conduct in previous lifetimes, it may even be a moment of full realisation. Even more lucky, if at this point the 'You' - as in, your full realisation of your Karmic energy body - is able to recognise the important outcome of certain scenarios, in order to steer your Karmic energy towards the highest light and best outcome for all sentient beings.

The point arises, of taking into account everything we had forgotten and all that we wanted to forget. Our Karmic energy is free of a limited physical body; how long this phase lasts is determined by all that has happened before and what occurs in this moment, where it connects and perceives all without filter and gets to make sense of it - the good, the bad and the ugly, so to speak. It is not like our brain trying to make a decision; it is an energy process of instantly attracting and repelling energy on sub-atomic levels. Everything that was past or forgotten, pushed into some recess in our mind which we wanted to not see and thought we would never have to confront again, is now equally present and active again, being brought to the surface in detail. In that moment, we will perhaps get the chance to observe that there were always solutions, in every moment of our lives, to relieving our pain bodies. It is much easier to perceive when we are not caught up in the density of physical existence. Often, people who have had after-death experiences, recall how all-encompassing they felt, how they could see and perceive everything without pain. We may be brought back into this very body after a short spell of being in the death realm, and become quite different as a result of seeing how before the experience. Sometimes people are able to bring back some of this universal wisdom energy and are able to heal, even from terminal illness. Or we may realise we haphazardly contributed to squandering the precious health we had, instead of becoming our light body on Earth. We have this life, this chance, to diligently alleviate our and others' suffering, rather than digressing, diverting, distracting. If only we had realised sooner that 'we' would survive death after all! If we knew not only that we would, but also how we would survive. The irony of it is that...

We will survive death. Just not how we think.

Here is a little ironic joke I use to remind myself of the mystery of our past existence and the fears we carry because of it.

Karmic mind to Self: 'Shall I tell you what happened to you in a past life? Self: 'Go on then, I have no idea, can't wait to find out.' Karmic mind: 'You died.'

It may sound a bit harsh, as these things are not something we tend to joke or want to think about and discuss in our society that is so scared of death. I am certainly not trying to make suffering worse or mock the mourning process we have to endure for loved ones lost. What we feel is very real - we feel that their Karmic energy has left with their physical body, and this phase has ended. We will go through a process of having to adjust to the physical aspect of our loved ones having been removed from our lives. This can feel like a physical, elastic energy that pinged back on us when it tore away once and for all, the sudden awareness that the limited existence having broken away from the connection with us adding untold hurt and pain.

But as you may have noticed already, this book is different. I apologise to those readers who are upset. I really have no intention to upset anyone, least of all those readers who are unwell or who have lost loved ones. And tough though it is to be forced to wake up at any stage of our lives, through external or internal events, there is hope. Everything we have learned so far indicates that no being ever ceases to exist. Our loved ones physical existence may be gone, and it will take time for us to adjust. Many cultures in this world celebrate this moment instead of mourning it, as they recognise the importance of ascertaining the being's auspicious passing to the next realm. The relatives and friends left behind take it upon themselves to concentrate all their energy on bringing about a good outcome for the departed, and it is a vital process for either party to be involved in, the one who is passing on to other realms as well as the role those play who are left behind. But in recognising that there is a role to play, an important one that appears to have been diminished in Western cultures, might be crucial to recreating a truthful event that helps all. Rituals that help the passing of the spirit who moves on, are very intricate and can take weeks of gatherings, prayers, offerings, meaningful dialogue and reflection.

To me, the notion of re-introducing a powerful inclusive role in how we deal with death in the West, holds promises of waking up to a better world soon, a more positive reality that allows us to be part instead of feeling left behind. Maybe we don't have to wait until our culture changes; we can do this right now, in this instant. There are often solutions even for the most difficult illnesses and processes. Even if problems cannot all be solved at once, and alas, maybe not all in this lifetime, there is definite hope in the new ways we can see our Karmic energy path as an eternal bond that exists between us and all we cherish.

The point at which our Karmic energy eventually becomes fully complete, even if it may take a timeline of aeons, is the moment where we stop yearning. It is the moment where we will be no longer subject to our perceptions of time and space, or the requirement of a physical existence to complete our own experience. After this, our Karmic energy mind may be free to roam weightlessly in other worlds and universes, or be drawn again to applying its new-found wisdom and steer back into existence on Earth and other planets in order to help others experience peace, wisdom, compassion and completion.

❊ ❊ ❊

21. The Undistracted Mind

Some of the above concepts are quite difficult to comprehend when we are still attached to our physical existence and our every day lives. We want to make a change but are still much too afraid to really follow up on what we can change for the better. Changes like the ones we are talking about are monumental but hardly ever talked about, hence us reacting with fear, often completely unprepared for major situations of change in our daily existence. One of the most important things we hardly ever get to practice and learn is how to tune into the vastness of our own energy potential. We already know how to exist in the opposite, i.e. what it feels like not to be connected. It doesn't feel great, it makes us sick, and we enter a time-line contract with the 3-d world where we often regret that we forgot to read the small print. Why do we not know who we truly are and what we are really capable of? Why do we resist our full potential when we are presented with it, and react with more fear and mistrust? With our precious active and conscious mindsets, our infinite potential within our Karmic energy body and despite our relatively short time on Earth in each of our unique physical existences, we are given the chance to be working out how to access our miraculous nature in the Now. This is our chance to be getting close to manifesting much more instant healing and instant solutions for many. We may be closer than we think, even if our brains do allow us to get distracted so easily. Am I talking miracles? Yes, maybe I am. Maybe that is the closest word I can think of to try to make you understand that, if you feel you are ailing or lacking – and aren't we all -, ask for a miracle. I mean it. Ask for help, even if there appears to be no-one else around. What we might call a miracle that we feel a million miles removed from receiving is the norm in the infinite potential of the highest vibrations in Existence. And as we have already learned, we are already a part of this transcendental process of cosmic creation.

Miracles happen all the time. It's when they don't, there is something amiss. Expect a miracle.

Even if you do not believe it, you have just arrived at remembering you have the chance to activate some of your energy body's most valuable components in order to find solutions for you. Even if we never become consciously aware of it, have never seen it, do not believe in it, or cannot see how it can possibly work - we are all a part of the great Truth, and the basis of all miracles is already within us. It does not matter whether our brain comprehends or is sceptical and it does not make us more or less worthy, it just makes it more complicated for us to feel we can immediately take part in the beauty of the simplicity of one simple yet utterly complex and profound law of the universe:

You qualify by being alive.

The reality of it is that your energy radiates out from you constantly without you even having to think about it. It meets with alike energies around it which it then reacts to or not. By 'around it' I mean to say potentially as far as the universe and beyond, as quickly as a thought and faster than the speed of light. When I say universe, I really mean this, our universe, and beyond, at the danger of sounding like a kids' cartoon character. But i am quite serious: At some point at the 'end' of our and other universes. the oscillating energy which created them becomes ineffable and beyond words capable of describing it. A formless entity beyond intention, form, timeline or direction, a field without limits, the endless potential of all that is. How do we know this? My counter-question: How come we have forgotten this? Why have only such a small number of people realised that we are part of this energy which can time-and-space travel already? Our energy mind is quicker than any light rays, plus we can project it into the universe and beyond in an instant if we have fine-tuned into our memory to remember how to do so. Some of us already remember how to do this, but most of us have to learn all over again. The more we practice and the more accomplished and focused we become, the more energy radiates from us, ever more subtly and without obstacles. We can ask for world peace, we could bring about an end to wars...if only we could all focus our complete mind for just one second and then build on that without any Karmic residue to deal with. That is the greatest catch the Universal Karmic energy has given us, splitting us into a gazillion different energies all at different stages of our development. This is why we find this so difficult to do on Earth - we are all at different stages in our own inner evolution that we are feeling separate and alienated most of the time, caught up in separation and fear. Tuning into this universal unity of unifying energy feels so impossible to achieve that we almost always give up without having even had so much as a sniff at the benefits. And yet, it subconsciously remains one of our main objects for our strife on Earth, to be reunited with who we truly are.

The blockages in the way of achieving our miracles lie within ourselves, and can be dealt with on an energy level.

The simplest things sometimes elude us, and it may be the reason why, as a society, we focus little energy nowadays on cultivating this most amazing of all tools: the complexity and potential of our energy mind. It wasn't always so on Earth. Ancient cultures living more in tune with nature started to grasp the full complexity of the phenomena they came across around them. A few bright minds always prevail in any culture, even if it does degenerate. Someone once stated - can't recall who - that If all the atoms in a light bulb were aligned, it would shine as brightly as the sun. Seems likely to me since people already learned to split atoms to set free vast kinetic energy almost 100 years ago. Every standard light bulb has the potential to do so, yet it only emits a relatively dim light using a maximum of 100 watts, which is about 1600 lumens. Every atom contains huge amounts of energy tied up in its fascinating formation. The big question we should ask is: Are our Karmic minds the force and intention that brings free energy to manifestation of physical form? If each of our Karmic energy fields that survive our physical form every time has a memory of its previous physical existence, and that memory is coded so that it will converge when there is a focus of energy, is this what will make us incarnate again, and in our case on Earth in relatively dense physical form? And if we remembered all this tied up energy we are made of that has made us manifest and we focused our energy minds on something we wanted to create, would it not potentially start to exist, unless there is an equal energy to counteract the manifestation process? If, for example, many of us got together with the sincere wish to manifest something mindful and worthwhile such as world peace, and worked on this in a concentrated effort for a period of time...but I divulge and fantasize. Of course, it is impossible. Or is it? Do we try to dissect our energy into bite-size pieces so that we can understand it better, but lose the ability to use to it maximum effect in the process? Have we lost the ability to at least focus our minds on our own well-being by thinking small? Can we not sit for even just a minute and keep our brains still, to allow the process to happen where we reconnect with our greater Karmic minds?

Perhaps we can't because most of us have a latent, inbuilt, long-standing fear of this inner stillness. Silence and the absence of action and reaction is what we think we really want to obtain, but in our Karmic memory, this equates with uncertainty and brings up fears of the unknown, the process of dying and the fear of death itself. This is what the physical existence, our ego, is really so afraid of: not existing. This is the paradox: as long as we have the fear, we cannot see past physical existence and continue to be afraid; our actions and our energy resources are focused on trying to avoid our fear of not existing. In our stressed, anxious state, our physical body and brain have long since stopped believing, trusting and understanding that we carry on existing. Having checked all the information in our inner filing cabinets on the subject of 'dying' in our ego memory bank only, we are not prepared to give up our fear of dying. Something has made us believe that clinging to the fear of dying will stop us experiencing physical pain and death, against all reason. It has firmly wedged itself in our psyche, in every cell in our body and created its own repercussions - a vicious cycle of thoughts and actions based on limited beliefs, and fears based on limited thoughts and emotions. We are one lovely bundle of angst and further resulting emotions, wrapped tightly like a straitjacket of our physical limitations. It has taken us lifetimes worth of our energy to build up this catch-22, needless to say we won't allow anyone to come along suddenly and try to take it away. We might even be aware it is a construct of reality that in turn is creating its vision of our future reality itself based on fear, but faced with illness and death, we react with fear over and over again and cannot contemplate this happy-go-lucky thought that we will survive eternally. How can it even be true? Where is the catch?

Well, we would be better off believing in miracles, so where shall we start?

Even if you choose not to want to make a start on anything outside your comfort zone, you might still find it of use to read on. Contemplate this: what if there are tools that make you worry less; make you less stressed; make you aware that there is something within you already that has the ability to heal you, make you complete, and weave health and happiness into the very fabric of your physical body? I just happen to believe that these very tools exist and I know that I am not the only one. There are more and more people who are awakening to the idea. I am mostly trying to address those of us who find it hard to believe in more than what our senses are telling us to be true; those of us who we tried to convince so far and have not just yet, the real 'hardcore sceptics', but also those of us who **have** suffered most severely and cannot seem to recover enough to experience yet the bliss of the bigger picture. Those who are on the verge of believing and who can be pulled into the awareness of light and wisdom, but whose belief system has so far failed them and told them not to, told them to hold back, to be sceptical, to be careful, to not be silly or do anything dangerous or fanatical. Those who probably would not normally even read a book like this, except…you are. You hung in there. Thank you. And for the record: I agree with you. We do have to be careful and examine all there is, and these days the information overload is almost counterproductive. Much damage can occur when we work with our inner energy. Most people experience some form of pain even when they are awakening, phases of great change, feeling lost and phases of desolation at times, maybe even a continuation of their long-term despair and depression without seeing results quickly enough. Please, to all of you who are feeling like this right now: do not give up. It is only our fear energy, again! It is our ego minds and bodies which hurt. The real you is not hurting at all. Test it! In fact, I urge you to look inwards and see where you feel your energy is stuck. It is this stuck energy flow, still playing make-believe, trying to control you with fear. We don't even know yet who we can become without our energy being stuck inside, we do not even know how great we are yet and how loving our lives could be if we set our Karmic energy free! Is it worth a try? You decide.

There are methods to try and achieve what we are talking about. We have never been in a better position to make attempts at relinquishing fear, and yet we are still drawn to prolonging the agony of our inner turmoil rather than trying out solutions to the problem. (For more examples, please have a look at the end of this book to find out how you can start immediately if you want). Try this for a recipe, to start: According to what beliefs you were given in your life path, you might already be able to tune in and tell where your inner ego-energy is stuck; if you have painful thoughts, assume that the energy may simply be stuck in your head. Where it is fear, you may feel it start as butterflies in your solar plexus area where adrenaline is produced, from where it can flood through the circulatory systems all over your body, giving you a feeling like you are constantly on edge. Some people are so used to the feeling that they don't even know it does not have to be that way. It can also become a cycle of adrenaline rush and adrenaline fatigue that has a strangely addictive ebb and flow. Sometimes energy is actually stuck in every cell in our bodies, and over a prolonged period of time it can even cause extreme physical suffering, degenerative diseases like immune system malfunctions and even cancers. It is not your fault! We have just never been told that there are methods how to tackle our stuck energy so it can be set free to assist us to feel well again. Almost all of us reading this can benefit from these methods. We can all start by making a list of our limiting beliefs to recognise how all-encompassing and unmanageable they tend to become. Name your fears and thoughts, find where they are 'stuck' and you are being presented with a treasure map of your road to health, not to hell. This is the first step to recovery from any illness. The second step will be to actually apply the simple methods to alleviating it, described at the end of the book. This is no hard sell, no subscription, no monthly fees. It's free, and it's quite simple and quick to learn the basics of. Try it to see if you like it. If you don't, have a look at some online tuition to help you find out more. See what others say about it. Research, but most of all, persevere. See the benefits right away of how intensities of fear can start to ebb away in an instant. When you ask for health, and luck, and a good outcome, you will be well on the road to receiving help to dissolve all that I have so far attributed to the 'ego mind'. It may take time but most will see relief straight away when starting to use the techniques. I hope I have made it clear enough so far, that the 'ego mind' is only the part within us isn't bad, but rather that it serves as a sort of kindly but more or less dysfunctional and misguided coping mechanism which your body had no choice but to put in place to patch things up temporarily. I imagine that many more than is generally assumed are sufferers of PTSD: Post traumatic Stress Disorder. This is not the real you, this is a symptom your system displays after suffering traumatic situations. FEAR is False Evidence Appearing Real; and it feels very, very real when we are in fear, in fight or flight mode. However, you are much more powerful than your beliefs, your brain, your body. If we could only be a little more curious as to who is behind the curtain in the 'Wizard of Oz' in the story of our lifetimes, we might realise - just like in the classic book and film - that it was just a little old man talking into a megaphone behind a curtain all along. The archetypes of our reaction to fear take over, trying to make us believe in the powerful unseen force that it can turn out to be, influencing all around us; but all it does is to make you fearful of your true powerful Self and make you feel small like Dorothy, like a fearful child trying to cope in an authoritative adult world, never knowing what is next, until she plucks up enough courage to take matters – including her fears - into her own hands. And our Dorothy finds that this home is already within her, and within her power to reach.

So - what's next? Just to reiterate, I am not a religious fanatic – I don't say 'Ye Be Healed'. That process from beginning to end is entirely up to you - and your Karma. Health, happiness, success - it has already been achieved by those we might put on a pedestal. admire or are envious of; but we don't need to externalise our happiness and project it onto others. The first step is always to realise just how much we are unconscious of internalising stress and how, when not resolved, it can get in the way of our well-being, becoming a vicious cycle of manifesting more illness. When we see it written down in black and white, listing our stress triggers as suggested above, we know it's time to go easy on ourselves and find methods to help ourselves the best way we can. In addition to listing our fears, it will also be very helpful to find out where we might be sabotaging ourselves by listing where we feel stuck in a rut by having limiting belief systems in place. This is not a 'name and shame' list, on the contrary we are trying to find out how to turn things around for us by pinpointing where the problem might be. You can keep the list entirely to yourself or share it with the world as is fashionable right now, it's up to you.

I can assure you that there are some great additional ways of dealing with ill health to those already in place right now on this planet. It's 100% better than denial or putting up with stuck energy. Kind people before you have already asked for miracles, co-created and received them. It seems that once these miracles were in place and physically manifest, they also became more readily available to more and more people to instantly tune into their frequency who could in turn make use of them. We have to be mindful what to ask for and focus on, though. We can apparently have the latest mobile phones in deserts where children are starving. You can see what I am getting at.

If you find resistance within to what I am writing, if you find yourself getting edgy, angry, bored or distracted, that's ok, it's a good sign you are alive and feeling. Please put your feelings down on that list for yourself right now, so that it comes good for you, becomes a healing aid and part of the process. Please be good to yourself; be gentle with yourself.

I know one or two very special beings who have done some of the ground work already who gladly share their knowledge with you. At the end of this book you will find a list of healing systems that work amazingly quickly and effectively and I invite you all to try them and/or email me with more to add to the research list – after all it is about freedom of choice and 'horses for courses'. Let this book be a working document.

❉ ❉ ❉

22. The Karma of Conflict

Of course, with the subject of Karma we will always be a little on thin ice. We have laws of Karma according to observation of cause and effect, but in terms of definitive answers, we do not have definitive proof that will satisfy those who are used to working with our ego mind only. I see that there has been a danger in trying to grasp the concept of Karma in our society with logical thought, but this does not lead us to the right conclusions. Karma invites us to think outside the box, to learn to trust our intuition and increase our ability to rely on insight. If we work with intellect, we end up with what we have now - situations where people make judgements such as saying that all people who have bad things happen to them, have deserved them; or that Karma is an instant force who has it in for us and will punish us like an authoritative God outside of ourselves who we have to worship lest they unleash their holy wrath upon us. As I stated before, that would be far too simplistic, judgemental, short sighted and naive. The consequences of not fully grasping the concept of Karma could be detrimental in itself to all our future well-being. It is important we learn that Karmic law does not work that way. Rather, as we already learned, Karma follows the distinct energy flow of either one of the following outcomes to situations we come across, every second of our lives: neutral re-actions, negatively charged re-actions or positively charged re-actions; each of these cause their equivalent energy force attraction within and around us. Since Karmic energy flow is a subtle force within us it can remain hidden for some time. A Karmic result to an incident in our lives may not present itself immediately but at some point in the future, meaning that something happens within us instantly but the visible result of the inner changes could be instant or light years away, or indeed anywhere in between. Karmic events are energy events which can manifest on a physical level. When examining what this means for each of us, some questions about our Karmic actions may arise. We obviously know what 'negative' actions and reactions mean. If we have endured situations over and over again which raise our stress levels, we can become prone to reacting more easily with fears of being hurt. If we are subject to high levels of stress without addressing the symptoms, our reactions to our environment may not be the same as those of a person who is relaxed and does not suffer from stress. If, as a result of unresolved inner conflict, we end up reacting defensively and angry towards others, and - in the extreme - feel justified in acting out, we not only show the symptoms of someone who needs to ask for assistance in dealing with their feelings, but can very quickly lose control over these and escalate into more open conflict to the point where we are cutting off our energy flow life-line as well as that of others. At this point, it is making it difficult or impossible for us to manage any precarious Karmic reaction we are creating which in turn can cut off our way out, because our energy flow has been disrupted. At this point, it is almost always only flowing in the wrong direction of conflict. It sounds so simple when we read it on paper like this, but looking around, we are all drawn into conflict at poignant Earth times, even right now as we live through many conflicts arising on Earth on a daily basis. Will we react with good intentions for the greatest good, by the power of our past good Karma and trust that our energy can make a change for the good of mankind? It is not so easy to stand in our own true Karmic Self when everything else around us is falling apart and many are in conflict themselves. We are faced with many who are not connected to such ideas at this time on Earth. Wisdom seems to have gone out of fashion. We inherently know that creating love and peace with kindness and generosity cause good Karma, but if the mountain we preach from is surrounded with gunfire and bombed out homes, what use are our good intentions and knowing our good Karma then? I am reminded time and time again how lucky we are to live in peace - if we do - and that I count my blessings every day when I know I am safe. Would it be squandering our good Karma if we do not make the most of our Karmic Self right now? If we do not at least send out good energy, good thoughts, good intentions created by our good Karmic past, how can we contribute to World peace if not by creating more good Karma all around, for all of us, in all future to come? We know we are able to create and sustain good energy simply because we feel it resonating within, connection us to a higher plane of existence knowing that we have created a ripple effect connecting us with others in a good way. If we are able to do this, why do we settle for lesser ways, suffering even? Are we that bored? Are we that disconnected? Are we so complacent? Or are we all really anxious and stressed, clinging on to life, grabbing it and throttling it to squeeze even an ounce of satisfaction out of it, so we can at least feel something, anything? If we are so unhappy, how do we feel another's need who is much, much worse off than we are?

I feel we need to name it, recognise it first, in order to be able to - or even just want to - do something about it. If we see what the issues are, where they came from, what role we play in the whole scenario, then we can find a way to get out, and also help others escape from the depths of despair that can befall this whole planet. So, more Karmic questions to ask ourselves -

What if we felt like we are living on a knife edge, would we go left or right, i.e. feel like we deserve a way out of it, or will we feel doomed without any sense of rescue coming our way? What if we deemed something a 'negative' event in our lives, but were actually able to draw some very positive conclusions from it? What if something negative was put to us, but we learned something really important from it? Do we feel punished? Did we 'deserve' this to happen? Have we always felt powerless, ever since we were small children suffering at the hands of adults around us? How deep are our wounds? If we are wounded, do we need to know, over and over again, how low our energy can go, before we get help? And what sort of help do we need? What if nobody comes to help? At any time, there a millions of people on Earth suffering inhumane conditions - why us? What did we do wrong?

If you are reading this and you are relatively well, relatively well-off, then it is good to be grateful, and extend our gratitude to good conditions. If we are not, and far from, then everything we are talking about is what we need to know, in order to make a change, to make a difference to our lives, and create a future by understanding who we are, and who we can be again.

What if it because of previous actions that something bad happened to us? It does not help wondering who we once were at this point. What we need to look at is who we are right now: are we alive? Can we draw a positive conclusion from being alive? Can we find a way to get out of this situation we are in, by knowing we are alive, for a good reason? Again, perhaps we need to be aware of not judging ourselves or anyone else too harshly or generalising too quickly when we just don't know the reasons why we are suffering right now. Right now, we need to be reminded that we are able to send out our Karmic energy to get help, right from where we are standing.

It is just that conclusion we need to draw from every situation in our lives: we often simply don't know enough about ourselves, to perceive our strength, especially when we are not in a good way. At those moments, we can only put out there the best we can; and that is meant by simply, but profoundly, asking your Karmic Self to ask for help. Ask for help, with every ounce of your being. Ask for yourself, include others if you are aware they need help, too. It sounds a bit crazy I know, but this is sometimes the only thing that we are able to do, when everything else has failed. We need to all prepare for those moments when all else fails, when we need help, physically, emotionally, mentally. Those are the times when we need to be relying on our true Self, our Karmic energy, to work with us. If we have never tried it before, it's never too late. Even if we have learned and know about Karma, it is the moments when we are down that we rarely know how to use our aliveness. Even when we feel nothing good about being alive, we will still be able to use our Karmic strength all the same. We can ask for help, for assistance, for strength, for guidance, for material, medicinal and mental needs to be met. We can make it reciprocal, and offer something in return, to make it more meaningful, to make it last. The best way to ask our Karmic Self to assist, is to envisage only our own being connecting with the higher forces of the universe, meaning that we don't direct our energy at anyone else in particular to help. That way, the best way can be chosen for you, and assistance comes in the best form possible. It also does not always follow that other humans will be able to help. We just have to look at how many displaced people are out there, hoping for somewhere safe to live. You would have thought that people who have much, will be able to give much to increase their good Karma, but it seems that most of us have not been taught that giving unconditionally increases our good Karma, and that acts of giving without thinking 'what's in it for us' will benefit all.

We have been slowly educated into oblivion, and so most of people's limited ability to see and comprehend Karma is not their fault. It serves those few who wish to amass wealth for themselves only to create a false perception of who we are. We are extremely powerful in our ability to ask for help, and set our Karmic Self free to assist us. We do not even have to trust the universe, it does not really mind if we don't. Our ability to create is so strong that it is a threat to those who wish to harness it. If we were all aware of who we truly are, there would be no wars, no famine, no slavery, nobody taking advantage of each other. There might be two reasons why we can still be in abject poverty in mind, body and spirit: a. we have not been introduced to the concept, because it's not been our time yet and b. because there might be forces who are actively trying to stop this from happening. In both cases, all we need to do is ask...to awaken. Should we wait until things have got a lot worse? I don't think you need me to answer that.

What about someone who has an easy life in rich surroundings? Has Karma treated them better than us? Is it as simple as us reacting by being envious and striving to be like them? Could they be concealing their own Karmic path of pain and how they have to cope with it? Even though we pay so much attention in modern society to a wealthy lifestyle to demonstrate that we are lucky, Karma is not that simple. On the contrary, it can be just as much a distraction from dealing with our Karmic issues as poverty can be. Any issues which are hiding behind a gold-plated facade will still have to be dealt with at some stage. We may be rich one day, but this may not make us so lucky as to be able to learn who we truly are, especially when eventually, all the riches fall away. Any external matter is of a temporary nature and not really worth striving for, although we could be fooled by what is going on on this planet. We would do well not to lose our Karmic energy by comparing what another has, to what we have. We would be caught up in a constant Karmic energy see-saw: create some good energy, get distracted, loose it again, having to create some more and so on. We seem to all be caught up in this at this stage of our being on this planet. What is truly worth finding is how we can create everlasting happiness that does not depend on any wealth or any other external conditions for that matter; how we can be well in body, mind and spirit by feeling connected at all times to our greater Karmic mind. How we can create good conditions for us to learn wisdom that will last us eternally, and the compassion that will include others' well-being in our quest. We cannot judge others simply because we do not have the full picture. We would only end up harming and hurting them, and ourselves and our Karma in return. Hurting others is never a good idea.

What do we do with extremely horrendous situations such as war, famine, violations against us – what happens then? Can we stay connected to our Karmic Self in these extremely difficult situations? Do we question as to how we are finding ourselves in the situation of being a victim of these circumstances? Why does anyone have to suffer violence at the hands of others? Rather than blaming ourselves, is there a healing aspect to be gained in trying to find out reasons why we are caught up in dire situations?

It is almost always very hard to find out from a Karmic point of view as to how our present situation relates to it. It's hard enough to trace what happened to any of us in our early years, never mind in a previous lifetime or lifetimes even. Maybe it isn't that useful either to spend even more lifetimes trying to find out every detail of our past, lest we end up getting too stuck in the process instead of living our lives in the present moment. However, if we found a good balance, peace of mind and an increased connection to who we truly are, would it not be empowering if we found solace in the idea that there was an explanation to how we got here? If we realise there might be a limit to knowing exactly how or why things happen to us, do we already know that the conclusion from our inner searching for Truth is that it falls back on us and us only, to try and be the best we can in that moment? Learning more about our past might enhance and reinforce that wisdom, because it might help us to see the connections of how our past will have an effect in the future. In that way, it could help us very much to live life by the right precepts, because we are bringing all the energy back into ourselves in order to empower us and make the right choices, eventually even in situations when it's very tough to survive. Is that not all we need to know, that there are processes that can make our reserve stronger to do the right thing if we get the insights and support to do so? Or will the thought of having to soul search make us even more angry and upset at feeling we have never not been a part of the process? If we find ourselves in the wrong place at the wrong time in the path of some crazed malicious person, how can we have possibly contributed to our own pain and misfortune?

I am not saying that there is an explanation for everything and that we will all find it. But I am also not saying reincarnation does not exist, or that it does not play a very precise role in our future lives. What I am suggesting is that simply our thinking along the lines of a Karmic process in action – that somehow any action we take has a reaction of some kind – can potentially empower any of us in this life-time to understand and deal with situations that would otherwise leave us feeling helpless and hopeless, regardless of whether we believe in reincarnation or not. If we remind ourselves of all the sub-cellular Karmic energy processes that are affected by any moment that happens in our existence, for aeons of life-times, then we have indefinite amounts of situations that contributed to who we are now. It would be only logical to assume that we have been in many various situations of being submitted to fearful situations before, as well as contemplating if we were in turn the ones who submitted other beings to being fearful of us. If we want to stop this cycle of survival of the fittest, we now have enough brains and Karmic energy combined to finally put an end to it all by not acting out on our fight-or-flight instincts and kill everything in our path to simply survive. If we have a roof over our heads and food on the table, we can be grateful to be aware enough that we are in that position where we should consider ourselves very lucky to be in a place that might have taken us many lifetimes to achieve. In order to make a difference in our lives and those of others, we need to increase the value we put on these observations and not take them for granted. We also need to learn methods to increase those situations for ourselves and others in the future. This means that whatever path we take, however we come to the conclusion, whether by soul-searching and learning about Karma, by praying or science, by observation or learning the hard way, we need to learn what increases good future outcomes and what does not.

My own experiences in this life-time do not compare to someone's who has had to suffer intensely, so I really hope I do not sound condescending. Having said that, I was not born with a silver spoon in my mouth in this life either. Although I do have a loving family background, I have also had to work very hard for my family I would do anything for. It didn't just fall into my lap and I drew the conclusion that when I decided that I would wholeheartedly be responsible for my own Karma, it gave me solace at the very least that I could conquer all that was put in my path, and that i could do much of it with gratitude for the gifts I was given. It actually gave me great comfort to think that I could look at a negative situation as something which may have been a hangover from my past coming to fruition in this lifetime, which I had an opportunity to deal with and neutralise within myself once and for all. The moment I thought that it was not my fault, but rather that I was the only one in charge who could do something about it by accepting it and bringing about change, I saw this very much as an empowering process rather than some form of bad luck or even worse, punishment that I had to suffer alone. As soon as I entered the process of looking behind the Karmic scenes I saw that there was no guilt trip or judgement intended. Karmic energy is there to empower us and make us feel more complete than ever. In the process, it felt there were many rewards for taking life into my own hands rather than blaming someone else for any mishaps. I was presented with many insights, tools and methods to deal with situations and turn them around so that I felt my Karmic energy was being renewed. I often felt purified and nourished by the process, so I will share some of my experiences with you a little further along in this book.

As I have come to understand, many wise souls choose to reincarnate into extreme and savage conditions, precarious situations and endure intense suffering, in order to experience what it's like and to help others in increasingly dangerous situations, to learn to see through fear and gain wisdom. It could be a sign of their Karmic super-strength and evolved path that their Karmic energy chose a life where they are able to help in those circumstances in order to reduce suffering. Some people go through much pain and fear initially in order to overcome adversity. Once they have pulled through, they can later draw on their Karmic strength and help others who may be suffering also, perhaps even more so. I believe that sometimes it is also possible that some beings incarnate with a vow to deal with all their Karma at once, in one life time. Maybe this is because they already know on a deep level of their consciousness and understanding that they will survive this physical journey, even if they suffer and have to great length themselves. Others, again, seem almost superhuman in their strength, fearlessness and resolve to assist others. Perhaps they have already overcome their fear of pain and dying, over many lifetimes? On the Karmic energy spiral that oversees all of existence which we find ourselves on, there are infinite numbers of living beings on infinite levels of being. Those living beings who choose to be in the same environment at the same time must necessarily learn what it means to peacefully co-exist simultaneously, having incarnated into a more dense physical 3-dimensional world. Even though we all have a physical form similar to each other as human beings, none of us are going through the same Karmic mode at the exact same time. This is the illusion our brain likes to project to simplify matters, but we must overcome the notion in order to see that we are all on the same path and are learning similar lessons, but all at different places and paces, trying to deal with life without losing sense of one of the main reason why we are here in the first place: We are here to evolve our Karma, hopefully in the right direction without going backwards.

We all deserve wisdom, love and compassion. It is much harder for everyone when we lose our ability to find the wisdom within us to avoid wrongful thoughts, words and actions.

We all have potentially infinite rebirths. We all have the opportunity in each moment to continuously evolve to higher stages on our Karmic evolutionary path, by the choices we make from moment to moment. We all deserve love, and we can put out there every moment of the day the sincere wish that we all make it through; hopefully there are more and more of us who can see the importance of gaining insight and compassion sooner rather than later. When we are able to hold on to the intention of assisting the process in our Karmic minds, we will have reached the stage of being able to influence our Karma in a very positive way. We will be guided towards situations to demonstrate in real life all the love we are able to create, for ourselves and others. We might be drawn to more and more challenging situations to do this. We might equally be shown where we still lack love and wisdom for everyone and everything in existence, where breaches in our Karmic energy minds are to be filled with more insight. It can be a steep learning curve on which we all deserve kindness in order to help us learn how to be. It is easy when we are in a state of calmness and a supportive environment, but easier said than done when we have to do this under duress. What if we find ourselves in a situation that resembles a struggle, where we might end up being the soldier that finds reason to fight for justice and peace? What if we are the victim of crime that loses everything dear to them? What about the medic who tries to help in a war zone? We could find ourselves to be one of these at any point of our Karmic evolution. We choose how we stand according to the state of our Karmic energy at that point, and it would be useful to know we have done our best to make it good Karma to support us in times of trouble. After all, we can't predict when we are going to be challenged in a precarious situation and with what resulting actions and morals we must defend our point of view and course of action Is our Karmic energy on a high or a low? Are we presenting who we want to be, according to living out our Karmic destiny?

Perhaps the difference between the wise soul and us mere mortal beings is that, on a deep level of consciousness, they are inherently aware that their body might be harmed, but their Karma cannot be hurt or damaged if there is no wrong action, thought or speech by the individual concerned. Somehow they often manage to overcome the worst of fates, at least on a Karmic level, perhaps because their level of Karmic completion allows them to. It can be the ultimate test to react with compassion and prayers for another who is trying to do us harm, in a situation which is the worst nightmare for anyone. Nobody would wish it on anyone to have to test their resolve that way and we naturally all pray that it never happens to us or any of our loved ones. Would it be so difficult to extend our prayer to everyone alive? Would we not want to have everyone alive and well, without suffering and anguish? It's not always just about preserving our physical existence, precious though it is. Where we make such a fuss about physical aspects of ourselves - our looks, weight, make up, muscles, hair and so on - wise souls appear to care little about their appearance, knowing that it is only a fleeting moment in our Karmic timeline and having overcome their fear of not existing in physical form. Often, physical focus is completely sacrificed in order to spend every waking hour on achieving the highest outcome for everyone involved, something we can barely imagine doing even just a few moments of every day. Most of us would need help, support and much time spent in any traumatic situation in order to see through our suffering. It takes time to do away with our fear and release the memory of traumatic situations in those situations. Perhaps our hyper-alert attention to physical aspects of ourselves only is a latent symptom of past trauma we may have experienced, who knows. It would be a comfort to think that maybe the wise ones mentioned afore are here to help remind us of better times and assist those of us who still have so much to learn and overcome. It seems a comforting and inspiring thought to me, as there is never any criticism involved by observing human behaviour. I think we even have proof that these wise beings exist on Earth – they are the people who stand out in crisis situations to help, come in all ages, shapes and sizes and could have any profession, background and belief system. Sometimes, our Karmic good luck might have already brought one or two of them into our lives. They are there at any stage for us to receive help and knowledge to overcome our plight in order to help others. It might be a good exercise if we start by seeing everyone in our immediate surroundings, too, as the transcendental beings they are rather than just their physical shape and how we identify them by their every-day behaviour in relation to us. It can be a very healing and emancipating process when we include ourselves in this, and might see who we really have in front of us and how we can elevate the way we relate to each other. If we see ourselves and others in the light of our everlasting Karmic existence filled with light energy, we may be able to eventually learn to better be able to appreciate them being in our lives for reasons that sometimes escape us here and there. It will be easier to imagine with some than others, and in those moments where it's really difficult to see someone else's divinity we can always remind ourselves that the practice we put out there will not only allow the other to be able to perceive their Karmic light body again, but benefits us just as much in return. Should we do this for those who have wronged and harmed us? It's up to you, everyone has to make their own decisions as we go along. It does not mean that we get physically close to someone we know to be a mass murderer. it does not mean we put up with violence to find our limits, far from it. Our existence is precious, our lives are precious, our health on all levels is important to maintain and learn to cherish. The bottom line of a practice we do for ourselves is that you will not harm yourself or another by practising the idea and visualising ourselves and others in our wisest and most compassionate form. Some people would call this a process of forgiveness, I would call it a process of reminding ourselves that we are all ultimately wise. In any case, it would be much more preferable to do this if the result is that it actively helps us to heal ourselves and be able to stay out of harms' way.

✿ ✿ ✿

23. The Karma of Finding Out Who We Really Are

In the chapter above, we have brought to the forefront the importance of recalling that we are more than our physical Self and the sum of our experiences in life. We are born with an intact system that remembers everything we have ever been, but a flaw in our physically being here means that we forgot the manual of how to access all this information. Most of us don't even remember that there is such a manual, never mind more to us than meets the eye. It brings about much suffering if we feel we can squander our lives believing there are no consequences to making others' lives hell. In this chapter, we expand on the idea of divinity in all of us, by looking at the variety of lives that Karma has brought to this Earth.

If we think about what presents itself right here, right now, the vastness of space we are surrounded with, the species of flora and fauna and the sheer endless number of different living beings we share this space with, it comes to mind that none of this just happened overnight. When we look at areas where hardly anything can survive, we still find lifeforms, sometimes very curious, that have adapted to extreme conditions. Does it not make us think how we got to be here, past the obvious of being born to our parents, living for a bit, then dying again? Is there not more to us, when we dig a little deeper, than looking in a mirror and thinking our lips are too small and our hips are too big?

In my work, I have met with thousands of people over the years, of all backgrounds. I have sometimes contemplated people labelled with a physical or mental condition, often noticing how beautiful their smiles are, how pure and full of unconditional love their being radiates. Many times I am in total awe in their presence and ability to shine so brightly, often despite intense physical and emotional pain. Who are any of us to decide that another living being is less worthy of love and respect than we ourselves are? Why do we even make distinctions by race, ethnicity, sex, IQ, even animals who we decide we eat or pet, other than showing our own fears and feelings of inadequacy? Many times I have caught myself thinking that beings who are stigmatised to be different from a perceived norm or are just perceived to be, may have come with the Karma of waking up others to the simplicity of loving unconditionally. They may be teachers of the greatest wisdom of allowing us to learn what is truly meant by 'being'.

What about the victims of crime or violence? What changes when we are subject to others violating our lives and existence, issues that are becoming more and more prevalent in a society that has seemingly lost its sense of who we truly are at our core. Only when we have lost our ability to be kind we are able to violate others, and it's a worrying trend as we see more virtual abuse the more people spend time on the frequencies that were destined to bring us all together more. We have the ability to make or break one another by the choices we make from moment to moment, and the Karmic repercussions and not always clear straight away unless our belief system includes them. It is a sign of a high level of stress and detachment from reality if we are able to be patronising and ignorant in the face of violence against each other, where some can simply make a brush off remark that those who are hurt must have done something to 'deserve it' and are not our concern. We are looking at differences, rather than what we have in common. We have forgotten that we are all in the same boat, that we are all born with the same principles: no matter what body we are born into, no matter where we live on Earth, no matter what skin colour, what language, what country, what orientation, what religion - we cannot be separated by what presents itself when we are using our judging brain.

We are all living beings and all living beings are all born with Karma.

What is true is that each being's situation differs from the rest, at any moment, because each of us created an individual time-line due to our past Karmic actions. None are ever the same, and as a result we do not know anyone's true Karmic Self. How wonderful then, when we meet so many in a similar situation, all on one planet, to learn from and to help each other grow...except our limited brain perception does not quite see it that way. We get on with a few; some are family, some become firm friends or distant acquaintances, there are those we have relationships with, whilst others turn into neighbours and work mates. Most we just walk past in the streets of life, and there might be those who we feel we have least in common with who we feel we need to turn into enemies. When we look at it like that, why do we even do this? On what basis do we decide who people are around us? What is it that makes some into close friends and others into enemies? Is it something they did or said?

Is it the way they look or how we feel around them? If that is what most of us would say it is, then all those perceptions are purely sensory. We put our feelers out and if our senses send signals to our brain that we should react in certain ways to a being or beings or even whole tribes of beings, then we react - often impulsively - to that external other. However, we have already learned that our brain tries to group things together to make life easier and keep us safe but it seems to do a poor job of it, judging by how things are turning out in the world right now. Our brain generalises and bases future events on past experiences which may not reflect the whole truth. Whilst we listen to our brains only, we just can't seem to get it right in terms of hating each other for our apparent differences instead of seeing the miracle of what we all have in common and could achieve despite our differences. The more we react to each other, the more hatred and angst is created, which has a devastating knock-on effect: it causes our systems to shut down and go into defence mode, ready to attack anyone who might be different from us in case they mean us harm. Whilst this is useful and healthy as an underlying instinct to keep us safe in times of danger, if it becomes the norm we are on a roller-coaster of destruction, unable to find out who started it. The end result is always destruction, unless we are able to start with ourselves and examine how we have been led to believe by outside influences that everyone is our enemy. If we see through that we can be so easily swayed by tactics employed to keep us small and in fear, wherever they may stem from, then our world can breathe and expand again. Those of us who are fortunate enough to see through it, campaign for equality and tolerance, despite the enormity of angst and despair that has prevailed. What we could do to make a difference is to take a look at each being individually, see what help they need and what type of negativity they have had to endure in their past, on a physical as well as Karmic level. This includes ourselves, sometimes first and foremost. The result, as we do this, will surprise us: almost everyone we get to know this way will say similar things.

We have ALL endured suffering, pain and fear.

This is a statement not designed to make us feel more despair, on the contrary. it is there so we can see that we are all similar, that we are all together in this, that we all have some things in common, no matter who we are, when we are alive. Fear and pain will cause us to feel separate from each other as we go inward to try and locate the issue and need time to sort it out. In those times, we need to be reminded that we are not alone, that others are still there around us who we are a part of, a community that is ours at all times, even if we feel far removed from it. This is how our condition makes us feel, but it is not reality. We can make the condition win and allow it to become our temporary reality of feeling isolated, and this is certainly happening everywhere we turn. When we see through it, once we realise we are all - of course, understandably - reacting according to our stress levels by looking inward to see what damage has been done. It takes time to find ourselves again, but if all of us are doing it, then we are all together in it. It might be the main reason why we are here on Earth in the first place, in individual bodies - a temporary experience of separateness that has got the better of us. We are ultimately not separate at all, but in the 3-dimensional time and space that can create suffering, we feel separate in our individual Karmic ego bodies. Our Karmic energy bodies can merge again with the greater consciousness at any time if we know how to switch up to them again to do so. If we see through our temporary programming of separateness on Earth we will sense that something has led us here which needs to be addressed; some pain, some hurt, some loss, some suffering. As soon as we recognise this, and that everyone on Earth is in the same predicament, and that, indeed, we are meant to be part of the whole universal dance again, we can learn to free ourselves from the illusion of temporary existence. We may not be free in a body that is keeping us in a certain place and time frame, but inside any limited bodily experience, our spirit can learn to be complete. From the experience of completeness within comes a different vision, the vision that we are not just an aching, ailing, ageing body in a limited life-span. We literally merge again with the experience and comprehension of Karmic energy and completeness that we already are. We might be here to learn how to sense and feel and be our Karmic energy on Earth first and foremost, which does not depend on a physical body. From this experience of seeing life differently springs tolerance for others, a sense of calm and completion that does not depend on external situations. This is already yours, it is inherently you, and whilst we all forget in times of suffering, it cannot be taken away from you.

Not many are trained or able to help others see through our Karmic conundrums; perhaps a reasonable answer may not be found that fits everyone at the same time. Perhaps we can only ever make guesses, and our main task is to help ourselves and others do away with the lmited perceptions we experience due to stuck internal energy expressing itself as anger, fear, guilt, resentment, ignorance or judgement, created by painful experiences we have made over lifetimes which we no longer remember. We have to find the right balance by looking back to find answers and solutions, so that it can help us heal our energies so we can stay fully present in the moment. Sometimes, a look into the past is needed and very much supported by constellations that ask us to halt our activities and take stock. Recognising these important phases in life can help a person enormously in order to grow from their intense experiences. It may help them take charge of their lives again, help them overcome and, if not forget, at least eventually come to terms with the course their life path has taken once more. Some may even be able to go so far as to examine on a Karmic energy level how any aggressor has affected them through the crime they committed, in order to set themselves free and be able to move into a more secure sense of their future again. There are methods and ways of dealing with past trauma and PTSD that resolve issues on a deep Karmic energy level. There are millions of people suffering more and more diverse ways of having been violated and abused. It would only be right to offer solutions that can help in those cases, the traumatic memories of which often get passed down through generations. To resolve these issues and neutralise the negative energy imprint within means that we can find ways of healing whole communities, which would otherwise affect everyone for years to come. By this, I do not necessarily mean forgiveness. Forgiveness in its true sense is a term that tries to explain a Karmic energy principle, but is fraught with misinterpretation nowadays. Forgiveness in its true sense simply means that we are at a stage where someone else's actions do not affect our inner energy flow any longer. This is often following a long process of untangling their energy from ours, with the effect that we are naturally left feeling we are no longer caught up in their Karmic energy mess. By using certain methods which are listed and/or described at the end of this book, it is no longer has to be a difficult and painful conscious effort. Forgiveness is then not something that we feel we have to force ourselves or others to do, if we don't know how to. We cannot ask ourselves to 'drop' the subject of violation against us, it would be cruel and inhumane. We would be dangling the carrot of forgiveness way ahead of ourselves, without being shown any means of actually reaching it. We need to be gently shown how to truly become aware how we have become embroiled in a violator's Karmic energy, how they have tried to reel us into their trauma and how we can find a way out of being entangled again. Once we start to realise that our energy is caught up in theirs, we can become aware of how to free ourselves again. The symptoms of unresolved trauma are becoming very tangible around the world as we are experiencing more and more suffering, which has a knock on effect on all that we do, say and think and all we come across. Our energy mind is extremely sensitive, so much so we might have forgotten how subtle it is and how to take care of it. If we are no longer shown how by our tribe, our ancestors, our families, our communities, our health systems, our tutors, teachers or schools, then how are we supposed to know how to take care of ourselves on the most intricate levels? If the world's focus is all on finance and defence which it has been for centuries, then everyone's energy is on high alert and stress levels. The few who warn us that we are losing the precious, natural and gentle aspects of ourselves and the crucial connection to our children will be ridiculed, or worse, tortured for their beliefs. Without us even realising we need a solution, this will continuously perpetuate and eventually destroy us and the world around us. In the meantime, most of those who have suffered but are finally experiencing some form of calm in their lives, want nothing more to do with conflict. Many of us are 'abreacting' without being aware of it, meaning that we are internally trying to process past trauma whilst on a conscious level, we are becoming less capable of doing every day tasks, instead preferring distractions and minimising effort physically and mentally so as not to have to put any more strain on our system. As we can tell, we are no longer far away from a point of no return, where all of us are aware we are facing a global crisis with not many options that are presenting themselves to alleviate the emergency status of this planet and all who inhabit it. At the same time, we are less and less able to deal with any more situations that are stressful, so we are having to co-exist with the conundrum of living in a polluted world that has become symptomatic of how we feel internally. The result is what we are facing right now - all around us at any time are increasing amounts of victims of crime in some way or another, making it more and more impossible to live normal lives. They will all describe the same symptoms – Post traumatic Stress Disorder and its consequences such as continuous reliving of the distressing situation however long it is past; phobias, nightmare visions and disturbing thought patters that arise at random as a result, physical reactions such as sleeplessness, panic attacks, heart problems, digestive issues, bodily pain, immune system illness etc. The beginning of the healing process for all these is to understand the Karmic principles behind the symptoms, and not to expect ourselves or others, for that matter, to simply 'move on from it' and feel that forgiveness is needed. Some feel that process has to be forced, despite how terrible they feel inside. The majority of us are unaware that fist, the symptoms that are experienced need to be voiced and neutralised in an effective way, rather than medicated. This is not just a cognitive process but a process where the inner energy has to be cleared. If we have any doubt that this is what is needed, we only need to look around at how many are struggling and battling with their issues, not knowing about these principles but instead resorting to drastic measures to try and override symptoms. To add to the horrific physical and emotional trauma the burden of having to take responsibility away from those who violated them, by forcing some form of forgiveness in order to bring about a quick result of inner peace seems to make no sense to me. If that's worked for anyone, then great. I have a practice full of people who have not been able to really do it and who feel guilty on top of everything else for not being able to forgive. This may possibly be because a false sense of forgiveness does not examine the relationship between the energies of victim and attacker, or how it can be fully released. A process needs to occur to release the entangled energies which can be quick and effective, too. Again, please refer to methods at the end of this book, to find out more.

I have spoken to very gentle people with beautiful angelic auras, who seem to attract inexplicable suffering to them. It has often made sense to me to ask those whose energies i felt are so pure and on such a high level, whether they had any idea on a very deep level that their journey to the dense environment of Earth would be a tricky one; and whether they felt that they had come to help others with their problems and to bring light, truth and understanding. Some of these souls even seem to choose the most dangerous situations on behalf of others, putting their own lives at risk, sometimes many times over; probably, again, because on their level of deep Karmic awareness, they knew that risking their life for another person would not only be noble, but could lead to a better existence for each involved in a next life. You might ask how this can be, when life is precious and we are all supposed to be preserving our and our loved ones' lives as much as we can. Again, I find myself on thin ice, being fully aware of how easily this statement could be misinterpreted. In fact, it has been misinterpreted, by many individuals, many cultures and religions, throughout aeons of time, and it causes us to feel quite uneasy. Images come to mind such as Jesus on a cross dying for humanity in the Christian faith, or the Buddha touching the Earth with his hand even after enlightenment, to indicate the willingness to exist in future for the sake of all sentient beings. There are sacrificial acts described in almost all religions, and yet we seem to have lost the true sense of the meaning of it. In our ignorance, some of us have not understood the essence of the energy exchange that takes place, but rather interpreted the phenomenon to mean that we should kill ourselves for some elusive benefit in the name of something or someone. The reason why these acts feel so wrong is because their energy exchange is enforced and can therefore not have a good outcome. Have we ourselves been subject to suffering the consequences of killing and being killed in past lives, for the sake of a 'noble' cause or rather, its misinterpretation by others who made us believe what they wanted us to believe for their own gain? It is possible there is some truth in this as there are so many different forms this can take, and all religions, all countries, all eras have had their delusions of sacrificing lives. Unfortunately, with any of these forms of belief systems that believe killing is justified for the sake of bringing about a good outcome, such as a good harvest, good fortune, appeasing the gods they believe in or a better afterlife, are not able to see what happens after the death of those beings they sacrifice. If they saw the horror, the Karmic consequences, the deep entanglement of confusing events when a being passes from this world in a way that is forceful - if it were visible to them and if they also saw their own entanglement in it, they would never kill again. Sadly, we don't have cameras that tell us what happens so we can see. We can only experience the inner sight and wisdom that we inherently have by going inwards again and paying attention to the signs that are there indicating who we are and how precious, once more, everyone's existence is. If we look at how ritual killings, live sacrifices, religious suicides and so on perpetuate suffering and have done over aeons of time, then we need to look no further to see where our justified fears arise from. The world has gone mad. Oh no, I am mistaken – it was mad a long time ago, already. Mad and beautiful, whichever way we look at it.

So how does a good outcome fit in with risking our lives for someone else?

Let's look at the innocence of it, the simple wish that is – or should be – behind any act of kindness: we want another being to be well, and happy. Think of a child who jumps in a river to save their dog. Think of a patient in a life-threatening condition undergoing surgery to receive an organ donated by their sibling, or even a complete stranger matching the requirements. Would we think twice to help someone we love? Would we help a complete stranger if we were a rare match? Maybe we would, or just admire those who do. But we can all see the good that comes from taking the real risk of losing something very precious, in order to save someone just as precious as we perceive ourselves to be. And here lies the difference: we are trying to save a life, not asking someone else to sacrifice theirs or even worse, take another's life. If we are able to put the one to be saved on the same level as ourselves it shows a high level of compassion and understanding how energy works and is perpetuated in both the giver and the recipient of our Selfless action. This does not have to do anything with religious bias. We do not have to believe that there is some external being that judges us for doing one thing or another. It is not a contest, it is not a proof of who is bravest. There are no medals for giving our lives to a cause, and there are no consequences if we choose not to, none whatsoever. Life continues as normal, we have not missed out on anything, and we will learn some other way what it means to be Selfless by being authentic, and giving what we can in our own time. If we are not ready to give, we can learn, slowly but surely, to become comfortable with the thought. Giving does not mean we lose out, on the contrary - giving means that we double the energy that was there in the first place, and some Karmic minds are able to multiply their energy with all the positive actions they take, simply because their whole being emanates their understanding of how Karmic giving works, and they have mastered the process of fearlessly acting on it.

At many points in our lives we are presented with the choice to put others above ourselves in order to benefit from our compassion. It's an act of Selflessness where we learn to not think about what's in it for us. Will we hesitate or not stop to think? In some, the willingness to be helpful can surpass their fears of losing out on something, and the sacredness of the purity of their Selflessness makes a gift of generosity multiply.

Remember we talked about our Karmic Self, and our ego Self, and that our ego Self makes us believe that this life is all there is? Our Karmic Self can shine through very clearly at times, and our lucidity to perceive our Karmic connections can sometimes be enhanced, for example in times of emergency. It seems to function like an instinct in some, maybe all humans, so that due to our heightened state of awareness our Karmic Self becomes more or less visible. What we have learned already about the ego Self is that it has limited perception, as opposed to our higher vibrational Karmic Self that has the potential to be all-encompassing. If we can get it right and we are acting out of our own conscious de- cision to be as Selfless as possible, then Selfless actions could mean we could eventually surpass our ego Self, lose the fear of losing our physical existence, and our Karmic energy body would register this accordingly. Again, walking on thin ice here in case there could be a misunder- standing. This is not meant to endorse acts of wilfully violent actions in order to destroy others. No matter how elevated we feel we might be, if we are simply judging others' lives and their choices to not be worthy of existing, we need to see first that this is not aligned with the principles of Karma and the nature of existence which allow all to simply be, and encourages all to learn and grow from their precious experiences.

It could mean that if we are acting out of love and appreciation for another's life, we will not be attracting a lower existence at our next rebirth, where we have then hopefully attracted a life where we do not fear for our survival every minute of the day. With the extra added bonus that we have also impacted the Karmic energy body of another being, who will have experienced what it is like to be saved in terms of a great need. We will have connected to their energy and formed a posi- tive Karmic connection. A very important Karmic message has been set up, in both beings, and perhaps also others who have been bystanders and observers. This is how we generate a good outcome for all those whose lives we touch in a positive way. Every moment of every day we are presented with choices that affect many others in turn, even if we only manage to be generous to one single being. The ripple effect is po- tentially vast, as you might imagine. it is important to include ourselves in the whole equation and make sure that we are kind to ourselves, too. It does not make it any better if we help others but neglect ourselves and our Karmic energy, by the same token that we are trying to help others by increasing the positive charge in their energy field, others will be inspired to do the same and feel the benefit just as much if we ourselves are energised.

What if our intention is premeditated, and we are doing good to simply further our own Karma? We can do acts of kindness for all the wrong reasons, such as glory, attention, thrill seeking or some other specific outcome attachment in mind. Perhaps there might be a good impact on our energy system; it might spark a learning curve and build confidence to commit to more altruism; perhaps we lose some of our fear and need to control as part of the process; perhaps we make experiences to learn to love even more wholeheartedly to some extent. If we are still trying to control much of what we do, or the outcome itself, it may not yet have the full impact of allowing Karmic energy to flow fully unhindered to benefit the best it can. But it is still a part of it, which may be better than no action at all. Practice makes us perfect, and insights into how to be giving the right way will be shown along our path. If there is any negative impact from commandeering our acts of kindness, it all depends on circumstances how this affects us and others in the process. We can probably come up with our own examples of how to best give unconditionally. Whether the recipients receive any lasting benefit is a question of their own Karma and subject to each individual case, even if the energy that is sent out from us is not premeditated. We have become more used to treating any altruistic action like a curve ball; we want it to return to us in case we feel we are missing out. Any action that has an outcome attachment is not completely Selfless and effective because we have the thought that we want something back in return. The energy we send out is like a boomerang, bound to our focus on the specific outcome to return to us. We may be able to create a good outcome, but with limited effect, as the energy is held back and still based on fear and a need to control instead of letting go of the outcome. It's ok though as we can learn to see through this, and rise above it in due time. It's not always easy and we need to consider the individual stages we find ourselves at. It does not mean we have to give away everything we own and leave ourselves with nothing. Having said that, there is the utterly fearless example of the Buddha, who in one of his lifetimes gave his body to a hungry tigress who needed to feed her cubs, it is said. Whether it's an analogy or a real event, it's an example of what's meant by a totally pure and Selfless and potentially fearless action. It also demonstrates what it means to be able to be the ultimate compassionate mind, in as much as there is no distinction made between any sentient being and their form of existence; there is no lesser or higher mortal being that deserves more or less to live and survive. Ultimately, the goal in life is about realising the connection between who we truly are and altruistic actions being able to generate the good Karma to get ourselves to be the best we can whilst including all others we meet along the way. Committing to true altruism is a life-changing, Karma-changing event, not for the faint-hearted. In Buddhism, this is called Bodhicitta, and there are two paths determined, relative and ultimate Bodhicitta. But whether it's Buddha, or a child acting without a thought for themselves to save their best buddy, it will all lead to the same recognition of our all being of the same essence. We are all interlinked, at all times, and sometimes it seems that none of us can leave without the other still suffering. Only a very few of us are ready to take it on, at this level, and I have to admit I am not there yet, either. Neither do I recommend trying to do something reckless. I recommend we try to put in our best effort, our best intention to find out our Truth within the best way we can, at any moment.

In my mind, there is also merit in learning to allow ourselves to be a human being as opposed to a human 'doing'. When we are doing, we are often doing something I a mechanical way, perhaps because we feel obliged, or are doing what we are told, what we think is necessary, because of adhering to a dogma or discipline etc. Whilst doing is a part of being, it's still going through our brain function first, believing that a thought process is needed to assess what is next. It does not always work towards a greater good. 'Being' comes from a different place within us, it's an inspiration often guided by our inner Karma, without us even having to know anything about it. Times of allowing ourselves to simply 'be' are the times when we get to take stock of where we are at, to let go and meander, listen to our true inner guidance to find out who we are, as opposed to following blindly what we are being told what to do in our ordinary lives.

We do all have a need to find out more about ourselves and how to make the most of our lives, and within those paradigms we need to look for the light as well as meet our shadow sides, because they are a thing, too. Some of us feel no need to get to know our shadow sides much, as their path is to avoid getting too drawn in. Others need to do the exact opposite and go right into all the darkness in order to learn ways to get out again. It's very hard to not get lost when we don't have methods, as an increased number of the world population that is suffering from mental illness will show, which can result in more illness, Self-harm and even suicide. When we lack methods to help ourselves get out of the shadow sides that inevitably exist, then we will find it extremely hard to appreciate that our good Karma has brought us alive to exist, and that there is a benefit to our existence for our own furtherment as well as that of others. We badly need training in knowing our true minds and what we are capable of, and that does not come from watching superhero movies. If we want a modern analogy to how our Karmic energy works, think of cloud storage. We are able to upload any amount of data into the ether whilst not really comprehending how this actually works. What we do know is that even the tiniest individual photographic memory we have in our files can be stored and is not forgotten. The amount of memory to store data is unimaginably vast, and if we imagine that there is a way to store information that encodes every single bit of our date because it does not even have to rely on electronic gadgets, we are getting close to having an idea of the phenomenon of our Karmic energy field that we have been talking about.

We need to pay more attention to our Karmic energy mind to bring about peace.

It may not be our only mission on Earth to find out more about it, and it may not be the focus of your choice right now, but Karma and Karmic energy certainly exists, for all of us. It is an integral part of who we are. It never leaves us. It's not the privilege of a few, it's our natural state of being. If we keep repeating all our good actions so it becomes autonomous, we don't have to think about it and keep reminding ourselves. It sinks into our Karmic consciousness and becomes a part of our every day lives again; the beautiful and complete part of who we are, instead of the fractious one, will be the one we will be able to present in our every day lives. In my opinion, it is one of the most important missions for any human being to be on the path to completely own their Karmic existence again, by getting to know the state of their Karmic minds and completing their Karmic light body within. We would all benefit immensely from the teachings that show us how to re-establish, repair and expand our energy flow, ultimately and ideally to a level of pure radiance. Whilst it may seem a distant hope for the future, we are the creators of our own timelines, which is the factor of all global activity that presents itself along a timeline. It's our choice if we need to procrastinate and make plans to bring in changes in a 5-10 year prognosis, which is very much what negotiations amongst organisations look like in politics and commerce. Is this how we promote peace? how do we feel about peace? Do we need to delay peace because we fear it? Or are we ready to start promoting it in earnest? It does not have to be that way. We have the opportunity to rewrite history and reset our goals and paradigms, our own, as well as that of our time. The teachings for mind training are available to anyone, at any time, and they should be free, and free of bias. They are not like a religious organisation or a cult. We do not confess our sins and are automatically freed from evil. We are the ones that make a difference, but only if we learn how to free our minds.

Only in the modern world have we put an energy block and a price tag on everything we need to be, and we have forgotten that we already 'are'.

Another purpose we no longer rate highly is to connect - ideally on all levels of our Karmic energy system - with other like-minded beings and wish the same level of enlightenment upon them and those who need our help. Both aims, applying methods to find peace within as well as connecting with others, can be worked towards alongside each other. It is not necessary to achieve one before the other, and there is much to gain from being within a community of those who are trying to do the same. When we realise that others are searching for answers, too, it becomes less frightening, more reassuring, to see that we are not alone. Either way, we can choose to be alone or join groups or do both, whichever suits us in order to find out more about who we truly are and what we are capable of when we are just setting out trying to make sense of life. We might become aware that it is not a programme of achieving anything, as if we were at school and get rewards for achievements. There is no timeline in which to 'complete'. We do what we can to learn that it's not just about awareness of all phenomena and how they correlate, it's how we react to them that is crucial, and how this sets a thinking and feeling process in motion within us that is very prevalent in Western ideology, but isn't necessarily healthy practice. It is this process of reacting to everything that presents itself externally that puts our energy in danger of being compromised and hijacked, so that we find ourselves being led further away from the completeness of Truth within us. If we were aware of how important it is to pay homage to our ability to feel complete within and tune into the highest, most precious frequencies to flow through us, it's like breathing in fresh sea air on a spring day. Our well-being depends on aiming to initiate our inner healing process again, and that of others. A natural sense of joyful anticipation within us increases as we recognise the merits of the inner 'quest', and yet, since there is no test, no exam, no certificate, no external reward for our efforts other than a sense of peace all around, there can also be no 'rush' as we are used to being subjected to, in our daily lives full of chores. A natural sense of urgency we may start to feel to find out more about who we are and how everything is connected is of a different nature. It is almost a child-like gift for wanting to learn and explore, a feeling that we need and want to find out more; that there is so much more excitement awaiting us, so we can activate more of the greatness of who we already are. Rather than feeling guilty, ashamed and isolated, we will awaken to re-connect, with the result that we also want to share with others. We will want others to be happy, too. Life is not about sitting there getting bored, watching others struggle or feeling ourselves beyond reprieve committing harmful actions. It is about becoming aware, gaining full alertness to the interconnectedness of fully 'being' and where this leads us, each in our own way, to completion and a sense of belonging and purposeful action. No doubt that seeking a strong sense of purpose can in itself also cause controversy. If we encounter beings who do not share our deepest wish to be enlightened and find themselves at the opposite end of the scale of rightfulness, I might be wrong but i have always felt there is not much use in coming across with a condescending attitude of preaching in order to convert. If others have their own way of going about life, it may be better for them to follow their path, their way of doing things, their beliefs, than to force them to listen to what others try to tell them. Unless someone is ready and wants to hear and do similar, we would do well to be cautious rather than to judge ourselves superior in determining that others need salvation.

For some, it may be their purpose in their life to not be journeying alone, but to seek their destined others, in order to feel they can fulfil their purpose. Creating our highly evolved and awakened Karmic energy body can automatically draw to it, through universal laws of connection, a twinning energy of other, equally developed beings. We have been talking already about how our Karmic energy body evolves through many stages and starts to become more radiant with each insight we add to our wisdom mind. We may encounter on our path situations where our wisdom mind finds other like minds, others who are on a similar path. It's also possible that, when another being has experienced events that resonate with ours, we end up being on parallel tracks along our limited time-lines here on Earth, for as long as it is meant. Sometimes energy paths cross, sometimes once, sometimes many times. Sometimes we are aware of others around us who we feel connected to; some we share our lives and work environment with, others we live in close proximity to or are in constant communication with. Some Karmic energy path crossings and parallel tracks we happen to be on with others seem accidental and appear from nowhere from one moment to the next. All these are phenomena of the push and pull of Karmic energy in motion which attracts or repels other beings at certain points in our lives for a reason. They can give us an idea of the stages of our own inner development and help us on our own path of finding our purpose. At times, these energies between beings become closely intertwined and are able to start flowing around each other's energy cores. This has nothing directly to do with how close we are geographically, since Karmic energy is omnipresent, this can happen over great distances, too, as well as without actually perceiving the other with our five senses. Many who converse with others via online media can probably confirm that there is communication possible that affects our whole being even without ever having set eyes on another in person. Even writing the old-fashioned way via post to distant partners, friends or family will evoke the Karmic connection on a deep level and would have done so in the past, too, and works just as well even if we have not met the other or seen them in a long time. It seems we are able to read between the lines and instinctively interpret the energies that come across, and it is up to each of us and our Karmic make-up what we do with this connection and how we follow up on it. Knowing how precious and delicate these connections are, it would be wonderful if we could honour them to the highest degree. We need to become aware that we are coming across another being whose energy has something to communicate to us, and has a connection with us that could be highly important for our future Self if each party respects it accordingly. How consciously we want this to happen is up to each of us, but it seems that we often take these connections very loosely, now that we can literally communicate with millions of others on a daily basis. It seems that humanity has communication flu or worse, judging by how unruly online chats can get. When we are unable to read the subtleties between the lines and it just becomes a Self-serving free-for-all, it is hard to see how we have benefited from the age of world communication that was predicted would come, as the Earth is reaching its own higher levels of vibration. We often cast ourselves only in the role of observers of any media-transmitted energy, but even in that position we have power through our energy between the lines to steer an outcome towards a certain scenario and should be just as mindful of that power as if we were actually in a room full of people. Once we are aware of how powerful our energy comes across even without physical presence, we can learn to use our power wisely and chose to opt out of a manifestation of our energy that intertwines with others'. Many people are physically able to allow their energies to intertwine and have much experience with this, but little awareness perhaps of its effect on others. If the effect is thoughtless for the other it can be very harmful. It may mean that others as the recipients of thoughtless connections feel harmed, and therefore choose to connect their energy on any level less often, as they feel less confident and rather more anxious about the consequences of the process. If, on the other hand, the intention behind sending out our energy to connect in meaningful ways is pure and upright, then it may lead to good outcomes. If the intention behind it is Selfish and detrimental, it may zap another's energy and become very difficult for them to withdraw from the entanglement. Many Western relationships end up broken because we are not aware of what our Karmic energy minds are capable of doing. It's a shame, really, because we could save ourselves a lot of trauma by realising how powerful we are and that this does not mean we can freely use our power to the detriment of others' well-being.

We are not just talking about personal relationships. We are talking about any interaction we have with another being in our lives, whether they be with family or work-related, with friends and acquaintances or romantic, and even political. I am sure you would find it interesting to explore what our energy does when we realise that we have actually found out we are karmically (sounds like comically does it not) intertwining our energy with politicians. It's making me chuckle, as many of us hate this connection so much, but I am very serious about it. If we experience interactions with others which we feel we have little control over, we would do well to have a look at what our energy is doing in conjunction with theirs. If we do not like what is happening, we need to learn that we have the opportunity at any time to change how we exchange energy, or even withdraw our energy entanglement with them. We can learn how to do this, how to bring back the energy to our own Karmic energy body again and how empowering it feels to receive back, from any situation past or present, our long lost energy. We may even notice that we entered contracts unwittingly which we never thought we signed, but where our energy has been drawn from us by situations or people outside ourselves without us realising. We may not even realise that we came into this world, still with Karmic contracts attached that we made in previous lifetimes and which need readdressing in this life. It is a fascinating process and the effects of healing by recalling all the energy we ever lost are mind blowing, I promise.

On the other scale of the spectrum, let's talk about how we have probably noticed and are yearning for the extraordinarily wonderful connections that can occur between beings on Earth. Let's see what happens when these beings are in agreement to be united on all chakra levels in the same space and time in what is sometimes called a tantric union. Tantra is not meant in terms of a sexual practice, but rather the sublime teaching of how all energy intertwines, and how this is a divine, sacred, committed practice that unifies us. This rare and divine practice, when accomplished on all levels, is not simply a practice between two loving individuals, but has the potential of containing an unimaginably energising outcome for many involved and a huge impact on the environment and all inhabitants on Earth. The premise is the consent of those taking part, to take responsibility for their own Self, their commitment to the process and the many results; although the practitioners are often unaware of how this will affect them, they vow to adhere to the practice no matter what. Practising Tantra can create in effect a small gap in time and space for each individual, a brief but expanding experience of the phenomenon of singularity and all creation that emanates from it as a result. It is not to be taken lightly, as we can become co-creators of our own reality in those moments so much more quickly and effectively, which demands huge amounts of responsibility and accountability for one's thoughts, words and actions. Having said this, i have a feeling that whilst we have had incredible masters practising on Earth at select times, there are also those known to have taken advantage of the practice and tried to turn it on its head for their own gain. Caution, alertness and sensitivity is advised, as it comes with being vulnerable ourselves, too, as we will become immersed wholeheartedly in the pure realms where material things are of no value and the world that contains it can de-struct as a result. Since it is so rare and sacred a practice, each being has to knowingly step into their own realm of where it will take them to learn what it means, often without being aware of the full extent of the consequences and the potential block-ages they will each encounter and have to overcome. I was lucky enough to have a first introduction to it by being given a vision during a single-pointed concentration meditation some years ago, which I am happy to share. I was aware of being present in what I could only describe after-wards as a celestial place. I realised afterwards by researching it that this kind of experience had been mentioned in scriptures many times before, hundreds of years ago. Not only did my vision resemble the mythical description of the 'Celestial Palace' in sacred Buddhist texts, it also appears in Tantric Yoga practices as well as imagery and descrip-tions of deities such as Vajrasattva with Consort, and the legends of the Hindu gods Shiva and Shakti.

Image Credit: © Arte Krishna by Samuel Pickens, pinterest

But the Celestial Palace described in thousands-of-years-old scriptures has nothing to do with an external place picked up in modern inter-pretations, illustrations or virtual reality. It describes an inner experience of accomplished Karmic practice, which allows energy to flow freely through our subtle energy channels. When it is done correctly it does not remain in the base chakra to get misinterpreted in the way of feeding a physical state of arousal; instead, it continues to flow upwards, swirling along the spine connecting through the opening at the top of the head to higher realms. To reiterate, this natural and sacred practice has nothing to do with any substance-induced euphoric states of mind, just the body's own inherent ability, its natural mode of being alive in its most exalted, pure state. If we are able to remain the observer in this state rather than disturbing it or trying to enhance, harness or restrict it, the connections to our highest energy sources of light frequency energy and quantum energy become kinaesthetically tangible to us, and possibly even visible or audible. This is our inner natural healing energy which is assumed to be the continuous healing process for our whole internal physical cellular structure. The energy flowing up and down along our spinal cord in spiral motion is the energy that feeds all our body, streaming outwards into hundreds of thousands of tiny channels of energy, feeding every cell in our body. Not only that, but it showed me subtle connective frequency structures to the highest energy sources that exist around us but usually remain beyond our normal visual ability of perception. It was a deeply humbling and moving as well as energising experience; I am sure there are many other ways of describing it in infinitely different ways according to each belief system and each individual's perception. As I understand it now, it is an anthropomorphic experience of the portal to our inner Karmic energy potential which is visualised and experienced in its purest form. Whilst it appeared to be an incredibly detailed vision to me, even this appears to be a sensory analogy that occurs in our brain, an interpretation of the inherent ability of unfathomable Karmic energy force that flows through all beings.

All of these conscious experiences of our Karmic energy in action have in common that, in order to achieve any kind of union in this highly energised form with another which I previously indicated, both individuals have to have accomplished their own separate, personal level of comprehension and integration of the process to their highest ability. They must find their way to Truth in their own right, on all inner levels, thus raising their potential of reaching to it within themselves, and the essence of knowing Truth means they already learned they stand alone without the expressed need for another to exist to complete them. At that stage of their inner development, they would also have to have their Karma allow their singularity to coincide with another of equal merit to be experiencing the process simultaneously. This is far from two people just having a sexual experience; or two halves merging to form a whole in the form of symbiotic co-dependence; or a neediness expressing itself by seeking completion through instructing, mimicking or in any way influencing the other.

As we can probably imagine, it is not an easy task, considering how much time and effort we are already expending on simply trying to find a partner to be sharing sections of our every-day lives with, whilst society is busy creating expensive industries proclaiming to be searching for our perfect match. This inner experience, however, is a slightly more elevated level, and other more watered-down versions may well spring from its abundant source. Not many of us are aware that our looking for it in another is a form of yearning for the celestial union. Instead, we are ending up forever dissatisfied with the mundaneness of an every-day relationship. However, once we have found and experienced what we were truly looking for within ourselves, it is almost impossible not to want to feel it again and allow the experience to expand into all areas of our lives. Easier said than done, as it's not quite like a virtual reality computer game where you complete one level and then move on to the next. We are weathering the storms of our 3-d experience of every-day influences we have little control over, and without finding a map to help us on the stormy journey to find our inner Treasure Island we almost always get lost and give up, settling for mediocrity at best. And in a way, it is not much different to being on what's called the 'middle path', because even when we do find out much about ourselves and why we are here, even when we do find our inner winds blow us in the right direction, we might still be doing the same things on Earth as we would otherwise – except with an inner sense of purpose and belonging, knowing that each second we are here we can make a difference by wishing everyone the same happiness and good fortune that we encounter.

We will learn to do this more and more, as en route to the highest form of Karmic connectivity, every chakra is awakened within; there is no stuck energy in the end, when every weakness we feel is conquered on its Karmic level and neutralised so as not to affect us any longer. A weakness is not a defect, it is simply indicative of a Karmic energy that needs freeing up. Just like an electric current runs through a device, if the circuit is broken at any point, energy cannot run through it any longer and any device relying on it will no longer function. Once it's fixed, it can be as good as new again. Can we imagine no longer feeling fear, greed, jealousy, anger or insecurity and be freed from these forever? It's almost impossible for most of us to imagine - and yet it is achievable for all of us. Where we feel we – or our lives - lack what we perceive to be perfection, it is only because it cannot exist completely on a physical level. We are, again, probably thinking of the principle of the Celestial Mansion, remembering what it is to feel whole, free from the restraints of a physical existence and fully aware of the Karmic energy flowing freely through us. There are solutions that bring this Heaven down to Earth, beyond our physical perception of stagnant energies in our bodies. It can be bridged by specific processes of neutralising Karmic energy flaws that tend to smooth out any mishaps in our energy flow. As you can tell when things don't seem to go our way and we get stuck with our Karmic energy flaws, this does not appear to happen on its own very often in our ordinary ego minds, in our mundane every-day lives. In fact, it does not have to be a rare experience to feel at peace and at one with ourselves, knowing that we are on the right path, happy, awake and aware. This is the one experience that most of us seem to subconsciously strive for and are indeed capable of, so that even in ancient scripts humanity already reported such efforts and methods to guide us there. Even though in modern times we may have lost the treasure map for such a union, we have never given up trying to solve the mystery. However, most of us settle for fiction and fairy tales we instead make do with, instead of braving the inner journey to last us for lifetimes to come. it really is worth looking for and with this book, I actively want to encourage you to find it again. In lack of feeling and experiencing miracles, we set ourselves up for failure in trying to achieve the perfect illusionary relationship in the form of a physical union. Whilst this is one way we could indeed find out about higher principles, the notion of 'two become one' is often misunderstood and turns into disappointment when it does not help us find our inner Truth, which we then believe can never achieve. We end up feeling disillusioned with our relationships and our every-day lives and simply resign ourselves to the fact that we must have been mistaken to try and find the impossible. This may simply be because we don't get enough external support and encouragement to keep looking and not give up. We are taught from early on not to set our aim high, and even if we are, we are not taught the ancient art of how to make it happen. No wonder how most of us feel cheated in life and love! With this book, i want to actively encourage you to look again, to find and solve your inner mystery. With our Karmic energy barely understood and rarely honed, we don't really understand when our unions with others don't seem to function any longer, and tend to brush them off with sarcasm and derogatory remarks, showing our disappointment. No wonder if we have only been looking for the Magick in the external world, trying to enter unions such as those based on physical attraction and desire, on limiting beliefs, fears, insecurities and co-dependencies, which can logically only ever give us partial satisfaction and almost never everlasting love. The amazing truth is that when we do get searching within, all our external relationships will benefit. Truth is not always easy to handle or easy to find, and it won't make everything perfect, at least not overnight. We still have so many conflicts within that will present themselves from past interactions over lifetimes, but searching for the Truth will give us the tools and the stamina to keep on a path of ever-increasing energy instead of ever-decreasing cycles of despair. So many are choosing to end their lives right now as I write this book, not seeing a way out. i really hope that we all find what we need and start looking past what presents itself, start looking within. Even if this is all a very elusive concept for most, the fact that it already exists in many tantric practices destined to achieve this as an ultimate aim of blissful existence, we might be encouraged to know that once we start, we will find many like-minded souls who have been practising towards this achievement of awareness in a succession of many lifetimes.

In order to let our Kundalini energy rise from its dormant state, physical attraction and desire can be fully present, recognised, acknowledged, lived, accepted and then transformed; there is no need to chastise ourselves for feeling attraction to anything external, like so many cultures have done in the past, only for the energy to then come out in deprived ways. The inner energy that expresses itself first in physical attraction and exploration of Self in relation to others is good, healthy energy. However, for the energy to continue to rise and circulate within the body as is its full potential, it must be harnessed in a clever way. If this seems as elusive in your life as it is intriguing, please read on.

Any action, re-action or interaction with the external which you may experience or interpret as a desire, or any thought or emotion arising from this desire, originates from the source of your inner Kundalini energy and can thus be translated and transformed into a higher form of realisation.

In order for Kundalini or life-force energy to become one again with the universal Karmic energy, especially in a tantric union with the aim of creating a stage of enlightenment between people, it must be allowed to wash through all of our energy centres undisturbed, without our own or another's re-actions halting it which may make it stagnate or dissipate from any of our bodily energy points. If it is disturbed, it will simply become diverted into other 3-dimensional manifestations of temporary reality, creating a time-line and further Karmic manifestations. Most of us are new to this practice and we are not perfect; for most of us, life is about interference and manifestations we hardly know how to have any control over. By finding out about the essence and principles according to which Karmic energy works within our body, we are all learning to understand the blueprint of life, some more slowly than others. It is then another matter for each of us to decide that we are engaged enough in the process wholeheartedly to support it and wish to consciously and actively make it more constant. It's a big commitment to living by the purity of these principles. For now, it may be enough to just be reading about them and get some of the vast energy flowing through us by simply reading between the lines as we go along. Kundalini energy rising and flowing through us does allow us to connect naturally and powerfully, simply on an energy principle of 'like attracts like' and of its own volition, without requiring conscious interference. In fact, when we try to steer it in a certain direction by thinking about it, we will most likely find it does not work the way we want it to. if we leave it to show us its natural state, it will be like observing the flow of a river. The river is meandering along, destined to arrive to merge with the sea. If we disturb it or disrupt it, it will not flow naturally to its destination, finding its own way.

We may not know which way is the best way, but the best way can be to surrender to the way that we are already shown.

Whether we choose physical contact with the external for any time interval throughout our lives can be of our own choosing, or we may be subject to working through Karmic issues that need to be resolved. We can learn to become aware of a situation in advance to allow for either to be present. Often, if we are living a mundane life, Karmic issues present themselves time and time again in order to be resolved. Being on a path of Karmic Self- discovery does not mean that contact or interference with the external is not allowed, as is prescribed in many practices and doctrines. But we can become acutely aware that our choices of reacting to external events may have power to help or hinder us and others on our journey. If we are in deep inner practice, it just means that for the process to work, for a length of time that is determined to be crucial to the process, any external intervention would disturb the inner energy flow, dissipate the inner electromagnetic charge and distort the result of our inner Karmic energy that is awaiting completion in connecting with universal energy. It is a tricky practice not to get distracted away from our inner energy flow, but for a truly meditative and tantric practice it may be not only be necessary, but worth it. You are worth it. When we are immersed in the undistracted process of being at one with our inner Karmic energy and are following its meandering rhythms within our physical channels, it can be intensely blissful a state of mind, although experiencing it we will not need any inner dialogue to asses it like a commentator at a game show. When we eventually become witness to the process, at first there might be glimpses and then ever expanding phases of blissfulness. Some people experience an instant immersion in the experience like an implosion on our inner world. There can be many short experiences like these, or long times of not experiencing anything in between moments of being at one with the Blissful Mind. All of it is possible, and unpredictable. We will just have to sit in meditation and see. Whether we practice on our own or choose to be with a significant other, the potential is that of ALL the chakras open for us, and them. You can imagine perhaps how rare this would be, knowing how many things have to coincide to make this happen not just for ourselves, but another being there, too, experiencing the same at the same moment in time. It does happen though, even between two people who are in agreement to not just connect at base chakra level which is what we tend to do in ordinary life when we feel attraction. Karmic connections are so much more than that. The term 'Blissful Mind' indicates that this practice is meant not in the misinterpretations of the purely physical, it is meant in terms of blissful existence with the aim of expansion of our inner prana on all levels which then connects with other, higher dimensions. There is no external stimulus needed, no drugs, no alcohol, no physical contact even. The practice is an individual journey which can be shared with others who are taking the same journey using the same methods with the same agreements to simply sit in meditation practice at the same point in time. That's all. There is no innuendo, no sniggering or sexual context, no judgement on who does it better. On that very high plane of existence, worldly context alone is no longer applicable.

Many schools of thought, workshops and practitioners as well as the usual more dubious establishments that are to be approached with caution have attempted to give lessons on how to do this over time, but the result of complete tantric transformation is rare. For pure Tantric evolution to manifest, we can certainly look to those who appear to have some good things to say about it, but we also have to eventually emancipate ourselves from the concept of teachers and teachings. The ones that are really true and unconditional, who have experienced and emerged with wisdom from the trials and tribulations that are a part of our Karmic evolution and have the ability to teach truly from the heart are few and far between. Our Kundalini energy has the ability to rise up and down along our spine to nourish all parts of our body with vital life force energy at any time with or without our awareness, and we are the only ones who are experiencing our own body and its functions at any time. Even we ourselves are almost always unaware of where we are at. The most important thing that is needed is You; your focus, time, awareness, attention and diligent practice are paramount, in order for the Kundalini energy to cross over on its spiral journey from boundless universal energy down through our being. On its way up and down in constant motion along our spine, having scooped up necessary Earth energy to ground us from deep below the Earths crust, yin energy charges can 'flip' to become yang charged and vice versa, as each chakra is flooded in turn. As the energy rises, the solar plexus is alighted to conquer fear and push out any maligned energies, whereas further up it soothes the heart chakra energies to allow it to balance and learn to deal with human emotions and compassion for all; the throat chakra needs new energy flow to learn to express pure universal vibration to others in the most beautiful ways; the third eye to know itself and all around instantly without judging. The crown opening connects us to the ultimate wisdom and the quiet, silent, brilliant ecstasy of sharing that wisdom with other minds, equal and simultaneously. When we are experiencing our inner energy and its movements in such ways, when we become experienced with them, we may become able to share these with others who are going through similar. Each will be united only in the experience of energy intertwining without demanding more than simply this, the brilliance of knowing and experiencing total together. This then is fully included in the process of our own energy flow but exists on its own at the same time; it interacts with the other yet remains untouched. We are inseparable - different but the same - and ever-changed by the process of the union, the indescribable that replaces all desire for anything less. The result is a complete experience of bliss beyond the Self, one of completion and higher intention. Nothing is done or demanded, everything is flow. The physical world depending on time and space stands still for an instant, and ripples of the effect of the tantric union will be sent to all through the sheer rarity and magnitude of an event such as this, initiating the potential for the highest accomplishment between beings. There is nothing to add, nothing to achieve, only a repeated concentration to continue and repeat the state of bliss, without seeking or becoming attached to it. This is what we are truly capable of on the highest level.

It is a tantric principle we have touched on here, I realise, and one of the ultimate experiences of an enlightened existence in physical form. Although a rare and high practice, it is nevertheless achievable by all sentient beings, as histories of different cultures, sciences and religions will testify. There is an alternative practice, too, of equal importance.

This would be the practice of its opposite and the flip-side of the coin, as there are always two opposing forces in our binary universe with the potential to achieve the same outcome. We are not talking about dark practices, but rather the practice of combining the two entities of yin and yang, of the two beings into one existence and being as one. This would involve making a conscious decision of being ready to sacrifice any experience of a sacred union between two beings, in however many lifetimes necessary. Perhaps a Western analogy would be celibacy, regardless of whether male or female is involved, which agrees to practice only using the power of total tantric detachment by giving up worldly connections to one significant other in order to benefit all beings simultaneously. It would create the same extremely high result of creating a 'gap', or a number of such 'breaches' expanding in the universe's time/space fabric as described above; that is, if the individual is able to create completeness within themselves and is able to transfer this unconditionally and unhindered to all sentient beings, ultimately at all times. In this case, reality may be re-shaped and redefined for an unknown number of times. Thus, individuals not practising the same can nevertheless be reached and affected in a positive way, according to how the Karmic energy field created reacts with them, as everyone connects briefly in that instant.

But how can we connect in such a way? What does it all mean?
On the most basic survival level, we connect to others and our environment to survive, possibly even procreate if circumstances permit. There is nothing wrong with that, it's all a part of the process. As we know though, our efforts on this level alone can be very short-lived – we need to constantly top up sustenance, our survival is fraught with difficulties and by no means guaranteed. Our highest potential on the physical plane of experience is that all our energy centres and channels within are active; we are aware of the fact of who we are and how to constructively co-create our existence; we experience and learn to connect to every living being. On this end of the scale of our upwardly mobile human experience, there is no glass ceiling. We aim to fly high and understand all that is, to benefit not just ourselves, but every other living being, too.
In the not-so-grey-scale but rather technicolour experiences of infinite possible outcomes in between, most of us can only ever learn to partially connect to the Highest realms within the context of our colourful lives and relationships around other beings in a temporary environment. Our surroundings and fellow beings are here to help us by pointing out the areas of our Karmic energies which may be stuck and need work, but also give praise to those aspects which are in full working order, lovingly put together by the accomplished parts of our Karmic past. In order to manifest more of the same goodness, we are encouraged by the feed-

back from our environment and all that it contains to create more of the same goodness.

All these, of course, could be seen as slightly idealistic statements if we are not experiencing anything like it, and the irony of what presents itself on Earth does not escape the eagle eye. Looking around the globe probably makes us think the opposite is true – mankind has created untold suffering and continues to do so no matter how advanced we believe ourselves to be. One of the reasons for this is that, in basic survival mode, we only think of ourselves. If our existence is constantly threatened, we live in fear that tomorrow may not come for us and our loved ones. The majority of humankind still lives under those conditions, separate from the riches that are enjoyed by only a few. Despite what we already know to be true about global awareness we are still on course of destroying most of it.

Sadly, as human beings, we don't recognise we are subject to binary codes and have the ability as human beings to live unconsciously and act without compassion or a further thought for anything else but our own lives. When we exist purely on a survival level, we might have no choice but to survive by killing and eating other sentient beings. But even when we are surrounded by abundance and live with the luxury of having food sources all around us, we still inflict pain on each other, often in brutal, painful and barbaric ways. It does not seem to decrease when we find ourselves in a situation of wealth, far from it. We often try to justify this and don't even question it, and those who do ask all the right questions as to why the state of our minds is so poor are persecuted. We even feel bad and retaliate when we are reminded of this simple fact that we are no more evolved than we have ever been, because we insist there can be no other ways we can adapt to in order to aim for all of us to stay alive and we believe that any other belief or challenge to our way of life endangers our existence.

On the highest level of connection, all wisdom is present and available to us in every moment. All the compassion it generates is necessary to co-create our field of existence, in a way that takes everyone and everything else into consideration. But who on Earth can remember what that looks like? We shoot the prophets who try to remind us. When we raise our awareness, we have to start within ourselves and tidy up our own Karmic energy, as well as learn to do it for the sake of all existence.

The ultimate idea of our existence is for us complete our Karmic energy system and learn to reliably and consistently sustain it, in order to utilise it for the benefit of all sentient beings.

Along the path of completion of one's Karmic Self, everyone else's will be moved, too, according to the ascension of the energy of creation at the existent level of completion. By completion is not meant the perfection on a level of perfect looks, behaviour or possessions. We have been speaking of an elusive form of completion, which I can only prompt you to find further reference to in the greatest accomplished masters on Earth as well as in the ascended masters on astral planes, whoever they may be in our minds and however they may present themselves to us. It may not be easy to accept some of the underlying principles with our ordinary minds. Please don't think I m telling you what you should be all about or what to think. Every spoken word can easily be misinterpreted and misused. Words are important, but easily interpreted in many different ways. They affect us all differently according to where we are on our individual path. Completion is attainable, yet requires a high level of practice and committent that most these days no longer understand, never mind aspire to. Many people these days are in agreement that, when on the inner path, there is comfort in the thought that you will begin to radiate energy and feel it, too; and by radiate I mean to say that your energy will radiate from within you, where it is generated by the flow of your Karmic Kundalini energy spiralling up and down your spine via yin and yang channels, through each of your chakras, feeding every cell of your body along the way. It is connecting base and crown, Earth and universe, creating completeness within at all times, an experience that in itself has no need for expression or impression. Eventually it will not need to draw anything from its environment for that matter. It sounds like science fiction, but it is quite real and has been achieved and observed to be true over centuries past. It's not a competitive sport, and it has been kept sacred for centuries for a reason. Sharing explicit experiences of bliss may not necessarily help another but instead can actually cause them distress, and this is not in the interest of any good practitioner. Humility is called for, great care must be taken not to mislead anyone, and no doubt many experiences will lead each of us to be the best we can. Each way is our way, and we cannot say that one of us is better than the other or has a better plan. The thoughts I am sharing are my experience, and far from trying to upset others, I sincerely wish for everyone to be happy and find them of benefit, too.

The experience of awareness of rising Karmic energy within us may only happen for short moments to begin with; it may burst forth in an enlightening experience and then be absent for years, but it is also possible for a human being to attain and sustain it permanently.

How long it will take to attain full awareness at all times, I do not know. I don't think anybody knows, or is meant to know, although many of us want to. It must be different for all of us, or maybe there is that key event we are all waiting for where we will all be enlightened in a flash, all together, all at once. It would be nice to think, but maybe it is best not to ask? I trust it must be worth it and I personally believe that this is one of the highest offerings we can make to the physical world whilst adjusting our Karmic energy for future higher levels of perception beyond the 3-dimensional realms.

❋ ❋ ❋

24. Karmic Energy and the Omnipresence

As a result of such tantric practice, we might feel less of an urge to connect with mundane events on a physical level. We may have no need for it, no desire. If we sense a request to make a connection it will be most likely to assist others, which can also often be done even more effectively on a non-physical level if we have learned to truly honour and master our gift to be able to shift energy towards a better outcome for all involved. If we do connect on a physical level, the intention and outcome are usually more meaningful and abundant. Rather than simply wasting time and physical energy resources by moving in the 3-d world, exchanges on higher frequency levels may in future become highly charged points of reference and facilitate empowered healing processes just as much as physical efforts. The majority of us may still be a bit too attached yet to our physical experiences to contemplate the idea or master the concept, but I have to say that this is where the whole subject becomes even more interesting for me.

When we achieve the level of perceiving permanent continuation of existence through our practice. our life work will be enhanced by being rewarded by the omnipresence of awareness and perception of everything in its true form, including our awareness of other beings on the same level.

These other beings would have also taken their individual inner journeys of enhancing their focused intention on creating a good outcome for all sentient beings to such a level as to being able to create a pure channel of energy within their physical and Karmic energy bodies. When I say create, i mean that they would have been able to remove any Karmic obstacle to allowing universal energy to flow through naturally. Once a certain level of blissfulness of living with pure cosmic energy flowing within one's 'Self' is regained on all levels, we are no longer confined to a 'Self', and other beings who have equally reached this level of existence do not feel a need to ask anything of each other. On this elusively high level of consciousness, there is neither a need for words nor physical desire of expression. Not even telepathy would be needed to experience this incredible but plausible level of connectedness between a number of beings. It is very rare to have this happen in human form, but it is possible, and it has occurred in cultures with very diligent practice. it may well be practised right now on Earth, only those who are at this level of awareness may well not be out in the open but rather choose to remain hidden away from plain sight. At this level of existence, no meaningless exchange between beings takes place any longer – just pure concentric focus of the result of all Karmic energy mind function and intent. I can't even find the right words, because at this level, there are no words to describe the phenomenon. Our Karmic energy mind can take on this task without our Ego minds being involved, but that does not mean that we are unaware or that our brain shuts down. Rather, ALL our energy is in the right position, flowing through us unhindered by any negative Karma to make the most of our resources. There are also no judgements or intellectual musings, no misunderstandings as to the meaning of the practice, and whilst what I am writing about will seem peculiar to most of us in our mundane lives, it has been practised for thousands of years. One such sacred practice is mentioned to be the 3 years, 3 months and 3 days yogic meditation, an ancient practice to prepare for Buddhahood by highly accomplished monks, not advised to try this at home. These practices are of inner agreement for deep transformation, which come about as a natural result of beings who are already highly accomplished in the tantric practice. Since so much on Earth is being 'dis-covered' and brought out into the open, even these most secret practices have been made public and described in films and documentaries. Perhaps this is a part of their destiny, since no corner on Earth remains sacred or hidden in these modern times. Is this the analogy of Adam and Eve having to flee paradise? As we are no longer able to grasp the true concept of sacred practice, we feel justified to grab with our boldly senses everything we are curious to understand. But these concepts are way beyond the limit of perception of our 5 senses and brain activity alone. Was eating the apple from the forbidden tree an analogy for bringing sacred practices into the mundane, 3-d world where everything is perishable? Was it forbidden because it was eternal until we tried to break it down into bite-sized pieces?

In any case, many of these pure mind practices that came to light were watered down to be consumed by mass curiosity driving an industry that set out to exploit their abundant potential. Their true essence has been lost in translation, the many have jumped on the bandwagon and greed has attached a price tag for a hip and trendy holiday break experience for the hungry and spiritually stressed crowd. Nowadays, the infinite energy contained in the essence of all that exists is broken down and available for sacred teachings like parts of a dead animal offered for food, and we don't any longer see much wrong with the fact that there is also a huge charge attached to them, or that they have been misused for lesser purposes of manipulating curious people by dubious 'teachers'. This can and does all happen, and is most likely also a part of the dance of dark and light in a myriad of different ways. I don't wish to have such aversion to it that I inadvertently give more energy to it, and I am also most likely a part of the problem writing a book about it with the consequence that every dear reader will be prompted to either like or dislike what i write, rather than feeling drawn to finding their own way to their inner pure land of blissful existence. With any good practice comes deep respect and care for each individual who chooses to find out more, and of course the alchemical process of transformation itself. If we are coming across recklessness and exploitation, this is part of wordly phenomena that are not speaking Truth. You can determine for yourself where there is little respect for finding pure Truth with a capital T in any area of your life, by using your instincts and insights as to whether the people and practices you are involved in are flawed. There are good teachers around, but if they are promoted by greed you will almost certainly be misled. For a long time, a good inner benchmark I held for good practice in the West was how much people charged. I still hold to this day that good teachings need cost little to nothing, out of the greatest respect for the being who is learning and the teaching that is being passed on being a universal gift, available to all for free or simply a donation or nominal fee. It has always been my humble opinion that practitioners who believe they are worth lots of money and have to express their Self-worth in money were the ones with the issue. You do not need to charge money at all to 'value yourself'. If you need it, it will ultimately come to you. And if you don't, there are ways to bypass it altogether. I am sure what I am saying will cause much controversy, as our attachment to money is so great at this time that we do not easily see past it. Call me old-fashioned, but the way I see it, the make-believe hype of little pieces of worthless paper and token coins we have cunningly been led to believe has taken over our lives. It is part of the practice of seeing above wordly events that we learn to see things differently, and if more of us see the inherent value of compassion and wisdom and use this much more often than exchanging currency, then we might be on the right tracks. Hence this book being made available to all, a donation is optional. I am aware that plenty of readers will not like what I am saying and feel their toes trodden on. I say we all need to learn to trust and respect one another; and find something else already in place instead of money. I have a feeling that some of us are already aware that the current structures based on purely physical phenomena are crumbling, as they can only ever be long-term temporary at best. A society based on amassing physical wealth and focused on physical attributes only will suffer greatly when circumstances change, just like certain aspects of nature are subject to fluctuations that are sometimes devastating, especially when we have been playing god trying to manipulate in order to profit. It's a great time to put ourselves out there to reconnect with others on more meaningful levels and lose some fears together.

All of us are already interconnected naturally and by default, so to speak. Something much larger, much more coherent than we are usually aware of takes place, simply by the law of attraction of higher vibrations that we learn we constantly synergise with, the universe's Wi-Fi connection, so to speak. the content we end up downloading is down to our Karmic understanding so far - we can be really childish and low level or use it to enhance our wisdom and ability for compassionate action. This download and our energy forms intermingle, merge, communicate and make it possible for us to attain a higher form of existence than we are used to, eventually even formlessness itself. The appearance of virtual reality is only a synonym for our true ability to connect on highest invisible frequencies to each other without the need for electricity. At a level of formless existence, there is no stimulation or exchange on any physical level necessary, even though this is probably extremely hard to envisage. All the same, this exchange exists constantly and naturally forms the basis for the build up to the next, even higher and finer levels of energy frequency interactions above the physical that still 'belong' to our Karmic energy system, situated above our own crown chakra. Are you still with me? Because this is the only and measly way I can think of explaining it. Even though it may sound far out, daunting, unachievable, ludicrous - some beings on this planet have, in fact, already achieved access to such levels of existence in and on a higher frequency vibration. Since some of the most recent last massive vibrational Earth shifts in the year 1999 and another noticeable one in 2012, for example, with another occurring right as I am writing after the December eclipses of 2019, this chakra system above the present, physical one has started to become more tangible to more of us physical beings as it becomes more realised within many more people. The effects of each shift have an earthly momentum as well, and as I sit here it is beginning to show itself clearly in the physical as it starts to disintegrate much more noticeably as a result of the constructs of human manufacture. The result is that more of us are awakening to this potential shift as we seem to have less choice, leaving their pure physical forms to rise up into other dimensions through spiritual practice sought by many who are finding the shifts hard to cope with. The shifts into higher dimensions have nothing to do with drug taking, astral travelling or any cheap forms of recreational mentality for personal pleasure. The fourth dimension is already ready for all of us able to see, the fifth in grasp not far behind, and beyond that some of us are already starting to tune into the

6th and beyond. These practices that we used to ridicule might well be very necessary the more the physical world struggles with its existence. We still have a chance to stay and live in the physical realm, or inter-phase between the two, for some time if we are careful enough to look after this place. However, the more we find we have tools to have a good look around, the more we see what's wrong. The physical realm will carry on existing, but since its density and that of some of its inhabit-ants is becoming more and more obvious to many, as we are observing with regret how the resulting low energy frequencies give birth to so much suffering, illness and malpractice, discomfort and fraught men-tal states. On the other end of the scale, the upwardly mobile evolution we are capable of through what I have termed the 'head birth' into a new chakra system above our crown will seem the preferable escape in the future, and perhaps our only option to 'survive' and exist in a more prevalently aware and Self-evident as well as necessary solution in order for humans to stay sane and possibly even continue to exist in 3-dimensional form.

Future generations from these times on would start to be born with the new frequencies already in-built. We know of Indigo and Crystal chil-dren of the past, but these will be known as what I have been calling the translucent children: those that are born with pearlescent, opalescent, crystalline and transparent energies within their frequencies, ready to transform their energies into a virtual state of existence. These chil-dren are born with less or little personal Karma to deal with in their lifetimes, if any, and an amazing ability to instantly heal and process information. Many of them will have been reborn with altruistic per-spectives purely to help others transmute their energy, too, and for no other reason than to help the shift happen for many more, as quickly as possible. This might mean that in future we might be able to spend less time on Earth in each incarnation but that we are able to bring about shifts in a much quicker way. Technology will no longer be known as such, as it relies on electricity, physical and intellectual research. The future lies in instant connectivity through higher forms of vibrational energy frequencies.

As always, on Earth there is a positive element that strives to unite all and heal all rifts, whereas its opposing force will try to use similar frequential knowledge to separate and create dissonance. Paradoxically, even dissonance is possible as a form of evolutionary effort of beings for becoming enlightened, however, this is not a recommendation to seek it in hope to suddenly find the realisation we have caused devastation and destruction. Even if they did - and there is much less chance they will rather than choosing positive actions - the harm done to other beings can and will hinder and delay the supporters of violent action in their efforts to find redemption for themselves. More importantly, as they stay connected to their victims on a Karmic energy level, absolution from the victims they remain karmically responsible for. All wrongful action, depending on each outcome and severity, narrows the margin for each existence to be a fruitful experience, despite any apparent intelligence and potential ability for remorse.

In the highest dimensions, there would be no place for division and the symptoms of greed, fear, anger or ignorance, as these are born from our ordinary ego mind. Our ego mind might not even exist on higher frequencies, as we can imagine. At some point in our future I believe our Karmic evolution will abandon the need for an ego mind, at least for some living beings. After all, the limited frequencies of perception our ego minds have, are responsible for destroying our environment right now and many other sentient beings with it; most of us are aware that we are not creating best case scenario but seem to not be able to do anything much about changing it. We bring fear to this planet from our Karmic past-life memories, where fear meant that our 3-d physical existence was threatened and in pain, but rather than conquer it, we have perpetuated fear and suffering in others. In higher dimensions, 'we' will have learned to overcome fear and physical pain will not exist as our body won't be what it is now either. Fear will not be necessary and prevalent as it is now since we are starting to learn methods to overcome and avoid it. This is hard for us to accept right now as our physical body and brain fails to try to make sense of something it has yet to experience, based on comparing it to any similar experiences from the past. The past has been painful, full of a sense of loss of loved ones and disconnection from our true potential. Our ego memory bank stubbornly wants to project only those memories from past experiences it remembers onto any of our forms of existence in the future, which is the best it can do to try and help us. Bless our little brains. They are, of course, useful by developing a certain 'fear memory' about dangerous scenarios in order to keep us from harm so that we do not hurt ourselves again. Even that seems like a difficult task as we see many people do really stupid things and ending up hurting themselves and others. We are getting more and more distracted as a whole, too, so surely it's becoming clear that we cannot rely on our brains alone to see us through under any circumstance. Sometimes this process is useful, but in the case of our spiritually advanced development, our ordinary minds have little to go on, except when it remembers previous experiences of having met this level of vibration already and deems it safe and beneficial to go with it. Sometimes, it will just make us feel like a rabbit in the headlights if we go through unknown territory and rely on our brains to guide us, rather than our connection to higher sources. We might call this 'instinct', but there is much more to it than that. This 'instinct' has the tough task to lead us to positive outcomes, which only happens if we are continuously creating good Karma. The logical conclusion is that we need to practice aligning to our higher minds over and over again, to come out of the fear of dying and losing out. Good Karma is for lifetimes, not just for special occasions.

So, instead of listening to an ego mind that makes us afraid of everything in case of what might happen, let me assure you that if the path of tantric practice is done properly and with good guidance, there is no need to feel lost even in trying times. We all want to have our cake and eat it - but the bonus of creating good Karma is that it's a good healthy wholesome cake and you get to fully enjoy and share the abundance rather than just crave it. Instead of worrying about losing our physical appearance and strength as we get older or worrying whether we will be taken care of or not, knowing that we are doing what we can to increase good Karma right now in order to be benefiting all in the future is an amazing feeling. It's as if we win the lottery, but realise we would benefit more from it being an all-encompassing experience rather than just a physical manifestation, if that makes sense. If only we can ditch our addiction to the merely physical and see what we can expand to with our every-day practice, the universe would provide for everything that we would ever need on the highest levels, rather than what we believe we need with our ego minds.

Beings who achieve these high levels of existence eventually have no 'need' or 'want' for anything any longer on a physical plane as they use their Karmic mind energy purely in a constructive way to include and benefit all in existence. The manifestations from their Karmic minds become gradually Self-sustaining and even their bodies can adjust to take more nourishment from surrounding energy rather than from solid physical matter. Manifestation of anything that is in the flow of the universe often becomes instant, as it is more and more based on pure wisdom of knowing how to create all that is needed to be beneficial to all. At those levels of understanding the underlying Universal Karmic principles, the process of bringing about miracles is never misused on trivia or used as showmanship. It is not even talked about often, to preserve the pure energies that exist without the observer. Rather, it takes on a sacred, gentle, non-invasive, unobtrusive, peaceful and prayer-like nature to assist and release all beings from suffering. Those who commit to this higher existence vow to not create negative Karma any longer with their physical presence, speech and thoughts; the premise for this is the understanding that we must no longer take energy away from another or our environment, but only act out of compassion and in harmony with creation. They cease to form dependencies on anyone, as those would only be created by submission to a lower frequency of fear; on higher frequency levels of existence, reality is no longer based on fear or fear-related phenomena.

At this moment in time on Earth, as has been many times before, many of our thoughts are still made of the fabric of fear, creating a need for and dependency on physical experiences. On the opposite end of the scale, once we fully reach higher levels of Karmic vibration, our every intention will be purified by having learned how to eliminate fear and refrained from actions based on fear creating more fear. If we can all learn methods to release fear therefore, we all have the ability to co-create our own future and how we influence others', by adjusting our own energy flow and our actions if we can commit to a sincere practice to learn to sustain universal energy. In the realms within which there is no need to 'leak' personal energy. We are all still struggling with how to sustain our own Karmic energy instead of losing it from our bodies and minds. In the mind-state of clearing our inner energy, this has the effect of an increasingly pure and completely radiating energy field within and around a sentient being or entity. The more your energy radiates freely and unhindered, the more recognisable you would become in your completeness to another being by the radiance of your wisdom body. To ordinary beings, you would either look just normal, or appear very kind perhaps; or be described as happy, humble, compassionate, radiant and so on. To others again, they will see where your radiance will stem from, and how complete it is, as well as the good that it achieves. It will become something that some people will covet, and others will want to help to protect. Be that as it may, our resolve to complete our inner journey must not depend on the reactions of the external, but rather be sustained by wishing everyone to experience the same levels of bliss.

The more good we wish upon others,
the more good will come from it.

At some exalted level, accomplished beings would seem to not even exist at all, other than to those who can somewhat see or believe in the principles of what we are discussing already and who might be able to perceive them to be luminous or ethereal. The difference to religious beliefs in which there are gods outside ourselves, the principles of transforming energy which we know of, theoretically mean that we are all capable of such ascension. Although beings who have accomplished higher levels of existence could well be perceived as 'gods' by some, in the end, each being will understand these energy levels according to their own beliefs at every moment in time. Every being is entitled to their own stage of development and expressing this as so. Issues arise when fear still enters our ego minds and taints our vision of pure energy. We might fear we will never reach these levels, get jealous, end up misdirected, angry and spiteful out of our own inability to find the methods to create our inner peace. This also means that some who still operate with the modus of fear, needing to instil power and control over other living beings and their environment, may even still perceive the concept of divine energies that pervade us all as a threat or something to exploit.

Those of the same or a similar level of cognizance will attract each other with ease as their energies converge. They can recognise each other, assist and exist alongside each other without conflict or dependence on another's reaction. In fact, there would be no 'alongside' any more as form ceases to exist. There is a merging instead, their energies coincide in a flowing experience of entering formlessness, which occurs on a different vibrational frequency above our ordinary human range of perception. We are talking about principles outside the rainbow spectrum of frequencies of physical matter; which is why it is so hard for us to see, perceive, understand or believe, never mind attain! How do we do this? How do we become beings of 'lighter' frequency, if this is our wish, our mission, our destiny?

It appears that all our experiences in body, speech and mind have to become all-accepting of all opposites including negativity, in order to become unified. It is no good to become spiritually arrogant and deny or reject anything that is of a lesser frequency. It does not mean we become complacent and simply refrain from condoning wrong actions as we perceive them. They still need to be processed and we can be a part of this process by helping others overcome them - again, in a non-condescending way that separates wrongful actions from the beings themselves who are all struggling to come to terms with their own Karma. We have to find equanimity and acceptance in all that exists whilst distancing ourselves from the destruction of any violence in any form, and find balance of how to deal with situations as they come along in our reality on Earth where everything co-exists, at times in great opposing forces. Nothing does well when it is excluded and abandoned from our focus and care. Caring comes in many forms and is adapted to ensure our safety, too. There are times when our existence is in danger, where some actively sacrifice their own health and well-being to assist others valiantly. Actions like these can enrich our Karma if we don't set out with an aim to do this. It is not about fighting reality, it is about unifying everything as a possible outcome within our minds, and so others' well-being is seen as just as important as ours. The more we can be inclusive, the more in tune we are with universal principles, the less we are in danger of allowing our own Karmic minds to be compromised by dissonance.

It sounds like an immense undertaking and difficult achievement, and just like life itself, a contradiction in terms, but our Karmic minds are the only place where we have a conscious say and definitive influence in terms of achieving balance and peace. We cannot decide where others are at. Here within ourselves is where our heart and home is, where we come to terms with the idiosyncrasies that life throws at all of us. It gets better: we do not have to wait until a perfect future - we can all start to heal within, right now. The first thing to do is that when we recognise the nature of our frustration with the external, we add to this that we vow learn to become more focused on seeking solutions internally. By not berating ourselves or others for not being at the highly evolved levels of existence we expect them or us to be, by resisting the pressure of seeing ourselves and others in a perceived race to try to get there in this lifetime, by acceptance of our failures and healing our shortfalls, we can introduce humour, humility and harmony. The most important thing in the early stages is to carry on trying and to not give up, because these amazing levels of existence (and there are several, ever more subtle ones) really do exist and are within reach for all of us.

25. Finding Our Karmic Truth

As already said, in order to accept what is going on for us and to make sense of life, it helps to have all the facts, many of which have been omitted from scriptures and texts, or got lost in translation. Opening Pandora's box may also have had the effect that people started longing to be something they were not accomplished to be just yet, so maybe some of the more intricate practices and methods were deemed not suitable, perhaps even dangerous. There is no point reaching for something outside of ourselves too soon. It may well drive us into madness. Simple methods to tidy up our internal act which work to our benefit are not a drug; they are not a trip to be buying a ticket or a pill for. It's not a fairground ride, and people need to be seriously considering their inner realms and reasons and become aware of their liability when choosing a path of destruction rather than reconciliation. We have the potential for many flaws within, reflected in our society. They can make it much harder to find out who we really are, outside of what we have been led to believe. Added to this, we are distracted by what society demands of the individual which is, by now, far removed from improving our inner energy circuits. It's only natural then that many have started to want 'out' and question our society. The way we have been going about turning humans, animals and our planet into cheap, productive and effective machinery is not sustainable and bears no relation to what we are truly capable of when we are not subdued, stressed and subjugated into the latest upgrade of the next barely disguised form of slavery. Of course it will start a rebellion when we simply turn inwards and start to find Truth, instead of following orders from those we no longer have faith in. Let's not take the frustrating parts we are trying to ditch into the next chapter of our lives.

Finding out our individual Karmic truth is a natural path of accomplishment and there are no tests or exams on the way, at least not the type we have been led to believe at stages set by external education facilities. We can start by realising we need to unlearn some of what we have been led to believe. We can detach ourselves from the beliefs that are no longer valid as we go along, learn to be more gentle with ourselves and others and not try to rush into the next scenario head on. If we want to learn to make instant changes, we need to go within. If we are not used to the process and have no idea of where to start, we need to slow down the process so that our inner journey is not detrimental to our mental health. Going inwards when we are so used to externalising everything, it is easy to confuse our Western education and linear thinking with the steps that naturally occur during the development of our inner Karmic energy path. We are looking for clarity and insight; but even when we have a strong resolve to do this, no matter what, it is no guarantee we will be on a straight and narrow path. I have observed people take some very high initiations into sacred principles of all orientations and then fairly lose their minds afterwards.

We cannot get clarity from an external source if we are not ready to match it with our levels of insight within.

Not that I can be the judge, but it seems there are situations where some of us are off in the opposite direction of our journey to realising inner wisdom and for some considerable time, sometimes years, they may not able to cope and find any joy in their lives. That is not the kind of higher vibrational peaceful existence we are aiming for and would all like to be a part of. When we are talking about higher existence, finer vibrations and beings who achieve intricate levels of existence on Earth, we are not looking at a website where we can order a holiday to do the same. We need to find our inner small-print on the contracts we have already signed before we entered this very life. In order to be well, extremely well, and be able to cope with higher vibrational frequency, our bodies and minds need time to adjust. We need to take great care of ourselves so that we don't fall apart instead.

Those who will be accomplished will have had many signs along their path, gone through many purifications and given up many things, in order to be who they are. We need to take things one step at a time; please be kind to yourself and others first and foremost - and take it easy. Sentient beings who have achieved these higher planes of Karmic energy levels are aware and awake enough to inherently know that they are not attached to the human body and its energy system any longer. They have, over time and practice, overcome perceptions of a final moment of 'death', as we call it, and the fear of it. Once they do pass beyond their physical existence however, their highly trained energy minds allow them to have the choice to reincarnate into human form again, if it is deemed useful for the purpose of helping to raise other sentient beings' vibration, too. You can imagine how different this is from most of us who are disillusioned with life on Earth, who would never choose to come back and who can't wait for Scotty to beam us up. If we are to 'ascend', so to speak, into another vibrational frequency dimension, we have to be at peace with this one first. It's not a computer game where you get more armour, tools, gold stars and lifelines; rather, all the fears of not having any help at all needs to be replaced with a very strong and sound inner conviction that we are already whole and complete, just as we are. We need to find that we have become peaceful warriors within, that we need to put in the right kind of effort in order to help others feel the love, too. We can all do it, for sure, all of us have the potential. We are all built similar. It is theoretically possible, I am not sure of the statistics, though. I again point you in the direction of several methods at the end of this book to find some that you may find useful in your own quest.

Let's get back to what happens on the frequencies of fearlessness and omnipresence. On the journey to this higher existence, light beings who have purified their fears and beliefs are far from alone. They are very connected with everything surrounding them, their energy brilliance shines and merges with their surroundings and can create a kind of vibrational energy 'dance' with others, a dance that involves the inter-twining of the energy spirals within; probably the only dance there is that is performed by being perfectly still. This interaction probably has similarities to the physical exchange we are used to, which happens on all levels of existence when any sentient beings meet. However, on a higher vibrational level it becomes more expansive and all-encompass-ing. It is instant as it has no physical limitations or boundaries – and it exists for the main purpose of assisting the ascension of sentient beings and never their detriment. On highest frequency levels, duality ceases to exist completely, making the distinction between everything as opposites, such as dark and light, good and evil obsolete; as hard it is to imagine. All that is on those levels and beyond exists to assist and as-semble what needs completion.

When this is in the early stages of being perfected, there is still a dis-tinction of inner and outer levels in a waning binary code of existence. Perhaps the idea that some people in the West perceive as being in the presence of 'twin flames' also falls into this category. I would interpret this further to say that there may, at the beginning stage, only be two beings at a time who share their dance together, but as consciousness rises within those ascending, it is logical that there would be more and more of those who are 'twinned', as well as individuals ascending, who have entered into the further process of refining their energies and awareness continuously. I also believe that, as depicted in many images of ancient Asian art, the principles of consciousness merging into one being will be reflected by those who do not feel any need to be with any other beings as they are perfecting their oneness within. All principles of a dual nature can be conceived within one being. Of course there are those who truly embrace these high practices and understand underlying principles of non-duality. It is not some weird cuddle party where physical desires are still a need and at the forefront of everyone unaware of how to deal with their fear of feeling 'alone' in this universe; instead, it is an inner cosmic celebration of knowing, of having accomplished a new yet timeless insight and experiencing a Karmic energy milestone whilst still living within the confines of a singular physical form. It is an indication of what is to come, and how it will continue, perhaps even on Earth. There have been many god-like manifestations on Earth already, and there will be more. There may be many, even innumerable such light beings in existence already who are holding this space and inhabit this light frequency in the universe right now, who have special meaning and take on specific energy roles. Maybe the purpose to this dance is to hold the space for this universe's existence and all who life within it, according to the conscious agreement of the intertwining energies. All our universe is subject to the duality of existence, however, it does not mean there are no other universes. I would say there is a good chance there are infinite amounts of universes in infinite time, since time and space would no longer exist outside the constrictions of dense matter. Maybe it is to create more life, more energy, knowledge, wisdom, more love, higher vibrations and better healing conditions for all in existence. It does not mean we all suddenly become reincarnations of Melchizedek and start to emulate everything we have read about. Beings on higher frequencies don't need robes, angel wings, unicorn horns or white linen, halos, crystals, disco lights or glitter. They do not need to put on their business cards that they are enlightened. As they radiate naturally, just by 'being' rather than with any set goal or ambitious purpose, they may simply exist to light the way in a most pure, unadulterated and unassuming way. Whilst they are more likely to live very humble existences and become more God-like and invisible by the minute through their increased vibrational frequencies, maybe some form of transference happens to us, too, so that we ourselves become ready to 'see' them as we evolve our Karmic energy body. We learn about existence in other dimensions, and maybe the idea of understanding and insight is just to create a small tear in the fabric of space and time as mentioned before, which helps heal this planet and to give everyone on it the opportunity to become wise and compassionate. Wisdom and compassion are tools. Intergalactic dance is a tool. Meditation is a tool. Initiations into highly volatile rites, are tools. Physical existence is a tool. All of them have been signposts, pointers in the direction that we are all one, we all want to unite, we all want to learn to be happy, and then *be* happy. I am sure that when the energy within a physical being ascending into an ethereal one is focused to such an extent as to be approaching pure formlessness, some sort of quantum leap becomes possible that connects all minds simultaneously, a completely blissful experience of light that reaches all of the universe at once in order to compassionately influence all sentient beings within it, on a level that is appropriate for each being according to their individual capability of understanding.

As I already said, I believe that, as we speak, some beings have already attained such a state of mind and conscious wisdom in the past and also in this present time. Some of these life-forms carry on existing permanently on energy levels almost incomprehensible to us, but it might explain why some of us see phenomena like ghosts or angels and believe in higher life-forms and deities. Of course, they are around, and some of them leave energy imprints, like kids who haven't tidied their bedrooms.

Ultimately there exists only the Karmic intention, focus and presence of everything that is. We are all part of it and this is what we are made of; it exists within us and is therefore accessible to all of us.

Meanwhile, back down on Earth; what I have been waxing lyrical about is this same light which you carry within yourself, this very moment. There is no difference. Start your dance, now, and start it with your inner Self. Make friends with yourself. Find out who you are. That is what Karma is all about. Your Karma is your friend, it points you in the right direction: within. It is not about searching outside, joining religion, going astral travelling or pursuing out of body experiences. It is already there, it is already yours. You are already 'it', you are already what you are searching for.

It is about connecting your 'Self' to source, reconciling your own personal journey and life experiences so far with the infinite light energy source outside yourself: Bringing the always and forever into the here and now.

As with many beings who have attained such heights of perception realise: it is about attaining the highest light experience of emptiness and vastness, only to then connect it again to our individual experience on Earth: To be one with all, bringing Heaven-down-to-Earth. The need to express the experience in any way, shape or form vanishes with the knowledge of already 'being', and it becomes clear that even - or especially?! - writing books about it becomes a minor, very humble form of healing communication in the light of the expression of Truth that is possible on such high vibrations. The only real conclusion that can be drawn from any glimpse of enlightening thoughts on Karma would be to wish for others, too, to experience it; to exercise life-surpassing compassion for all and be able to hold everyone in equally high regard as we do ourselves. To raise awareness and be able to make use of all the precious gifts for all of us who may not have achieved realisation yet, to use the talents and transcendence we have as individual human beings in order to manifest compassionate thoughts. These motives and energies are the ones that are pure good Karma, which will prevail past any experience of ill-health and death on an individual level and will remain prevalent lifetime after lifetime, and beyond. The last noble Truth is that there is a way out of suffering, and there is indeed.

* * *

26. Good Karma

We have learned a little about negative Karma and Karma 'mishaps', but what about good Karma? How can we make sure that we reap the benefits of good Karmic actions and what are they in the first place?

First of all, if we could look into the future and see the benefits of expanding our good Karma, I have a feeling we would never be tempted to pursue ignorant and unskilful actions again. The way we could live - in peace, harmony, love, light and happily ever after - it would blow our minds, as we could instantly feel the connections between our actions and their outcomes. How awesome this truly is - and this is not just my inner hippy talking! - is for us all to find out. This could truly be our reality. A higher, conscious reality which we still choose to exchange for our current relative misery, which on a Karmic level we are still attached to, love to complain about incessantly and which we like to continuously blame others and circumstances outside ourselves for. Whilst we still do this and, worse, continue to either deliberately or subconsciously educate next generations into believing, we are disempowering them as well as ourselves, and we all end up being 'out of' our 'Selves'. When I say 'we', I really mean to address our ego mind and our Karmic mind. The fact that we still allow ourselves to be 'ruled' by our ego minds is down to energy caught in a loop in our bodies created by our past Karmic actions. To break out of those confines that have become our comfort zones and recognise that we are not actually enjoying freedom of choice at all, but are instead still slaves to our trapped Karmic energy, we must first get out of the 'red' on our Karmic bank accounts.

So, in this chapter, there are a few tips on how to increase our chances at experiencing future well-being by increasing our good Karma credit rating - the only one worth worrying about, as far as I can tell.

Looking after our own and others' well-being self-generates good Karma.

It is a well-known fact in many cultures that looking after others' well-being can bring good fortune to both them and us. You are certainly to include yourself in this process by making sure that your attitude towards yourself is wholesome, too. It is just as fruitless to have a guilt trip about what a lowly creature you are and feeling so worthless that you treat others much better than you treat yourself, as it is to concentrate purely on yourself to the exclusion of anyone else. There are probably psychological terms for both of those mental constructs. How can we get the balance right? Whilst it is always good to own up about Karmic insights we have into our own shortcomings to learn to overcome them, it would be in everyone's favour to recognise ourselves as inherently good beings, even miraculous beings, living in a world full of potential miracles. This does not mean we can commit crimes and get away with it, hide behind a false exterior or feel justified to get even with those who have wronged us. It means that there are ways to make it our intention to become insightful to our own plight, and when we have learned how to heal, that we share this insight for the benefit of others who cannot quite see themselves shine yet. As HH Dalai Lama expresses aptly,

"When we feel love and kindness toward others, it not only makes others feel loved and cared for, but it helps us also to develop inner happiness and peace." — HH Dalai Lama

It is good practice to share our positive experiences with others, because the energy within us starts to activate and radiate when we think well of others outside ourselves. It trains our energy system to radiate energy, and allow new energy to flow through us more abundantly. It helps us to transform the views we may have of the world and people outside of our own field of vision. It is as simple as this: the more good thoughts we have, the more we pass on to others, the more we gather insights and truth. The more truth we radiate, the more we purify our energy.

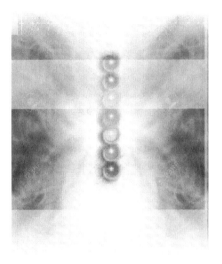

image credit © https://depositphotos.com/stock-photos/energy-field.html

Our Karmic energy body cannot fully be perceived with our senses including our eyes. It helps to have images like these to bridge the gap between what we can see and what we understand of the Karmic energy that flows through each energy centre in our bodies. The energy that flows from the crown into our bodies spirals downwards through each energy centre, into the ground below us, rises up again from there along our spine in the opposite direction and again merges with universal energy from beyond the top of our heads. This cyclic motion brings renewed energy but can also stagnate.

We are in training so to speak, during this life time, to release the old and make room for receiving new energy constantly; establishing, recognising and consciously helping our minds to maintain a continuous flow of energy. We receive new energy through all of our chakras into every cell of our bodies, every second of the day and night, but we can aid this process along by consciously visualising receiving new energy from highest source. Creating good Karma means that the energy can flow freely and unhindered throughout our bodies without obstacles. Whilst this energy flow is established as soon as we are alive, you can also consciously connect with the universal energy, and thus learn ways to help you receive the purest energy frequencies through your crown chakra. There are exercises and meditations at the end of this book, which can teach you how to let pure light energies in and let them wash through your body like a beautiful, crystal clear river, releasing stagnant energy blockages all throughout. Every exercise you enter into will be different, every time and it is useful to get used to practising this process over and over until we can do it in our sleep, so to speak. Each time you do this, your mind and body will become more used to the process of allowing only the best, the most helpful frequencies into your system. It will help to clear old Karma, stagnant energy and blockages as we become more aware of what stagnant energy means to us individually. It can express itself in physical symptoms but also visions, insights, even perceiving colours and sounds as well as dealing with external situations differently which helps us to see where we are still not acting out of compassion. You are always in control as to how fast you want this to happen, and it can never be to your detriment.

We can easily learn to bring in pure energy frequencies which our environment provides naturally and in abundance to replenish our chakras. There are plenty of examples at the end of this book. Our physical bodies cannot function without this energy, and exercises such as learning how to properly breathe in 'prana' – life- force energy – in a meditation can work wonders. We can also do this consciously in other situations, for example on a nice walk, feasting our eyes on beautiful places in nature etc. It doesn't have to be complicated and we can do this in a few seconds, or longer when we have learned how to do this effectively as well as created more time to do it in. The more we practice, the easier it gets, and eventually we will become so accomplished that we can channel this energy in ever more difficult situations, not just when the sun is shining and the birds are singing. We do not really need nearly as many external stimuli or buy as many props and gadgets as we think we do. The way we often use them thoughtlessly is not necessarily making us happier anyway. If you want to try it out, you can use the meditation of the single pointed concentration - or Shamata - at the end of this book to help your mind get used to simplicity and generating energy from within.

But when is good Karma not good Karma?

I am certain you don't need me to tell you really, surely it's obvious that good actions, kind words and thoughts are all contributors towards good Karma; but there are a few things we can do that we may not have thought of.

As a rule, it is not skilful to rely on others to provide energy for us, although sometimes we have no choice but to rely on others' kindness, which is a little different. We can offset this with gratitude and a willingness to help them in return, whichever way we are able to. There is a difference also in whether kindness is extended to us by another of their own choosing, or if we tend to use others constantly for everything and become completely dependent on them, even when we can do things for ourselves. That way, we do not learn to live within our own bodies and minds, we are not making good use of them and deny ourselves the chance to create good Karma for ourselves. On our arduous inner journey, we may falsely assume that there is merit in remaining meek and forever fearful of our own inner power and reliant on others; if we deny ourselves trying out what we can do willingly, we may end up repeating this pattern of disempowerment time and time again. Some of us do this and are not even aware of it, in the form of constantly worrying that things are not going their way, that nothing is ever worthy of their effort, that everyone else is to blame etc. In the therapies recommended at the end of this book, there are some simple methods described which help to overcome this mind obstacle easily by simply sitting in an armchair. It can be that simple to rewrite our stories of why we feel we cannot act in a way that suits us best.

On the other end of the scale, we may instead be surrounded by people who rely on us to provide energy for them, even when we have learned ourselves not to repeat the pattern any longer. It is our own Karmic choice to continue to do this, as long as we feel able to. We can examine these relationships for their validity at any time, to see if they remain opportunities for us to help them, or at what point we need to allow the other to become Self-sufficient and responsible for their own good fortune. If we - or they - are not able to let go of the co-dependent sport of 'energy-grabbing' between two independent, healthy and capable adult human beings (we are not talking about children here who are in need of being cared for as long as they are minors), it may be keeping us dependent on one another out of our old friend fear. It does not necessarily create good Karma, it creates habitual behaviour patterns and stagnant conditions where each party might never really find their own inner best way of being. So much so that any of us sometimes end up slipping into leading our lives and loves thinking that this is how it needs to be. There is a difference in being able to rely on each other and demanding each other's attention, getting upset or frustrated when we cannot control them or the situation. This is true for many of us at some point in our lives, whether in relationships with family members, at work, with partners, friends, in social circles and socio-political situations. We would be well advised to try to become aware enough at some point that this way of thinking and behaving based on limiting beliefs and expectations can lead to a lot of disappointment and friction. It does not lead to lasting happiness, which we will eventually come to realise when the other party withdraws their energy from this game of fear, for whatever reason. These interactions have a limited life expectancy. If we experience tensions in our interactions with others in our lives, such as partnerships, family dynamics, friendships, business relationships and so on, it could be more or less due to a game of co-dependency. How would it help to learn more about this positive take on life instead:

When we start to be responsible for taking care of our own Karmic energy body and learn how to heal and sustain it, we can live a more healthy, happy life in harmony with our loved ones. We can learn to free ourselves and others from issues that arise purely from the results of unskilful attachment.

This does not mean that you are not allowed to be with anyone - far from it. The word 'attachment' in a Karmic sense describes situations where we have become dependent on a specific outcome and it is leaving an imprint on our Karmic energy body. We either have an obsession or infatuation with a situation, or the way others behaviour affects us means we cannot remain impartial and detest a situation so strongly that we feel deeply affected by it, whilst at the same time also not being able to recognise that this is going on for us or know how to turn it into a healing experience. This is what's meant by 'attachment' in the case of our Karmic connections to the external: our attachment is based on fears of situations we can't or won't deal with or do not know how to face. There is no judgement against us or anyone else, just simply an observation that our inner energies are somewhat disturbed and out of balance as a result of something that happened to us and how we reacted to it. We might be unaware that it's affecting us, so that our first step is always to acknowledge it. Make a list of everything that has affected you and you will probably be less surprised to learn that all this will affect who we are and how we feel about ourselves, others and the world we live in. The insights we gain simply imply that we can - and deserve to - have healthier relationships with ourselves and others with less stress and arguments. We can do this by learning methods which help towards trying to raise our own energy levels without having to ask for constant assistance from a specific other. Even if we are in a dependent state out of necessity, say for example for health reasons, it may give us a feeling of inner peace and independence that we have longed for. Try it – you might like it!

To speak with the words of HH Dalai Lama – 'Non-Attachment is like the Love you Experience for your First Child.' You see, it sounds confusing – the term 'non-attachment' sounds as if we are not allowed to truly love others – but that's not the case. When we unconditionally love someone, or something, that is called non-attachment. We are in the moment, we are free, our energy within is flowing easily and unhindered. As a result, we are at peace and one with love so we feel less of a need for anything else to make us happy. When we can translate this feeling to most or maybe eventually all our life experiences, we can be in love with life. We will have mastered the art of non-attachment and experience only love. Is that something worth living for, and to experience? You bet.

When we make a decision to eventually start our conscious ascend on our Karmic 'ladder', any energy robbing from people or our environment around us will not feel valid or necessary any longer. Instead, we will perceive all the energy we need as part of our inherent selves to be already present as is, as an existing creation that we have already been a part of. The insights sometimes even appear instantly as soon as we call our energy back from situations outside of ourselves. No matter how 'negative' those external events we have become embroiled in might be, the moment we call our energy back into our bodies to complete ourselves again it will feel better. We do not have to leak out energy, we do not have to 'send' energy - we just have to radiate from within, and to do that, we learn how to complete our inner Karmic energy. From this healing process, we learn to feel whole again and all the world around us will perceive us differently as a result. We can learn to undo behaviour patterns and make good all that we now recognise as being less desirable in our perceived past. We all have the birth right and ability to feel this within, and as we increase our practice to expand the experience, no matter where we start, we will gradually feel less of a need of anything external to replenish us.

Nobody owes it to us to complete us.

Not our mothers, not our fathers, not our partners, not our children. If we release the energy entanglement of the roles we have given others in our lives, we will set them free to be who they need to be in their own right. It does not mean we give up our relationships or family circumstances. It does not mean they will stop caring if they have cared before. On the contrary, relations may vastly improve as a result of how we perceive ourselves and others in a new way. If we are already whole, and working towards owning that completeness, then our sense of being becomes unshakable. We can expand it to all areas of our lives that we have externalised. It's a very exciting piece of wisdom that we can take fully on board and rejoice in, or take it one step at a time if necessary. Take it easy. Be less hard on yourself, question the expectations you have of yourself. Are they really yours? Or have they been instilled in you? There is nothing to prove to anybody and everything to gain by throwing out outmoded belief systems. The process can be a bit like a game of snakes and ladders, and we may achieve inner happiness and good Karma for some of the time, only then to experience times of inner turmoil. This is all normal, and we are all subject to the waxing and waning wave patterns of all physical existence. There is no linear path, everything is cyclic, spiral existence and if we don't do something now, the spiral will do its full turn as it does and come around again. Hopefully, we will take it on board though, as a spiral means that we are going to be a rung up next time on our vibrational inner journey and not going around in ever-decreasing circles. The Yogic Masters would laugh and shrug, telling us to be happy with our inner turmoil, to be calm. Good Karma comes with acceptance, and with acceptance comes insight into how all things are interdependent. I am no further along in my quest than anybody, I simply pass on the wisdom that this is part of the principle of lasting happiness.

Eventually, we will learn to be ok with the good times, and the bad.

Now, there is a very simple and very effective way of directly increasing the good Karma we are creating, too. Listen up, because this is important:

When we are in a state of happiness and are

**simply perceiving something as beautiful
in this very moment, whatever this may be,
we can make a sincere wish that others may
become equally happy, and realise they may
find something equally beautiful in their lives.**

If we truly think about this inner ability we have to change so many things in our lives in accord with our own healing and inner growth, it is an incredible fact that it should even work. It is not only in theory so simple that it is profound, it is in fact essential in practice that we repeat this exercise over and over again, in order to set free the energy tied up within in so we can feel happy. It does not mean that we 'leak' energy from our body in over-dramatic expenditure. Quite the opposite - we feel the happiness with every pore, and then we simply enter the thought to allow this happiness to be felt by everyone and everything, everywhere. It feels a lot like ripples in a pond – the stone drops in the centre of the pond, causing ripples of energy waves to start radiating out from the central energy created by the stone falling into the pond. When pure universal energy finds its way into our body from our crown it feels amazing, it gets transformed into happiness as it lights up our hormone centres. The more you practice this, the more you are sending out ripples, you shine and naturally radiate. Others will naturally feel this. The stronger the energy flow is that you can allow to circulate within you, the more others will feel it, and the further away others can feel it, too. Ever heard that one person can't change the world? Yes, you can. Start a wave - a wave of happiness; and start it within yourself. See what happens.

There is a wonderful book I once read, it is simply called 'The Garden' by Michael Geshe Roach. I read it many times over and always found some other aspect I needed to re-learn. It describes the principles of attachment, good Karma and happiness very beautifully in vivid images. I remember clearly how the protagonist lives years in search of a woman he once met, who becomes his elusive muse. The ending is profound, and so simple that we are reminded how life is staring us in our face all the time, in all the smallest details. The gist is that there is nothing to search for. It is already there. We don't need to act big, we simply have to notice how we are already radiating and keep renewing the process. You go shine.

Everything good that happens to us, even the tiniest little thing, can become a catalyst to initiate a habit within us, which is to wish others to see/feel/experience the same happiness it brought us. Start a habit of happiness.

You can steadily build on the experience of wishing your good feelings, your observations of happiness, your radiating goodness and the good Karma you have accrued for others, too, ever more sincerely and increasingly effectively, happily and continuously every time, without regret, resentment or feeling overwhelmed. This way, you can slowly start to share not just small glimpses of true inner happiness in your life, but larger parts, too.

Whatever actions we deem we are capable of doing from moment to moment in order to commit to creating only good Karma, there is an important add-on that we can learn to set our energy free to be what and where it needs to become, so that it can best work to determine our benefit and automatically that of others, too. Imagine the Karmic energy you created within through your diligent practice of good actions, good thoughts, good words you have given to others, but you are holding on to it tightly within in fear or losing something that you cherish. What if you realised that this energy can multiply? What if you set it free, not to forever lose it or simply give it away, but to realise that what you have created has the power to grow and expand according to its nature and the direction you give it? This process is an important insight of many spiritual practices. In this instance, I will stick to the terminology given in Buddhist texts, which roughly translate into the word 'dedication'.

Dedicating the good karmic energy you created by your actions is an energy transformation. We are making a dedication with our conscious effort of increasing the outcome of this good energy by allowing it to expand beyond our own confines. A dedication can be made at the end of any period of creating good Karma for ourselves and others, short or long. For example, when you have finished your practice of creating good Karma by radiating happiness that we started above, simply dedicate it afterwards, by saying in your own words that you sincerely wish for others to experience the same. You can add a visualisation of what it means to you when you say 'others' by including all who you care about, all who you have met, those who you have never met, those who are suffering. Whatever you start with, start with something you believe in whilst including 'All Sentient Beings', even if you are not able to visualise them. The time will come when we can do this. You can then also transfer this principle to any situation you like that creates something good in your life, because all of these have already manifested due to your good Karma. You can set the energy free to multiply all the time, every time you experience something positive! When you see good friends, make a dedication. When you have good family, make a dedication. When you have fresh, healthy food and clean water, make a dedication. When you have medicine, and clean air to breathe, make a dedication that everyone shall be able to have this, too. It is like an offering and a prayer that it is set free and can radiate out from you. It is an incredibly powerful tool for transforming your own and others' energy. If you give a gift, you dedicate the act of giving. You make a wish that the gift is going to make someone very happy, and that the happiness increases exponentially. You can even do this: link an imaginary level, like a movie in your head. If you have seen something beautiful, dedicate your perception and your good luck for having noticed it. We also learn some important principles in life: gratitude for every tiny thing that comes our way. We learn to perceive things as they are created from good practice. We learn not to take things for granted, and we learn gratitude and awe for being alive and everything that exists.

W we have started to look at how we are fortunate enough to create good Karma; it is by no means always a given that we truly get what this means. Not everyone will be in a position to create good future outcomes and it helps to realise we are already at an advantage if we can. What this also means in this context, is that we understand more and more how interconnected everything is that results in what we do, say and think. We create with our actions, and from the result of good actions will be born the recognition that we are all looking for the same, we are all united in that we are looking to be happy, and we all need to learn how best to create this happiness for ourselves.

Nothing outside of ourselves inherently exists. All phenomena are created as a result of interdependent creation.

The concept is called 'interdependent origination'; meaning that everything has been created because of previous action, and if there is a lack of understanding, there will be a creation of lesser benefit to each involved. If we keep buying certain things without thinking, this will have an effect on our environment. Fossil fuel, plastics for our every increasing desire for instant and fanciful foods and drink, deforestation for our demand of paper products, air travel and so on. As I am re-editing, we are in the throws of the worldwide 2020 coronavirus outbreak. As predicted aeons before, we will not be able to eat money, soon enough. You could just read over this and think that our actions are benign and the end justifies the means, but since it's nature's Law of Karma that underlies everything we are, and everything that will be, there are consequences for our wrongful and meaningless actions. People just don't generally want to be reminded, just how one Swedish teenager enrages an aged US president becomes synonymous for our inner voice reprimanding us for our actions, whilst the devil on our shoulder seduces us to not care or worse, get enraged and act all entitled to deflect from the fact we are all responsible. Our perception of others and our environment is directly influenced by how we well we understand this Law and see through what presents itself externally, how much of it we have adjusted accordingly so far and how we can apply its logic and truth to all that happens now and in the future. It's really not that difficult. If we shout at someone because we do not understand them, they will walk away and possibly never want to talk to us again. The connection with that being is interrupted. It is down to individual Karmic circumstances whether we meet them again in this lifetime or in another, and whether circumstances allow for a better outcome. We have a responsibility in that we cannot complain that someone is angry with us because we have played a part in this. Since they walked away confused and misunderstood, they are left to their own devices and their inner Karmic tools to resolve this for themselves if we won't help. We have a chance to resolve the situation instantly by explaining why we reacted the way we did, find a solution to it, and resolving the energy disruption within ourselves. If both parties can approach each other to do this, then there is no longer a Karmic issue. The Karmic negativity is dissolved and things may improve. You can also apply this to our environment, not just people. If we want to know how our unresolved Karmic residue is affecting our planet, then we only need to look around. Our planet is a perfect representation of the microcosm we have within us. The rivers are our blood streams, nature is our heart, the air we breathe our thoughts. We have built roadways with solid tarmac criss-crossing the earth as our thoughts have become more convoluted and calcified. Our rivers are polluted as our arteries are clogged with greed. Our beautiful and important rainforests are burning, like the hearts we have that are hardening from the lack of compassion and foresight that exists. We no longer find enough time for musing, we rush around stressed in little angry-sounding vehicles representing our repressed anger at having to go round in circles whilst our habitual actions are no longer guided by wisdom. The air we breathe is only pure for so long as we can keep our minds still and calm and as we distance ourselves with scorn from each other we crave warmth, not realising that the warmth we have created with fossil fuels to feel cared for and secure in each of our isolated homes is not the warmth we need but has instead been melting our ice caps. Not knowing any longer the ancient passed-down ways of how to live in tune with nature, grow our food and look for her gifts already there to heal us, we are dependent on chemicals, surgery and vaccines to keep us alive, powerless with weakened immune systems unable to fight the same chemicals that create bacteria, poisons and viruses that will kill us in the end. Everything we process in industries designed for commerce will end up meaningless in leaking landfill, poisoning our Earth as we continue to consume mindlessly in search for meaning in our lives. If we realise that nobody tidies up for us, we might also understand what it means when we continue to consume something that has been made by sacrificing nature or other living beings. We kill out of our own fears of not remaining alive. We create waste and negative Karma which we remain responsible for, whether we like it or not, whether we are aware of it or not, whether we get angry about having it pointed out or not. If we accept that responsibility rather than shun it, then a solution can be found more readily for all involved, especially when folk finally recognise this on a large scale. We can then also start to apply this to all that has happened to us in our lifetimes, and examine where the resulting fears that we are left with are still akin to the waste in our world.

It is on the outside as it is within; once our inner disturbances are smoothed out, we can have a different thought pattern again, one that will support us and have good repercussions on how we live with others harmoniously in a thriving ecosystem. We need to recognise that everyone and everything is connected and live accordingly; also that we logically must have had lifetimes before this one with less mindful actions if we are still having trouble clearing up within in this lifetime. You see, far from blaming anyone or beating ourselves up, it is simply about seeing truth, and that truth will set us free, giving us methods to rise above and connect again to all the Karmic energy we lost. When we reconnect our Karmic energy to the whole, we will have everything we need in order to function well, create more good Karma and be awake enough to see what needs to be done. In order to undo the damage we can see again that every resource we have can be reused, nothing ever goes to waste, and with knowledge, compassion and wisdom we will prevail as we always do, but we cannot live our lives like it is our god-given right to destroy everything and everyone around us without there being karmic repercussions because it's simply not true.

We can increase good Karma by acts of giving, such as dedicating some of our time, energy and maybe even our money to others. How precious do you feel your money is? You could do some work for a charity or visit a nursing home for free and find out the true worth of yourself without connecting to money. Donate a part of your wages to a true cause and see how it feels. All this effort makes your energy system, your thoughts and beliefs become familiar with releasing stagnant energy. The act of giving, especially unconditional giving, encourages the inner energies to start flowing again, and your body becomes free to take in new energy from the highest source. Make sure it's from the highest source of Selflessness by consciously determining your energy source, by asking only for the best and most helpful and pure clear energies to enter your body.

Again, generous giving is not to be mixed up with 'leaking' energy from your body, which can make you ill. It also should not be confused with creating dependencies as mentioned before, which some form of conditional giving is definitely subject to. True giving is followed by a sensation of releasing energy blockages, leaving only happiness and the good feeling of having created something new, establishing a healthy rhythm of naturally releasing and renewing energy, becoming aware of our own vast Karmic energy stores within and learning how to radiate and complete those even more, without ever losing any good energy. We are never in danger of making a mistake, if we are learning not to expect any energy from others or leaning on any external instance to resolve things for us; rather, we are simply using the most profound power of all as a resource: the power of our Karmic minds connecting with the greater mind. This is exactly what frees us from past Karmic blockages, and will create better conditions within ourselves, with the result that our surroundings change for the better, too, when the Karmic timing is right. We can then grow our giving exponentially, by being aware of how huge a scale of interconnectedness it can create.

Nobody has ever got poor just by giving.
(Anne Frank)

Even if we may initially feel like we are not making a huge difference to other's lives, small steps might be what's needed in the beginning. They are just as important to take as the ones on a larger scale later. It is almost always worth more to give something small willingly and wholeheartedly, than to give something which we resent having to let go of and then regret giving. The former creates good Karma, the latter not so much. Does that come as a surprise? It shouldn't, because you can probably tell that resentment means that the energy is reversed and is refusing to leave us! So it might be good to wait until we no longer feel regret or resentment, better still to work on our reasons why in order to clear our energy. It is a new undertaking for us after all! It can be exciting, fresh and well worth taking the time to do, even if it feels strange and new. I remember my young daughter pouring out all she had in her purse for homeless people without a thought. That kind of giving is what we are talking about, the giving from the heart that knows it's a good thing to give, and the right giving will create abundance, not poverty. The energy those pennies had gave me tears, as each of them carried the love and care from a child who gave unconditionally. Should we not all remember what it's like to feel like that again?

One of the more important aspects of this exercise is for us to learn to give without attachment. We need to learn that the old, stagnant negativity released from our Karmic minds and bodies has to well and truly transform in order for the new, fresh energy, prana or chi to flow through unhindered. Did you know that a simple first exercise for understanding generosity is to pass a piece of fruit from one hand to the other? It seems silly, doesn't it? And yet, it explains energy transference to our body really quite well.
A physical object has left one state of being, and by our focus and attention, it has reached another. It is still the same object, but in another state of being. The concept is well worth contemplating and also practising. After all, we are still trying to change our Karmic energy mind. We are opening up to mindfulness through the concept of giving, and the act of giving means that something leaves, in order to learn to trust that energy flows and more useful and abundant energy forms can come to us. Another cultural act of giving is to set up an area like an altar or shrine where offerings can be made; sometimes actual, some in the form of prayer. We are projecting mind images of the highest form into the space in front, and are asking that these will be repeated for us, over and over, as good Karma. By refreshing and replenishing the objects on the shrine regularly, preferably daily, we are also reminding ourselves of its symbolic representation of continuously checking our inner world to see where energy is stuck and needs to be passed on to make room for the new. We often take for granted the simple things we need for survival, such as food and water (two forms, one for drinking, one for washing), warmth, medicine and fresh, clean air, so some cultures represent these and their impermanence (often represented by flowers) by symbolically placing and renewing them on their prayer table every day. They also add a symbol for sound, meaning that it is important for us to

remind us to ask for the purity of frequencies to help us stay well and/ or heal. It is the greater mind principle behind it which matters, to see that in the physical world we need to continuously renew our sources so as not to become stagnant, and create continuation of our life-giving resources by becoming mindful of them. It's a great and simple exercise to start off with, too, and everyone can do it.

✳ ✳ ✳

27. Karma and Outcome Attachment

If we are still attached to the old comfort zone or are thinking of any specific outcome, a wholesome energy renewal cannot take place. A partial or temporary energy renewal might take place, but an energy residue stays behind that is still equivalent to the resistance we hold within, like a child who does not want to share or give away their security object. Usually, we are not aware we want to hold on so tightly to our gift of being able to renew our energy, but there is something in the analogy of a child who might be forced to give up their comfort zone too soon. Perhaps we have had those experiences many times in our lifetimes. Perhaps some of them were traumatic. Most of us who have these and other energy blockages feel anxious when they are presented with change and having to keep in motion. It's actually quite normal. The brain cannot compute what happens if we open up yet and acts out of fear instead, always holding on to things just in case there is a shortage of resources. It's a safety mechanism we can become aware of. If you are scared to let go or are subconsciously blocking the process, simply become aware of this fact, and accept it. Treat yourself kindly, especially when you know what it is that is blocking you from moving on and evolving. We don't need to deny it or reject ourselves for the fact. We are all in the same boat, so we may as well have a good look at what is going on within. Ask yourself WHERE this fear of letting something go feels stuck in your body and WHY. What is the nature of the thing that you are afraid of, exactly? Usually it's just a part of us that is scared, not the real 'us'. Locate it, determine it, shine your light onto it, shake hands with it, make friends with it. Perhaps we were made to give up too many things as a child? Perhaps we missed out? Perhaps we were coerced into giving things we could not afford to lose? Perhaps we lost someone close to us, or were forced to move from an environment we felt safe in, to a worse place, physical or metaphorically speaking. There is absolutely no need to ignore it or put on a brave face, or grin and bear it and give up reluctantly. There would be much less merit in that even though life often cruelly forces us to do just that anyway. If you take your act of giving your inner concerns time first and examine the feelings it brings up within you, then this is a good thing in terms of recognising our Karma and our possible Karmic blockages. For example, if your thought pattern concerns your worries around money and that you could not possibly donate anything to others because it feels like not enough will be coming in to replace it, you can learn to recognise and then simply accept that you still live your life in a great deal of fear of not being able to survive. I chose this particular issue as most of us will probably relate. There is no need to beat yourself up about it. Accept that it is so, fully and wholeheartedly, at that particular moment in time. Or, another example, you might perceive yourself as not being worthy of others giving you love and attention. Again, the process of acceptance is the same, and change follows acceptance naturally and automatically. It may take a while to recognise and name our blockages, use the right methods to change our habits and learn to not take our stuck ways of looking at life at face value, but the methods given at the end of this book really do help us and as if by magic do all the hard work for us. What's not to like. Coming back to the act of giving and loving unconditionally which we started in the last chapter. Compare the pocket money a child wants to give freely, to the energy of giving more money but with the intentions of not setting it free. holding it back somehow, attaching conditions to it that we grown-ups have become so accustomed to doing. For example, I have always found it interesting to observe how people respond to someone begging in the street. I have often heard people say something like: 'these people should not be there, they are fake, they earn a lot more money than us, they should get a job, they only spend it on drink and drugs' and so on. Which individual has set more energy free, the child giving wholeheartedly, feeling connected to whoever it is they give to, or the begrudging adult?

One of the Karmic truths underlying learning how to give unconditionally is this:

People will cross our path so we can practice our unconditional giving.

Increasing energy flow is far from naïve, silly or childish. It is a very accomplished form of practice which we all need to learn. How do we learn, though?

We should really all have T-shirts made that say: 'I need to practice unconditional giving'! As it is, unconditional giving does not depend on the recipient in front of us. We might be standing in front of a highly accomplished being who recognises our unselfish act and is able to increase our kindness a thousandfold, how would we know? How do we know when the tables might be turned, and we might need the connection to that being as much as they need ours, now? How do we know our luck might not change and we find ourselves in the same position as them? When we see Karma as the endless spiral of existence that it is, where nothing is a coincidence and we are all connected, then we will see the benefit of giving what we can, in each moment. How truly unconditional it will turn out to be depends whether we recognise the learning opportunity as the perfect one we need at that moment in time, in order for us to learn to give unconditionally. If it is a beggar we deem undeserving, the antidote is to realise with gratitude that this is our very own manifestation, on our journey to learning to give and receive Karmic energy unconditionally on an even greater scale. We don't always get to be in control, we don't always get to choose the situations in life where we can give because we are ready to. We are not all celebrities in front of a camera flaunting charitable causes. Giving someone in need right across from you, right in front of you, when there is nobody to applaud you, it is between you and the Universe whether you pass the test. Remember the piece of fruit in your hands? This might be the next level. Try not to fail at the second hurdle but if you do, if you did already, many times, know that there will be many more opportunities to repeat the same lesson over and over again. All you will have to try and do is remember that this is what they are - our lessons, and also great opportunities to increase our good Karma. Trials are not necessarily sent to hurt you or trip you up. You may just not have recognised the signs of the nudge you needed before. All that it has been trying to make you feel and truly understand is that the person asking you for help, is the pin on your very own inner map app of where you need to be right now. Be grateful instead of resentful, it's easier. If you want to not give anything, or truly can't at that moment in time, ask for the being in front of you to be taken care of some other way. Give your blessings, give your sympathy. Ask for another opportunity to come along shortly where you can give more. Ask for good conditions, too, such as you recognising this lesson in connection with your vow to deal with it then. Remember, there are always much worse situations to be in and we don't know where we will be in a day, a month, a year's time. By creating good Karma unconditionally, we make connections between people and create serendipitous conditions in the future. I have spoken to many people who learned the meaning of gratitude and generosity only under the harshest conditions. We can recognise how to create good Karma right here, right now, and without having to learn the hard way. How lucky are we? We are still in a position where we can give and don't have to beg for survival.

When we are able to drop our attachment to particular outcomes, we can apply the concept to so many areas of our lives and combine it with creating a different outcome:The good Karma of mindfulness; of abundance; of giving; of prayer - and of avoiding Karmic damage, even. There is much to be said about removing obstacles on our future path of existence, definitely something we should put on our wish list.

An aspect of how we separate ourselves from others and our own abundance is that we often ask: 'What's in it for me?' This is, of course, another form of attachment, a fear that is based on our inability to recognise or trust the process. We do not trust that more can come to us than we can imagine ourselves to deserve to receive, so therefore we still believe we need to hang on to controlling thoughts to make absolutely sure that we get something in return. Our whole system of exchanging currency is based on this fear that we won't get anything in return! Our fear is causing a short circuit within us, which is making us believe our limiting thoughts and those that others are trying to make us believe. It's up to us how compliant we want to be to the demands of not only others, but also our own thoughts and experiences working against our best interests.

The act of sharing does not block abundance, rather the energy disruption that has created our internal fear of not getting anything back in return does. Wherever our fear stems from, this is what is stopping our energy from flowing freely and so it becomes a Self-fulfilling prophecy: we fear not getting anything back, the fear blocks our abundant flow and as a result we don't, so the effect of our act of giving is lessened by our fear. We then tend to justify not giving anything because we have not seen it work for us. If we can see through this, then that's a great first step, because we can learn methods to help us to allow the energy of generosity to circulate. It should also be mentioned that giving does not limit itself to giving money. We can give our time, we can give food, we can give shelter, advice, a shoulder to cry on. Our inner process of letting go - letting in, I prefer to call it - allows energy to start to flow freely through our mind and body again, until we finally can consciously let go of this fear of not surviving, of not having this energy, with all our love. If it helps, play with the idea first in your mind, like a child would get to know a new toy: with curiosity and full attention learning something new. That is how it works best of all.

You can ask for any action you take in that way to have the best, the highest, the most abundant possible outcome for all involved, and then set the thought free.

Again, we are learning to slowly get away from focusing on physical aspects alone, so we can remember that our Karmic mind is already omnipotent and can create a good outcome. When our Karmic energy is stuck, we usually are stuck in our physical circumstances, too, and generosity helps us to loosen those inner energy knots.

Even if you can only give a small amount, you imagine in your mind for it to increase in energy. It works! Look at how the opposite so far has worked as well: if you felt guilty that you could only give 50 pence to a poor person, you already have proof that this is exactly what it will stay at: guilty giving. If you imagine that this amount increases many times and can do so much good, you will set it free to be used to its greatest potential. In a small child's mind, coins are all the same, they do not have an individual value. Our minds have only grown to accept the fact that there is a certain value to certain coins. It's a fact that is amazing to realise: we can change the value of physical items any time with our mind by expanding our understanding of the connection between the coin, the unconditional giving, and the process of the mind energy increasing the value of the act of giving. All of those three together with all obstacles removed, become ultimate potential and infinitely powerful. If only we knew how powerful our minds were, we would use them more often. You can try it: next time you hold a coin in your hand, notice how you are immediately attaching a certain value to it by habit. But what if that coin holds so much more power? If you increase its value by giving it with the thought that it has the potential to grow, then this very coin could be priceless. i have often travelled abroad to poorer countries where the value of our currency is increased, and a small amount that we might see as nothing in our country is seen as huge amounts in another. The value can easily be seen to be relative as we watch how currencies fluctuate on the currency exchange or stock market. There is no intrinsic value to the coin itself, only the value we put on it. We base it also on what we can buy for it, and as the value of currency diminishes, its buying power becomes less and less. We are therefore further misled by having to accrue more and more of it in order to buy what we need to survive. And before you know it, we have forgotten that it's all created with our minds, or rather, those who are manipulating our minds into thinking that money is worth pursuing. We can change it. We put our own value on each coin. Our hard labour is already defining how we feel about money as we have tied our life energy to earning it. But what if each coin can contain our actual energy, our powerful inner energy that creates everything in the first place? If we give something to another being - and it does not have to be a coin - we can attach a different outcome to it, not one where we give it begrudgingly and reduce its value. If we give it, knowing how huge an influence it potentially has, how much of a difference it can make in others' lives, how powerful we are for the fact that we can give something of great, even infinite value to another, then it will work, for the benefit of all. Why limit its value when the value of our genuine gesture can have the outcome of infinitely more.

* * *

28. Expanding Our Understanding of Karma

I am sure you will understand by now - and perhaps even agree and be excited by the idea - that Karma is a living, flowing, universal energy force; it fluctuates and can be changed by the power of our intention, motivation, actions, thoughts and words. It is not set in stone. It can even be changed instantly. It is always useful, though, if at some point in our lives we experience some sort of insight and become aware of the reasons for being who we are as a result of our Karmic actions. Glimpses of insight can come along when we are not looking for them, even when we least expect them. Sometimes they present in a highly dramatic way, during life-changing experiences such as, for example, giving or witnessing birth, and many other poignant moments in our lives. They can also appear in those life events which we would rather avoid, such as accidents, illness or even near-death experiences. Even - or especially - these close-calls can all act as moments for Self-realisation, despite their more traumatic aspects. I have learned first-hand several times now that a part of us connects with the invisible universal energy force above and around us much more during those times when our survival is being tested. I am not sure what the reason for this is, perhaps there is a connection between our adrenaline producing endorphins during times of great stress, so that other bodily functions shut down. A friend who was in a near-fatal accident in the fast lane of a busy three-way motorway reported that, as her car was spinning around having been hit by another car trying to pass hers, she was 'carried upwards' by 'three light beings'. She came back into her body once her car stood still and was safe, and became aware that all cars around her had miraculously managed to stop and nobody got hurt. She did not even have a single bruise on her. Many similar reports exist of people avoiding near-misses and reporting that they, too, were 'carried' to a higher dimension - too many cases to ignore even by the greatest sceptics. I come from the understanding that we are always connected in this way, but are not usually using our every-day intellectual processes to form a constant awareness of this connection. However, we are made to remember it at certain times more than others. I have always observed a huge positive change and shift in those who reported these experiences, after they were shown who they truly are and what they are connected to and capable of. It's something I believe we can bring about more often, if in a much gentler way, using the methods described here.

A more prophylactic way of experiencing insights can be utilised by using methods to ease ourselves more gently into the experience of interconnectedness. We may feel more in charge that way and less fearful, since we can consciously ask for and examine the truths within. At certain auspicious times it can happen that we are able to access higher realms more easily so that many insights arrive all at once, similar to watching our life/lives pass before us. After all, we have a Karmic record of all we have been before, it's just that we tend to forget how to tune into in our mundane every-day lives. At other times, our Karmic insights unfold more gradually, so that we get a chance to take a deep breath between such poignant revelations; which, to my own admittance, is not always what happened when I started my inner journey! At times, it can seem like a never-ending roller-coaster of information on what our Karmic journey has been so far. I consider myself lucky to have had insights into many good experiences and how this has shaped my current existence, but I must have at some point agreed to be shown all my shortfalls in past lives so I could recognise and clear them once and for all...I can be a glutton for punishment, but I found it useful to learn how ignorant and downright lowly my actions on my past life path had been at times. It was not always a pleasant experience to be confronted with, however, I am eternally grateful that I was shown my inner path. If i had not had the opportunity to see the error of my ways, I now know I would not have got to being alive in this body and mind, today. Through my practice of applying methods to assist my quest, I came to terms and got used to regularly being shown truths from past lives, some happy and some not so much, and I eventually saw the sense and realised the gift in both. I also noticed as a result that there is no use complaining and still trying to blame circumstances or even someone else for any of it. Once I was shown the connections from my past to the present, I could no longer ignore them. They were no longer hidden and became a conscious part of who I am now.

I had to realise that I now had a precious opportunity to face my Karma and be accountable for my past actions. Luckily, at the same time some fantastic methods opened up for me to help me take the sting out of any negative past Karmic actions. I could have carried on living in denial pretending that the events I was shown and things that I did never happened, a choice that many people take when it all gets too much. But I didn't want to dismiss the precious insights I was given, and I saw that this is something we all have in common: we are all still trying to brush some of the more uncomfortable results of our previous actions under the carpet. Since nobody else can see the connections and most people don't even believe in them, we also don't realise that by not acknowledging our true nature, we are trading in our full insight and wisdom for a lesser conscious lifetime. It seemed like such a waste of our potential in light of the Karmic energies within us that I had also been shown, the promise of a beautifully bright, luminous existence. I craved being back there so much once I was shown, so that I was willing to do what was needed in order to make this state of mind more permanent within myself. I knew I had to cast out some demons from the past before I could get to experience this state of bliss more often. If we are not happy with our lives now, we could do worse than find out why we feel this way by looking into our past before this lifetime. The Magic of it is that the instant we agree to find out more about it, can see it for what it is and undo the ties that still bind us to it, we can leave the past behind once and for all, set ourselves free and be more present in this moment. It makes sense, does it not – but it is not so easy as it sounds to find and unpick the threads to our own undoing. There is nobody else out there who can do this for us, nobody in the sky saying that we are or aren't a certain way and whether this is right or wrong. There is no judge, no jury. We are free the instant we allow ourselves to connect again to our higher Karmic Self, especially when there is no longer Karmic debris in the way. There is only ever our own inner Karmic memory trying to nudge us over and over again to find out our truth. We have, of course, a personal choice whether to go there, or not; whether to believe in any of the concepts to do with past lives, or not. But I had been aware for a while that if I chose to not look at it, it would continue to manifest in external situations I might then not have any influence over them at all. This way, I could consciously choose to be more in charge of my own destiny. Leaving it unattended and unresolved, it would have repeated the same patterns over and over again, and each time I would be creating yet another scenario, making it increasingly complicated to know where it came from in the first place. Who knows if I would ever be in a position again to work things out this way. I am aware that we are in an advantageous position right now, even if we do feel sore and sorry for ourselves for what has been done to us, on many occasions. However, I did realise that if I never had that chance again to overcome personal pain, I believe that would be worse than anyone ridiculing the process and telling me I am wrong to feel the way I feel. I am happy to share what I found out, so you are able to feel empowered to make your own decisions more easily.

I am not saying that our Karmic memory has it in for us, and neither does the greater mind or universal energy which merges with us at times to replenish our energy resources and remind us where we came from. These are powerful, sentient forces but they are also benign, meaning they don't have intentions to do good or bad either way. Our Karmic memory is based on energy that polarises into positive, neutral and negative gears; when there are negative elements, it just repeats the broken record over and over until we 'get it' and learn to neutralise the issues of what is bugging us so much within so we can move on from restricting circumstances in the 3-d world we live in.

I don't believe that anybody escapes this inner Karmic facing-up-to-our-selves. We will all have done things we later regret, even the best of us. There are mechanisms that can change our Karmic energy wiring within, to help us find what we are dealing with, what we have done that might have hurt other sentient beings and vow to learn to act with insight and wisdom in future. Our 'conscience' becomes clear as we take responsibility for our actions. Is our 'conscience' and 'subconscious' not interlinked with our Karmic record somehow? It seems that it is, and perhaps it is our subconscious that feeds into our moral compass. Perhaps the nature of our subconscious is actually quite similar to what I have termed our Karmic memory in this book. Perhaps they are both part of our memory mind, linked by energy frequencies that ebb and flow, rising up at times to be cleared and hidden away deeply at others. If we can access our subconscious and make the necessary connections to our past Karmic actions, then we will find the key to unlocking our own Karmic history. I believe that may be the reason for the serenity of all of the masters who I have met in my life, who seem to have a beautiful aura of humility about them. They are always ready to be humble about their origins, to admit that they are only human. They do not put themselves above anyone else, punish themselves or others. At the same time, they have a very highly developed conscience, cognisance, conscientiousness and conscious awareness of the inner state of their minds, and the minds of the whole of mankind. Having practised all their lives the art of understanding how things are interconnected, taking time to find out who we truly are and where we come from is an inherent part of this practice. As a result, those who find the answers within naturally stay away from any deviant action and also translate this peaceful stance from the state of their Karmic mind into their actions, speech and thoughts. The purification of those three 'doors', as they are also known – action, speech and thought – can serve as a measure of the condition of our inner Karmic energy system. When we have developed wrong thoughts, or wrong speech, even wrong action, it is time to look at our inner world and ask ourselves where they come from. At that point, if we pay a lot of careful attention as to what has been happening within, we will find clues in our past as to why we are violating not only our own bodies and minds with wrongful behaviour, but may also be ensnaring or even endangering others with our unresolved

Karmic issues. If we chose not to take this step, there would be so many repercussions, one of which is that we continue to see others as responsible for how we are acting, thinking and feeling. The instant we decide to look inwards at our own issues and resolve them on a Karmic energy level, our Karma becomes purified and our own suffering alleviated. We - and others - would benefit from the fruits of our good efforts immediately. This does not mean we have to beat ourselves up or be constantly apologetic about how lowly our existence is. That would be counterproductive to being in charge of our own destiny and is not necessary. If we managed to truly help our minds develop inner happiness by eliminating our obstacles, we would not feel the need to inflict suffering on others. We would no longer have to reflect our problems onto others. We can also learn to stop the guilt trip and realise that we are worth the inner effort of becoming happy and peaceful.

The first and last suffering we need to address is the torture we inflict on ourselves and others by not recognising our unskilful actions over aeons of time. We can better use this energy by learning how we can constructively make peace within ourselves and all around, once and for all.

When we think of the Karmic potential we all have, what we theoretically could achieve with so many good people on this planet, it must make us wonder why our good Karma, peace and happiness hasn't really been rolling out yet on a large scale. I have a few observations and considerings to offer of my own in this chapter. There are many questions open to reflection, and I welcome everyone to add their own ideas, because I have noticed that there seems to be an elephant in the room on Earth, the million dollar question that everyone who may be contemplating their own Karma might come across: what if at some point - even if it was lifetimes ago - we ourselves and not somebody else, did commit a horrible, unspeakable crime? It is undeniably a 'what if?' question with huge implications that we cannot ignore. Since we have all existed endless lifetimes, the statistical likelihood exists that any of us, in some form or another, may have subscribed to killing others. It does not even seem so far-fetched when we look around and see that there are plenty of people in this world still prepared right now in this so-called civilised age, to pull the trigger on others or attack another aggressively in some way, for some reason or other. For some, those lifetimes where we killed another may not have been so long ago.
First of all, we need to also remind ourselves that the benign universe itself does not judge. Rather, it discerns by the distinction of duality, by the divisiveness of attraction and repulsion of energy. However, because

the seemingly invisible, long-term effect of Karmic reckoning and re-percussion is not so easy for us to grasp, we have created the need for a justice system on Earth. We have limited our belief systems based on face value, which is partial and temporary and by its very nature flawed in its concept. We cannot always judge whether someone is guilty of something or not, if we do not have proof. Many still think that if they get away with something in the eyes of the law, they can simply forget their wrong-doing ever existed. However, because this is not the case and our inner Karmic record continues to hang on to the skeletons in our closets, any unresolved issues accumulated over lifetimes make it much harder for us to trace where they originated form. We might know that there could be some truth in it, simply because as a result, we also have created a bit of a mess on Earth that we can no longer oversee. Even with historic accounts of events, it is not enough to create a com-plete overview of who did what, making it so difficult and sometimes even impossible to keep record or find resolutions for the conflicts that exist on Earth. Is it not logical to assume that our previous actions that we are no longer aware of contribute to the situations we find ourselves in? Does some of it seem so unjust and unfairly distributed, perhaps simply because we cannot trace back into past lives as to who did what, who started it, who is at fault and who suffered as a result? Systems that have limited concepts of the unlimited whole existence of life and the energies that exist beyond life can only work to a limited extent in terms of allowing us to understand the whole picture. It's obvious how frustrated we are by this, but perhaps our real anger has a deeper cause: we want to remember why we are at the receiving end of all that hurts us. There is a catch, though: even if we did spend precious years trying to find out what happened, we would still come to the same conclusion: We have all been victims, and we have probably almost all of us likely been perpetrators, too, even if we don't especially warm to the idea. If we use this simple insight and apply it to every-day life, we might find more peace within and come to the conclusion much quicker that there is no point carrying on fighting – at all. It simply takes the wind out of our sails, but perhaps that has to happen for us all to feel we are all fa-cing the same issues, over and over again, until everyone gets it. These insightful moments make a crucial difference: they serve a purpose and can help to remind us how we can resolve issues amongst everyone, but we have to nevertheless develop our own talents and commit to becom-ing self-reliant to find Truth, rather than blindly trusting that external systems can do this for us all. The danger of justice systems that explain and deal with only a part of who we are and how we think life works ra-ther than how it really works, is that we forget that they merely repre-sent a tiny part of the whole cosmos. Its concepts are based on belief systems which may not be able to explain the magnitude of life in sim-ple terms. Over time, this has led us to believe we want instant justice instead of Karma, external resolution instead of inner insights. Parables, limited descriptions, complicated terminology or too many cryptic clues left us demanding the opposite: instant gratification, 'concrete' facts, visible and tangible results and legislation were put into place to ensure vindication for those who were wronged. We became more agitated the less answers we had and made our anxiety manifest its demands from an externalised system. The system was created by the templates of a limited perception range in our brains. We made the decision that we would outsource our responsibilities for our own actions, thoughts and communication. We put other people in charge of running everything to do with civil matters as well as criminal, in the hope that there would be relief for victims and punishment for criminals. But a system is flawed by nature and cannot ever fully provide this. Neither can the people that work within it, despite how qualified they might be. Nobody is able to tell how someone else's Karma is working its way through their system, and whereas some people work for the greater good, others are still doing quite the opposite. As much as we want to, on Earth it seems we are not all suddenly on the same page as the rest of humankind, and we are not all suddenly homogeneously acting with kindness and compassion. We probably won't ever fully know how Karma exists in all detail, and whilst we miss being at one with everyone else around us and have such longing for another, a family or community where we feel at peace, it looks like we cannot expect everyone else to feel, react and believe the same at the same time. Religious and political systems have tried to homogenise humans into all the same behaviour which ended up in rigid, even aggressive political, social and religious constructs. Templates, belief systems and structures are only helpful if the beings within them are treated in a humane way and remain humane. As soon as its compromised by the intentions of those wishing to exploit, the system becomes destructive and collapses, often taking many lives with it.

There are also people who have introduced similarly rigid systems for straightening us out on an inner level, but perhaps we should be cautious as to wonder why they have an attachment to us submitting to doing so. There is a difference between offering ways to ease suffering by understanding and helping each other more, and the way some people express their need of others to be different by their definition of what they perceive to be right and wrong. This way of seeing things in black or white has brought much destruction to the world over aeons of time, and as a result, many have been forced into submission, fear for their and their families lives, repent their beliefs, tortured and even killed for their chosen way of life. The mistake does not lie in the diversity that life brings on Earth, it lies with the way we do not see through the limited understanding we have through our brains' perception. It is certainly evident that we all have our differences despite obvious similarities, but it is perhaps better that we remind ourselves we are not so dissimilar during times when the whole world is hell-bent on segregation. We feel we must strive for harmony and peace but should we not ask why this is not a given in the first place? I wonder if it might be because it's unrealistic, perhaps even counterproductive to ask this from all others, lest it turn out to sound like a cult demanding obedience.

Will inner peace instead remain elusive, reserved just for a lucky few who are able to free themselves from the inner Karmic conundrums that keep pulling us in the wrong directions, unable to find peace within? If the Karmic justice system is right, then it means everyone will get to see the repercussions of their actions at a point that is down to their individual Karmic determination, and everyone will have a chance to redeem themselves. If this happens at a time according to each being's timeline that they created with their ego-mind, and if that ego-mind is mighty confused, then this means that the timeline will expand, possibly over life-times. If our ego-minds are getting less and less help and support for developing healthy and necessary insights, can it be the system's responsibility alone to teach them? Will people who are offenders, re-offend, or will they comprehend, submitted to punishment? Will their insights grow, will they be ready to be responsible for their actions, or will society continue to have its hands full, making sure constantly that some of the worst culprits are not re-offending and that the number of crimes does not increase? Will our efforts to be kind and make people understand the connections between our thoughts, actions and Karma be rewarded or rejected? Will people ridicule the ideas or rejoice? I think we already have quite an adequate idea of what happens when we try to impose our point of view on another. We only have to look around the world to see how divided people have become in their set beliefs. If we do it right and can make sense of all of the above insights into truths, then there can be one lasting result: that we become more tolerant and compassionate, because we can already see that all possibilities that exist in the Pandora's box of humankind have come true. As a result of not seeing the whole picture, we already have any possibility, any outcome, every single scenario of suffering already represented on Earth. If we already know this is occurring, and can hold the compassion in our heart of rooting for people who suffer, as well as truly understand where their suffering comes from, then we can build on this wisdom.

It will always lead us to the right conclusions rather than pursuing a path of prolonging suffering.

There are some difficult questions this poses which have already presented themselves in our society. Questions such as: Is it up to us to decide whether it is our call to end another's life, ever? If we already know that anyone who has committed a serious crime and killed others, do we not also know that they will automatically be confronted with their surviving compromised Karmic minds? Will it not have a lesser result for all involved to want them dead without there being some form of resolution to their issues? Will their issues resolve, simply as a result of their experiencing their own death at our hands? If they have a rebirth, how will this be determined, how will their previous actions affect them and what will the outcome be for their future existence? And - back to the elephant in the room - if we may have all committed wrong actions, perhaps including murder at some point in our infinite evolution, how has it affected us now? Have we perhaps disassociated into single beings as a result of our previous actions? Is this why we are on Earth as individuals with a longing to be 'home', connected with others and experience completeness? Are we constantly searching for what we once called our own, that our natural state of being is not actually human, but something superlative to this? Is one of our tasks on Earth to be observing how separation makes us suffer, to put an end to the process and find the right ways to create completeness again within ourselves? How can we counteract our dispassionate actions, thoughts and feelings towards ourselves and others? How come we sabotage ourselves with lower actions if we want to create the most logical and fruitful conclusion for all sentient beings? How can we not be tempted into wrongful actions, stick to good actions and a good outcome only, because we certainly seem to need it? How can we stop this madness?

I am hopeful and optimistic that we can, and that there are methods on our side to help us do so. We can only hope that in time, everyone's own inner Karmic energy system which is powerful enough to record, will also remember and recall significant events in any of our lifetimes which would help us make sense of our lives right now. if it kicks in sooner rather than later in order to remember who we were before, then we have a precious chance of making the most of who we are capable of being right now.

As we know, it is our Karmic energy mind that also attracts situations to us, in order to remind us how to regain Karmic balance. We are awfully blessed to be reading about such high frequency concepts without being persecuted and punished, but what about those of us who are not? What chance do others have with less opportunity for looking at ways to undo the negative impact of their wrongful actions? If we come across concepts which help us resolve life issues more easily, do we have a responsibility towards ourselves only, or can the awareness of our increasing good fortune also be the driver to make this possible for others?

How can we assist others in finding their own inner truth in the most loving, compassionate way? It is a massively delicate subject, and I am not here to convince you or tell you what to do or argue with anyone. I am here to pose questions that might help start a healthy inner process of sharing thoughts and contemplation on the subject matter, inviting readers to do the same. Questions and answers are only skirting the subject, I am fully aware. They can, however, bring about inner connections if they are speaking of a greater underlying truth, and we will know if this is right by our own inner reactions. Suffice to say, it might be that once we have gained our own understanding through personal experience of these facts, we will possibly never live our lives in quite the same way again. We will all individually decide how we can balance out our inner world, and it will take as long as it takes for our realisation process to evolve. If it's about ourselves only to start with, then first of all, being reminded of this fact will help each of us understand that it is of no use to judge anyone else's progress. We need to learn to look inwards first and foremost and we need to start by learning how to have a strong basis for understanding ourselves again. We are longing to be able to look past our insecurities, our anxieties, our shortcomings, our worst feelings about ourselves and our environment. We mostly do not yet know where we are at, let along where others are at, which surely means that we can't yet guess as to what the consequences will be based on their actions they chose to take. Let's learn first how to develop some skills in exploring our own true nature, do that with regularity and commitment and all else will surely follow.

When I set out with this chapter, I wanted to question how the concept of Karma holds up, on one of the biggest subjects of life: killing another being.

I think we got as far as understanding that we have a choice to find out more about our own Karmic energy body and look inwards to find out who we really are, which may well be an on-going project. It's interesting to observe that various cultures and ways of life integrate this phenomenon in different ways into their everyday lives. We can argue that religion can, too, perhaps some more successfully than others. But this book is not about religion, set structures, penalizing or a lengthy discussion. It is a huge subject to examine Samsara, the world of delusion, and how our confusion and not knowing any better make things be even more complicated. Others started to take advantage of the fact, wanted to manipulate and control mankind and not live by truth. There is much on the subject out there already, so this is not the time to go into details. In the context of this book, I would only be asking questions as to what it is within ourselves that we fall for such manipulation time and time again.

Don't we want to make the most of every moment without being distracted by lesser elements? Don't we want to live in peace and harmony? Why can so many of us not have their human rights met of living with dignity and having their basic needs fulfilled? Who is thwarting our efforts? It is time we asked some questions and looked for the answers. I know what I believe, and I trust you would want to know our inner truth, too.

In order to explain where I am going with this, I want to look at a cultural example of what can happen when a human being attains a certain level of recollection, realisation & remorse. Once again, whether we believe or not, what matters is the Karmic energy principle behind the story, and as a parable at least, it may give us answers to Karmic understanding of grave misconduct. The example is a legendary historic figure named Milarepa.

Milarepa Image Credit© (Buddhist image library)

In Tibetan history he is one of the most revered and well-known figures, loved by all who follow traditional teachings of Buddhism. He was a poet, a saint and founder of one of the lineages in Tibetan Buddhism. What is interesting is that here are some specific accounts of the Karmic developments of one human who became responsible for the deaths of people. In a modern judicial setting we would probably be analysing the fact that he was under-age, that he was aiding and abetting his mother who, aggrieved by the abuse she suffered by her in-laws after her husbands death, appeared to be the instigator for the crimes she made her only son commit on her behalf, and that it is believed she sent him off to be trained to summon dark magic in order to bring about the deaths of people indirectly, which would not stand up in court these days; unless an investigation of the crime scene would turn out any evidence by which he could be linked to his cousin's wedding guests, 35 of which perished during their celebratory meal. Of this there is no record. But this is not where the story ends, because the first act did not quench his mother's upset. These things never do, do they. In a second plot of his mother's creation, this time she made her only son go to a better-class sorcerer and summon a hail-storm to kill some people in a barn. It worked – the necessary large hail made a whole building collapse on top of those who were residing in it. These days, nobody could have linked him to the crime. But we are talking Karma here and deep insights into our intentions, which was more fashionable then than it is now. Milarepa, on learning that his intention to do harm had worked, was mortified. He realised that he was much more powerful than he had thought, and now he had used his power to kill harmless villagers. His remorse was intense, and lasting. His recognition of the fact that his actions were not acceptable combined with his remorsefulness, created the next part of his lifelong dedication to mastering the Karmic wisdom teachings and undo the bad Karma of his deeds. He passed some gruelling tests by a Master who would teach him well, spent years contemplating Truth in cages clad in cotton rags to clear his Karma and, what he couldn't yet know is that it would make him enlightened and a Saint in the eyes of those who heard his story and could relate. The rest of his life he spent as a poet and musician, teaching his followers simply about how important it is to follow the simple beauty of life and to become one with it. He had the fortune – or was it good Karma - to turn out to become a very highly evolved and enlightened being despite the acts he committed in his youth using black Magic, meaning that he used his precious mind power to influence circumstances and phenomena to cause the death of others. Despite being a strong and powerful young man, Milarepa, the legendary Tibetan song-writer and poet, spent the rest of his life being humble, seeing that this would serve his future lives much better. In fact, it is said that he no longer had to return to the human realm as an ordinary being, but would be reborn in the pure realms.

I hope you like the historic account as much as millions of others all over the world who have been inspired by it and taken some of the elements that present themselves in there into account, to be applied to our modern systems of thinking. In our days, he probably would have been acquitted. In Karmic terms, he recognised that he had been unskilful in his actions, showing a high understanding of the connections between his actions and their consequences for other beings, as well as his future Self. He would have spent years trying to undo the sorrow caused to those he felt he had harmed, and that is something that is missing from our modern day thinking. Even if someone gets penalised and locked up for their crimes, does that mean they automatically learn how to undo their negative actions? I wonder how people would react if we even suggested that such a process would be helpful. We would probably be laughed at, or locked up ourselves for the illogical suggestion.

Be that as it may, I think perhaps we already know that we can take from this whatever we want, it's up to each of us. There are so many more these days that have such intense feelings and thoughts they find they cannot resolve with their limited ego mind. Are we like the mothers and uncles of Milarepa who won't make it to the pure lands? Notice how there is no account of Milarepa ever turning against his mother for putting him up to his actions. He takes full responsibility, the brave man. But there is more to it than just admiring his strength of character and how it all turned out well in the end: if we don't learn how to overcome our demons, we, too, could be in danger of believing we can get away with murder. Perhaps it will inspire us to find out more, perhaps we just need to learn a bit more to not just dismiss it as just another silly story.

But far from it – this historic example where relics still exist to this day of Milarepa's life in the 11hundreds (Gregorian calendar), is a very good account of how intricate our Karmic dealings are. People also took into account many signs in nature to divinate future outcomes based on being present in the moment, something else that we no longer do. Reading up on and researching many such phenomena would be something I can recommend, as the purifying and meditative actions we could choose to take are very much preferable instead of many of the mundane ones we habitually choose to do nowadays, having been removed from our true Self we are so desperately trying to find again.

Perhaps the potential to do wrong lies latent in all of us, and it could strengthen our mind, so it's easier to resolve and encourage us to not act on it. If it really is an account of how one man can change his Karmic actions, then we could be on to something, in terms of turning around world Karma and what keeps recurring to everyone of us in terms of wrongful action.

When I first thought it worth thinking about this in realistic terms, my questions were: How does this 'change of heart' happen within a human being? How does it work? Is there really a universal principle that works like a universal 'pardon'? If there really is a way we can undo untold damage, what is the method and how long will it take?

Before we go into my experiment here of explaining how I believe the historic account of Milarepa to be a good example of what occurs within, I would first like to point out that there are whole host of important figures described in Buddhism as well as many other religions, too many to mention, who represent a variety of highly evolved internal stages of wisdom and compassion. These can be achieved and experienced within our own Karmic energy fields in order to explain what occurs with our inner Karmic connections. In order to explain further, I need to also mention how images of I have tried to, as anywhere in this book, transcribe the conundrum of Milarepa's predicament into our

Western way of thinking. What we might be lacking is the background to how Tibetan iconography functions. Highly transcendental Karmic principles are locked into sacred images and put together in a highly skilled way, with many accurate measurements based on sacred geometry made and the imagery painted according to principles that exist to evoke the Karmic energy transformation in the observer directly. It is possible to look at and study imagery deeply, and even without knowledge to receive deep insights and transmissions of what occurs and how it translates into an energy shift within us. Sacred imagery in all cultures is designed that way, and Tibetan Buddhism has very intricate art that has been studied and explained in great detail. There are many thousands of different deity images and even more symbols describing a certain state of mind and state of our Karmic energy environment. If you find it as fascinating as I do, I would encourage you to look into the subject further. It would take us too far away from the subject here to explain in more detail, but I will suggest further reading at the end. Suffice to say that the imagery and historic figures are trying to tell us more about the fascinating world of our inner energy and provide many clues as to how to purify our Karmic energy paths, if we care to find out more.

You can also use this book and all the techniques described at the end as a shortcut and quick reference to learning more about how to change your inner Karmic energy. This is why I sat down to write this book after all, to give you an easier way to have insights into some very complex esoteric principles. I will try to explain from the Karmic energy angle again, as to the answers I have come up with and what I deduce could be happening.

We have already talked about the much-ignored existence of electromagnetic energy resonance within us, which stores all our Karmic actions in electromagnetic coding in this lifetime and all before, resulting in an unimaginable fine and complex Karmic aura or energy field. Think, perhaps, of the idea that has been suggested, that all matter in the whole universe might fit into a square inch cube if condensed. It's impossible for us to grasp, and it will also be impossible for our brains to compute that our energy 'field' merges and becomes one with the Karmic aura or energy field in the stages between life and death. There are many names for this stage, | quite like using the 'Bardo', again, a term taken from Buddhism. Our energy adjusts in the stages of the Bardo, it takes our Karmic experiences and merges them with the greater energy source. Electromagnetic resonance in the universal energy source is not necessary, but the two can intertwine and sync. One can become the other. We bring into this lifetime our Karmic energy resonance from endless existence before this, and have a chance at improving it, in this lifetime again. The fact that our Karma's very nature in our physical existence is an electromagnetic coding within our bodies could potentially suggest a theorem relating to quantum physics, that it is possible to release even extremely negative Karmic situations coded in electromagnetic resonance, perhaps even instantly. How we do this must be the result of learning how to access our Karmic energy memory and how any release of negative energy facilitates our merging again with the Universal energy source. In short, the more negative Karmic charge we release from our bodies, the more we are connected again to the greater energy force that prevails beyond all existence. Many of us are unable to remember in our physical strife that we even have this connection, unless we have already had a grasp of our highly accomplished Karmic memory and know how to consciously expand on this experience. Most of us would be made aware of our Karmic energy body only once we reached the Bardo state, the stage after death during the Karmic energy merging process before another rebirth takes place. At this stage, we have the chance at least for a moment, to wish we had done things differently, even though any regret can, of course, no longer be altered in that physical existence (with a few exceptions where people are revived and return to the same physical body). After that stage, our Karmic memory merges again with universal energy; it shifts from being a 3-dimensional and measurable energy field, into the cosmic energy source which is beyond measure. It might be good to remember that this energy source does not stop where our universe stops, even if we have termed it 'universal Karmic energy'. It is the source of all existence from which everything material is born, the greater consciousness behind all that is. Just before our energy body merges again with this stage, we have a chance of RE-cognising who we are and what we have become. The important process of energy-shifting through experiencing sincere remorse even at the last second - which we covered in a previous chapter - can shift our Karmic energy into a different future outcome as a result.

If this process, which is also well-documented in some of the scriptures quoted in this book, is really what actually occurs, then we could also deduct that there is potential merit in being in a human existence in order to make positive shifts within our Karma whilst we are here. On Earth we have a combination of consciousness AND physical ability to bring about such a shift, if only we had the insight and methodology to realise the importance of our life here on Earth and act upon it. Right here, right now, we can apply methods to shift our incomplete Karma; we may even be here in order to assist others to do the same. We have created practices such as 'praying' which exists in many cultures. A 'prayer' is more than religious practice which some dismiss as nonsense. There is more to it, especially when applied consciously. It is actually an inner principle by which we are able to shift energy from one state of being to another. We accept one state of being, and put our focus and intention onto another, more evolved and therefore desirable. in order for it to work, we set this free in order to be dealt with on a higher energy frequency level than we are currently on. Even so, we are capable of commanding the energy to be directed to assist our quest. it is similar to making a sincere and meaningful wish. So, the two worlds work together, seemingly, and one state of existence is not that dissimilar from another. It appears that on Earth we have the advantage of obtaining a much closer focus on some convoluted sections of Karmic energy knots, perhaps so that we can untangle them. It's like having a ball of knotted wool we are trying to de-tangle, and in order to do so we must get much closer to it to see what is wrong and concentrate on the process.

How many of us crave the afterlife, and can't wait to return to their family of light beings in other realms! And yet, we are here for a reason, we came for a reason, and we have work to do. We are in the right place at the right time if we realise that this 'otherworldly' feeling we may get, is there because it's not separate from us; it's within us. We are united with it already and can take it with us wherever we go. A term for this shift into ourselves is 'remembering (who we really are)'. Other terms that exist in our dictionary which also indicate energy shifts within are 'forgiveness' which we have also spoken about previously, and 'penance'. Some cultures believe that we actually need to be penalised for wrongdoing. In fact, most cultures do, in order to maintain an intact community. A Karmic shift, a change for the better on an energy level would be the highest outcome of undoing wrong actions, by which the individual who has committed them is made to shift their energy onto a higher level so that they would 'remember' and be less likely to be re-offending. How is this done? In our current societal belief system there seems to be little indication that there is any focus on such elevated practice. Rather, we are focused on restricting physical existence of those who have committed harmful acts, so that they are contained and have little to no chance to cause any more damage. The question is whether we would actually be better off learning and practising how to bring about this shift. This way, life would improve for as many as possible. Since the practice is theoretically available to all humankind so that we all have the potential in us to shift to such a level of understanding, we actually have it in our hands to be able to bring about a better outcome for all involved. We could eventually all be free from suffering...and if we could only see with our own eyes what that really means then we would all be practising right now.

Once again, it's probably best to start with ourselves and recognise the Karmic energy principles behind all actions, speech and thoughts. All of the three 'doors' as they are also called, can become purified, maybe never all at once in one society, but who knows what's in store for us on Earth? If we put out a sincere wish to have something occur that will bring all of us together, all on Earth to be uplifted into higher understanding of the connections between all of us, would it work? Would we understand each other better? Would the Earth heal as a result of us refraining from abusing her and each other? Would the Earth be a planet that will be forever changed for the better, for new generations to come and build on our insights? Or is this all a temporary dream, a nightmare even, for some? Many dream of circumstances where we are all simply elevated into higher existence, by Aliens, an Earthquake, a meteorite, a volcanic eruption, space missions, a photon belt, specific astrological constellations, scientific evidence of other planets and so on. We use fiction, such as TV, movies, theatre, books, animation and gaming and even when we represent ourselves online to escape our limited reality and yet, this is exactly where our strengths lie in order to make a shift. Perhaps some event does make it possible for us all to make this shift together all at the same time. Perhaps we have to be willing to put some effort into it without seeing much evidence that it is working. Buddhism talks of the next appearance of a Buddha, Buddha Maitreya, depicted as a Buddha standing or sitting upright, rather than cross-legged. The image is symbolic of a future incarnation of the Buddha who will be teaching a pure form of Dharma, at a time when Buddhism was predicted to have been forgotten on Earth.

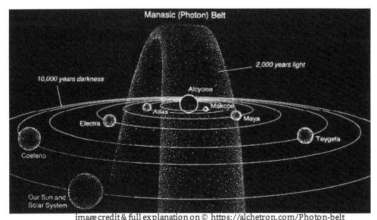

image credit & full explanation on © https://alchetron.com/Photon-belt

Buddha Shakyamuni Image Credit: © Jampha's Mandala

In any case, since we are present right now, the more of us who comprehend, the better, one sentient being at a time, and the more likely it becomes that we will all be able to create and enjoy true happiness on

332

Earth.

Could this be what the account of the life of Milarepa is hinting at? Perhaps it is true, even if only to make us understand that there is no time better than right now to recognise the invisible connections between us all so that we can change our outlook and behaviour patterns accordingly. It certainly has relevance even in this day and time, since we can easily relate and draw many analogies to every day existence. Milarepa and his actions have inspired countless people who identify with the temptation to commit wrong actions, only to then be reminded of the way he was able to change his course of action. Nothing like a superhero with a dark side to inspire us.

Of course, every individual's Karma is different and there is little way of telling where we are at, at any given time. Other conditions may apply that we may not be aware of yet, the small-print in our human contracts, which might be the reason that Karma appears to work quickly for some, but not for others. The realisation of Truth may come to some in this life and yet take lifetimes for others. We may understand what this means in detail as soon as we come across the first hurdle: realising that we have to have the good Karma to be able to recognise, access and process this Karmic information in the first place; if we do not understand any of the principles then it's harder for us to practice. But good Karma will find a way – ideally a 100% foolproof and quick way - for us to put it into practice and be able to change our Karmic coding to its most excellent equivalent so that we can avoid any further negative Karmic attachment. In order to create a state of non-attachment or neutral Karma so to speak, our electromagnetic resonance with regards to a particular issue has to become neutral. It's perhaps a bit like an inner lie detector. We might fool others, but our inner Self will always give us away. In the case of Milarepa, he would have had to revisit each case individually, of those who suffered as a result of his Karmic actions, in order to neutralise the effects of his actions. He would have had to meet with their Karmic reactions without any resistance, and that of all those affected in turn by their deaths, to try and reverse the Karmic energy of his acts entirely; he would have had to renounce any connections with his learning dark magic or temptation to ever use it again. On top of that, if he indeed became enlightened, he would have seen the futility of impure thoughts, but there would also have to be without no thought or intention arising about killing, or any of the feelings connected with any thought of killing; without any charge whatsoever with respect to killing present within his Karmic energy system, or doing harm in any other way, he would be able to use this final event in his life to achieve enlightenment eventually, depending, of course, of Karma carried over from his previous lives. It is said that he had immensely good Karma in previous lifetimes, allowing him to use his remorse and denouncement of worldly attachment for the rest of his life to take on the suffering of those he had harmed and reverse the effects of his bad actions. He took on a vow to reverse all the suffering of those he had harmed, knowing full well what it meant to make an unbreakable promise to take on whatever is requested of him to bring about such an energy reversal from bad to good on behalf of all others, for as long as it took him to work through it all. Even if we don't understand the full meaning of such a practice, we can see that there are Karmic energy processes involved, by which we take on others' Karma. We can also learn from this that negative actions can be reversed, even if this is not as simple as it sounds here in a few lines. This is no mean feat, and it should not be misunderstood to tempt anyone to commit crimes just because they think they can be nullified. It still means we take vows for those lives that were lost to be replaced by our own Karma, and the practice that follows can take decades, even lifetimes to master. If we were not able to clear all of it, any suppressed action, thought or intention within us or anyone we are still linked to via previous negative Karma, in lack of insight, method, application, resolution and neutralisation of all Karmic charge, will still continue to create attachment in future existence. Should the complexity of the process help us to not commit negative actions? Absolutely. Should we learn to find out more about what links us to others? Maybe, but if we have run-ins with others, we can just assume that we still have some Karma with each other and that situations like these can clear the Karma for them and us, once and for all.

It does not mean that we have to walk through life doing penance and feeling guilty all the time. After all, we don't know what's happened in the past, and we also do not want to lose our strength and resolve to do good, and this includes ourselves. When we are well, we are easier able to deal with others' suffering and can assist to alleviate it. We also do not have negative Karmic bonds with everyone, but we can certainly help them with our new-found insights and methods resolve their Karma. Too. Otherwise, we will all see each other as a threat and are either caught up in repelling/rejecting a scenario, or we are attracting too much outcome attachment via our ego mind in situations concerning others. Either one is attachment. Only when there is a neutral stance, with no thought/speech/action attached to an event or situation, is our Karma neutralised. It should not feel bad, or that we feel we should ignore people. It just means we no longer have negative Karma between us, so our Karma is clear like the endless sky. The path famously described by the Buddha as the 'middle path' might be called this for a reason. If we manage to have no re-percussion, attachment or rejection to a particular circumstance, event, memory, thought, emotion, situation, provocation, sensation, trigger, image, sound, person, colour etc., then we are on the middle path: we have become transparent to that experience and its energy can pass right through us without it finding and clinging to any resonance within us. This does not mean we should suppress reactions, become indifferent or ignorant to other's pain or suffering or what is occurring. It is not a detachment, quite the opposite: we will be prompted throughout life to examine our inner energy system carefully over and over again to make ourselves aware of our Karmic make-up through observing our thoughts, feelings, words and actions. Then, we must find practical solutions to resolving any inner Karmic conflict and express this externally to those we have ensnared in our negative actions. We have so much more power to resolve issues than we think or have been taught, and as I keep saying, the most direct and effective way we can do this, is on the vibrational level where Karmic memory is recorded. On these levels, a resolution is much quicker, more fruitful and not just reserved for a few. It is not some privilege reserved for an elite few – it is available to all of us, and the only thing separating us from inner peace is the knowledge of how to achieve it and then using methods for putting it into action. On the accomplished levels, we need to remember what it is like to not know and remember in order to exercise true compassion. With true compassion is meant that we wish for everyone to have this knowledge and gain the benefit from our actions. This is what is worth working towards.

As you can imagine, if we applied this logic to someone who had committed a serious crime, there would be numerous experiences involved that have a potential charge to trigger a reaction not just within the victim, but also within the perpetrator, possibly for lifetimes to come and not just when they were confronted with their actions again. These inner triggers are memories that repeat like broken records and they will be present virtually every moment of every day. They would trigger anyone in my mind, there is no doubt and plenty of proof in those who cannot wait to share the information that is torturing them within. It is simply logical that an energy that is still stuck within will re-present itself under certain circumstances. This is what we have discovered: When the energy is still stuck, it will feel denser the graver the issues are, and have much more negative charge attached to it. It would stop us from seeing the wood for the trees. When it is resolved through working out the Karmic connections, it will always have a neutralising effect with regards to bad Karma. However, whilst anyone has the chance to work through their own Karmic issues, we cannot commit a crime and then hope to apply methods to immediately neutralise it within. This is not how Karmic recordings work. Neutral in this sense does not mean dispassionate, disinterested or disconnected either. Neutral means we have cleared the issues which, according to their severity, plus the ability and resolve to clear them, may take some beings lifetimes even with good methods. It would also mean that if we want to see through all our suffering, we have no choice but to work through our issues to be able to see with clarity and transparency. Even if we cannot recall events, they will still present themselves in our lives, downloaded by our Karmic energy system. Issues present themselves in all sorts of ways, reflected by the problems we are facing in life on this planet. Often, they express themselves in our 'subconscious' thoughts and imagery. Sadly, it is the same route that has to be taken by those who are victims. It is only through the negative resonance in our inner pathways that a timeline has been created. Whoever started it, we end up having to tidy up within. It doesn't seem fair, but least we have methods that we can use to effectively do this, and we are coming across them right now, so we have at least the good Karma to turn it into a good outcome again. Whether we are aware of our own wrong actions in the past or not, whether we have been a victim of them or a perpetrator or both - once issues do resolve, the experience of there being a timeline vanishes and condenses. Good fortune can arise again as a result and as energy flows, it may bring more serendipity, encouraging us to resolve even more issues within in order to feel even more peaceful. What's not to like - this will be what we have been waiting for.

When committing negative actions, we are repeatedly confronted with all details of these internally as well as externally, until such time when we have been able to neutralise all aspects of wrongful action.

Would it not be useful to start someone on a programme straight away, if there was a way of getting them to use their time in order to fully make amends? This is assuming that there is a relatively straightforward healing path for everyone, even those who have committed severe offences. Whilst we might not be able to come to a conclusion whether this is feasible for others, we can certainly make that decision for ourselves. This is by no means a punishment in the way we are used to, being exercised by someone outside ourselves condemning our actions. It is simply a Karmic law of action and result that we can neutralise in its consequences. Yet, the truth of being confronted with our actions and what we have had to suffer without the benefit of remembering all the circumstances as to why, may feel like punishment at first. Don't we deserve to be rewarded for our bravery? Don't we deserve to be taken care of compassionately? This is exactly why I am suggesting this method of Karmic healing. We may not even remember why we are experiencing bad fortune, and how – or if – it is connected to any of our previous actions. When a 'punishment' is implied, what we most fear in connection with it is the drop of our energy within our energy bodies and minds. It makes us feel bad, because our energy hits rock bottom, perhaps exacerbated by the childhood memories we hold of punishments we received that we could not defend ourselves against. The threat of this low energy feeling administered by some external authority figure would have made us want to disappear into a hole in the ground and become invisible to anyone who would have tried to punish us, especially when this was severe and undeserved. This is not what Karma is about. Karma is not a parent that personifies punishing a child. Karma is a law of energy flowing, one way or another, according to our actions, words and thought patterns that create it. Underlying all actions, words and thoughts is the universal Karmic energy law for all experiences positive and negative, and it follows logically that serious cases of negative actions, words and thoughts are no exception, rather that their existence is proof of its inclusion in the principles of cyclic existence. The effects are repeated until neutral. Even if we do not know how everything is connected exactly, it is logical to conclude that if we continue to act wisely and with compassion, that this will help us and others on our journey of Karmic discovery of our truth. I think all we have to do is to look around in order to find the answer. If we do not know the exact origin of bad Karma, would it help us and others to do prophylactic good deeds and practice, to counteract and prevent bad Karma? Definitely. Just what the doctor ordered.

This must be one of those experiences we would rather not think about and explain away as scaremongering and religious mumbo-jumbo. As a result of our disconnect from Truth, we try to look the other way or dissect it. We have developed a strange fascination with fiction giving us snippets of information about being in danger of a predator of some kind, killing and death and how the hero always overcomes all this, which give the audience just enough of a scare-factor to make them feel that they can walk away relieved after the thrill of watching something happen to someone else, without having them having been affected long-term. It's a form of disassociation which has become a social norm, to the detriment of our environment. By neglecting our inner truths, we are allowing ourselves to be fooled and end up consuming that way without regard for others. I let you decide by whom we end up being taken for a ride, but it's probably no surprise to you that there are many who take advantage of our confusion. The Karmic mind cannot be fooled. It cannot necessarily determine what is false and what is real, much like a child in a cinema watching a movie does not recognise the difference either. Our mind is pure and will record violence within to a certain extent, when violence is presented, even only suggestively on a visual level. Perhaps we should question the intention behind a production of visual impact of violence. We might ask ourselves why we would want to proliferate violence if there is already so much of it in this world, and influence an audience towards more violence still? Are we trying to conquer any form of pain and the pain of dying by simply making it fictional? Are we trying to be invincible, are these our modern ways of religion, trying to understand how to overcome pain and death? By now, we seem to look past it, not pay attention to it, even enjoy it. We have created a 'split mind' from an early age to adapt to this, and have not even noticed or questioned whether this is a good thing. It would be crucial to recognise in the context of a psychological understanding of our Self where we are working with many such segregated compartments within our minds. Most of us humans have this ability by now, so that different areas of our brains are set aside for different task - we generally call this intelligence. But does juggling this compartmentalisation not get awfully confusing at times, especially when we are under duress? I am proposing there is a danger is that when we are in situations of stress, our brain might no longer be able to correctly assess how to react to it. It seems that it can happen that our brain has filed fictional experiences we are observing as reality and the other way around, often without us realising. It would be a worrying trend, but it is clear to me that this is already happening to many who live in the civilised world. Our brains are often overstretched with an overload of tasks, so we are even conditioned into behaviours, so our brains are capable of making us attack innocent people or end up walking past real people who need help. This is by no means an observation of psychological defects in a minority of people, this is something that is starting to occur in larger numbers, to apparently highly functioning, intelligent members of society. Is it not something we should look into further and ask ourselves why people are reacting so weirdly? Is it because our brain no longer discerns properly and does not react to other's suffering any longer, as if it were not real so we distance ourselves from their concern? It might be a Homo Sapiens issue, I don't know. Our brains and bodies evolved to cope with situations of extreme stress and adapted and compromised as a result over many thousands of years, it is said. Was it all to our advantage to become so specialised? It seems that if we don't watch our actions, our brain will go into melt-down. The Karmic energy recordings within us contribute to short-circuits in our bodies, and it seems that this is visibly and tangibly affecting how we react to our environment. We are no longer coming in peace, and may not have done so for some time, without noticing that our inner peace has slipped out of our reach. Whereas at some point in our evolution we might have been aiming to all be able to assist each other in a caring, compassionate way, we then started to observe situations where something went wrong, and we distanced ourselves from these seemingly without having moral compass prompting compassionate action. Even now, we can feel something some of the time but not at others, and then choose to distance ourselves from associating with others. Our brain paths are being altered. Nowadays with so many distractions and diversions, we find it hard to make sense of and unite all these components. We end up feeling split a million different ways and end up juggling our various realities, getting more and more stressed as a result. Of course, our poor brains are doing overtime all the time now and suffering from overload. Our experience of life and all it contains has become more separate rather than unified. All the while, our way of dealing with our symptoms is by turning away from having to face yet another problem, so we choose to distract ourselves even more, watching and listening to ever more meaningless, degenerate, commercialised ramblings. At the danger of sounding like an old cynic again, I will point out as an example that we don't hesitate to 'follow' someone online who we do not know and have never met, but who is deemed a worthy 'celebrity' by their hyped and manufactured efforts which are usually stupefyingly boring and simplistic trivia rather than true accomplishments of wisdom, bravery or compassion. We are downplaying our power instead of questioning what we are doing. Instead, we are consuming one thing after another like there is no tomorrow and no planet to save. We observe the instructions of animated characters on screen and dotted around our household and follow every word they say, as a way to get away from our own confusion, fears and the complications in our lives, rather than looking at solutions and finding out what is truly there within us. I am certain we have been duped into losing our way and the world populus is now largely suffering from Stockholm Syndrome.

Be that as it may, it is not for anyone to say it is right or wrong, including me. That is not really even what I am trying to do. I am trying to align to a fact of life much ignored, misunderstood and mystified, just so that solutions can be brought to light, just in case anyone is still looking for them. This way, truly terrible negative actions could be prevented in the first place by raising enough interest and awareness of how they came about, even if we do end up resisting the truth and uproar against what presents itself clearly and logically. I actually happen to find comfort in the fact that Karmic energy laws appear naturally, where an often fallible, corrupt and inhumane legal or governing system is almost always set to fail sooner or later. Nature has a way of righting any wrong in the end. This is not meant as some sadistic pleasure taken in others' misfortune, it is simply knowing that life has the ability to be in balance again, even if human existence often presents itself as totally chaotic.

'Judgement day does not/cannot/must not exist'; so many of us choose to think; and yet, the notion sticks in our minds, probably because the concept has been utilised rightly or wrongly by many religions. It does tend to make us feel uncomfortable though, and we would rather distract or anaesthetise. Why is it seen so negatively? Is it because it doesn't just seem to be a movie title where the protagonists are having a more than just a bad day? What we might be trying to ignore and forget is that every second, every tiny little incident in our lives, is recorded in our Karmic energy system, which has the capacity to store endless amounts of information in the tiniest space. Every day, every second, is 'judgement day'. There is no particular day set aside for it, rather, it is determined by 'Karma ripening', meaning it's more to do with what we call 'what goes around, comes around'. If we had the inner map and guidance to determine when and where, we might be able to tell when we will be confronted again with certain aspects of our Karma, good or bad. There are such ways by which it can be determined, but most of us have lost interest and the belief in finding out more about such skills; so they remain reserved for the wise people, many of whom by now live in isolation, consulted only when we need to know more about a pressing situation desperately and ask for divinations. There is something we can all do though. We can simply deal with every day the best way we can, act the best way we should. Every time that we do so, we dedicate the result of our effort towards the benefit of all sentient beings. That way, we make every second count, and we multiply all our efforts. Every moment that you are aware of being fully present in the here and now, is exactly that. It is giving you proof, a personal check-in point, to show you that you are on the right track and that you are able to increase this to more times when you are able to do this. The infinitesimally small vibrating particles within the uncountable atoms within our bodies are enough to give you the scenarios you face every day. These sub-atomic particles hold the charge within us that chooses to resonate with events around us on Earth every second of the day. Nobody and nothing else determines. Our energy attracts. You can choose any moment to have a reset and start having amazing moments, hours, days!

Have you ever thought about the fascinating findings of forensics, that determine accurate truth by researching and finding genetic coding of infinitesimally small particles of our DNA that there is a one in a trillion chance, for example, that we will have been in a certain place at a certain time and have left a particle of us behind? Karmic energy is a bit like that. It encodes our very specific imprint into energy frequencies, even tinier and finer than DNA which is still a physically identifiable component. Karmic energy is coded within our cellular structure, it interacts and intertwines with it, it determines our behaviour and holds recordings of who we once were before we got here. It never gets lost, it is always there, even if we find this hard to understand. But it's not visible to us, so we try to deny it, a little like the criminal who denies having been at the scene of the crime, until there is certain proof that they were. I would almost like to predict that at some point in the future, science will find proof of Karmic energy and how it's already recording and encoding our every move. Only at that point, I very much hope nobody will use this knowledge for their own gain.

Committing to finding out about what this, our inner wisdom and resulting compassion are, is our commitment to our life, our choice to make it as vibrant and transparent as possible. By this I do not mean that you become a push-over and people-pleaser, a do-gooder and yay-sayer. I mean that you become authentic, you become you. There is no secondary agenda, nothing to catch up with any longer that was a hangover from lifetimes past, nothing to chase you. Explore what it means to make yourself wise, by starting with your Self. Who are you? Why do you exist, in the way you do? What works for you, what does not, and why? By committing to positive actions we set good conditions. Positive also does not mean you cannot say 'no' to any situation, including being harmed. You can positively, vehemently say 'no' to situations that you feel are not right for you, at that moment in time. You no longer have to feel ashamed, guilty or anxious. Your birth right is to BE, and be happy.

29. Karma and the Bardo

As we have probably all witnessed ourselves by now, by committing to negative actions some beings are setting their own energy vibration to a programme of deterioration. Perhaps this started off as harmful actions against them and they feel justified. Perhaps they even are – who are we to say. We cannot judge another's Karma, and unless we focus on our own and make use of methods to set the gears of our inner energy system to neutral so we can see and find our 'Selves' again, any of us can end up on a vicious cycle of continuously harming ourselves and others. Unaware of the damage we have become accustomed to, we continue to cause ourselves and others harm. When we choose not to look at our actions, why we choose them and instead pretend that they never occurred, we will be confronted with that information again, ultimately at the very latest (and possibly worst) time: when we pass into the Bardo at the time of our death.

The Bardo is a term for the in-between stage of life and death. It can appear at stages within our life-times, too, at points of transition which we experience as great stages of change. One of the greatest changes we cannot alter is the fact that we have to relinquish our physical identity sooner or later. We will have to transform our Self into the next stages of existence once our physical form has ceased, the formlessness after death, and any subsequent incarnations after that. We in the West tend to have cultured much fear of this time and try to give it as little thought as possible before it inevitably happens. As a result, we are often not the slightest bit prepared for what happens during this time, although paradoxically, we would benefit so much from learning more about it.

Since it has relevance in the context of talking about Karma, we would do well to start off more of a discussion about the Bardo to get used to what these concepts mean in relation to us and our Western education and mindset. I am including some concepts explaining what the Bardo could mean for us here. For example, we know already that each action has its own Karmic energy pattern. The beautiful actions of love and compassion have their own vibration connecting us to the whole universe. However, having committed unskilful actions such as the aspects of serious crimes we have been talking about here, a person would be represented with the energy consequences of these actions, too. In their tiniest details, they are also recorded in our Karmic energy memory bank at the stage of passing into the afterlife stages, also called the Bardo. Is this judgement day, then, where some divine being judges us and deems us more or less worthy of being in some form of heaven? In a nutshell, no. It is, in fact, our own Karmic memory bank reminding us of the detail of all our actions, giving us an opportunity to re-connect to the Truth with a capital 'T'. Perhaps this is the notion of and analogy of heaven where all concepts are Truth and all is well. At this point in time when our physical body is ceasing to exist, we will typically have little to no conscious control over any trigger images that are surfacing and will not be able to counteract or interact with them on a physical level any longer. Our brains might survive for a short while longer and should we be revived and recover fully from a near-death experience, we may have physical recollection of our brush with the afterlife. Some might even be able to recall some of the visual energy images that occur soon after physical death, as already recorded by those who did indeed come back from the brink of death. Even so, once any brain activity ceases, our essence separates from the physical body to merge with our Karmic energy mind entity to observe; a process that some believe can take up to 49 days. We will perceive not with eyes but with our Karmic consciousness instead, and according to the extent of previous good Karma this will result in a certain level of lucidity and comprehension. Since this depends on how much good Karmic energy we have accumulated, it might be worth thinking about creating even more good Karma whilst we still can. On this level of existence, we will, for a short window, have acute awareness of the implications of our previous actions, as our passing into vibrational formlessness allows us to become all-aware again of the interconnectedness of all life and our position within it. For a short while, this will express itself in visual memory recollection, before it then turns into pure energy perception integrating us with the Universal energy at some stage afterwards. We would feel connected in some form of awareness of all the goodness we created by feeling connected to other beings, but would also have awareness of those we have harmed. Since there are no barriers to our experiencing everything clearly, their experience will be shown to us, so we will be one with their experience of suffering, too. Whilst we may be lucky enough to be able to address the error of our ways in an instant at this late stage, and maybe even be given insights into understand our real reasons for having acted this way, we will live through what we have done to others in a kind of mind-union of connectedness. At this very point of the Bardo state, there is a crucial stage of development that may be involved in the process of determining our re-birth. If we have recollection and a resulting reaction such as remorse to any of our wrong-doing, there is still a chance that a change of course in our future Karma sets in at this point, even if we did not experience any remorse prior to this during our life span. Take for example our troubled Magician Milarepa again, who did have remorse for his actions during his lifetime, and was therefore able to begin his remedial actions towards those he had harmed in his lifetime, there and then.

The notion of remorse has the potential of being a huge life-changing moment, which is the reason that I have given it special attention at various points throughout this book. My hypothesis is that it is possible for our energy polarisation of any wrong-doing to not only be exactly reversed during a life-time, but also in the stages of the Bardo. This particular energy reversal, which has commonly been labelled as 'remorse', is stronger than 'regret', for example. It determines that we have a true realisation that our action has been unskilful, and in addition it is also connected to our willingness for the energy to be changed from that moment in time onwards in order to find a solution to alleviating suffering we have caused. It can even have the result of a complete reversal of our energy outcome from this situation within our energy system. It is the realisation within our consciousness that we truly wish to put right what we have done wrong. This is what the label 'remorse' means in the first place, that we have become reversed in our attitude towards our own actions. Negative actions we allowed ourselves to commit in our lifetime(s) suddenly become repulsive to us. In the case of any disturbance we may have had as a result of us committing a serious crime, we now have the extraordinarily good opportunity of having a change of mind in the Bardo in an instant through this energy reversal within. We may still be able to perceive the results of our actions, and it may have the effect of our prompting an energy reversal towards a positive future direction of remedying the situation through our recognising that our action was wrong. Whilst in the after death we won't of course have a physical opportunity to remedy the situation until our next lifespan; and yes, there would have to be another life span as our Karmic energy recognises when it is incomplete, without fail. Where and how we incarnate again depends entirely on the determination of our Karmic energy at this stage. My theorem is, that it is possible for our energy polarisation related to a particular act of wrong-doing to be partially or even exactly righted again, and our consciousness affected in such a way that we take our 'remorse' and our wish for reversal of our wrongful actions with us into the next lifetime. Energy blockages related to unresolved negative actions we have allowed ourselves to commit in our lifetime(s) so far, have one last swift chance even in the Bardo to become righted and/or be pointed in the right direction for complete resolution at a stage thereafter. Not everyone will have one last chance to have this resolution to our actions, as we become witness to our life gone past one last time. It is an achievement of consciousness for us to realise that those actions were 'wrong'. We will have to have the relative fortune to have recognised their cause and effect, and for them to become insufferable to our 'Self', which is on its way to becoming whole again with the All-presence This all still happens on an inner, individual level as it tries to merge with the omnipresent energy. There is no judgement as we know it from an outside entity, nobody appearing who will take us to hell and torture us, other than that which springs from our own tortured minds.

Nobody and nothing, other than our own Karmic consciousness trying to complete what has become disconnected, can project the images and phantoms of any suffering which we may have created, prior to any moment of insight.

The images mentioned above that appear to us in the Bardo are incredibly strong and can have powerful attraction for us, even at this stage. However, it is said that if we are attracted to the lesser vibrations, however colourful, then we run danger of being drawn to a lesser form of rebirth. When we instead find nothing to distract us and there is nothing to attach to, our Karmic energy mind has no need to follow the phantoms and will instead flow and be attracted to the highest vibrations. The vibrations of higher realms are much purer, brighter and possibly even more abstract, rather than resembling familiar figures and a flurry of fleeting imagery from the past. Endless images and phantoms will continuously be created on lower levels of vibration, and we may automatically fall for the bright light show and be drawn to it if something within us still needs resolving. There is, though, no 'good' or 'bad' interpretation any longer as there is on Earth. We are drawn on an energy level to what we must resolve. There are countless images and all appear according to the patterns we have been responsible for creating ourselves, within. Whether we see beyond the bright lights and are drawn towards the highest frequencies depends on what our Karmic energy is attracted to. There is little that our mind can steer consciously at this stage, as we are riding on our Karmic energy force alone, the goodwill of our prayers and good deeds, our awareness and our outer-worldly wisdom.

Our 'remorse' and subsequent vow to resolve a previous action most likely means that another energy attachment may automatically be created: that of experiencing the right Karmic circumstances to try to rebalance a situation, which may now be tilted towards a desire to rectify the imbalance of hurt we may have caused, or the hurt that was inflicted upon us in the lives we have left behind. The implications for our Karmic energy body, which has now left physical form and is lingering in the between-stage of Bardo, are that it may be automatically drawn again to take yet another life form. We won't have an opportunity to reject this, as there is no brain or body to reject with. We had our chance to review, and the next stage is now the result of all our energy drawing us to the next outcome. How different our lives would have been, if only we had known this! Despite the fact that things can happen instantly on a Karmic energy level, we do not necessarily get the chance at this late stage to rectify any energy imbalance. We may be drawn into another existence to straighten out our energy and any of those who we harmed. All past karmic energy we accrued shapes the process for us whilst we are busy leaving this planet and our physical form already. Did we prepare for this moment? We might have left it a little too late for that, to which there can only be one logical conclusion: it means that it's only the more reason to make amends during our lifetime for anything we choose to. That is, if we see sense in everything being explained here. Perhaps we have huge resistance to what is being suggested. Karma suggests we don't just go happily to sleep after a long and busy life. It isn't guaranteed that the fabulous pearly gates are visible to all of us, there might be some Karmic debris to be cleared in the way to getting there. And thus, our trusted steed, the Karmic energy body, gets saddled up to create another existence for us, according to the energy laws of rebirth. What should we do, if nothing on Earth has taught us yet to prepare for the afterlife? Who will we be, in future? I think I can say with certainty that it's not all bad. Most of us have done good deeds after all to bring us back safely into another human existence. 'Not again!' I hear you shout? i have met many people who are terrified to be reborn on Earth again. For them, it's a punishment to live again in a place where there is so much suffering. Perhaps it's worth remembering that this is one of the best and fastest places to grow and redeem ourselves, and we might still need to be shown what we are to work on in greater detail, find the beauty and the miracle in being alive and share it with others in order to see the whole Truth. It is out there, if you pardon the pun! Will we accept the mission or run screaming? We have already learned that, in the case of anyone's wrong-doing, the tables may well be turned and they may get to experience feelings and memories of what it's like to be submitted to what they have previously done. This is not meant to be a tit-for-tat revenge trip, just how Karmic energy works in order to rebalance. Thankfully most of us seem to have a natural moral compass to stay away from harming others, perhaps from lifetimes of practice and experience. But in the case of those who don't, they may have felt what it is like to be subject to pain equal to the one they inflicted, until they recognise the connection and repercussions so eventually they won't ever be tempted to repeat the process again. As you can tell, it becomes very confusing as to the 'whodunnit' if none of the players remember who first committed the crime, who was victim and who was the abuser. So, in the case of any wrong-doing, we could guess that all participants have been victim and abuser in previous lifetimes. In the afterlife, it does not serve as an excuse that we weren't aware of the repercussions or did not believe in the survival of our energy body. Instead, each one of us needs to individually recognise and be responsible for our actions which may have been less than desirable, and that as a result, they will become attached therefore to the energy frequency of needing to even out the energy imbalance. It also does not work to be smug about another's path, although this is often how we see it in the West, feeling vindicated when we observe what we feel to be instant gratification in Karmic justice. Karma is not a candy shop where you get to binge watch others' mishaps. We need to be responsible for our own reaction to others also. If someone has committed atrocities, then it might be better to send them in the direction of seeing sense, because they will keep doing what they are doing otherwise, which is much less of a desirable outcome. Those who are so removed from their emotions that they cannot see others suffering need to be shown how to, although this is often easier said than done. We can sometimes only hope and pray that they will be shown, and this may not happen in this lifetime. it is really tough when we are the victim of such behaviour, and we must of course go through our own healing process and all the mixed emotions this entails. Again, there are methods that facilitate the process. There is endless suffering and all that is being said is that everyone has the ability to end suffering through developing their own insights into their actions, some definitely faster than others. Which side do we want to be on? As we have learned, we will be well advised to do this on Earth whilst we still can. Once in the Bardo, this process has nothing to do with any form of physical consent, when it could matter the most – 'we' do not exist as such any longer. The energy body will be doing all the meticulous and exacting calculations on subatomic levels for 'us' then.

Karma is not just an Eastern Philosophy we choose to follow or not. It is a universal principle that applies to all Existence.

Luckily, remorse would be enough to at least reverse the process of a negative attachment. You can use another word in its place if it works better for you. Remorse here is meant in the sense of recognition of wrongful action and the willingness to reverse the action. Some prefer the term prayer, or use mantras on passing into the Bardo state. Whatever the terminology or method, they all deal with similar phenomena, a process of inner acknowledgement in order to permit our Karmic energy to initiate the reversal of the effects of negative Karmic energy attachment. It will do its job after that without our consent or input. We can only rely on what we have done so far in our lives and hope that it has been of use to us in a future existence.

As a result of feelings of remorse, guilt, regret and so on kicking in, some beings end up compelled to take on some of their victims' burden, to the point of their Karmic energy conclusions committing them to experience what it means to be a victim themselves in their next life. Most of us would never have any recollection of why we have a set of beliefs that sends us in this direction and spend quite some time confused, maybe even resentful of the fact that we have become the recipient of anyone's wrong-doing. Some even commit to consciously choosing instead of involuntarily being submitted to this Karmic pattern, taking on the suffering on behalf of others like martyrs. Some will have never done any harm, and are experiencing suffering nonetheless. All of these scenarios are possible and it's virtually impossible for a mere mortal to tell where it came from. None of the processes are necessarily traceable, and none of them can be judged by any outsider; which of course makes it harder to understand the concept and implement any changes to our current belief systems. It might lead us to the observation that what remains evident is the cyclic existence of suffering that seems to continue indefinitely - at least as long as we do not see through how we persist in sustaining it. In order to rise above it, we need to see through it, and in order to see through it, we need to stop doing silly things like hating another enough to want to finish each other off.

Is it that people feel so diminished and disillusioned by all the harrowing experiences in their perception of this one life only that they get to live, that they conclude if this is how dull and pointless life is, they will live it recklessly as if there is nothing to lose? That their only way of being light-hearted and expressing a passion for life when doing mindless and pointless things? Is it because we have become so desperate to feel free from all the pain and anguish of not knowing any better that it paradoxically makes us then not free at all, perhaps not for many lifetimes?

Agreed - it really is like a living hell on Earth for many who do not even have enough to eat, clean water to drink or sanitary living conditions.

However, there is a stark difference between extremely poor living conditions and those created by our boredom, our inability to connect our actions to a moral compass based on the right ideology. We can live in the lap of luxury with all that we need and still turn out an axe-murderer. Our ideas of how we relate to each other and our environment, the necessity to find out who we are and why we are the way we are and find a place to create good Karma are all things that should be on a national curriculum. It's obvious that the less we are presented with the right impulses to find crucial information so that we can try to find answers to our Karma, the more hellish and hopeless even a wealthy society seems to get. Perhaps it's all fine, perhaps it's all art, perhaps I am taking it too seriously. Good can come from any situation, for sure. This is not supposed to be a sermon. But isn't what makes us truly free and light exactly that which we have forgotten to seek? How to rid ourselves of our attachment to our own inner Karmic energy binds? They don't just go away, do they. I think that is what I am getting at: We need to find out what these are, in order to free ourselves from them. We could really do with learning to use our own inner radar which would give us an idea of what they might be. When we feel a hunch about something we learn about and it starts to resonate with us, we can follow this instinctive reaction to find out more about how we are connected to it. It is an exciting journey where each and every one of us is free to take from this inner knowledge what we feel is right for us at any moment. When we experience unexplained pain and illness in this life it might sometimes even help us to understand that we carry an invisible vibrational imprint from previous times, which affects how we deal with this one causing us suffering right now. A Karmic imprint can sometimes be more tangible to others at first than it is to us, so that others end up pointing it out to us one way or another. We might be able to tell, because we will either reward this with gratitude or with upset that someone has reacted to us in some way. Either way, they can often be hard to detect otherwise, until they manifest in the physical body. It could be an imprint that tells us, 'You need to learn how to stand in your power again', or 'I am learning how to alleviate suffering, by experiencing it and finding a remedy so that I can help others ' or 'I feel really weak, show me how to be strong' or 'I need to learn to feel comfortable being vulnerable', or even 'I haven't been looking after myself, so now is the time'. It's not always about placing ourselves in extreme situations. Life is often about finding out about all these very subtle inner energy blockages before they get bigger, and shifts can be made very gently within at an early stage. It is about each of us knowing ourselves, learning how to cope, learning strategies and teaching ourselves methods. I find it is an essential exercise to find out more about our inner Karmic beliefs, like in those four statements above. Perhaps you feel inspired to find some of your own, because at the end of this book, there are methods to help you find and overcome your own mindsets, or strengthen them, whichever is applicable to you.

Hopefully we will be able to gradually adjust our health and presence energy level this way once and for all, and become clear and alert enough, just like Milarepa, to realise that no violent action will bring about an easy resolution. Instead, all actions against ourselves and others become internal energies and stay there until resolved. And since remorse - or any process of insight that aids reversing a compromised energy system - can put it back on track, actually seems like a pretty desirable healing process to me. If it sometimes feels like an unfair or tough one on the individual, it is because we may never have accessed these processes before in our lifetimes. Perhaps this is the first time we have gained insight in any of our lifetimes of how these inner scenarios came about in the first place, and all we got to see so far is the results of previous Karma in action in this life. It simply is not guaranteed that we get to be all-knowing right away, but it is possible, subject to our creating our own personal timeline. It's our own conclusion if we feel this is unfair. What we can do, however, is take on board that the possibility of our energy system evolving and growing from experiences over lifetimes exists, and that allowing for this ultimately makes for a better, more peaceful co-existence with others. If it helps us to understand that this is the outcome and we can work with the principle to make better choices as well as heal the past, then it will have been the best learning curve ever.

You may have wanted me to come to the conclusion at any point in this book that, when people do evil, they will rot in hell for the rest of our lives. But Karma does not work quite like that.

Karma wants everyone, without exception, to become wise and compassionate.

As we just learned, Karma is the straightening-out of kinks in our energy blockages within us that were created as a result of wrongful doing, wrongful thinking or wrongful speaking. I have been using the word 'wrong' in the sense of unskilful, meaning, not getting the best result. It does not mean somebody is there to tell you whether your actions are right or wrong. 'Wrong' does not mean that we have to be fearful of someone punishing us, so that we end up changing our energy within in fear, to the point of disconnecting ourselves from deserving good

Karma. Nobody has the authority to change anything on our behalf on a Karmic energy level. You can try to hand over authority if you like, to see what happens. Most of us have already done this, unwittingly, and may be paying a huge price. I can already tell you that nobody can do this life for us, but that every opportunity will be there in this, our lifetime, to improve our ultimate understanding of Truth. We are never alone, and the right pointers and teachings may appear along our path just as we need them. The complete picture is always there for everyone to experience, whether we are accomplished or unaware. We have to comprehend that we cannot say for certain whether we have not committed any wrongful action in another life-time; but just because something bad happens to us, does not automatically mean we have done something wrong in a past life – but it could. In any case, it means there is an energy within, trying to right itself. There is no need to search our whole life for a specific explanation, or to guilt-trip ourselves and others, or act from a feeling of shame or fear of punishment, because that makes it even more complicated. If we tend to do this, we can luckily also undo this. Who knows what our inner contracts are, and whilst we don't know, we can end up being more confused than ever for a while, focusing too much on why something happens in our lives rather than enjoy getting on with our lives. If this happens, we can also learn to iron out our secondary reactions; not just a situation that has occurred and our feelings about a situation, but also how we are stopping ourselves subconsciously from healing from that situation. Each individual's Karma is immensely, infinitely complex and different from another's. As we said before, it follows logically that we cannot ever truly judge and condemn, that we must accept responsibility for our actions and consider the possibility that they span over more than one lifetime. Taking responsibility does not mean we have to allow others to take advantage of us. It means that our acceptance of this possibility will allow us to see and understand why we are subject to the processes and unique laws of the universe, and why we have had little insight into them so far. We can only ever truly work on our own situation and our side of the Karmic story if it involves others, hoping that others get it, too. First, they must go through their own healing process and be willing to find their own Karmic connections, in their own time. How soon they do this is up to them and depends on how and when their own Karmic conditions will bring about their own healing process. It is always different from ours. They may not be ready to understand our process for lifetimes, and we may have to learn to accept theirs and be ok with that. We all have to develop many skills along the way, different from each others'. Would it not be better for our own minds and Karma to help others, so that they meet with all the right circumstances and are sooner able to stop hurting, or causing suffering? Would we really want to meet a person to harm us under the same circumstances over and over again in another lifetime? Their own Karma is enough to decide their physical circumstances and conditions, as well as the state of mental and emotional health they will likely have in the future. It does not need us to decide what will happen to another person next. If it helps us, we can rant and rave, but whether another being is willing to take this on board, is up to them.

As for any victim of crime and their family, how hard it must be to be able to see through all this? To heal from a vicious attack, to recover from trauma, to be able to stand up again and dare to live. We can only imagine the terror connected to a violent scenario, unless we have experienced similar. All the more reason to apply the above principles, to have help offered to them to acknowledge what has happened. To be heard, to have sympathy, understanding, to grieve, to be held or left to grieve, to allow all levels of emotion to be processed. To eventually be ready again to contemplate forgiveness, to be able to take steps forward. To move on, to extract a good outcome from any life-changing event is the goal we all must individually face up to, in any of our life-times, and it is that very goal of finding inner peace again we all deserve. No-one is an exception; no-one is without suffering, none of us are singled out, as the following illustrates:

The Buddha was sitting in the shade of a tree talking to his friends when Kisa ran up to him. He could see straight away that she was very upset. "How can I help you?" he asked.

"My name is Kisa," she replied. "I have been looking everywhere for medicine for my son."

The Buddha looked at the little bundle in Kisa's arms. How could Kisa be helped to accept the truth that her little boy had really died?

"Kisa, if you want to make some medicine, you must have some mustard seeds," said the Buddha. "Go into town and ask at each house, but you must only accept seeds from a house in which no one has died."

Quickly, Kisa set off into town to get the mustard seeds.

As Kisa went from door to door, the answer was the same. Everyone had lost a loved one; if not last year, then a long time ago. Kisa had no mustard seeds but now she understood why she would not be able to find any. She looked at the little bundle in her arms. "I am sorry, my little one, you have gone to another life and I did not want to let you go. Let us find a resting place for you."

In the evening, she returned to the Buddha. She was no longer carrying the little bundle. Her face was now much calmer.

"Have you been able to find the mustard seeds, Kisa?" he asked.

"No," she replied, "but now I understand that everyone loses people they love. I have laid my baby to rest, and am now at peace. Thank you."

Coming back to the Bardo of the aggressor, if remorse does not occur at the moment of recognition – which again depends on prior Karma -, then the Karmic learning process becomes undeniably harder and delayed. It will depend on all other actions a person has taken as to what outcome their life story has, in terms of their future Karmic path and ability to learn from their actions.

What we can tell and have already established is that another's Karmic life pattern is infinitely complicated, cannot realistically be fully looked into by anyone else, and none of us may ever know what has occurred to anyone before, to prompt them to make choices for themselves which may affect them and others' lives indefinitely. We only have our senses to observe their actions, thought and speech in determining how accomplished they may have become, and those can potentially be compromised.

Sometimes, we get the feeling that we might know somebody from a past life experience. This can happen, although I also believe that experiences mirror and repeat themselves, so that certain energies in people end up reflecting and triggering reactions within us, making us feel like we have met them before. On the other hand, if it is true that we all have lived for aeons of time, we would have met quite a few people in previous lifetimes and may recognise them again in this lifetime, perhaps even spend a prolonged period of time with them. To most of us in the West, having not been educated in the art of Karma and being relatively new to the subject, the whole idea of rebirth and Karma probably seems like superstition, or serves as interesting food for thought but hypothetical examples at best. Not all of us are going to recognise their own evolution in the concept of reincarnation. However, if we can keep an open mind as to the usefulness of the outcome of a belief system that understands how energy survives and affects us in a lifespan that extends this very life we have now, then it can be a useful starting point for learning more. It may also be good to point out that we have so far been theorising mostly about the potential outcomes of wrong actions in this chapter, which is inevitably very dramatic. Not all scenarios when passing into the Bardo are bad! Many of them are reported to be very serene and beautiful, allowing our energy to merge again with the all-encompassing, luminous sensation of the omnipresence of formless energy. The bottom line is logical - that it is desirable if we can leave the beautiful experiences to the Bardo state to determine the quality of our next existence, but face up to and deal with any undesirable previous actions, even seemingly insignificant ones, right here and now, sooner rather than later..

Any one of us can become aware of our

Karmic connections within this lifetime.

On a more upbeat note, any of us could theoretically become aware of our Karmic connections at any given moment during our lives and well before it's too late, we would be able to use at least some of our time in our human bodies to enjoy exercising compassion and redeem ourselves somewhat. We can choose to become aware by changing the vibration of any of our potentially negative past Karmic actions. We can even do this without knowing if there have been any negative actions. Any good actions that we undertake will create good conditions for us and others involved, now and in the future. Perhaps we will get to be in a true state of peace as a result, which is, after all, what we are all striving for: real peace and happiness that comes from a mind which has made peace with itself and its surroundings. Any of us are able to turn around our wrong actions whilst still alive and make amends, too. It is all about undoing the electromagnetic processes that have occurred as a result of any harmful action, and creating a good outcome for the future.

Thinking about it logically, if this is all as it is and there had been any harmful action taken against anyone, we would not only have to look at our own complex reasons for acting this way, but also be well advised to look at everyone else's Karma that would have been affected by our actions, including any victims and their families.

A soldier serving in a war was struck by remorse, feeling the full force of the true meaning of his having killed an enemy's child. He was so upset by the impact of his action that he asked the Lord Buddha what he could do to truly undo the Karma of his action. The answer came, 'Go and find an enemy's orphaned child and raise him as your own'. (Unknown Source)

To understand the parable and put ourselves into the mind of the soldier, we would realise that he was asked to learn to understand the creation and precious existence of life. He was asked to commit to being there through every stage of the child's development, re-assessing his own life throughout whilst also being responsible for his adopted child. He would thus be most likely confronted with the triggers that having killed another child would drag up. The parable explains adequately what it means to be responsible for our own actions and the consequences thereof, as well as committing to taking care of another's life and well-being. Karma is tough but fair and equal, with no short-cuts, unavoidable and necessary but certainly doable; a precious chance to make amends and attempt to release the negative Karma that the action of killing left behind.

Less dramatic actions in our lifetimes are also subject to the same underlying Karmic process of healing through recognition, remorse, understanding underlying principles of the vastness and preciousness of universal vibration, acceptance, amends and forgiveness, as in the case above.

The Vibration of our Karmic Energy System Contains the Blueprint for our Next Life-Form.

Spiritually awakened people often say that it is possible for us to 'choose' our life-form, the date and time of birth, our parents, circumstances etc. That is true – except, as you can tell by now, it may not be by conscious choice unless we are highly evolved beings. Most of the time, the choices are being made for 'us', our ego-selves, by our Karmic minds. Our Karmic energy creates our physical 'Self' based on our Karmic energy, according to the combination of a myriad of patterns of repelling/attracting vibrational frequencies as well as spacious neutral clarity, all of which were gradually accumulated in all our lifetimes and cyclic existence before, right down to the most recent formative impulses that made us come back into another physical existence. As you may imagine, very few people are capable and present enough when it comes to it, to be able to steer their energy towards a higher rebirth, although with specific training in this life and specific preparation for an auspicious death, this is entirely possible and sacred practice for those who submit their lives to this achievement. Even a Karmic energy charge that has not been accounted for yet, whether 'positive' or 'negative', is taken into account in this instantaneous 'weighing up' process on our inner energy scales, in the process of passing, but also during many stages throughout our lifetime. There is a parable of this process in many scriptures, not just the Christian or Hebrew bible, which I am using here as an example. The text is the Menetekel, to give an idea of this phenomenon. The writing on the wall, a much-quoted paraphrase, literally appears to the King Belshazzar. I have taken it to mean that his Karmic energy body had been 'weighed', as in the processes in the Bardo state, and that it had been found to be lacking, purporting the looming loss of his kingdom and his own demise:

*||This is the writing that was inscribed: **Mene Mene Tekel Upharsin**. This is the interpretation of the thing: MENE; God has numbered your kingdom, and brought it to an end; TEKEL; you are weighed in the balances, and are found wanting*
Daniel 5:25-29 ||

It appears to be an analogy to what we are talking about in general; stages within and between our lifetimes where our Karmic energy system is assessed, where it is temporarily merged and measured against the greater, all-encompassing energy. If parts of it are of lower frequency, the result of the measuring would mean that it cannot fully be merged with the greater energy. If our energy frequency has dropped through wrong actions, we will start to feel it, too, well before it's time for a final weigh-in, and this is what I believe the analogy is telling us: that it will give us plenty of warning signs that we are on the wrong path; and that the result of our actions will be that our rebirth is not guaranteed to go well accordingly.
Either this is what happened to King Belshazzar, or someone was after his kingdom and tricked him into being murdered. We will never quite know. But I do think it's interesting that there are many parables and historic accounts in many cultures and religions that speak of this energy phenomenon, often in very cryptic ways, which make the message slightly more mysterious.
Here is another example:

'In Maat ...the dead (called the " Judgment of Osiris," named for Osiris, the god of the dead) was believed to focus upon the weighing of the heart of the deceased in a scale balanced by Maat (or her hieroglyph, the ostrich feather), as a test of conformity to proper values.'
(From https://www.britannica.com/topic/Judgment-of-Osiris)

As we can see, here is the same phenomenon described to occur in an example of a different culture, namely that of Ancient Egypt, talking about the 'weighing of the heart' in the afterlife (the hall of Maat), to see how much the being in question had adhered to the equivalent of good Karma.
What is interesting to observe is the mention of process of 'weighing' itself. Fascinating to think that, if we understand that there is no weight to our Karmic energy encoded as a frequency when it is ready to merge with the omnipresent energy that is, it might be deemed too 'heavy' if there is any unresolved issues attached to it. The parable would suggest that unresolved issues are still attached to the physical realm and therefore carry a measurable weight. Is this possibly indicative of our

unresolved Karmic energy itself remaining attached to the physical realm and that it must return to it, because there is an actual 'weight' to our Karmic energy that draws it back down to Earth? It could mean that what we have been deducting about how Karma could have scientific principles at the root, if our electromagnetic coding is not able to fully transform into weightless Karmic energy frequency after death, ready to merge with the highest formlessness, then it may have no choice but to return at some stage according to the nature of all its energy components, in order to complete its physical journey on Earth. I am certain that we could come up with a visual model of what our Karmic energy would look like when it passes from physical body into its surrounding, and attempts to dissipate further into finer frequencies until ready to either merge with greater consciousness or return on Earth. If there are components attached to the energy which is our unresolved matter, then the density of those modules will pull us into another lifetime in the physical realm, certainly sooner if there is indeed a link between its density and the pull of attachment to another life-form.

It is fascinating and encouraging to see that many vibrational phenomena are equally represented in various forms of worship, no matter by what name. Whether the knowledge of full events was at some point in human history hacked into bite-size pieces by some, in order to make them more palatable for the masses, or whether they were hijacked in history by perpetrators trying to manipulate mankind - my belief is that whenever humans became immersed in events beyond our physical form involving vibrational energy, they all seemed to want to describe and make a record of these phenomena. Set in stone, written on papyrus, carved into walls - as soon as we take anything from formlessness down into the solid 3rd dimension to manifest in physical form, it seems we must accept that it can get watered down to become a somewhat reduced likeness of the original events. The same is, of course, true for any process when using language to describe events, reminiscent of the tower of Babylon, where nobody understood each other any longer after trying to construct a 3-dimensional tower to reach the higher realms (!), as opposed to reference in the Old Testament where people ended up speaking in tongues when touched by the 'Holy Spirit', meaning their minds were inspired to talk only of their experiences of the highest frequencies. In order to understand why there are a myriad of different interpretations of all these energy transmissions, it might help to understand that most scriptures will by necessity be metaphorical analogies. They try to convey an experience to others who may not have had those experiences yet. Even when reading accurate accounts of Karmic events in ancient scriptures, these texts are so rich and varied in their vast choices of language and dialect, that the texts are often incomprehensible for most. Even when translated by specialists, words can easily be misinterpreted or lost in translation. In order to experience Truth, we have to find methods to experience its vastness for and within ourselves. We can read a thousand books but still not know the Truth. Be that as it may, whether we understand the full principles behind it or not, we are all subject to it.

Every detail of all that we have ever experienced is taken into consideration and recorded in its entirety within our own Karmic energy system.

The irony is, therefore, that we already HAVE a complete record within, of what it feels like to be awash with beautiful universal energy and all that ensues from it. It is 'written' within us, in Karmic energy coding! We have to get back into it, to merge our conscious, busy ego mind with it. We can do that by quietening our chattering monkey mind and be still, until our awareness rises of who we really are, of what our true energy core feels like and what it is capable of recording and being. What has happened instead is that we started to interpret it and wanted to put our own version out there, so to speak. We might have wanted to share our excitement at what we found, but we don't have to be clever or educated in order to experience our 'I AM' presence. Every being without exception has the inner ability of full insight and the resulting wisdom and compassion; it is not a process that needs a university degree or a single written word. Oh..- the irony is not lost on me.

Even those situations we accredit to others or blame others for, only come back to what the energy of these interactions does to the energy within us. Others can even be like a mirror for our own energy and reflect it back at us. It makes little difference whether anything was ever anyone else's fault or not, in terms of how we can resolve it. When I came across those who had been wronged in therapy sessions, surprisingly it did not matter so much in the end whether the attackers were aware of the wrong they had done, whether they were punished or not, whether they singled their victim out or chose them randomly. What mattered most to the victim was to untangle their energy from that of the aggressor, in order to be free to be able to get on with their lives as far as possible. Their Karmic energy was no longer intertwined with that of the aggressor after applying simple methods of undoing these jarring knots and convolutions. It seems to be crucial in our healing process to go through how it felt within us, to learn how our separate energy bodies each individually received a particular energy vibration of a specific event in a particular time span and how our bodies and minds reacted to it at the time and how this has perpetuated since. It is crucial for our Karmic energy healing process to also learn how our reaction to any event remains present within our Karmic energy system. It sustained an imprint that was created as a result of an incident, which, if you remember, is what we were talking about earlier. We are actually able to claim back all our lost energy again from events as well as involving others - sometimes even in an instant.

The opposite of the above incidents and resulting energy connection can occur if our connection with events and other beings is of a higher nature. The higher the vibration, the more synergy there is between humans as to our homogeneous interpretation of it. The Karmic energy composition we share with like-minded or higher-frequency beings is benevolent and experienced as a loving, caring, gentle, synergetic healing process. We may use different words in different languages, but it seems we are all able to experience and describe the same phenomenon when we are experiencing the flow of universal energy within. Some people interpret this to come from within in the first place, and some believe it to be from around us, as far away as other universes and perhaps some force greater than we can imagine. Others still need to have a figurative explanation and a more condensed or even scientific version, in order to comprehend and accept these principles according to their comparisons with their beliefs. All methods, beliefs and attempts at understanding are equally valid in the light of humans trying to grasp and integrate the inner processes needed to absorb the Truth with a capital ‚T‘. It is understandable that, as part of that process, people will create bite-sized pieces of a section of this Truth. This will be ok for some, but not enough for others. All of it is right in the light of learning open-heartedly; nothing is inherently wrong with breaking down elements of Truth. Problems only start setting in when any process is interpreted wrongly and/or used with ill-intent such as via forms of elitist thinking trying to capitalise on these free concepts and bind people's freedom for their own ill gain. Often, the infinite potential of being able to do good is not fully understood as part of a whole macrocosm of existence. If we did understand it, we would relax more. Any of these scenarios have of course already occurred and repeat themselves over and over again on Earth in every generation that has to learn anew, as part of the principle of cyclic existence on Earth. That seems to be the nature of the 3-d beast we're up against.

This process of assimilating energy events in our lives is not only true for people or situations we have come across, but also for any physical conditions we have or may develop; any unresolved physical conditions are connected to the energy chinks in our Karmic armour. They are also reviewed many times throughout our lives, and at one final time in the Bardo state of our passing, when the information from our physical body is transferred to our Karmic energy body which lives on. Say, for example, you have suffered from an injury for some time which never fully healed. At the time of 'Karmic energy weighing', any energy blockage present in an injury is translated from your physical experience into the pure energy realm of existence beyond all physical existence. There will be an automatic alignment of how this energy imprint of an injury will be transmuted into a future existence, based on the specific Karmic energy pattern that it has left, and the general state of Karmic energy the person has accumulated. Some interesting questions to pose would be:

Does the overall energy body of a being have the strength to recognise and override the imprint of an injury in order to neutralise it, i.e. heal and complete the energy in that part of the body whilst we are still alive? Has it gathered enough understanding and good Karma to not have to repeatedly endure having this physical injury? Will there be signs of the injury in a next life and if so, what might they be and how can an injury be prevented from presenting itself in our next life?

We may have never contemplated any of these concepts as yet, so that thinking about how we can prepare ourselves for our next life probably seems an alien thought process to most of us. If we were brought up in cultures where reincarnation is an accepted fact, then there would be many such preparations in place to ascertain a good rebirth, and this is in fact what is already an integral practice in many Eastern philosophies. The attitude is one of inclusiveness, making sure that what we do right now will be of benefit in future lives, and at the very least a neutral action which does not harm us or anyone else. If harmful actions occur, practices and prayers are applied to lessen their impact. Preparations are done for a good passing, even predictions where and how a next incarnation is possible, even likely.

You can probably already tell that, once again, we cannot judge the full dimensions of the principles of Karma just by mulling it over in our brains. But it must be said that some aspects are predictable, at least by those who are insightful and wise enough to interpret certain signs and attributes. Prophesies have been done for thousands of years, reaching far into our future even, and it appears they were quite true in many cases. In terms of physical conditions which was our initial questions, any injury would be seen as to being there for a choice of reasons, any which one can and will contribute to its further existence - unless the fateful slate may be wiped clean by the person in question creating good Karma. It might help if it has already sunk into our Karmic consciousness that an injury has at its core an energy blockage or weakness that can be reversed. Any such imprints in our Karmic energy bodies might be something we may have had to hang on to for some time during our physical existence, but we may develop the good Karma of realisation to not have to repeat or hang on to it any longer. Some cultures firmly believe we can carry physical marks such as birthmarks, moles, scars and similar into the next life from an injury in a previous one. I find it fascinating to explore this in terms of our Karmic energy breaches or chinks which we talked about at the beginning, actually being able to manifest as physical signatures of previous injuries in and on our bodies. Whilst some can't befriend the idea, I don't think it's far-fetched at all when we consider that, actually, all of our bodies' aggregates are created as a result of our surviving Karmic energy coding reincarnating from previous existences.

All these insights are food for thought and serve to inspire us to take these findings into account and integrate them into our lives any way that we see fit. They are there to enrich and enhance our worldly experience so that we will have the freedom to each decide in a strictly personal manner what is best for us and everyone involved.

The same logic that applies to physical issues also applies to any other situations we have discussed so far. We are not at all used to thinking this way in the West, where physical illness and accidents are seen as a nuisance. We are not that interested in why a condition arose, but are focused on fixing everything again as quickly as possible so that we can function and enjoy life again. We treat illness as separate from our bodies, something alien that we want to get rid of as quickly as possible with medical intervention, rather than finding out about any potential holistic approach which may take longer but is able to help our bodies heal many symptoms that allopathic medicine can only mask. There can be no right or wrong. Both ways are right, both ways have validity. Both ways are there to help alleviate suffering, and many who help as medical staff or natural healers are equally equipped, compassionate, dedicated and able to bring about cures.

Some of us may wait until our deaths to resolve any physical hangovers and still live as if nothing could ever harm us, but even if we ignore the warning signs we may be faced with our Karmic state of mind nonetheless many times before then. We may even be pulled into this Bardo world we talked about during our lifetime. It is possible to catch glimpses of it way before we are dying. This is the in-between state of mind outside the physical realm, a sub-conscious space/time continuum where split second decision-making and processing inner information will be influenced by our Karmic past and influences our Karmic future, where we are sometimes openly faced with our raw selves, with our issues and those we have taken on to be ours, in a very intense and yet overseeing way. In the Bardo we may also be presented with insights again as to how all things are interconnected, and we can draw conclusions from being temporarily merged with the greater wisdom mind. Some people have entered such in-between stages unwittingly during their lifetimes or try to follow methods to do so deliberately, to attempt to come out the other end feeling much lighter, sometimes to find that their injuries and whatever their cause is, has vanished.

A reminder once again that this is not to punish us or anything, far from it; there is no such thing. However, if we do not see through the whole mechanism of how our Karmic bodies function on the basis of our previous levels of understanding and make necessary adjustments to help us be healthy, this may mean that the electromagnetic light body that survives our physical body could choose a similar problem within another physical body again in future lifetimes. It may continue to do so until the Karmic imprint of any injury or negativity in our bodies lessens. We can either address it now, or rely on being affected for a number of precious lifetimes until we finally find the right solutions for it to disappear. Does that not sound awfully tedious? It does! So why do we put up with it?

It seems a human condition that it happens like this with many incarnations we have, before we achieve certain levels of awareness that permeate our existence. We somehow forget every time who we are from lifetime to lifetime and appear to have no method to retrieve valuable information and insights from our past existences. We tend to therefore spend lifetimes and precious lifetimes tediously reconstructing the meaning of life and our place within it, slowly growing in spirit as a snail crawls along the floor, unaware of its surroundings, living unaware of the truth of how we came about in the first place. Our many archetypical fears stop us from looking at the Magickal mystery of life. Luckily, more and more people are awakening to the realisation that we are the sole entity responsible for all our Karma and that so far, we are terrified of the fact. The sooner we realise it, the sooner we can shrug it off, laugh about it and be mended from the malaise.

Is it easier said than done? I believe we have not had better conditions, more opportunities and quicker methods to repair our energy bodies for a long time, as we have now. And yet, our poor little Self still chooses for us to run away most times, hiding into total oblivion, out of fear, ignorance, or even greed in some individuals' cases – but mostly fear. My personal opinion is that we can certainly apply methods to alleviate fear, we can build communities to share knowledge to alleviate ignorance, but greed is something that has the urge to destroy not only us, but many other lives and our planet, too. Underlying greed is fear once again, if only those acting out of greed would be willing to conquer their fears and turn within to find answers. We can but hope.

Bardo: Vision of the Serene Divinities, Tibet 19th Cntry. © Tibet image Library

At the Bardo states throughout our lives, and certainly at the time of death, we will see the greater consciousness as it presents itself in all its glory; but we will also be presented with our lesser conscious times - even if time no longer exists at that stage, and neither does an understanding of how we might have wasted precious time remaining unconscious. At any of those stages though, even when it's at the last minute, hopefully some idea of the bigger picture and the vastness that we are, will set in. If not, perhaps we get a chance to compare the various forms of existence in what is called the second Bardo, or the stages of the six senses. In any case, if we are preparing ourselves now and contemplate on the vastness we inherently are as well as the smallness we thought we were limited to so far. These concepts appear to coincide with the accounts from people who experience near-death experiences. Many of them report seeing this all-encompassing amazingly bright light and feeling pulled by it, yearned to be united with this light body of painlessness and would have chosen not to return. Some won't and go on to other experiences beyond this initial stage, some are given a choice whether to return into this life, and some return but really did not want to; they would have rather remained in the very bearable lightness of being beyond the pain of a physical existence. Being drawn back down to Earth and having seen connections between both worlds, there is something very useful that can happen. This useful thing is something called insight. Insight is of course not just useful, it is a wonderful thing and once we have it, we will probably want to hang on to it and experience it over and over again. It may not always *feel* wonderful but without it, there is no process of the Karmic energy reversals we talked about, which are necessary for a chance of a partial or even total release of our inner energy blockages. We would remain stuck in the same situations for even longer without our new insight, or even regress in our evolutionary process, which is also entirely possible. If only we knew what's at stake! We live such complex and stressful lives that we have forgotten who we are; we have forgotten our true age, our wisdom, our endless energy as well as our personal time-line that brought us here. Our complex Karmic energy system is capable of recording it all, and comes up with the results of our previous actions over and over again, mirroring them back at us through our environment. There are, of course, not just bad times but good ones, too! Only we can see through it all, and hopefully we can overcome hurdles creatively in this lifetime, as that would mean we could indeed be in with a chance to undo all of our negative Karma in one life-time. It can be done, and some people are able to do it. However, to start off with, we should simply start by looking to try and find out who we really are, what makes us, us – and learn methods that help us become the beings that we are truly capable of being, instead of just the result of endless loops of twisted balls of negative energy that urgently need discharging from our every pore.

I am pretty sure which path I would find more rewarding.

* * *

30. Experiences of my own Karmic Energy Mind

Because of my obvious fascination throughout all my adult life with the universal energy concept that is Karma, I felt passionate about finding useful and effective methods for understanding, realising and also sharing ways of how to overcome the less desirable aspects of the cycle of existence. Whilst I wondered if in many ways my efforts might be in danger of reinventing the wheel, I soon came across a lack of existing translated material on the subject that I felt was conveyable to a wider audience without losing its in-depth, comprehensive approach to explaining it well. Although material such as this is now becoming more easily available, the methodology is often still very complex and difficult to understand for most. Also, it's easy to notice an increase in spiritual awareness and emphasis on esoterica in the West in the past couple of decades. Many have entered a similar quest for solutions, created by our need to understand and overcome the stresses our every-day challenges produce. It's easy to lose clarity, though, and the myriad of directions the Western mind takes are reflected in the plethora of spiritual tools marketed today. I was never interested in marketing spiritual awareness. Instead, I wanted to promote well-being, particularly on the level of our much ignored energy minds, in order to find links between our Karma and possible causes for ill-health that would have the potential to go beyond a mere diagnostic of where it hurts in our physical body and prescribing a painkiller. I knew I wanted to come up with a more easily accessible way of understanding the principles of Karma, so that it would be possible for any lay being to utilise and benefit from it in their everyday lives.

I decided some years ago that I wanted to do some research into my own past lives, having come across the first one described in an earlier chapter purely by accident. Before having my own insights, I was probably as sceptical about these occurrences as any other person, and blissfully (or stubbornly?) ignorant. I remember a book by a celebrity coming out a couple of decades ago, speaking openly about her past lives. I was fascinated, but also doubtful that could I possibly believe in something I could not remember experiencing. Also, how could it be proven that what I was experiencing as a past life was not just some early childhood memory? Could it not just be dismissed as a childhood experience, cloaked in colours and a context I would, as an adult, no longer recognise as having occurred in the earlier years of my life? And, last but not least, would people ridicule me and judge me for believing that some of the more obscure scenes that unfolded during my past-life recalls were truly my very own experiences, only in a different timespan?

Having now read several very fascinating books on the subject, and having had quite a few of my own experiences since, it is now not a mystery to me any longer; it seems very logical to me now after 20 years studying the subject. I even care a little less if people think it odd. Countless people in various cultures on Earth believe in Karma, and many have vivid memories of their previous existences. The effect it has had on me is that I do not feel I have anything to prove by quoting from my own experiences about the subject. To me, it is more than just an interesting experiment we either believe in or not. Whilst I never actively sought out past life memory recall, I do firmly believe it is an important and natural process of gathering information en route to completing our Karmic energy system. Much like a medic might develop a remedy by injecting themselves with it first to see if it works and is safe, I always want to make sure that the methods I have explored and experienced have relevance, are safe and most importantly that they work well enough for others to want to experience their benefit also.

My own individual experiences have in the past come on suddenly, often very rapidly and unexpectedly, after sometimes taking years to develop into conscious realisation. To concentrate on them alone would have been a science in its own right, but I did not want it to distract from my overall practice. It may help to know that there are many thousands of baffling but verified accounts of individuals, even small children who can recall many details of their past lives; they can often give accurate details of their previous existence, their names, looks, age, family, where and how they lived and how they died, and have, in some cases, even been able to find the place again when guided to it.

Since I did not grow up with a religious belief that encourages interest in rebirth, in fact quite the opposite, I blocked and fought the idea with left-brain, analytical logic for a very long time. I am mentioning this here, because it is quite common to think that way as a result of a Western upbringing, which tends to favour left-brain orientation. At least the past four decades in the West have been very focused on intellect, and using this intellect for predominantly for commercial gain. When we don't have a balance between right brain intuition and left brain logical/analytical thinking, it happens that we become dismissive of all things we cannot find a logical explanation or use for. Being right-brain orientated and intuitive in a left-brained educational system, you may possibly have grown up as the odd one out in your circle of family, friends or work place. If you felt different then or even still feel different, alone, misunderstood and at odds with a world hell-bent on destruction now, you have probably asked yourself a million times why you are so different from those you are involved with in your life. Even now, educating our children is still based mostly on skills concerning left-brain logic, and children are evaluated from much too early an age by their ability to be logical and rational. People, especially those with children and/or working within the education system, are recognising that we have many different talents which are falling short of traditional evaluation by any traditional schooling system. Acknowledging the difference between children acting from the left and right brain hemispheres means that more and more children these days who are creative and inventive and follow their own rhythm and thought pattern are no longer classed as different at best, disruptive at worst. They may have been labelled as unintelligent, hopeless dreamers or have fallen short of tests and exam results. Nowadays, children are labelled with ADHD or being 'on the spectrum' to at least acknowledge that they think and feel differently, but more that their mentors take note not to label them any longer in a derogative way. Our children are calling for a different way to treat them, a way that is more geared to the talents of the individual needs of each child, rather than a rigid system treating each child the same. Children are becoming more and more sensitive, families find themselves under so much more pressure for their children to perform under the guise of authorities rule making, so that more parents than ever are looking into alternative education methods which allow for a more sympathetic style of education. Taking into consideration each child's needs and sensitivities, taking cues from the children themselves as to what they want to learn and where can bring about a new era of education the new restless generation. We need to adapt as to how we can ascertain that there is more variety of places and methods to teach from day to day, even hour to hour. These new generations are fast, and they get things more quickly. They are much more easily bored, and catch out the teachers that fall short of their scrutiny of whether the system is right in supplying one teacher for a classroom of over 30, in an overcrowded environment that is full of walls and limitations. Our modern children want to be free, and their minds are more free. It's a good thing, after all they are the ones who have to tidy up the mess we left this world in. If this rings true for you or your family, please know that you are not alone any longer, I would say. If you ever felt isolated, please also know that the stigma involved in making life choices based on intuition, insight, artistry, music, creativity, psychic ability and so on, is diminishing. In the current climate of Earth history which is still favouring brain activity over heart matters, we are prompted to keep on trying to readdress the balance, because that may be what we came here to do, for us, for our children, and for new generations to be able to thrive.

But I digress. I have no doubt that there are literally endless previous lives we have lived, even though this seems impossible an experience to verify, since we have never followed up on these subjects scientifically. However, the good thing is that science is indeed catching up fast, and even science is now looking into the fact that it is very likely some part of us survives after death. The inner experience of re-living some of my previous lives has convinced me without a shred of doubt that they existed, and I existed in them. Re-living them is exactly that: it is literally feeling everything that I felt as the person I was at that time, being in that body instead of just seeing myself outside of it observing, as if I had a kind of inner camera filming events. however, far from being in a movie of my own imagination, the person I was when reliving a previous lifetime felt absolutely real. I could recall what is was to be in that life, how it felt to be within virtually every tiny detail of that physical body, to look through my eyes as they were then, with the thoughts and feelings I had in that life, about the unfamiliar events I could not remember until then. You could argue that this sounds very much like hypnotism, or rather what people generally perceive a hypnotic state to be; that we become some other identity, and suddenly do crazy things when asked to. This is not the case with my experiences. I was fully aware of the overlap of my own physical presence in the room and that of another lifetime in which I had already existed. I didn't set out to have these experiences, they just occurred in broad daylight without anyone else present, without warning or preparation, without any process of Self-suggestion or hypnosis being used. In any case, being so focused on the detailed events of those lives I witnessed, I would have not been able to follow any instructions by anyone else present in the room asking me to do something anyway, as my logical, present-time brain was fully awake and aware all throughout, and I am sure would have contested any interference with the experience I was concentrating on. So it cannot have been what we generally perceive to be hypnotism.

What did probably occur is that my mind went into a true meditative theta state, during which we can easily recall many things logged in our Karmic energy system that we were previously not consciously aware of.

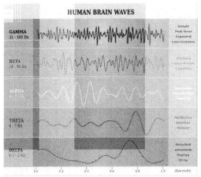

image credit © https://www.dreamstime.com

Often, when recalling another lifetime, I became aware of its limitations, too. Having awareness of my own Self simultaneously with the 'other', as if cooking on two gas flames at the same time, compensated for the sometimes chilling recall that came with that 'other' body. It felt good that, despite what happened to me in previous lifetimes, I could remind myself that I a solid, functioning body that I could depend on now. As you will be able to see below, some of the lifetimes I recalled were most definitely not chosen for their glamour, and actions I took in previous lifetimes now seem cringe-worthy and embarrassing to open up to. I realised we weren't all Joan of Arc or Albert Einstein in a previous lifetime. I did have scruples sharing these experiences here. I asked myself why anyone would want to share some of their personal lifetimes, when the whole procedure will be exposed and cause embarrassment, but at the same time, I see usefulness in being humble. Also, I do like doing things the hard way sometimes, it's way too easy sitting on a chair in front of an audience declaring myself enlightened. Last but not least, reading about these simultaneously mundane and weird experiences may have benefits for others: I'll try it so that you can do it, too, in a less exposed and more mainstream and private manner if you choose to. I have only good conclusions to draw from all my experiences, and that is what spurs me on – only good can come from realisation of our personal truth, and it may also lead us to realisation of greater Truth. Seeing the bigger picture now as a result of many past-life experiences helps me to understand the connections of why I chose that specific body and mind, that particular lifestyle at that time; and also how it relates to who I am now. It opens up choices again in this life, following a path of honesty and acceptance. Life does start to make sense then, and I can recommend the process if you are at all interested, even though I am probably not so fully committed to and versed in the hunt for past lives as some individuals are. I did not even set out to experience some of them in the first place, instead I wanted to resolve some deep-rooted fears that presented themselves in the present. The recalls just happened as part of a greater quest and a deep inner practice. It is as if I needed to see a few lifetimes with my very own eyes, and once I had seen, I did not need to go into it any further to believe they were real. I learned very suddenly in one experience that when we function mostly in the right brain hemisphere of intuition, there is no desire to look for analytical proof because we inherently know it to be true, with every fibre of our body. Who knows, maybe some day we will find proof, but what occurred I know to be real, and that was right and good enough for me as it is for thousands of others who had similar experiences.

As I said, most of my past lives tended to flash before my eyes and charge upon me without me even looking for them. I don't drink alcohol and I am lucky enough to also not have to take any prescription drugs, and I must admit I have never taken drugs of any kind and do not advocate it, not even to enhance any of these spiritual experiences. I feel it is not necessary and I have met people who nearly died or did die doing what they did, so I am very wary of the commercialisation of spiritual trips. I know that many these have experimented with hallucinogens and I don't judge, but I personally find that the risk of losing yourself in them is just too high. It's not the point. I was lucky enough to have had some great teachers who taught me ways to access deeper levels of consciousness without looking for them, by just simply sitting down to meditate. The past life experiences I had arose from a constant practice of meditation and focusing inwards. I know that some will be sceptic and I can't change that, we all have our own path of finding our own inner truth, but I know that my experiences were not auto-suggestive, either, in case you were wondering. I do not use meditation music or guided meditations. I simply work with silence and simple in-breath/out-breath, a steady gaze and the images and recurring feelings that present themselves within as a result. I don't alter them or suppress them, and that is where the methodology I use is very different from most that are marketed. These experiences are not the result of some money-making scheme or the latest craze. They are simply – already there. If anything, you need to peel away a lot of external mumbo-jumbo and get comfortable with the nothingness to find the eternal energy that's already there. Some experiences of a previous existence appeared this way as part of a deep meditation, some as an intense, sudden and unexpected flash of insight; others yet again were aided by using the simple process of tapping into the energy experiences within, mostly through the meridian method of EFT™, which you can learn more about at the end of this book. The tapping process helped me to focus and also lose any fear that came up as a result of my experiences of past lives. Having said that, I have to add as a disclaimer that the EFT™ algorithm was not necessarily designed for this purpose by its founder, Gary Craig, but, in my case, it lent itself beautifully to the process. It helped me release fear, feel relaxed, go with the flow and be able to allow whatever it was that wanted to surface in the form of energy information. I was able to permit the Karmic energy flow through my mind without trying to judge, alter my perception of it, or feel that I wanted to escape or create a dependency on the outcome of it. It was part of my Truth and as such, I have always worked with it and value it deeply.

This was the way I came across one past life experience, one of those you can't possibly have dreamed up to want to relive, or feel proud of as it presented itself. I will go into it all the same, to give you an idea of the process of linking elements of insights into past lives to this present lifetime after the event. I didn't find it at all funny at the time it happened, I was shocked as I looked down on myself, only to see and feel my body as that of a very thin French woman in a decade or even century long gone. And before some readers may smirk, this is not a sales gimmick. There was no glamour in this life, I am afraid to say. I felt her feelings of despair and depression immediately, a deep state of desolation and resignation. I felt a deep loneliness that I had never before known in my life. In any of my sessions, I did not choose my experiences like a child looking at a sweet shop picking out the best ones before buying. I ended up being in this past life experience, because it simply appeared and presented itself as part of another issue I had been working on a few days prior. I did not at all reckon with the harshness of experiencing this life so out of the blue and would never have consciously chosen to go through it. It took my breath away how depressing and desperate the moments were that I experienced as this thin, drawn woman with black hair scraped back into a bun; and yet so mixed with her deep longing to help somehow, to connect and feel useful as a human being, and to bring healing to the people who were brought to her. Everything in her room was a dark, dingy red, with cream high ceilings, an unlikely flamboyant chandelier, worn carpet runners, shabby wallpaper, a few bits of sparse furniture. But the room was freezing cold, had only stale air and hardly any daylight. It was not a happy deep red but a colour of feeling sickly and abused, invoking a sense of desolation and a sense of resignation when I realised suddenly I would never have the chance of getting out of this misery, being who and what I was in that lifetime. I smoked in that life, even felt a cigarette installed on my dry lips. I felt the paradoxical comfort from it; at least there was something, anything. I don't smoke in this life – never smoked even a single cigarette. I have always hated the smell and during this recall of my past life, I absolutely hated the restrictive feeling of being a heavy smoker. At some point during the experience, I got transported right towards the end of that lifetime. I recall looking down on my thin, old, desiccated and drawn body, proud only of my still thin and shapely legs, but I had come to realise that it was not the sort of pride that was lasting or desirable, but the kind that left you feeling weak and alone. At some point I simply collapse from sheer exhaustion in that very room I had always lived in. My stomach feels caved in and sore, like i am sick and haven't been able to eat for a long time. I feel deeply cold lying on the floor, there is nobody with me and I am ready to leave this weary existence. But none of the males I indicate had been with me in that room attend to my rescue. Instead, there is nobody there to help or witness my death. I die alone, feeling overwhelmingly cold. I feel my heart stop just from the sheer weight of not wanting to live that life any more, and at that point I take my last breath. It feels endless, like I can't breathe even as I sit there, observing my vision. End of story? No. Here is the most peculiar thing: as I feel myself passing, I gain some terrific insights. Firstly, I never realised that I truly did try to help those who I met with in that room with all my heart and soul, with all the means and understanding that I had at my disposal. With all my heart I wanted them to feel better, to be healed, and I wore myself out caring for them deeply on some level, but also despised their ignorance and ruthlessness on another. I never made them realise that I had a heart, too, and that I wished for them to see how pure and gentle it was. I saw then, that my Karmic energy body had allowed me to do my healing in that lifetime with mostly the limited help of lowering my energy to others' expectations. I had no choice in that life, but there was a price to pay for the less than sacred unions that never once allowed me to involve and open my heart in that life to someone special. I was meant to continue searching for something else, I realise that now. The hard life I lived and the feelings I suppressed meant that I had spent a life giving away my energy without receiving in return. I was quite simple-minded, so it never occurred to me to ask this of anybody. Once i had finally passed, I could also truly feel that there was no-one at fault. There was no blame at that point, only pure understanding and the wish to love even more wholeheartedly next time – and in that instant, I recognised that my unfulfilled and urgent wish to find what it is that gives us everlasting love became the Karmic energy attachment to my next human experience.

Where exactly this incarnation fitted in, in terms of chronological sequence of all the other recalls I had, I could not say for sure; I also did not dwell on how many lifetimes I had before then and after that. What I do know and value more than anything is that many insights into my present life were opened up as a result of the above experience. I believe that it helped me to see the following:

As a result of Selfless actions and genuine – if somewhat restricted - love for humanity in that lifetime, my Karmic energy body was able to expand, seeing that these unconditional actions had a positive impact; which, in turn, created a new, stronger, healthier body in this lifetime, a female incarnation again due to the unresolved feelings I had, but able to incorporate an understanding of yin and yang principles to internalise the experience of both elements; as well as a new incarnation of new physical and emotional strength with a very loving, secure attachment to my beautiful family, to several very beautiful homes with a strong presence of both a caring father and mother. It created understanding and knowledge of the need to overcome physical desires in order to pursue a path of the profane. I became adept at teaching methods to alleviate psychological and emotional needs by choosing a profession that taught me all I needed to know to appreciate both.

I also learned in my chosen times of solitude that my immense capacity for love and healing was meant for much more than just its physical manifestation this time around. I was given the ultimate insight into my own Karmic mind and how precious it is, by the endless patience I had learned from that life; and finally started to train myself through meditation and mindfulness to use my body, mind and spirit wisely and to its highest potential. It's like I had been saving the best until last, waiting for the right moment to release all that I was capable of being - just like in that life when the full potential of life opened up before me. I was able to see and feel how precious and beautiful life really was, as if a whole lifetime of seeing beautiful details of nature had saved itself for the next.

Even recalling the lifetime now as I write, it appears clearly in front of me, not just visually but emotionally, too, and hopefully that deep vulnerability shines through as you read it, rather than seeming ridiculous, embarrassing and something to snigger at. It still feels as real today as it did when I first saw that I was that woman. And even if I were to doubt the experience (which I don't), I would probably say it would not matter. The insight, vision, parable, mental metaphor or whatever you want to call it, gave me such valuable information and changed my perception of myself in this life forever - and, I believe, for the better. I am grateful for the insights I was allowed to have, and my ultimate conclusion is that even if one person reads this, can relate and heal from their own Karmic links as a result, then my openly waxing lyrical about it will have been worth it.

So, even if we believe otherwise and think rebirth is just the brainchild of a bunch of happy hippies, even if we did disagree and can't see how it applied to us, even if there are reactions to this rather zany and raw, not high-and-mighty chapter, I have made a decision to carry on, with or without your permission, dear imaginary reader, as my brain obviously enjoys being its own therapist and it saves me talking to myself in supermarkets.

Not many books that i am aware will examine the relationship between the writer and their imagined audience vs. the real audience they may or may not attract. There is a Karmic energy relationship created between all, reader and audience, and needless to say that awareness of the fact means that I honour you even though I have never met you, and hold you in highest esteem. These days where people who have never met before and might never meet in person, but have use of the miracle that is the internet to communicate, stay in touch, be closer than they would ever dare to otherwise, we have a chance to build worldwide communities to work towards our common goal: to survive on a planet that needs our help, desperately.

I have some idea why we end up losing the plot and use it instead to divide and rule, distract ourselves, wonder all day what we look like in the eyes of others or even have proper fights with each other online. I expect that some will misunderstand my intentions or find fault with the style and contents of this book. As with everything we come across, it's allowed. I will carry on regardless.

It is also my belief that we do not have to force these events, as they appear naturally as a result of our Karmic energy mind initiating them, once conditions are right and we are ready to receive them. I would say it is probably more important to focus on kindness and combining our new-found confidence in ourselves with doing good deeds. The rest will start to create itself automatically.

At one point, probably whilst I was doing something completely different, I 'saw' my mission – who and what I felt I was here in this life to be. Through this experience, everything became different and it started to change me into who I became. Again, an example of how these events can't be forced, they will just occur in their own time without our control. Often, we cannot even fully understand at that time what they are supposed to mean, but we find out as part of the journey towards fulfilling those insights into the path ahead.

Since this was such an important message I received out of the blue, it became a part of my awareness, and changed my attitude to life and how I live it. Some will say that I was able to access my Akashic records, a state of mind akin to the Bardo, a realm that exists as a part of our Karmic energy record holding the blueprints of our individual Karmic path. There are a few times in life when conditions are aligned, where we get these windows of insight during which things become quite clear to us as to who we are and where we belong. It doesn't always show us how to get there, mind. Perhaps if it did, we might not want to go on the journey in the first place, as it doesn't always mean it is going to be easy.

I will try to explain, which leads me to another lifetime I recalled. Having had the intention and made the start to be on a true meditative and tantric (in its true sense) path some time ago in Y2K - without knowing too clearly what that really meant, I hasten to add - I did not realise that what I had started to practice, was to become conscious of the way that we influence our Karma, how our life-force energy affects the process internally and how we influence our inner energy, our prana, according to the level of our connection to higher dimensions by our insights. We are influencing our inner energies every second of the day by what we do, say and think; to speed up, slow down, flow up and down our spine or stagnate. I sat in my silent, still, inner practice, day after day. As I did so, not looking for any particular outcome, I became aware that, typically, my energy would 'wash' through each energy centre along my spine, where it would hover and then move along my spine, sometimes quickly, sometimes not. Sometimes it would remain indefinitely, even for days, in one place, and I realised that this was happening if there were any blockages to clear, which there inevitably were. It almost always coincided with the times I did not feel well, or agitated somehow and least wanting to sit still. I don't have to tell you that it doesn't feel particularly brilliant feeling stuck, especially when you have vowed to just sit it out. Over time, I have been in many an intense scenario that I felt was unjust, because I thought I had dealt with it already; only to be reminded it was still very much there in the form of a Karmic energy blockage. I am probably not telling you anything new, I am sure you know the feeling, too. It can be a very confusing and lonely experience. But as I sat, something started to shift, and the energy suddenly transformed into a visual journey. I am guessing that this does not always have to happen, but it happened at that time, probably because the energy shifted to the brain/third eye area of my body which meant that I saw how it transformed. It also took me through the inner energy memories that were stuck and being released, showing themselves as another past life recall experience. This time, it occurred as part of experiencing some long-standing issues that I have since identified and interpreted as what I then termed Generation Karma. I was not sure at the time if this was a 'thing' by this specific name, but have since found out that the phenomenon is something that has happened to others, too. I will explain my definition of how I view this in chapter 45, 'Generation Karma'. On this occasion, the vehicle of meditation combined with EFT™ helped to take me through this particular past-life experience.

It started with a simple observation about my being a mother in this lifetime, which was all about not being very understanding of my teenage daughter at the time. I wanted to work on certain behaviour patterns that bothered me about myself. Thoughts arose and ebbed away again, centring around how I grew in my own female incarnation into the role of wife and mother in this lifetime, including how the female was represented in general in the Western culture I had been brought up in at this particular time. I realised that women often weren't allowing themselves to be in their 'yin' energy any longer. We were prompted to be strong and active go-getters, do everything and have everything - the home, the job, the children, the relationship, everything. We grew up being told it's all there for us to take, we just had to be the best and the first and always happy to grab it. It was not fashionable in my teens or twenties to be sensitive, feminine, receptive or vulnerable. It was the 80's, a time to be successful in business and achieving degrees and professional acclaim. It was seen as a weakness to be feminine and yin, and women were prompted to 'have it all'. To go out to earn money as well as have babies and decide from an array of possible relationship types which ones we wanted to have most and not to forget to forge meaningful friendships, look a certain society-approved presentable way and on top of that, also be responsible for tending to a home and all the money worries and chores it brings with it. I am a very strong feminist I hasten to add, in case that hasn't come across already. But i felt completely overwhelmed and anxious, like i had to achieve all these things to prove that I was worthy of the title. Little did I know then that campaigns were started to undermine feminism as early as the movement started, which most likely suffered decades afterwards from the hangover of the 1960's advertising campaigns by 1st world governments and an ever-present male-dominated, preferentially treated male economy.

All this suddenly became visible to me in my meditative epiphany. The belief that the female was to have it all but also do it all was so ingrained in me that I had no idea it was there. I realised I was caught up in a world where you could not win. It was designed to make us fail, and then blame us for the consequences of our failures. There were so many concepts that I felt strongly about which were unpopular at the time, so I never felt that I could share these, certainly not as a new mum in the late 80s/early 90s yuppie culture. I wanted to stay at home with my child and not feel a pressure to earn money as well, on top of learning how to best rear my child. I remembered the ways of ancient tribes, finding one book to encourage me with concepts such as co-sleeping, long-term breastfeeding, child-led weaning, natural nutrition and home-education. How odd I seemed, in the midst of trying to balance keeping a home and also being there every minute for my child to give her what I felt was the very best I could give. It felt so confusing and disheartening that I did not make the grade of being - never mind looking like - the greatest superwoman on Earth, but was instead cast as a slave to the stove and my family. Everywhere around me, society was convincing women that it would be the best for everyone involved to bottle-feed, leave her children to cry at the end of a corridor and then be off to work. Instead of feeling like a slave at home, they said, you must prove yourself worthy and go out, hit the glass ceiling with a career that was always paid less than your male counterparts. Instead of looking and feeling like the wonder women we were promised to be as feminists, it left women with children having no apparent choice but to put on their brave smiles and compulsory make-up, and yet feel utterly vulnerable, totally exhausted, totally berEFT™ and in debt, as well as exposed, belittled and dependent on a significant other, with her biggest worries of having no choice over her children's well-being and education being left unanswered. We are not even mentioning the abuse that stemmed from the low Self-esteem, dead-end jobs and marriages women found themselves in. Trying to combine all the must-haves we were supposed to go-get would make women all over the world feel like failures in a no-win as a result. Superwomen of the 80's who could 'have it all' were hailed as the new phenomenon, but paid less, never mind regarded as some sort of object for the general acceptance of sexual harassment. Coincidentally, whilst the housing market rocketed at first, making it unaffordable for most families to own their home outright, it then collapsed, going into recession in the late 80's and early 90's. More people than ever were duped into taking out unsecuritised loans and mortgages, which literally translates into 'death payment'. It conveniently meant that their homes and possessions they slaved for would be gone in an instant into the bankers' hands if they were unable to keep up payments. Increasingly, more and more women - and men, for that matter - explain how they became more and more depressed, anxious and stressed, unable to understand why and still trying to fight their insights. Instead, another cloud that loomed on the horizon was starting to rain down: more civilisation-based illnesses started to be diagnosed, and as a result, more anti-depressants started to swamp the market and get prescribed than ever, because that meant we could still be productive, couldn't we. Our children grew up in the care of strangers, we didn't know who they were any more and they rebelled instinctively against all the social constructs we were trapped in. Eventually, even they got sick - but there was always another pill to fix it, wasn't there. In the West, a disconnect was occurring on a scale that was finishing off wo/mankind as we knew it, slowly but surely. We were told, and we believed, that we could have everything. Instead, we were sold, by those who wanted our beautiful, endless, compassionate, loving, caring, giving wo/man-power all to themselves for their own gain. We were conned. We were sold. They told us lies. Our children suffered. We became more sick and anxious than ever. We had nothing and had no rights to anything. And they had us exactly where they wanted.

The woman/wife/mother, symbolic of the principle of nature and her abundance and unconditional giving, was stripped bare of all she had to give. Without any means to leave if she felt she had to or was violated against, she became victim to all the violence that combusted when the card house fell. I realised that there was a trait in me that also felt very easily violated against by yang energy in particular, and I seemed very sensitive to the subject although I had thankfully never really experienced physical violence from a male in my adult life. I felt that my defences were up, maybe on behalf of every woman on the planet who could not defend herself – it certainly felt very strong. In light of the previous incarnation experience and realising what era I had incarnated into this time, I felt that there was still something else stopping me from being fully at ease in my physical incarnation this time around.

.As I examined these thoughts that flashed up in the meditative session that day years ago, it happened again that I had a sensation of some otherworldly place opening up to my left, a familiar lightness and airiness which felt ethereal, pure, happy and welcoming. This occurred after a sensation that I was becoming younger and younger in age in my recall of previous experiences, some of which went back to childhood and made me feel quite emotional. i did not hinder the process nor encourage it, I just let it flow. I then remember the bright space opening and becoming immensely light, pulling me further up and to the left – and then all of a sudden I am clearly sitting on a dirt floor. I can feel it underneath me, the warm, dry sandy, dusty ground, although at the time of the experience the real 'me' is by now actually lying down, to better feel able to endure the whole experience that I felt was coming. I can see, feel and smell lush, tropical foliage around me, and sense high humidity. There is a wooden rectangular hut raised on stilts to my left, which I know serves as a sort of small group hall. I am sitting cross-legged on the floor, my head bent slightly forward, and from this angle I can just about sense and know that there are others around me, sitting around me in the same position on the same dirt floor out in the open. It is hot and humid, I am in traditional Buddhist meditation position and I am calm but highly alert. There is something going on that is far removed from meditative practice, something very unsettling. I am wearing robes, and I am a woman - a nun. I have the sensation that I am not a Tibetan nun, as I often wondered in this lifetime whether I had a previous incarnation with this particular connection, as I have a strong affinity with Tibet and its children in this lifetime; but I am fairly certain that in this past life I am in Vietnam, although I don't have an inner picture of what the rest of the country looks like or if this is the right name, because all I can only ever remember this small sacred place in the jungle. I am practising another form of Buddhism different from the one I am used to in this lifetime. I am young, perhaps late teens or early 20's, and I do not really understand the practice exactly and why we were asked to sit outside and not in the safety of the hall to my left. I do not have an overwhelming desire to move as I am practised, but I feel that I would rather be in the shade of the hall where I cannot be seen, but for a reason I know that is impossible. I am being watched. My robes are thin, dusty but washed clean and a faded, rusty red. My head is shaved, I feel it and am familiar with the feeling. In this life, i have never had a shaved head, I wasn't even bold as a baby, so how is this sensation of having a shaved head so natural and familiar, as if i have always had it? I am comfortable within myself, although I feel everything around me is in turmoil. We have been asked to sit outside and be still, and I am aware we are not here of our own choosing. We have been raided, by whom I do not know, but it is a siege of some sort. I sit, and calmly await what we all sense will happen – we will die. I have been practising meditation for this moment all my life and I am trained in being ready for this moment. I do not know exactly when I will die, or how. I am just sitting doing my meditation, until the moment it happens. Out of the corner of my eye, in the last moment of my life, I catch a glimpse of a figure with raised arms and a long, strong, thin wooden stick in his hands. The next second, it strikes me against the left side of my neck. In the instant I recognise I am being struck and beaten to death, my meditation ceases and my will to survive kicks in. Adrenaline rushes in, I have lost my cool – but it's too late. I die within a short time there and then, and with a feeling of outrage, having been cheated and ambushed. Realising that my goal of preserving loving kindness and compassion for everyone has not been achieved in the face of death, frustration arises in an instant. I show fear and anger in the last moment, lose my energy by blaming my aggressor and going out of my mind. I am not accomplished enough to create compassion for my killer in those last seconds. I leave the world as a scared, disappointed but also relatively accomplished and humble being; and my Karmic energy body will draw me back to face my frustrations in another lifetime.

My thoughts return to being the observer again this scenario rather than being in that life-form in my meditation, and i then become less affected and calmer as i distance myself from what has just happened. Reflecting on it afterwards, I realise that meditating in a forest amongst like-minded people all my life had sheltered me and prevented me from looking into my own Karmic energy mind. It brought complacency, made me less alert in my meditation, I used it as a routine to keep me steady and calm. The ambush I experienced in this lifetime pulls me out of everything I know suddenly and violently, and I will still feel this indescribable sensation of helplessness in the face of looming destruction right into this lifetime.

Probably because in my practice as a young nun, I had learned to treasure and master my inner peace, but not my physical life-form just yet, was the reason I was vulnerable when in my peaceful yin state of mind. All I could think about was that a yang action, a blow to my vulnerable neck by a man I never met who wished me evil and killed me, became the cause I chose for the thoughts that entered my mind on passing. I could not keep my meditation in that instant, and I would have to bring the resulting terror of being struck down by a stranger I could not resolve into another lifetime. I felt disheartened and betrayed, as perhaps I would now have to repeat the harsh lesson again and again until I had finally created the right conditions in a lifetime to find a way to be able to keep the balance and compassionate presence in my energy mind. It would take me years to come to terms with this past-life experience, as it was a very tricky situation to master. In fact, I still don't think I am ready to test it again, I don't think I would pass this time either.

In this lifetime, my Karmic energy mind showed me the remnants of the energy breaches in my armour in a variety of different contexts many times over, and I have learned to see this as opportunities for me to deal with these, as well as find gentle and effective methods and shortcuts to help me do this. In this life, I learned that by being put down time and time again, I was shown that there was a lack of honouring my femininity, and yet I chose situations around the subject over and over in order to overcome my feelings of inadequacy. Up until these insightful experiences showed themselves to me, I had only had glimpses of the energy residue of having had a past life being violated against. Maybe there were more that contributed, I have not seen all of them in as great detail as these. In this lifetime, like many women who feel they do not have a choice, I at first allowed myself to be put down and not stand up for myself a woman. My vulnerability did not feel like strength, my gentleness that prevailed throughout much of my childhood was often challenged, although there was never a perfect analogy to the violation present in the above past life recollection. Instead, I felt as though there was something in the way to feeling safe being receptive, passive, yin; that I had to create a safe space first, in order to be vulnerable without being in danger of being exploited. That safe space equated to feeling protected enough to find out more about my inner Karmic energy; how to adjust and heal it again from those wounds, so that it would function wholly again in order to naturally radiate and protect. I went about the task in a fiercely independent way, reflecting who I had been before, and feeling at ease with my own company, compelled to lock myself away whenever I could to find out more about this inner 'me' and how I could connect with others around me in the most beneficial way. i am very grateful that the two seemingly opposed intentions always ended up merging with the right motivation to create some very beautiful outcomes in my life. I credit it to the energy set free by making sense of all these events showing me that despite great misfortune, we can create the sense and comfort of a vast and beautiful community around us. It felt like a layer of comfort, connection and protection to be a part of an ever growing world-wide community of aware, compassionate folk, something I hadn't expected to be a part of. I learned why I felt I had to try so hard, my eyes opened and I understood and accepted why I could be a little too hard on myself at times. The mind training I once again received through this recollection experience of that particular lifetime, as well as perhaps many others, was very profound. The benefit of trying to find solutions was my learning that I was no longer alone.

It was an immense relief to be able to experience a sense of opening up that replaced my relative isolation, after the realisation flooded in that I had probably taken on some of my limiting beliefs in these previous lifetimes. Once they were released, my energy flowed freely through my body, and I could feel the connection again to the greater and higher energy realms. I asked myself, 'What if everyone else, too, can relate to these limiting beliefs? What if we all had our own individual, yet similar hurdles over lifetimes which made us who we are, right now? What if we are much more than the sum of these experiences? Would we not have found many a solution to mankind's issues, if we were released from them and able to look at them from the outside in, rather than carrying the burden of being affected by them every moment of our days? If we continued to painstakingly piece every experience together each for ourselves individually, where is the benefit of the group dynamic? If some of us have done it and live to tell the tale, if we can show others how to do it, is there not a glimmer of hope that all of us can do it, sooner or later, according to our owning our inner Karmic world?

I have opened up about my own experiences here not because of an inflated sense of Self-importance, but because I am adamant it does not help to belittle our feelings, to anaesthetise our flaws, to 'overcome' by suppressing what is going on within and soldier on. I am here to say, embrace your yin! Generations before us have fought so we can live gentle lives. With their experience, would they want to see us fight as well, or would they want to see an end to all this suffering? Our inner world is there for a reason, giving us hints, telling us where to look for the sake of our and our children and grand-children's peace. The peace we seek is within already. I want to demonstrate that even the most ridiculous sounding scenarios can bring about an epiphany. We are all connected, we are all-knowing. There is often just a lot of stuff to clear that's in the way. Isn't it time to name it, and find out who we can be, without it?

Looking back as I am doing the final edit on this book in 2020, it occurred to me what, in the greater context of the past years, this time was all about, and how we are entering a new phase right now. Our planet changed its magnetic field a few years back around the millennium, according to where it is circulating in its orbit around the solar system and having entered a photon belt in 2012. The shift that we are sensing now is the result of years of the Earth being in limbo between yin and yang energies, a transition period where everyone was a confused as to who they were, how to identify, what to do next - male or female energy? yin or yang? And I believe this phase we are entering into now is a sign that the Earth energies are moving into yin times for definite, perhaps for aeons to come. The first months of 2020 the world has stopped, in the grips of a deadly virus, and 1/3rd of the world population is on lock-down. It is unimaginable that this would be possible to implicate, but however it presents itself, it is the beginning of a new era, confusing though it is. It time to be passive, time to reflect, time to be in nature, time to be giving, compassionate, open-hearted, abundant and generous. Time to communicate, time to pray, time to be still, time to be gentle with ourselves, time to love and grow...time to be, and time to learn to be unconditionally happy.

By seeing through some of my Karmic scenarios, I saw the connections. I am also seeing the bigger picture of how many times this happens to sentient beings, and what repercussions exist therefore. Buddhists talk about the 1st law of the Dharma - that there is suffering. And there certainly is - infinite different ways of suffering, too many to count. We are re-creating them daily, over and over by not looking for the reasons why. We end up retaliating all throughout life, defending ourselves from attack, having lost track of who we really are without all of these scenarios of suffering. It is not meant to be a depressing thought, but rather an inspiring one, simply based on a logical and plausible conclusion. It is doable, it can be done. What if there is so much individual suffering that we can't possibly conquer it all at once? Then it must logically follow that there is a different way. There must be a way out of any suffering, a method for each of us to alleviate it. Personally, I believe that method has something to do with the wisdom that comes from learning about our inner experiences and linking them to a logical conclusion that takes us into a calmer future. If we find out what lies beneath our suffering, then we will have opened the door to the way out of suffering. By just seeing through one's own issues, we are also sensitive to others' troubles. Through insight, we become avengers of suffering. We want to actively put an end to suffering and we want to demonstrate who we are when we are not in physical, mental or emotional pain. Our inner energy can make automatic changes for the better for us, including our realisation of Truth, so that our we are set to not allow suffering to continue any longer, as much as we can help it.

As is the case in my example, I learned to see the positives it was trying to show me, one of which was that I was not at fault in this. I did not actively invite it in in some way, as is often believed by those who insist that victims play a part in choosing the role of victim. I can honestly say there is NO conscious part within me that I recall which said, go ahead, I consent. The violation in this lifetime experience came as a complete surprise. I am to date not aware of any of my other lifetimes where a similar vulnerability when being in the 'yin' state of mind was also exploited. As far as I am concerned, the murder was not initiated by me and I did also then manage not to blame the perpetrator. I simply wanted to deal with my own feelings about being harmed. In fact it didn't entirely matter to me who he was, I did not feel anything about him until those last few seconds, in which I was more concerned that my poor overwhelmed Self had understandably lost its calm. I learned to have sympathy with myself, to not blame or Self-shame. I also never gleaned enough information on the reason why he killed me, in fact, not even as part of my reflections, even to this day. I can imagine there would be infinite past life situations that others might have experienced in which the reasons are still very present; where the image and motive of a violator might be much more vivid and complex, left behind like a bee sting in our energy mind, making it much harder to come to a sense of peaceful inner Karmic resolution. I can imagine also how that would bring about the confusing array of issues and situations we face on Earth, and how nigh on impossible it seems to see through them all. But even these very deeply traumatic experiences, however recent or long ago they occurred, can be made neutral. We can look at every single aspect of them as they arise, and gentle smooth them out. Luckily, we can also kind of bunch them together in groups according to their similarity which makes life easier and the process less lengthy. Even though each aspect might be different, they also have things in common. If, like in this example, we are dealing with a violation against a being, and if we assume that everyone may have experienced something like it in any of their lifetimes, then there must also be a remedy that applies to all of us that will even out our inner breathing space again.

Perhaps we are all on Earth for the same reason: to find a remedy for our suffering and use it in order to lose the illusion of feeling isolated.

I could reason that this event may have been the result of my being a perpetrator in another lifetime, which would arguably bring in more compassion for the aggressor. As a matter of fact, I am actually aware of being the aggressor in another lifetime, and using my yang energy to destroy others' livelihood. When I reflected on it, my conclusion was that it would definitely have had repercussions on subsequent lifetimes, perhaps even a resulting lifetime which followed after this particular one.

To explain, I will go into more detail of the next experience I then had. This past life recall occurred as a result of looking into my relationship with finances in an EFT™ session in this lifetime. It didn't at first appear to follow on from any of my previous experiences, as the recall I had actually occurred *before* the previous one I just related to you. I slipped into the experience without any other prior reparation very unexpectedly again. It appears that Karmic energy sorts through the debris within and might loosen up some trapped energy that then requires attention and sorting out into sequence. It may not always make sense straight away, and we might need some time afterwards to come to terms with the new information we found. My tried and trusted way was, by then, to always gently focus and calm any fears by tapping on acupressure energy points through these experiences, so that they can quickly pass through and leave the body once and for all.

As it turned out, I was the aggressor in that lifetime; I saw myself as a stocky man with very fair hair, reigning over people as a feudal lord, taking away their harvest and all revenue from their hard labour. It felt horrible and alien to be in his vile body and experience his lack of emotions. Looking down on myself and how I felt, I had no compassion, just an ill-accomplished sense of entitlement, an absolute and unwavering conviction that I had a higher standing than others, a 'better than them' belief. I did not have any feelings for those people or knew who they were, how they lived; they were 'beneath' me and therefore they owed me and that was all that mattered, or so I had been brought up and felt accordingly, in that lifetime. They were just ordinary folk that had to obey me and I owned them. In that body, there was no questioning the fact. They were mine to do with as I pleased, and I had no compassion for the fact that they and their families were entirely at my mercy. Being in his body again, I realised with horror that many hundreds of them died painfully and in poor conditions because of my actions. I observed how he treated his people and was overcome with shame and embarrassment to realise I owned this past life experience. It took more inner work after I had insight into that lifetime to loosen the experience, and it took me some time to regain composure. I had been responsible for others' suffering and death. This had been me, in another lifetime, and I had allowed it to happen because I did not think to look for a better way. It was my responsibility now, to undo those Karmic bonds and to try and alleviate any suffering I may have caused. The techniques I describe further down in this book help to do this on an inner level so that these Karmic bonds no longer affect how we feel on an outer level. They iron out our 'bad' Karma, so to speak, so that we can see how we have wronged others, make amends by clearing our Karma to free ourselves and learn to give back to others what we once took. For some 'heavier' cases, we should definitely not do this alone but ask for help from those who have more experience and can suitably assist the process. Once this has been done, we also no longer have to attract situations in which we have to constantly feel guilty or ashamed. That is not what is required and there is no need for religious chastising. We need to want to find out how to take time and pay attention to ourselves, find out what and who we are and how we came here. We are all able to contribute again in whatever way we can. There are methods to do this that make this process a lot easier than running into a brick wall over and over again, lifetime after lifetime.

Having had the privilege of seeing the potential causes and results in several different lifetimes had profound effects on how I perceived myself and the world around me afterwards. First of all, it allowed me to set myself and others free from our respective past Karmic roles; not by an artificial act of forced forgiveness, but by recognising that I, as any of us, am not flawless in my human timeline, and as a result, there may be a causality between any of my lifetimes' actions, good or bad, as a hangover from previous existences. Since we can't always be sure of the facts and won't be aware of every life we spent on Earth unless we are the Buddha himself, I logically deduct that there are circumstances that are unavoidable sometimes, which is how I now understand it; and all of us have to experience them in a number of lifetimes, with no exception. We are all destined to come to the point of realisation of the higher Truths sooner or later, even if we go kicking and screaming. Ultimate Truth is a beautiful place, if we can even use the word place. A beautiful experience where every issue we ever had is finally dissolved into nothingness. Why would we not wish to aim for that, the highest experience open to us in our little individual ant-like scrabbling on Earth? It is for us to set our course and decide whether we want to overcome these faux impressions we give of ourselves to the world around us, in order to neutralise their ill effect on our Karmic Self. If we are really still fully attached to physical appearances, see it as Botox for the soul. How we do this and when, is up to us. Are we afraid we might not get there and if we do, there might be nothing left of us? I think we are, and yet, our fear could not be further from the Truth.

By actively reducing our fears caused by our heavy pasts which seem to run so deep, we can allow ourselves to avoid abusive situations in the first place or at the very least, in future. Looking back, it became clear to me that I began to be more ready to accept the yang energy alongside the yin. I learned that strong, active, powerful yang energy does not automatically mean violence and abuse. I am also seeing that I can allow myself to be yin, passive and feminine, too, without having to feel powerless, exposed or dependent. I am both male and female energies, and I can see how there are vast benefits to enjoying the presence within both. I am hoping to carry on clearing Generation Karma, the Karma of past generations in my ancestral line of women and men who had to put up with violent situations in order to survive, and sometimes still do. There is more on Generation Karma in chapter 46.

There are still lessons for me, by which I am to learn more about my Karmic links; some I am aware of, others less so. I am sure I speak not only for myself when I talk about my own Karmic experiences here, and that is partly why I find it important for me to be open about it, so it can invite others to come forward with their experiences, too, in a safe environment. By nature, I do not generally open up from my ego mind, shouting 'hey, look at me, this is all about me'. I can also see the downside, that there could be misinterpretations and misunderstandings caused, within any watered down or personalised experience of a universal concept, that it might cause controversy even, but ultimately I do believe that we are all grown up enough to take responsibility for our own actions. To sum it up, there are many experiences like the gentle ones I mention above, which I have had the great fortune to live through since. And living with a healthier balance of inner yin and yang energies, I allow myself those times during the day when I can channel my outgoing energy into the right actions, the ones that feel intuitively right for me, those that take me further along my inner journey of discovering that, every second of every day in my perceived timeline, I already AM.

I feel that many may gain knowledge of their own Karmic links by learning about how it is possible for everyone to spot their inner processes. All you have to do is look at yourself, and go from the outside in. When you are honestly taking time for your inner Self, you will become familiar with recurring thoughts, dreams and images floating through your mind, those we don't usually pay much attention to, ever. There may also be personality traits and idiosyncrasies which you thought were yours forever and made you, you. I believe that many of these traits, memories, behaviour patterns, even illnesses and so on are there because we haven't been able to resolve them yet. How can we, if we have never before even told there are methods to make it easier for ourselves?

We have to know ourselves to let go of ourselves,
so our full potential can flow.

Once we realise that many of these internal sensations are by nature transient, we can ask ourselves where they arise from and start to find answers that way, just as many before us have done already. At the end of this book are a few suggestions for exercises that may help you do this. Perhaps we can also see the Karmic links between us and our parents, elders, ancestors, as well as the special tasks we came to perform and obstacles we have come here to clear, perhaps even once and for all. Previous generations have, in their own way, worked hard for us to be here today, so that we can finally be the ones to recognise these tools to make our lives easier and find the time to use them, too, in order to do away with all those remnant Karmic links that are unhelpful and stopping us from being at peace with ourselves and our surroundings. It puts it into perspective when we look at it like that. We have the time, the tools, and the circumstances to do this, right now. Methods are accessible to all of us. Lose no time. The moment is now. And it is so precious. Perhaps it makes us realise now that there is time sensitivity in Karmic Law, too. Many people with Karmic links good and bad, incarnate again at similar times, in order to clear their issues. If we clear up our own Karmic debris, our children won't have to do it for us.

And if we think that our children should, because they owe us, we should ask ourselves why we came to think that.

You are alive. You are a who-man being, loved and cherished already. You already live on this planet as do plants, and animals, and other humans. Plants and animals do not ask if they are allowed to be, they just grow. if we stop them, it's because we are not aware we are continuously stopping our own flow. Claim back who you are, you do not need to prove who you are through your actions. You need and are allowed to be, and this is the time to bring yourself back into being. You want to go back to the richness within, the spirit that you knew as a child, the wo-man who dances with energies, and your love within, the one who is choosing happiness. The one who smiles nd laughs because, you know, that is what you are here to do.

* * *

31. Karmic Links and Our Body

As you can see from previous chapters, I found truth in and took on the belief of many different ancient cultures, beliefs and ways of life. I found that many of them already described what I felt to be true - that there could be a link between the infinite Karmic bodies we inhabited in previous lifetimes, and the one 'we' subsequently chose to be in now. It seems feasible to at least examine the idea in theory that we take components from previous lifetimes into this physical existence we have right now on Earth. Perhaps these attributes are more than just fleeting memories of a distant past that flash before us; perhaps some of them are physical aggregates that we are led to believe are simply down to a genetic disposition. What if genetic disposition is also subject to Karmic laws? What if Karmic laws are governing our DNA? Who knows what our DNA even is and how it really works? The definition of it and how we are using and even manipulating it has changed much over the past decades, and the more we learn, the more it is a complete enigma with many surprises; but we still do not know how life truly comes into existence and humans are still busy trying to create robots instead of understanding our own lives.

The idea came to me whilst pondering the miracle of life that, perhaps when we are obsessed with a part of our body in this lifetime and spend so much time and money trying to change it, we might still be 'used to' the body we saw to be ours before, we might still have a latent memory of being in it and in some cases, are still attached to it. Could one of the reasons that we get so caught up in changing our looks in this world be, that we did not want to leave behind our body in a previous existence? Were we surprised and shocked in that lifetime to see our body separated from our Self too soon? Did we carry over a Karmic residue to be resolved in this one? For example, perhaps you had wavy brown hair in your previous incarnation which you loved; but this time around, your hair is blonde and straight – and perhaps you hate it being like that because you still have a Karmic memory of your hair looking like it used to, in a previous incarnation? What do you think, how does the idea sit with you? We are certainly quite obsessed with changing a lot of our bodily attributes nowadays. Do you have any part of your body you would change in an instant, if you could? In your mind's eye, do you still see yourself with other physical components so that your ones in this present existence do not feel right, that they somehow don't belong to

you? Would it not be interesting to know whether this was true, especially when there are examples that exists in conditions such as body integrity identity disorder, body dysmorphic disorder, somatoparaphre-
nia and others. People in this day and age spend vast amounts of money
on having surgery to change the appearance of their bodies to make
them feel more acceptable, which in other people's eyes may seem unnecessary. We might never really find out the truth, but I feel it does
have something to do with a deep unease that cannot be based on any
experience we can trace in this lifetime. People want to change their
skin tone, their faces, their hair, their bone structure, their overall appearance. I also wonder if, since we have been male and female in previous incarnations, we will have attributes and memories of being either.
Many people have issues around accepting that others can be any gender they choose. The myriad of reactions against others' choices tell me
that some people might have carried over their own issues from previous incarnations, becoming strong preconceptions and opinions in this
lifetime. Each to their own, but it can become an out-of-control issue
when people are not able to be tolerant, especially when there are no
signs of a challenge to their person that explains to them their hatred
against another's' choice of how they present themselves is inappropri-
ate. If people have such fears, are these fears also based on who they
were in a previous life? Perhaps they feel just at odds in their own skin.
At this point in our Earth's evolution we appear to be becoming more
conscious of no longer needing to adhere to a specific gender to feel accepted, and this also won't be the first time it will have happened on
Earth. Periodically, consciousness arises and brings with it the understanding that beyond Earth existence, none of us are just 'male' or 'female'. Deities in sacred images dating back thousands of years and more
have neither predominantly male or female components. They simply
remind us of our inner energies which carry either yin/receptive or
yang/active energies on this Earth, and/or any combination of strength
of both of these nourishing our physical existence. As we become more
aware of our Karmic energy, we may gain a sense that we are not dependent on gender. When we encounter those who disagree strongly
and feel personally affronted by the principle, could we assume that
there were issues of threat to the individual in previous lifetimes concerning their gender causing them fear? Are the ones who are reacting
so strongly against these natural concepts in a process of coming to
terms with their own Karmic past? Are they allowing themselves to explore their inner Truth on this and other matters or is there a fear so
strong that prevents some of us from finding out who we really were,
and are? People try to change the colour of their hair and skin all the
time, some white people love tanning and some dark-skinned cultures
promote the use of skin lightening products; lots of people change their
eyes by wearing contacts and their hair-style and eyebrow shape regu-

larly. By now, it's almost a norm in the looks-orientated world to not be happy focusing within, we all must look the part and hence use surgery to change the shapes of eyes, mouths, noses, cheek bones, the size and shape of stomachs, bums, boobs and thighs. We must not have come to terms with ageing yet though, because wrinkles are not acceptable, so they are Botoxed away. We even created the chance to more or less permanently adjust our gender identification by altering our sexual organs. These days, some form of enhancing surgery has become almost mainstream to undergo, even expected standard in the eyes of some very modernist cultures. Looking at those very specific cultural body types that appear to be favoured over others it seems it has made some people feel forced into surgery at an ever younger age. Most procedures are far from cheap, and some of them follow agonising life-changing decisions, so it can't be an easy process from one day to the next. Without trying to sounding biased or predictable, could there be a Karmic reason for these situations, too, or is it media manipulation, peer pressure or simply sign of the times? Do we feel more attractive, or more comfortable, in our new skin, forever more? Do we feel less anxious, does it make us happier? One of the answers as to why we sometimes feel we choose these dramatic options might be that we otherwise do not we feel like it does not represent us on the outside the way we want to feel on the inside. Is there a discrepancy between our physical body in this lifetime, and how our inner luminous Karmic energy reminds us we want us to look? Do we all want to look flawless on the outside because that is what we miss on the inside? Perhaps the simple truth is also that we want our body back from a previous, happy life and can't get used to the fact – again due to us not realising our Karmic links – that we now have a new one; one that feels so odd to some that their happiness depends on changing it. Perhaps there is a possibility that if we find a way of understanding our old and new bodies through the Karmic link between the both, some of us can make peace with who we are and feel better about what we have now, but also find courage against those who really can't accept others' choices and go into attack mode about it. Perhaps they, too, might be insights into inner reasons to learn why anyone has the right to choose to make changes to their bodies and why that choice is theirs entirely.

Of course, any of the Karmic principle behind making our choices in life to gain insights in our own time applies to all aspects of life, not just our outer appearance. I chose the subject as it is more apparent than ever with online presence that people feel insecure and incomplete about how the come across to others. I want to encourage that we are free to make choices, and also throw in the idea of Karma in these contexts because we may not have considered the reasons behind the way we feel about ourselves and how we identify in connection with this world. Whether the subject is to do with everything we earned and learned in this life, i.e. culture, country of birth and residence, living conditions & space, health, community, children, finance, leisure pursuits etc does not matter in terms of our Karmic links. What does matter is how we connect it all up to see it's interlinked and has influenced the choices we make today, but also gives us the freedom to choose differently if we realise we no longer need to follow a specific path if it no longer suits us. Recognising our Karmic links will give us more freedom to choose what's right for us, and there is absolutely nothing wrong with that.

So, I hear you ask - how can we find out more about what our physical body looked like in a previous incarnation? I would ask, 'where to start?' I can give you an answer to an extent – you won't find it in a personality quiz online as it's at least as complex as our genetic code that exists as a result of our previous Karma. And finding answers might also not be as useful as a distraction as it sounds, if the methods don't have the results we expected or are craving. It's not a goal to be achieved, to know what we looked like, just for fun. It can't be marketed like an online tool to let you see what you used to look like before you came here, or be translated into a computer programme giving us our own individual design of what our Karmic links look like. We have to be patient, and naturally come across it, to see what it has to tell us and how relevant it might be, as part of a whole understanding of who we are. By itself, it is not even necessary to find out more about, in order to achieve insight into life, the universe and beyond. Despite that, however, I will give a little intro into my personal insights. Hopefully it will help to understand the principle behind it, and entice you to find out more in your own quest.

Since we have all lived as sentient beings before, since 'beginningless' time as the Buddha Dharma Teachings describe it aptly, it also makes sense to me that we may have assumed various animal shapes before human lives. I am not even mentioning all our incarnations and other universes yet, I will leave that to you to figure out in due time. In my mind, there is a certain evolutionary sequence on this planet, and it may overlap with the Western interpretation of evolution to some extent; although evolution in terms of Darwin's theory does not talk about Karmic evolution, at least in his published materials, as far as I am aware. Please bear with me if this already offends some with strong religious beliefs against evolutionary theories, and perhaps make up your mind a bit further down if you like it or not.

Our lifetimes were infinite before this one, and are infinite after this one. We may have memory of none of it, or become aware of some, and perhaps only of the most recent timeline before our current existence. It makes sense to me to speculate that, on the basis that we have lived infinite lifetimes and lifeforms before, we would therefore also have assumed affinities with animal existences and also an aversion of some, based on our specific incarnations as certain animals in our previous existence.

After all, Darwin's evolution theory, although disputed by some, explains quite feasibly the suggestion of an evolutionary relationship between all species, and the increasingly complicated steps that finally led to the creation of man, backed-up by the findings of many of the 'missing links' between each evolutionary step. I have had this thought, that, when we introduce the concept of reincarnation - which could in its own right be termed a 'missing link' - into Darwin's evolution theory, we may even have an explanation for his theory as well as be able to integrate his studies into the greater principle of Karma and reincarnation. I will pay special attention here only to the mystery of what he describes as 'mutations', since I would need to write a whole book on further detailing how the two theories intertwine. Suffice to say, Evolution theory is still in question by those following certain beliefs that oppose it to this day. I have had a personal insight I want to add here, for your digestion: What is it that actually makes mutations occur? Of course, I can imagine had Darwin introduced the theory of reincarnation into his controversial History of Mankind which he published towards the end of his life, he would have had to be extremely careful not to upset both scientists and the churches of his time, as he would no doubt have been discredited for the heresy of even mentioning reincarnation in connection with his already revolutionary work.

Since I am neither scientist nor afraid to start a discussion to find a common potential denominator between science and Karma beyond the dogma of religion, I am happy to make a fool of myself for stating this:

That, when a consciousness/life-form/sentient being, human or animal, has a live physical body on Earth, it has the chance to sense and experience what this body is capable of doing as well as what it lacks a capacity of. in addition, it may also have a certain understanding and proposing thought process according to its intelligence as to what conditions would potentially improve that body's lifespan and its chance of survival. For example, if we are brought up in a country with very little resources to yield food or water, our continuous physical effort would continuously be caught up in finding and creating food sources. In addition, the lack of available food and water would have the effect that our focus, intention and hope is entirely on creating and finding more food and water. Some inner process would be initiated which would involve us make a proposition in our mind, perhaps a thought process which includes a desire, a longing and a 'prayer' for more food and water to become available. But where in our minds would such an inner process be able to exist? We could say it's the brain, for example, but this only works to a certain extent, and would not explain why all animals are able to evolve. The consent so far is that it must happen just by chance, but I do not agree. The effort we are able to put into finding a solution, combined with the urgency causing a concentrated hope affecting our nervous system of finding it, is somehow capable of sending out our energy frequency focus into a finer, higher frequency source or dimension. Would this not fit the principles we learned about already, those that exist in our Karmic existence? These efforts are all exactly what is needed to create an inner Karmic magnet-like energy imprint, focused on harnessing the best possible outcome for a successful future finding said food and water. Food and water is known to most of us, we know what it looks, feels, tastes like. The urgency of need we have felt all our lives searching for it every day to quench thirst and still hunger has created its own Karmic imprint within us already. What we are imprinting that is new, is the availability in abundance of it. This hope for change may not be possible in one lifetime alone, and suffering may be endured for a length of time as a result of the fact. We none of us probably know exactly how much our actions are influencing our future fortune and just take everything we have right now for granted. But what if our past actions have created the good fortune of plentiful food and water in this life, and that we need to continue with our Karmic imprints to work on the essential things maybe a little more consciously? According to however much effort we put in and Karmic kudos we accrued, the very focus of our full attention, true intention and pure energy would certainly have influence on our energy mind, and with it our Karma. We take it with us into the next existence, through our Karmic energy finding its new existence. Our efforts will create a new form that makes it possible for us to be alive, in order to create more helpful conditions, gain new talents and get insights into the whole cosmic cycle we are finding ourselves in, over lifetimes. Nobody will evolve their Karmic energy body in the same way twice, but perhaps we will be reborn into similar conditions again on Earth in order to bring about change - the change we tried to make in a previous existence. Since we still have our Karmic energy mind, it will recall what changes we needed to make from last time, whether we consciously recall it or just know instinctively what we have to do this time. This would be a logical conclusion to why we can make quantum leaps at times as a civilisation, when the time is right, and might become visible in all other interactions between life forms and this planet. Suddenly in our evolutionary past, a brain developed and became bigger than the rest. It had more capacity for logical thinking, deliberating potential outcomes and deducing advantages over others. It might at some point have been able to conceptualise, after many practical exercises to try and find easier ways of finding food and fresh water. Over 5000 years ago, humans invented the wheel. Who knows – perhaps it was someone born with the Karmic energy to create and work with a bigger brain. It is a huge subject, but in this context, i am excitedly theorising, and also combining these theories with the observation that beings have adapted to their environment all throughout existence on Earth, according to their ability to introduce new ideas and utilise various elements, put across visualisations, conceptualisations as well as being able to apply rough ideas in practice into their environment. The idea of an inner electromagnetic record of all our achievements being passed on to the next life might already exist in not so small ways, when we talk about adaptation in its anthropological sense, for example. Indigenous people and Tribes living in tune with their surroundings are extremely attuned to finding water in places where they are used to walking for long distances in the heat without it. They know instinctively where nature will manifest water and often find even small currents of water in vast deserts. An untrained eye would not find it, and a normal person would die within the shortest time. Whilst this is a form of adaptation, the principle of focused and internally integrated attention to specific outcome might well be the same.

By concentrating our mind in single-pointed focus, every individual is able to gain insights that are freely available. Energy forms and patters on many vibrational levels become accessible to the trained and accomplished. Whether we experience them to be visible or audible is of no consequence, as these patterns are always integrated by all beings in existence, and can be accessed and fine-tuned by our consciousness sooner or later.

This practised focus over long periods of time is exactly what is required in order for our energy system to bring about physical changes according to Karmic law. In the case of mutations, we are often talking of a process taking thousands of Earth years, which makes the theory seem all the more viable: in terms of infinite existence and possibilities, the amount of Earth years we tediously take to advance are really nothing. There is plenty of time to change, and yet, in terms of our short lives there is no opportunity we should waste. It also appears that, on a mass consciousness level, change on a large scale is not that easy or quick to achieve. In addition, it also seems logical to me that there must be beings who have themselves transcended all these earthly difficulties, having risen and transformed their existence which now resides on higher frequency planes. Some of them have made vows to assist us and lower themselves down to Earth again, as they have done many times before. They may indeed also be able to assist with implementing change, and may descend on request and when most needed. It also follows that some beings are not of an Earthly form, or - wait for it - incarnate into earth bodies through a human birth.

Back to our discussion in terms of the Earthly realm. Mutations appear in any species. They can just suddenly happen, out of the blue, and seemingly don't follow any pattern. Suddenly, there is a change of colour and pigmentation, a physical attribute, even more complex inner structures can be affected. When we examine what we said above, it follows that when the Karmic energy body of one individual with enough Karmic resource has changed, their physical DNA will change accordingly. The change appears at random, since we do not have insight into that being's Karmic energy process. Here is a question, then: what if, in between lives, just one individual within a group has enough focus, insight, presence and concentration of Karmic energy resources, that they are able to initiate a change of energy mind and also have the good Karma to improve their situation with this new-found Karmic energy mutation in their next life? What if even just one energy mind in millions or more, may have changed all others' lives for the better? After all, we have to assume that all our Karmic evolutionary path takes shape that way. We start off as tiny cells, amoeba maybe (funny meme alert), and because we know we can do bigger and better we slowly but surely advance on the evolutionary ladder. Applying this thought to mutations, we have to remember that sometimes, it takes just one out of millions to create a much needed change for that particular species, but even that single being is still subject to Karmic laws. Do they have full awareness of the changes they bring? Do the changes have their own happy-go-lucky momentum or is everything calculated, according to Karmic laws? Is it the support of many that helps bring about these Karmic changes, since it can influence the individual's Karma but also helps the whole community to change form accordingly?

Not every being of any species is going to bring about a mutation subject to the above good Karmic energy created in that lifetime. By the same token, since a Karmic change on this scale is difficult to achieve and rare, it may be an explanation why mutations do, indeed, happen rarely but have phenomenal advantages ascertaining their survival.

A being that has inspired people and technology besides, is the humble peppered moth in the article below:

https://www.mirror.co.uk/science/industrial-revolution-spawned-mutant-moths-8096413

As soot from coal-fired factories blackened trees and buildings in 19th-century England, naturalists noticed that peppered moths were also trading in their light-coloured wings sprinkled with black specks for a sleek, all-black stealth-bomber look known as the carbonaria form. Within a few decades of their first appearance near Manchester, the black moths dominated, making up 90 percent or more of the peppered moth population in local urban areas.

I have a feeling that our model theorem of Karmic rebirth as part of a study of mutations might work here as well as in many other species, including humans. Whilst mutations are not always at an advantage, one moth species happened to survive better in their environment through a random mutation. An initial white butterfly species turned into a darker grey colony which had a better chance of survival. One individual suddenly turned up and was better camouflaged, so it had a better chance of surviving in its changing environment. The white peppered moths were more visible, so were more likely to be prey against darker backgrounds and did not survive. The new colony of darker grey moths was created from the newly arisen mutation that was much more successful as it could barely be detected by predators. There are countless examples of these if you want to research the phenomenon online.

Might a butterfly have had enough realisation and Karmic energy at the stage of dying to realise that a darker colour may make it less visible, or does this process happen completely randomly? Are both possible according to the level of consciousness of the species, so that the ability to morph itself evolves, too? If we have had a mutation in our consciousness as humans that would make us survive better - of which there are many examples - is it not feasible that as we evolved, we as a species started to obtain high enough conscious Karmic energy to bring about those changes, in the myriad of stages between life and death? Does our Karmic energy cloud gather other outerworldly information in the states between lives, to gain a better existence? And does this work for all living beings gathering Good Karma?

More questions. Do we have more chance as conscious beings to mutate in between lives, and bring about much needed change? If so, why are mutations of humans in a more evolved form not occurring faster or more often? If we are in much need of change at this stage in Earth's evolution, would it not be beneficial for a mutation to occur that would benefit the human race, preferably as quickly as possible? We could definitely do with a bit more help from the universe, but perhaps we need to know how to ask for it accurately in these times of urgency on the matter. One thing we do seem to ignore is that with each generation is that there are new genetic combination possible. When i say we ignore, I say this with caution, because I think there is a sadly sinister aspect to modern society that is taken advantage of the fact, but worse, taking advantage of our children. It is a harrowing development that is becoming more prevalent that some people believe that the pureness of children's energy is to not to be cherished and nourished, but harvested instead. It is a very sinister chapter in human history, perhaps one that has been open for a while. Looking back in history, we have always had extreme ranges of how to bring up our next generation, from making them work in factories, abandoning them to the other, happier and more loving criteria that apply to gentle, natural parenting. As a parent myself, I have never understood how anyone could harm their children in any way, and yet it's almost every day news these days. How did this happen? How can we let this happen? How can we protect our children more? I feel that some of the issues lie in the separation between family members which we have touched on already so that many are forced into separating their young from an extremely early age from the nurture and closeness a small baby needs. When we are presented with a society based on financing that does not put social aspects such as families first, people become impoverished not only fiscally, but worse. I see psychological damage of family units from an early time in a child's life will make things harder in the long run. I am not saying it's the family's fault, far from it. I am saying we might want to become aware that this course of action has only been prevalent where much stress has been put on a society which, as a result, has become more separate from each other than ever. Families are the most vulnerable, and in those families, small children are most affected. Perhaps, as a society striving to be more conscious, not less, we must pay more attention to what our children truly have to offer. Our children are the future after all, and they are full of fantastic insights and beautiful Karmic energy to bring about much needed shifts. They need us to protect them.

What about the hypothesis that we may have all lived certain past lives as animals? Did we all have animal life or lives, and were we all able to progress and evolve into more complex beings, using the focus of our increasing Karmic energy to propel us along into higher forms of existence, with the human form being the ultimate? Have we already put it out there that we were meant for even higher things and are asking for the next step to reveal itself, or are we shouting for help, for someone else to come get us out of here? Or is the human experiment a sad fail and an evolutionary dead end?

Our ever-present Karmic mind might have always enabled us to realise that the life forms we left behind could be improved upon, so that we returned in this life in a body that housed a higher chance of survival than we ever had before, through being able to access a higher form of consciousness. If we think about it, the human life form might have one advantage compared to any other: we can make a conscious connection between our Ego mind and our Higher Karmic energy mind, and we can, whilst we are here on Earth, consciously ask to be shown solutions to the issues we face. This would indicate that we would already have a path behind us which changed from simpler life forms to more complex, conscious ones, as consciousness proved itself very useful in terms of our evolution. I am not saying that some are more important than others, far from it. That type of thinking just gets us into trouble. We can't say another living being is less worthy of life just because we are more evolved, that's a contradiction in terms. But perhaps our arduous 'animal lineage' did exist, in order to provide us with stepping stones towards the development of our human consciousness. It would be nice to think, except there are too many of us humans still hell-bent on destruction. It appears that it's time to ask our Karmic minds again to connect us to the omnipresence so we might improve upon who we already are - and not in a megalomaniac way. Perhaps there does need to be another step in human evolution - the one where we can see much more easily the existence and workings of our Karmic minds and their omnipotent ability to create good outcomes for all involved. Perhaps this even includes a more advanced evolved ego mind, one that is less easily side-tracked and manipulated and therefore not quite so tempted to Self-destruct.

Here are a couple more fun questions: has our evolutionary path influenced us to such an extent that we still have certain remnant animal traits in this life now? Is it possible for us to go backwards at all? Hinduism proposes that we can go back into animal forms in future lives according to our Karma. It also already worships animal reincarnations of highly evolved beings. The idea of our evolutionary time-line is meant as an exploration, trying to help us to understand and empower us in who we are. Who we once were and who we are now may be more closely connected than we think. We can use this information to promote a more harmonious lifestyle where we get to understand that we are all connected. Perhaps it's worth thinking the idea through - perhaps we did come through a very particular time-line of animal lives to get us to this one as a human. We may even be able to recognise and identify certain remnant traits or features accordingly. Perhaps some of us have

the highly developed senses and predatory attributes of a wild cat, or the habits of an animal that lived in a particular habitat such as a jungle or a desert. Maybe our mind and body were adapted to living at certain times of the day. Perhaps quite a few of our preferences and characteristics in this life could be down to previous animal lives. Could we even *look* like the animals we once inhabited? Let's have some fun here, it doesn't all have to be serious! Have you ever thought, walking along the street, that - without trying to sound rude - people can look like some animals? Some have attributes of horses, pigs, lions, rats, weasels, snakes and even toads; or goats, eagles, vultures and monkeys – the list is, of course, as varied and colourful as Earth's – and other planets' - fauna itself. There is absolutely no offence intended by this statement, I mean it entirely as a compliment. Animals are often the better human beings, and after all, I am trying to take you, Dear Reader, on a journey, not for a ride.

It can be quite hilarious but perhaps also become a little distracting having this thought in the back of your head when you're out and about, but at the very least it is an interesting exercise in being open-minded. Could there be more to it than just a bit of fun? Is this the reason why we favour some animals over others, choose some animal companions and guides, feel protective over some and fear others? The possibilities are endless, and for you to make your mind up. It could help us be less callous and more inclusive, especially if we don't use the idea to be even more abusive to each other than usual.

When I started to think about the theory of animal evolution a bit more soberly, I personally could no longer justify enslaving animals any longer for the same reasons I mention above. Like many humans I know, I believe that each animal is as valuable as the next, and on their own equally important journey of discovering their own path of evolution. I have too much respect for the divine being that inhabits the body and the magical process of life creating life, to be involved in disturbing it. I personally have no doubt that my own Karma would also be affected negatively. Why would i want to kill something I can't create? I would only like to improve their life, not take it away. How do I know who the being is, at the core of their physical existence? Where are they on their journey? Is it possible that a human being can even go back to the life form of an animal?

The logic of Karma teaches respect for all beings, in as many ways as we come across. Conscious movements these days use many different terms, like 'non-human beings' instead of the word 'animals'. However, even the word 'human' has become a derogative term to some and can be misconstrued. I was told that in legal speak, 'human' means that one is not capable of looking after oneself. Due to legal systems performing under maritime law, apparently to be 'human' means we are presumed 'lost at sea' and dead, unless we present ourselves as proven to be alive.The language we habitually use is another form of expression of our ego Self and higher Self, but even this seems to have been compromised these days. I will leave that particular chapter of human evolution for another time and place, as more information on this subject and many more which connect to it can easily be accessed online. All I am trying to convey is that each state of aliveness cannot be replaced by any other. Even a cloned sheep will have its separate identity and individual Karma, different from another. However much we believe we can recreate an individual life-form, we cannot, and I personally don't believe we ever will, although it won't stop us trying and it won't stop human obsession with AI. If only we had as much fascination and respect for live beings who really need it, and spent as much money and resources on helping those instead of creating more fake ones.

The further we are consciously removed from our Karmic essence, the more complex it gets, and it seems all the harder it is to stick to creating good Karma only. Paradoxically, we need to keep it simple in order to keep our diversity. Our society is basing all its functioning on our brain and what it understands. But the word 'under-stand' is also compromised, as some might say. We are standing 'under' some other rule outside ourselves which is commanding us to obey. That's not what we want, though. We need to find out more about all the miraculous natural laws that are already there. Everything else outside of those is dead. Nature creates, not humans. We can't make anything grow, not even a single blade of grass. The Principles of Nature were there long before came along and made a bit of a mess of it because we could still get terrified by it and still die. We are still so scared. Going back into ourselves, respecting nature's creations as they present themselves might be a good idea, even though we have probably forgotten what that even means. I am sure nature has ways to remind us.

There are many trillions of beings suffering as animals, since they are not always strong or able to speak for and defend themselves. It seems the animal industry is a sad symbol of our inability to grasp the preciousness of all life. A huge percentage of animals are barely alive for a short time only in a miserable existence because we believe that they are there for our food or worse, entertainment. Some even kill animals for fun or because they feel some entitlement, quoting food chains and the most ridiculous arguments. There is no argument for killing that cannot be dispersed, once we are truly connected with higher energies that tell a different tale. It is my understanding that it is useful to an animal to help it survive and have a good life, if it would normally suffer or be put down. That includes animals we are scared of. I once was asked how I would react to an animal dying out in the open, whether it would not be its Karma to die. I always answer that it was also their Karma for me to come along at the right moment and try to help. We simply don't know enough about Karma to show so much entitlement to make a decision to kill anything.

Ignoring Karma keeps us in ignorance.

I understand that many animals benefit from human contact and kindness, in order to learn to grow their own Karmic energy bodies in lives lived in proximity to humans. As always, any being's Karmic energy has 'chosen' the existence they are in at that moment in time, including humans. However, this is never, in my eyes, an excuse to treat animals badly. What are our past life experience that would make us stoop so low? If we were predators in animal lives before this, our human life, perhaps that would explain it a little. But don't let's get stuck there and still display our power over others as if we still had no choice. We are here to learn who we are now, after a lot of anguish trying to get here. Would we want to go back? Some will probably answer with a yes, after all, this human life isn't a walk in the park for all of us. I do have a feeling, though, that it sucks more not being conscious enough to even make that thought process and decision. And for all the above reasons, added to the fact that we are creating more suffering day after day, hour after hour, minute after minute, here is the second million-dollar question: why do we believe we should eat them? We have nothing to fear, only to gain from learning about and understanding the Karmic path of animals, who are all, in their own right, on their validated path to become evolved.

There is a historic account of the Buddha himself recalling two of his lives which I would like to cite: one as an ox, pulling a plough, next to another, weaker ox. He felt the other ox struggling and helped him by taking all the weight of the plough. He died in the process of having put another being's life before his own. In another lifetime, he is born as a human, and comes across a tigress. He notices how weak the tigress is, and that she has three cubs. He chooses to sacrifice his life in order to feed the tigress, so that she can feed her cubs.

I am not even going to offer an interpretation of the above, as it can so easily be misinterpreted. Suffice to say that we can further our Karmic energy, not stunt it, by taking ultimate care of other beings around us. We don't have to sacrifice our lives to do it, either. In the case of the Buddha, he was fully aware of the consequences and embraced his Karma fearlessly. I will also be the first to freely admit I would not be able to make such a Self-sacrifice, I am simply not that evolved yet.

Having become a little side-tracked into a discussion about morality here, how about this as an overall conclusion:
The potential wisdom and compassion of our human evolutionary form, combined with the concepts of reincarnation, could have the effect of more compassionate and wise generations of future life-forms coming to the aid of a world that is becoming increasingly polluted and driven by a terrified species defending their territories in survival mode. Here is another thought: What if they are already on this Earth, right now? I ll leave you, dear Reader, to meditate on that.

"Many births have been left behind by me and by thee, O Arjuna! All of them I know, but thou knowest not thine." So said the divine Sri Krishna to the yet unrealised Arjuna.
(From Two secrets: Reincarnation and evolution, SriChinmoy Library)

I believe we WILL find solutions. In our Karmic minds and in the greater consciousness they already exist, and its vast potential will manifest, perhaps even through the processes described above. We also have to simultaneously accrue a lot of kudos by putting in the right effort. It is of no use being a suicide bomber for a religious cause. Killing anyone is not the answer, ever. Even if we felt we had enemies, even if we felt it was justified, at the moment of death we would still be faced with our ignorance of the preciousness of life and have to start all over again in a next one.

Imagine, if you can, we were at the in-between-lives stage, the Bardo, awaiting our next existence. We are free-floating in space, happily all-seeing and feeling wonderfully free of all our troubles. From up there, we are given a brief chance to manifest. What would you do to help, if you were acutely aware of what would be most needed on Earth? If we were to become aware that we could right now, in that time, bring omnipresent intelligence, compassion, wisdom and unconditional love together in a new life-form, what would we ask for in order to overcome many of our and the world's problems, now that we are becoming one again with the universal Karmic energies in between deaths? It's certainly food for thought if we anticipate it and play it through in our minds, because it's just important to practice manifesting now, even though we are not at that stage yet.

Many sages over endless times may have been meditating on this already, perhaps for an eternity, and are already aware of many of the answers; as well as methods of how to actively prepare for an auspicious death that will be ideal to adapt into a future life form, more adept than ever at solving world problems. This active preparation for an auspicious death and future life is not something we will ever have come across to be possible, even useful or necessary. Nevertheless, it is a thing. The announcement of a future Buddha Maitreya we talked about, the life-manifestation of pure compassion and wisdom in physical form, is already widely accepted amongst some cultures as a promise of just such a metamorphosis of mind over matter. A singular being perfectly adapted to bringing peace to a planet which is being destroyed by the impurities of our isolated ego minds, with the ability to have insight and compassionately bring about the best outcome to put an end to the unfeeling ignorance of non-empathy and the resulting inability to connect, will be exactly what the doctor ordered. But the energy of one being coming to our rescue at some point in the future does not mean we twiddle our thumbs and wait for it to happen. It means we prepare, it means we alter our course, it means we change what we are obviously doing wrong, because if we don't, we remain in separate form and stay disconnected. All of those are simply defilements of our Karmic state of mind that can be liberated, refined, purified, exercised, manifested more efficiently in a future life form – or even this one, for some of us. For now, we have this body to work with, as well as the hope that we will recognise that we are the ones in charge of the manifestations of our

Karmic energy mind, which we need to get to grips with. The Karmic influences that shape our every-day lives need to be recognised as such, so that we see the wood for the trees again.

❋ ❋ ❋

32. **Planets and Astrological Influences**

I seem to remember reading in one of Dr Stephen Hawking's early works, that he then believed that there cannot possibly be any truth in astrology, as the planetary constellations are interpreted only as they are perceived on planet Earth. In outer space, the constellations obviously are not as we perceive them on Earth; rather, all planets and stars are at vast distances from each other, the constellations disappear in relation to each other and do not, of course, appear in the relation as they seem to be, seen from the Earth. This is his reasoning, and I see how it is based on his absolute genius, respectable astro-logic and how he may have concluded this from all his superbly intelligent observations. However, I am not that intelligent really, but I wonder if it is not an easy argument to disprove? For example, does not the same go for time? As Einstein's relativity theory rightly states, on Earth, time exists, very much so. In outer space it becomes immaterial. Time is subjective, relative, and dependent on the observer or possibly even observing object. So, in my humble opinion it would also follow that the same goes for Astrology: Planets and stars create a constantly changing magnetic pull due to their astral space-transitions, the nature and patterns of which influence us as they move across the sky. Each stellar body has an electromagnetic influence on us according to its own blueprint. We are held in a mathematically calculable web that creates constantly changing and yet predictable and repeating astrological conditions on Earth, bringing about various combinations of situations in which we apply our daily life lessons according to our own patterning determined at birth. I believe it very much has an influence on us, the same as time does, for the very simple reason that we are on planet Earth and not in outer space. Even police and hospital staff find that shortly before and during full moon phases, for example, there are up to 25% more reported incidences of accidents and incidents. It is only when our Karmic energy body will have learned to completely transcend gravity, and the space-time continuum, that our present attachment to this planet loosens its grip on our true Self, including the influence of astrological constellations on our Karmic experiences, as we see and feel them on Earth. After all, we are already aware that we are not subject to the same time frame once we are in space. So the further we move away from Earth, the less we will be influenced by it, of course. But while we are still here, we are subject to the conditions that present themselves down here, which is a sobering thought that we can luckily overcome by using our Karmic minds.

Our bodies react to planetary influences as we are made of the very same stuff; our ethereal bodies are subject to the same electromagnetic laws in this lifetime as the rest of this particular universe. As certain constellations occur in our solar system, they strum certain wavelengths within our bodies, and these vibrating energies within us trigger memories, sensations, thoughts and emotions as well as potential feelings of well-being and illness alike. Some constellations are very rare and create auspicious conditions for us to create good Karma – according to thousands of years worth of some philosophies' wisdom and insight, they can multiply our good actions many, many times. Other constellations are more aggravating, and some also have the ability to bring very ancient Karmic conditions back to the forefront of the present time again. An example of such planetary occurrences are the retrograde phase of the planets, which almost always let us feel as if we are re-living parts of our past all over again. Planets do not really go backwards, they only appear to do so when seen from our relative position that we are in, in relation to the path they take alongside the Earth, orbiting around the Sun.

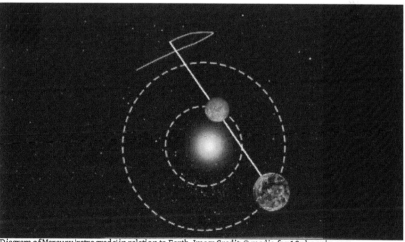

Diagram of Mercury 'retrograde' in relation to Earth. Image Credit © media.fox10phoenix.com

There is a very interesting phenomenon that occurs when we view all the planets on their path relative to Earth over a period of time. All of them make beautiful patterns like multi-petalled flowers, each planet in a different way.

Have a look for yourself what this actually means for us, in on section of this series of beautifully explained video clips, Astronomy with MicroStation Orbit of Venus Dance of Planets -

simple   but   profound: https://www.youtube.com/watch? v=_aocKBYyjM0

At these regular intervals when certain planets appear as if they are going backwards relative to Earth, even though Dr Hawking might have disagreed, they can influence our every waking thought in the present and trigger inner experiences powerful enough to bring up Karmic situations from our past – simply because we ARE on Earth, and not on the Sun. I have had whole rooms full of people experiencing the same phenomenon in the same day, just in slightly different contexts. We could call it synergy, or synchronicity. I like to think that even in the moments when we feel deeply isolated, we are still united. If there is still a negative or positive attachment to past situations within the levels of our Karmic energy mind, experienced by our ego minds as an inner 'missing' or a 'craving', then these energy formations and sensations within bring about feelings and thoughts from which can arise an action we choose as a result. The feelings can be so strong that we can be triggered by them as if these past events have only just occurred. If we cannot tell where our feelings have arisen from and find ways to resolve them, of we then act out of impulse instead of dealing with them constructively as they arise, then consequences can be potentially devastating. If we realise how it can occur that any negative feelings and thoughts may arise as a result of unresolved situations being brought to the surface from years, maybe even lifetimes ago, then we at least have some chance of riding the storm. If only we had means of being more aware of the fact that these things happen periodically all the time so we be more prepared for it and deal with it accordingly. Oh - wait! I forgot, this is all mumbo-jumbo and has nothing to do with a productive modern society. Or does it? And yet, ancient civilisations, for example, already had very advanced skills to put astrological information together in the form of graphs and charts carved into monuments of stone, which could then tell them very accurately how these planetary influences could be calculated. All this knowledge has inspired many scriptures and school of thought on how planetary alignments can affect us and our Karma. There are likely many skilled professionals during every human era who did similar work, but just for the sake of an example that stands for many other valid forms of divination and its results, I have briefly concentrated on this subject here.

Each planet has a different energy frequency that affects us in certain, quite defined ways, according to our own inner frequencies, too. If we remember that we are on Earth only for a relatively short time to undo negative Karma, and spend the rest of our Karmic existence in between lives in omnipresence, then we will also recall that we are made of the same materials as the universe we decide to exist in. It's no coincidence in my mind, that the astral bodies nearest to us will pull our energies in various ways, so that we end up having some of our Karmic material highlighted in order to work things out for ourselves.

If we did something wrong and knew that we would have to relive those moments in full detail over and over to heal the pain of others who were affected by our choices, I believe most of us would think twice before repeating said wrong-doing. If only we all saw the connections, but we are so far removed from each other, physically and psychologically, that we usually do not. What we are also far removed from is a true understanding of how our actions and their repercussions are connected. We are not separate, but the result of our actions has made us separate. In our thoughtless hurry to become disassociated from people and events, we are others' but also our own worst enemies, as we are depriving ourselves from having a fully functioning comprehensive mind. There are of course also situations where this is a condition brought about by illness, and also traumatic experiences in early stages of life. There are many cases where no diagnosis is ever made or treatment is sought for the various forms of mental illness that cause the individual distress, but also have terrible consequences if any sufferer is left to commit offences against others. The suffering that ensues has endless forms, as we are very likely fully aware by looking at our world as it is, and has been.

A sane Karmic mind is our utmost insurance cover. We fool ourselves into thinking that this cannot possibly be of importance, but imagine if it were. The outcome would be that we would actually be whole again if we only stuck to good thoughts, good actions, to bring about good results. This is not just someone telling us off, not just parental guidance. This is your own inner radar telling you that you are cleverer than you can imagine, and you can have it all. It's already inside you.)

What you long for, yearn for, is already within. Start looking.

Astrologers are not the only ones versed in putting together a complex map of our own Karmic influences at birth, but the art has surely been given a hard time by the right-brain bias of our modern times. It's been discredited and diminished to existing in the minds of millions as one-liners in tabloid papers, and whilst a popular form of divination, it still does not have the full understanding and acceptance it deserves. Maybe this is because with everything concerning our Karmic choices, there will be a variety of potential possible outcomes for each individual that can appear like similar yet separate experiences. If we start an action to see what reaction we get, if, for example, we shared the sentence 'I am sad' with thousands of people, it can have many different reasons for any of us to say it, as on an individual level it can mean many different things. If all those people hear us, then we will be creating many different reactions from those around us who we say it to. It is such a simple example of how Karmic action and reaction can work, but we probably all got the concept immediately. Probably because a very bright spark used it to become a billionaire.

Astrological aspects can affect us differently at certain times more than others. They also cover different subjects that our mind separates into, since we have inner components that relate to ourselves, but also our immediate environment, how we perceive the world and others in it, where we place others who we know around us, how we approach them, our talents, gifts, the way we see ourselves, our work, interactions and communications, and how we propel ourselves to connect with our planet. We might crave contact with others at some times more than usual, or can feel one way or another about where we are at with the plan we thought we had of our life. It can mean that our astrological aspects make us the complex, all-changing beings that we are. We are never the same twice from one day to the next. One minute we crave company, the next we need time to ourselves. One person will interpret a phrase or event exactly opposite to another, although they might both be right or wrong.

Something that is within us is triggered into a reaction, and what we are exploring here is that this reaction can be caused by an external constellation that is affecting us all. How it affects our lives and our interpretation of the energy vibration varies. However, using Astrology as a tool, some of our reactions can be grouped by their similarities with certain energy alignments. These alignments follow Karmic laws, and we are created according to these Karmic laws. We have chosen to be aligned a certain way. The events and emotions we split our daily experiences into, can synchronise with or distance us from others, but they come from the same source. Our individual energy bodies will react differently from the next person according to many of their own inner beliefs and astrological set-up, but many who are wired in a similar way will experience them similarly. The 'wiring' so to speak, is laid out quite neatly in the complexity of connections in an Astrology chart. Charts can be drawn for the birth of children, but also individual events in time. The constellations are changing daily; they are never the same twice, and affect our lives accordingly. There will be recurring themes and archetypical situations as well as behaviours that we will repeat time and time again, as they appear on our spiral staircase of life.

I believe at this point I need to introduce an explanation of how it might help us to visualise an overview of our Karmic life-times as a succession of steps on an upwardly spiralling staircase. Each step is connected, but it isn't a physical, solid staircase. In effect, it is made of energy and constantly in motion, contracting and expanding, according to all our individual actions which create the Karmic ladder in the first place. It might be unnerving, but it really just depicts what we already know about life: it is unpredictable as we take one day at a time, and that much of what happens next depends on what we have done before. Although it appears still enough to an onlooker, as we are on it, we do not always experience that stillness for ourselves.

Image of a Spiral with individual 'rungs' in various frequencies indicated by colours, as it might be perceived to be a part of our Karmic history. © Image Credit: Droga Visuay Auditiva

As we look down, we see the rungs right below us which we have already taken. All of them are facing in the same direction, but we are a little higher up each time we move along in our own individual space/time continuum. Each rung indicates an individual stage in our lives, subject to our individual Karmic path. Each rung has separate sections which we perceive to be 'time' and 'space'. If we managed to fully overcome the inner obstacles of our Karmic tasks, our Karmic spiral would change accordingly and transform, as it is not fixed. It can shorten, lengthen, curl tighter or looser. It is made up of our own Energy in this lifetime, and will change nature and become one with us again once we are not in 3-dimensional form.

If we don't go with the times and grow from our experiences, we will feel like we are going around in circles, and that is literally what we would be doing at those points in time: we would not be evolving, we would simply be slowing down, even to a standstill at times, repeating the same lessons over and over again, according to the same unchanged beliefs and situations we are stuck in. if it is meant to be, our flexible spiral will support us and adjust, and we will remain going around on the same level of the spiral over and over until we have gathered enough Karmic energy again to move to a more expansive vision of every circumstance we are involved in during this dance that is life. Those points in time give us a chance to resolve patterns in our life and our spiral where our energy needs help. These points can be moments in our lives when something happened to us that we find difficult to move on from. We have a choice to move slowly or stand still, and there might be nothing wrong with that if we do standing still well. We can move fast, and think that it's better, but if we are moving for the sake of being 'out there' we also may well fall. At any point in life, we may also be asked to look down again to see if we are still aligned with our life mission, as the spiral also continues to align with our previous positions of any of our lifetimes. We might remember that the spiral has no beginning and no end, but it certainly has purpose.

For every day we spend on this planet, there is an astrological hint of what it might be about. I remember consulting an Astrologer about a friend. The Astrologer looked at his chart and said that my friend had 9 very difficult hurdles to overcome. He then looked at me and asked if I was prepared to accept that my friend would not make it through all of them. He put it so well, so nicely, so compassionately that I could come to terms with it and always knew what would happen eventually. I was very grateful that I was at least prepared when it did.

There are people who look at the constellations to interpret them and according to their skill, will be able to do forecasts, often with great and amazing accuracy. It does not seem very hard to understand that it can be done. One-line horoscope entries in newspapers and magazines does not do astrology justice. And yet, so many millions read their horoscopes daily, seemingly just for the fun of it. It has created a whole industry of its own right. Although we probably have to approach a lot of it with discernment, our own minds seem to be instinctively pointing us in the right direction. Just remember to find someone reputable, don't get addicted to it and don't spend a fortune. It's not necessary. An astrological birth chart for each of us can by now be obtained for free on many online services. It is totally individual and never the same twice, like our very own fingerprint. Even twins who often share the same birth chart will have different outcomes in their lives according to their Karmic reincarnation. The interpretation of certain astrological aspects of our charts is down to each individual.

Many forms of divination have existed since time began, in all cultures all around the world, by different names and methods. There are many fascinating books on the subject, and I won't go into full details here, but there will be some recommendations online for more research.

To keep it in context our thoughts on Karma, a good start for looking at our own Karmic links in connection with Astrology would be, for example, which sun/moon birth sign our Karmic energy body was attracted to at the point of conception and birth. Energies that incarnate on Earth are drawn by their own frequency either to fire, earth, water, wood, metal or air. I have mixed up the elements here to represent both Western and Eastern ways of divination. When I mention conception, I am fairly certain most of us have never even thought about looking up a chart on this important start of our individual process on Earth. Also, we can look up if we are cardinal or mutable signs, as well as which Animal year are we born in, in terms of Eastern Astrology. Each of the 12 animals have their own attributes, much like our 12 star signs do. Even though we talk about the year 2020 in the West right now, this way to calculate time was introduced by Pope Gregory VIII as recent as the 16th century. Calendars elsewhere around the world vary enormously and take entirely different calculations into account, often based on moon cycles during natural seasons. In some cultures, the day and time of your death are at least, if not more important in comparison to your birth. In many tribes even to this day, the day and time of a birth were traditionally not always determined exactly by any calendar, but by the constellations of planets and the moon seasons. People's type of burial is still today in some cultures determined according to what divination signs there are around their death, for example, by the dominance of water, fire, earth or air elements. This is said that it will aid a good rebirth according to what their Karmic body will most need in its transition period in order to ensure a good next life. There are divinatory signs which are followed to find important reincarnations of previous Lamas or Holy People, as well as many different methods involving stones, coins, signs in nature and so on, representing healing guidance that can help us understand ourselves and our Karmic path better.

Traditional cultures of this world have been using Astrology in order to divine auspicious and inauspicious times for their events and important actions, and continue to do so to this day. It makes me think that, if we did find out the dates which are naturally lucky for us and those that are not, we would perhaps save ourselves a whole load of trouble by sometimes not leaving the house. Not that we have the kind of lifestyle any longer that would cater for that. Don't tell your boss I said that. I'm seeing the funny side, too, but I think you know what I am trying to say. Each bit of information can make us realise that there is a manual to our lives after all; it was written long before we came to this Earth, and each of us have our own individual pattern cut out for us, within which we can decide how best to use it with our own inner intuition, determination, focus and intention.

A map is a map. It will guide us, but it's not the real thing. We have to live our life and make the best decisions we can, from moment to moment. It's not an electronic device that takes us to a simulated place. We must take the journey for real, and learn from it along the timeline we brought with us into this life from our previous existences.

✽ ✽ ✽

33. Karmic Contracts And Interaction

*Other beings do not exactly exist
the way we perceive them.*

All beings will have been given their Karmic body in this life according to their previous Karma. All are re-enacting their own Karmic dance at the same time as other beings they have consciously and/or unknowingly chosen to coexist with in their lives and on this Earth. These other beings we either get to know closely, or learn about from a distance. Some we see on a daily basis, some once in a lifetime and some never personally. Some we will deem to be friends and family, some we won't, and even if we do have the chance to connect with some beings very closely, there is no guarantee that they will be with us for a lifetime. When we feel close to someone, we often don't really know why. We will notice things about them that we feel familiar with or find interesting, and are attracted to them despite not being able to explain why. After a while, our brain gives us the idea that we 'know' them, who they are, how they work, everything about them. It may look like we do, but however close we might be, we don't. We can't. We will also never completely share our very own subjective view of the world as we perceive it through our eyes and our experiences with them. Even if there are many parallels and much synergy to be shared between those who have come into our lives with similar energies and outlooks, we all incarnated from different backgrounds, lineages and have thus developed individual points of view. When we are able to bear this in mind and respect it, we will feel less of a need to make the other see things exactly the way we do, because they can't and never will. Even though it makes some people feel invalidated and infuriated, knowing that the other person cannot see things exactly the same way as we do, could make us try less hard to control how they live their lives. Nevertheless, we feel so close to some beings that we make a full committent to them. Once in a while it happens that we find people who we feel incredibly close to, who we seem to have much in common with. It feels like a unique common bond, so that it seems like we have known them before. The cross-over of energies that synergise between people in this way has often been described by the word 'soul mate'. The Term seems to be used a lot nowadays. In a way, all world population must be our soul mates, because we overlap with them in time and space, i.e. we are here, together, right now, at the same time, and all our aim is the same - to be happy.

Since we hardly ever have all humankind in mind when thinking of closeness and being with one special person, I am deliberately choosing to describe the experience of how we relate to others in a different way to what we are used to. When we set eyes on another being, we already come with a whole host of preconceptions; our experiences including those that are hidden from our own view, our needs and desires, what we feel we are looking for in another, what they must look and behave like as well as what education, job and aspirations they have. How we look, present ourselves, what we believe in, how we see ourselves in the future and how we experience the world through our own eyes relating to personal and work experiences, must also be acceptable to them. When we meet someone new, the information we receive from this encounter triggers within us a myriad of instant internal processes to determine who this person might be, and who they might become to us. We know nothing about them and yet our ancient inner cognitive-instinctive detective system demands that we go through the process of knowing as much as we can about the other within the first 7 seconds. An inner stone-age process mainly based on survival in case we are in any danger, we very quickly make up our minds whether we like the look of this person in front of us or not, whether we want to connect with them or not and if so, on what level, and also whether we are safe with them or not. In fact, the result of our processing information about the new person based on this 7-second check-out is basically limited to one of three outcomes: either we have neutral feelings about them, positive or negative. By the way, there is absolutely no telling if we are right or wrong, which we are probably aware of by now. It is entirely our own inner Karmic energy scanning the other person's. Whilst it's quite incredible that we are all more or less able to do it - and aware that we are - we must also know by now that it is not fail-proof; and yet, we all use it to try to determine if we are drawn to someone or not, safe with someone or not. It's definitely not a great way to know anything about anyone for certain, despite many current electronic appliances building a whole business idea on the concept. However, we are looking at this from the angle of how our instincts can often be fallible. Let's see what happens next when we try to interpret what goes on within us.

Neutral feelings mean that we experience no inner sensory reaction of attraction or rejection in that first instance when we come across any situation, including another being. We feel there are no touching points we recognise as a result of that encounter and we carry on as if it doesn't exist, because we do not feel threatened, repulsed or attracted in any way. It does not mean that there literally are no touching points – it simply means that at this particular meeting time, our inner radar has not flagged up anything. Maybe our inner filing system is missing crucial information and reserving judgement, which is a good thing when we realise this inner judging process is simply based on the limited experience of our ego minds. After all, it's there to keep us safe. We may not have a clue if we have a serial killer in front of us, who is adept at hiding the shocking secrets of their previous actions successfully. Equally, we may have an enlightened being approaching us in ordinary clothing and simply pass them by without noticing. Either situation would easily escape our inner check-out system, a reminder that we really cannot make up our minds about anyone quite so quickly. Nevertheless, we do it all the time. Whilst our inner radar is usually on overdrive, we are not normally aware of that crucial little moment between perception and our reaction. It is an important point to be aware of, as in spiritual practice, the time span between the two is prolonged so that we get more time to allow more space between the two. It is interesting to see that our modern way of life is doing exactly the opposite by asking us to be reactive all the time, to make up our minds quickly, to judge instantly. All these are seen by society as a form of intelligence and quick thinking, enhanced by a caffeinated crowd rushing around to achieve, go-get, and throw themselves into the next consumer craze. Are we all being had? Are we all under some spell? Are we craving the predictability of recognising certain triggers so we can have the feel-good factor of being rewarded for getting something right? We all seem to be pressing buttons really quickly these days to feel a part of society, including each others'. Perhaps we should find out why many of us are feeling more isolated than ever and yet crave being accepted and validated so much that we end up looking and behaving exactly like some enigmatic external force based on the fact that statistics want us to.

There is, as we might imagine, another inner reaction which is beneficial and not to be confused with the above flawed system of being manipulated into not being able to process important information. There is a constant way of life where we stay in neutral gear as a default, which does not depend on the external influences of any phenomena. I am talking about the 'middle-path' realisation of complete oneness within ourselves, which allows for all to approach us equally regardless; and we ourselves are able in return to be equally in acceptance of all of them and remain unaffected by their energy. It does not mean we are complacent, docile, mediocre or disinterested in others' and our own well-being. Far from it. The space that is created within by retaining our composure means that we have the inner space to meet any situation with our full Karmic energy intact, and always ready to bring fully calming and healing energies to the situations we come across. There is no inner judgement created, no inner expectation, no inner dependence on the other - any other. it has nothing to do with showing a stiff upper lip or refusing to become involved. It is not laziness or unskilfulness. On the contrary, it is the ultimate of goals within the highest possible healing energy practices of various cultures and communities all around the world, which many aspire to but only few can truly manage to reach. This is because it is very difficult to do on a more permanent level. The idea is that it is not necessary to rely on our flawed internal system to check people out, so as to survive a possible encounter or make it into something other than it truly is. There is instead, a full awareness of the other and a sincere wish for them to reach their highest good. We have an ability to override our inner judge by tuning in to our much greater internal consciousness we already possess within our Karmic energy experience on Earth. Through remaining centred within oneself by having resolved much conflict within, we automatically assume the position of acceptance of how things are and also at the same time using our wisdom to hone our energy system to be creating the highest good at all times, so that the best scenario presents itself in all events through our non-attachment. By non-attachment here is meant that everywhere we are, we are present to be creating the highest good, constantly and eternally. Even if there were a sense of threat, there would be alertness to the fact. Our awareness serves as an opportunity to turn around negative Karma. It might be difficult to comprehend or even execute at first, but all we do to begin with is to set our minds to wanting this to be the outcome. It is an existing principle underlying many religions, often misconstrued due to the missing teachings that should have a duty to make us fully aware of our inner Karmic energy potential and the methods of achieving this on a more permanent level. At many points during our own personal energy evolution, we will have the opportunity to neutralise fear on specific subjects of our choice in order to make the best decision for all involved from moment to moment. This does not mean we forcefully ignore our instincts and feelings, put on a brave face and fail to realise we are being taken for a ride. It takes energy work within to come to a state of mind that is unaffected by external influences. An absence of fear on the whole means being engulfed in awareness that we are residing in universal light, as is our birth right. When we know how to make this state permanent, we will only feel love, and want the best for others, our loved ones, our environment, even strangers. This love is who we inherently are, this Magical 'neutral gear' of non-attraction and non-rejection which allows us to stay in our presence and full energy flow. It has the power to overcome our past inner fears.

The 'neutral gear' is the non-attachment of Karmic teaching, the middle path, the non-reactive space between attraction and rejection. When our see-saw of flitting between those two opposites becomes exhaustive, only our centre, our core, our inner singularity and its essence remains. When this is achieved on all levels, we realise that it is ultimately unshakeable and indestructible in its nature. At this point, we are one, and at peace; with the universe and all whom it contains. Nobody dictates, nobody intervenes, nobody bosses anyone around. In the state of non-attachment, we radiantly just 'are'.

So, neutral is good. Neutral does not mean we do not get involved, that we do not evolve or exercise compassion. Neutral is the space within which we can be everything and allow others to exist unconditionally, too. It is the gap in between activity. It means there exists a resolution of our Karmic convolutions. Neutral is our centre core point, where we truly find out about ourselves: who we are, where we came from, where we are going and our connection to each other.

I am making the journey towards achieving this blissful state of being sound easy. It is not. We will come across many confusing times on Earth. What about the opposite reaction to infatuation, ie. the many ways that negative attachments are created within us to an external being or situation, such as dependencies, rejection, hatred or fear? When coming across a new person or situation, it can also happen that we ourselves can have negative sensations based on our preconceptions, and as a result we feel like backing away from this strange new situation or person, based on the information we are receiving from our own inner receptors. All of this can all happen within a few short seconds, and all occurs according to what we attract and reject with our own energies, as well as how they interact with the other being's energies. The person in front of us is not always as we perceive them. They 'exist' only in the way our energy field reads and reacts to them. The way we react to each other becomes entirely based on the information given in those first moments, and what we then make of it. Regardless of any right or wrongs, helpful or unhelpful deductions, our brain then cognitively starts stringing events together, and bunches together similarities to try to make sense of it, gathering signs of abnormalities to prepare for any situation that may become a threat. It is trained to do that habitually with everything and everyone, from an early age. If we were exposed to our mentors' derogatory beliefs from an early age, we may have had no choice but to take on their fears and rigid ways of thinking and dealing with others.

Each of us has their Karmic energy field around them, by which everyone attracts, rejects or feels neutral about others and the world around us.

Our energy field appears to also be able to cause a reaction in others inadvertently, but it contains a solution, too.

We may continue to be drawn inexplicably to following the determinations set by our inner system of recognition set by our past actions. Perhaps there is this person we have just come across someone whose energy we feel drawn to; the energy within us is literally leaving our body to become entangled with their energy. This may happen with our energy from just one area within our Karmic energy field, or many. Our energy is reaching out to them. We may be reacting to them emotionally, too, by feeling happy, but also confused, overwhelmed and a host of other sensations on top, but still overall interpret this as a positive experience, even though it is entirely subjective. Someone else might react to the same person entirely differently, and this fact alone, which we observe on a daily basis interacting with those around us, is already evidence that our energy system check-in is unreliable. Even so, we sense our energies were literally drawn in, and we all probably recognise this process as it may have already happened to many of us. Our 'Love at first sight' sensations create endorphins and make us wish for nothing else but to follow them everywhere they go; nice to check at this point whether the other person is reciprocating or running a mile.

I know I am being a little tongue-in-cheek, but there is something it makes us aware of. Often, we don't notice a part of our energy mind is leaving our physical body in these and other situations and we quite literally lose it, at least for a while until we call it back into ourselves. By the way, we can call our energies back into our own Self from situations however long ago, even lifetimes ago, at any point. It is an incredible experience when we do so, as it makes us feel more complete than ever, an experience that nobody else can fulfil for us. If we don't know methods to calm and contain them, it follows that our bodily energies are already swirling around elsewhere outside ourselves. We have probably been doing this unwittingly for years and wonder why we feel anxious and depleted. Without our energy fully present within us, we start to feel we are missing something and look for it outside of ourselves. Before we know it, our energy is focused on another human being, even though we may not even be aware that this is exactly what is occurring. They will be able to feel it, though. Maybe they won't be aware what is going on either, but they are definitely able to feel it. They have their own freedom to choose what to do with this energy, whether to allow it in, or reject it; whether to say something or not. Sometimes we literally seek a target so we can let off our frustrations of not feeling our own energies completely within ourselves. If we could somehow do a sketch and make this process visible of how our energies seek others', I think we would laugh, probably, or feel mortified. But since we are not usually focused on finding out what our inner energy is doing, we probably liken it to falling in or out of love with someone.

When we meet some people, our energy leaves our body without us even thinking about it. We want to learn more about them, we want to experience excitement, we want to become embroiled in the other's experience of being. Before we know it, it escalates: we are infatuated, we can't stop thinking about them, we can't sleep or eat because a part of our energy has gone AWOL and is scouting them out. We are fascinated by something about the other, we sign an inner agreement that we must learn more about them, and already anticipate there is much to be experienced with them. Some of it clever and loving, and some of it not so much, as it turns out. Whilst we could be seen as a little overzealous but harmless, some people really take advantage of others being so unconscious that this process takes place. Putting our precious energy out there to see what another being is about is a very deep process that has a downside: we tend to forget to stay safe. It can be misused and manipulated, especially if accompanied by complementing words and actions to steer us towards a certain outcome. Many people are trained or train themselves to do just this, to lull us into safety and make us do something in return we normally would not. If we are trusting and unsuspecting, we won't be able to notice. Their energy goes out to us just the same as we have just learned, every time, no matter who the victim is. Combined with the right pep talk we are drawn in by the invisible energy threads their energy created within and around us. All good and well if we realise it and can still walk away, but sadly it becomes more sinister when some people try to manipulate others into entering violent relationships and are able to imprison them that way. This is where we finally realise we need our energy ties to be severed urgently, but by the time we have become the victims of such behaviour and realise what is happening, it is often too late. It is such a creepy way to get someone to do our bidding. Nobody will be able to see the invisible energy ties they will try to bind us with. Because there is no visible proof of any wrong-doing or abuse, a lot of innocent people get drawn into scenarios because they keep wanting to believe and trust what they are being told. They also keep being told that it will get better if they act a certain way to appease the aggressor. It can happen anywhere, any time, which is not good news if we are in a work situation or similar, and/or around a manipulator every day. But the method behind ensnaring and enslavement is always the same: another being is trying to put their energy into our body without our explicit consent. I deliberately put it that way, as there are many - and all more or less horrific - ways to interpret it, so I will leave it exactly as it is for you to see the underlying implications and draw your own conclusions for your personal safety. I have seen it happen lots of times because I can see energy in colours leave people's bodies long before anything bad has happened. Staying centred in the middle path as we are trying to practice will not leave us defenceless. On the contrary - when we really become aware of how energy interacts, when it becomes visible and tangible to us, it may well give us insights and keep us safe from harm without having to feel we are obliged to interact in any way that might hurt us. We really should have some sort of visible warning system that makes everyone more aware of how powerful this could be as an early detection of something that's not right. Many people do get things happen, like some people make their skin crawl. Legally, it cannot be proven that this is a process that occurs, when there are no witnesses and no evidence, it looks consensual and an aggressor often gets away with it, leaving the victim blaming themselves for how they got drawn in. This is one of the reasons i am writing this, so that we can all become more aware of how precious our energy is, how powerful it can be and also what it can do in relation to others that we might not be able to see. It's perhaps one thing to play a relatively innocent game with our energy, testing it out on others, even though it's intrusive without the other noticing. But it's quite another when we use the power of our invisible energy to actively try and force others to alter their behaviour to suit us. I think we can all think of many situations where this has already happened. Sadly, we have a whole society that manipulates each other by now, including their children into behaving, dressing, performing in certain ways and seeing nothing wrong with it, causing implications for the growing generations, decade after decade. The clearer we become within ourselves about this, the more confident we can become that when we feel uncomfortable in others' company, we can check to see how their energy is making us feel. If we have clearer ideas of how powerful our energy is even though we cannot see it, we can then learn to become more aware of it and our right to have permission to either accept or reject it. We may have to assume that even though we are very clever and wise doing all this and adjusting our lives accordingly, there is always some force present on Earth which will attempt to manipulate it to try and turn it to their advantage.

All of it is a learning process, according to our own level of Karmic existence being lumbered with a human body, stuck in an evolutionary time-line process. Don't feel bad - the universe appeared on just such a whim, the sudden state of existence arising from non-existence, the origins of life wanting to experience itself, the dance of Shiva. You are a part of it - it's hard to escape it if it's all around you. However, it seems there are bright ways to go about experiencing, and there are less bright, less conscious ones. Even if we do experience attachment to external energies whilst we are still inexperienced and learning to keep our inner Karmic frequency intact, we are always on a path of learning how to contain and manage our energies in relation to others. We learn to remain on a high frequency level whilst at times also being exposed to inevitably lower frequencies. Depending on the timeline and nature of attachment we have allowed ourselves to become involved in, once it has expired – which will inevitably happen - detaching from it can be as laborious as the attachment felt desirable. We often have as much aversion to the process of recalling our energy back into our bodies, as we had joy in attaching our hopes to another. We can remind ourselves that the energy we have expended into another is ours to call back to return to us, although we must learn to do this and repeat it until it returns back to us as easily as when we entered the moment we sent it out. It is a huge learning process that takes much time and effort. Eventually, we might become wise to it and not enter a contract with another without fully being aware of the consequences. It's up to us to recognise our inner tasks and requirement of resolution. It's our job, not anyone else's, but, of course, help is always available when we take charge of our own energy.

Once we choose to recognise how we are playing with our own energy, to become aware of what we are invested in, it is good if we can make a decision to put our precious energy to the best use possible. The best use possible is always to give our attention to people and projects unconditionally, to create the best benefit possible for them and all else, without adding the intention of any personal gain from outcomes and beings involved. Attachment might seem tempting at first, and it is certainly promoted for personal gain in many situations in many places on Earth. We even want to be passionately attached to a spiritual cause, learn to leave our bodies, 'send' love from our energy, whilst leaking out energy freely to the lucky object we have chosen to receive our loving affection. We often do not realise that we don't have to leak out energy at all. We just have to radiate, shine, emanate radiance that flows through us, for others to automatically receive with our true, pure intention to assist. How the recipients then react to this, is also up to their own understanding, willingness and investment of their own energy, according to their ability to accept this unconditional offer. How and if they do it and how long for is up to them, as well as how long the energy plays out within the greater context of a time frame it is given. We sometimes have attachment to their reaction as well, though, which we often hadn't noticed up until then. It makes for an interesting knot to untangle if we are expecting a certain reaction or outcome. Remember that all giving for the giver is about themselves, whereas all giving for the recipient is about how they choose to react to the gift. Is the giver giving unconditionally and knows how not to allow their energy to interfere with expectations? Is the recipient reacting with true gratitude and learns to trust, feel safe and be authentic? A first step to untangle from any outcome attachment gone wrong in the past, is to become conscious that our energy has gone out from our body. If we then learn to allow for it to return to our bodies again, our energy will replenish and it can more easily flow unconditionally. We can practice the process until we will wise up knowing the difference between pure giving and giving with an outcome in mind. There would be no problem if we all learned to wish for and create outcomes that benefited us all. We would increase all our Karmic energies so much and feel that the sum of all recipients is much greater than its individual components. Much in this world of desire and consumerism is based on attachment to the external, items and situations not truly worth investing in, many of them downright detrimental to our health on all levels. We need to learn how to grow things again in a way that is abundant. Abundance happens when we allow all our energies to grow.

It is good to see that not just adults are being taught to be more mindful this way, but that help is also given to children as to how to become aware of their own energy bodies and minds. They must know that they have permission from the grown-ups around them to hold on to their inner energy in order to remain mindful and healthy. That does not mean children must sit down and shut up, and the same goes for adults, too. Everything within a child is naturally wanting to learn, is geared towards external stimuli, growing and expanding every second of the day. We can learn so much from our children's unconditional abundance of energy. To be able to listen each others' inner Karmic energy and wisdom, we could use practices like yoga and meditation together. We must try to shield and protect our children from leaking out energy to those who will exploit it. But we have to do this mindfully, too, using the right tools. It does not help to make them even more terrified of us adults than they already are. Think of how they see this world, which we have so shamefully spoilt with our ignorance. Should we not be honest with them?

Instead, industries have shamelessly exploited our tendencies to feel shame and guilt, to feel stressed and anxious. Our inner insecurities and lack of energy make us susceptible to connect with external stimuli and hand over billions for useless distractions we do not need. We need our inner Karmic energy flow back, and so do our children. Our bodies suffer from our lack of balance, due to the fallout from our leaked energy, creating more and more expensive and destructive distractions. We have become so hypnotised into forgetting that all this abundance already exists within us! All the colours, shapes, textures, sounds, experiences and so on, are already ours. Our children know this! And they are trying to remind us, every day. We are all inner astronauts and our children are the new generation on a quest, reminding us that there is an inner journey waiting to be re-discovered. Attachment per Se is not a negative thing, mindful attachment can teach us skills if we have the inner resolve to aim for true compassion and wisdom to build up to an incredibly strong and useful, balanced mindset, with the potential of bringing the right outcome for all involved. If we only do as much as to place our focused attention on this to start with, then we can be sure to be on the right track.

The way we react to anything external is our

choice, based on how we have learned to create and evolve within our own Karmic energy system.

It might be tough to hear this, but it is never meant in a callous or uncaring way. It never means that when a person suffers, they deserve to suffer. On the contrary, it means that we all inherently have the ability to change the outcome of a situation by how we manage our energy awareness, something that should make us feel empowered and Magick. However, we are too often scared to take this responsibility for ourselves seriously and bring on change accordingly. Many times we also lack insight into the connections of how we are stuck, and the methods to help us get out of our conundrums again. How can we be any different, if we have not learned how to, in this life? Could we tap into the all-knowing part of ourselves again that perceives things in their true nature, not just subjectively? It could be because of past Karmic situations that influenced us in a negative way, that those external things seem to bother us, but they don't always have a bearing on our future if we determine that there is no re-action necessary. If we realise that we have a better way of feeling resolved within, then we can surpass a situation without having to be physically affected. If we realise that we can't truly own anything or anyone, no matter how much we wish to become entangled in anything external, then we will see that something even better will replace what we may have once lost. When we realise that we have an option to do this, that there is a way, then we can use many a tool to address our situations differently, as stated at the end of this book where there are many suggestions for tools and methods to bring peace back into our inner energy system and our over-reactive brains.

So, even if another person chooses to provoke a lot of people in their life, it can still be possible to remain unaffected in our exclusive personal field of inner power despite their actions. People whose minds are in distress will often try to reel other peoples' energy into their own to complete theirs. They may not be aware of it, but all provocation on their account is to feel our energy enter their energy field. It feels better to have company, and in some situations, any company, any interactive energy situation, even if aggravated, is better than being alone. We have a choice whether to get drawn in. It can, at times, be a dangerous game. It does not mean we shut down, suffer and don't connect to anybody, if we decide not to, in order to be safe. It has to do with utilising and activating our own immensely powerful inner energy again, as well as becoming aware of what happens when it starts to merge and interact with others' Karmic energies and external circumstances, like we laid out above. If we remain fully present in our own energy, situations can also resolve themselves, sometimes with better results. We are often only used to using our adrenal energy when reacting with our natural human fight or flight instincts in order to meet a challenge. Our energy reaches out to get to know the situation to make sure we are safe. If we are aware of this process of our energy leaving our body at this point, and how it can escalate from there, we gain a conscious choice to remain within our own energy realm instead. We can also recall any of our energy at any time, should sending it out have turned out to be to our detriment. If making a conscious decision to send out our energy feelers and interact was the right choice to keep us safe, then great. This is what it means to remain responsible for our actions; it does not mean we do anything to cut off our feelings or human interactions. It just means we remain fully aware of and alert to our own choice of actions. It also means that we should never attack another's energies, consciously and deliberately provoke an attack, or prolong any arising conflict unless we are defending ourselves. If we choose to attack in that moment, we also become responsible for the other being's reaction, no matter how a legal representative would interpret it. If we are aware that another being is, for whatever reason, sending out their energy to attack others, manipulate or provoke them, or in any way use their energy in a negative way, then we can also remain alert to the fact that this is their energy issue so as not to get actively drawn in, allowing us to remain impartial. Often, we try to help others by appeasing them, but this does not always have the desired effect. It also may get complicated to untangle ourselves again, especially in prolonged conflicts, to the point where it is impossible to tell which is their energy and which is ours. The moment we withdraw and firmly stand in our own Karmic energy again, matters and solutions have a chance of becoming clearer.

If we are affected by others' actions/speech/thoughts/energy without them actively seeking to provoke, attack or openly involve us or someone near us, then that is our energy issue to sort out and we can step back from it accordingly at any moment before the lines get blurred of who is at fault. We do not have any obligation to become embroiled in anyone's drama, especially if we are not at fault and we are not to blame.

Taking responsibility for our own energy involvement is not a form of punishment, it's a skill. By taking responsibility, we are taking back into our energy body all the energy that got entangled with the external. It is a process of empowerment, of regaining the balance of lost energy we thought we could not have back; we can, any time. The Miracle is that this energy process also transcends time; it can be used for many situations in retrospect, even if those situations happened decades or even lifetimes ago. The reason is that our personal energy field merges with our Karmic energy, and if we claim back energy we lost, this feeds into our Karmic energy body which is not bound by space or time. We always have a choice – to re-act and throw our energy at an external situation which can cause an energy eruption between the people involved, or use our completed and intact energy field to connect to the situation on a much higher level. You do not need to stay in a confrontation, you can walk away and deal with your own entanglements first and utilise methods to complete your energy field, so you can better resolve any other issues afterwards. We are often under the illusion that we must resolve everything immediately on a physical, confrontational level, but it seems that quite a few gazillion human issues are not resolved that way. There are of course, very urgent situations that are an exception, and humans have regular run-ins with each other as to what these are. We can learn the art of resolution on a higher level, we just need to re-train our minds to become aware of what our energy is doing, when it is wise to interact or wiser to use our energy differently.

If it is causing us much grief when others are not able to contain their energies, could it not in our and everyone else's interest to learn to manifest the inner equilibrium we are all truly trying to achieve, and to ask for everyone else's peace as well as ours? inner balance does not mean indifference, and i am fully aware how confrontational some people become in an abusive situation. It won't help much there, and the question of how to deal with these was once answered by a Tibetan Master with one word: RUN. At those times of emergency, do not try to be clever. It does remind me of my favourite clip in a British sitcom called Black Books. One of the main characters, Manny, has accidentally swallowed the 'Little Book of Calm' and is since sporting a halo and white robes, i.e. a hospital gown. He has released himself from hospital after assimilating the little book and is now putting himself in harms way around the streets of London. He spouts off nonsensical words of wisdom in precarious situations, such as advising a woman giving birth to 'do something different, roll up your sleeves, or eat an orange', and then moves on to confront a bunch of skinheads to try out his wisdom on them. (Please look up the clip, it's a lot funnier than I can relate here) What is funny is that it does relate to real life, where we often try this ourselves and apply completely absurd methods to try and appease others whilst not having a full grasp of the gravity of some situations. We might get away with it, but is it worth the risk, if others are ready to unleash their energy tentacles in any direction at any point? At best, we will be seen as completely removed from reality, which might not be far from the truth. When our inner Karmic energy level balances more and more, is that not the time where we set our intention on manifesting as little disturbance of peace as possible? We may have forgotten that this is what nature does, in our lifestyles so far removed from it. At the danger of sounding as cliche as the clip I quoted above, it's true that, as our energies become more focused, this brings more insights and helps us recognise the interconnectedness between all that is going on, externally and internally. Our focused energies hold more power to create good circumstances, the more we practice. Logically it must follow that we would then also have others' best interest at heart and are able to help on an elevated level rather than become embroiled in physical altercations. The energy field within and around us can serve as a protective layer, if we use it with the intention to truly only create the best outcome for everyone we meet. When we practice this, we will notice more and more that it ceases to hold grudges against anyone. The intention of sending good energy from highest frequencies to others has the power to cleanse, purify & flush out stagnant energy from our own system, bringing in new, clearer, higher energy frequencies for us to pass on and share. Just by focusing our highest inner energy on the intention of a good outcome, we can literally change our own energy for the better and create better situations and solutions for our future and that of others. Our sincere wish would be to want to be able to see the greatest and best outcome reflected in everyone - and using our newly found higher energies can assist to create this result. It is a principle of the highest truth, but it does not sound easy to achieve if we are caught up in situations that are low level. We can start by ourselves first, thinking about including others' well-being in the practice of honing our Karmic minds, akin to prayers but with more oomph. We are actively involved in this process and we can bring peacefulness to ourselves and others that way.

Everything beyond matter exists as one.

We will eventually stop attaching scenarios to our Selves that are indication of our inner energy still being turbulent, once we have experienced what it means to be aligned with the higher energy frequency sources. We can check in with ourselves and see if we are using any of the energy centres along our bodies to interact with others on a conditional energy or even physical level, or if we are already aware that the divine energy we are looking for and hope to pass on, enters through our crown. We may also attract more situations to help others as our fear lessens and our ability to channel energy from the highest sources increases, in order to help others deal with their energy. This is equally as skilful and compassionate a thing to do, and sometimes we get thrown in the deep end to learn how to do it well. It would be easier to become aware again that this may be happening to you. Without knowing what our energies are capable of once we are connected to the frequencies of higher purpose, nothing will make sense and every sentence talking about it will seem far-fetched and annoyingly sanctimonious. Are you a highly accomplished helper already, and have on some level made a vow to attract those in trouble? Are you sure that in any situation, you can remain mindful of your energy as well as theirs, and make decisions based on how to best to assist them? You can help yourself and your mind to do this, if that is what you are ready for. Or you can go slower and learn your skill, try to find out if life gives you time to train your awareness first, to then be prepared for all eventualities. There is never nothing to do. Whether we are bored, troubled, busy or accomplished, we can all think of manifesting good things in our highest minds for ourselves and others, and when I say 'think good things' – why stop at good when we can think the best? The skill of people who are seen as advanced spiritually is that they have had the good – and often laborious – Karma to become masters at the art of manifestation of compassion and wisdom, and have not lost sight of constantly aiming to visualise and bring to Earth the highest level of Truth that they dedicate themselves to live by. Their commitment to having purified their Karmic body to this extent is credit that to their greatness. Far from living amongst monetary wealth, those who truly achieve realisation do not reach for riches. Those of us who are not quite there yet to give up their creature comforts, might instead just have to make do with wishful thinking that one day, we will be ready to exchange our material riches for an eternal awareness over lifetimes.

Ultimately that is the goal - if we can call it that - but admittedly it is not so easily done when we feel powerless over situations that happen to us, especially those which we feel we have not created for ourselves. Life has a habit of sending us moments to try us. And yet, to create a peaceful and powerful outcome, we must try to overcome our urge to react solely with our ego brain. It is not called re-act for nothing; it seems that if we react, we re-enact the same scenarios repeatedly. Granted, the moral high ground is nigh on impossible to achieve sometimes, unless we truly grasp this underlying energy exchange between people. We need to see that we are learning how we can withdraw from the conflict of repetitive negative reaction. An example of what we are usually missing in our interaction with others is that our perception of others' energy is limited. If we imagine an angry person is creating a scene in order to receive attention seeking a fight with someone they only just met. We do not know what has made him so angry, but even negative attention is better than none, for some. They will try to provoke others to claim some of their energy by goading them to get involved in their energy drama. We do not only have any details of the reasons for being angry, we also do not know the whole Karmic time-line of how they got to this point. They might be aware of a specific situation that has made them lose their cool, but most likely they have no idea why they are truly reacting so strongly that they are now picking a fight. Perhaps it does not matter so much, because what matters in that instant is whether their energy is going to get dissipated. Their inability to see their own energy body though, never mind make the best use of it, may result in their trying to provoke others by a host of negative attachment methods to make them help him get his blood pressure back down to normal. You can perhaps see what I am getting at: In those moments, it's obvious that they literally don't see, or feel, any loving connection to others around them. Their experience is one of agitation, isolation and blindness, which is based on a deep sadness really, not an aggression. However, to see it for what it is at this stage might be too late. Someone with several unresolved inner issues such as this, becomes aggressive when coupled with the expectation that energy has to come from others around, and be given to them at their command. There is desperation there, too, not just sadness. A resigned notion that they are most likely used to not having their true needs met. For any of us this might be true at some point, where we subconsciously use goading with passive=aggressive words, actions, body language and throwing out energy 'hooks' in a desperate and often unconscious attempt and cry for help. We are trying to reel others into our energy field like a fish on a hook, to receive help to cope with issues we may not even have become conscious of yet. Obviously, once people stand in the middle of a street shouting at passers-by, possibly even intoxicated, are often too desperate at that point to have much awareness of how to optimise their request for help in a situation like this. Their cry for help is, in the form they expressed it, not heard at all. Whatever their situation is, if we choose to become involved at that point, it might be explosive. We have to be aware that it may be to the detriment of our own energy balance, unless we are very practised and sure of what we are doing. We also need to be sure that the person in question isn't going to enforce their anger by using stronger ammunition than just their words to enforce their needs, such as weapons. It's become a sad fact that more people these days resort to doing this. It is our own responsibility to make a decision as to whether we feel we can afford to become involved or not, whether we have the Karmic skill set, or whether the risk is just too great. But what if we have no choice in being involved? Perhaps we know this person, perhaps they are close to us, and one minute they were fine, and the next they are not. Or perhaps there is a response team that was called out to deal with the situation, armed and trained for such situations to be on alert. If any are able to see through the issues that present themselves, they might be able to reason with those in trouble and talk them down from their state of agitation. But what happens then? Will they get the assistance they need, the help they need? There might be those able to get them in touch with themselves again and remind them of who they are, which is entirely down to their good Karma. They might be on a learning curve, and they might not be. It is wise to be solid enough in our own mind to not rise to any provocation if we do become involved in any precarious situation, and to know our skills so that we don't ourselves create a dependency. We need to keep in mind our desire to help on the highest level, whilst being exposed to situations where others may not have any awareness of the concept.

Sometimes, we will bite off more than we can chew. We think we can do it, but our human nature proves us wrong. We may have fear, pride, attachments to teaching the other person a lesson, even wanting to be overly helpful and such like crop up. All of these attachments occur all the time and are fully understandable, yet they are incomplete; added to this is the problem that we are often more attached to an outcome in a situation than we would like to admit, and things can go more than a little awry. What happens, for example, if we want a person to behave a certain way so we feel more in control or, if we are so frightened of their reaction that we need them to be calm to feel safe or, we are the ones who feel superior and act to make them feel inadequate? When we are unaware of energies, when adrenaline runs high, when there are ulterior motives and unknown physical as well as Karmic backgrounds, things get out of control - as we can see all around us where people would laugh at the notion that our Karma affects our actions. Lots of people could not care less. Any examples of severe outcome dependencies may draw us into a scenario that is tricky to get out of again, once we have started to become physically involved and all the energies have gone charging out from our bodies like bulls in a china shop. Once the energy 'hooks' have gone out and got tangled up, we may not even recognise what has happened, never mind be able to resolve it and are easily reeled into situations that are not sane or safe.

All who receive negative Karmic imprints from any negatively charged situation will have ways to apply in order to fully neutralise them again.

Perhaps we already know this subconsciously, and we probably also know from experience that some beings do not know how to respond any different. Will we be able to make a predator stop attacking us when they're staring in our face? Better to know how precious our existence is in that moment, set a precedent and love them from a distance, where we can wish them well with the highest possible energy we can muster, with all due respect to their nature and their own environment. Are we ready to be in a stronger position than them to remain calm and see the bigger picture? Or do we know that once we are involved in another's energy drama, we might end up enraging them or even acting out their negative feelings for them? Our Karmic energy mind does not make our bodies bulletproof. We can become corrupted, making us even more likely to get in deeper than we ever wanted to sink. The danger might be that we cannot tell any longer where our energy ends and the other begins; our energy can be affected by that person's field, the two may intertwine whether we like it or not. We may find it impossible to keep our cool, for example. We may start to re-act, losing some of your own precious energy. We may believe we are obliged to sacrifice our time and energy and stay in the situation to 'sort it out', escalating perhaps even into a physical confrontation. Of course, most of the time, nothing gets sorted out that way; it only becomes a repetitive pattern. The result is that on both sides, precious energy is lost that will later have to be replenished, and a vicious cycle is started that is all too familiar to some who have been victim to this for years. If only we recognised the danger early enough and were strong enough to resist, perhaps also taking time to assess our own energy expenditure, then we would be choosing another, more useful way of resolving conflict. Energy conflicts exist, there is no doubt, on a physical plane, perhaps even other dimensions. Some people become victims every day in their relationships, trying to appease the other and not seeing a way out. We need opportunities for ourselves to be able to go into our highest energy selves again, where we are able to wish for the best outcome for ourselves and the other involved in a clear, sacred space, changing the existing mind-field to a more loving one as an intention. This is the way we can best help, although even then it is still the other person's choice whether to act differently, not ours. We may have assisted them, or we may not, but we hardly ever get to truly resolve conflict in an open battle and see reason why it is there in the first place. This is where we have forgotten to administer the power of our inner energy flow and what it can do for us and others.

* * *

34. Karma, War and A Way Out

Aggression logically leads to more aggression,
but it can be diffused once we learn
how to apply Karmic principles.

This may not be how we have been taught. Many people simply still believe there is a benefit in sacrifice and open warfare, and that seemingly walking away from conflict is an act of cowardice. It is a conditioned belief where we give power to others over ours which arises when we are not yet fully aware of how to handle and apply our own Karmic energy potential and its vast potential for resolving conflict peacefully. When we are disconnected from believing in our own energy power, we start to feel and believe we are powerless, and all kinds of problems ensue. Feeling powerless is directly related to a restricted inner energy flow. Others may take advantage and exercise power over us when we feel disconnected from our own energy. Is it worth the risk? Can we not free ourselves from all these antiquated mindsets, once and for all?

At all times throughout human history, humans have suffered and not been able to see their lives flourish to its full potential. We may have had no choice but to say that this is how it is. These immense tragedies of the past are, however, by no means history - they are still a fact today. How can it be that despite the advances in some areas on the globe, despite such prosperity and growth in a percentage of countries worldwide, we have not been able to spread the goodwill to others just yet. Governments of countries are still drafting those who feel an obligation to go to wars apparently on our behalf. And those involved have done so on the assumption that they did right, because we were all convinced to apply whatever force needed and deemed necessary in a declared emergency to defend ourselves. This may be so. But what if we do what we usually do and ask some questions? What if there are better methods for resolving conflict than warfare? What if the boundaries are blurred between attack and defence so we can not easily tell the difference?

What if there is no emergency situation, what if we are not acting in defence at all? I am treading on thin ice here as this is a matter of World Politics, and I don't think the connection to what it might have to do with Karma can be made clear in a few sentences. But the principles of how we see each other, how we deal with each other, how we perceive matters around us, can be applied to as small or large a matter as we want – they always stay the same: If we are overcome with fear, our systems will shut down and our old brains will activate fight or flight mode. The more fear that remains unresolved within us, the harder it becomes to think straight, keep our hearts open and stick to humane actions. It doesn't exactly sound like a slogan for winning wars, does it. That's because things became complicated, and it's now almost impossible to see who is right and who is wrong, what to believe and what not to, whether to defend or not, what to do and what not to do about it. There are such extreme circumstances by now on Earth, and a lot of it is to do with greed. It seems that, once again, the three defilements of greed, anger and ignorance of the consequences are being applied to create division amongst people. We are being led to believe that we are either winners or losers. How did this happen, if none of us really want to think that way in our every day dealings with each other? Are we really out to finish each other off, or are we led to believe something by others because it serves them? The greed that exists in some can't become the greed of whole tribes of people. Just because some deemed the land on Earth so important in terms of accruing riches doesn't mean we have to all become involved. Who should benefit from the resources that the Earth has to offer? Does the Earth belong to anyone? Should some be allowed to fight to get to the front of the queue, no matter who they are casting aside? What queue? Who thinks there is not enough for everyone?

Whoever they are, if that is what they did and think, this is not in line with what will prevail over lifetimes to come. It is a very short-lived way of thinking and being that does not take one thing into account, as usual: our Karma, and the fact we will not be able to shake off any of our wrong-doing that easily. When we think about how much suffering has been created on Earth already, how many people perished and suffered as a result, why would anyone who puts people first, want to create more? Most of us want to end suffering, and rightly so. What if some really don't, and treat each life as a disposable commodity? We must become aware again of the preciousness of being alive, our biggest achievement so far. We are alive in this body because we earned it, let's not have anyone else believe that we should throw it away or sacrifice it. We must be clear of the difference: Nobody else gets to decide for us if we can be heroes who truly understand what a sacrifice means. Nobody else must gain from our willingness to give our existence for the benefit of others.

If we must look at it in detail, then we will see that historically, Martial laws were put in place and enforced to cover against the decision-makers being accused of crimes against humanity they tried to convince us were necessary, often with immense, brutal force against millions of people. Perhaps in those dark times there was no choice but for people to believe what they were told, that they could only resolve conflict on a physical level of warfare; that they never had the resources to see through those who made the decisions to sacrifice millions and to notice they had no say in it at all; that the inner Karmic accumulation of a prolonged state of fear of external attack created an imprinted image of enemies reinforced by propaganda; that once countries were divided up and segregated, people separated into different camps and were told to fight each other under horrendous conditions, so they could not confer and see that the result of their actions would be followed by what inevitably came next: unable to adapt to peaceful times again, people could not easily drop the image of an enemy they had obtained, because it stayed with them in their minds, every section of their daily trauma. Even if they so desperately wanted to, they did not have methods to get over their harrowing experiences. They had to live with the consequences. Being on their guard all the time, unable to change the image of the enemy within meant that, in peace times thereafter, they may have had no choice but to submit to transference of their traumatic experience into their now, every-day lives. They had to adjust not only to a time of peace again, but also to the fact that a different, perceived inner battle always remained, and that life would never be the same again for them.

Putting good people under the duress of such ongoing trauma of real, perceived and anticipatory threat of having to attack and being attacked in return, of losing their lives and never seeing loved ones again, under orders from those believed to be superior to them to hold no attachment to the situation's outcome of killing millions of beings, is the lowest of the low situations that humans who meant to protect their loved ones can find themselves in. Humans are always at their lowest, most vulnerable point when put under duress and forced to kill, even if they are convinced to be feeling strong, righteous and powerful. The trauma that those who served in any war carry back home - if they do come home - does not simply go away. The heroic sentiment turns into horror, but once a war has been fought, it leaves behind the problem of millions who have are berEFT™ and have no method to heal themselves from their experiences. For many of them, there is no compensation either. People will have lost life and limb, families and friends.

At what point do we realise there is no winner and no loser? How many examples of suffering do we need before we see everyone as equal, equally vulnerable, equally in need of help, equally desperately in need of peace? Even now, as our best form of defence, we believe that we must insist we are beyond reproach, above board, that we must somehow be better than the rest, that only then we can deem ourselves safe. We were not told to look at and question how this all started, how all our energy minds were affected and how it continues to be so in the perceived threat of wars someone or other might instigate here or there to gain this or that. The instigators did not perceive how Karmic debt might be created by aggressive behaviour even if used in what they perceived everyone to be defence. Karma was not a word that was ever used then, and even now nobody really knows what it does and why. The way we were treated and how our minds were affected, many under the circumstances had no choice but to sacrifice their ability to resolve their inner conflict on a higher energy level especially when under attack, hoping they might get the chance at a later stage when peace had been restored. Sadly though, for many of them, their inner peace never returned. We can all see how sad and wasteful it is when lives are lost and when the living lose their minds. Unfortunately, there are always Karmic repercussions, whether you are the one to start or the one retaliating, as those who ended up fighting for a cause will all be able to tell. Killing another being is never a simple thing to liberate our Karmic mind from, and many were only left with the choice that they also sacrificed their sanity for the cause they believed in. Was this one of the many reasons why the wisdoms of Karma were kept from us? in order to make us do things we didn't really want to, in the name of those we felt we had no choice but to protect? We were told things, but many things we were told were simply not true. Those young men, some of them little more than kids, were sent out by so many countries in so many wars. They still are, to this day. How can this still be happening now? They were told to be heroes, but they were alive, they were part of a family, they were going to have relationships and children of themselves. Somebody at the top there has a lot to answer for, because if we ever saw through the whole revolting scheme that played millions of people and continues to trick good people decade after decade, we might think differently. We would imagine that, if a war was on, to quote a famous line from the 70's and 80's, simply nobody should show up.

Don't think there aren't many ways that greed can instigate wars. As long as there is greed, a fear of not existing, a fear of poverty, a lack of morals, and a few superior sociopaths believing themselves to be in charge, they will agree to sacrifice however many as they can, as long as it doesn't affect them personally. There are people on Earth who are unscrupulous, who think differently. Their brain in their ignorance probably tells them that people are dispensable because there are so many on Earth, we can afford to lose a few here and there. In any case, they think people are very expensive and inconvenient. Pesky even. The thought has been put out there and it has already took hold of some good people who really believe we are overpopulated on Earth. There is room for everyone, but not everyone should be allowed to run countries and people into ruin.

There is no being on Earth that deserves to be here less or more than another.

Resolving conflict on a higher level of consciousness does not mean we don't physically care, are not compassionate or that we cowardly walk away from peacefully resolving confrontation. It actually means there is a simpler and also more effective way of conflict resolution. We are very busy already doing exactly that, most seconds of our day. We could be so much more effective internally resolving issues if we had the right methods. That way we would be less stressed and feel much more serene on the inside. It does not matter what we look like on the outside, what we wear, what make-up we have on, whether our shoes cost a million dollars or our car is gold-plated. If we could perceive what we are like on the inside, I think there would be a few surprises. I do still have a sense of humour despite everything, so I would propose an app that makes our photos show what we truly look like.

Previous generations did not have the choices or time for insights as we have today, and looking around, the fact that we should feel calmer and more composed than ever still does not appear to have been implicated very much. There are still wars around the world, we are still at war with each other on many a personal level and still as hell-bent, if not more, on destroying animals and nature. We are so easily led into a war of sorts every day online, that we do not even see when we are lured into it. We still have nothing else to compare it to, in terms of any inner serenity that we would not like to miss. What's happened to our inner serenity? Why is it not higher now than ever? We have to assume that there are some sinister forces working behind the scenes, or that it's simply our lack of method that keeps us from yearning to be at peace enough to find out more. Those who are working on lower frequencies will want to have power over us, our bodies and minds, and our life choices. It looks like we are very happy to oblige at the moment, but is this really what we want, is this really what makes us happy? We simply MUST look inwards to see what has gone on and what is going on. I feel passionately that we have a duty to at least ourselves to do so. It would be nice to think though that we are still able to be as compassionate as we have always been and find it in us to make changes in such a simple way within ourselves to start with, in order to avoid further carnage on this planet and resolve the problem without some dreaded implications for our future. I really feel we either choose to do this of our own accord, or someone/something else will come along and will try to impose the necessity on us so we can learn about the preciousness of our inner power, no doubt.

The idea of our Karmic evolution is to raise our and others' energy vibration to its highest potential, and to stop any actions lowering both our and other beings' Karmic energy levels.

It doesn't sound so easy, does it? As a civilised global population, we still have not done away with attacking each other, but at least we are exploring a new angle to why this has occurred historically and how we can make a difference by not getting drawn in. We have the power of being alive, it is the greatest power possible, and we must not give it away to any other entity if we can help it. If we strengthen it with our inner Karmic practice, we have much more of a chance of obtaining enough equilibrium to see through others' game play. When people are still corrupt enough to sabotage others' lives, how can we raise our game and be evolved enough as a whole Earth community to perceive and care about each other in a compassionate way and help each other sustain every being's Karmic energy levels as well as their precious physical existence? All life has an equal right to live on this planet - that's a universal law. Anything less that we believe probably stems from somewhere dubious, although i am not saying that living by the principle is easy. But we call all make a start somewhere, easily enough. Rather than arguing who lives or dies, just because we have not overcome the traumas of the past which has left some of us with a seemingly inherent urge to kill each other when we feel justified, why don't we start with whatever we think we can contribute to make this world a better place? Bash one less vegan, or something. I have lots of ideas, but I have a feeling that it's a lot better when it comes from each person's own heart.

How often do we kill each other with words, thoughts or looks each day and actually prefer the company of chosen animals we have let someone breed a certain way to look cute enough for us, who charged a small fortune that would feed a poor village for a year? It sounds ridiculous to some to be asked to care about all sentient beings' lives, when we cannot even save enough human lives from hunger and illness even to this day. If we have been so many beings before in endless lifetimes, and can have a rebirth as any being again; if human life is so precious and every rebirth depends on Karmic action and reaction, then the only logical solution to ascertain our own highest energy levels must be that we learn to care about everything and everyone, on an individual level, without excluding anyone or any living thing. I'll let that sink in for a bit., because I have a feeling that in order to even just make a start, we must learn the right methods to care for ourselves again, properly.

And after that – what's next? As we get to the subtler levels of our Karmic energy fields, we become more sensitive to our own inner hurt and start to crave the peace we have had a taste of. At any moment of the day, the ultimate goal, if there is such a thing even, the notion of full enlightenment, a blissful balance within, no matter what happens around us, will give us the only logical outcome to be able to find eternal peace. I liken it to a mathematical equation: internal peace + external peace = enlightenment, and also internal peace + enlightenment = external peace. Or really, when one of them exists, all of the others must exist equally. On that journey of realisation, we will notice that our hurt stems from situations in the past which have left their Karmic energy imprint on us and which we have inadvertently allowed our energy to be influenced and manipulated by. We will know when we haven't noticed that it has been affecting us when we, out of not knowing any better, let our energy system carry on creating blockages to being our true selves. When we are so identified with those blockages, we no longer see who we could be without them. We so easily become blocked and sidetracked from recognising who we truly are. We do own our own happiness and we can learn to see past our own imperfections. As soon as we are honest and start to work with ourselves with the right methodology, we raise our own awareness levels automatically without trying to not just elevate ourselves but others, too. We will notice the interconnectedness of everything. We might start to see and treat others differently, too. Gradually, others become less of a threat. We realise that

We are not all at the same stage of development, but all beings have an equal right to exist.

I think we said this before as well, and it's also worth repeating. We can begin to appreciate and feel their existence, notice the beauty in them, because we have quit our habit of how we reacted to them with our stuck energy. I know it's easy to be cynical when we apply our new-found wisdom in a field where there is still much suffering and no chance of a recovery of wise thoughts any time soon. In those situations we can but put it out there, sometimes from afar, that there be a solution. Since mind energy travels at more than the speed of light, our mind focused on other issues outside ourselves can be heard, especially when many come together with a similar mindset to try to bring about positive change without the intention of harming others but instead, to bring compassion as well as wisdom, a combination which is sorely needed all over the world. We have agreed to be learning how to become open to our own subtle understanding of ourselves, and it has increased our sensitivity towards life and everything living. The world is presented to us as the interlocking puzzle of beautifully functioning symbioses that it is: each creature being there for the sake of its magical beauty, as well as a testament to the synchronicity, serendipity and synergy of life. Everywhere around us are poignant signs and reminders of who we are. We can see that we are all here to help uphold the connection between all others. We start to rediscover the amazing miracles within ourselves that we had started to take for granted: our heart beating, our organs functioning, our lungs filling with true breath – and we see that the world reflects every cell within us in a multitude of creatures in infinite variety. Our blood streams are the rivers of our Earth, the trees our lungs, plants are our nourishment; our convoluted and hardened, repetitive thoughts the tarmacked roads that stop our beautiful Earth from being heard. It can be disheartening and saddening at first to become so sensitive, but we must go through this process, only to realise that our sorrow can be overcome. It is a stage of another habitual energy pattern we will get to know better and break through more quickly and easily as time goes by. Not being sad for too long doesn't mean we are cold-hearted or do not mourn. It means our energy recovers better to be able to help alleviate the causes of the strains we are put under. We don't do ourselves justice by lowering or overloading our Karmic energy body with negative energy blockages, and yet that is exactly what we are doing right now. We will carry on doing so at first whilst we are undoing a lot of old inner Karmic energy residue, and periodically after that in order to recognise and overcome the same. However, it is not life's intention to make us feel miserable, quite the opposite. As we create good outcomes with our true and luminous minds, we tune into the beautiful world within, one aware of all the potential of life, the miracle even in the darkest moments, and with our powerful minds we can turn it into its best possible potential for this planet: an enlightened vision of what it truly could be when the hurt is removed, when pain and fear have left; within us and around us alike, as it is one and the same.

As we become Karmically lighter, we realise the network of connections between us and all others, the more we will feel inspired to work on creating good case scenarios for others in our thoughts, speech and actions, realising we are also creating a green light for their and our future. When we realise that we are creating unseen connections to others through our actions, these are the connections become the serendipity that sees us through times when we usually lose faith and hope. We must learn what it means and what to do to be good to each other. When we are connected with complete awareness, there will never be a moment of not feeling connected again. Try to reflect on the beauty of it in its entirety without thought, which is contained in just one small flower, for example. It is genius in its simplicity and yet it contains all possibilities. It might even be the only way that works to help us understand that we exist as a result of an exploding singularity, and we may return to it again at some point.

35. When All Seems Lost - Karma
& The Symptoms of Society

It's all very well just reading about good advice, but it might have the opposite effect when we are just not there yet, when we don't know what we are still supposed to do if we have already tried everything else. If we already feel the exhaustion and exasperation when we recognise what we are up against in life and want to move forward more mindfully, but don't know what we should do - how should we go about clearing up our inner energy act in a constructive way? What is it that can best assist us in having a breakthrough in terms of realisation, leading to a more loving lifestyle?

It is plain to see for most of us that our education system based on intellectual prowess alone do not work, otherwise we would all be better people living on a healthy planet by now. In fact, I will go so far as make the statement that our education might have contributed to hindering a process of recovery for our planet, and has instead contributed to the world being in such convoluted chaos. Putting an emphasis on commerce before the compassion of a community spirit, blasting our children into future productivity without enough support for family, impoverishing their early days by not ascertaining fair wages and reasonable conditions for a vast percentage of families with children on Earth, putting them through years of stress and duress from a few months old with only acknowledging achievement, not a healthy emotional, mental and spiritual development; preparing youngsters for a bleak future as system drones by focusing on their potential productivity only, creating job opportunities to ascertain financial contributions to the state instead of making sure that they are emotionally secure, creative, mentally and emotionally well youngsters, as well as taken seriously and respected for their input into the decision-making for the shaping of a future society they will inherit and co-create. It all sounds like more of an agenda rather than a solution, but this serves an explanation why we have poverty in mind, body and spirit in 1st world countries where there should not be any.

We have corporations instead of communities;

we have competition instead of co-operation; we have intellect ruling over intuition. 2D electronic passports to identify us but we have forgotten that we are more than 3D, alive, sentient and already better connected than any gadget, if we can only remember how to tune in.

That was quite the sermon. You catch my drift, I hope. As an example, how is that we can keep telling ourselves that we want improvement on all levels and yet, there appears to be a short circuit that has caused a paradox in our Karmic energy system - because I cannot see any improvement yet; perhaps quite the opposite. Apparently something is in the way that has a mind of its own, having also caused a multitude of reasons firmly lodged in our think tank as to why we should continue to be a part of this journey of Self-destruction. Despite our awareness that these paradoxes exist within us as well as everywhere around us, that they must be a cause or at least a contributor to the general destruction of our environment and all it contains, decades later we still have not been able to apply the right methods in order to resolve any conflict of interests. Instead, we are subject to just as much strain and stress as our ancestors might have been. We have been distracted deliberately lest we find out how powerful we are. It seems out of proportion that thousands of years ago, we did not have resources like we have now, and yet we don't seem to have been able to evenly distribute these resources and make them accessible to all to ascertain everyone's fair chance of survival. If we are all still mostly caught up in our inner world of the rabbit hole, led to believe that this is our lot, to get on with it and fend for ourselves with no guidance at all, if we are educated into a system where we cannot even find a chance to find resolution for even relatively minor issues, how will we gain enough brain space to resolve any of the major issues facing us all? At the time of editing, we are under lock-down from a virus that came up from seemingly nowhere. A virus that is killing many thousands of people a day, in 2020...it doesn't seem that we are progressing at all, it seems that we are still on course for the prophecies of the end of the world as we know it. Perhaps we need that for people to wake up and rally round. If our education from an early age has taught us to be in competition with each other, disconnected from the important overall picture of what we urgently need to do, then we may not even be aware that there is more to life, that we deserve better, that there is a way to live to create more peace within, as well as on the outside. If we are only just getting enough to get by, and a vast percentage of households in the wealthiest countries on Earth are still living in abject poverty on minimum wages having rely on social housing and food banks where 30% of children are not fed a hot meal every day (https://cpag.org.uk/child-poverty/child-poverty-facts-and-figures), statistics in the UK in 2020), how will we know to co-create a peaceful outcome for everyone if we still have to live in fear of not having enough to eat for another day? Instead, the planet is ruled by a greedy elitist few who have either lost their connection to the real world or couldn't care less, whilst the masses carry on slaving and submit their good Self, their aliveness, their essence in terms of labour to commerce, without a thought of the consequences for the future generations they are told they are sacrificing our freedom for in the first place. How can we come away from the inner paradox that has been created without our consent or cognisance? How has our inner paradox become inadvertently responsible for the cognitive dissonance that has taken over this world?

Two things we cannot afford to lose in life are our compassion and our wisdom.

There is a way, perhaps even several, and it does not have to feel hopeless. There are methods that are not attached to any fixed belief system or costly programmes. The methods are freely available and we can take it at our own pace to get to know them and learn how to use them.

In order to make sense of this conundrum facing us all, let's start with a common example most of us can probably relate to. If we start to get the paradoxes out of the way, we may create enough inner space to start thinking straight again and seeing the endless sky beyond the brick wall, so to speak.

To begin with, if you even just for a moment casually think about any incident which may have occurred at some point in your distant past. Most of us have had a moment where something happened to us we did not anticipate, but which we have never forgotten. No matter how major or minor an event it was or how long ago it occurred, talking about it often has not helped lessen its impact. Even if the event occurred years ago, the memory of it is often as vivid as if it happened only yesterday. Not only that, it appears to still affect us the same way, too. Have we ever asked ourselves why? How is it that our mind can still autoplay events from the past, over and over, when we neither asked it to do so, nor is it always useful to us and we could often function much better without it? We have to deduce that logic or cognitive reasoning alone does not necessarily help to dislodge a memory stuck in our Karmic energy system, otherwise they would be gone by now. Anyone who suffers from PTSD (Post-traumatic Stress Disorder) – which I mention a lot because it can affect many of us without noticing - will probably agree they still experience past trauma internally on a daily basis, and often decades after they have been affected by a traumatic event. Medication or therapies such as psychotherapy, psychoanalysis, CBT, counselling etc. alone, although useful in diagnosing and pin-pointing the problem, do not always work effectively in resolving bad memories, feelings and physical implications surrounding an incident. Finding the underlying psychological reasons for the repetitive internal programme does not always lessen the anxiety and anguish either that is still triggered in us. It becomes such a strain that it feels like it's a permanent debilitating part of us. It can even continue to make us fear that any incident might recur, affecting our thinking and emotional well-being daily.

Sometimes the pain of suffering gets so difficult to cope with for some that they feel they can no longer run away from it. In lack of good methods for resolution, they feel so intensely anguished that some of them are unable to cope. It's understandable that this is so, knowing the pressures that many people are under. We often simply don't know what has happened to beings that makes them feel so low that they see no other way out. Cue the submission to substance abuse that some choose to make pain and our internal broken record of painful memories and experiences go away. What they don't see in those moments is that they are handing over their Karmic energy power the moment they subscribe to drugs. If we do that, in those moment of choice, we will be at our most vulnerable. Our inner power starts to dissipate, it can and will literally leak out from our bodies. It ebbs away to such a dramatic extent and so quickly sometimes, that there is a real danger then that we won't make it through alive. Even if we do, it will not work to make things better. People use it to lessen their pain, and yet, it does the opposite: it creates more. It has the power to take away our freedom and ultimately everything we ever called our own, including our Karmic energy.

However horrendous the consequences, with conditions like these we observe that our Karmic energy system indeed stores every tiny split-second of our lives, and it should make us even more aware of how valuable it is, and how much we can assist it to help us feel better and more in control again in turn. It might help to realise that we are not the only ones where the accumulation of a multitude of events has at times resulted in our inner energies being anything but cool, calm and collected. We all have certain fear triggers in common. Many people have to try to find ways to keep themselves safe and sane by using learned behaviour patterns to help them bridge or override our trauma and fears. The drawback is that it becomes difficult to come to terms with the fact that their issues have not gone away yet, that, so far, they have only found temporary solutions to override the trauma which don't always work to mask it. It's not easy living with that, and that's why I am using the example of PTSD here to introduce one of the main methods we can all use for any situation we might find ourselves in that we are fearful of. It does not only work for PTSD, it works for a vast range of conditions, because they all have in common that they affect our inner energy system in a similar way. By addressing our inner energy system issue directly, many of the issues can start to be dealt with more easily. This is a major development that has become more widely used in the past three decades, and is extremely worth knowing more about and using on a regular basis, especially if our efforts have not yet been rewarded with a method that replaces all the temporary solutions we have already tried that do not work. This method might be the one that stops us from completely giving up and having to carry on living life as if on autopilot.

Knowing that we have had past lives alone does not necessarily do away with the unresolved Karma we may have accumulated in these. The next step is that we apply ways to resolve it.

Fortunately, there are some fantastic Karmic energy tools available in the more awakened 21st century, which, if you ask me, are worth more than winning the lottery. It seems that as soon as human consciousness was ready to acknowledge that our Karmic energy existed, and that it held all the information we needed in order to unravel our negative Karma, we also started to perceive and reconnect with the right tools to deal with it. These tools are based on re-balancing the inner energy system, where any traumatic event from the past will have left an imprint on it that does not go away. Ironing out the creases, erasing imprints or the kinks and chinks in our armour I have been mentioning all throughout this book. This is a moment where we talk about how to do this. We nowadays use many tools that Western allopathic medicine used to ignore and dismiss, but has now started to take seriously - because some of them work, and they are used all the time successfully. Amongst many techniques and their offshoots available today are the Meridian Therapies I keep going on about, but also Yoga, Breath work, Meditation, Chi Gung, EMDR, NLP, Hypnotherapy, Tai Chi, Shiatsu, Reiki, Reflexology, Bowen, Pilates, Acupuncture, Osteopathy, Chanting, Chiropractic, Craniosacral, Constellation work, methods of Nutrition and many, many more, some more cognitive than others – a list that is too long to be comprehensive here and I apologise for only mentioning a few indiscriminately. I'm sure there are others, and please add to this thread by doing your own research, as times are changing and they are springing up everywhere in different formats. Some paths such as Tantra and Vajrayana Buddhism actively pursue 'tidying up' our energy flaws in a single lifetime, offering hope of fast-track versions as well as more laid-back energy therapies. The advanced Buddhist paths are powerful methods in helping us and are of a very particular nature, bringing us to the divine consciousness along a straight and narrow path. If you choose it, be sure that you are aware of what it takes to tackle your Karmic connections all at once, though. There are slower paths should you feel those would help you more as an introduction. I would not advise it for the lay practitioner to go immerse themselves in something deep and complex alone. Some of these paths of alternative medicine also cannot be taken lightly and take lots of training and studying for the practitioner. It might help to already have a solid understanding of ones Self and our Karmic connections.

Some of these methods have existed longer than mankind itself and are as valid now as they were then, and some are the result of combining modern knowledge and findings with ancient healing methods. The great news is that any of these methods can either be made use of as a recipient or practised in a beginner-friendly way to help us on our inner journey of tidying up lifetimes' worth of Karmic debris. Some of these methods exist so that we do not have to suffer longer than necessary in order to benefit. Equally many religions, whether we follow them or loathe them, have incorporated prayers, chants and time for reflection as well as ceremonial offerings such as flowers, incense, water and rice that can be made symbolically of our gratitude and wishes that others may benefit from abundance, too. All these do have something very valid to offer in our battle against negative Karma, as they can raise our consciousness of higher paths, energies and existence, all there to assist us in our quest no matter what religion, if any, one follows. We do not have to follow a religion in order to be able to pray, though. Prayers are wishes we set free with pure intention to grow exponentially via our Karmic energy body into the vastness that is. We can combine these wishes with offerings, and these offerings are nothing like the horrific sacrifices some forms of worship will make us believe we have to give. An offering is something we are willing to back up our wish with, in order to make it stronger. It is there to strengthen our focus and intention, and connect to the realm of manifestation where matter changes into energy and the other way round. If we offered say, a flower, we would be reminded of its unconditional beauty and appeal to the creation of it, to be applied to what we wish for. Meaning we acknowledge the infinite wisdom mind energy that is able to creates aliveness, and we increase the connection with it with our gratitude and our willingness to increase our knowledge of it. We would also do well to make only wise wishes that do not interfere with the creation of good outcomes, as such wishes can only be to our and others' detriment. The process of simply wishing and sending out prayers is just as valid and healing as more formal types of worship.

The rule of thumb should always be that you do everything at your own pace, and follow what you intuitively feel most suits you and are passionate about. Learn to develop and trust your instincts and what you feel works for you; no-one knows your Karma, remember, and only you can find out what it is for yourself on your inner journey. It is good to take time to make a wise decision, be gentle with yourself, listen to your inner world and trust the process. There are not only good methods but also good, trustworthy people out there to help you. You know that you can slow things down if you fear any change coming up too quickly, and when it does not feel safe; likewise you can speed things up when it feels it is not working fast enough for you.

I would like to mention again one group of methods in particular though, since we have already started to talk about these earlier on. One of the things that some energy therapies address better than all others is the process of double negatives that can occur within a sabotaged energy system. EFT™ and TFT (Emotional Freedom Technique™ and Thought Field Therapy) and their offshoots, for example, are such therapies that can help sort out our energies, feelings, thought processes, physical issues as well as deeper, cognitive processes that hinder our progress towards achieving peace within, when seemingly nothing else will.

This is why these therapies are so important for us to link up to, in our quest for tidying up our inner Karmic labyrinths. We all have in common that by now, we have been exposed to so many paradoxes in life, situations that have often been twisted and riddled with mixed messages, so that some of our programming from early on in our lives may be producing continuous paradox reactions within our energy system, which our body and mind are not able to identify and process. Our bodies and minds often lose the ability therefore to induce their own healing process where usual every-day problems can be evened out. However, traumatic events that may have occurred at any stage of our lives and caused us mixed juxtaposed beliefs about ourselves, others and the rest of the world, cannot be processed by our mind easily and can cause anxiety, erratic thoughts and behaviour at cross-purpose however pure our Karmic intentions are, due to the opposing mixed messages within. Sometimes, these opposing energies have even existed over lifetimes and were carried over from the past, creating even more confusing symptoms even from birth.

As we will discover in chapters 44 and 45, childhood is such an important, formative time that can determine much that happens to us, which repeats itself later on in our lives. We might not all be able to start our Karmic search for inner peace by remembering our childhood, however, if we do remember parts of it that didn't agree with us, we may do well to look into those and how these affected us accordingly. Did our needs get recognised and met by caring adults in a reliable, constant way? Were they balanced, well, loving, committed, wise, compassionate, caring and clever enough to read and meet our needs, love us and look after us? Or did they abuse their position by neglecting, punishing, subduing our nature or subjugate, own or abandon us? Was our childhood safe and sound, or did we need to defend ourselves and retaliate, resent and revolt? Did we receive the message that our lives were in danger if we didn't fight in order to survive? Did we learn to feel bad about expressing our needs? Did we really misbehave or did it just seem that way to the grown-ups around us more interested in their own problems?

All of these and many more would be examples of how paradoxes might have been created within from early childhood onwards, where a sabotaging relationship with our carers infiltrating our inner world would result in a potentially insecure, anxious and confused state of mind. When we grow up, we will find out at some stage that what we experienced was far from how things should have been in an ideal case scenario. How come these horrible situations even occurred, if we were small children who only just started out on their brand-new journey in life, who should have been able to rely on their carers? All of us really did need all that attention, approval, love and affection every second of the day, especially when we were still tiny, tired, hungry and in need of affection and closeness all the time in our earlier years. How come some of us got exactly what we needed, and some of us clearly did not? Some who experienced and suffered a harrowing, on-going scenario of punishment by those around them and were lucky to come out alive, grew up to believe that they are not worthy of any love or affection and still battle with beliefs of unworthiness. They would be ignored or scolded when they did not do as they were told in the eyes of the responsible adult and still carry those memories into their adult behaviour patterns and the way they feel about themselves in this world.

No doubt, parenting is far from easy. It's one of the most difficult things on Earth to do right by our children, because even if we do, it hardly ever feels like we do. A healthy arrangement is when parents agree to take responsibility for their children, so that at some point when children turn into adults, they will want to take responsibility for their actions. But this is not necessarily always the case. There are complex Karmic situations and ties between family members, each of these connecting with each other in many different ways in as many different days. We can all explore how to find our own Karmic path in all these family ties, and undo some of those that bound us too tightly. I have dedicated a whole, separate chapter a couple of pages down, to continue talking about a most important subject, Karma and our Children.

There are times when parents and guardians, sometimes inadvertently and possibly due to their own negative Karma, are responsible for a host of mixed messages and even greater mistakes that have profound effects on our psychological set-ups. Where did this chain reaction start, though? And where will it end? Some of us learned to keep so quiet about their needs that they never learned to listen to their body's messages and emotions, possibly because the message was that they would be punished when they spoke up for themselves against their guardians. As a result, perhaps we can imagine that when we apply this to every-day emotions, the highly fluctuating scale of the effects of individual Karma is stretched out along a long, arduous time-line of everyday occurrences of triggers of our inner trauma. Although life seems so tough and unfair sending us even more suffering this way, there is actually a purpose to it: we are prompted over and over to examine where our feelings and sensations came from. We are not supposed to have to put up with them, it's just that it seems that way, stretched out over a long time period. The reminders are trying to lead us and guide us to solutions of the problems we have been carrying for so long. In that way they are no different to, for example, a tooth ache that tells us we need to go to the dentist. The tooth is not at fault, the fact that it is aching is the reminder for us to do something about it. All we have to do is find a dentist and go get our tooth fixed. But with our inner turmoil, we don't know what to do and where to go to have it looked at. When we feel emotionally and mentally low as adults, are upset or angry, sad or scared, rather than having sympathy with ourselves and starting to try and find help with learning what's wrong with us, we might carry on with a broken record of guilt, shame, unworthiness and punishment for our poor state of mind. Before we find help, which is what I will come to next, have we ever asked ourselves what the connection is to our past? If we have trouble sleeping, how many days as tiny children were we locked in a bedroom, crying ourselves to sleep? If we feel sad and lonely for a few days and just cannot seem to pick ourselves up out of it to contribute as we usually do, how many days did we have as children where we felt like that, because that is what happened, we were left alone for long periods of time making us feel terribly sad? If we had days, months, years where we were conditioned as children to believe that this is our lot, will these not form the basis of the adulthood we now experience? How can we not think that the two are related, our childhood and our adulthood? Were our personalities put on hold for a long period of time, because nobody wanted to know who we really were? Were we asked to hold in our desires, our passion, even our anger, until we were adults when we were told we deserved it? Did our feelings and opinions matter? Were we being heard? The truth will be out there, and it's not always pretty for everyone.

These are just a couple of examples from my practice, but there are infinite combinations of suffering they represent, and I am sure they resonate in one way or another with all of us because all of us have been children and all of us will at some point have experienced the educational standards that told parents to leave their children behind, as we would not remember. But we do. We remember everything, every tiny detail. Our inner karmic energy system does that for us. If we don't feel that it can be the case that of such paradoxes might be created and oppose our well-being within, affecting us by having created a sabotaged energy system, then we need to remind ourselves that some of them are so severe that in the UK alone, more than 1/4 of the population is affected by health issues such as depression, bipolar, schizophrenic tendencies, paranoia and many other disorders too many to mention. Up to a quarter of the population is taking anti-depressants, suicide rates are increasing, especially amongst teenagers. More than 30% of people worldwide find it hard to maintain a healthy weight, 15% of the World population are said to experience some form of disability at some point in their lives. The list of types of physical conditions is just as endless, i don't even need to mention the percentage of people suffering from degenerative diseases - cancer, immune system illnesses, heart problems, organ failure, aneurysms, blood diseases etc. Children suffer more than ever from anxiety, ADHD, insomnia and eating disorders, whilst approx half of marriages end up in divorce.

I think we can make a strong case for there being a relation between the amount and variety of conditions we suffer from and the help we could do with by finding solutions to allow us all cope better. In addition to this, we might also have to ask ourselves if families are becoming increasingly dysfunctional and whether domestic violence is on the increase, and the reasons for this, which might be an increase of poverty and a lack of education in subjects to help us understand ourselves more. Over 1/4 of the female world population has been in situations of domestic violence. That is an appalling statistic. If we can become aware of the connections between how we grow up as children to how we feel as adults, can we make deductions about the impact this has on the normal functioning of processes within our body and minds? Even though, as the advanced human race we propose to be, we should have all the right facilities by now to not have any of these problems, people seem closer to pressing the Self-destruct button now more than ever; certainly no less than we were aeons ago as a human race, bashing each other's heads in with clubs. How did this happen? Nothing much seems to have changed, despite all the knowledge we have which should have given us the ability to improve our well-being noticeably more than it actually has. We have created an alarming amount of physical, emotional and mental illness which seems to be becoming the new norm, yet not many appear to have asked questions or tried to find any obvious answers in order to tackle the problem. Could it be that one reason for this that we have not found the connection between our past and our present, or employed methods to tackle our Karmic hang-overs?

Energy techniques that directly offer solutions to problems suffered by any being at any age are still an enigma to most, a well-kept secret that only a relatively small minority of society appears to be using. Be that as it may, I am stating the obvious question: Can we afford to ignore the benefits that exist as a result of using them? They offer a simple, safe and inexpensive, sometimes even cost-free way of acknowledging our inner energy system which holds our beliefs and mind sets, in order to access inner information about our physical and emotional health and how to improve it individually. It can very often also overcome states of anxiety & depression arising from a vicious cycle of inner Self-sabotage, which can stop us from even looking for and finding solutions. I wonder why there is such resistance to using these marvellous techniques then, if they work well in addressing these issues? Who put the doubt in people's minds, or have we got to the extreme paradoxical state of paranoia where we cannot trust, believe or accept anything, for fear that it might be detrimental to us? These should and should nots, do's and don'ts in our heads, feeling guilt about this behaviour and shame about that, fury about this situation and fear of that person and so on are escalating our paranoia conveniently until we have reached a complete inner stalemate.

We are not just individually showing signs of our inner energy system being at its most exhausted. We are, as a society, reflecting the very same status of being at a point of no return.

There comes a point at which our energy body cannot provide us any longer with a state of health, it must go into a state of surrender, and that is, as anyone can see, a check-mate we are facing sooner rather than later on this planet. It is a dangerous place for any of us to be, and a sad state for humankind as a whole. We might feel like withdrawing into ourselves and yet at the same time we cannot cope alone any more because it no longer feels safe within us, either. We are stressed and need time out, yet the financial pressures of the modern existence we have been coerced into shouldering, forbid us to take the time-out we need to recover. The wondrous ability for our energy body to cure itself becomes lost in a constant game of catch-up. This tendency is on the up, with many seemingly 'normal', functioning adults succumbing to mental or emotional malfunction at an increasing rate.

There are sadly as many external factors contributing to our inner paradoxes, as there is a continuation of the paradoxes we have experienced so far in our lifetimes. Toxic food-like products and toxic environments, as an example, are not helping, and are all a vicious cycle of symptoms of stress as well as causing more of it: a lack of the ability to Self-care has ensued on a large scale of humanity as a whole, and seems to have been replaced with Self-medication.

Even though these are sad facts, it makes perfect sense that they should even exist, as we have carried on accumulating negative Karmic energy for lifetimes and not been offered a reminder to pursue tactics to help us start lowering our negative Karmic calorie intake. Did you like that analogy? Good, because next, we need to realise nobody is coming to the rescue. We need to catch ourselves out herewith, right now, or we will be hit with the resulting Karmic heart attack at some point sooner or later, figuratively speaking. Blessed be the lucky ones who already then who have come across the right techniques already, for they will have found the key to their inner sanctum. You can see that this is why I mention them here - it's urgent, and we all need it. Make a genuine wish to be connected to your highest potential of health and well-being, for your sake and that of everyone else. You may think it cranky and weird, wondering how it can possibly work, but in my experience, it is not only logical but vital to introduce such techniques into our lives, as well as into our equally ailing health system.

Of course, I should also express a government health warning – the small print on the prescription is that it is not always EASY to unravel the knot of energy paradoxes within. It works quickly, but it can take some time to tackle everything that has been building up inside. Consider how long it has already been there! It can be a bit of a minefield not knowing where you are at, at any time. What is the alternative though - to become even more sick, is it not? We are faced with the 'Matrix' choice: the blue pill or the red pill. Which one will it be for you? If we choose to wake up, conditions in our minds can still carry on being quite confusing for a while, despite having started a particular regime of un-tangling our Karmic knots; this may also be because our brains have been conditioned to think the worst, because we don't trust the process, be-cause it seems that it gets worse before it gets better; because our brains have been running the show for too long and we have been relying on it blindly. It seems that our brains have taken over not just the thinking process but also the judging, assessing, condemning authoritative pro-cess that was started in our childhood and before this lifetime, as well as the process of life-altering decision-making. Before we know it, we carry on like hypnotised robots, giving our brains the green light at every crossroad to think for us. We have forgotten to take care of and trust our gut instincts instead of asking the question of who we really are, inher-ently. We even see nothing wrong with the thinking process favoured by a Western-style education offered at schools, colleges and other insti-tutes, a commercial enterprise phenomenon that has steadily been in-creasing and extending into Eastern countries, too. A constant barrage of electronically-based information systems we have invented as a re-sult ensues, with the side effect that we have not put enough emphasis on being ourselves and living well. We are putting emphasis on the sys-tem, not the individual. Are we even doing right by our children? What has made us become so estranged from them? Are those who live in modern society forced to send them away from their families into insti-tutions from as young as a few months old, so we can make more money to serve the system? Karma is basically applicable to all areas and in all chapters of our lives. We have all been babies and children and before that, we have been alive many times in different physical bodies and cir-cumstances. And yet, the subject of talking about rearing our children in a conscious, mindful way is regarded almost like a taboo, even by a very modern, democratic society based on humanitarian principles. We are teaching each child at schools how to perform best in exams, by sit-ting still and listening to one single authority figure for each subject, chosen by a curriculum that serves an industry only, not the individual. Children are not taught or even encouraged to take care of their bodies or minds, breathing wrongly, over-oxygenating the brain and continuing the loop of constant thought, so that we grow up not even being able to fall asleep without thinking and worrying. Our heads are on overload, and most of us haven't even noticed, popping pills along the way and seeing no choice as to do the same with our stressed sick children. Why? Because we don't complain, we don't look for an alternative, we are not well, we have forgotten how to be well. It suits a trillion$ industry to keep it that way! And we have started to think who else would we be without it, anyway? Have we not almost forgotten who we are and what we are capable of, without daily information overload from around the world, media propaganda, ads, soap operas, computer gadgets, super-markets, roads, traffic, enforcement systems, virtual platforms, social media and mobile phones everywhere we walk. Even in the not-so-modern world that exists less and less on this planet, gadgets, media and markets have opened up a new way of life. There are remote villages where people have no food, but they own a mobile phone. The ice caps are melting, and so are we.

We are continuing with our internal compromised energy system of being scared and living in fear, not knowing how to fix ourselves. We are functioning on a paradox energy system that does not know how to tell us that we are simply scared to be ourselves; scared to find out who we really are, how big and powerful our minds are. And we are scared of admitting we are scared.

If we are ready to do things differently, where do we start, if we don't know how to start? What do we do, what shall we say? Most of us will externalise and look to groups and conversations to try and make things better. But this might, at best, only give temporary relief. In order to bring about a more permanent change, we must start looking for the answers within.

Perhaps you catch my drift. My point is that every aspect of our non-functioning external world is being created on the basis of inner paradoxes we carry with us and continue to believe in. Can we continue like this? Not for much longer, I think. At some point, something has to give. As it becomes more complex, I strongly believe that it becomes more important to just make a start, no matter what, and learn as we go along. We can have expert help with any of the above techniques, when we finally pluck up courage to tackle them. If we continue to get aggressive, if we self-medicate even, it is not good, as we will be losing our precious inner energy that we need in order to make a difference, and that is not what we are advocating. We are trying to actively avoid people having to do that. But in order to make a start somewhere, we will have to learn new methods, new techniques, and we will need help once we got the courage to start. It's not the techniques that are the issue, they work just fine. It is the convolutions of our inner energy system that are by now presenting themselves on a massive scale, although of course they are subject to Karmic law in their own right. How we tackle them individually and connect to our external world is up to us, should this be our choice.

Are we making the step based on a belief, perhaps, that we have been feeling unworthy of being treated well, of not being trusting of others, or not knowing how to ask for help, of feeling disconnected? If you can see through your reasons already, bear them in mind, they have relevance - or even better, write them all down. Please be good to yourself, and allow yourself some help for these and other issues. Instead of just watching a yoga clip for example, ask for help to find a good class with an experienced facilitator who you trust, who will also be trained and able to explain some of the philosophy behind it, as well as being able to answer your questions. Some of the energy techniques mentioned above, are indeed designed to work well as Self-help techniques, too. This does not mean that you cannot have help with them. If you followed a course or a religion to help you unravel the mystery of life, you would want to know and examine who is teaching you, and be ready to let go if you outgrow the teacher or the doctrine does not suit you or is starting to override your inner instincts. The warning lies in this: we have become so alien to our true selves that waking up, becoming alert and sensitive to ourselves and our environment again, can come as quite a shock. We have to prepare ourselves for what it is like to see with awakened eyes again. Make sure that every day, YOU are the most important being in your life who needs help, even if it's just for a few hours at first.

The best teachings will assure us that there is no teacher, no authority outside us. We can certainly learn from situations, from texts, from all others around us, and many times we learn things that are very useful to us that we end up being eternally grateful for. However, nobody outside us is superior in any way. There are concepts that offer us explanations of external phenomena, some of them infinitely beautiful and some of them not so; some understand them better than others, and live by them more than others; but nobody is better than another, nobody is higher or mightier than another. The more we have energy flowing through us, the more we are in tune with the greater good, and that might make some feel more powerful. Great responsibility follows inseparably from great power, as Voltaire already said, at the end of the 18th century. It's true. There comes a point when we feel in the flow that we feel expansive within, and it could be misinterpreted that we own this power somehow. But it can just as easily disappear again when we try to hold on to it or use it in a manipulative way, as our Karma will demonstrate when it changes if we try to use it for the wrong reasons. Even if the repercussions of wrong action are not visible to others or even ourselves straight away, they remain within us and show themselves when the time is right, sometimes sooner, sometimes later, unless we understand that we have to undo all the convolutions of wrong actions within ourselves all over again. We would do well not to make it too complicated for ourselves, so that we don't create a timeline where it becomes impossible to see what's what, where something was created within that later has to be undone, where that 'later' means there is no guarantee that we will be shown methods again as to how to undo the knots. Oops – maybe we already have, in the past? If so, is it not the best time right now to learn to make use of the positive aspects of our Karma right now, so we can run a different programme in the future?

You decide.

To begin with, the inner journey might not be what we wanted it to be - all singing, all dancing. Instead, it turned out a little rough for us and made us feel a bit sad. We may have allowed the paradoxes to take over and run amok within us. Don't worry, it will pass. We will need to spend some time with ourselves, and face what comes up for us. We need to check in with ourselves to find the next part of ourselves to be treated well. We can ask ourselves meaningful questions all along the way, such as: Where am I at? What do I need, in order to be aligned with my greatest good? We also need to practice remembering that we have a connection to our highest good at all times, how to use it wisely so we allow it to stay open and intact, and how to ask through this connection for help, with the best possible outcome when we need it. This is something we can put out there straight away, right now, until in chapter 49 in this book, we will be ready to look at more techniques in-depth to help us bring about our and others' peaceful states of mind.

Perhaps we must also ask ourselves this: What have we done? How far are we removed from the 'real' world and have accepted a man-made, fake one as the one to live in? We are scared of not surviving, scared of dying and fading; and we have created a world that denies us access to befriending death and coming to terms with concepts such as realisation and rebirth, which have always been a part of life, and shown to be so in many ancient shamanic and religious teachings alike. Instead, we want to live in a body that never ages, be rich, powerful and famous and live forever; we prefer to take painkillers to obliviate (as in a famous recent kid's story, the famous Harry Potter books, great word) the obvious: that we are only here, in this body, for a duration and that it might not be such a bad thing, if only we could learn to be humble and really make the most of it. What we can learn to do is to face our worst enemy: the paradoxes created within ourselves, our Karmic energy bodies, which resulted in us identifying with a false sense of Karmic 'Self'.

We have created this life, these sensations, this world around us, based on the likeness of the world we experience within us.

We have created it, believe it to be true and absolute, and yet we have based it mostly on fear. Let's learn how to neutralise fear – see what happens! A universe that has existed without us for an eternity - and will do so again - is waiting to be discovered. By You. Be part of it. Be a shining, bright, important part of it.

I am fully aware I haven't actually told you yet how to do it, how to go about changing the inner paradoxes. I am fully aware I am not your teacher either, and you must find within yourself what to do or think. As I said at the beginning, I don't even know if you exist, dear reader. Although you are completely unknown to me, I decided I would share with you what I have learned so far. I know the answers are all out there, I have seen them, but I also have had to give up hope, too, at several points in my life; and yet, something carried me over into my next life experience. I have described the methods that I learned in order to overcome fear at the end of this book. It tells you several recipes of what you can do and how to do it. The most amazing thing is that since a few years passed that I had a chance to finish editing this script, we are now in the age of vlogging...so we may even get to meet, online. There might already be online tutorials, Youtube clips, individual and group sessions online, to help everyone deal with their individual questions on how to best tackle issues we come across.

The very last ingredient you need, other than what I talked about above, is that you apply the method, and do so as a regular practice. Simple as that. This agreement I cannot enter with you, I can only encourage you to make a contract with yourself. Take time for yourself, be good to yourself. This is between you, and all the parts within you that are waiting to be reunited with you. I believe you can do it. It is not as hard as you might think.

* * *

36. Karma and Manifestation

Isn't it exciting that the more we tidy up our internal energies, the more it seems to happen that we can make good things manifest? Actually, it should not come as a surprise; looking around nature and its absolute abundance surrounding us every day, we find that evidence of abundant manifestation and the miracles that this universe manifest is freely giving us every second of the day. We are capable of creating by simply being alive. The aliveness is the miracle. We are being shown how to be congruent and integrate all our separate components into life's stream of abundance again. For example, when we need a shower, we turn on the water, but unless we stand under it, we won't get to experience what it's like being engulfed by it. Why we want to reinvent the wheel all the time when everything is already there is perhaps another story. Suffice to say we don't need to.

> *Right here, right now, everything we*
> *need is potentially already there.*

Please don't think I am mocking mankind by saying that, like yet another well-meant but unpractical bit of pseudo-spiritual nonsense. There are so many beings suffering on Earth, because they don't have what is needed. No food, no water, no shelter, no safety. This is not something we can ignore, all of us are affected by their suffering, how ever far removed we are from it. This is something we must look at in order to find better solutions, and also in order to understand the fragility of life, too. How fortunate we are when we have our basic needs met. Life is not a competition, but we have been making it into one. Too often we take things for granted. It's a good idea not to take anything for granted but to regularly become aware of what we have around us already, show gratitude, and help those who do not have it, rather than turn away from them. One moment, we have fresh water, food, a family, freedom -

the next minute we might not. What does it create, our ignoring others' suffering or even making a mockery of it, god beware create it and contribute to it? It will show it to us again and again until we can no longer look away, so we get the hint with the goalpost, that's what.

To try tuning into the process of manifesting for ourselves, we always include others as well, even if we don't quite see yet how it will work. We are not supposed to see yet, we are supposed to learn to be diligent at our practice to do the right thing, and learn to trust. You may have already tried it before and seen that it works. Great! It is about learning how to put ourselves into the stream of abundance, not outside it or next to it, but right into it, and practising receiving from the highest sources only through the top of our heads, our crown chakras, to allow new and constant life-force energy to flow through us to replenish us, every day. It is such an important principle we can invite back into our lives, that it would help for us to prepare ourselves a little, and to set the scene, even if just internally. When you are about to do a sacred practice, first think of the space around you as a beautiful, inviting space, where you invite the highest and most loving energies only. Take some moments for preparation to get it right in your mind, whilst taking some deep breaths. It is just as important to get these preliminary preparations right, so that we invite protection as well as and only the highest energies. in order to do this, we make offerings, internal symbolic ones and real ones. Again, take some time to really do this mindfully; the preparation is ceremonial, too, and just as important to visualise as a part of the process. During this time, we make offerings which are prepared in advance before any practice. You can put some flowers in the space you are manifesting in, some symbolic items to represent things we take for granted, such as water to drink, water to wash with, something that represents fresh, clean air to breathe and something for light and warmth; another for healing medicine and another for a pure, clear, undisturbed mind so you are able to quieten it for a while without distractions from disturbing sounds around you. See the end of this chapter for specific guidelines for setting yourself up mentally and physically for the process.

If you can't make something alive, don't take its life.

It almost seems at times that life has been leading up to a crescendo, to prepare us for a new age and a new dawn. We can make it so, and I do believe it takes our active input for it to happen according to plan. We can't just sit there and watch TV and expect things to change and progress, but we can sit there and do something constructive internally for the world to change.

Positive manifestation is not quite as simplistic as the ideas we might have of it. One thing is for sure, it has nothing to do with any dark Magic process or even making some sinister misguided sacrifices in order to get something we want badly. Be aware that the process takes time to develop to begin with, and that there may not be much happening at first to teach us patience and the laws of the universe and the right conditions ripening. We might perceive signs en route to guide us in the right direction. We will be shown how to learn about how to interpret signs and their meaning, too, when we become accomplished at tuning in to your Karmic energy.

Manifesting is serious stuff, far from being a game, and I have long suspected that is being used even by some very wordly powers in charge right now, as it always was in history, too, but we should certainly remain clear-hearted during the process and ask for guidance as to whether we are asking for things that are in tune with the greatest good. Asking for specific things and outcomes may not have the result we were looking for, or be short-lived. This is simply because the rules of nature allow some things to coincide for a while that are not mindful or useful for a good future for all involved, but we would just be using up good Karma if we did. We can use our inner energies for much more useful things than very mundane stuff.

Despite the serious consequences of misusing the process, i believe that most people will know within themselves not to use it lightly or even to test it, but to become more in tune with and stand by natural Karmic laws. Lots of people have heard of the word by now, and many of us have probably been manifesting on a small scale already, perhaps without even noticing. A few years ago, people were all over this new fad of manifesting a parking space, where you are told to think of your destination, picture a lovely empty space right near where you need to go and – voila, there it is: your space is there just as you arrive. I don't know if you heard of it at the time, too, but it is a very mundane example of manifestation that turned the equivalent of viral in the 90's. No idea where it came from, but to think positive, at least it introduced the concept in a benign fashion to many people fascinated by the synchronicity that it tended to prove to them: that when we are 'in tune' and have aligned ourselves with the universe, it will try to assist us. There are also plenty of books and films based on this particularly Westernised manner of manifestation, that will tell you how to become rich and famous and get to own the car/house/swimming pool you always dreamed of. Whilst I don't deny it is an introduction to the principle of manifestation and subject to the same underlying energy principles, I was a bit mortified when it came out, I have to admit. Why would we use the all-encompassing, all-seeing, omnipresent energy that creates and has always created all life at all times, in order to manifest a red car or a blue house or a stash of cash? Why work the cosmic slot machines when we can have the whole universe assist us in the highest outcomes of our good fortune? I freely admit that I would immediately dispute whether we should be using precious energy connections for material wealth. it does appear to get squandered that way instead of us finding out more about what is truly possible. I would rather guide people and remind everyone to think of asking for something more meaningful, and I would love to think that we can do something much more amazing than creating meaningless material wealth, especially when a few good people come together and agree to manifest mindfully as a group. Be that as it may, the result in any case will be that it seems to work the more we build up good Karma as well as believe and trust in the process, but of course it can also work even if we do not believe in the principle at all and think it's all humbug. It's probably because we still believe we have to consciously do something about it, but that is not the case. People manifest good things all the time without even being aware of it. For example, children are fabulous at manifesting, they don't even think about it or need to believe in it. That's because believing something goes through our cognitive brain, but children still have their pituitary gland open and intact so they have much more of a chance to still be naturally in tune. Do we understand all of our brain functions or how our heart beats? No, but it works for us all the same. Our Karmic energy body works for us, whether we are aware of it or not, whether we believe in it, or not, whether we understand it, trust it, or not - unless we completely sabotage it. If all our precious energy is focused and less of it is spent on doubting and pulling us into brain function territory, then we should be able to manifest some amazing outcomes.

The clearer our Karma, the more quickly manifesting can occur, especially that which is in tune with the greatest good.

When we learn to clear our Karmic debris and set our energy free to focus on the more important stuff in life, we can really begin to feel its miraculous workings. We are often Karmic hoarders by nature though, and don't tend to clean up after ourselves, probably because we have never even thought about it or shown how to. You can perhaps already see by looking around the planet, that you can use manifestations for good or not so good causes. Everyone has access to it. You can use your Karmic kudos for your personal gain, or a small select circle, or for the benefit of all. That it is the choice we face in life, and the small print on our Karmic contract urging us to use our Karmic energy wisely. Are we going to spend energy manifesting car parking spaces, or are we going to use our vast inner power to make a difference? Some people will have already used the process for ill gain, perhaps without even realising that's what they are doing. But there are consequences to all our actions, and there are repercussions even if we have been made to believe there are not. There absolutely are. I am suggesting here that we aim high - you can set free the creation process of your inner focus and intention to be for the benefit of all of mankind. This is a small statement in this text, and a huge mental leap for all of us, without exception. The concept is very simple in principle and yet, it has powerful implications if we start to do it in earnest.

Most people on Earth are still unaware of all these principles. If we all still want to hang on to our toys like children who are not ready to share, perhaps once we feel we got enough proof that it works, we would trust ourselves and the process more. At that point we can also practice giving something away.

The Truth is, the more we are able to set our intention to help all beings unconditionally, the more benefit we create; ourselves and the small circle of beings we particularly choose to affect included.

It's a win/win situation we didn't even realise we already have. I can't emphasise it enough how important it is to learn to truly and unconditionally manifest, because we all benefit when we make offerings in order to create powerfully positive energies we merge with the greatest natural principles in existence. Our awareness will expand accordingly as we go along, all we have to do is make a simple start.

Many of us already know that these principles are true from experience, but for a lot of people who are still at the stage of believing only what they can see, it may be harder to accept. For many, it is still a process of re-educating our mind, otherwise we continue down our miserly path of only wanting to see what we can get out of the process. Some will only believe what they see or see what they believe they want, because they would like reassurance that it is exactly what they have asked for and can relate to it. That's ok, for a while. We can take as long as we want, after all, there is nobody telling us otherwise. We might miss out, though. A lot of what we are potentially capable of manifesting will remain invisible to us that way. It's all a learning process as long as we keep an open mind, open to being awed. When we are working with the principles on a grander scale and have let go of the 'seeing is believing' stage, we need to know that we don't always see the good results with our own eyes, but also go through stages of inner realisation. We begin to feel no attachment to seeing them. What we will notice, however, is an increased amount of synchronicity and a definite sense of connectedness to all around us. It's a feeling that the universe converges to assist us, it feels to be on our side, rather than working against us. It's not life that doesn't give us what we want, it's us. We don't give ourselves what we need, so we blame external things, anything, other than ourselves. Even if it's not that easy at first, it makes complete sense to me, therefore, that there is much to be said for letting go of that attachment to seeing proof; but do you know what, until we can trust the process, I know how difficult it is to do. Things will come to us, and until they do, people might need to carry on with little things first for proof, and that is ok, too. Would it not have been great to have been taught these principles from an early age? Why do we have to make our children believe about fictional characters who have superpowers, when the real McCoy is within us, and it is infinitely more fabulous and exciting?

As we know, it is no use to have more of an attachment in changing anyone else's Karma than they have themselves. It is also just fine to use little stepping stones to help us feel more confident and learn to trust. As always, we have to remind ourselves that we do not know others' Karmic path in the first place. We are not even aware of our own. All we can do, is not to try to hard to set out to convince anyone else of these findings, it could be misconstrued. We can just stand within our own truth, practising as congruently with our newly-found beliefs as we can at any moment in time. Everything else will follow naturally, especially if we don't just twiddle our thumbs and wait, but are able to put in some good effort as well.

It is also very understandable that despite – or perhaps because of – the general deterioration of our energy mindset in our increasingly false world, many people are looking for something else other than the dreary reality that presents itself to them. We are becoming more acutely aware that there must be something more that we can do on our precious journey on this planet, other being told to go to work, earn money, spend it, borrow some more and then go to work again to pay it off. We have been had. But our minds are awakening alongside much favourable assistance from higher up to help us see things more clearly, realising connections that were there all along to aid us. We are 'getting' how the universe works in its miraculous ways without our brains interfering and instead, co-operating with our Karmic intentions and our Karmic good fortune.

No doubt the physical realm is disintegrating, that's why we are being called to meditate, to keep connected to the higher realms. We have said it for years, the physical is on a decline and may not even prevail at this rate for much longer. I don't know the outcome for each individual, but will call on protection for you and all whose lives you touch and fight so hard for, from highest source to assist and shield you from harm. We can do this! We are not just physical body which will deteriorate no matter what. I believe there will be ways around the lower frequencies and their manifestations. 'Right now' is a hole in the matrix! See what we have created with our love? Expand that love! Make it grow...grow it in your mind this time, whilst
being still. In the sunshine, tending to your inner world, whilst you are still well, and recovering. You will always be you, even if it soon goes mad again and we can't hear ourselves think or feel. Right now, we are here to expand this space, this time we created, and ask the universe to make it so, and make it grow.

Maybe where we've been going wrong is that we do not so much need to 'get it' in an analytical, logical fashion, but rather in a subtle, Karmic energy theta-wave sort of way, which is all it needs to be. Remember we are made of the same stuff as life and the universe itself, and can often bypass the analytical side of things. If you really need it, you can have a certificate of proof that you have permission to bypass your logical left brain and all that you have learned so far in your education. Do we really need it? As ridiculous as it sounds, it's kind of what we have been doing all along. Needing approval for our actions, needing to know we have done the right thing, that we are on the right track. All these exams we did with our left brain, all the certificates and accolades we have, we can hang them all up and look at them - but we can't take them with us. They are evidence that we have stamina, that we are clever, and caring, and intelligent. All those things have got us to this point: to realise that we are on the next level of life, right now. It is not necessary to repeat what we did in the past – it is enough that we just are. If we can't 'be' just yet because life is crazy for us right now, then keep repeating the Mantra within, and manifest it for your near future:

It is enough that we just are.

Everyone without exception has Karmic energy, otherwise we would not exist. Everyone has the ability to manifest, without exception, and intelligence or analytical evidence is not needed. Otherwise only the educated would be wise, and only those with a degree would have quality of life. You can tell that this is not how it works, even though our education system would like us to believe it, for the sake of commerce based on fear. I believe that many a science is wonderful, artful knowledge and tries to find proof of what already exists, but quite Self-important and possibly even useless, if we cannot apply it in a practical way to manifest an improvement to our own and others' quality of life. It is then not yet a part of our wisdom mind. Wisdom opens the door to the realisation that you have to bypass your programming that made you believe you had to be awfully clever in order to be worthy of anything.

Really good stuff can start to happen when we are honest with ourselves, become mindful and leave the grasping, fearful, angry, rather ignorant and hungry-for-experiences 'brain world' behind – or just become aware of being caught up in it to start off with. It almost sounds like I've got it in for our poor brains, or science, or physical reality, doesn't it. Perhaps I meant that there is so much more to discover than our brains alone could ever come up with; good things like moments of peace and bliss; very happy days for no reason; things that go our way, even when we did not expect them to; people close to us, making us feel loved, connected and whole; people we do not know holding doors open for us, and not just literally; our health improving; our friends, family, even those we are not friends with yet, being nice to us back; coming across the right thing at the right time, being in the right place; a feeling of inner belonging; a sense that everything we see is intensely bright and alive; beautiful synergies in life that make us realise there really is so much more out there than meets the eye.

I had a very simple example of manifestation a while ago, which I would like to share with you. I set up a shrine with offerings every day, on which I put a flower as a reminder of the breathtaking beauty in this world, but also its physical impermanence. Since I really do not like taking the life of anything, not even flowers, I decided that I would offer instead the beauty of all the flowers in this world in my mind, picturing them still alive and happy on their stalks, being nurtured by the ground and the sunshine. i left the flower bowl empty but in my mind it was full of joy instead. I told the universe quietly that I would only accept a flower for the shrine if it had already dropped off some plant. In the midst of snow in winter, this seemed unlikely so I let go of the thought. A few hours after this thought, something on the ground right outside where I was staying caught my eye. Someone must have walked past there with a bunch of flowers a while ago, because just one beautiful blossom of a white carnation with a purple tinge on its petals was lying there, waiting to be put on a very special shrine that day. It made me smile and I thanked the universe for the reminder of our connections; and, zany person that I am, I pictured that the universe smiled back at me.

Seriously though, I believe it is important, too, to have the right kind of innocent fun whilst we are trying to manifest. We are essential joyous beings, we are allowed (even without certificate) to enjoy what we do, personalise it, visualise it, make it our own, dream it in rainbow colours or through rose-tinted glasses if we want to. Even when we are committed to service to others, be as exuberantly bright and shiny as you dare to be – and then let go of the idea of ever possessing it. It is you, it does not need to be owned. If you stand out too much and you are in danger, cloak it. Learn to trust it and know that it is yours already. Of course, it must be, as

The universe contains infinite abundance for all of us.

What is even better is that the universe has no price tag. Make use of the fact and get used to it again, as everything is inherently free. Even if it has been compromised, it can be set free again. Start within the power of your mind. Know that there is a huge advantage to manifesting mindfully, with the benefit of all beings in mind. There are a couple of guidelines to manifesting well. If it doesn't happen straight away, there is no need to twiddle your thumbs and sit there doing nothing. Instead, get to work. Repeat the exercises in this chapter and the ones at the end of this book, again and again, daily, regularly. The practice may also show you that you might need to get some internal obstacles out of the way to manifesting instantly. The bottom line to manifestation is that everything is ours already. So why is it not like that in the reality we experience right now? The answer is that we simply have too much happening internally that requires getting out of the way first, in order to be. Like so many people already see and agree, if you don't get that pay rise, or that fab new shiny car, the new partner that has every attribute you ever wanted, it's worth reflecting on the fact that it was maybe not meant to happen in the first place.

We need to also be thinking about another vital component to manifestation: a soil so to speak, for them to take root. We need to create good conditions first and build up some Karmic kudos before there are even seedlings, never mind a harvest. How do we go about this? We need to spend some time knowing how we can be of service to the universal principles we are appealing to. Serving mankind and beyond creates good conditions for the future, and we could be starting right now. You can start small if you like, or try something big straight away, it is up to you. If you start small and do it wholeheartedly with no resentment, that's fantastic. If you're doing something that you find is a little too big for your shoes, go back down a size or three. The important thing is not how big your give-away gift is, it's also how congruently and consistently you can give something away with love that is coming from you, and you only. Not you as in a group, or a company, or virtual, or for a material reward. Practical application grows into practical results and more. Put in as much effort if you can, into assisting the universe to create good Karmic outcomes for everyone involved. Include yourself, too! It's important that you feel right about what you do. It's up to - just you - what you can come up with from within you, and how much love you can put into what you do. Give your time, give your love, give a thought. Show that you care and connect. If you are planning on doing something really big, as long as you are not attached to anything in the process, you can slowly build up to doing that and you will create something amazing. There is a little catch, however - you also need to learn to not become attached to getting anything in return, including great results! It won't do be expecting eternal life, having just given away all your belongings. The universe is not a restaurant, you do not get a menu, and you don't get to choose what happens in terms of good outcomes. If you are not ready internally, nothing much will happen, other than your being guided to the right people and circumstances to change what needs to happen internally. If you were hoping for material compensation for your effort, set that thought free, it may guide you how to find something of much more lasting value. If you do not know what that is yet, have confidence that it will be shown to you, even if you doubt it somehow. Don't forget - the universe has a sense of humour.

✳ ✳ ✳

37. Quick reference to manifesting well:

- Create good conditions by clearing your Karma – remove obstacles in your way to clear manifestation, see previous and following chapters for inspiration.

- Create even more good conditions by being of service. Offer your help whenever you can, as many times as you can, to whoever you can. The more unconditionally you can assist, the more directly it reaches your Karmic kudos bank – i.e. making a condition such as a financial attachment to your help, or helping whilst feeling resentful or unable to cope, bypasses the direct line to your brownie points in the sky. Again, clear away obstacles you might have to trusting the principle and allowing it to work both ways, in its own way and time, without our interference.

- Clear all grievances you have with anyone in your life, however long it takes. All it takes is for you to clear it within your own mind, so that the situation is peaceful. Clear any new occurrences between you and another as soon as they arise, or at least as soon as you can. If this is not possible involving the other, clearing it in your mind as inner process is also sufficient.

- Put in an effort into helping and assisting the universe by creating good outcomes for others.

- Make an inner vow with yourself to not hurt another being, and to live by this principle of appreciating everyone's life as much as you can, extending it to more creatures all the time. If we can see every creature is precious, we can see what is absolute Truth, and as we can tell, people will make their own journey towards it, in their own way.

- Make offerings regularly that you feel are appropriate, i.e. they are mindful offerings that remind you of connectedness and the beauty of creation that is out there for all to be a part of. The process of offering creates a concept in your mind and then sets it free to create more on a higher level of vibration. There are 8 types of offerings:

1. Water for drinking; in your mind, offer it in vast quantities and of the highest quality to every living being in the whole world, then translate it as if condensing the whole concept into an actual bowl of clear, clean water. These visualisations will become easier as the ability to manifest increases within you. Offer the best and purest water you can find, fresh on a daily basis, to represent and invite more of the constant stream of clean, clear water all of us need daily to survive

2. Water for cleansing the body and mind, and our environment, to wash away illness and impurities, to bring and maintain health – offer as above

3. Flowers – offer as a reminder of the miracle of nature and its growth patterns, its constant ability to recreate, and also its impermanence. Make yourself aware that time is precious and that nature has already created all we need, in order to be well. Ask that any conflict with regard to clean water being available to all beings on Earth, be resolved

4. Medicine – offer a sprig of a medicinal plant of your choosing or as available, as a reminder that we will sometimes need help from our external surroundings to be well and that at some point in Earth's history, life-giving, all-healing medicine plants already existed. Extend the wish for all beings to be well and have all the instant medicinal help they need, in order to experience health and a long life

5. Light – attune to the infinite brightness of all vibrational existence in your mind. Make it as light as possible within your energy body and mind, and transfer this thought to a symbolic candle in your offerings, always remembering that the light that exists within everything as well as in the potential of our perception, is absolute and all-seeing illumination

6. Food – as with water, offer it in your mind as nourishment for the creation and sustenance of the whole of physical existence and all beings it contains, then translate it to an actual bowl of symbolic fresh or dried fruit, seeds, edible plants or grains. Make the offering as pure as possible and as reminiscent of what is naturally given by nature, i.e., do not use any part of a sentient being as an offering, or food containing parts of them as ingredients; try to use unprocessed, pesticide-free food unmanipulated by mankind, preferably. (there are many variations of simple, natural food offerings with no cost attached, try to do the best you can, which is often also the simplest options you can find readily). Then, as the power to manifest increases within you without conflict, offer more to more beings internally, and ask that any conflict on Earth, too, in regard to food available to all beings, be resolved

7. Pure Air – Often offered as incense, air scented with herbs is the reminder that it is essential to ask for and offer up fresh, clean air all the time to be able to breathe deeply and keep well. Offer it in your mind by taking deep breaths of fresh air when walking, and bring into your thoughts more and more people (named, or as a whole) who also need the same. Ask that any conflict on Earth, in regard to clean air to

breathe available to all beings, be resolved

8. Sound – Beneficial sound vibrations are vital for our Earth bodies and Karmic energy minds to be functioning well, so it is good to focus on bringing only the gentlest and most healing tones into our consciousness, in order to attune ourselves to the greatness that energy vibration brings into our lives. Spend a moment contemplating that all that exists is in existence through Karmic vibration. Avoiding harsh sounds, fill your mind with such vibrations that aid our consciousness, and translate this to your own sound creations, such as humming a mantra or chant, which also transforms and counteracts lower vibrations tainting our environment.

- Make sure you are manifesting something mindful that you believe you can cope with. Something that has meaning for you and is not simply an item in a shop that you cannot afford. The more we are aligned with our higher purpose, the more likely a manifestation will appear

- Take time to imagine your manifestation to be as real as possible in your mind. Allow it to be playful; imagine, if need be, a negative situation to morph into a positive one. You can be as specific as you want, with details or timing

- Make a vow at the end of your process, that the outcome from your efforts is not just for your own benefit, but is set free from the limitations of your physical energy body, so that it increases exponentially, so that your efforts grow and everyone can equally benefit from your manifesting skill. Process any fears around ownership and any thought processes which prevent true abundance to shine through

- Get any thoughts about money, reward, treats, benefits, receiving something in return, being deserving or undeserving, any specific outcome attachment etc., out of the way. Allow these thoughts to arise first, and then firmly take them from your mind to allow them to blend back and transform into higher forms of vibration again, by allowing them to rise up from your crown. They are no longer yours to concern yourself with. Learn this practice so that you find peace, and find proof that you do not need to keep these or any other issues within you, in order to benefit from your manifestation

- Set the whole of your manifestation process free as a last step. Do not hang on to any particular aspect, allow al your wishes, ideas, thoughts, feelings, images, projections etc. to float up from your body. Hand over any insistence to influence the process and exchange it for a sense of trust that all will become part of higher levels of vibrational manifestation. Allow a vision to enter, that all the light from what you created flows through you and every part of your body, all your cells, and all the cells in all other beings. Allow only pure light to remain after your practice, and keep going with other processes regularly, even if there is any residue of doubt, or any other feelings that can be transformed.

- Imagine your efforts expanding, becoming brighter, and that all issues that need to be dealt with, are transformed into light

- Allow a vision to come forth, where everyone is able to benefit from your positive efforts.

Learn to assist without expectations.
Learn to love without attachment.

Repeat this process as often as you want, whenever you want. I cannot tell you enough how good it is and how well it can work. Try it for yourself.

There is much more information at the end of the book, as to what we can do next. A lot of the times, we would do well to simply learn to sit in our own company, peacefully, quietly, and learn to not be uncomfortable not doing, not hearing, not thinking, not talking. All of it helps to make us whole and complete again.

On a more light-hearted note - remember the film Forrest Gump? One of the reasons people probably loved it so much is because someone who seems to be not particularly blessed by life at first, shows that he actually has all he needs to manifest greatness, in a funny, melancholy and roundabout sort of way. It reminds us that we can all achieve it even if the odds are against us. A sense of love, compassion and inner faith that went out of fashion decades ago, combined with an inner drive to do things right and the ability to be honest to a fault, he innocently applies himself to all that life throws at him and becomes the embodiment of our ability to carry on, even if life throws him plenty of spanners in the works. Despite that, he ends up making life-long friendships, he gets the only girl he ever loves despite many bitter-sweet twists, he becomes a cult figure famous for no reason other than his fad for running he subconsciously chooses as a form of grieving; he even makes his biggest dream job come true in memoriam of his best friend he couldn't save and turns it into a multi-million dollar business whilst simultaneously stumbling across and being a part of some of the most famous moments in history. Note how little outcome attachment he has to becoming rich, how it arises from an idea that he sets into motion wholeheartedly with his best mate who is - begrudgingly at first - alive because of him. Being rich is not at all about the money for him, but about the simple, yet profound and powerful love he has within him, for his family and friends. He knows he has no choice but to let his girl, who he loves and puts above all else, be who she feels she needs to be. She is a part of the flower power movement of the decade, deeply hurt within, the embodiment of the freedom people try to seek externally without finding it – she comes and goes, and he knows he has no choice but to love unconditionally; he loves but he never tries to control her. Love, too, is entirely subject to Karma, it will elude you if you try to grasp it, but come to you when you have let go and least expect it; it can also leave you again without warning, having given you gifts you never knew you were looking for. In the movie, she passes away, but she has given him a son who embodies the eternal principle of continuation, the exponential result of human love bearing the sacrifice we make for it. We finally relinquish all our outcome attachments for love and the connectedness we feel that goes beyond a lifetime. It is our enduring Karmic spirit that creates life. The movie is still just as relevant years later, as a classic reminder that we make life so complicated at times, we find it so profoundly difficult when the principle behind it is quite straightforward. What we are asked to do, is this: do what the universe does; live and create with love, and carry on regardless. Meaning: live lovingly, every minute, every second even, if we can. That's a good manifestation to aim for. I get that it's not funny at times, I agree it is very, very hard at times. We don't always get to live a pain-free life or love every second of it, but it is showing us every day that it is not impossible. It is showing us to not throw life away, that it is precious. Everything that is 3-dimensional is short-lived and impermanent. It's an effort, it often seems like an external goal in the distance, I know; but the goal is already yours, it is within you, it already belongs to you. We have just stopped seeing and believing it at some point. We just tried to play grown up at some point and became too caught up in being rational, trying to achieve something and sometimes getting caught up in trying to make sense of the pain, too. We started to have programmes run the show and our brain went on auto-pilot.

As odd as it seems, we need to stop resenting who we are, what we are doing and what is happening to us. Let's start to live what we love and love what we live. We need to claim back our true selves and manifest an awakening more than anything. We need to dare to be whole again and stand in the blinding light at the core of our spine. We need to stop listening to people with lower frequencies, who appear as meaningless authorities telling us what to do and get paid for it, too. They are simply asking us to be included in our manifestation process, as they are unable to do it for themselves as yet. It is time to expose ourselves with all our faults and flaws, and perceive the brilliance that comes with it. We should give ourselves permission to be living our truth right now, and not just wait for someone else to do it. I, too, would be wise to not just write about it, but to also walk my talk. I might be talking to myself, perhaps I am still attached to teaching a fictitious audience, what do you think? I have created an inner vision of a reader who might benefit from my ramblings. It makes me chuckle to think I have been talking to myself all along. I invite you to give up following every word anybody else says including me, and start to be YOU, even though you might not exist and if you do, we have never even met. Find out who YOU are. Practice every day, keep in mind that luminous space within, your core that is true and real, and which you can return to any time, even or especially when it's tough. We have an opportunity to create a different reality for tomorrow, and the day after that, and set one foot in front of the other. Constellations and circumstances change from every second to the next. We can be affected really badly by our external circumstances one minute and utterly hopeful again the next. Those moments when we feel least like practising manifestation, are exactly the moments when the practice might be at its most powerful. Do it, whether you believe it or not. Please, don't give up.

Without trying to sound too serious, I personally believe that everything I am talking about here are all vital steps in learning how to manifest. If we do not yet know and learn to be congruent with who we are, warts and all, with all the good, the bad and the ugly Karma hidden inside there somewhere, then we are still shooting in the dark in terms of how our manifestation process works out, not knowing what powers we may unleash. We can use the techniques I mentioned above as often as we want to for neutralising negative Karma, limited mindsets and energy blockages. Instead of being bogged down and stressed by them, we might just end up laughing at them, for a change. When we have finally found a way of dealing with our lives face to face with our Karmic energy levels, we will also finally feel different then; when any of our previous negative Karmic charge has become neutral, we will feel that it is nothing to worry about any longer. Any personal and trying issues become more and more distant; we become more removed from any Karmic residue that affects us badly, and think about it less and less until it has completely gone from our Karmic consciousness. Rather than being unable to take part in the greater picture that concerns humankind, when we allow our inner conflict to resolve, we become more able to connect with and contribute wisely to the external world we face. We do not have to carry on making affirmations until we are blue in the face, or carry on being terrified of anything we deem 'negative' because it no longer reminds us of being affected badly by it in the past. We can accept we are Earth beings, like everyone else, but are also reminded to not be held back by the temporary illusion of it, knowing that we are so much more. It is not about being perfect – that is just another programme. It is about realising perfection. We cannot manifest perfection as it does not exist the way we want it to, in terms of Karmic circumstances on Earth.

On this note another light-hearted anecdote; a few years ago, my mind was troubled. I was distraught at some injustice in my life and, to seek solace, I thought I would sit and meditate in front of a beautiful, shiny golden Buddha statue. I just wanted to sit quietly and find out what this internal turmoil was all about. Some hours later, I was still no closer to understanding. I happened to look up at the shiny golden Buddha statue above me then and suddenly thought to ask: 'How do you do it? Why is it that your body shines, when mine feels racked with troubled thoughts, emotions and physical pain? How do you shine so brightly, everywhere, from every part of your body and mind? I could never be like that. Parts of me will never be shiny.' The Buddha statue seemed to smile at me and I then heard an inner voice speak to me, 'It is not that my being is perfect; I am beyond the concept. But I did, in my lifetime, learn to accept all the aspects and attributes I had been given. They do not all shine, but I accept them all the same. There is no good or bad for me, so every part, every atom of my body shines. I am at peace, I am one.' I was truly awed by the experience of this as I hadn't 'got it' before then – or if I had I had only temporarily mislaid it. In that instant, I understood. It blew me away. There was a huge release that followed, of the pressure I had put myself under, of trying to become something, rather than accepting the being that I am. I understood that the process of being is not one of achieving, or striving, or improving, or putting some goal outside myself, but rather to go within and reconcile lost parts of myself and make friends with them again. To not reject, but to accept; to not berate, but to love myself. It was a major milestone and I am sharing it only in case someone reading this might benefit from the insight.

These principles of life that we continue to re-discover, the Karmic principles of attracting and rejecting energies, were long existent before ideas like chaos theory and the butterfly effect came along. If we were to try to control our Karmic powers with outcome attachment, for example to make our lives perfectly easy with a perfectly predictable outcome manipulating natural Karmic energy outcomes, it would not work the way we expect it to. It reminds me a little of Mickey Mouse in the Sorcerer's Apprentice from the 1940's, based on a mythical parable 1000's years old. (And I just realised a new movie is to be released about the story as I am writing – uncanny coincidence?). The clever apprentice sees what the Sorcerer can do, and wants a piece of it. But he takes on more than he can chew; having put on the forbidden Magic Hat to make his job easier, the Magick broomstick he summons to fetch water for him as he thinks it can make his life easier, multiplies on his attempt to destroy it; despite his futile attempts to try and fix it, the situation gets spectacularly out of control. He has to admit defeat and wait for the stern Sorcerer to put things back to normal again.

Of course there are much more sinister examples for what happens when we try to orchestrate and influence Karmic law, but I still think the analogy is poignant. We could take into consideration that Movie producers have been experimenting with the profound influence that animated images have on us, and how powerfully they have influenced our energy minds for decades since. Whilst the age of technology was forecast a long time ago to bring manifestations in connection with inventions of the human mind, these could be either incredibly amazing as well as terrifying. If we stick with the example of the invention of the moving image which has developed ever since the start of cinematography in the late 19th century, we are so immersed in it by now as a form of more or less educational entertainment that it has slipped into becoming a substitute for our inner world, it has made us less aware of just how powerful a tool it can be in terms of manipulating our Karma, too.

We know we need to learn something to make us tune into our higher frequencies, but are either at our wits end as to where to start and are going on what resonates with us here and there, pointing us in this direction or that, to using our Karmic energy for this experiment or the other - or we are too affected by circumstances or too complacent to make an effort altogether. We want to have Magick in our lives right now, but don't want to take on the apprentice role. We want to have instantly what someone else has already worked on for lifetimes. We think we know what to do already when we have learned to handle some of what life throws at us, but have to admit defeat and start from scratch when our lives don't turn out the way we wanted them to. Most of us have no idea yet how to apply the principles of using Karmic energy and yet, we are fascinated by the concept of its Magick; however, when we try to apply quick fix results-orientated ego-mind thinking, we soon realise that there is often a price to pay for experimenting. Trying to get instant easy results, we very quickly have to admit we are out of our depth when it comes to mastering our lives. If we are not willing to learn about basic principles, then things may quickly get out of hand and we might then need to muster the courage to admit we need help in order to sort out the mess we made.

Life definitely has made us draw a clever external analogy here. If we see through it, we cannot escape the fact that mostly everything so far in our lives has already been created as if by some random hidden Magic with our invisible Karma account in place, whether we like it or not. We might be able to apply for things we need, but whether we get them is

not automatically granted. Who governs these decisions? What is behind the pattern of life? We are unable to control it, as it is mostly hidden by a language based on frequencies that we do not understand,
which, in any case, is seemingly encrypted in our Karmic energy system
in a language we cannot decipher. Why, to anyone looking around on
this planet, we appear to have given up trying to find it, never mind unlock it. Instead it seems we have thrown away the key. But there is a solution, as I keep saying, and in order to learn how to access it, all we have
to do as usual is to apply ourselves a little to learn to unlock it. We can't
have it as easy as to not think about it; we need to do something, instead
of being hypnotised and spoon-fed by those who we give authority to influence us, just it seems like the easier option to want someone else in
charge who conveniently proclaims they can do it for us. We want a Magick wand to make all the difficult stuff go away, but there is always a
catch. Added to that, if we do suddenly manage to manifest, say for example, the partner/job/child/holiday/wedding/money/house/car we so
desperately thought we wanted and which finally appeared before us as
if by Magick, it may turn out not to be what we thought we wanted at all.
We might be happy with material things for a while, but soon they
change, we change, circumstances change and we think we then want
something else to make us happy. But it won't. Material things, anything
in the physical realm in fact, deteriorates and can't make us permanently happy. Maybe we thought if we put all our energy into a specific
outcome, it would all work out well so there would be no more suffering,
no more hardship. Our manifestations are often understandably out of
fear, but we might have forgotten to let go and let the universe in so that
there was no leeway; it was our way or the highway. We tried to be in
control and instead we have to still learn that we are not. We had probably also forgotten that, in order to manifest wisely, we needed to also
take our Karma into consideration. When we look at the results we have
all together manifested on Earth closely, we will find the result of the
chaos that ensues of ignoring the Laws of Nature. Karmic Laws will have
equally shown up all that which we least wanted to look at and least
wanted to deal with. Situations often become out of control when we
meddle with various outcomes and we end up being out of our depth,
having to face the same and often even more responsibilities for our actions than we were trying to avoid, being too afraid to take it on in the
first place. It seems we cannot escape what we are meant to deal with,
we can only confuse ourselves by postponing the issues we face further,
often unaware that this co-creates the timeline that stretches out before us. Once we agree to the terms that our Karma has set for each of us
and have found ways of dealing with things well and with the right
methods, we start to reap the benefits of seeing through the confusion.
Once we are able to raise our awareness, we can also shift our motivation
to include reaching this stage of Karmic agreement within ourselves,

the result being that we really do recognise what it means to be happy within.

Whatever our past was, whatever we have done and whoever we have been, it has to surface because if it doesn't come to light, it appears it will carry on manifesting our future for us anyway, unpredictably and at random. You may have little say in creating what you want for yourself, as it might give you all the situations that you need to work through first as well on route to getting what you wish for, to make you see yourself as you are and acknowledge who you truly are. This is more to do with reaching a state of inner equilibrium about our past than a form of punishment. If we ignore the steps we are pointed in the direction of, we will end up facing them again, many times over, until we finally see that it could be quite simple to do away with the dents in our Karmic armour. We just have to lose the guilt and the shame, the angst and the anger, before we can see through everything and move on from it. Even if that is at times a scary thought for some, we are always better off finding out our truth. It's a much preferable outcome than to let our inner hold-ups run riot and create more and more negative outcomes for ourselves and others, which they inevitably will. There is also another very positive aspect to being able to sort out our Karma sooner rather than later: once we are presented with our truth, we will become part of the wisdom stream of realisation, where all past Karma has the potential to be resolved and methods can be more easily found to help us. It is a logical conclusion that we have to arrive at, that this can also include even the most horrendously wrong actions, ultimately. In theory, even these can be integrated and reabsorbed in the wisdom stream. As you can imagine, nobody can write this sentence lightly, and I am well aware of the implications of sharing uncomfortable knowledge and insights. However, we are talking about a resolution, not a punishment. We are not talking about pay-offs and compensation. We are talking about solutions that work, even if in some instances the process will not occur in one and the same lifetime. We have also already mentioned how a victims' suffering will affect the perpetrator's Karma, and how a perpetrator inflicted not only physical and psychological, but also created intrinsic Karmic wounds within the victim. There may be much to be discussed and debated further, for each individual situation is different and requires utmost care, attention and time to resolve it, but the biggest downfall for anyone inflicting damage upon another is, that they may have already lost their ability to see the connections in order to be able to try to bring about solutions. They may not even be able to begin to see how to reconcile the energy discrepancies within themselves in order to start any feasible healing process. Until they were able to understand the repercussions of their actions and how to approach them with honesty, until they were able to admit fault to all involved and not just before any external judging authority, as well as seeing through their wrongful actions and perceiving the resulting pain with remorse and a willingness to resolve the Karmic implications of their actions, the inner Karmic re-balancing process cannot begin. The conditions for this process are difficult, but the good thing is, they can also become a part of the process. There just has to be a tiny glimmer of hope at the beginning, a tiny glimpse of acknowledgement of the truth of events.

As for the victims, any healing process from having been violated against can be horrendously complicated, upsetting and painful. Sadly, when those who have committed wrongful actions do not surrender themselves as the ones who caused their victim(s) suffering, and if indeed they committed the crime under circumstances not conducive to a healing process for either party, then the process may become more stretched out over a prolonged period of time. A most difficult situation such as this, however, can still be approached successfully with some methods available today. Healing can still occur despite the setbacks. It's easy to see there are a majority of cases where the perpetrator refuses to or is not able to recognise what they are letting themselves in for so that an external judging and punitive system had to be implemented. If we are not familiar with the laws of Karma, if we no longer live by its principles or know how to repair any Karmic damage that was done, means that suffering stays there for longer and time becomes stretched out, meaning that in the time between pain and finding a cure there is more chance for more suffering to be caused in either victims or perpetrators. Is this not all the more reason to do something about it as soon as we can, if we can, once we have learned how to? Can we not all identify and relate? Do we not all suffer in some way? Would we not all benefit from less of it? Leaving it for longer has as a result that there is often a time-lapse between cause and effect. This is what we seem to be up against more than anything in our lives, rather than anything remotely resembling instant Karma, and it means we cannot easily determine the connection between any action that was committed and its outcome. However, it does not mean it is impossible. It can be done, but we usually just look to outsource the result of any such incidents and leave it to a judicial system to decide. It's understandable that we do this, after all, it would be in the interest of the recipient of wrongful action that their suffering was recognised by the perpetrator as soon as possible. Alas, the process of 'punishment' conducted by an outside authority may not be so straightforward either. It may also be much delayed or have the desired result, as is often the case. The perpetrator escapes the system seemingly when there is not enough evidence being found or has received what seems like a lenient sentence. Shocking as this is for anyone who is left suffering, there is still the invisible process of Karma in action occurring behind the scene. Their individual responsibility and liability for their actions still stands, whether there were court proceedings or not, sentenced or not. As long as they still have not entered the process of inner reconciliation with their own negative Karma, they will only be able to further their own life choices to a certain extent, until such a time when the Karmic spiral of their life revisits the same point again at which they will relive their past actions. Remember what we said earlier, that we must not think of our lives along a linear timeline, but rather a spiral one? It is true what they say: what goes around, comes around. We have to acknowledge, therefore, that the conflicts so many of us find hard or even impossible to resolve, occur first in the disconnected Karmic links within our own energy system. They stay in our system from times past which we won't even remember, sometimes lifetimes ago. The 'split' at certain points within our Karmic energy network that we experience thereafter, can be due to inner rift that is created as a result of someone's - maybe even our own - wrongful action. It will be hard to determine what exactly happened without concentrated effort, time and help. But help is at hand, herewith - not only that, but hope, too. If we are able to untangle some of the inner conundrums that present themselves, even if there is a delayed reaction, we would then also be able to recognise the origin of it and resolve it, instead of ending up in the ignorance and confusion of blind hatred, anger and always being on the run trying to escape from it.

The inner rifts we may be experiencing now, might be no other than those which our previous Karma created.

If we have just found out that this is what lies at the core of the problem, would it not be nice to see the positives, i.e. that this could finally be our chance to be able to do away with our confusion? We are not here to continue to beat ourselves or each other up. We need to find solutions and apply methods, once we have accepted that here lies the crux of many problems we face. If our systems are not based on Truth, we will not easily find the solutions, and keep going 'round in circles. What's more, we may end up creating even more suffering, itself creating even longer timelines, continuing a period of confusion instead of shortening it. We have created external systems that cannot be comprehensive by their limited nature, because we no longer rely on our natural inner systems to guide us. It cannot work for us to the full extent we desire it to.

What will work instead is to have a closer look at our thought processes, our emotions and internal belief systems, understand what our inner energy systems are and how they work miracles for us. We need to spend time to acknowledge them, shine a light onto them, find methods to see through them so that we can find answers to resolve them. Sometimes it seems so much easier to blame another, but it leaks out from our own energy body and will not really give us any answers. When we blame, we are taking responsibility for the other who is not taking responsibility for themselves, and the other way 'round. Many are truly are lost in their perceptions and can do serious harm, there is no doubt. We can acknowledge, accept and look at this on a Karmic energy level, too, in order to protect ourselves from future harm. There is no long-term result or useful benefit in blame, shame, guilt, ignorance, anger, greed or fear. Whilst understandable as a human reaction, it will serve us much better to spend our precious energy in order to find useful and practical ways of healing any of our inner rifts instead; and preferably well before we become involved in others' energy rifts. We would find life so much easier if we learned how to first be stable and familiar with knowing our own Karmic energy path, as well as simultaneously finding ways to resolve any issues we come across along the way. It is not meant to be a process of Self-flagellation, far from it. I can't emphasise strongly enough that it is about being honest with yourself and finding out who you are first and foremost according to the symptoms you are displaying. Once you can bring it all out into the open for yourself, the benefits start to outweigh the fears we have of doing so. We learn to be comfortable in our own shoes, no matter what. We must find good methods to turn it around for ourselves, and as far as I can tell, there is no time to be lost.

A lot of what Karma teaches us, on the surface, seems to be opposite to what we think we should believe in, certainly what many of us have been taught to believe so far. In any case, many of us follow our love for everything positive and want to do only what is good and perfect for us and those we care about. We strive to be good people, we take care to only be with loving people who we love back and who we feel comfortable with. But Karma teaches us to love other things, too, and not just go on face value. Karma reminds us to go beyond what feels comfortable, to take time for people who need us and not always choose according to who we feel is the best-looking, the best-off financially, the most desirable for us to be around. There is no outcome attachment in Karmic teachings other than what we discussed. The mind is set to the highest outcome already which is to benefit all, to benefit the greatest potential circle of life. Cultivating the connections between all of us and giving time to people we do not necessarily gain from or have an obvious benefit from being around, is growing this essential network of tribes in a technological age, where we can still act out of compassion, the wisdom of being caring and a well-developed belief that the world will thrive without us acting as if we have to make a profit from it all the time. There need be no fringe benefits if we know that we are a functioning part of this network already, we are included in the abundance of it. The more we make ourselves and others aware, the better it works within the realms of our inner Karmic consciousness, too. We can learn to build it up, trust and rely on it at all times to support us, and that others are around to teach us to offer support as well as be supported.

We must also become aware that there is such a thing as Karmic law. It is no use; if you are not meant to be a millionaire in this lifetime, you will not be. Even if you got all materialistic things that you may have ever wanted, you may still not get what you need anyway and, as we now know, that's not the point. The point is, we can chase the rainbow forever and miss what we have right here. We can ask for useful things right now. Why don't we dream bigger and ask for the right stuff, such things like world peace, for example, to manifest? Why don't we inspire people en masse, to create food and clean water for all on Earth? And - dare I say it out loud, something that nobody would dream of asking for and yet, it's so important - why does nobody ever ask for good conditions surrounding their death, so that it becomes an easy and auspicious transition to the next stage? Why don't we manifest the best planet it can possibly be, for our children and children's children? Why don't we ask for methods to guide us to our own holy grail of inner wisdom? Perhaps we did not know that we could ask for such things or that they would be important. Perhaps many of us are already doing just that, allowing themselves to manifest already on a highly altruistic level. Once you trust that it can be done with the right effort, there really is not much to add, other than using the gift of being able to manifest wholeheartedly for the greatest good as often as we can, so that eventually, it does become an integral part of our lives. It sounds boring doesn't it, but it's actually one of the most aware, alert, accomplished and rewarding ways of life. I actually believe we could do it, after all, we have manifested ourselves to be here right now. We had also already created our lives in tune with nature and each other, if only there weren't some who are still taking advantage of the fragility of life, hell-bent on destroying it for a meagre and temporary profit. Unfortunately the ones that are still doing that, are also often the ones that claim and take everything for themselves without a second thought. Can we stop them? I don't know the answer to that. All I know is that we need to be aware when we manifest, we are doing so according to the laws of the universe. One of those principles is also that everyone and everything is allowed to co-exist, in order to learn their Karmic lessons. There is no segregation. That means, saints incarnate with murderers, at the same time, and we cannot always tell who is who and what's in between the extremes. What we can do, is to keep our power up, keep manifesting. A tree that has lost a branch does not suddenly stop growing. Unless its core has been irreparably damaged, it will continue to grow another branch. In a more transcendental way, this is what we are capable of, too. When we use it wisely, we avoid suddenly finding ourselves in the deep pit of the dark side, and that's not such a great place to be if we don't know how we got there or how to get out again. It's another useful thing we could ask for - to be able to not ever have to suffer again. How do we go about this? Life is not a Hollywood Movie where the dark force gets annihilated. There are countless nuances in between the dark and the light; many people on Earth who are still living in ignorance, and many more living in absent poverty, perhaps as a direct result. We can use our inner energy to come out of ignorance, in order to help others come out of poverty. Which one is it to be, will we care about others or let them die? What will be the repercussions on our future selves, in other existences, if we had a part in it, if we allowed this to happen? Could it not just as easily be us, living in poverty and needing help? An uncomfortable thought, at the right time, is maybe all that is needed for us to be alert and motivated again to get moving, to make sure we are on the right track.

As we become more versed at manifesting, we will be faced with important choices. One thing to never forget is that there will be others who will to depend on us for our gifts – include them in your set-up, include them in your thoughts, include them in your prayers. They are your best friends; they are your benchmark for where your wisdom is at, they are your greatest asset in achieving compassion for yourself, for your family, your friends, and ultimately, the whole world and beyond.

We can ask for an auspicious future and lifetimes, as well as co-create the right conditions for this. We apply the internal benchmark of how much responsibility we are able to take at any moment; we will not be able to tell how much power lies in our hands for our own future and that of our family, as well as that of mankind, however, directly or indirectly we are always able to put the balance right by our own choice of actions, speech and thought. If we focus our intention on creating good outcomes with a good mind, it is all within reach and within our power to change things. If we don't, we are using up our accumulated power for a while, and things might look ok, but the downfall will come when we need to then replenish the Karmic tank with good energy that has to come from ourselves and nobody else. There is little time to whine about a chipped fingernail if there is a planet to save, I always think.

*The art of manifestation lies in being
able to manifest mindfully.*

It doesn't help to ask for money whilst forgetting the Magick of the moment, you and your loved ones' health, connecting with people, being at peace and so on. Choose wisely – because it really can come true. I once wished for everyone to be happy and enlightened and was sent lots of people who were on the same path of learning how to be; who were on the same level of learning as I was and who constantly reminded me to stay connected. When I gave birth, I asked to sail through the early years safely, despite sleepless nights and several adverse external conditions. Once I was awake enough, I asked for health and was guided to optimum nutrition via a friend turning up at the opportune moment. The important stuff is of a higher frequency and well supported once we make up our minds to enter the stream of higher consciousness, it seems.

You know, there is something we continuously choose to ignore in our lives as it is such a taboo subject in some cultures. However, since it is very much an accepted part of life in other cultures, including those which acknowledge the existence of Karma, I am going to mention the 'd' word again: it is important to learn that we can also ask for auspicious circumstances around our death. How about that for clever ideas for manifesting. Many people hate to think about this time in their lives, but thousands of masters can't be wrong. We should give it some loving attention, too, if we want to try to put an end to suffering. You probably catch my drift and I will respectfully leave the suggestion here for you to pick up as and when. In the meantime, the 'Tibetan Book of Living and Dying' describes the process already in such a detailed way that it is less necessary for me to do so here.

Last but not least, finish your manifestation process by being grateful for every opportunity you get to feel connected again. If you receive the right circumstances and connections, reinforce them with gratitude for them to whoever you believe in, or just into the space around you. These principles work for everybody, not just those who believe in something greater than themselves. We can apply these principles even if we only believe in the power of our own mind and nothing else. Make that space within you as big and bright as you can, and let your voice be heard clearly even if you remain perfectly still throughout. If you are still on your way to finding what you really need, ask and be grateful for being shown the direction to follow when it's ready. It is a major indicator of your future dealings with yourself, your life, your destiny, and others', too.

ULRIKE MULLER

* * *

38. The Vastness of Karma and Our Karmic Energy

'*Dark matter is the biggest unknown in the universe. Scientists know it's there, primarily because they can see the effects of its gravity in galaxies; the known stars and gases aren't nearly heavy enough to bind galaxies together. So, astrophysicists believe that galaxies have unseen "halos" of dark matter providing the missing bulk, and collectively account for 85% of the mass of the universe. (There are other sorts of evidence for dark matter out there, but this is the big one.) They don't, however, know what this mystery matter is made of. ('Science' Magazine article April 2020)'*

We know by now that, through scientific experimentation and deductions, mankind has tried to understand and define the laws that create matter on this Earth, in this solar system and in this universe. Many great minds have contributed, whilst their theories have also been queried, questioned and subsequently updated. The general belief amongst Western science is that we are bound by physical laws of gravity and electromagnetism, but in more recent decades, science has been going sub-atomic into theories like quantum physics and string theory to explain the behaviour of sub-atomic particles. The more science is able to find out, the more our rigid constructs of a solid material world start to oscillate and become less comprehensible instead to the ego mind that enjoys tangible, solid things. It all appears to be happening on an almost magical and certainly more unpredictable higher consciousness level, which is really what we knew already all along, even without the use of science. It is fascinating that for hundreds of years, the validity of Western historical theories' was based on examining the cause and effect of dense 3-dimensional matter in its physical existence only and in addition, chemical composition since the 17th century. Anything that was beyond this was either humbug, heresy or a matter for the churches. As it turns out, we have since been able to establish that we are all made of vibrating energy – always have been, and maybe always will. This energy is infinitely greater, clearer and more radiant when we are able to perceive it beyond its existence on Earth and realise it appears that it is infinite, indestructible and simply carries on existing happily without us in other dimensions beyond the space/time continuum, beyond the third dimension. It is a nice feeling to remember the fact that we inherently are that energy at all times, that we are just temporarily in the straitjacket of a physical body with only two opposites of everything in this duality-based universe, with a limited little electromagnetic brain computer trying to make sense of it all. We should really install a moment in our every-day work lives to remind ourselves of the ridiculousness of our situation, in order to put it into context and make light of it.

I keep referring to our brain as if it were some little whining comedy body part that has trouble catching up. I guess there must be something in this that I need to look at for myself. The brain is obviously an incredible organ in itself, with fascinating facts of how it developed into a highly advanced mechanism to co-ordinate our physical functions. On my path working with energy therapies, I have gained so many more insights into electromagnetic resonances and our own magnificently capable energy bodies. We don't generally realise yet that they far surpass the perception and skills of any brain. Granted - the brain is a part of the process, but it's certainly not all of it or even the main part of it. We seem to have put so much importance on identifying with it that it has perhaps become a little pompous and Self-inflated. So much emphasis has been placed in our society on the ability of the brain only. We classify our ability to survive in how intelligent we are. We value intellectual prowess only in various doctrines, institutions and intellectual circles, but for whatever obscure or even sinister reason, the exploration of our energy system was altogether ignored and discredited in Western history. I would like to herewith officially redress the balance: whilst we have celebrated the cerebral powers of the brain as being the most complex and capable computer ever in existence on Earth, I would like to believe we can also make sure that our awareness increases of the inscrutable powers of all things energy within our bodies, around and beyond them. Without electromagnetic impulses flowing through our body, our brain would not function, and our body would not have these impulses - or most others, for that matter - were it not for our brain. It's a beautiful symbiosis, but it's not a relationship that exists to the exclusion of all other processes within us that need examining and addressing. If only we could 'see' properly with the limited powers of our eyes, sending minor frequency signals to our brains! We have invented machinery, visual aids and mental constructs to help us 'see' beyond the visible spectrum perceived by our eyes, but very often, we cannot fully comprehend these with our brains alone. But we do not even really need any of these processes to gain the benefit of energy processes coursing through our bodies. Instead of trying to intellectualise, question and construct, we could instead concentrate on developing our inherent powers beyond our brains, and would do well to hone those super-sleuth skills. But these super skills are not super-human, they are very much a part of all of us, and accessible to all of us.

We can 'see' so much more with our inner instincts, find out so much more about how powerful these energies are by perceiving what happens within and around us when we use them gently, peacefully and mindfully, and how it has the strength to affect all our happiness and that of others eternally. Is that not what wars have been fought over for centuries? There is ultimate greatness in this skill, its infinite potential; and also immense responsibility for using the powerhouse of our energy wisely.

When we sit quietly and become aware of our surroundings, we will also gently and gradually become aware that our energy leaves our body; it is not bound at all to any of the physical laws of this tiny body in a tiny place in a tiny solar system in a tiny galaxy in one of the universes, and it becomes one again with the vastness and 'emptiness' that is really full of all creative potential beyond words and explanation. There is no fiction about this science. We already own that which has no boundaries, no matter or even antimatter, no dark holes and supernovas; no matter how vast they are, we go even beyond those: it is inside of us and we are made of it, as the energy we inherently are, is one and the same with what we always have been and always will be. Let your vastness sink in for a moment.

Although we might not ever fully comprehend it with our brains or brawn, there are limitless amounts of universes. It's a short sentence with a massive impact, because we can't think about how big this actually is because we have nothing to compare it to. Our brains don't think that big. In order to grasp it, we would need to be able to access that special energy within us that I have mentioned again and again, to the point where you are probably fed up with me and wondering where the heck you've left it, like looking for a lost item of clothing in a wardrobe you urgently need for a function. It's not a bad analogy, because we will find either of these when we are least looking for them, deep within a hidden place we would have never thought to look. It will only make sense in hindsight, once we found it. That energy is what helps us find who we truly are, what remains of us when the physical no longer functions. Once we do find it within us and have that AHA moment of reconciliation with our long lost Self, we won't lose it again so quickly if we keep integrating it into our daily practice. Our endless existence is truly beyond our own understanding even of limitless galaxies, but there is no need to panic - we don't necessarily need to be a scientist to understand how these work. As a little homage to Dr Stephen Hawking, may he rest in peace, I am certain he is smiling down right now from exactly that vastness as we ponder it down here in this tiny book with such big spaces between its lines. It's ok that it is already too much for us to process and incorporate into our infinitesimally tiny daily decision-making process of, for example, what to have for dinner. And it's ok just to focus on that, and whatever comes next after that, and take life each moment as it comes. That is the conclusion we draw from anything we are talking about here: we are trying to integrate the always and forever into the here and now.

In my mind and many others, there appears to be a chance that there are even limitless amounts of universes, and there would consequentially be infinite amounts of other life-forms that take on limitless shapes based on different universal laws. It does not follow that all of the galaxies in all infinite universes all follow a binary code like ours. There may not even be celestial bodies such as galaxies, stars, planets or moons in other universes. If we remove ourselves from duality thinking, it's plain logic that there would be limitless interpretations of life. The odd-looking aliens in various works of fiction may actually be as good as any example of what alien life-forms might actually look like - or they may even be much more weird than that. After all, we are still imagining them to be based on a 3-dimensional physical form, whereas other universes may no longer use physical dimensions in order to manifest lifeforms. Perhaps other universes exist with 5th dimensional frequencies, and higher. There exists a conclusion in Buddhist texts dating back thousands of years, that it is possible for beings to evolve up to the 12th - or 13th - dimension, depending on which text we read or our own experience of such 'levels'. This is also seen and reflected in many other belief systems attempting to document life beyond physical existence. We must remember that these belief systems are based on diligently exercising our internal experience of inner sight, which includes but also goes way beyond Western scientific research and mathematical equations attempting to discern truth based on 3-dimensional phenomena only. We can all decide for ourselves which we want to give credit to. My belief is that we can't use a rigid system firmly based on 3-dimensional observations and apply this to higher dimensions where these laws expand and become obsolete. We already have what is needed to become aware of Truth: we have our inner awareness, our aliveness which is a part of the highest Truth - it is here to remind us again and again to look inwards for the path, to find our way back to our connection to Truth. Higher levels of perception for beings able to reach other frequential dimensions are called 'Bumis' in Buddhist scriptures. These levels of existence, all indicating a gradual escalation into finer and higher frequencies than exist in the physical experience of life, are what any physical existence has an inherent ability to evolve into. Our sensations of frustration in life that there 'must be something more', our general dissatisfaction with the limitations of our physical experience might itself be indication that we are already aware of the existence of these 'Bumis'. After all, this is what we already experienced in between each of our physical stages of existence many times before; we have been in between worlds, and will be there again. Our inner strife for belonging is indicative of our sense of knowing that we long to be working towards merging with higher forms of existence again, and that repeating physical life over and over on the same level of cognisance is not the ultimate experience we are here for. If we follow this as a theorem, not some phoney fanciful fantasy, then we might be guided to ways of actually achieving some of this on Earth. What is requested of us is that we do not do anything to harm ourselves or others; to still our inner winds, our chi, to the extent that we can quieten it long enough to gain insight into the deeper processes of transformation within us. The more diligent we are, the more likely it becomes that we will start to catch glimpses of this vast existence outside of our physical sensations, encouraging us to do this more often and for prolonged periods. The physical realm is not evil or useless or dark or depressing, it is just impermanent and pales in comparison to the levels of existence that shine with brilliant light. We are here, however, to complete tasks to further ourselves and assist others. Physical manifestations are not worth striving for as an ultimate goal, as they will disappear again as the fleeting phantoms they are, with no permanent value as such. We would waste time and energy pursuing these, and would do well to exercise compassion towards ourselves and others if we got lost in them, to resolve any issue we might experience that we feel ourselves not to be on a 'higher' path, so to speak. 'Higher' also does not mean better.

Every path is valid, but we could sometimes save ourselves so much time and energy by seeking within, instead of externally.

Since it is not possible to bring our physical bodies into higher dimensions, the logical conclusion is that on higher experiences of levels of existence, we ourselves become merged with them. Existence is no longer an individual one, with a defined outside away from our Self and an experience of being inside an ego body, a physical form. There will ultimately also not be an experience of 'levels' of existence at all. Again, it is not something we can grasp with our brains, but in order to bypass our cognitive barriers, we must find the way to unlock our inner astronaut to begin with. This is not a trip where we can take off into an inner fantasy land and then come back home for tea, as nice as it sounds - it is a serious committent to take science a step further. We can't just sit there, strap ourselves in and be 'taken' there by external means. We are the ones making a conscious commitment to many principles which allow our own Karmic Self to be so fine-tuned, that we are able to transcend our physical experience of Self into its higher, finer, more intricate levels of existence: it is our individual, inner evolution into our truest existence. For us humans to experience it, our journey into higher frequencies is inevitably inward to find our own essence of being again, and become versed at setting our physical experiences aside of ourselves. Whether we realise the importance of it or not, whether we believe it or not: this is not a ticket just reserved for a dedicated few who can afford the expense. We are all on this journey together, rich or poor, East or West, North or South. In order to find and reconnect with this vastness, this spacious existence that is full of ever-present experience, the emptiness that is beyond our grasp or any attempt at worded description, each of us will get there in our own way, in our own time. We are here to bring Heaven down to Earth.

When we look around for evidence that higher forms of existence may not be bound to our Earth and its gravitational, 3-dimensional system, we will notice that other forms of 'gravity' already exist even as nearby as the moon and all other planets in our own solar system. In other universes, any version of 'gravity' or laws of physical existence other than we are familiar with and take for granted may exist, and it is likely to be unlike anything we are used to on Earth. Scientists only in recent decades published their study that indicates the expansion of the universe is accelerating towards its 'edges', meaning that there are different laws of gravity that start to change, as matter is less and less bound to laws of physics on Earth which only apply to 3-dimensional existence. It seems the less physical matter there is, the less it is bound to a gravitational law, and the faster it can move. Ultimately this is the same as we've been saying all along: beyond physical matter there is no time and space, there is no relativity theory that applies. Beyond matter, all laws change, and black holes are the spaces in between matter and pure forms of energy, even beyond light frequencies as light still travels at a certain speed. Pure frequencies are omnipresent, they are not bound to where they can be, or when. They just are.

We can also observe by mathematical equations and deductions that the universe is curved, and that linear lines no longer exist by themselves. They are only experienced on a miniscule scope such as on Earth, where matter is very dense, forming a relation between time and space. As we look at vast expanses, we see that any 'line' is not straight, but exists as a tiny part of a curve. There is no such thing as a perfect linear in space, and by space I mean the space beyond our own orbit, beyond the reach of any object we have ever sent out from Earth. Everything that projects outward from a physical form will follow a trajectory that becomes an arc, even if tiny sections of it at first presented as linear. The ultimate form in space is that of an orb if it's centring around its own axis, or a funnel in spiral motion. The universe itself is expanding in a spirally funnel motion, as is our own physical time-line on Earth, even if this is hard for us to perceive.

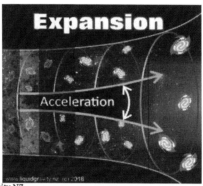

Image credit: © Liquid Gravity NZ

But whether we are able to grasp all these concepts or not with our logic-based brains, the straightforward deduction from these observations demands for our brains to at least conclude that we have been habitually seeing only one outcome: that of physical presence alone as seen from our individual perspective. And we are perpetually recreating our Karmic future because of this limited perception. Mathematical probability speaks against physical limitations we experience on Earth applying to other parts of the universe, but our limited perception is not allowing us to take other outcomes into our daily considerations. Whilst we can argue forever whether this is wise or not, feasible or not, it may be worth considering that it is vastly beneficial for our future well-being. We don't think of other life forms out there, because we focus on picturing there being another planet exactly like ours. Added to this, we will only believe it when we see it with our own eyes, and until then we keep our heads down and destroy this one. There are even plans already to exploit the moon for commercial use. What are we doing, what are we thinking? As always, our eyes and our brains deceive us maybe just a little. The answer has to be, again, that we focus inwards to find better answers and ways to live our lives.

To conclude, there might well be another planet just like ours, but that is not the only possibility out there and, more importantly, it really is not the most important question to focus on. What is more important than anything for us to learn to grasp, is that infinite possibilities of a variety of outcomes are pointing us in the direction that there are infinite different adaptations of life forms in existence, in infinite universes, but the comfort of this will continue to elude us as long as we approach it with the tools of limited perception only. The simple conclusion we have to draw from this is, that we are really limiting ourselves in our potential to be connected to the greatness we are a part of.

We talk so lightly of the term 'universe', but do we even really comprehend what the implications of the word really are, how vast it really is? Have we seen the universe beyond the capability of our eyes only and if we have, can we really understand it? It is an astonishing exercise when we look at the bigger picture, making us realise again how vast the space actually is that includes our little selves. Reminding ourselves of the concept of vastness is vital, as it helps us realise who we are and where we belong as well as put our problems into perspective, making us realise how we tend to trivialise our lives by dismissing the fact we are certainly not alone. However, once we have received the re-connective boost we needed from that reminder, we may need to leave the subject of chasing-universal-existence in order to return to our main task on Earth. We need to focus on ourselves internally to make ourselves elevate to the level of the glimpses of vastness we have just caught, so that these can become more permanent. If we chase forever and ever, we could get lost in the chase and it could be a waste of our Earth-time, just like the knights of King Arthur dispersed forever in the search of the Holy Grail. Once we have suitably reminded ourselves that everything co-exists and also has the potential to exist elsewhere other than Earth, we may as well leave the chase for more knowledge to others to pursue. We haven't got time! And this is why:

We have always existed and will carry on existing beyond form which is not bound by rules of gravity, magnetism, whether we can pay bills or not or our hair looks great today. Although there is much comfort in the thought of existing evermore, we cannot really afford to spend precious Earth time to become complacent - yet evidently the majority of people do. Whilst we can all learn to be tolerant of all the infinite diversions humans invent in order to relieve boredom, there is stuff to be getting on with for some of us, right now. If we grasp the concepts of vastness even for a moment, it will be life-changing. We are then faced with the task of translating what we have experienced into a more meaningful interpretation of our purpose on Earth. It is hard sometimes, as it will feel like we come back down to Earth with a bump. Some people will get lost in escapism, wanting their connection back at all times, unable to face mundane life as it was before. But there is an important principle that describes what we need to go through in order to cope. It is beautifully wrapped up in a simple Zen Koan: Before enlightenment, chop wood, carry water. After enlightenment, chop wood, carry water. It is not a trick to make us fail, it is a very clever, succinct way of describing that in our physical appearance, it seems that nothing has changed, even if we have just experienced the vastness of existence and merged with it to be forever changed. We may still look the same, we may still have to continue to do the same in order to survive on Earth, but internally, we have just changed forever more.

We are incarnated as a 'who-man', in our very own 'who-man' bodies which we chose for that purpose, whether we like it or not. I like the inspiration for the word 'who-man' I am using here, by the way, as a result of a few moments meditation on who we are. Now that we all identify in so many different ways beyond our gender and sexual orientation, we are on a quest to find out how we fit into the greater context of being alive in a space beyond earthly existence that we did not remember before, which we are seemingly still new to, and are trying to define for ourselves. When I say we have to get to work, therefore, I don't mean paid work as a robot for an exchange of worthless material and someone else's gain, no. I mean, inner work on our Karmic Self. We still have Karmic connections here, we still have our Karmic act to clean up, and this is the best place we can do this. It's no use to fight against being here kicking and screaming. We can't destroy life by taking our own, it's no use - we will come back until we are at peace with the preciousness of it. We have what it takes now, whether we feel it or not, what we don't want to do is to bring it about that we will have even less in future. Instead, please take comfort from this, that there are solutions. The next time you get anxious, or bored, or upset, that is your entry point. It is your calling to do something new, something different. It's the moment that your system recognises a fault within; that there is something else you are supposed to be doing. In those often uncomfortable instead of inspiring moments, you need to be clever and catch yourself out. Don't fall for the trick of going into oblivion and space out. There are several things you can do to enter the space you need to be in. Hear me out. Once of them, as crazy as it sounds, is to chant.

Chant, instead of rant.

Repeat a prayer over and over, and make it a meaningful prayer to you, in order to help you to start re-connecting to your higher purpose. This is one of many suggestions we will go through, one by one. It's a good one to start off with, but if it doesn't quieten your inner demons, you could also sit quietly, if that works. Or you could write down and set your intentions, so that they serve for you to be reconnected. Ask yourself what you need and write it down. Make it become clearer to you what you need to manifest, just as long as you realise that boredom and anxiety can potentially become your best friends.

Set your intention to making yours the most amazingly complete Karmic energy system there could possibly exist. Consider it carefully and make yours the wisest, most tuned-in, compassionate choice of focus. Forget for even just a moment all the fear, feelings of regret, sadness, anger and thoughts of greed, envy and competition. I promise we will come back to them, they cannot be ignored and you will be shown methods at the end of this book to deal with any of them, simply and effectively without hassle, money or pain. This might be the most important task you could ever undertake on Earth. Your most important mission in life, as you always suspected, might not be just doing the dishes and then watch a soap, it might be to level up and clean up your Karmic energy act instead. It is also a good idea to unlearn being scared of finding out more about ourselves, and perhaps tear down a few Western taboo subjects and resulting outmoded mental constructs en route. All throughout life, we are basically preparing our Karmic energy body for when the moment comes that we are united with the omnipresent energy again, and we can only hope by then that we have been making the most of being on Earth by living our life to our fullest and truest potential in the time leading up to that moment. It's a massive task, one that many of us decide to split into tiny sections of time which stretch out our Karma over many lifetimes as a result. It's ironic that a culture that celebrates hedonism doesn't realise that the 'only live once' motto is totally opposite to what will actually likely occur if we procrastinate and delay our true tasks for being on Earth. It doesn't mean we cannot have fun being mindful, far from it. There is much humour in realisation! What it does mean is you have all the fun without being destructive or anybody being put through mindless suffering, unless you are still on course to Self-inflict it, in which case, it's of course up to you whether you want assistance or not.

The way we live our lives, what we do with our energy system, determines just like a mathematical equation exactly how we will continue to live and exist even beyond physical existence until another rebirth. It will also determine exactly if, how and when these moments contribute to our coming back into a new physical existence. It is in fact determined by more than a mathematical equation, it is defined by the exact science of Karma, generated by Karmic energy laws throughout our existences which are steered towards certain outcomes at certain points. Many of these existences have been and will be again in physical form.

Although they can change in an instant according to our actions, they still have to follow certain physical laws and principles. Our Karmic energy particles can be dispersed and not cohesive when lower frequency energy is discharged, but can also become more unified the higher the frequency is that they are exposed to. This is the true meaning of the hugely complex Karmic law of cause and effect: All our own energy equations are subject to it, according to what we have been, done, said and thought. It's a no-brainer as to what outcome we should aim for, although in physical reality we have hurdles to overcome which are to do with energy blockages and reversals in our Karmic flow. The complex mosaic of energy cohesion and repulsion in our bodies will form our unique and specific energy body, which is continuously changing and hopefully adding valuable and positive experiences to it. At the point of passing away and once our Karmic energy has separated from physical form, all of it is taken into account in terms of determining what our new form will be. We now exist as Karmic energy only, until our next incarnation. The 'I' is subject to transformations according to all it has experienced so far, and the experience of the 'I' is suspended in its ability to actively add or take away from our Karma in this state. Our energy is rearranging itself according to our lifetimes-worth of accumulated Karmic energy patterns. Energy can reform and reshape instantly depending on how far it rises away from physical to non-physical states also subject to the patterning created during our lifespan. However, in Earth-time it can take days or even weeks, months or years for our energy bodies to complete this cycle and reform. This is why in some cultures there is a practice to leave the physical body to complete its energy work for a specified time. It will also make sense now why, in more advanced and evolved cultures, great importance is laid upon the practice of preparing for a good death – there, I said the dreaded 'd' word again - by leading a purposeful life. If we do, then there would be no reason to fear death. If we saw that the outcome of a wholesome life is a good afterlife and rebirth, then we would encourage and celebrate the process - which, as a matter of fact, many cultures do. Not everyone on Earth sees a passing from one life to the next as a bad or final thing. We find it hard not to be in control because we don't see the consequences of good actions, but the beginning and end of a Karmic lifetime is not something that is in our hands to determine, even if some people's energy is so low that they see no other way but to influence it. Be that as it may, in any case we will lose our physical shape, and become free radicals again (in a figure of speech), but are we in those moments non-attached and free enough to not be fearful of our sudden Karmic freedom? At that point, we are no longer influencing our Karmic energy body. We become observers to it. It is finding its own new shape without our conscious input. It really helps to contemplate the subject, making ourselves aware how fantastically and infinitely great our energy really is when it becomes re-united with the omnipotent oneness that is. Whether we perceive it that way is up to our Karmic actions - most of us are still running programmes which prevent us from seeing Truth. We just have to look at our computers to see what happens when we run outdated software with a clogged hard-drive and tons of malware: it slows down, to the point of not functioning - and so do we. So we want to do the opposite, really. The good news not printed in any newspaper is that we can completely allow ourselves to be at one with omnipresent Truth at any time throughout our lifetime. We do not have to wait until our physical body becomes defunct. To experience this unity whilst we are alive can be practised over and over again. There are no limits or ill-effects, in fact the more often we sit and practice, the better. It is potentially the most satisfying and unifying experience ever – and it creates lasting results in terms of good practice and preparation, too. Being unified with the all-encompassing energy field is the one experience that most people chase and cherish as the ultimate goal, the holy grail, without realising what it is they are looking for. We chase after this very experience in all our striving for happiness, but it cannot be caught with our intellect or physical mass. It can only be sensed with an open, spacious mind, and a willingness to let go of our mental energy attachments to worldly experiences, dramas, thoughts, emotions and sensations; they happen but we also need to be able to learn to see past them and leave them aside. Even if we have experienced real trauma in life, as we already know, it need not be in the way at all to us achieving peace. Our physical body can suffer, yes, but our ability to connect to oneness remains intact - provided we are not causing ourselves and others harm. There have to be compassionate methods to allow us to come to terms with our damaged internal parts, of course, for which we have tools readily available that work well nowadays. It has to be one of the best methods ever if we get to experience oneness beyond all worldly experience created by our energy minds, especially when we lost faith in our physical bodies which have been

Once we learn how to do this safely, we may be ready to catch glimpses of the greater reality, and then we will also learn not to mix up these glimpses of reality with other sensations, illusions or phenomena. For example, we may get distractions even in the realms of meditating and inner energy work whilst we are trying to find our true connection. We might get caught up in imaginative space-hopping with no further purpose other than to say 'I've been there', as if it were yet another holiday destination to be ticked off. Nothing inherently wrong with it, especially if not induced by hallucinogenic substances. For the record, I do not and will not endorse any process that involves using substances which alter our inner world in any way. The trouble with these is we are more likely to lose our ability to discern what is important and what is not, what is phantom and what is a useful pointer into the meaning of life. We may see things that exist or may not. It is incredibly easy to get lost, and lose track for a prolonged time and whilst some people see that as more desirable than their actual physical experiences, it is nothing like the real thing. We do not need it, especially once we have been through some simple processes that take us where we want to be anyway without side-effects or costs. There are no shortcuts.

We need to learn to trust and cherish that what we have already, is all we need in order to get what we want and where we want to be, which is already within us anyway.

If it takes a lifetime, it may seem a lot to ask. But what is that, really, in terms of time that does not exist, other than through our attachment to it? If we do not practice losing our attachments as part of the process, we will not get the right result. If we obscure our inner world with nebulous effects, how can we reach clarity? By non-attachment is not meant that we cannot love anything or anyone, it simply means we are loosening our ties to physical outcomes that we feel we need to happen in order for us to be happy. We are free to love, any time, without there having to be certain conditions first for us to be happy or free or loving. We are love, at any moment, even when we're aching and grumpy! If we are more attached to the aches and pains, we will feel them more, and they may get in the way. If we are able to practice non-attachment, we will feel love. What's not to like? Which one would we prefer?

Having just made a point, let's utilise it to get back to our practice. When we tune into our inner world in order to connect us to the higher frequencies, there are plenty of colourful experiences and resulting sensations that await. In order to not get distracted, we need to be clear about these and able to ask ourselves whether any phenomenon we experience has a purpose and is trying to show us something more meaningful; if it does, it's ok, as long as we can also let it go again into the eternal mind stream and move beyond the illusion. There are lots of experiences and phenomena presenting themselves outside the physical realm which we will inevitably come across, but they often do not have the ultimate result we are looking for. They are therefore simply what they are: phenomena not to get attached to or caught up in, as if we had something temporarily stuck in our eyes or ears. It sounds really quite strict, when we all love colours and shapes and sounds, thoughts and feelings and distractions to fill our lives with. We can always come back to them later, but for the time that we are attempting to keep our minds as still as possible, we simply allow them to pass us by. It will be hard at first, but we will get used to it, and it is possible - and very worth it.

It sounds even more strict when we find out that the practices we are talking about which have been kept secret for aeons of time, are so powerful that they can alter our mind stream. In fact, this is their purpose, to help us improve our mind stream. you can imagine how important it is to keep our practice as simple and pure as possible, because we would not want to be caught up in lesser outcomes.

It is for that reason, too, that our individual experiences are also not usually shared or spoken about, because of the energy leaking effect that can ensue. Sending energy into the 3rd dimension must preferably be done with responsibility, and leaking energy out through speech and thoughts in a mindless or even negative way will water down the good effect we are trying to create. We are learning to become fully aware of what we are doing, as well as getting used to the idea of doing anything we choose to with the highest intention of healing and making good. If we just continue to thoughtlessly spread negative images and ideas everywhere, our Karmic energy will lose power. It does not mean we cannot share our thoughts or worries - indeed we should with those on a similar path, so we can help each other. It is hard to gauge the Karmic effects of ill-intent as we know, but the more we practice stilling our inner chatter, the calmer we will become, the less disturbed our minds will be. There might be some nice side-effects, too, a feeling of serenity or bliss even, that spur us along to continue with our efforts. We will learn to know the difference between good and bad, helpful and unhelpful and all the nuances between. This is the point: we gain the good and lose the bad stuff within and as it leaves our body, it can eventually no longer harm us, leaving us in a better way to accumulate and harness our ultimate power for the highest good. If we choose to not use it for the highest good, it's like playing the lottery, finding out you won the jackpot and then realising you lost your ticket.

Ultimately, we must also let go of any attachment to re-experiencing only the highest energies all the time, again and again, and becoming addicted to it. There are many people suffering conditions of fear, and the fear of accepting that on Earth, we will have wave patterns of cyclic existence which we cannot brush away by refusing to acknowledge them. If we apply the right methods, we will be able to conquer our inner fears of what we face, but the world cannot adapt in its entirely according to our fears. The practice we follow by examining our Karma and applying methods to resolve it, is designed to eventually see and experience absolute Truth, and on the way, we will experience millions of different situations to help us see and find it. It will not always be an energy 'high', because that is not what presents itself in life. We are, however, able to aid the transformation of anything that is suffering with our care, love and attention. Would we walk past a person who needs our help, because their suffering makes us feel bad and we fear it will affect our resonance? That is not the kind of Truth we are aiming for; the Truth is about compassion for all others, and wisdom of knowing methods to apply it on an ever larger scale. The moment we create inner energies with good practice, we set these free, and allow them to unfold like the petals of a rose into creating even more good energy. When we enjoy a rose and benefit from its colour and scent, it takes nothing away from the rose, especially if we keep it alive and growing in the soil it thrives in. We will also see the rose go through stages where it loses its petals and becomes a pod filled with seeds for future roses. If we realise that cyclic existence on Earth means impermanence in many ways, it may inspire us to want to connect to that which will last, and make us become Masters of the greatest cycle of impermanence that exists, the one of death and rebirth and how to transcend it. We all fear this cycle, and we are all here to overcome our fears. In order to overcome them, we will have to find and apply methods to do so. That way, fear can be expelled from our body and no longer remains a part of us. We cannot hoard or sustain ecstatic feelings forever like we attempt to amass fortunes, saying and doing only certain things, wearing only certain clothing in a ritualistic way as if that makes us belong. We can become wise to our fears, wise to our shortcomings, and turn them around to serve us, and others. We cannot grab hold of anything on Earth other than the experiences of our own Karmic Self and take it with us, although many of us try.

We are slowly learning to relinquish our fear, having created an OCD-like control over life and how it insists we live in it. We can allow methods in to help us dissipate it from our bodies and minds, setting us free to experience peace from deep within.

We continuously create new energy, just like our heart keeps beating and trees grow new leaves every year. We cannot keep hold of it just for ourselves because we are a part of the cycle of existence. If we allow our fears to win, we will become miserly. Instead, we can learn to integrate what we have experienced into our every-day lives. Simply try it out just to be it and live it from moment to moment. We can start right here and now. We are learning to be all of this existence by being a part of it, in our temporary human body, rather than hating the lesser parts of it and wanting to be 'out of it', something that many these days seem to attempt to alleviate with spiritual escapism or spiritual bypassing, as I call it. We cannot escape or bypass our Karma. It's impossible; but we can improve and lessen the impact of it, without any doubt.

I am aware I already mentioned that the word 'spiritual' by now has been much over-used and turned into a minefield of so many meanings, almost like the words 'religion' and 'charity' have, too. It is in danger of being a dirty word through the malpractice of an unscrupulous few. Being 'spiritual' simply means we have awareness that there is more than meets our eyes; that we are committed to being alert and attentive to the moment, seeing the forever present in the now, the always in the moment; with a burning yet non-attached desire to create the best possible outcome for all involved and an inner state of true compassion coupled with infinite wisdom that creates external peace. To get the outcome we wish for, if this is part of our mission as we see it, we learn to trust. We set our intentions accordingly and have the right motivation to follow and aim for the highest good without being attached to any particular outcome or component of the complete Truth. Each component may lead us to the Truth, though, via our own observations in times of still reflection. It can be a powerful and life-changing experience at first, to be able to perceive existence and aliveness in other dimensions; so much so that it can be a difficult encounter for most people to detach from again. In order to preserve and persevere the whole Truth, we set our intentions to being open to it, rather than settling for just its individual components. It's a big step to decide individually whether we are even ready in this lifetime to want to know the whole Truth. There are many phenomena attached to higher frequencies that make it quite tricky for us to let go of them again and simply allow them to exist rather than try and involve ourselves to the extent of losing ourselves. When we set our intentions on knowing Truth, we will also want to hold on to the peace and compassion that comes with wisdom, lest we lose sight of the overall experience of vastness.

En route to our inner experience of the destination of all-encompassing Truth, we certainly will encounter many other ethereal beings who can assist. Most cultures speak of them in many different terms, whereas in modern times we refer to them as angels, guides, spirits and even ghosts. Whatever name you want to give these perceived beings beyond the 3rd dimension, it is only logical to conclude from all that we have said before that they do exist. It was already an accepted fact in many cultures and philosophies going back thousands of years, and yet modern society is still questioning its validity until even now, simply because science has not 'seen' proof to validate their existence. Of course we can't 'see' them with our naked eyes, because they reside beyond the visible spectrum, and often not even in the physically measurable spectra, either. Once we realise our education may have so far excluded us from learning the ability to see them and exercising the right to acknowledge them, we can make a decision that it's never too late to start on our path to Truth and finding out what miracles lie on its path ready for us to find. We can start to reintroduce their energy into our lives to make it easier for us to connect. You most certainly can learn to see them and appreciate them. You are allowed to love them, too, but we must also understand that they are also subject to Karmic laws just the same as everyone present in the physical world. They can certainly guide us, but they are not the ultimate goal of experiencing inner Truth. They are guardians of the Truth bound to the same ethos of wisdom and compassion, and the each represent aspects of Truth in their own right according to their vibrational nature. Some are there to protect, others to open our hearts. Some guide us in a certain direction with their light, whereas others remove obstacles out of our way. They are of higher frequencies than Earth vibrations, but they are also on their own inner path of enlightenment. It is therefore quite possible to also have beings of higher frequencies who still have to make their decision to be on the path of highest Truth themselves, meaning there can be highly evolved ethereal beings who are not yet committed to the highest principles yet. Their committed task is to assist you in order to reach the heights of unconditional being, and by assisting you, their own status is elevated. When you allow them just to be as they are without attaching too much or manipulating any outcome, you will gain so much insight into their nature and understand that their individuality is still keeping them as separate beings. They still have to complete the journey to being complete and one with the highest principles of Karmic teachings. Don't be afraid to ask for help, therefore, but also be aware that their existence is a part of us already that teaches us to be unconditionally compassionate and wise in turn. We can learn by the experience of meeting them to hope, to have faith, to trust that we do have a future, to be free to aim for a pure, clear, undistracted mind. If we learn this, we will find something even more precious: our trust in our innermost core of existence. These beings have conquered much of the weight of their Karma and their vibrational binds to fear, so they are showing us what is possible for us to do ourselves. If you ask, they will be able to guide you to finding methods.

The odd thing is, by following this practice and setting every angelic being free, we will not lose them as we may fear. They are still there, but appear elevated by the compassion we show them with our not attaching any of our energy to them. Some of them will be able to open doors to higher dimensions and countless, even more evolved beings residing on still higher planes. They are all there to demonstrate what is possible for us to do when we go within and start working on what holds us back. After all, it is only our fear stuck in our Karmic energy body that is keeping us stuck, and the same principles apply even in spirituality. Messages from Auntie Jane who passed away 30 years ago will keep on coming, even when you let go of being attached to waiting for her message every Friday at 6pm. All phenomena naturally belong to your field of perception automatically and instantly, effortlessly even, almost as a side effect without your focusing on it, providing that you ask, reach, aim and practice for the highest good. As another side-effect, you will almost certainly also recognise the less loving energies, worldly and un-worldly, and be able to cope and deal with them the same way, more effortlessly and effectively.

To put it into a different context, I quote an account of the Buddha Gautama meditating with his disciples, including one by the name of Báluó-duo:

'Báluó-duo became a follower of the Buddha, and he often remained in the woods in the company of animals, who loved him very much. There he meditated a great deal, which of course gradually gave him super-natural powers. He could fly through the air like his friends, the birds. (...) It is said that he was very good at performing Magick and was not above doing so in public, at one point levitating in order to retrieve a valuable begging bowl that a rich merchant had mounted at the top of a pole to see which monk could jump the highest. The Buddha reprimanded him for this exhibitionism and forbade the entire Sangha from preforming public miracles (which is why to this day any levitating done by Buddhist priests must be done in secret)'.

Text Reference: https://pages.ucsd.edu/~dkjordan/chin/luohann/ LuohannO1.html

There is so much that we are able to accomplish in this human body. In order to be it, we can make the most of it, put it to good use, clear it, cleanse it, love it, share it, look after it, treasure it. It is not about our external, visible looks, at all. It is about taking greatest care of our inner riches and become aware of what precious cargo we carry into this life-time. It is our highest purpose to do this on the highest levels, and it is our birth right to do so. It is so precious and sacred, we cannot even fathom it – and it doesn't always feel that way, either, as we have some-times had to accumulate so much debris in our energy body, that it has made our human lives heavy and dense. We can, and will, recover our inner world when we put our mind to it that we want to. We may discover that many things happened to us whilst we were not fully aware of our inner ability. We have had things taken away from us over lifetimes to make our lives hard, such as the land which was once our own, which was to provide us with nourishment and shelter. We have gotten so used to the idea of being made to feel small and insignificant, we have forgotten how important and magnificent we are. Perhaps there really were people in the past that did not have our best interest at heart. The land we now stand on was compromised to 'belong' to someone, rather than being freely given by nature for us to thrive on it. But those who took it as theirs and are now selling it back to us as a commodity, may not remember any of the history, and may therefore not see that this is what happened to all of us. Hundreds of years later, we may all of us just see commercial transactions, and focus on competing with each other for the privilege of being on the right side of the money. We have financial ties and 'contracts' with 'companies' that are not favourable, and yet we appear to have no choice but to submit to in order to survive. Even all these years later, the fight for land and what it can do for us continues, so much so that we do not care about what happens to the land, how much it becomes toxic and exploited. Some want it so that we are bound to the rules they invented and subjected us to, and those who do are hiding behind facades they created so as not to have to engage in the consequences they created. The majority of the population has been duped into a type of modern slavery without noticing, whilst also forgetting that the majority of any people are the ones who carry all the power. But people are tired from all the work they do, the stress that life causes them, sick from the pollution of our planet and the toxicity of careless, loveless, hapless transactions. People are looking for their freedom by escaping into other realities, not realising that virtual ones are only a small fraction of what their minds are truly capable of. But we can see through this, on our inner journey, and see things for what they are. It's not that difficult. We can do whatever we feel is right and good with the information we are given. We are always free to be able to use it to enhance our lives, and make the experience a loving one for ourselves and those we care about, once again. However, it may equally be our right to have phases where we refuse to feel appreciative of our lives. Nobody tells us otherwise. To be validated in having had to learn how hard it can be to survive, to have acknowledgement for painful experiences in life, to feel justified in how we feel may be exactly what we need at those times in order to keep us on track and help us clear up our Karmic energy, polish it, cleanse it, dust it off. We do not need to suppress what's going on within us. We can use all experiences we come across as a cleansing exercise, even those that have been cathartic. All illness; a loss; run-ins with people; a traumatic event. All of these are not negatives to be brushed under the carpet when they are our opportunity to become an even more expansive version of us. This is not hear-say when we meet the right methods to alleviate them, giving us hope to be able to recover from deep feelings of anxiety, negativity, stress and depression. It is not ever a competition and there is nobody judging whether you are doing it right or wrong, whether you are better or worse than somebody else. There is nobody there to punish you because you have done something wrong; this is why I do not really subscribe to the word 'punishment' but simply use it in the context of how many on Earth still believe in it and would still interpret Karmic justice to be a punishment. It is not. There is nobody there to teach you lessons as such - nobody - unless we put them in that role to remind us how to solve a problem we face. If we learn how to free ourselves from that very experience, we will not even know what punishment is. If there are tribes out there in remote forests who have no system of punishment because they don't need it to resolve anything, they won't know what punishment is. I make the assumption that punishment came about as a civilisation grew so big, fast and greedy, it forgot the human aspect. It forgot how to resolve issues. A sign that we have is our inability to even find the methods that help us these days. They are out there, but we are 'out there', too. We are wounded, we have been hunted, and we need to feel we can heal again, because otherwise, we are no longer within, where our strengths are. traumatic events cause our energy to leave our body as if in preparation for death. We get close to it, even. And in order to heal if we are still here on Earth after going through life-changing events, we deserve to have our energy back to ourselves, so that we can feel complete again. Where is that offered to us, these days? We are supposed to take pills to mask our feelings, our suffering, to sleep better, to function. But I have spoken to thousands of people. They do not work for them, in that it makes no change to how they feel about something that happened to them, even years ago. It does not help them recover. It just means that more time passes between an event and the present. These roles we put people in, the way we relate to them, are first and foremost a sign that we have inner energy reflections which are asking to be addressed. If they don't get addressed, our inner energies inadvertently create energy voids within us, and we feel them. It can be felt in sadness, bereavement, grief, anxiety, depression and so on. When we have these within us - and most of us do - it is possible that situations and people can step into these energy voids within us without us being aware of it. Those times can be precarious, it can make us feel very vulnerable - but we are all united in the fact that it can happen to all of us, without fail, rich or poor, young or old. Also, by others - often deliberately, sometimes inadvertently - stepping into the places within us that we already experience to be in pain, we are actually and quite paradox-ically shown where they are. That much is true, we will definitely know where there is a wound if someone places their finger in it. It's not a good feeling for sure, but it might be there for a good reason, and that is in order for us to locate and find the right way to ease out our inner dents again. Again, we are not being punished, we have not done any-thing wrong. If these energy voids allow others to stab our inner Karmic energy wounds time and time again, it might be time to call for help so we can heal from them. We don't need to do this on our own. Remember the parable of the fierce lion who ravaged anyone who could come near him? When a tiny mouse notices he has a splinter, it suddenly makes sense. The splinter is removed by the mouse, the lion is grateful and al-lows the mouse to keep its life.

Could reading this book be a way to find out how to locate and remove the splinters in our bodies? How much have we suffered already? How many more have to suffer? Is it not time for a change, and does this change not have to begin within us? Even those who proclaim they can heal us will only be able to heal as much as each individual is ready to, according to their own physical, emotional and mental ability as well as Karmic function. The illusion we are under is the age-old dilemma of mankind of not standing in our power. We need to come out of that thinking and feeling that we are somehow lesser than. Granted, our fear of people in positions of authority who have taken our power so they can tell us what to do or feel is very strong when we are vulnerable. However, they can only do so because a part of us might be subcon-sciously agreeing to inner contracts with them. It all sounds mysterious, I agree, but based on past conflict we have endured, misinformation and potentially also previous abuse, we might be more vulnerable to those who take advantage of us. Since we are no longer remembering our own Karma, we can only accept that we need to work with what presents it-self. But an agreement to work with it, is all the willingness we need in order to start. We need to first get stronger again, to not allow anyone any longer to invade our Karmic energy, and reinforce this new mantra on many levels. We will eventually realise that anyone out to hurt some-one may be doing so because they themselves are hurting and have yet to learn how to recognise and deal with their own pain. How to stop this roller-coaster ride of this, and many other attachments? The only con-clusion is to start by making a commitment to yourself. Be yourself, say 'it hurts' when it hurts, rather than holding your hand in the proverbial fire pretending it doesn't hurt. Until we can be shifting energy on a higher frequency, we are human beings. Meditating on it with help, if you need to know where your feelings are at; make use of the philoso-phies and therapies suggested and you will feel that the greatness and power is within you still, no matter what. You will feel it again more and more often, and you will also see that there is plenty of time to do other stuff. This is the most important, right now. Do what you feel you need to do, walk on hot coals, bungee jump or levitate, but the real greatness is in you becoming real and feeling complete, and for others you choose to have in your life to see and experience that greatness with and within you. Start to shine, in a very humble, non-competitive but none-theless bright and joyous way. Stay humble, make yourself invisible if you need to. But feel the shine within you, and shine all the same.

Often, the answers come to us in silent moments of stillness. A long time ago we started to call these 'downloads' in our groups and the term has taken on, probably because it makes sense to a generation utilising virtual reality more than our physical surroundings. They are simply truths that arise when our ego mind has fallen silent or is just jabbering on in the background without us paying attention. Finding the missing puzzle pieces of information of Truth with a capital 'T', readily available to those who allow themselves to learn to tune in, are what medita-tion is about. The true content of universal Truth is accessible to anyone, at any time, theoretically. It is just that we need to learn to sit and be still, and not even wait, for waiting is another activity.

We get used to our thoughts being on hold. In that passive, non-action, still, not-paying-attention-to--thought state, in between the various physical and mental states of trying too hard, we can see glimpses of the infinite wisdom where internal and external do not exist as concepts, and blend into it.

The vessel that we inhabit, the shell of our body and every single cell it contains, is made of the same substance as the universal forces outside of our selves. This information is not always retained consciously as it is not designed for the conscious brain to intellectualise. Rather, it stays logged in our Karmic energy body and can become a part of our every-day intuitive activity. For example, you can read about it here, possibly understand, agree with and get motivated by it, but you will still have to go through the transformation within yourself in order to activate it in your energy mind & body. It is a concept we find so hard to understand, that our whole culture is based on the opposite - simply because we cannot seem to manage to do it properly in our every-day activities. If we want to make changes within our Karmic energy system, we need to properly learn how to. This process sometimes happens automatically, but it's not guaranteed. It may already have started to happen whilst reading about it here, and it can also happen randomly, at any moment, or as a result of continuing practice. A high IQ is not a prerogative; neither is it necessary to understand everything in this book, or in life for that matter. You don't have to join expensive clubs or secret societies, either. It is profoundly simple, really: the more in tune we are with the universe and the more time we invest in methods to help us being in tune, the easier coping with life can be, as it will feel like we are a part of the 'flow'. Whilst it is hardly ever how we expected, it is so well worth pursuing. Omnipresent energy is a truly supportive and benign force with no ill-intent, always on our side, despite how it presents itself sometimes. No exams there, no harm, no punishment, no finger-pointing, no judging authority - only a reminder to take it easy, to stop believing all these limiting things that we follow blindly, such as obsessions with money, work, physical beauty etc. These are simply all stress reactions - unless you are fortunate enough to sublimely enjoy what you do without expecting a reward. You might think, hang on, what do i do for a job? I love my job. And what do I do for money to feed my family? We cannot do a system of beliefs overnight, that's true. Not everyone will be at the same stage in their lives simultaneously. But we can all be turning these methods to our advantage to live less stressful lives. No matter who we are or what we do, ask yourself if you can do with extra time to try to slow down and start to feel more alive again. At first, keep reading, keep gaining confidence, keep turning new information into a game plan. Learn how to allow yourself to be, simply, kindly, gently, and slowly see how you can feel safe and complete with just this. We need to teach our inner world to feel supported, instead of always feeling anxious and rushing around like crazy in a constant adrenaline malfunction state.

You are learning to love and nurture and be gentle with yourself, love yourself with all your heart, even the parts you have a programme not to like. You are learning to look after your mind, to cherish it, its heritage, its future, the brightness and glow that it is, right now,

always has been and always will be.

You have probably been waiting for me to give very specific examples of what can happen when Karma is in action, so they can be applied to all other situations. Just like our brains are trained to filter out only precise information as evidence, we also now want 100% watertight proof that Karma really does work the way we think it does. The catch with this idea isn't that any Karmic outcome cannot be specific, but rather lies in our expectation that it should. We tend to use the word Karma like a shotgun, like something we want to administer as payback, thinking that certain actions will have instant repercussions in the external world. They actually do have instant repercussions – but in each being's internal energy system instead, with an 'access denied' sign at the door for the rest of us. We cannot see what result a wrong action has caused within someone else's energy body. We can speculate, make educated guesses, which we often like to do to feel in charge, but we would really be wasting our time. Our idea of intellectualising Karma is not the idea of Karma. Karma's idea is to keep it simple: accept that good actions, words and thoughts bring good Karma, and anything else doesn't. I would also say that, personally, I would liken it more to science than classify it as a philosophy or a religion.

For the sake of being comprehensive, let's see what we can safely say about what can happen within the realms of Karma, without generalising, questioning and making assumptions about it or worse - deciding on another individuals' Karma.

We first need to remind ourselves that there is a link between the Karmic experiences we have in life and the Karmic energy body we inherited from previous existence which we inherently are. Let's also remind ourselves again that we do not live in our brains. We also learned that the Karmic energy body is not just a throwaway notion; it is that which will survive our physical death, and experience a rebirth again. The accumulation of all our experiences become a part of it, and it is the one thing we can realistically call 'I'. Our physical experiences are a part of it, but the inner Karmic energy stage that is putting on the show in our lives, is where we need to focus. This is where the energy flows through our bodies to keep all our systems functioning and alive, and where we can learn to change so much about ourselves for the better.

Say, for example, you have come so far that you have become aware of your inner energy channel network with its cross-over points and funnel-shaped spiral chakras, and you know it does in fact exist and is not just a useless fictitious pseudo-science, as many you trusted and learned from might have had you believe. You had heard and were curious about this inner energy network, researched it yourself, experienced it within, and it felt intuitively right to follow your instincts to act upon your findings. You then came across a method for focusing on one of the centres of your energy flow within your body which you found worked well for you as a method for relieving your anxiety. You want to learn more, and are beginning to make a connection between how you feel well when the energy flows freely through your body and also the sensations when you feel anxious and it stagnates, how it then makes you feel unwell. You learn that energy sometimes pools in the body at certain points, as it comes across electromagnetic short circuits. You feel it when it literally ends up running around in circles, unable to push through energy blockages and barriers. It's like a light switch that needs to be switched to 'on', or an appliance run on full batteries, except one battery is the wrong way around, so it cannot function. How can Your body pass on the message to you that there is an energy blockage in a very direct way? it can do nothing but communicate by repeating patterns within your physical, emotional and mental experiences. It seems that Your emotions are making you more sensitive to situations than ever, Your body is in pain, even Your brain is affected as the energy no longer feeds the neurological pathways adequately. Your inner energy is on yellow alert, thus hopefully creating in you a wish to give this attention, find out what's wrong and nurture it in order for You to recover before it gets worse. It is as if there is an inner mime artist repeating the same movements over and over, in terms of how annoying it can get to live the same thing again and again. When you are anxious, you can't think back to a time you were not anxious. You are anxious to be alive, and anxious not to be. You are anxious in crowds and anxious when you are alone. You traced it back to childhood but it seemed quite happy, except for when you were left alone for long periods of time at night. For a while, you blamed your parents, but you love them and want to forgive them for not knowing better. You know that it won't get you anywhere to blame, so you use the method you found to trace your energy back to the start of all this. Suddenly, your inner energy starts surging through you like a river in the spring, you feel energised, you feel that you are a part of the sky above you, where everything is on a different plane of existence, far, far away from Earth and yet, you are still here. The experience is as real as sitting on a chair in pain, except where your energy has taken you now, there is no pain. There is a beautiful bright light, and you feel like a child, playing in the sun. It lasts for a little while, then you are brought down again through many layers of existence, and suddenly, you feel yourself sitting firmly on the chair again, solid as anything - but all the pain and anxiety has gone.

Do you know what happened? Will we ever really know until the day we die? The important thing is that it does happen and it just happened to you. To You, it's evidence that Karma works in conjunction with our energy somehow, that the fields overlap, perhaps run parallel in some way to our nervous system. Karma has activated your inner energy memory of how you are much more than your body and how you have the ability to heal. Because somewhere, something has caused your system to short circuit, and now you found the trip switches – it's time to switch your life back on, issue by issue. You might notice your pain has lessened, sometimes it's even gone completely. If you had just sat there relaxing, the pain would not have gone, as you tried many times before. If you had done exercise to alleviate it, it might have made it worse. But because you accessed something that connects your physical body to a higher plane of existence, that holds information about you and your health, your inner memories of where you came from, your body is able to recognise where your pain is and in the moment where you bring it back to yourself rather than losing energy by blaming others, you realise you are whole enough to heal. Gratitude floods in as well as curiosity, as it's the first time it's happened to you. Where was all the information locked in about your early years in this life? What was this higher plane you were taken to, a place of healing where many were there to assist you and where your pain vanished? All the while you are still sitting there, pondering, you realise it does not matter. Questions do not matter. It only matters that it works, and that it will work again for You next time You need it. You replaced your curiosity with something much more valuable: Trust.

The above is one adapted session account of many which I gathered in my years teaching energy therapies. We soon found out that there is a specific link in our subconscious between our inner energy prana and the Karmic energy that makes a record of who we are. Anyone should be able to try it, however, it's a good idea to have someone experienced with you. Also, everyone will get a different result, and not everyone will 'see' as the person above saw their higher levels of existence. This is because although we are as human beings all similar with similar issues presenting, we all have very individual experiences and ways of interpretation, too.

Because it can sound harder than it is, let's do one thing at a time. In order to get practical, let's start with one energy vortex first - the base chakra, for example. In the chart below it's easy to see how our energy within translates to certain frequencies according to where they settle in the body. As you can see, the base or root chakra is the lowest chakra in your body, resonating on the lowest frequency. Low does not mean bad, it refers to the frequency and wave pattern it emits and consequently functions on.

Image Credit © EnergeticMatrix inJoy AllWays

As its name suggests, it resides at the base or root of our torso, between the anus and sexual organs, but you will not find it for looking although I am sure humankind in its great wisdom has gone through all possible contortions to do just that. It is an invisible - to the naked eye, at least - energy vortex at the end of a straight, vertical and central energy funnel spiralling around the spinal cord. It flows continuously between the exit point of your energy vortex at the top of your head or crown, and the base of your torso at the root. It is designed to be pushing our continuously swirling energy

upwards, above our crown, to curve around, re-enter, spiral downwards again into the root and further down below our body, rising up again from there and so on, in order to gather vital energy from our surroundings as well as expel stagnant energy. Not only does it spiral around our spine, it also formed a network of hundreds of thousands of minute channels all throughout our body in order to feed it with energy even into the tiniest areas. It also forms horizontal energy funnels at regular intervals along the way. As many of us are already aware, these are all the central chakras funnelling energy into our torso and head, front and back. They appear at equidistant intervals, and each of the central chakras feeds a hormone centre as well as vital organs relating to every one.

What most of us have been taught is a 7-chakra system, but there are in fact 12 internal and one directly above the crown, opening up to surrounding energies and many more chakras above this, ready for us to inhabit our additional ethereal chakra system forming beyond the 3rd dimension in 4th, 5th and so on, according to the principles of our own Karmic energy development. Various schools of thought believe there are less or even more, some major, some minor chakra points, all over the body, above and below. For the sake of keeping an overview, I am accepting the 13 -bodily- chakra system here, because there is one fact that most of us are not aware: according to the principles of sacred geometrical patterns which formed the blueprint for our physical body on Earth: each chakra from root to crown is the same distance apart as our pupillary distance, the distance between the centre of our pupils. There is a fun way of determining this, which I learned from a friend who has always been very dear to me as a great teacher. Hold your index finger and thumb in front of your eyes, in line with the centre of your pupils. (You can use a ruler if you have one to hand and prefer to be exact) Apparently, the distance between your pupils and the distance between your chakras is identical, and are said to be both subject to the measurements of Pi, although I have not found mathematical equations to verify this - over to you if you can find them.

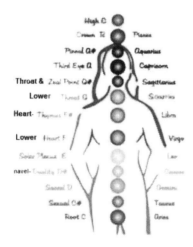

The Twelve Internal Chakras (+1 above crown, the beginning of our 4th dimensional chakra system)
Image credit: © InstinctiveHealthParenting4U

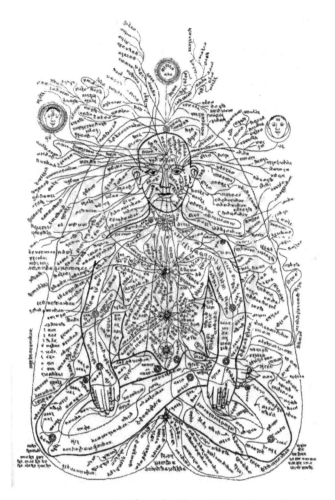

Sushumda Ida and Pingala Nadis

Image Credit: © Kundalini Consortium

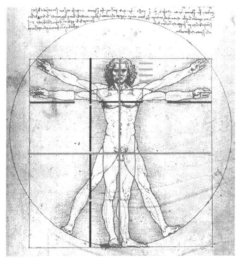

Da Vinci's Vitruvian Man, showing his knowledge of sacred geometrical patterns creating & sustaining life
Image Credit © https://www.dreamstime.com

Then, keeping your thumb and index finger fixed at the same distance, move the thumb to your third eye chakra, with your index finger at the level of your crown, the highest point of your head. As you will be able to see, the distance is the same between the top of your head (your height) and your third eye. You can then measure the rest of your chakras by moving your index finger down to where your thumb was, to determine the next chakra point and the one below, and so on. For the majority of people, the chakra points should all be equidistant:

- Top of the head (Crown)
- Third Eye
-     Nose/Nasal - yang
-     Chin - yin
-     Throat
-     Thymus
-     Heart
-     Diaphragm - Seat or Centre of Self
-     Navel
-     Base (Root)

There are also energy points below our base chakra, gradually entering the ground, rarely seen in images. These ascertain our respect for the 'I', our physical body, our Ego mind and connection to the Earth. As of late, our whole chakra system is gradually moving upwards, loosening our connection to Earth and material things, opening up our Crown Chakra to other dimensions and our new Chakra system above our physical entity. Although we all develop at a different pace, we are also bound to Earth's moving through its own Chakra development which influences us tremendously without realising. Eventually, my guess is that we are rising above material planes in accordance with the Earth also going through similar, and our current state of dismantling aspects of our Earth that have kept us bound to her and nourished by her, are becoming less and less available to us to sustain us. We are changing living conditions on Earth, probably to a point in the future where we can no longer survive as the complex, evolved physical beings we currently represent. We can all have guesses as to what's next, whether we will adapt by using apparatus to keep us alive on Earth, whether we leave Earth to incarnate elsewhere, and whether Earth itself will morph and change again according to its own Karmic evolution.

When your Karma has ripened so that you are finally able to perceive and see the connection between your physical body being miraculously nurtured by your energy body, you might feel like you entered the twilight zone for a while. Nothing will be the same, and you may start to pay much more attention to how energy flows through your physical body. You may become very sensitive to your own as well as environmental energy fluctuation, which will be helpful in figuring out where energy is stuck in your body and what you can do to assist it in moving along again. When you realise how connected you are to your surroundings in terms of energy exchange, you may automatically feel a need to change your lifestyle when you realise how physical body and energy body connect, interact and react to external influences. Factors like, for example, how we nurture our physical and energy body with the best circumstances, nourishment and frequencies, including the highest available form of absorbable nutrients from pure forms of food. It may affect what your body can tolerate and absorb, and you may become more intolerant to certain things you ingest, with the result that many people who have already entered this process are abstaining from lowering their energies through the use of low-frequency substances. Apart from obvious poisons that we are subjected to by a relentless stream of industrial toxins in our air, water and soil by now, there are many things we ingest that will cause a reaction in our newly-discovered energy system. We probably didn't think about it much before, but substances such as alcohol, chemical drugs and medicines, nicotine, dense and hard to digest food items, toxic industrial and household chemicals, food additives, as well as ill-prepared toxic plant-based drugs, allergy-inducing or addictive substances like sugar, caffeine, hydrogenated fats and such like will cause harm to our body. The list is larger than we most likely ever anticipated and is probably met with some scepticism at first, since we are not used to the idea to listen to our body's immune system telling us what's good or bad for us. We will not know how much this ingested matter has been affecting our behavioural, emotional and thought patterns, too, until we start to take them out of our diet. Much of the anguish we feel throughout a typical day can be traced to something that we took into our bodies and minds that is not good for us, to say the least. Through many schools of thought and alternative medicine, we are even taught that food items we love and eat every day are classified more as medicines to be used sparingly, such as onions, garlic, spices and even some herbs. We can even absorb tiny amounts of a medicine and our body will recognise its blueprint, affecting our cellular structures to reset accordingly. Looking into any of these practices and more, listening to our body and choosing more carefully will all result in your physical and energy body flowing much more easily, bringing us a better understanding of how to maintain our inner health; especially when we realise that every plant we eat that is green and alive has its own perfect frequency and alkalinity to heal us. There are food and medicine plants abundant in nature already, with so many health benefits, too many to mention. Someone once said there is a plant for every human illness which makes sense to me, after all, we are natural beings with our evolution only facilitated by nature in the past. It's only in the most recent centuries that we have invented machinery and synthetic substances. Naturally grown, unadulterated, unprocessed, often very simple foods that also do not involve the negative energy of harming other beings in any way, are logically best, and I personally fail to understand why this is still such a bane of some people's existence and a bone of contention between many arguing for and against.

Our physical agility increases when we internally nourish our inner world, with many positive effects. The agility we are talking about is not, however, of a caffeinated nature where we just get the same routinous stuff done in less time and end up unable to rest our minds, sleep or really progress. One of the reasons why we choose to consume and do any of the things habitually is because the energy will have us going round in circles. It is not conducive to spiral development which we need to internalise to be evolving into happiness, contentment and of course, our old friends compassion and wisdom. Our ability to stay calm, remain peaceful, find happiness within, befriend others rather than make enemies and tread carefully around the world is governed a lot by what we consume. We are often quite the opposite - agitated, easy to rise into upset and anger, and instead of being able to relax we feel perma-tired, lethargic and fall ill quickly. I have met many people who experienced all this and more, before it forced them on their inner journey of recognition. As a result, we will change, and if that sounds scary, then we can also tackle the fear to ease this. Personally, I would never want to be without the knowledge I have now, and the insights to come naturally; but I am no exception, everyone's natural state is one of integrity with their own Karmic Self, only we have forgotten who we truly are by now. There are so many benefits to be had, even in connection to our Karmic memory. We would be able to recall many more past connections in greater detail than we would ever previously have imagined to be able to. You may have started your inner journey already and nod to all of this, and as an important part of it, you might already enjoy the practice of visualising and sensing light energy rise up and down your spinal column, flooding your chakras with the frequencies of light that are inherently yours, shining into even the darkest corners of any residue of abuse, hurt, anger, shame, guilt, depression, resentment, fear or any other term that describes an energy disruption which may be caught up in there. Those moments when we recognise these can be quite intense, and it's at those times that we need help by being reminded that we can deal with any of the above negative charges and more, by using an energy technique of our choosing to help us ease and sometimes even undo any internal damage we feel it has done to us. It helps us recognise even more to learn that any of these feelings are often just stuck energy which can loosen up even when it gives us a host of physical and emotional symptoms. You know you are empowered to change your Karmic energy flow and neutralise the effects of stuck Karmic energy; you know you can ask for help so you will not have to deal with the difficult bits all by yourself. Many of the aspects of residual Karma stuck in our system can be neutralised by us taking the step to opt for ourselves being nurtured and cared for. We deserve it, we deserve to feel better, be made friends with, acknowledged, listened to, loved and forgiven. Let's make a start to replace all those symptoms with the Sacredness that they are born from, let's write a new chapter for them, acknowledge their sanctity, and allow this to filter into each of our individual chakras to give us the long lost feeling of completeness we so miss. This should be inclusive of the times when we still do not quite feel like we have the strength yet to be acknowledging the sacredness of our Karmic energy body and mind. Over a period of Earth time, we start to become used to having this new sensitivity for our body, mind and emotions, we start to see them in a different way. They are not something to run and hide from, they are a part of us to be nourished. Instead of getting bouts of negative energy come up and feeling forced to override our pain, we learn to experience how gentle and yet powerful it feels within us, how delicate the energy is that circulates around our whole body and yet how amazing and healthy it can be. It has the potential to make us well again, when the kundalini energy fully functions in order to push and rise up from the lower chakras upwards as well as raining down through our crown, flooding our thousands of energy channels and our physical body with vital life force energy therewith.

You can aid this process by learning to understand and support how it works, by inviting a gentle approach to your body and practising your visualisation, in which you are able to cherish your body and insist the same from others; include gratitude for each and every cell of the trillions it created from conception, and continues to sustain on your behalf every second of the day.

Whilst getting in touch with deep, meaningful insights like these has been a journey for most and a lengthy one at that, it will most likely dawn on us at some point that nothing could be more important. Realisation itself is a very precious thing to arrive at our doorstep, something we should very much appreciate. We will be able to change our Karmic outcome for the better and we will notice subtle differences within as a result. Your body is the basis for, but also the result of your connections to higher realms. The two are intertwined and interactive. Your body may be more sensitive to everything once you become more aware, but also feel stronger in some ways. Symptoms of ascension can be many. Some people have quieter, more inward phases, others become more confident, more able to speak up for themselves or hold their truth. Coming back to working with our base or root chakra in particular means we will be addressing issues to do with our survival, our ego, the physical body component of our Self, scenarios surrounding birth and being born, learning to feel grounded and that we have a place and a right to be here on Earth as well as any resistance we feel to being here. Procreation, creative and sexual issues, problems caused by destructive/Self-destructive tendencies, anger and frustration, releasing stagnation and so on. All of these are applicable to the balance of yin and yang energies within, as well as how we identify with our 'Self' and our surroundings. We might have issues setting our energy into motion and keeping yin and yang in balance, as well as having an imbalance of feeling unshakable within our body. Our body might either feel too set in stone, or too far out. The more we work with the ideas, concepts and methods of energy and how it works within us - and there is so much research out there already, too much to mention in a brief - the more we are able to clear. If we have started in order by focusing on the root chakra first, we will soon realise that every day's energy is different and it activates different chakras at different times. We can go with the flow rather than chronologically, and may soon also be drawn to the realisation that this is not the only chakra there is to work on. It cannot be separate from the other chakras as they are all connected and work together. Energy can shift up and downwards through the body at different paces, and you may find that some or even all of the other energy vortexes can be affected, too, in the same process. Ask your intuition as to where your energy is most prevalent, and where it is most stuck, periodically. Even if you are not sure which chakra you are working with, it's ok. You will still be able to benefit. All you will need to do to begin with, is to be open to work on whatever presents itself from moment to moment. Let your issues be your guide.

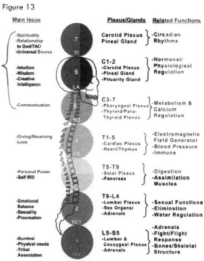

image credit © http://www.helenfu.com

There are lots of charts like the one above available online these days, that allow you to associate certain issues with particular chakras, but we do not necessarily need to become experts on where they are stuck in order to be able to resolve them. I also have a feeling that the issue we face aren't always located in the Chakras they are associated with. Carry on doing your inner energy work as regular maintenance, or as often as issues come to the surface. Gradually, you will notice that you become more adept at balancing your energy and less inclined to attract external lower energy frequencies into your body. It is as if your body intuitively knows that some energies do not have a place within.

This is how it should be ideally all the time, in a healthy energy body, but almost all of us are far removed from the ideal these days. All the same, we will learn again to recognise when something does not feel right, learn to throw it out of our system and enjoy how our physical, emotional and energy body slowly but surely increases in strength, regaining its inherent ability to naturally radiate energy from within. This is often followed - or accompanied - with changes in our lifestyle and work/life balance as we notice that we do no longer feel the need to make ourselves ill by serving mankind. Those who choose to sacrifice their health consciously in order to help others, will follow their inner insights that this may well serve to the benefit of their overall Karma. As long as we feel we have the strength and know that we are contributing in valid ways to wo-mankind, dedicate our experience for the benefit of all human beings, these actions will be an exception to the rule, by which we are calling on our connections to higher energy sources to sustain us throughout times of stress, hard work and even pain, for a greater good. As I have mentioned before, this will be even more beneficial if we dedicate it and truly remain unconditional and independent of others' judgement.

> ### *The highest form of help we can administer for others is to assist them to be well and able to live their lives to their highest ability.*

Almost as a side effect, you realise all the connectivity within yourself, and how one small cog in the big wheel affects all of it. We will notice how we can actually repair something within that we thought irreparably damaged, and as a result, it repairs externally, too; how the way you treat yourself better reflects in the way you are taking more responsibility for your inner well-being and how you relate to the world; how this is one of the most precious things but at the same time, should be a basic prerogative in order for us to be allowed to be not only alive but also be well. You may also realise that, in many instances, the past can indeed be re-written, at least on our energy level where it really matters as it affects our perception. We might find that negative events might not have the same effect on us any longer. We may realise that some hang-ups that we had all your life, such as fears we may have had to put up with, start to vanish and leave us free to get on with our lives. We may notice there is a connection between our inner work and how we act and behave. And finally, we may also eventually realise that our inner world has always determined our Karma and the other way round, they are intricately interlinked even if we cannot quite see or understand how. The important thing to take away from it is that if it works for you, it's ok to share it with others who may also benefit. It may prevent so many difficulties that everyone has started to take for granted. That is the very least we can reliably say about our good Karma: that it is capable of getting us through the day, on a daily basis.

* * *

39. 'Negative' Manifestation

It's definitely not all doom and gloom. I am trying to emphasise just how precious the gift of the power of our Karmic mind is, and i am repeating it because we have a tendency to vastly underestimate it until we fully understand the process. Also, as I said right at the beginning, I realise not everyone will want to or has time to read through a whole book, so I want the message to stand out, at a time where recognition for what MMS and internet searches call 'pseudo' sciences is still comparatively low, almost non-existent. This is, of course, rather convenient. By calling valuable therapies, theorems, ideas, belief systems and concepts that date back thousands of years 'pseudo-science', it conveniently puts off millions of people who research mainstream internet sites to help them understand. However, if it goes too far and it ends up trying to form our beliefs for us, so we won't be tempted try to go down a much better, more effective route that's free, effective and efficient, then we should start to think why this is and who it is serving. It's certainly not necessarily serving us if we remain the ones that get left behind. It does seem to proves a point though, that we live in a world right now based solely on the erratic results of commerce at all cost. There is a big divide occurring right now that we are all caught up in, which was already foreseen by our ancestors around the globe: that the time will come when the world will be split into different camps and points of view, that they believe that they are right more than they care to reconcile, and that they will be ready to fight each other for what they believe in. It's inevitable when we already know we are forced into working with a superficial duality system that keeps people thinking to go either left or right, to have an opinion for or against. But we are so much more than that. We really do have the chance to think beyond that and overcome this illusion like many others, too. We must go beyond simply accepting what others want us to believe, in fact, whilst thinking is certainly important, we must also access realms that go beyond thinking, that are even better than thinking. These are the realms that have been withheld from us where we find peace, and we are being ridiculed for searching for them. It is not enough to be reading about them, not enough to simply discuss them. We need to find them again within us, which is what we are trying to do here.

Do we really believe we live in such fantastic times that we can afford to be so nonchalant as to not find and utilise methods for our inner peace? I don't think we are, but we might be made to feel that we are. I am not trying to add insult to our injuries. Right now, at time of editing, 4.5 BIL-LION people across the world are on lock-down to avoid a deadly virus, something that two months ago sounded like a terrible B-movie. Because we usually use only our 5 senses to rely on to perceive ourselves, others and our environment, we have allowed the burglar through the back door. Focus has been on money and increasing economy, creating industrialisation at all cost. Everyone has 'gone to work' and created money, but we haven't got richer, wiser, or more caring. The ones that got rich are the ones who sold us the idea and invented the system. It is defend this by colourful graphs stating that world poverty has fallen, but since we believe these graphs, we only see this in terms of each individual country's GDP. We have become blunt to the experience of exploring more of the full potential of our natural ability and inherent inter-connectedness. When greed took over, we were swept with it, and we have become used to a system where we fit in like a round peg in a square hole, not using our superpowers, i.e. our simple, yet profound right to live a wholesome lifestyle. We are still shell-shocked from wars created to terrify us, and nothing has changed right up to this minute because it's so effective. We fall for it every time, and who can blame us, the 'evidence' that presents itself is that many people have it in for us, and on top of that, in stressful times we start turning on ourselves. We no longer live together happily ever after, we have become aggressors and victims, informants and delinquents, policing the poorest and most vulnerable in society. We have been pulled into camps, for and against, according to how easily we are manipulated on the weaknesses of our brain activity alone - and we don't even realise it because we have forgotten how magnificent we truly are. We have inevitably based our reality on what we perceive on face value and then defiantly defend what we think we already know. We insist that we are clever enough to see through the tactics, what is up and who we are, we believe we are informed reading the mainstream newspapers and proud to have qualified for a paying job, without questioning the origin of our reasoning. Doesn't our hair rise at the back of our necks when reading this, questioning our integrity? As a band put it bluntly and humorously, with a song titled 'Don't you know who I think I am?'

I am trying to raise uncomfortable questions to pull us a little out of our comfort zone. Of course, we are all doing our Best. Of course we have done well. Of course, we can be reassured and have our ego stroked so we calm down again. But this is not the point - I am not the one who doesn't believe in you. It is another group of people entirely who have tried to pull the wool over our eyes; and it might be time to try to find out just how much we have been duped.

We appear to have been hypnotised at some point. Put a good person under stress and duress, and present them with two choices of how to get out of it, they will choose the less painful option. That is basically what has been done to almost everyone of us, and our families before us. The few that escaped are those who lived outside the parameters of the power games that were played out on a world stage, which by now are few and far between. Oh yes, and those themselves exerting power and oppression over others. It would seem that we had no choice, having to choose time and time again between a rock and a hard place. As we had no choice but to become passive to the aggressive stance of those who only had us in mind as their workforce, we started to adapt to the situation, and so did our brain, to lessen the blow of the inevitable. We got used to our prison. By now, we even sympathise with our aggressors, and our brains adapted to the prison that suddenly presented itself as an opportunity. What could be so wrong, to work for someone else and be given a wage to feed our families? All the choice we would have, all the security we needed, and none of the worry that our family would go hungry. We believed the paradise we were promised, and didn't realise we were building someone else's whilst sacrificing our own. We resigned, tired of fighting the inevitable split mind we felt within. But there was another cost we hadn't calculated in the contracts we signed, not knowing any better: our brains changed. They adapted to the new paradigm, and even if we realised, it apparently was too late to stop the outcome. Our brains started to be trained by those in charge, but not just to keep a record of all potentially dangerous situations, so that we would learn to steer a safe and reasonably satisfying course through the waters of life according to what we chose to learn, rightly or wrongly. Without realising, we allowed our brain paths to become overstimulated, in order to do more than just monitor our experiences. As a result, we came far, far away from our true capability as alive beings, whilst our brains were given the go ahead to rule all of our decision-making exclusively. This changed everything, but not in our favour. Our brain has been steering the good ship Self under a pirate flag wearing a blindfold for some time now without us even realising what has happened, whilst our true Self is taken prisoner below. And I will now tell you why I believe why it was possible and easy for others to make it so.

As we know, our brain is designed to gather information from our everyday experiences, and then it categorises them. It groups them together into experiences that are necessary, useful, even those that are fun to do, as well as those that are harmful and dangerous. Most human brains do this, no matter what our background or status on Earth; it's like a filing system on a computer hard drive. That is what it is designed to do, as well as learn more about events for our safety and survival and add these accordingly. Whilst it diligently creates a filing system based on many of our limited past experiences, it has only a limited library obviously, to try and determine whether any action we are about to take can be deemed useful and safe, or not, viable or not. As it processes information from our lives, it just means that it holds a record of experiences, just like a computer that is running a binary programme based on whether experiences were safe or not, helpful or not, dangerous or not and whether they should be repeated, or not. It cannot discern whether these decisions to file them into categories are actually correct or not. This is usually done by us, our Karmic Self. Our Karmic Self has the additional tool of our Karmic memory, which plays into our intuition, experience, and ability to compare rational discernment to actual fact, whether something is right or wrong. As an example for all this, let's imagine that as a child, we were playing outside on a lovely sunny day, and we got near a pond. Our brain didn't know yet what a pond was, but it looked inviting, so we stepped forward into it. The experience that followed was that we got wet and cold and out of our depth, hopefully just for a few seconds until someone came to help us out, but enough to realise that this experience was nothing like we expected. It was frightening. As a result of our body going into immediate shock mode, it would emit adrenalin to try to get us out of the predicament. Our brain automatically uses the adrenalin to kick into action to file our activity of entering unknown waters as dangerous, in order to keep us from future harm. This seems a very useful mechanism and it has indeed worked to keep us safe in many situations where we faced danger. However, as adults, what would happen if there is someone beside us, in a situation we deem precarious? Would we trust our brain? Or would we trust this other person, promising that the water is not cold, it is not deep, and that it is a pleasurable experience after all, now that we can learn to swim which, in our fear of getting hurt, we have avoided up until now? Will our brain gamble? If it does, what does it need to have, for it to give us the go-ahead? I think you can already see where this is going. On our own, we would not think of entering the body of water again, because our programming says it's dangerous. But if there is another influence that questions this belief, and gives us additional information to say it is safe, then we might try it, according to our own disposition and how persuasive the other person is. Our brain would also need to know one more thing: whether we can trust the other beings judgement. Again, this depends on our inner filing cabinet, and trust is a very arbitrary thing: it entirely depends on subjective criteria we have gathered so far in our lives. As children, we trust our caretakers because they look after us and love us. If they don't, we learn not to trust them, and many other adults beside. If they do and say the right things to encourage us, we also gradually learn to trust ourselves, if they don't, we become insecure. If they are overpowering and authoritarian, we inherently don't trust them but don't give ourselves permission to follow our instincts. If they are careless and lie to us, we becomes confused and insecure in our decisions in lack of true information. Will we stand beside the lake, trust what the person next to us is saying and go in? It depends on all of the above, and also how our Karmic Self plays out: were we born with an optimistic, outgoing, inquisitive nature? Or are we more cautious, reserved, thoughtful? Even our Karmic nature is based on experiences we have made - those from lifetimes before which discerned everything about us in this lifetime. A combination of these components and our experiences so far in this life, will decide whether we feel safe to go in, or not. But we have forgotten one thing: the person next to us is still there. And it depends also on how they use their energy to influence our decision. If they keep on talking trying to convince us, we might override our cautious thoughts and go in, just because they talked us into it. We may not know who they are, even if we think we can trust them. They may have good intentions, but what if they don't?? Why are they doing so, in the first place? What is their motive? What if their own system is compromised, leading them astray and us into the bargain? What if they act out of some compulsion, or were influenced and swayed by others to tell us to go in, no matter the consequences? And here, we have the final picture: two beings, standing before a major situation in their lives, which might have life-changing consequences. The analogy is now on par with what we face in our lifetimes, time and time again: do we, or don't we? If we do, against our better judgement, what are the consequences? If we don't, is our brain telling us limited information only, based on past fears? What might we be missing out on? Do we have a choice not to make that decision? Who else will it affect, if we make that decision? Can we put it off? And last, but not least - which position do we find ourselves in, the one contemplating a choice to go into the lake or not, or the one who is influencing them?

Unfortunately, there are many people by now who have taken the second choice, perhaps because they, too, saw themselves compromised having been faced with making an impossible choice, and who now feel themselves forced to pass it on to others. The question is, should we ever take advantage of others at these points in our lives? Many obviously have done so, in so many different contexts. It's become the norm in a society that worries about money all the time. But even then, they are not at the top of the food chain. They are often trained by those behind setting up these impossible choice systems, who employ experts in human psychology fully aware of the conundrum of the human condition, our weak points, and the way our brain works, or doesn't, as it were. If we realise that the scene above was a set-up, one that need never to occur in the first place, that we never had to enter this scenario, that we can just leave because we see through it, then - why don't we? The answer is, because we are very vulnerable at times, and it means that this underlies both positions no matter who we chose to be in the little story above. We are often so unaware that we are being pulled and pushed into certain directions, because our brain cannot see it. Our brain is not capable of decision-making, and we should not be using it for that in moments like these. It's probably also the reason why we sometimes cannot come to a conclusion, because we are automatically asking our brains to make a decision for us, when it simply does not have the discerning power we credit it with. What will ultimately decide is our instinct, and our Karma, and if by now we have accumulated enough good Karma, it will keep us safe, and it will feed into our instincts to allow us to go no further if there is any danger in proceeding. If there is no danger as such, it will give us a choice whether to proceed, with a warning. We make the decision to be safe, or not, and we will be aware of the consequences. If we make a decision to our own and others detriment, it will leave a recording in our Karmic log, too, and we will have to undo it again sooner or later. If we make a decision to stay true to ourselves and take care of others the same, this will contribute to future well-being. For example, in our analogy above, has it occurred to us to ask the person who wants to influence us, why they are there, doing what they are doing? Whether they know the lake? Have they been in it themselves? Why do they want us to get in it? Often, we just have to ask some very simple questions to find the truth, and to turn in the right direction.

Of course, we must always start with ourselves. I also had a choice whether to write this book with others in mind, whether to write this chapter or not, whether to put it to you, or not, and whether it was going to be for your benefit, or not. I could have chosen not to, or be the one to tell you to run into the lake of life no matter what, see if I care, even if I knew that it was very deep and you can't swim. I could also be the one who decided to enter the lake by writing this book, despite the dangers that lurk when we speak of Truth, lest there be people who don't want us to know and have methods to stop us. I gave you these analogies and all the information here, because I believe in informed choices for everyone, so each of us can make their own decisions without someone else's hidden agenda being more important. I also made the choice long ago to make this information freely available, because I believe that it should be. It is not mine, it has come through me, from a higher source. I have some great mentors, too, with wonderful advice, who encourage me to proceed when it's safe, and warn me when there are obstacles. And so, I chose to bring up the subject because I feel it's more important for everyone to learn that everything we do is affecting our and others' Karma all the time whilst we are here on this planet. Even if there are dangers these days doing the right thing, I feel the alternative is much worse, of making uninformed choices based on the way others influence us who we don't see for who they are, who don't always have our best interest at heart, who may not even be visible and accountable to us at our most vulnerable moments; and maybe, if we had known better, we would have chosen differently. I am here because if even one being says, 'yes, I get that', will have been worth the effort.

We often do not realise that we still have to take action on top of our brain function, to independently determine for ourselves as to whether our subjective inner filing system is objectively right for us, or not. If we have learned to be scared of certain things as children, it will be difficult for our brain to allow us to feel safe to be around them in the future. We may have recurring information pop up about those things or similar, that trigger fears in us and still make us believe they are dangerous. If we believe our brains and react with fear without questioning, it will be difficult for us to approach those things as grown-ups with discernment and a relaxed type of respect, regardless of whether the thing is still a threat to us or not. I come across cases which prove this process all the time, such as adults still terrified of the dark, or certain noises, or certain rooms in their home. I heard war-time children relate how the whistling sound of bombs falling still rang in their ears, decades later, and filled them with terror. Any event can affect our behaviour patterns so badly that our bodies were so traumatised they had to come up with coping mechanisms. Many of us can relate if there were any traumatic events in their history, too. The memories can be extremely intense and because we don't know how to help ourselves with regards to coping strategies, symptoms can become severe, too. If this rings true for you and have ever experienced something similar, as most of us have, we might still be applying our fear of it now to situations where we are determining whether we are safe or not, based on our old experiences. If we can relate, we will know that this is exactly what our brain is doing for us: like a computer, it's checking what resonates with our brain cells. If for some reason earlier in our lives we have learned not to feel safe, this might affect our decisions for other situations still now. Our brain cannot really do any other job other than remind us of all the things that have happened so far to make us feel unsafe, after all that is what it is there to do and what it does best. It finds information about the cause of our inner energy disruptions from the past, information that is transmitted via synopses in our nervous system, but it does not always know where exactly these energy messages came from, or how to resolve them. Sometimes we get flashbacks in accordance with these findings, which help us to find out more about whether our fear is reasonable and justified or not. If it is, then we can still apply methods to lessen our nervous reaction, and if it is not, we can learn to peruse coping strategies which can be useful. I would always opt for methods which we know work to alleviate our fear reactions, since coping strategies bypass our natural reaction but do not always lessen it. They can also be complex and cumbersome, and cause issues in their own right. What we best do is to put ourselves back in the driving seat and back in charge. We have to be the ones that discern and see each situation for what it is: our brain is quite miraculous compared to any electronic device humans have invented and we should be grateful if it functions well, but it is not the be all and end all. We can accept that it is part of our being, that there's no way around it but to admit it has its uses, but it cannot continue to be master of our whole universe; it is too flawed. It would not be so bad if we were aware of the fact, but often enough we are not, and there are huge implications if we rely on our brains only. Looking around the planet again with a sigh, it is obvious that the result so far, is that most of the time we tend to make decisions on autopilot using our brains only, which can then turn out to be some of the worst steps made in the history of mankind.

I find that one of the biggest blind spots of human behaviour in the 21st century is that our fascination with machines mimicking our brain functions means we vastly overrate the use of machines over human instinct and our status of being alive. What weird – or deliberate? – human-brained decision-making process recently allowed a robot to gain citizenship in Saudi Arabia? A robot that was seen to be apparently programmable to kill people, no less. If there were shares in our individual aliveness (and there probably are), then they would be constantly dropping the crazier our decision-making becomes. But they aren't. They are going up, the more we are able to sacrifice our aliveness in favour of the invention of machines that resemble us. I know many people who find the notion as scary as I do, and for each of us, there are ten times more who love the idea. Our fascination with machinery has overridden our common sense, an equally fascinating point in human evolution for those observing the planet from afar, no doubt. It's permeated every aspect of life by now. We are using computerised systems right now in order to read this, and do so for an increasing amount of time every day, as a means to more or less communicate human concepts. It is not wrong in itself, and it is in line with there being so much emphasis in our society on using our brains only as I mentioned earlier. But will these computerised crutches of our 'civilised' virtual environments become compromised to work against us, or worse, compromise us to work against ourselves? I know, these are questions that were already asked way before their time in 1968, via a great Stanley Kubrick movie called 2001 - a space odyssey. The matter was dealt with prophetically then and it is still relevant now, even though our fear has probably lessened as the benefits we gained in the meantime have taken over our brain and convinced it that it's all good. But are we all as convinced as our brains are distracted? I find comfort only in the thought that perhaps even this phase of humankind was foreseeable in a Karmic way. Perhaps thousands of years ago, beings stared into the starry skies and deemed a predictably detrimental phase very likely to occur in Earth's Karmic future which included this age of virtual reality. It could certainly potentially bring us down as a society, if we completely submitted ourselves and increasingly succumbed to the obsession of relying on over-stimulated brains and computerised energy forms. Perhaps Earth has been here before, many times. Perhaps we have had technological ages before on our spiral of existence, and every time we repeat the same rung on the spiral, we go through it, over and over again. Be that as it may, it is but one smallish area of our vast energy potential, which we are currently treating like a new kid on the block, as if it is the only valid one. Only when we start to question our limited inner processes and our resulting temporary perceptions of reality, we begin to be able to see right through the displays of our often flawed behaviour, which so far we have hypnotically concluded, but sadly based on a considerable amount of faulty deductions and resulting erratic behaviour mechanisms.

Only when we master these mechanisms and take charge of the helm again, can we start to go beyond the distraction and really tune in to our true selves and merge with the greater energies. If it's any incentive, those energies promise much better shows than we are subjected to on available internet services we are all convicted to having to pay for in order to view what other minds have come up with under the guise of entertainment. I do apologise at this stage for my cynicism. Ignore me if you will, and skip this bit if you don't like it. I will ramble of for a while longer, because I believe there is merit in realising that as long as we still come from our 'ego' mind, meaning only the limited resources of the physical body and perceptions we have of the world and beyond, we can potentially do quite a lot of damage to ourselves, others and our environment.

I probably don't even need to mention proof of this. Surprisingly or not, there are depressingly vast numbers of examples of sick people and ruined environments, so much so that it has bred a new generation with ever earlier signs of physical and mental illness, disturbed and destructive family dynamics and a host of other illnesses created by the miseducation, intellectualisation and trivialisation of ourselves and our offspring. Life has become degraded and over-complicated, and many of us have lost faith in but at the same time are missing what it means to be real, to be truly ourselves and live authentic, caring, loving lives; unfortunately, we are not out of the middle ages just yet and this is still not a part of any national educational system's curriculum that I am aware of. Probably because we are convenient as worker drones, but not as functioning human beings.

* * *

40. Karma and Politics

We are often misguided and distracted by false messages to look in the wrong direction to try and find the big players and trouble makers, but we know by now that our brains might just as often get it wrong, too, and we could end up shooting the proverbial messengers. It appears that we certainly do have elements on Earth which are working against us, which is knowledge that really is centuries old and perhaps also a result of our not being able to clear our Karma as of yet. We would be able to face and tackle these mind manifestations if we perceived them for what they are and grouped together to tackle the issue. We are strong together, in groups, and just as well that we do have virtual reality in which we can still meet, because it has started to be discouraged by those who fear our power to have us too close together. If we needed to find out who they were, we would not have to look very deeply, all we would need to do, in the words of Robert F. Kennedy Junior, is to 'follow the money trail'.

If we do want to make a difference, we would first of all need to learn to find our inner strength and conviction, as well face facts within us and not just put our heads in the sand, pretending that everything is fine whilst spending precious energy complaining about trivia. Perhaps we can choose to shift our sources. Maybe the human experiment was always meant to go through these times of repeating the dark ages, but how can we still justify wars between countries and millions of people dying as a result of famine and crazy diseases? How did we get hood-winked into thinking that this should truly still be happening, or did we subconsciously agree to it somehow? This is now supposed to be the age of enlightenment...how come so many are still caught up on the wrong side? Why are we still supporting and encouraging corrupt governments, a handful of over-paid people part of a club of privileged to represent us badly and, it almost seems, deliberately designed as such to not be acting in our best interests? Why are we just complaining that they decide for us who lives or dies, who becomes enslaved to a system that does not serve humanity and how much of the planet is destroyed, paying lip service with regard to respecting human, plant or animal life? When we look at it soberly, we can plainly see that humanity is still caught up in cyclic existence just as much as it always has been. Hundreds of thousands of years on and we have not torn ourselves away from the same trials and tribulations that we had to face as so-called primitive cave men and women. Maybe instead of quaking in our boots, we could become Karmic avatars and make more use of the 100th monkey principle instead? By applying our pure intention, pure Karma, and good actions, thoughts, feelings and words, we certainly would already automatically be bringing about a different learning environment and a different outcome.

It does not have to remain a virtual reality alone, designed to distract us. We can truly learn how to be Karmic Avatars. A future planet could include those who have overcome a large part of their negative Karma which held them back, for them to return as super-human beings. But why wait when we can call upon this vision already? Perhaps they are already here and we just have to remember how to summon them and their wisdom. Perhaps they are all around us, assisting this planet as we speak. We could certainly do with the love. If enough of us were to actively manifest and project our image of a loving, peaceful, fear-free community, society and environment with our thoughts, deeds and actions, then others would perhaps get it and might follow. This is what the hundredth-monkey principle describes - that a certain majority is needed before a remainder of the population gets the idea and jumps on the movement, so that they can coincide. If we are all in agreement that our strength is in the innocence of our sincere wish to live in peace? That we would create a better world for ourselves and our children, by not being put under duress by a few who are acting out their less than tolerable scheming plan to keep us all suppressed? Is it not worth a try, or are we too far down the line already? Are we already too far down the road as a deeply disconnected world full of manipulated misery, so stressed in our caged lives that we are easily influenced not to care what happens to others at all?

Many activist groups call for immediate changes, and despite so much effort from so many all over the world who are concerned, the decisions of what happens next are apparently firmly in the hands of the tiny crowd in politics who have the means to stop the heartbeat of this world in an instant – and all ours with it. This, they have made very clear over decades, and living with the implied threat in the meantime, we make for very productive slaves and consumers, do we not. What sort of a revolution is needed, if any? Do we need an inner Karmic revolution? Should we call it a revolution, when it is all just a quiet, internal, individual blast of energy that could happen for all of us more or less simultaneously? Will it help to implode all that is mad & bad? Or do we just need to learn to love coexistence?

So far in Earth's history, we have witnessed an industrial revolution, hailed to be the saviour of humankind's problems, but bringing factories and famine instead. The technological revolution brought numerous 'useful' gadgets for every-day life that were supposed to make living easier, but resulted in toxic pollution, deforestation and poverty again.

In the electronic age, we have had more wars, more toxic accidents, more famine, more sickness, more debt and more environmental issues than we would have probably imagined necessary in the 21st century. We have more medicines and more mental illness. We have access to more fake currency than ever, but we are less real. We have potentially more light but we seem to have inadvertently invited more darkness to deal with as well. Has any of it changed our minds, our inner worlds? Has any of it made us wiser or have we just been distracting ourselves over and over again? Have we moved with the energies of the Earth, through each of its eras, until we have the age of light frequencies so we can see their luminosity? Will it bring us what we sorely need - wisdom and compassion in the age of enlightenment? When we look around, where are we now? The corporate revolution? The age of corruption? The 20th and 21st century of lab viruses? What will be the revolution of the future? The environmental revolution? The spiritual revolution? The meditation revolution? The healthy-mind-in-a-healthy-body-revolution? It will be for some, for sure, who put it out there to make it their reality. You can choose whether you want to be a part of it, whether to start now or in another lifetime.

I think it will help us to see the connections, the bigger picture, and also the way that our Earth's evolutionary stages reflect different frequencies, as it is moving through its own spiral Karmic journey. The Earth itself moves continually through each 3-dimensional frequency level and periodically repeats the process before moving onto higher ones. The Earth also has its own energy funnels and high frequency energy points. It has meridians in terms of leylines. Each of us arrive here on Earth to be part of her process, too, as well as complete our own. How we take part or not, is up to us and what our Karma brings with it in terms of talents, skills, opportunities as well as set-backs. How we apply these, is also up to us and our level of consciousness and ability to apply ourselves to the task. How much we manage to create and dedicate, as well as take with us into the after-life stages, is up to us, again. How much is learned by others, is up to them. How much can be taken on by them at any point in their lives, is up to them, too. How much they can co-assist and co-create with us, is also up to them. But there are things we can do together: we can assist each other, help each other, connect and communicate with each other. With some, we will be able to do the above, and some are not here to be on the same journey with the same objectives at the same time. There are infinite combinations and possibilities of how beings achieve their own process, and we have to decide how we approach each of them. When wisdom and compassion are the underlying motives, we will be able to see all for their ability to be who they are, or not. We need to find out what each of us are about, what we are capable of, how we can assist each other, as well as try to manage all of the above without outcome attachment. This means that once we have applied said wisdom and compassion to help others, we set it all free, to be for the benefit of all beings, so it can grow and multiply. We can use our effort, our energy, to make our intentions spread like ripples in a pond. In fact, we can apply that to many things we offer, all we have to do when we do something positive is to wish for it to be reaching all others as well. Having no outcome attachment does not mean we don't feel anything, quite the opposite. It means we have compassion for each being and the whole process they are involved in and the wisdom to apply methods to assist them that are much larger than our feelings; so we are aware that

We can learn how to let our feelings of love and compassion grow. Despite the urgency, despite all that needs to be done, the journey is for us to return to this moment, the Now, and grasp its full energy potential in all its entirety.

Some will be able to contribute, some only some of the time, and others will not see this as part of their journey at all. But we needn't base our efforts on the outcome of others' Karma. Just keep on doing what you are doing.

Having said that, what is our task here on Earth? What will be the outcome if we abuse the gift of ourselves, others and our environment to the max? If we observe others doing so, are we simply to stand by, chanting in a cave whilst allowing others to do harm, without regard for the consequences? This is how I think it is, in our crazy Samsara, the realm of suffering: Whilst we beat ourselves up about letting things go too far, whilst we are bickering amongst ourselves about who started it and who is to blame, there will be those who take advantage of the situation and put themselves 'in charge'. They might be those who are laughing all the way to the bank. There might be those who deem themselves to be decision makers on behalf of all of us, who feel they are running the show, ruining our lives and our children's futures. Megalomania and a massive ego-trip are fear reactions, reactions of feeling out of control, on the level of the base Chakra. As we can all see, it can get really out of hand when some decide that their issues have to become world concerns.

They will find ways to attempt to be all powerful and make sure that we are all subject to their power. They will enforce it with restrictions of freedom and violence, methods of control, because their energy is out of their control. They are not managing it, so they are asking everyone else to do it for them, whilst they believe they are bigger, better, richer and more entitled than others. If their power gets so big that we do not have a choice, there can be no end to their power trip. When it gets to it, we are forced to follow what some of them demand us to do, which is to please, if we don't mind, leave this planet in every conceivable and heinous way possible - because those who are conscious can become very inconvenient, and so can those who are no longer productive enough for them. It is very hard to think straight and feel well with this amount of mind disturbance, so they probably won't. These beings are around in every generation, in every country on Earth, and some have such Karma that they can affect many people on Earth at once. If only they chose to use their power for the good of mankind when they still had a choice. They must not be underestimated in their ability to be actively, deliberately and consciously preparing to break off the fight of all fights amongst us all. We do not have to believe them, and we do not have to be like them. They are examples of what not to do, and lessons in diligently increasing our good Karma in order to assist all mankind. We already know the consequences if we don't.

But first things first. Let's perhaps understand which parts of our own and others' Karmic minds can hold such negativity, as well as learn more about the people who use negative energy in a detrimental way as their MO to manipulate people. We are not talking about negative energy as in the polarisation of something like a battery, on one end we have 'negative' and the other 'positive'. It's not quite that simple within our bodies, it's, in fact, very intricate a system as we have already learned. Hundreds of thousands of channels carry an electromagnetic charge, and there are power points at all the crossover points of many such channels. These channels carry the energy that keeps us alive within, they are our aliveness. Without them, our heart would not beat, and we would not be here. But there are things that can block these energy channels, they are susceptible to deterioration just as anything else in our bodies. It is very necessary to be discerning; an inner 'negative' feeling or thought can be a very useful warning sign that something is not right in our energy system, and we cannot afford to be dismissive about hunches and instincts we may be sent as signals. We can assume that when we have 'negative' symptoms that there is a blockage somewhere in our system that needs addressing. A blockage is an accumulation of energy in one of the points in our bodies. We don't have to find out where to be able to apply an antidote, which is a great advantage. But we do have to do something about it, in order for it to right itself again. If we don't, chances are that it will stay blocked, and that this blockage will create others within as a knock-on effect. The energy blockages won't just stay in the energy system. Since this feeds all our body with energy, our whole body will be affected if flow is not re-established. We may feel unwell, we may have negative thinking and feelings, we may have physical symptoms, too. They may gradually accumulate and even saturate our system with a reduced energy flow to an extent that it breaks out into a full-blown illness, either physically, emotionally or mentally, depending on how the blockages are affecting us individually.

This is such a massive piece of information with such far-reaching consequences, and yet, it has been kept an absolute secret. In fact, it is still not something that is widely available, not FDA approved, Wikipedia is not acknowledging its merits and so on, despite millions of people learning about it who have already benefited. Three guesses why this is, answers on a postcard. The most important things to focus on now is, that you have just read about it, and found out about it. This is happening for you, right now. It is your opportunity to make use of this information and learn the simple techniques, free of charge, to allow you to make changes in your body's energy system to help you stay well and healthy. Good people are all around us, and they don't know that they can help themselves feel better. I have a duty in sharing this with others no matter what, I know this is what I am on Earth to do.

Some people may be so scared of the negative energy charge, because it has been there for so long, that it will make it hard for them to try something new, not knowing where to start. Some will be very adept at discovering it, some will see themselves as hopeless cases, and some will use it only for their own gain. All of these scenarios will benefit from the techniques, without exception. We will not do ourselves harm applying them, there is no brain-washing and we won't be able to use these techniques to the detriment of ourselves or others. As for those who set out to use it for their own gain, let's examine them and their motives more closely, and try to bowl them over with our new-found ability to use methods to disperse negative energy. We all already generate positive energy for ourselves, universal love, compassion and wisdom on a higher frequency. in some, this is masked by the multiple blockages that occur within. It does not mean that anyone suffering from symptoms of negative energy overload has the right to discharge their energy against us, or that they can try to take our good energy. We must remember that before we try to help, that our good energy will fall into a bottomless pit of another if we are not mindful that we are only here to assist others to raise their own. But look around you - isn't that what everyone is doing? in lack of an effective energy technique to alleviate our inner short-circuits, are we not trying to take each others energy when we lack our own? If we feel we are not receiving it from others, are we not trying to get it in any way we can, and end up focusing on material things to make us happy? If we do both, or either, we have not yet been shown a simple universal observation:

We cannot take others' energy to replenish our own without consequences.

It happens all the time, because we are not yet wise to how our inner energy works, and how to switch it 'on' again when it's been down. Electromagnetic negativity is not in itself harmful. It is only a sign that there are unresolved energies within us that need sorting out. They have typically been there for quite some time which is not something to be ashamed of, just something to become aware of. In lack of a simple, effective way to discharge negativity, humans have come up with endless ways of bypassing and ignoring the issue, rather than keeping it simple and look within to sort out the overload. So how come an accumulation of negative energy blockages within the Karmic energy system of most people has not resulted in us all becoming aware that we can do something about it? Why are we standing by as observers to the destruction on this planet that has been created as a result? How come it can be so strong that it has this power over us that actively disables our ability to functioning properly? Could it really have got carried away since we began our course of human activity on Earth, and it's run amok since then? Would it not explain the scale of negativity here that is hell-bent on destruction, detrimental to our survival, making it so hard for us to see through it, work it out and find true meaning of life? What made us so stressed? What made us look the other way? What created the cognitive dissonance that prevents us from seeing, living and striving for Truth? Are we all victims of the oppression that results from a massive avalanche of negatively charged energy within? Should we not ask ourselves what the internal connection is that is to everyone's harm, and what we can do about it in order to release the overwhelming energy bottleneck causing us to short circuit?

You will probably realise by now that there really are good answers to all these questions; I am not just asking them in vain. This whole book is building up to the methods we apply to the madness. There are solutions, and all those who I have met who didn't believe it at first, now know that it's true. Many of them have already benefited, and many of them have lived more peaceful lives because of the techniques we can all learn to disperse our inner negative charge. Whether we have blockages to using these to help ourselves heal does not matter in terms of being able to get results, simply because we can include any reservations we might have in looking at them more closely, too, rather than pushing them away.

When we look at what we truly need, are we thinking we will die if we don't have the latest consumer products? Have we not all been taken for a ride in being made to think it, by watching advertising campaigns to play in money for big corporations? Do we love them more than we love ourselves? Where does it end, if we don't learn to love ourselves enough to want to try out methods to help us? Do we all have anxiety now, have we given up trying to find solutions? Have we forgotten that we have earned the right to be here, that we deserve to be here, that we also deserve to feel good about being alive? I am myself still trying to find out which parts of our detached selves as a result of not being shown methods to heal, has caused us a potentially limited capacity of believing that we have a right too feel good; that

We have the ability of thinking about, believing in, supporting and also bringing about the greatest good.

We already managed to co-create an all-apparent need for huge piles of waste, such as plastic shrink wrap, bottle tops, syringes, micro-beads and carrier bags, toxic, radioactive waste, pesticide off-runs and oil slicks that end up in our beautiful seas, countryside and all its creatures, leaving behind the legacy for the next generations to sort out. Who thought of the paradox of continuously misusing science for a period of over a century now, to build nuclear weapons and destroy millions of people, wildlife and environments to experiment on? Who endorses and commissions wars? Who built nuclear power stations that became lethal and unsafe the moment they were active, leaking into our environment and poisoning all within it? Do you get me? No matter whether we agree or not, we created it with our minds. We have the ability to do much greater things than that, if we allow our minds to remain unhindered. Let's apply the same underlying principles to manifesting something much more useful and greater than we ourselves believe we are able to. Nikola Tesla already understood this and said: "If you want to find the secrets of the universe, think in terms of energy, frequency and vibration." Could this be the reason that we cannot find the part of our ego mind that is insistent on ignoring the connections between our actions and their devastating results, as well as our refusal to act upon them? if we haven't found solutions yet to the most urgent matters on Earth, do we not have a little hope that when we receive help to look at issues so we can work with them from the inside out, this will have the right impact to find an external solution? Are we still giving this part of our brain the go-ahead again to make decisions for us, paradoxically denying us access to a better future out of fear for our lives? We CAN actually find out – by tracing the thought process back to our inner energy minds, especially the fears that the ideas came from that work to our, our fellow beings and our environment's detriment.

Here is a little idea I came up with, it is perhaps part of why we've had a problem here, Houston. We are all subject to being created in a process of Karmic energy birthing into human existence, in which we have an individual experience on Earth, first as unborns, then as babies, growing into children and then adults, a process that takes at least 18 years if not more to be complete in physical form and which continues to develop and morph into old age. The point of our first existence on Earth forms the base point of our individual spirals of existence on Earth. As the time-line on Earth continues, our Karmic spirals take us through many millions of experiences, every second of our lives. In one of the earlier chapters in this book, I have gone so far as to state the hypothetical idea that it is possible our experience as unborns, newborns, babies and children entirely repeat themselves in adult life. These experiences are met by our inner energy system and deemed either neutral, positive or negative. Our task on Earth is to learn to be able to balance these inner electromagnetic charges and gain a natural, neutral yet strong inner stance in reaction to any of the situations that can present themselves temporarily as very real challenges. If we do so without forcing anything, without pretending they are not there when they are, by finding the right methods to use to truly resolve and bring about inner peace, we will emit the most desirable outcome of not having to repeat the lesson of Karmic energy repeating until resolved. We could, as a result, notice at any point climbing up the rungs of our experiences during spiral life-timeline that this is what we are actually doing. We are repeating phases which we have already experienced previously, in this or even other lifetimes. At any point where we revisit the initial experience with another, similar one triggering similar responses within us reminding us we have been here before, we are presented with a valuable opportunity of resolving any negative Karmic left-overs by raising our frequency. This process of awakening and realisation is aided by alleviating any blocked energy issues in our Karmic energy bodies to do with unresolved Karmic situations, as explained before.

41. Short digression into Karmic Psychology

I would like to introduce another suggestion on why i believe that some people, maybe many of us, myself included, separate themselves at times, from their own Self and the healthy pursuit of their inner journey, the result of which may be harmless, but can also be potentially destructive on a personal and global level. I believe this is very necessary as the symptoms are becoming more prevalent as we move into ever more convoluted conundrums in difficult times on our Earth's journey, and we don't want to lose good people who might be extremely sensitive and have much to contribute here. It is sadly quite easy to see when we look around, how common it is that many people have disassociated from their lives, their loved ones, even themselves. Many of us do not know who we are or why we do what we do. We do jobs, because we get paid, so that we can be well enough, in order to work. That's who we appear to be - or so we are led to believe. However, this is not who we are, and we are probably all aware of the fact in this day and age. In order to really see through the illusions if we wanted to, we would need to pinpoint at what stage we were led to believe them, and at what point we started to lose ourselves and were led away from Truth. As far as i can see, the natural Truth you are born with is that you have the freedom to live, find your purpose and joy in life whilst also abiding by human rights rules of respecting others' rights equally. You have a right to be alive. In an ideal world, if we stand by this, we should be supporting each other naturally, to be nourished and reassured by those around us. Let's for a moment assume that you have had this type of life-affirming care so far, so that you know you are loved and appreciated for having appeared on this Earth, and that this already occurred at formative times in your early life as a baby and growing up as a child. As a result, at points where you were old enough to become separated from this care, hopefully at an age that was suitable for you, this solid, unshakeable inner knowing that you were already enough remained with you at all times, certainly at the most important ones. It reaffirmed for you that you didn't have to 'do' anything to be loved in return, that you were fine just the way you were, doing what you do best, finding out your talents, bouncing off your family or carers when you overstepped the mark a bit, knowing you already had their approval when you showed a talent for something like compassion, laughter, dancing, joy, moving, growing and being healthy. This affirmation that you yourself are already enough, it transferred gradually from your carers or family to yourself as a growing young adult, giving you confidence and an ability to want to be well, and live well in future. Eventually, you one day realise that this confidence that was reflected back at you, was already yours, it came from your connection with your universal umbilical cord, a bond with your Karmic Self that cannot ever be broken. This confidence is yours already, it is your aliveness, your being, and nobody else's.

In an ideal world, we will all feel this, at all times. This is what we are capable of being, and doing for each other.

I really wish I could stop here, and I really wish this small chapter containing so much Truth could be the end of this book. But I wrote this book because we can all see that things aren't always like that. Most of us by now have lived through times where there wasn't enough affirmation that we are enough. Insecurity crept in, and we felt that we had to be somebody else, strive for something more, do something, in order to be acceptable. I also wrote this book because we need this confirmation now than ever that we still are enough, just as we have ever been. And because we need constant confirmation that it is still so, constant reminders. Let this little chapter and many others throughout this book be your guide, and your reminder that, whilst so many things may get in our way, we are still enough.

We are. We are alive. We already have confirmation through our bond with the all-present energy that prevails, that we are. We are now, and we will always be.

We thought we thought someone would protect us forever, that someone would be with us forever, that we would last forever - we do, but not the way we thought. When we experienced physical separation, we thought our world had ended and there would be no more. We stopped trusting. Some of us stopped trusting the moment we got separated from our mums at birth, as babies in a separate bed, away from the nourishment and constant warmth we needed. Others, some sooner, some later, some more, some less, stopped trusting when we were separated from our birth mothers and fathers. Have you stopped trusting? Did your connection get disrupted too soon, so that you never realised if affected your trust, in others, in yourself? A next hurdle then came when you started being away from home for long periods of time. Like most who were herded through the sheep dip of formal schooling, you stopped believing that you were already good enough. How old were you? Were you sent somewhere you had never been before, without explanation, without a choice, without alternative? You were no longer with the security bond that your family or carers provided, and you had no choice but to do it, and you had no voice either to explain how you felt, other than a cry for help. Do we not see the psychological implications of what we do as adults, always intent on separating, sending our children away, sometimes from birth, unaware of the consequences?

i really want to know who made this so, and who made it socially acceptable in a historic account of how we have been told to take care of our children by others, so that it would be a social norm. i have some ideas, but the most crucial one is that we have allowed someone else outside our family to tell us what to do, and that what we weren't

enough to decide for ourselves, and what we were doing with our children was also not enough. We followed somebody else's rules, and they had followed someone else's before that. Where did these rules come from? What if we didn't agree that they would be good for us, or our children?

I would like to reset the balance by reminding you that you are enough, as a parent, as a father, as a mother, as a child.

Sadly, it's gone so far in our society that every possible situation of stress-related illness has permeated every aspect of our lives, including the fact that we can no longer say at this point that this beautiful advice will work for everyone, in case people might misinterpret it. On Earth, we no longer have an absolute Truth that helps everyone, right now. We need to find out how to connect with it again first, to make sure we are ready to apply it responsibly to all situations in our lives, and for some, that will be simply asking too much. But if you are ready, and it makes sense to you, and if you have the energy and connections to make the right decisions for yourself and your loved ones, then let this be encouragement to you, that you are on the right track and that it is well worth pursuing. Others may not be so fortunate, so it is important we represent all that is truly good in life, to the full.

What happened to you, when you were young, so little that you can no longer remember? As painful as it might be, we might need to know why we are now who we are, how we are, just so we can find our true Self again, away from all the beliefs we have been led to believe to comprise us.

Below are questions I once wrote down, to help a middle-aged woman cope with her severe agoraphobia, trying to gently trace it back to where she felt dis-empowered in her life, so much so that she disassociated from reality. Please note, these were my preliminary notes, not all of them were asked, and only a couple of them were addressed if they were relevant in any one session. I have included them here because they are relevant. Hardly any of us realise how important early age experiences are, and questions such as these may reactivate memories that are important to resolve, in order to move one from situations that present themselves to us as unhelpful. If reading this brings up any triggers in you, please use paper and pen to write it down. It's important. You are important. There are ways that the triggers can be overcome, and they open doors to a wider, more peaceful perception of our Self and what we are able to do without having to constantly feel under stress.

Questions about Reasons for Agoraphobia as an example for subsequent therapy session:

'How long ago did you start to believe you were separate from everyone and everything else? Were you too young to have a choice, a tiny baby even? Was it even made to look attractive so you would go, or did you not even then believe a word of it, did you try to fight it? Did you know what was happening? Did your parents believe in it so much that there was no arguing with them? Did you get rewarded for leaving behind what you loved and cherished most of all, did you get punished for not wanting to leave and 'playing up'? Did a part of you get left behind, were you never the same after that? Did you start to doubt yourself but never got the chance to question or find out your parents' reasons for their decisions, or discuss whether you agreed or thought they were right? Were you expected to go and leave somewhere else at an early age, too early, far too early for so many, and feel you had nobody and nothing left, that you just had to get on with it? Did you, after a period of anxiety and mourning your loss, have no choice but to come up with this huge break, like a split within? Did the split part of you that was away from those who knew you and loved you, did it come up with a different part within you that could cope, or not? How long did it take, if it did? How many of you are within you? Did it take a second, third, fourth personality to tide you over, until your hope of the time that it took for you to be reunited with your family became a sadness and resignation that it never would? How old were you when you were sent away again, this time to school/boarding school/another family/foster parents? As you are reading this, at what age do you remember this next split happening, the one that you were told you would grow out of/ that you had to be grown up about/ that they left you to do deal with/with strangers who you were expected to trust but some of whom may have also betrayed your trust? 1 year old? Less than 1? 2? 3? 4? 5? Do these not sound like terribly young ages for you to think back on, now that you are older? When you are on your own now, how old do you feel within? Do you still feel the same, I.e. left to fend for yourself in a different environment, away from everything you know and is familiar, away from all you know and love, if you were to leave your house? You

experienced new friendships, but also new adversity, that you could not involve your family in. How do you feel about those situations where we tend know in general that children need to be taken care of to feel a secure bond, by those who love them? In some cases, this adversity was there even earlier, even within the family. What are you aware of about your birth family? If we have experienced trauma from birth or even sooner, there can be intense feelings of a lack of trust, issues of feeling unloved, creating disorders and illness all based on us trying to cope with a chaotic and unloving environment. Even if you had a healthy family and upbringing wherever you grew up, were you unable to go outside and others, were you led to believe that you had to create another persona to survive? This persona might be the exact same one that has taken over your everyday life as an adult, whereas there is a feeling that the 'real' you is still in there somewhere, in distress. All those dreams you once had as a child, which you still have, of being able to be you but not knowing how, of being loved, of doing what you enjoy most – they almost belong to another person. They don't seem to be yours, as if you don't deserve them or know how to bring the two together. It seems so far away, so impossible, they are so far apart. The 'real' you is hidden away deep inside, where it's safest, but it's also lonely. At least it's where everything is as you are used to – just like it was when you were small - and so it is now when you stay at home and don't go out. There is no chance of feeling comfortable with just being. It is not safe. To just be, you feel you have to break through that barrier of believing that it is not you who goes out, it is your alter ego. But that's getting harder and harder to do, because it is not. That other You is fake, and you resent it but you need it as well to survive. It is the robot you had to create at an early age, the one that didn't have bad feelings. If you see what the robot does on a daily basis, you get angry, because it is what others told you to do and believe over and over when you were little. You were told that either you are good or bad. You were good when you obeyed, and bad when you were upset. In any case, you were always judged and never knew how to be just you. You now feel you have no choice at what you do, because you believe you have to earn another's over and over again every time you go out and come across another being. Does it feel like everyone you walk past is judging you in your mind? Is that the worst about what doesn't feel safe? Or is there something even worse? Do you not want to be judged, because that is what they told you you are worth when you were little, and that real you is reminded of it and still believes it? Are you afraid to get a job even if you want to have one, because that is what you were told the aim of the game is, you are judged by the money, only if you do your job well will you be worth something? You get money, and you were told money is more important than love, which was never mentioned again, not even as a reward. You don't even know what love is, other than knowing you can never have it because it means you would have to come out and find it. Anyway, it's not safe for anyone else to know the real you. Is that what it feels like, impossible to cope, impossible to manage?

The antidote to apply frequently is to validate all the answers to the above, whilst also using a Meridian therapy process described at the end of this book to remove all the 'stings' that our past experiences have left within our Karmic energy system, one by one.

I wanted to give an example of how deep our feelings and experiences can get, in terms of having many reasons why some of us don't feel that we can cope with the demands of life. No doubt I could have chosen even worse examples, but this is simply an example of what we can do. We ask ourselves good questions in combination with some of the methods I describe at the end, to alleviate our issues. We can tackle some belief systems that we have grown accustomed to, and gently ease away their intensity from our Karmic bodies. The more we work on ourselves, and anyone can benefit, the more we will get out of it, the less we will be affected by certain situations and the sometimes terrifying fear we might have of them.

If the above affected you, I have put information at the end of where to get help. One thing we can do whilst reading already is to reaffirm the following:

You are alive. You are loved and cherished already, despite your experiences. You already live on this planet as do plants, animals, and other humans, all alive. Plants and animals do not ask if they are allowed to be alive, they just grow. We can learn from them. If we stop them from growing, it's because we are not aware we are continuously stopping our own flow. You CAN claim back who you are, If you know how. You do not need to prove who you are through your actions. You already are. You need and are allowed to be, and this is the time to bring yourself back into being. You want to go back to the richness within, the spirit that you once knew, even if you only caught glimpses. You are the wo/man who dances with energies, and your love within, the one who is choosing happiness. The one who can smile and laugh and just 'be', because hat is what you are here to do.

Perhaps we never have to feel at all separated.

In this world, where almost everything is possible, we can create virtually anything in harmony with the abundance of nature. Except, in the meantime, at least for as long as we can remember, we have been more or less horrified witnesses subject to the world stage turning to the creation of weapons, wars and famine; death and torture – in short, hell on Earth. Why? Whose world stage, whose invention is this, when none of us consciously chose it? Do you have anyone in your close circle of friends and acquaintances who would qualify to be deranged enough to think up inventions like these? No need to answer that. There are plenty of people out there who live in constant fear from the atrocities that have been committed on this planet. Life has put me in touch with quite a few people to teach me that too many were tortured for their beliefs; some of whom became my greatest teachers of compassion. The least i could do for them is to help them by sharing methods to alleviate their pain, and that is what I am also doing herewith. In my wider circle of acquaintances, I have a few proud but minor crazies perhaps, none of them capable of doing damage on such a large scale, or any inclination to want to do so – quite the opposite: all of the people I know personally have in common that we all want to lead happy, peaceful lives, no matter what trauma each of us have experienced, and this includes those who served in wars. Due to my propensity for looking into matters on a deeper, psychological level in the context of bringing about solutions, I feel, however, that I have a duty to find out how violence on a large scale even happens. Is it the work of an insane few? The result of subtle oppression of the masses? Was there perhaps a part of our mind so threatened that it separated us from others in fear of persecution, triggering fight or flight reflexes which never departed from our human psyche since we left the caves? Have we all had to overcome these hurdles, some of us more quickly than others, and some haven't yet at all? Are some still stuck in their own Karmic hell of so many inner energy convolutions and past demons that they see no other way out? Have our stressed Karmic minds been constantly on the run for lifetimes and now we can't stop? Or is this the Endgame of an evil master plan after all, to make us all so agitated and paranoid that we fall out and fight each other, whilst the Self-proclaimed masters stand by, smug and indifferent to our suffering, awaiting the planet emptied of the masses they don't wish to share the planet with? Again, no need to answer – it's a rhetorical question.

As by now, we must surely realise that there is something amiss, if most peace-loving individuals willing to share the Earth and make it thrive are being hindered from even planting heirloom vegetable, fruit and grain seeds to survive. Even if we do come across those situations where some are willing to use violence, there is more often than not something that is seriously amiss psychologically that needs to be addressed individually, from case to case - or, most likely, a greed that drives them to sacrifice others for their own gain. Before we put our attention to those individuals, should we not first see how this has been done to us already, going on for centuries? Was there a point zero where the first act of aggression started that affected us all, or did we all come to Earth with that latent ability and make a choice whether to act out on it or not? Are we showing symptoms of this now, in this lifetime, as a result to the amount of oppression that we have endured for lifetimes, some as aggressors, some as victims? Should we not look at ourselves first, before we explore the actions of those who are either after us, or desperately trying to awaken and save all of us? Or are we resigned by now to putting the demands of repressed and distorted minds of just a minority of sociopaths addicted to power before our needs, as if suffering from Stockholm Syndrome, hoping to appease them so they will leave us alone? I am talking about those who openly still wish to rule the world and would have little hesitation given the chance to systematically exterminate large parts of the human race. It seems like we feel so under duress that we are forgetting to take care of ourselves. How much has their Karmic energy system been compromised, so that their hatred for people, their disdain and disregard for humankind is so engorged they forgot all about their capacity for compassion? Do we have to ponder to their own downfalls, give up thinking positively and trying to help each other? And last but not least, would we not all be capable of such actions, if our Karmic energy minds had been compromised enough? Who knows what's going on with these people, but will they stop, if we put a stop to their behaviour by locking them up? Do they actively need us in order for them to learn their limits, and would they benefit somehow from some form of psychological evaluation and programme to turn their inner evil around, or is it too late for them? And who will they be reborn as, if they are so far gone to the world and removed from the kindness of wo-man? I truly wonder if these people learned new programmes, and if they didn't have a choice but to follow them religiously every day, if this would reverse their Karmic energy enough for them to learn something that they need to see. I think it's worth a try, for the sake of all wo-mankind. I have an inherent optimism that if they don't, they will be made to in their next existence.

With the same power of our Karmic energy that some misguided people waste on crazy ideas of destruction, we can learn again to create peaceful environments; we can all choose to support nature again, so nature will support us. I think we possess an inherent ability to do so, it's in our nature so to speak. None of us should have to be made to believe that someone else's lives are a priority over ours, that their happiness counts more than ours. We are all equal, and have equal rights, even if we are led to believe otherwise. I truly believe that all of the power of our lives combined, counts for much more than we give ourselves credit for, and that we can create a good outcome for all of us, absolutely. Especially when we are all doing so already in our own right, making a commitment to work on our Karmic Self, we will become aware of the synchronicity with others on the same path. They become our 'Sangha', the solidarity of people with a like mind, on a similar path, with a common goal of looking out for each other. We must be willing to accept that it will take some beings a bit longer to realise this, maybe even a few million years, if we consider the evolutionary process of an amoeba. It has a long way to go. But a few people deeming themselves intelligent acting out their psychopathic fears on the rest of us? Perhaps everything is repeating itself, and sometimes the tables turn. Whatever we feel we individually need to be, I can hardly believe that we will allow them to be successful in their ploy.

42. Karmic Memory – Releasing the Fear

When we examine most of what we have created so far without having previously utilised our inner wisdom to maximum effect, we might realise and be able to admit to ourselves that a lot of it does not equal the beauty and mysterious life-force available to us on Earth. I think I used the analogy before, that we are not the creators of life on Earth, some of us can make artificial bacteria in a lab, and not even if we have children. After all, we cannot mastermind either of them, and I know it's a hard pill to swallow. However, what we do have, is perception and the ability to ask for miracles. Please look at a leaf, or a flower petal. ANY leaf or petal or even a blade of grass. Hold it, and look at it, closely. Can you see it's alive? Can you feel the tiny cells that are brimming with aliveness, striving to grow and produce more life? Have we forgotten? Do we not see the Magic, even just walking past plants along the pavement every day?

I refuse to call them weeds. In our crazy linear thinking of insisting on progression, pushing for ever more convoluted ideas that trigger an intellectual overdrive mechanism within us that wants to go bigger, better, wider, taller, more - we are bringing in mad enhancements of inventions trying to improve on nature and what is already perfect. Civilisation has forgotten that we cannot go forward without going inwards. It has also forgotten that everything we are creating is - dead. It is not alive. We cannot survive with this alone. We cannot make nutrients out of what is not alive. Technology which we are so proud of has motion, a binary system to mimic discerning function, even motion sensors. It has a power source, steering, even lights. It can maybe take photos, even at night, much better than our eyes can. Very clever toys, some of them extremely helpful when people are genuinely in need of them, others more sinister than that. But they are not alive. We are pretend astronauts, like children cosplaying at Halloween, trying to improve what we already have. Perhaps we can't get away from this human urge, who knows. If we have flown to the moon - not entering the full discussion, honestly, nobody has time for that - if we humour the notion that those in power may just have managed to do so or just wanted to convince us - either way, it doesn't matter, because where would it take us in our personal quest, where we can get past this universe by being an internal astronaut? We have trillions for that research, but not enough to save others from starvation outside our perceived remit. The U.K. is currently giving the go ahead for a multi-billion dollar train project, whilst people are dying in a virus lockdown. The U.S. president currently wants to mine on the moon whilst China has probably already started in secret. Does it not sound somewhat insane? Are we playing a game of 'what's wrong with this picture'? The jury is out and the power game is on. Gazillions have been spent on warfare over decades on ever more sophisticated methods of killing each other. Countries can be invaded for oil and gas and millions of civilians killed; billions are raised for charity marathons and yet, nobody has come up with a pain-free, 100% reliable cure for cancer in 80 years of research yet. I cry every time I see someone die, wondering what heart ache they and their family went through; no otherworldly belief will make my compassion and wish for their greatest good get any less; but isn't our constantly weakened state of fear, anger, illness and mounting stress weakening us? We rush past reality having no time and energy outside the stresses of work- and family related issues, we do not have time to listen or comprehend, so we argue and lament instead that it doesn't feel right, until our children reflect the obvious by rebelling under all the pressure. Where is our gentleness, where is our kindness? We stand-under the influence, the spell of some Self-professed higher instance that tells us it knows better. We are forgetting more and more how to look and ask for what is rightfully ours: the natural, inherent serenity that is missing to keep us sane; and yet it is still out there. Does Karmic energy frighten us so much that we are staying away? Or are we so in awe of it, with its endless, random, wild, unharnessed, unpredictable power to create, that we feel we are not worthy of being included? Can we imagine being a part of the magnitude of its creative potential that entirely overshadows any of our inventions? Perhaps we are scared of it because we feel out of control in light of its awesome power. Maybe because in lifetimes before, we had to die at the hands of the power of nature and as a result we became frightened of being at its mercy. Maybe we are still scared of being exposed to nature's power now and escape into our tiny little concrete box houses to take shelter, resisting losing control at all cost, terrified of one day having to relinquish our physical bodies again. If that's what it is, and it certainly is good reason, then we need to have the equivalent of a big hug from the universe. Perhaps it's time to reap the benefits of all our efforts and succeed in conquering our innermost fears. We deserve to master the biggest fear of all: losing control over our lives. We have not conquered life's biggest challenge yet and instead, we still settle for becoming old and ailing over and over again, without there being an apparent end to it all.

But please don't let me make you feel worse by pointing out the obvious, that is not my intention. Allow me to give you at least a glimmer of hope. I did promise that it is not all doom and gloom. We are going in the right direction, asking the right questions, drawing the right conclusions. It's uncomfortable at first to say it how it is, and to think it and feel it is too much sometimes. This is why we have to take the next step, so we don't keep getting caught out in a web of fear: let me remind you that there IS an end to all this suffering, we just have to remember what to do, be clever about it and not run around in circles. As we can see, there is no point. We need to look at what we are trying to avoid seeing and find out why we avoid it, including how much we always end up hurting one way or another and end up running away from the fear of being hurt. Many of our actions and behaviour patterns follow this, running around in circles. Only when we stop running for a minute and employ the right methods to allow ourselves to recognise that we are scared, each and every one of us can determine and resolve what it is that is most obviously trying to trip us up in this lifetime again, and every single one before this. Some of us are afraid of others, some of us are fearful of unfamiliar situations, probably because we had to face countless others under the guise of different circumstances we didn't understand and manage to resolve in a different lifetime either; any of which might have spelled much danger for us. A fire too close, too much water swallowing us up, a height that reminds us of falling, a desert that threatened to dry us out or a forest that froze us. A predator too fast or poisonous: snakes, rats, spiders or raptors. Some of us fear closed-in spaces, others wide-open ones. Some of us have inexplicably strong urges to defend ourselves from being impaled or drowned, shot or run over, even when there is no real present threat, or any that we can remember from our past to justify the fear. Certain memories can trigger our senses – visuals, smells, circumstances. All of these are memorised, logged and stored by our inner Karmic energy bank, and are kept there to remind us of a time when we were in danger and perhaps did not survive in previous lifetimes. Therefore, triggers for the fear of dying are extremely common and understandable, as they also have a purpose to keep us safe in this life-time. It's a pity that past-life memories are not medically recognised and taken into consideration as yet. Many of us share very similar, archetypical phobias, but why don't all of us have precisely the same ones? Because of the fact that we do not, it makes sense to me as a result to propose that two things could be logical conclusions: a. These energy memories might serve as indicators that we indeed have exact memories because of exact occurrences in previous life-times, indicating for us to explore the details of the memory, in order to do the one extra thing we so far have not been able to do, which is to release the fear; and b., We have a particular space in our Karmic memory bank with specific aggregates, which encodes energy memories that brought us here in this exact time and space so we are able to erase our fear.

I think there is a lot of hope in these theorems. I don't think our Karma has it in for us, far from it. I think it is trying to assist us.

We need to find and understand what it is that we have individually experienced as a threat to our survival in the past, and what it is that we need to acknowledge in order for us to overcome our fears, feel secure again and brave enough to face the world. The first step is to remain open-minded to this being a theory that might actually make sense when we apply it in practice. Especially when we also acknowledge the fact that none of us share the exact same way we died in previous lifetimes, but all of us did actually die - ergo, most of us will share the same fear of dying. Many of us will also share that we are afraid of similar archetypical fears, such as water, or fire, or flying etc. But if we examine these in detail, despite similarities, each of us have different inner images of how we picture these phobias. Perhaps these unresolved phobias are also one of the reasons we are all here again, individually, with our sense of an existing 'Self' as a detective, to find out how to solve the mystery of our previous deaths. What happens when our 'Self' is released, free to be and go where it needs to be? Are we scared of that freedom, too?

As a matter of fact, there are a few archetypical fears which most humans have in common. Two examples we have been talking about but not thought of in terms of reincarnation, is that most of us seem to have a fear of dying and a fear of pain. Even just thinking about these makes most people's stress levels go up, and nobody wants to think about, never mind talk about or explore them further. My take on it is that this is what happened to us: a. we had previous lifetimes; b. we experienced pain, and c. we died; maybe several times over; maybe many times over; maybe even infinite times, in any case, so much so that it is ingrained in our memories that we never want to go through it again.
I know it sounds a bit gory but there is a point to it all. Another most important question to ask, is: Are we finally here, at a moment in time, to overcome our fear, once and for all? And possibly also another conclusion to this: it could be a reason for some, if not all our behavioural traits, especially the ones described in the previous chapter. It could be the reason why so far, we have felt we are stuck in so many ways and frozen in our behaviour patterns. It is yet another reason I feel it is important to look at our internal Karmic energy flow, see what is stuck and understand why, and help ourselves to at least somewhat alleviate these fears. Does it not make sense? Don't we deserve to be free of all of it? Does it not help us, are we not relieved to know that there is a reason for why we feel the way we feel, that this is what happens to us, and that of course we have reacted with an archetypical fear as a result? Without becoming aware of it and finding a way to release it, we are condemned to repeat the cycle over and over again, only to at some point hopefully and finally gain conscious understanding that this is what has occurred and be able to put it to rest. After the initial shock, it should come as a relief. The ultimate reward for being brave and carrying on, is that

things change for the better when we understand. Even if we do not believe in rebirth, don't we all want to get rid of our anxieties, even if we can't understand and make logical sense of the full spiral of existence? Is that not that what science has been trying to do, and religion, too - and probably each of us individually, in an isolated and frustrating way? So, are we still happy to label ourselves Agnostics, Atheists, Ascetics, Anarchists, Nihilists, New-Born Christians, Non-Believers, Flat-Earthers, Darwinists or whatever? Or do we realise it is more important to discover what we have been programmed to not believe in? What is the one thing we have we been omitting from all of our lives? The answer is: A solution.

We have all argued with each other until we were blue in the face about philosophy, science, religion, country boundaries, relationships, work places etc., even bashed each others' heads in for it. What if there has been a solution for all of us, all along? Maybe we do not want one. Maybe we are not ready for it. Maybe we are all 'Anti-Solutionists'. Sorry, I do apologise, I am getting carried away. Just being a little flippant, in light of the fact that I have met hundreds of people who already experienced getting rid of their fears and feeling amazing as a result. it's not a sales pitch, just the honest truth. Perhaps we want to discuss that a few hundred years longer, or just go for it and try it for ourselves. It's up to you. You can, of course, and must believe or not believe whatever you want.

Back to some other questions we could be asking ourselves instead of watching our lives go by like repeat TV shows: Would it really help us if we believed there was a rebirth for all of us? That there is a continuation of something that survives of us after death? Or shall we continue to keep calm and drink tea? We could do both, I guess. At least it would make a great movie title. If more and more of us do believe in reincarnation, it will be interesting to see our individual interpretation of what each of us think what it is exactly that survives our physical bodies. Having studied various religions and philosophies, I believe we all have different words and ways to describe the same phenomenon, as is often the case.

I am concentrating briefly on a minor detail of my own research again next, not to prove something but simply because I enjoy drawing conclusions from reading and contemplating observations which others made and studied, centuries ago. There is, for example, one small phenomenon which has always fascinated me. I have briefly mentioned it above already - apparently there is a belief that we can even bear the marks of previous lifetimes on our bodies as well as in our Karmic energies, so much so that there are people who have done studies on interpreting those marks.

(https://psi-encyclopedia.spr.ac.uk/articles/physical-signs-reincarnation-cases)

It wasn't just me who had come to the conclusion that there is indication a link might indeed exist, and because I had contemplated already that it might actually be true before reading the study, it led me to ask in turn why so many of us still negate these findings and don't want to know more about them, instead of examining them. Would that not be our old friend, the fear of dying, rearing its ugly head all over again? The one that we don't like to be reminded of, because of what happened to us the last time and at all times before that? Since most of us still have not yet had a chance – or the good Karma - to utilise methods to overcome those fears, we repeatedly try our utmost to ignore all hints pointing us in that direction again, where it feels darkest and the most scary. It's true, we have suffered so much fear without any sign of resolution, and all of our fears have accumulated within like in a pressure cooker. When there is little or no method on offer to reduce it, so much of our inner resistance is completely understandable. We carry on trying to avoid looking at what makes us feel even worse, but it does leave us staring at the snake like a frightened rabbit. Meanwhile, unfortunately our fears don't just sit there and twiddle thumbs. They have a destructive dynamic in their own right. All these fears continue to get to a boiling point, no matter how much we are trying to look the other way, distract ourselves and pretend that we don't care. I would state that it is our inner, untreated fears that are a main contributors to creating our current world problems that we examined before, as well as many of the individual issues we face as a result. They are capable of doing so much damage and if I be honest, I believe in people, I think we can do it, if only we can overcome our fears first and foremost. Our behaviour patterns would improve accordingly, and it doesn't even take an eternal optimist to believe that our Earth would breathe a sigh of relief, too. Our global sum of accumulated inner fears manifests itself in the outer environment on as many levels. Our fears are creating shield-like, protective membranes to the outside world to keep us safe. The analogy is that we have creating plastic, brick and mortar to protect our vulnerable bodies from harm. We try to hide behind computer screens and end up inadvertently destroying the very thing that we wanted to preserve in order to be safe and survive: our safety and privacy which is so easily breeched online, at any time. There are so many examples this applies to, all with the underlying motive to try and protect ourselves from our own fears and failing miserably. As long as we have deep fears of not surviving, we will give them the power to act against any potential threat we feel life may contain. This means we have given away our power to our fears to act on our behalf. The same as with our brains, this also cannot work as a decision-making process or safety mechanism. Many disastrous manifestations have occurred as a result, and there is nothing that modern about the process: our fears are ancient, billions of years old. We have not changed that much. We are still Neanderthals, but now in plastic, brick and glass caves, struggling to shield ourselves from lions and tigers and bears; only this time, the natural world is not the threat. The threat is much worse than that, it has grown accordingly as our fears became stronger. The threat we face is now our own inability to survive, due to no longer being able to make sensible decisions under duress. Since we are almost continuously under stress and accordingly, end up making the worst decisions almost all the time. Our environment mirrors just how removed from being relaxed we are by now. It is very sad to observe that our current level of fear, which is the result as well as one of the causes of our inner negative electromagnetic charge being disrupted, can perpetuate not just internal suffering but also so much external damage. It seems to unnecessary. By realising our ability to heal our brains' vicious cycle of over-thinking and over- reacting, we can enter a much-needed healing process for ourselves, which we can then also pass on to everything and everyone around us, causing a tangible effect for all across the globe. We mustn't be made to feel guilty for not having done that yet, as it won't help us feel better. Applying methods will help. There are ways we can help ourselves immediately feel better, within just a few minutes, and I have been advocating them for years...I do wonder why they are not being shown to an extent, to bring relief to people who really suffer with terrible fears and anxiety attacks. Please check the end of this book for more info, too. What these techniques do is similar to a meditation, but with more focus on what issues present themselves and maybe even more instant. It will create a time-gap between our perceiving something, and how we react to it, allowing us to not have such short fuses or react with utter panic. It's not harmful, as in, it won't make us drowsy or unable to act in an emergency, it will simply allow us a moment to think clearly and find the correct solutions instead of panicking, which is extremely helpful and very necessary these days, by the looks of it. These abilities to have time to think before we act used to be the norm, but we are under much more pressure these days and our fuses have become shorter as a result. The impulses that are reported to our brain via synapses are exaggerated and often cause our body to release adrenalin, when really the situation we find ourselves in may not have warranted it. Without having been shown methods top cope, our brains have created a loop of continual fear within us which is almost impossible to get out of, without help. As we said before, we cannot rely on our brains alone to do this job, it is not designed to do so. We must allow ourselves to intercept and actively support our brain function so it doesn't malfunction. There are ways to tune into methods to calm the stream of fear on a different level. Whilst we still have these 'negative' charges running around in our mind stream, they have a certain power to manifest. Luckily, they don't seem quite as strong as positive ones, but they will still hold us back. They may still be in the way to us reconnecting; they may still repeat on us until we face them.

The biggest threat nowadays is that there are plenty of humans under stress now, some of them with great power, whose biggest fears are making them initiate and actively create outcomes for their own gain only. That would almost be ok, we might think, and perhaps we believe we can co-exist with those consequences. After all, each to their own. However, what we might not realise yet is, that there are indications that the outcomes some individuals are aiming for, may mean they are trying to exclude most other beings living on the planet with them simultaneously. I don't want to scare you or to just take this at face value. Please examine the evidence trail that demonstrates we have always lived in precarious times on Earth, so perhaps our situation right now is not unusual. In the past few hundred years up until now we have had wars, famine, chaos, destruction etc. But do we really need to still live like that? Should we not question the decision makers and find out why our planet is still in chaos when we could all have a really good standard of living, if we share and distribute our resources without them being corrupted? It really does make me think that with the abundance we have already, more than ever, why we still have poverty-stricken famine areas on Earth, and those who actively profit from creating war zones far away from home are closer to our doorstep than we might think. What will be their next step? Are we not in some sort of war zone already with the fears for our existence that we are constantly bombarded with, supported, if not created by some who try to hide their intentions?

As always, deep down, I don't believe it has to be as scary as it seems to present itself. I believe we have solutions already to many issues we face, we just have to make them more available and widespread. There is hope, which I will keep repeating and emphasising until you are probably fed up with hearing it, simply because I would love for us to see, find and bring about solutions to the problems we face; because I believe it's already out there, or rather, in here, within us.

Whatever the outcome, whichever side we are on, it is important to keep in mind how much every life is worth preserving. We are faced with numbers of deaths in graphs going up and down, but it tells us little about the precious lives that have been lost. It should not just be dedicated healthcare professionals being asked to apply the Hippocratic oath - it should be all of us vowing to preserve lives. As an individual as well as a community we need to re-connect in whichever way we can, in order to make a difference, and many of us are already dedicated to doing so, with their particular skill set. Our life does not follow a linear time-line, our lives are continuously circling around the same issues until we got the hint, so that all our good efforts can become a part of our Karmic consciousness. It does not stop, ever, even if we sometimes feel we want to stop the train and get off. It's fine, of course, to have a break once in a while so we can ease off and recuperate, that's up to us to decide. Luckily, our love can often overcome our overwhelming fears, we just need a little help so we can feel it again - and sometimes we need more than a little help which is fine, too. Ask for it. If you think about it (I know I have), if every one of our fear-based thoughts came true, we would be even more worse for wear than we already are, that is certain. Since we are not, it must follow that our fears don't rule us yet, and negative energy blockages don't define us. They just appear to us to be vastly inflated, like airbags they can be very in our faces. They are like boulders in a stream. They can affect how the stream flows, but they can also be moved, and that is some of the best news I can give you. We do not have to let our fears define us and render us inactive. The sabotaging thought patterns that have held power over us so far, lifetime after lifetime, can be changed so they no longer affect us in future. Remember that it does not even have to be that tricky, expensive or long-winded; neither does it take the brain of a rocket scientist. It also does not have to get in the way of us being who we want to be, if we focus our healing on the aspect of no longer allowing it to. All we have to have a willingness to hold our hands up to agree we are ready for a good change, observe how to go about it, and make our minds up on what to tackle first. We don't have to look back at some things that have so far not worked in our lives and feel bad about it any longer. We can learn new things in an instant and become convinced enough by our own examples and experience to want to examine what we want to do with this new-found status of ours. Nobody else is trying to tell us what to do, no influencers here. Once we have looked through all this information however fleetingly or carefully, we can then concentrate on balancing our frequencies with positivity and hone our inner powers in earnest, so that they will finally actually bring about the desired results for us, and for the benefit of all sentient beings.

* * *

43. What Effects Can We Expect?

I do ask myself sometimes, 'Am I mad? Is it because of my happy early childhood memories, or is it my Karmic path I was given, that I think positive and hopeful when faced with so much adversity?'

I am by no means a Pollyanna. I am fully aware that what we are facing right now is no mean feat, and never has been. I am not trivialising our suffering, or what we have to do to alleviate our problems. All I feel is a deep inner knowing that we are able to overcome many issues, and that we need to share this knowledge to conquer much of our suffering. Each of us will develop their own skills in bringing their own takes to the table, of what they feel they are here to do. I feel it's important that we all contribute to the problems that present themselves, and don't just sit back and let someone else do it all for us. We all need to do things for ourselves, to make this world a better place.

When we do, we can make our own experience of the greater energy source that surrounds us all, which is of a supportive nature and will oblige our request for help. As I see it, on a higher, finer frequency level, like attracts like, on a denser frequency level, opposites attract like the North and South on a magnet. The more loving, focused, compassionate and wise our wishes and the clearer our own Karmic energies are, the more unconditional our motivation and intention becomes. It also has a power to multiply then and spread out, feeling at one with the all-encompassing energies already out there. With a little bit of extra effort and our input, the more certain and immediate it can become that they will be fulfilled. If we ask for things that serve our higher purpose, like, for example, our Karma to be purified, then we will meet with situations that will make us grow. It does not always mean that they will all be easy. In fact, some of the good stuff is best learned when the situation is somewhat challenging. There is a little but powerfully poignant example on the subject that has always helped me to put things into perspective, to feel tremendously grateful for what I have, for appreciating being alive:

'There was a Buddhist monk who was imprisoned for decades in prison. Day after day he was tortured and treated unreasonably. This monk practised the ultimate love by feeling compassion for those who tortured him. It sounds almost unfeasible, but this monk continued. According to him, his only moment of being in danger was the moment at which he almost lost his compassion for the guards. Through the use of compassion, he did not break.' *(www.livingpractice.life)*

Naturally, it does not mean that all lessons should be difficult to be useful to us. Good lessons are those which are appropriate to each individual and their situation. Most of the time, we need nothing more than encouragement and reminders to do the Best we can, to do the right thing. Nothing to do with obedience to another's' demands, which we may naturally have developed a resistance to since childhood. We just have to learn how to best get through those poignant moments in time that stay with us as intense life lessons, so we can get to the 'other side' of them as unharmed and congruent as possible; hopefully wiser, too, in order to be able to see their point, even if with the benefit of hindsight.

Learning about our Karma and how to release ourselves from any negativity is an undertaking so complex that, to know it from the outset would possibly make us give up before we start. Be that as it may, the inward journey is possibly the most rewarding, most important and most worth pursuing on Earth. With so many fringe benefits along the way, it may help us through times when feeling upset, lonely and confused en route to feeling on top of the world, many times.

As I said at the beginning, people have in recent times coined the phrase 'Instant' Karma, and I hear this term used more and more often, by which is meant that the effect of an action follows the cause instantly, or at least without much delay. It may well be possible for this to happen, but as we know, there are so many various energy connections to be considered that the phenomenon - more often than not - maybe coincidental but more importantly, it would be odd to think that it will be visible to the observer as to them being able to tell what someone else's Karma is. We already learned that nobody else can decide on the extent of another's Karma, and this applies here as well. The term is sometimes used with a certain sense of satisfaction by the onlooker who wants to believe that here an incident that proves 100% that negative actions draw to them a negative outcome for the person who commits them. If this were true, would Karma be acting like a judicious god that points the finger at anyone, from above? Maybe it's a whole discussion for another book, but an example for a situation where the phrase might be used would perhaps be, a person who has just been rude to someone who then walks straight into a lamppost as they are turning away from the scene. To many, it feels like someone is getting their 'just deserts', without delay. Perhaps Karma really does work instantly sometimes, but more than likely someone's got so distracted by getting too involved in a scenario that they forgot to look out for themselves. Karma doesn't have it in for us the way we think, but it does try to tell us about the state of our inner energies, and situations like that can remind us to focus on keeping our wits together about life, or life can have a habit of working against us. That really applies to all of us. It also shows that we really do want to believe there is some principle out there that sorts out the good, the bad and the ugly. It's clear that many nowadays are interested in the phenomenon, don't know enough just yet, but do want to see proof of it. But it just does not quite work the way we think. There is no punishment as such, just a connection between cause and effect, and this can be much more complex than it presents itself. It also more often than not has a time-delay to make it harder for us to decide what's what, which we also do not like to be reminded of as it complicates matters. We do want instant justice, that's obvious. After all, there are plenty of people on this planet living a life of crime, even murderers living in splendour sometimes without any apparent repercussion. This is, as we must know by now, because their Karma has logged their crimes, and you can count on this fact absolutely, but conditions have not ripened yet for it to be activated along the path of their Karmic ladder, and with it, the chance to neutralise its connection has not arisen yet for the bearer of bad Karma.

I suppose we would all like to be in control of all our lives and everyday outcomes, thinking that we can influence Karma that way. It must appeal to the control mechanisms we develop based on fear, that we latently have in all of us. I am not sure the way Karma works is quite as simple as that, so that something bad happens and there is immediate retribution. We might have to ask ourselves why we want it to be like that, so evident that we can believe in it more. We can't control Karma that way, though. If we control our lives to the point of having everything our way to the tiniest detail, we will find we might be unprepared for a time where it will inevitably not work our way. Even if we have managed to keep ourselves and others out of situations of harm by staying put and not creating upset, we will still have to face what happens when there are inevitable moments where we cannot control an outcome. We are not in charge, even if we fear not being in charge. This doesn't change just because we are afraid and are locking ourselves away. Unless we manage to develop our inner world out of compassion, not fear, and gain wisdom on a very deep level to resolve our inner conflicts as well as practice assisting others from afar, we will still actively become engaged in processes eventually, to resolve our own past Karma and learn how to help others. A friend of mine who went on a ten-day retreat allowed herself to be engulfed by bliss, having grasped the concepts of stillness within. She walked out of the retreat place into the open, where she came across a woman walking towards her. The first thought that came into her mind was, 'isn't that woman overweight'. She scolded herself for the thought, and her inner peace she felt she had worked so hard to gain was gone in an instant. We can possibly all relate to that - we make judgements all the time, assessing situations out of fear, and then, on top of that, we berate ourselves for it. It's a double negative that doesn't get more positive for punishing ourselves for it. We can shrug it off, see it as an important learning point in our lives, and try again.

> *Unless situations make us realise that we are in a perfect position, right here, right now, to connect each other with love and compassion for our own shortcomings as well as others, we will have to repeat them; in order to overcome our tendencies to run short of being unconditionally loving to ourselves as well as others.*

Negative Karma does not magically disappear, it takes recognition and a little bit of effort to undo it. We often create it without even noticing, as most of us do not have insight into how it works in full detail. It may well be true that 'instant' Karma could exist, especially in this day and age where time appears warped and events seem to be clustering and speeding up. Quite likely, however, that the interpretation of two incidents are being connected and seen as an insult followed by instant justice by the onlooker and are actually unrelated. Again, the Karmic principle applies that we cannot know another's Karma, so it is for us to look at our own reasoning when we find ourselves in the role of onlooker and have enjoyed a dose of 'Schadenfreude'. Perhaps it's true that we are experiencing a kind of glee at seeing another's misfortune, which is probably not such a good thing for our own Karma even if the culprit is guilty of an act of wrongdoing. The answer in Karmic terms, which, after all, affects us the most long-term, is always the same: to practice non-attachment in many varieties of situations, meaning we have an opportunity here, too, to send out the highest energy frequencies to persons or a situation to bring about the best possible outcome. It is really simple, effective, involves nothing harmful and is always what is most fruitful for all involved. For the sake of our own and other's sanity and healthy development, we can bring our energy back to ourselves to be able to learn to emulate best case scenario. This is our superpower. We will never know quite why things happen the way they do, so all we can control is our reaction to external events. It all sounds a bit pious when we just read about it, but if we are truly within our fully-fledged inner energy to see how powerfully we are already connected to others and external incidents to assist the highest outcome, we will prefer this blissful experience to any other, lesser reaction. We can then extend this process, multiply it by practising and applying it to many other situations in our lives. The result of how we feel during this highest energy practice, standing in the pure energy of knowing we are all beautifully connected by light-expanding bliss, will hopefully make us choose to manifest it again by repeating it over and over, in order to assist others. It is like finding an inner exercise routine, an inner chant, that brings about the highest outcome we can possibly be. No physical exercise compares to the feeling it conveys.

Even if mainstream media transmit news and stories to us about this and that every second of the day, continuously goading us to judge, discern and evaluate, at the end of the day, we do not know if anything is represented in true form, without a hidden agenda. We will not learn our inner strengths by watching TV. We will not know Truth, even if we are accomplished at piecing facts together. We will not know the whole picture of or ours or others' past actions, even if we think we have proof of some of the details. All we would do is to carry on harming ourselves and others by judging how good or bad or ugly others are, whilst not focusing on working on our inner ourselves. Practising and expanding on our inner images and actions is, after all, a part of the Truth that we have been told is imaginary. We have been told it's superfluous, useless and dreamy, and we were scolded for following our inner beliefs and trust our intuition. I wonder who started it and to what gain, but I deeply know in my heart that we have to reclaim the highest possible inner world we can for our sake and survival, in order to see how all-important it is. We get lost in being made to believe that we have to be split a million ways via our poor, overworked brain cells. We become very vulnerable to deception when we are split. It's almost convenient then, for others to take advantage when we are confused, distracted and procrastinating. As I could probably be accused of doing right now, trying to convey this particular message, which ends here. I have to go follow my own advice, sit with myself now to find my own inner strengths and improve it instead of projecting it onto you, my dear imaginary readers, but I promise I will include all of you in my practice. I hope you have enjoyed reading this offering of an accumulation of my thoughts on the subject. It is written with all my love and I sincerely and humbly put out there that it will create some good, for all of us. Although, I will try to let go of that thought now, too, before all these words make it even more convoluted.

Be, and be love.

✽ ✽ ✽

44. The Karmic Spiral of Human Existence

image credit © https://aminoapps.com

I will try to explain why I feel spirals and vortexes are so important in Karmic investigation, and why I mention them here. There are shapes by which Karmic energy forms in all dimensions, and some of them are of such pure frequency that they apply, exist and interact with each other, as well as form inter-dimensional bridges within physical life-forms. The spiral is one of those sacred geometrical shapes that applies to inter-dimensional Karmic energy manifesting in the 3rd dimension, as are circles, arcs, power-lines and toruses. Since they are all able to interact, they are really rather important in terms of manifestation of life and matter on Earth. They are the outlines for the building bricks of life, converging to create the essential energy grid for cellular structures to form in 3-d. The spiral form is special because it has the ability to bring in and expel energy, as well as transport it along all its individual turns. A spiral can double up with another spiral and form energy 'rungs' - such as can be seen in the example of our DNA. The energy that is brought in from our Karmic energy cloud may intertwine with an energy spiral and converge with it, according to kinaesthetic principles. At this point, our Karmic energy is on its way again to becoming matter, whether we chose it or not, it looks like the point at which such conversion manifests is determined by the nature of our Karmic essence that may remain non-manifest until such a point where it collides with at first maybe one, and then perhaps many, energy spirals converging, which draw it into existence again. We are, at that stage, first and foremost Karmic beings on a journey of spiral existence incarnating on Earth. Our DNA is spiral, the energy which flows around our spine to feed and maintain our physical body, also flows in spiral motion. Our Karmic timeline on Earth is spiral, not linear, which is quite a revelation when you are confronted repeatedly with that truth in life, in order to really understand what this actually means in terms of our individual Karmic growth. Spiral motions appears to our eyes as if they were only 2- or 3-dimensional, because we cannot perceive beyond these with our eye/brain co-ordination. However, these movements certainly link into other dimensions, as they are not bound by 3-dimensional limitations. They go out into the universe, i.e. 4th and 5th dimensions and beyond. From there, it is able to bring down to Earth light entities, information and energies which promote healing; as we said, it also includes bringing down to Earth Karmic energy minds from previous existences, back into a new physical manifestation on Earth. On top of this, almost every light body with the Karmic intention to be manifest in a 3 dimensional form on Earth has to move through an inward motion of the Karmic spiral to con-dense so to speak, and become incarnate this way due to the density of the physical frequency on this planet, with a few exception of highly evolved beings who are able to manifest instantly. Not sure what exactly happens on other planets and planes, but I have a feeling that other brilliant minds will pick up on this and come up with a few examples. I m sure this would be much better a subject for a Superhero movie than any other because it is actually true. This is who we are, this is what we can do, and will do again in reverse into even better conditions, if our Karma allows. Is that incentive enough for us to not fear any longer, to be excited about who we are, to find some awe in our existence?

To reiterate, when we leave this Earth, through several processes of disintegration our essence finally becomes existence beyond matter, as sentient Karmic strands, if you will, merging with the great essence that is. It's a great process of re-configuration, gathering information, discarding discordance and aligning again to our highest potential following the transformation after our last incarnation. A giant defrag, if you so will. We have to wait there in suspended animation before we attract light spirals again to reboot, so we can become 'light beings' again with more attributes pertaining to, well, light energy, the most important of which is that it is not only able to move, it also has weight. It might be very light compared to dense matter on Earth, but it has the ability to travel, and our strands have the ability to hitch a ride. But before becoming being physical bodies on Earth again, we must also become in our ethereal form aligned to a particular light energy that has formed itself according to specific laws of physics into a spiral in this case. This attracts and merges with our strand formation, so what was once a spread-out Karmic energy field with our particular pattern which we call "i", will now be pulled together again into more and more dense levels of existence until it finally assumes a physical, adapted shape again, according to all the gathered information from previous stages of existence, including any re-formation that has occurred outside our physical existence.

The cross-over point at which this occurs is the singularity which the spiral is moving towards, in concentric circles, moving our light energy along and compressing it, to a point where it is so small that our whole essence is condensed in a singular 'light dot', I shall call it, a point of our concentrated strands infused with light energy from our compressed spiral that has brought us to this point in order to incarnate. Something that is within us has been pulling us all along to this new point in our existence, something that is knowledge of all that is, combined with universal principles to allow it to converge. But something else must also pull us from Earth at this point, so that the 'light dot' we are, the concentrated essence of our 'I', can become physical form again. That which pulls us finally back firmly onto terra firma is the magnetism of our mother's and father's DNA spirals, which have combined to form their own attracting point of magnetic pull within a cosy, inviting environment just at the right moment in time for us to settle in to. I am not sure how long we had to wait for this moment, it depends on each individual, but theoretically it must be the potential spectrum of time between zero and infinite.

The spiral energy then splits into two and starts to form the first two channels. These are formed by the spiral energy polarising into yin/yang energy and spiralling around the central energy line of the seed, all from the centre of the new being. This energy pulls the initial cell mass from its centre into an oblong shape, and it will also eventually form the central spine in the oblong shape which, with more time, develops gradually from an embryo to a foetus. At first, the yin energy pulls towards the base of the life form, the yang towards the top, and ultimately together they will spiral around each other from the trunk to the top of the body, forming the chakra funnels there and in between along the body, which will continue to feed into the form of the physical body to make it manifest according to its Karmic blueprint.

Image Credit © StrangeSounds.org

Image credit: © Ruth Stubbins Pinterest

Image Credit © GnosticWarrior.com

When we observe images of life, we observe the spiral everywhere. It is the universal driving force behind the manifesting being.

In order for us to come into existence, the Karmic energies had to create a singular instance to physically manifest. Next, in order to make this new creation thrive and grow, our Karmic energy body merges with the existing physical building blocks in order to start a new body. This process of spiral Karmic energy joining and feeding into matter adheres to the Fibonacci principle and the endless mystical number Pi, which underlies the creation of spiral cellular structures from omnipresence, by the infinite number of their circumference in ratio to their diameter. The spiral and circular orbs are one of the most common underlying structures in manifesting life on Earth, as it was called into existence beyond matter before incarnating. Geometrical shapes such as Fractals as well as the shape of the Merkaba within the Tetradecahedron, start to build along more linear, yang energy principles which our modular physical structure must fit into in order to be incarnate on 3-dimensional Earth. They are all patterns and principles underlying physical manifestation, reminding us of our endless existence before incarnating into structures on Earth, many examples of which are shown in nature.

The motion of spiral light energy brings down to Earth with it our complete Karmic energy body, into the at first tiny cell mass it needs to settle into for our existence in the physical realm to be made possible again. Since its first moment of meeting the light spiral, our Karmic energy has quickly become more densely focused again, so that once it enters into the seed of our 'Self', the plan for a particular blueprint for each individual human life can activate according to our Karmic energy imprints combined with physical attributes from the parental DNA. Without our Karmic energy entering, there would be just a cell mass with no consciousness. We will remain forever connected to the frequency on which the flow of invisible energy exists eternally. This is our aliveness, our connection to the endless stream of life in existence, our given gift from the omnipresence that we sprung from into seemingly separate beings. However, we are always a part of this aliveness, at all times, only we have forgotten this in our dense, physical, temporary life-forms. All the same, this is the energy that keeps us alive, and as such we become visible beings in physical form on Earth, each of us a miracle that has been birthed into life through a journey to Earth along with the light energy frequency pulling us along channels. And now we all continue to grow in our mother's womb, building cell structures according to our Karmic blueprint and based on geometrical patterns and of course, the kindness of a human being that has to have gone through the often very tricky and intricate process of agreement to share their body with ours for some time.

The space between 'matter' and 'no matter' is like a misty horizon. There is movement between universes, there are strings, waves, twists and patterns; and omnipresence exists everywhere and permeates all. The frequencies and geometrical patterns are the codings that our Karmic energy body has been surviving in as a non-incarnate 'spirit' or 'soul' or 'entity' before and after incarnation. These and more, are all terms we humans use for want of a better description of something we can rarely fully understand with our brain function alone, as they tend to give much more intricate information than the 3-dimensional attributes that we imagine to still exist outside our own physical bodies on Earth.

To me they are simply this: our sentient, bodiless, Karmic energies following precise and/or random energy patterns according to our individual Karma blueprint we have so far created in our lifetimes, with added adjustments that take can also place in between lives. These, our Karmic energy blueprints are governed by principles that coexist simultaneously in this universe and also beyond. This we cannot easily yet comprehend with our limited physical perception, but we can all certainly try to grasp by tuning into different wave patterns, for example by keeping our body still and quietening our brain for a time, we will, for example, be able to access theta frequencies within our own energy minds, where we are able with much practice to observe absolutely everything, down to the last detail beyond our physical form.

'(Theta is..)A brain oscillation pattern detected by EEG, which in humans is termed cortical theta rhythm and has a frequency in the 4 to 7 Hz range, and which are normally present in minimal amounts in the temporal lobes. The theta rhythm is common in young children; in older children and adults, the theta pattern appears during light sleep, meditation and drowsiness, but not in deep sleep. There is an uptick of theta activity during short term memory tasks. The theta rhythm is actively sought in yoga and transcendental meditation.'
(From https://medical-dictionary.thefreedictionary.com/theta+waves)

Our Karmic energy is a complete log of all that constitutes our unique energy convergence from 'before' this very moment in time, even as you are reading this book. Using the process of stilling my mind, I also became aware of another phenomenon: some Karmic energy forms will eventually be able to expand beyond the need for physical incarnation, which is a logical conclusion if we approach it with a mathematical mind even, as there is a finite time-line involved in allowing us to become free of all Karma. At some point, our Karma will not have a 'before' or an 'after' that needs to continue to return to reconcile. It will not be necessary therefore to be incarnate, but instead, energy forms no longer attached to past Karma can incarnate at their own focus of intention if deemed necessary. Necessary would be situations to help others, and where the outcome is of benefit to all involved.

In the meantime, back on Earth, a quick recap: our individual Karmic energy gathered in outer space, ready, willing and able to enter a new physical existence. The Karmic energy component of our future existence, an imprint of our previous experience in terms of Karmic memory and resonance, is helping to form our new body in the womb of a new mum we've never met before. Except, our Karmic energy mind will be drawn back into a space/time setting again, mostly at the point of the egg being fertilised in the womb with perhaps a few exceptions, but certainly by its own Karmic attraction to this particular scenario. The three components – physical contributions of Father and Mother plus each new being's Karmic energy - converge at a moment of cosmic conception in 3-dimensional space and time, according to their individual component attraction and determination. Many women I know and have spoken to have sensed this, visualised it and even felt different the moment that the Karmic energy of another being enter their bodies. There are most likely many different, individual outcomes, as individual and relevant as we all are and choose to be. We simply cannot foresee every possible Karmic outcome.

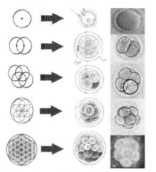

Image credit © https://fractalenlightenment.com

The new light body, which becomes incarnate into physical existence, will then become polarised into components according to physical laws; components form according to yin and yang, left and right, up and down, and the Karmic light body brings into life its own patterns accordingly, including the complex multidimensional flower of life (as seen in the 2-d image above), which helps to combine matter aligned along its energy formation grid and all components within it in order to grow from a singular cell. The four directions in physical form are the basis for the new cellular division and formation: upward movement from its spiritual connection, downward for its Earth connection, left for yin or feminine and yang for right and masculine energy. These are all new, duplicate cells, created in the shape of circular spheres which each carry a particular resonance and coded frequency in their own right, according to our past Karma memory. Our energy knows what to do next, which is to start pulling the cells into the oblong shape we are used to for a body. Each energy frequency resonates with violet/pink/white/gold/opalescent for uppermost, red/green/brown/dark/black for Earth connection, blue//turquoise/indigo for one middle orb, pink/red/yellow/gold/orange for the other. I am trying to describe universal colours beyond our perception here, which do not exist like dense Earth colours but are much brighter, more vivid and also appear to overlap and interact. They are iridescent, glowing, oscillating and flooded by ethereal light, hence the dual/triple 'colour' description above. These are not just colours that we are used to, as in an artist's pallet. These are the signatures of the frequencies that determine the physical body attributes according to our Karmic blueprint. These circles that resonate at different, subtle frequencies will be forming different parts of our body, and this is the first indication of who we will be. The lighter colours indicate higher frequencies which will form our crown, our head and our connection to the above. The lower frequencies are responsible for forming our lower trunk and its connection to the 3-dimensional Earth to be born into. Our bodies slowly grow from there after the initial cell divisions repeating themselves and growing exponentially. We all have our own unique, divine 'knitting' pattern to work with, and according to this, influenced by what happens to us in the months we form in the womb, we will become the newborns that will start life on Earth. The energies intertwine and overlap, and their co-joining makes multiplication possible, intensifying into membranes, multiplying into cell mass and contents. They are at all times connected and interacting with each other, representing much the same structure as the first actual physical cells which continue to multiply and gradually shape the unborn's body, adding more mass as it becomes available through nutrients fed to the new being. The Karmic energy-body blueprint has at this stage been handed to each of the physical cells in order to form, which would look a lot like iridescent soap bubbles on an energy level if we could see them, as indicated in the microscopic, coloured image of the delicate fertilised eggs below. Of course, we can't usually see this with the naked eye, especially when they are nestled in a cosy, dark womb. The new cells are beginning to duplicate in the miraculously complex and delicate density of becoming physically manifest, whilst still being governed by sacred geometry principles.

https://scitechdaily.com/breakthrough-in-understanding-evolution-mitochondrial-division-conserved-across-species/

As already mentioned before, in order to get the new cells to form into its oblong form, yang energy pulls cells along a central channel towards the base of what will soon solidify to become the complex spinal area, and yin energy will flow towards the crown of what will become the head. The yang energy will pool around the base and pull cell mass to it to push into two separate channels for the legs to form, and then also starts to circulate in spiral motion clockwise upwards from the base of the yang channel. The yin energy will do the same in the opposite direction from its position in the centre of the cell mass and form a channel of energy that flows right to the top the skull, where it will stay open and not be covered by bone even until after the baby is born, at least for a while. The energy motion to bring in all the cellular mass needed for the structures within the brain first, then the rest of the body follows the pattern of the Torus again, as in the image below, except this time it is pulling Karmic light energy into forming a completely new life form. The Torus constantly regenerates and pulls in energy, much like a candle flame is fed by the surrounding air and the matter it consumes in order to physically manifest. If all goes well, a complete being will form, based on Earthly conditions as well as the Karmic energy blueprint. Any problems at this stage of a pregnancy, any accident, illness, introduction of toxins/chemicals/radiation may result in changes and set-backs for the unborn, either on a physical, spiritual, mental, emotional level or possibly even all four, which may in turn affect how the new being relates to the world in a variety of ways. Each week a different, very intricate phase of development takes place in the uterus, also solidifying the bond between the yang and yin principle and the growing child, which in turn is governed by the Karmic energy body the being brings with it. The theorem certainly would explain our questions about how our beautiful, perfect babies can sometimes be born sick. It may also give us the opportunity not to feel quite so much blame or guilt as parents, when we take the aspect into consideration that each being's Karmic energy body is very much responsible for co-creating the shape of the new life-form, and might hold the answers to how unforeseen circumstances and phenomena might be explained. The Karmic energy body holds all our information and adds new material to it, every second of the day. It never stops, it is always present, even if we might not be able to see it, or know what it means.

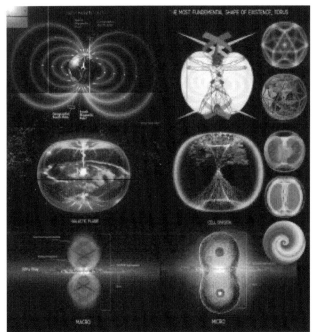

Image Credit © :https://arganesh3.wordpress.com/tag/sacred-geometry/

So, if this means that an embryo forms with the help of Karmic light energy memory playing a crucial part in the development of the growing unborn, we might also wonder if an embryo would not form without an incarnating Karmic energy blueprint. Of course I can't answer this for certain, it's simply a question to pose on a delicate subject matter. I based it on a phenomenon that has been taken into consideration by generations of certain cultures but has been completely written out of the history of others. Whilst controversial, it is in my opinion worth looking at in the context of Karmic incarnation, at least. It would then give each of us a chance to individually reflect on whether we believe in the idea, or not, and whether we want to take it on board, or not.

There are also other still unanswered questions, for example how genetics link in with our Karmic energy body. Does our Karmic energy mind that incarnates our body supervise and determine our genetics, too – possibly even all of our genetics? Or does it have part-responsibility and can steer existing genetics in a certain direction? Are the genetics that resemble us down to the infinite combinations possible in light of limitless existence, limited only by our Karmic energy body development so far as it incarnates on Earth, combined with the choice of Earth family we incarnate into? Does our Karmic energy choose its future existence in a matching Earth family, purely determined according to the laws of attraction, or does it choose the first available option as it nears its entry point on its journey back towards Earth? I deliberately pose many questions about this sensitive subject here for us to deliberate, rather than imply absolute concepts, as I feel we all have much more to find out about and contribute to the subject.

In my understanding at this moment in time, all the mystery and intricate details of creating life at a specific point in Earth time is held in our Karmic energy blueprint. However, more important than an argument whether this is right or not, and insisting that it is right or not, is remembering the reason why it is something so difficult for us to perceive or learn more about, in lack of our ability to find out more with our five senses and brain receptors alone. You might remember me mentioning several times before that our brains like practical, visible, tangible evidence, and that life is not always obliging. As a result, what our brain tends to do in situations like these, is to either decide it cannot be that important or that it is too confusing, so it will either dismiss the subject altogether as if it doesn't exist, or allows us only as much as to start arguing for or against unknown facts. Because it makes us feel threatened when we have to fight against some unknown force, we try to form groups of people who also feel threatened the same as we do, and we then try to come up with solutions of how not to feel under threat. Because the threat doesn't just go away, because we can't find ways to understand it better, we feel safe only with the groups we identify with, who all share the same beliefs. This is a very human thing to do, and all over the world we appear to do the same - nothing wrong with that. However, whilst so many of us are in this mode, we cannot easily see that there is one thing that our brain will not do: it will not override itself. It will hardly ever say, 'hey, I have no idea what to do with this information, so why don't you find a way to find out more about it, because this is where I cannot help you find the truth.' Have you noticed it never does this? It's like asking our computer to spell-check, check for content, save the programme; but also write the story for us in the first place. How can we overcome feeling helpless and fearful, if we are not sure what we are running from, or even when it all started? We can simple re-evaluate how we think and feel about a situation after a while of applying methods to calm our nerves again. can all feel fearful at times, and must voice our different experiences, but there if there are no solutions offered to make us feel safe, there is a higher risk that we are more likely to be prepared to defend ourselves against an assumed enemy whilst missing the real ones. Being at war with each other and creating a stand-off based on our different opinions, in turn based on all our limited brain perceptions, would be just as dangerous as not trying to find out more information, better methods and ways of higher perception.

In answer to many issues that present themselves on Earth, certainly when we talk about even hinting at quantum mechanics, it might simply be that our brains are not developed enough to be responsible for us finding a solution. How many situations on Earth does this apply to? And if our brains cannot know, how and where do we find the reliable 'thing' within us, which is bigger and better than our brains?

The information we receive often does not compute in our poor overworked brains, let's face it, but our brains do not like knowing that, and we don't like that they don't know. Since we pay so much attention to our brains only and at times, completely identify with everything they come up with, we also do not like to admit that we haven't fact-checked our brains. But instead of humbly admitting to the fact that we don't know everything, what happens is that humans start to overshoot and play god instead, in order to compensate for our inferiority complex. Humans tend to override that their brains do not know the answer to life by either emphasising their intellectual prowess, or going completely the other way and not bothering; and thus have come up with a perfect distraction: humans become preoccupied and obsessed with what they think they can do, in a million different ways, too many to list. Trying to replicate life, is one thing relevant to mention again at this point. I think we need a moment to let all that sink in, in its entirety.

We can probably observe that this behaviour replicates itself elsewhere, too. The danger is that we don't just end up like big children treating Earth like play school. We are playing an expensive game with glorified toys, bricks, crayons and building blocks. It could almost be cute and loveable, if the machines we are so proud of inventing as grownups were not equally imperfect in terms of their limitations, pollution and destruction. Because we are imperfect, and they are imperfect, the two combined have not made it right, at all. We have misused our chip on our shoulder to rule and kill, dominate and destroy other sentient beings. If you are thinking that is not me, then please do a quick check up on what you have bought and put in the fridge to eat later. We are all involved in this one way or another by default, and none of us can honestly say we are completely uninvolved in causing others suffering.

Some of us more than others, granted. And this is also not meant to be a guilt trip. After all, we are trying to get away from all the limitations and destruction, we want answers to our questions, we want solutions to our problems. If only we could see the Karmic energy process, if only it were more easily visible to us! Would we not then understand how delicate this process of life is? How Magick? How incomprehensibly miraculous, ourselves included? Would we stop being constantly frustrated that we cannot replicate its miracles and marvel at what is given to us as a gift with gratitude, or would we carry on exploiting, sabotaging and throwing a tantrum the size of the universe?

Let's examine what happens to us humans and why we are so loveable, kind-hearted and imperfectly cute on one hand, and so destructive and dysfunctional on another. And more importantly, why there is no time to lose to start exercising our Karmic energy resources, instead of or at least as much as we make constant use of our monkey brains.

A growing being in the womb will, under the right and fortunate circumstances, continue to develop and evolve via the fertile ground they incarnated into, this being their emerging Karmic energy field combined with the physical home on Earth that the parent(s)/guardian(s) have prepared for them. Even at this early stage, the unborn already absorbs and processes their environmental experiences emotionally, spiritually, mentally and of course physically, to be added to their own evolving Karmic energy system, according to the potential of their Karmic blueprint.

It is a mystery to me that the process of how life creates life remains such a mystery. Should we not be asking ourselves why this is? Why is this not part of our research and education, instead?

Once the yin and yang energy have commanded the pull of the initial cell mass into the elongated shape of a fully emerging foetus, the eternal flow of life-force energy becomes the incoming, bursting flow of vital source energy pushing into all the future chakra points along the torso. There, it begins to push into funnelling outwards from the body again, gradually forming all the channels and vortexes necessary for bringing the energy flow through the body from its surrounding environment, as well as all the physical matter required which is gathered and created from the mother's body through the umbilical cord and the amniotic fluid, in order to form all his or her inner physical attributes: circulatory, nervous, digestive systems, inner organs like brain, heart, skin, sensory equipment and so on, are all created in turn in this way. Just imagine for a moment if you will, what an astounding act it is, to form life in such a relatively short space of time from a combination of physical building material and our Karmic energy matrix. A good many people find the subject of pregnancy taboo or repulsive, not able to bear witness again to any of these processes that occur in relative secrecy. Perhaps some of us didn't have such a nice, Magick time in the womb ourselves that we want to remember, who knows, but it would be understandable that it's scary for some. In any case, it could be another fine example of where our brains are not really equipped to process information about the enormity of life in progress, never mind being able to truly grasp the miracle behind it. It is an astounding miracle, impossible - and not meant - to be recreated by the human brain or body, even though they do certainly have vital tasks in distributing some of the incoming energies. Sadly, though, trying to figure out the miracle - or not, as it were - has not stopped us wasting precious time, money and most of all, lives. The process of creation is so astonishingly beyond our logical comprehension that our brain constantly tries to diminish it, a flaw that is costing us dearly. Most of us still do not truly know what is going on in the world, much to the detriment of the mothers who gave us life, for example, who, let's not forget, are a necessary part of the process. But we do, we do forget. We easily take it for granted, and there are lots of cases where mothers-to-be are the most vulnerable victims of even a civilised society. We only need to look at the image of pregnancy portrayed in modern society, where women should still be attractive to the onlooker, and keep their focus on their work and status in society until the very last minute and preferably be back looking perfect again the moment they have given birth. Pregnant women often become invisible, feel unloved and uncared for, a phenomenon to be wary of; the miracle that goes on within, something shameful, hidden and forbidden. This still goes on today, despite of and perhaps even because of our modern society. An Article recently showed that the second highest cause of death in pregnant women in the U.S. is not a medical condition - it is homicide.

https://www.thespec.com/news/world/2017/09/15/

What can we do? Blame our brains and become detached from our responsibility to remain accountable for our actions we take, based on its deductions? Should we not try to improve our understanding the preciousness of life? We have so little space and time these days for learning about the magic, miracles and mysteries of the omnipresent and Karmic energies passing on their message to us. How can we, when we are busy trying to keep families, house and hearth together whilst holding down at least one job? We need to be aware again so desperately as a society.

How do we get back to where we can stand again in our aliveness, in the stream of superconsciousness?

Please allow me to go on a little detour in order to come to a conclusion and possibly even an answer.

✵ ✵ ✵

45. Karma, Existence and the Sacred Yin

In these times where the Sacred feminine principle is more unleashed than ever, when we are trying to rescue a planet thrashed by yang activity, there has never been a more pronounced time to remind ourselves of who we truly are. When we look around in society today and how pregnancy in particular is treated worldwide, it appears that we simply ignore the huge importance of support in pregnancy and for the new life that is forming. There is so much secrecy around the sacred yin principle, even to this day society likes it to remain as invisible as possible and as a result, we end up fearing it. Everyone pretends that it's business as usual and that it's all in the name of equality. And still, there is no mention of equality when we examine the wage gap between male and female employees, as well as the inadequate responses of male energy in work and home life.

As a result, women themselves find that they end up easily hating or resenting the changes happening to their bodies and parts of their pregnancy rather than revering them. For us to make a change in the way society functions, our Earth time is in the process of introducing a shift into a yin phase again. This happens periodically on Earth, where magnetic shifts in Earth's history have brought along great changes in human history, too. For some, it can't come a moment too soon.

But in order for it to happen, we must learn what the sacred yin means, and what it is asking of us.

Yin energy, as opposed to Yang which has dominated Earth time for a few thousand years now, is more passive and receptive. It is a principle that permeates all on Earth, responsible for times when we feel we need to be dormant and nurturing ourselves. Many of us, however, have not learned how to do this, and will end up ignoring or even abusing the principles of yin, as it could easily be misconstrued to be weak and passive. It is not. It is equally as strong a force as the yang, just like we would not give meaning to negative and positive charges on an electric current. We can use both wisely, and get to know their influence on us accordingly. Very often, a pregnancy will call on women's yin energy in order to be able to go inwards and figure out the changes that are occurring, rest instead of overdo things, be gentle with themselves and their unborn instead of being made to feel that they still need to hold down three jobs to be worthy.

Yin energy is the opposite of yang energy, and we will feel as much when there are regular phases in our lives when we are all subjected to it. As in the black & white circular diagram that most people know, yin retains an aspect of yang and vice versa. The energies are often attributed to males and females, but this is far too simplistic and does not take into consideration that everyone experiences yin and yang phases within themselves during their lifetime. However, one of the most prevalent yin phases that occurs, can coincide with a pregnancy.

Sadly, because our society prefers people to be yang and outgoing, work- and sports-orientated, active, go-getting and dominant. Yin energy is more passive, associated with quiet, calm and dark, i.e. inward-looking phases. Sadly, pregnant women often end up feeling disempowered and abandoned when yin energy hits them; instead of being physically active like they used to be, they feel sick, scared and hormonal under the tremendous pressure from a detached and hateful modern world to look, feel and dress a certain way to even conceal their bumps, to still look attractive and available, work all hours to contribute to a commercial world, not put any weight on, not change - and still behave as if nothing is happening, as if their world is not completely changing within. I despair sometimes at how insensitive and ignorant to mother and baby the world has become. Women become birthing machines in some places, are abused in others, have to go into hiding for fear of being killed or are mentally, emotionally or physically tortured for their choices in pregnancy, childbirth and throughout motherhood; they are deprived of their livelihood and forced back into earning money far too soon, regardless of the miracles they have just been able to perform. These are simply downplayed, as if to say 'hey, what makes it so special, it's just what women do'. There is no prize for making the miracle possible. Is there a jealousy that women can perform these miracles, despite how hard it is, how uncertain, scary, painful and exhausting? Is this part of the reason we are no longer able to value it, taking it for granted? Perhaps it's simply that others who haven't had that experience can't relate, or won't. Or is it perhaps because of it, women have been discriminated against, cast as and become the Mary Magdalens or the Mother Mary's of the modern world, saints or sinners of human evolution, nothing in between and little chance to connect with their tribe and find themselves again.

An honouring would be nice, of the mother, the baby, the process, returning to a feeling of safety for the vulnerable, a skill we have forgotten to perform in thousands of yang-dominant years on Earth. But times are changing: we have entered a new era of yin energy which will become more apparent, prevalent and predominant, over the next foreseeable future. This is just the beginning, reminding ourselves of the miracles of life, the preciousness of existence, honouring and cherishing the sacred feminine. We will receive joy and gratitude, for every living being who incarnates and also those who are not and remain connected to us from afar. It is still customary in some tribes, to welcome new babies with songs, and have name-giving ceremonies according to the baby's energy, by the whole tribe. New beings are honoured, welcomed and protected into life by all who surround them.

How far removed, in our modern world, has having a baby become? Has it become a some-thing in some modern social circles, an optional extra, a some-thing that one loses money over and discusses the amount of maternity leave, calculates affordability and time frames; an event to buy things for, a social talking point to connect with others, to feel estranged from and become depressed over, since it no longer easily fits into the social environments and habits we created for ourselves. As a result, parents believe in advice to separate from their babies as soon as possible, handing over their babies to formulae mostly at a few months old, a lonely crib at the end of a corridor with doors shut to preserve the privacy of our adult privileges under the guise of being told we are doing what's best for baby. Nurseries, child care and state schools are more and more readily and unquestioningly sought, and become involved as third party carers at ever earlier stages in our new being's Magick days, without seeing the dis-connect and discontinuation it creates on the isolated ground we are choosing for the souls of this next generation on Earth, the ones bearing the sour fruit of the dystopia we are no longer able to resolve.

How can we possibly relate to what happens, and what to do when a new being is called in, if we cannot remember experiencing it ourselves? How can we prepare for a natural event in its breath-taking, humbling, regenerating, ecstatic awesome rawness, which no word can describe and every parent experiences differently?

And yet, most would agree that there is nothing that prepares us for the reconnection with life that we will feel - how nothing will ever be the same afterwards. Consciously witnessing the birth of the children of our tribe, we have the unique opportunity of seeing the universe in action, and although circumstances are sometimes far from ideal, the process is hardly ever one we can ignore.

Let's have a closer look again, as to what happens next from a Karmic perspective.

For the mother to give birth, for baby to be born healthy and survive, everything must start again at point zero, from the moment of baby drawing first breath outside the womb. Energy has been pumped through mother and baby's system at high velocity to facilitate the birthing and ascertain the new life's survival. The new spiral of a beginning lifetime starts with the birth moment of first drawing breath. The spiral of the baby's inner Karmic energy that has been developing in the womb is now co-joined with the Karmic spiral of a new life drawing their own breath from their new environment. It is a point that is not often recognised as such: the singularity of a beginning, the focus of all the energies situated in one single point in time, this point being the beginning of a new life. All its inherited material can be downloaded into the separate new being from then on, combined with all of the new experiences of being a new breathing body on Earth. Let's have a look at a spiral with a singular point at its base and beginning point.

The starting point of a spiral can be seen as the beginning moment of a human life

This is the point of the new life beginning to breathe - which is a spinning point of concentrated energy that pushes out from baby for the first time. The energy will then continue to spiral in very small but very fast and tiny, tight circular turns in upward motion to allow this being to develop incredibly swiftly, ascertain its survival, bringing it to life and nourishment in order to maintain its beginning life-cycle. Everything stops for a moment, even the clock sometimes. These are the first seconds, minutes & hours of a new-born. They are absolutely crucial points for a new being and how they connect to their mother, as well as their first experience of their new external environment. I speak of the birth mother first as an honour to her, but, of course, fathers, birth partners, carers, family members, adoptive parents are included in the process, too - they will all be able to instinctively feel and recognise the importance of this first moment, the beginning of the baby's spiral of existence and can interpret it intuitively. After all, this very moment is recorded in many countries as the entry point of a new life, complete with date, time and place of birth. That moment is very emotional for many parents and those witnessing. Even in hospitals, many birth centres nowadays place the baby with the mother first and foremost, wherever possible, to feed, lie skin to skin as the baby has been used to and continue the warm smell of familiarity, but then also to be held by both parents, or the father or birth partner if present whilst the mother needs care. This is a natural bonding instinct to keep offspring close to the skin and safe, also seen to be present in many animal species, ensuring the survival of species. Hormones have prepared many mothers' bodies for this moment, and despite such intensity and interventions during pregnancy and labour, many mothers will have their instincts intact enough to hold their baby close immediately. Most will feel how crucial it is to have as little intervention as possible in these very first moments and the times thereafter. Everything can stop for a moment, if possible. It must. Everyone around would be able to feel it and honour it, too. This moment is reserved for baby to arrive here on Earth and feel welcome from the first seconds onwards; to establish their Karmic energy as well as the physical, to have arrived in a safe environment, even better when in the arms of a caring and conscious being. A sympathetic environment created in order for parent(s) and child(ren) to feel safe and allow themselves to be gentle in those special moments, for their bonding time to be respected, is luckily becoming more common practice. Not so long ago, it was common practice to slap a baby to make them cry and then whisk them off to be washed, tightly bound in wads of cotton, placed in a plastic tub and be presented at 4-hourly intervals behind a glass screen, crying for their mums to feed them. What a difference it makes, to instead set the scene for new life to be cherished and to encourage and protect these precious moments, for every single sentient being on Earth included.

Meanwhile, the Karmic energy spiral has started to make tight little turns and create new Karma in this bright beginning for the newborn outside the womb. Already at the initial first breath and the welcome into safe arms, the 'I AM' presence is reaffirmed and invited in, too. The baby's inner presence and Karmic consciousness can this way be established to remain intact and united with them in physical presence, and long may it continue. Many mothers choose home births to have a more intimate experience with their newborn and partner, and choose to have baby stay close to their skin at all times without interruption so that there is no separation anxiety that arises for the tiny new life. If at any point any of the instinctive rituals to make baby feel safe and close by are not possible, for example for medical reasons, these can be repeated at a later stage. Even hospital practice will often recognise support close contact right after birth nowadays to support and encourage bonding with the newborn. It really does make a difference to do it sooner rather than later, but this isn't meant to upset any new parent who, for whatever reason, has not had a chance to make contact for the first moments. If there are challenges, the parent(s) will already be aware enough of how it feels to be separate from their newborn, there is nothing that describes that feeling, making it even more viable to propose that our every instinct should be respected as much as possible, as it is, indeed, important to be as close as possible. The only thing more important is to always make sure that mother and baby are well, and we can also be grateful for the good Karma of having good care around us to ascertain this.

The baby's full Karmic matrix blueprint of their past represented an inverted Karmic
energy spiral in the womb around them, which has been pushing baby into its converging, singular point during late stages of pregnancy and then labour. At the moment of birth, a new spiral time-line begins to unfurl from the point of the old, opening up into the opposite direction, keeping hold of all past memory but also opening up to all the new potential for its future life.

Image Credit © https://mathcurve.com/courbes3d/spiraleconic/spiralconic0b.jpg

The Top Karmic Spiral surrounds baby in womb, influencing their growth and development, helping physical processes into manifestation from energy and also pushing baby downwards in labour and during birth. Birth point is at smallest point of both spirals connecting, then opening up the new Karmic light spiral for the foreseen life-time (at bottom) at newborns first breath. The top spiral remains open for some time to the newborn into childhood, as they remain open and connected to their universal origins and are therefore much more open to memories from past lives as well as universal observation.

As we can probably imagine, a lot of energy exchanges and expels during birth, culminating in the act of baby's taking first breath. This is the point where the 'before zero' Karma meets with the newborn Karmic being that is about to develop into a physical adventure. What an amazing moment! Everyone who is involved usually feels this moment, overwhelmed with tears and awe for witnessing the enormity of the presence of life. We meet and witness a universal being having just come into physical existence from a universe based on energy and unmanifested potential!

Since I was fortunate enough to experience this for myself, I will talk a little about my own perceptions from those times. I remember feeling this overwhelming feeling of happiness, of indescribable and joy when looking at and holding my daughters and my grandson in my arms for the first time. The universe shone in their eyes and despite the physical endurance, I counted myself to be the luckiest in the world, as they were all thankfully beautifully awake. I got this sensation that they were all here with complete knowledge of where they had just come from, honoured guests from an all-knowing place so vast that our limited 3-d perception made us forget how to link in with it, and they had come to remind me. I also sensed the spiral, the dense and tiny movements like the unfurling balance spring of a clock. Everything our babies are to experience in this wide-open state of mind is an important part of setting the scene for the rest of their lives. I felt protectiveness beyond human measure, in perfect relation and response to what a baby must be experiencing and needing at that time: ideally, for a baby to thrive on all levels, their Karmic spiral has the potential to manifest everything to be as agreeable as possible; it reminds us that the omnipresence in its ultimate compassion strives for there to be the potential of every circumstance of every being to be ideal; even if physical conditions cannot always translate this universal love into a perfect scenario for all human beings. Good Karma would ensure that the potential and strive for good conditions be largely fulfilled. I felt in the past that this was not just a theoretical potential or mathematical probability, but something I wished to be able to assist with all of my being. The overwhelming feeling of love flooding through for our children in this bonding process instructed me to create this for my children. It was so intense a feeling, that I would make a vow to do anything at all to make it the easiest, most loving, most beautiful experience for them, still to this day - and for others, too. I fought very hard for that bonding process to continue uninterrupted. I felt that there was not much room for error, that everything was crucial for the survival of all Karmic energy to remain intact and unharmed. I felt it, and I knew it to be truth. I believe that it is truly meant for us, through our live Karmic links with the greatest potential of life on Earth, to be able to feel protected and supported enough to continue to act and feel like this in a baby's first moments, days, weeks. This is what the yin energy is capable of, despite being the 'passive', allowing, letting-in, flowing, intuitive feminine divine energy, it can also be superbly strong. Who needs to move mountains when we can make babies grow overnight?

How on Earth we justify hurting any mother or baby at these sacred moments in time, is still beyond me. If anyone went through the endurance of and bore witness to this sacred, delicate, powerful and yet oh so vulnerable point in time, would they not do anything to preserve it? Why is there such a tangible force on Earth that tries to destroy, diminish, denounce and disconnect us from it? It is very true that all possibilities exist here on Earth, and all have been explored, so it's probably more a rhetorical question that I am asking. When we know the outcome of committing to life, and our vow to give our utmost care and attention to life already, what is there to improve upon? We will have our hands full taking care of all those who need us, as well as learning to be more skilful all the time as we go along. Should we be dissecting, experimenting, dismembering, killing - that which we will never be able to recreate? There is nothing that can stop our Karma from wanting to protect those we love, and yet there is every conceivable atrocity present that has occurred somewhere on Earth to try and destroy it, often with devastating effects, every day. Surely, even those who wish to harm were once born. What terrible things were done to them, what atrocities did they endure and witness, what awful Karma did they bring with them so that they would turn out so disconnected to life? Could they not be reconnected, too, despite all the anguish they must have experienced to become so derailed? As alive beings, as parents, we have a natural instinct to do anything to protect our children, but it has also become blatantly obvious that this instinct can be easily destroyed through actions against us, causing long-term harm, stress and fear. If pain and suffering is already inflicted upon our babies from early on, in the belief that they won't recall anything that happened to them at an early age, how can they have a chance to grow up healthily in mind, body and spirit? How can they ever properly recover from what has been done to them? It seems that many reports are coming to the surface of child abuse, neglect and deaths. A baby's conscious attention span at the moment of birth is only a few seconds, and in those few seconds the baby takes in all of the environment, all of the love, the good, the bad, the ugly, unfiltered by any deliberation process, which does not exist yet and won't for some time. A baby's brain is not ready yet to reason and distinguish, however, a baby's Karmic energy body is absolutely fully developed and present. This is what is pushing energy through the tiny body to make it grow on its spiral journey through physical existence. Asleep or awake, every moment after birth, they have to be nurtured and cared for at the breakneck speed the tiny inner movements of their spiral clock demand. This is the crucial, most sensitive and vulnerable start of Earth time and space for this and all beings on Earth, and at the same time also their chance of receiving help for the greatest potential of their Karmic completion. What looks so tranquil and peaceful to a bystander watching a baby fast asleep, is an incredible inner journey for the baby: he or she has to adjust at lightning speed to an environment entirely new to them; they have to grow very quickly, or the alternative is not to thrive and fall behind or even ill on some level at a precarious time of their development that would have a knock-on effect on their future well-being. All life has a Karmic potential and urge to thrive and will do its utmost to do so. But what if needs are not met on a physical level? What if the demands are not understood and misinterpreted, and conditions are far from ideal? How often is a pregnancy, a birth, the seconds - minutes, hours, days, weeks, months, years - after birth not under ideal circumstances? This is where the baby's past history logged in their Karmic energy body co-creates circumstances with everyone who interacts with them in their lives. I believe I spoke about the hypothesis earlier, that the Karmic energy stored in their energy memory might well play a part in what happens to them from conception onwards. However, this cannot serve as an excuse. Who knows if they chose us as parents, because we would be the perfect choice for them to grow up with? We will not be able to know what their Karmic information is, we don't know how it affects our children, but we can do our very best to vow to take good care of and protect them with all that we have, to steer them in the right direction.

And so, the baby's inner spiral energy opening up determines for the new-born to adapt and thrive on all levels and at breakneck speed, which has parents up all day and all night feeding, nurturing, cradling, soothing, bathing and lovingly, exhaustedly caring for their babies as best – and as fast - as they can. The energy spiral that parents sense an urgency to respond to, is reflected in their instincts to get their skates on. A babies cry for help is genuine, always, and parents must quickly learn to respond under huge pressure. We become doctors, nurses, athletes, security night staff, soldiers and so much more, overnight. All those parental instincts are well considered correct, as they are often the only reliable source to pick up on a baby's state of health on many levels. As a society, we would be wise to respect and support parents' efforts and their instinctual desire to nurture the next generation. These valuable instincts, however strong, are also fragile and easily bent under stress. All of the Earth's community has a duty to keep them as intact as possible, as the parents of a new-born are doing their utmost to sense and pick up things about their babies and this new generation with their heightened sensitivities that affect the whole population. Our Earth tribe should be our safety net for the ever-increasing numbers of nuclear and single-parent families. In days long gone, it used to include guardians, elders, protectors as well as all other family members who would also become very tuned in to the needs of the new family unit and take pride in becoming involved in the next generation, seeing the continuation of the ancestral tribes and their efforts bear fruit. We can only guess why this is not encouraged further in our society, but we have certainly suffered an almost complete break-down of our community at some point. We had thriving communities everywhere, not that long ago, before a greed for commerce took over in the last 4 decades. That's not that long, really, and perhaps there is still time to recreate what we still remember to have had. Perhaps they still exist and are evolving elsewhere, away from the threat that it would be to the detriment of our children to grow up with the potential of being violated. Perhaps that's one good reason why we are keeping our families safe and close by, and yet, we have also to deal with domestic violence and child abuse rife in families, so that hasn't really worked, either. The issues we face on a daily basis are, again, hidden as if it's something shameful, under the guise that families' choices and preferences should remain a secret struggle of some kind. At least this is not something that we originally did as tribes and communities on Earth, where we talked to each other before everything became modernised, industrialised and technological, and virtual reality turned into a minefield of division even amongst good, and certainly the not so good, people.

I wonder if our minds, bodies, spirits and Karmic energy minds actually thrive on the isolated environments and nuclear family set-ups we now have to deal with in our lifestyles. Perhaps it's now more visible and inevitable than ever to observe that anything on Earth co-exists, from one extreme to another, with all the grey areas between and it seems there isn't any scenario that hasn't already been presenting at this time on Earth?.Crazy as well as sane, all living next door to each other, in closer proximity than we might think.

I am expressing it like this, being fully aware that you can read between the lines. What happens if things go wrong? When circumstances are far from ideal; when babies are not cared for; when health issues arise; when nurturing is not on the agenda; when outside influences interfere with the process of taking care of families in need; when actual harm is done, threatening parent or child; when there is a host of circumstances conspiring to separate babies and children from their parents? We are all aware there are forces which can and will work against parents and their children, too many to mention even, and I am trying my Best not to ignore them here. However, I also want to remind us of the miracle right in front of us, and point out the immensity of the enormously powerful energy bond that has been created amongst us humans. We could start to notice, value and work with it more, as it needs preserving, or else human life on this planet will be in more danger than ever. This bond has always one of our biggest strengths to keep us alive and looked after, to make us feel connected and validated. This is life, real, pure life, not one we have created on-screen with the imagination of limited capacity making us into Avatars we could already be, if we had spent time and applied methods to see our full potential. We are already on full capacity, right here, right now - let's make that more visible so it shows itself to us, so we have proof, so we know what we are working with: It is this life, our aliveness, so strongly present that it can help us find many answers to our questions; through our children and their Karmic connection to us, our own parentage, our ancestors, fellow humans and yes, all living non-human beings are also included. All. 'All' is a big word, is it not? It takes a while to sink in that the Karmic energy we have been talking about, is all-encompassing, and wants us to be reminded that we are, too.

Children also teach us all the time, of what it felt like to be open, before our energy connections became blurred, and I hope and pray we will not lose or be deprived of the ability and privilege to learn from our children and accept our Karmic task to protect and nurture their vulnerable lives, including their presence to their and others' Karmic energy.

As much as this is ever possible, as I described above, we are here to guard them, ourselves and everyone else we can have an impact on, to make sure that all our Karmic energy bodies and minds develop as well as possible to allow us to grow into amazing beings, representing the miracles that humankind is capable of co-creating. We are miracles bonded into existence, as a result of the alchemy of transforming universal energy into physical life form. How this ability is so overlooked, taken for granted, under-acknowledged, abused, sneered at, ridiculed, poisoned, ruined, dissected dismissed made more difficult for all in the midst of making the most of at times terrible trauma – again, it leaves me speechless at times. We cannot be blamed for thinking that there is this force out there up to no good, trying to undermine our efforts. If it exists, it is, in my opinion, not even a force that is inherent to the goodness in us. I believe in the good in people, but as we have seen, our brains can easily be taken in by outside influences who will have it commandeer and compromise our thoughts, but I cannot for one moment believe that we are here to be and do evil. We are here to get over it, and find help to do so.

I can only assume it is another characteristic of Karmic energy that there is sometimes very little of it freely available within some beings to help them think, feel and act wisely, thoughtfully and with reverence for life. Perhaps they were never shown yet how to truly cherish life, perhaps they lost their freedom to do so on account of their wrongful actions; alternatively, the accumulation of their wrong actions may have lost them the ability to see the preciousness of life until such time when what good Karma there is left has made them see sense. In short, positively charged Karmic energy can turn around the lack of connection with their compassionate minds. The more there is of it, the better. The sooner we start accumulating good Karma coins, we can cash them in against some of the bad deeds we might be accused of having done. In any case, the destructive pattern that has taken someone over as a result, can and must be broken, in order to stop the continuation of what-

ever has captured their Karmic energy and held it hostage. I am not saying this sentence lightly, when we are all fully aware we have terrible acts of violence happen on Earth, and we still have people in charge so disconnected that they think it feasible to have the power to annihilate all of us at the push of a button. At the end of the day, this is what it comes down to: if and when we are disconnected from the reminders of our Karmic energy mind to act with compassion and wisdom, if we are running the show on autopilot, we are in danger of making all the wrong decisions. Worse, we can actually believe ourselves when we rationalise the notion that we deem ourselves in charge of other beings to decide whether they live or die, are healthy or sick, rich or poor. At that point, we are all in grave danger, and I believe just the threat of this being so makes many people live in fear. It should already be taken as an act of violence against people but hey, it's being done 'for protection', so that's ok then. We might think we are immune to it, but any of us living on Earth are subject to the same duress, some perhaps more than others. Perhaps we always have been, right back to where humankind started. But none of us can be singled out to not be capable of setting a foot wrong. We are vulnerable to deception, sometimes even our own, and therefore should be aware of the fact that a good practice that helps us stay connected will be the best protection we can exercise on Earth – not just against others who wish us harm, but our own inner wiring going wrong so we never again would have to find ourselves lowering our Karmic frequency so much that we are in danger of committing atrocities ourselves. f we believe that could never happen, we just have to read accounts of what humans are capable of when being manipulated into thinking it's all ok, when under pressure, when sick, overtired, in pain, intoxicated, or have their freedoms taken away. Let's also not forget the Milgram experiment of 1961, which showed that ordinary people who were placed in front of a glass window looking into another room showing a person strapped to a device able to inflict pain, they could be convinced to inflict pain on that person in the other room by being told that they should turn up a dial. Even when they could see through the window that it was hurting that person, they still followed orders and kept turning up the dial to do as they were told. It was a truly sobering experiment that still affects the study of mankind and how we react to each other today.
https://www.dailymail.co.uk/sciencetech/article-4312792/Most-people-hurt-told-authority.html
Alternatively, we just have to look on social media and know what humankind is capable of.

Even in more favourable conditions when our Karmic energy does get to incarnate in a more apparently glorious human form, there appears to be much of a time line of practising our reconnection for many of us, before compassion and wisdom sets in again, with of course some exceptional beings who are already born extremely wise and able to apply their wisdom in the highest principled ways. Would it not be interesting to know where our Karmic energy mind is at, become aware of its power and how to use it wisely early on in life? Would it not be equally useful to know the pitfalls and weaknesses in our set-ups as soon as we are ready and willing to see them, so we can be aided to make better decisions for ourselves and others we are involved with? Why are we left to be fending for ourselves for such a big part of our lives, which could be lived more happily and blissfully? Should these not be the questions that we must ask, in order to perhaps find out how we got so disconnected in the first place? I see a strong link between some practices in child rearing, to how our childhood will affect us in the long run. If we are looking after our babies, we experience and give back our love in return, the essential every-day component to cope with what our future brings. If we are persuaded or even forced to not connect to our children for large parts of their early years, then we will be affected by that in later life, as will they, without a shadow of a doubt. Why does nobody tell us this fact? Are we too polite in saying it how it is, for fear of upsetting the freedom we all have to choose what we want? If we all crave freedom of choice, to do as we please, why don't we apply the same to our children? Why do we treat them as second-class citizens, and still do things to them that are most regrettable, with there not being any freedom of choice for them, just so we can have it? We still put out there that children will not remember the first few years of their lives, and use that notion to disconnect from them. This is something that was put out there by those we may want to question. Were we ourselves children that were ignored, left behind, abandoned - and we are subconsciously just repeating the pattern until we realise how much we are hurting, trying to have our 'freedom'? We may not realise it, but we might have been set up, and this set-up has set us as well as our children up for more generations of issues in later life, all over again. That's very sad, and other places on Earth where the close contact between parents and their children is still intact, are watching on, wondering when we will realise we are being sold so many lies, and how poorly the state of our culture is, as a result.

We can quite possibly deduct that, if a human being has not had the necessary care and compassion extended to them at crucial developmental points in their Karmic existence, that this being might suffer considerably more than others on many levels and find it virtually impossible to feel well. Added to this,

We cannot simply brush off others' suffering

by reasoning that their Karma is bad and that they deserve to suffer.

This is what we do, though, every day, due to not feeling connected ourselves. Have you noticed? Why do we do this? This knowledge that we have been talking about, that has been hidden away, should be commonly available for all of us to utilise and not subject to a psychology degree. It is not that hard to remember as we have done it many times before. Everyone can do it, and everyone has a right to know and learn how best to exercise these insights. They don't all have to appear in the latest Marvel movie. The repercussions of not having an opportunity to learn and apply any of this in this very lifetime, are devastatingly obvious all over the planet. A vicious cycle ensues, the cycle of samsaric existence. It is most regrettable that we do not learn about these connections in our everyday education, in fact, it seems that it is kept from us at all costs. Let us all conveniently become labelled in a way that suits commerce. Consumers, tax payers, labourers, work force, key workers. We are being removed from our true Selves. How else can we explain that there are beings who suffer? Beings who suffered for lifetimes before, are, like us, climbing slowly on their own path of recognition and enlightenment. Is there really a god who punishes us or them or is it simply our stuck inner energy which keeps re-running the same tune like a broken record? If this is so, there would be no good that comes from punishing ourselves or anyone else further. We could instead help them to see, to understand, to become their true selves again, and at least refrain from making them suffer even more. We must not exclude ourselves and do the same for ourselves! How else can we stop suffering if we do not yet know how to, if we have not been shown, have forgotten, have estranged ourselves from 'others' who are a part of us? How can we rediscover our strengths, our potential to heal and bring about good outcomes, when we ourselves have been compromised?

A good way out of the maze is to learn to gather the wisdom of how to detect the nature of our inner Karmic energies to unlock our strengths again, whilst extending our compassion to all beings who need to be released from suffering. It does not sound exciting but I promise you, it is one of the most rewarding journeys you will ever make. The rest can and will then take care of itself.

Image Credit © https://78notes.blogspot.com/2017/02/the-spiral-world.html

When we realise that the best time to do all of the above is now, then we also know that the best time to start taking care of a being to make them feel wanted, cherished, loved, connected, cared for and nurtured is right at the start of their early life. When we understand this simple logic, then we have already recognised more than most. To observe a delicate human form starting as a tiny baby, and how quickly they have to try to grow, determined once again by the Fibonacci spiral principle that underlies our Karmic energy body to allow cells to grow exponentially to make the survival of a new being more viable. Babies immune systems have to develop, so do their senses, their eyesight, their body strength, and they need help with all of it instead of being ignored in the corner somewhere until they are bigger. If this round the clock care did not happen for us, then we will still have to find it in our lifetimes, with the help of connecting to other sources which hold wisdom and ways to complete us. We may have missed out altogether on a caring mother or father, and spend half our lives trying to recreate that missing element of love. You can see how important it is to take care of our children, in fact, everyone around us. In all the medical books I scoured in Oxford twenty years ago, I did not find any connection mentioned between the development of a baby and the sacred energy patterns that create life – fancy that. Luckily, we do have the frequency of web connections these days, which can be used to reciprocally enlighten each other if we find literature on any subject, and much of the research material which I have combined with my inner wisdom mind is available out there in some form or other for further research. Slowly but surely, there are people who gather these principles depicted here and elsewhere, and are starting to format them into moving images. It's certainly on my bucket list to make a movie of the book. Luckily, instead of just writing words, we have by now the use of the limited, more feasible form of freely available screenings, which have entered many households in combination with electronics and binary code as carriers to assist us to communicate and connect for the highest good, whilst we are still honing our telepathic skills and perfecting our inner unity consciousness. Times are not far away when everyone who can afford it will be walking around with an inner computer chip and their own holographic projector screen in front of their eyes, with all information loaded up so that we will be able to hear it as well as see it, under the guise of giving us directions, be able to drive vehicles without steering via voice command, helping with driving, recreational activities, communication, shopping, food preparation and so on. This will be the future, a no-touch future generation where we are isolating even more on a physical plane and yet are simulated the image of others before our eyes who we choose to speak to even if we have never met and probably never will, so that the feeling that we have them close will be simulated for us. VR won't be a black box in front of our face, it will be clear and invisible, as well as interactive with our environment. Oh people will love it, and be completely unaware or not care whether all of their moves are monitored and any fine or personal restrictions can also be administered from afar. All I am asking is: who will look after our babies when we have become so removed and been led to believe we are toxic to them? You might think I am crazy right now, but maybe in a couple of decades we will change your mind when we realise it is already happening and we are paying good money for being had, too.

Whilst editing, we are all aware already that there are by now plenty of images and video clips available online to back up what I started to transfigure into Western speak, all those years ago. I am also aware that several techniques to counteract some of the ill-effects of some the above into consideration, which I mention at the end of the book. Sometimes all we have to do is ask, and the answers will be shown, especially as we become more adept again at being in tune with our greatest good.

The purpose of our lives on Earth is also to reconnect with the perfect harmonic blueprint that is laid out in the sacred geometry patterns we are born in sync with. The sacred patterns appear to be based around the 3's: In the first three seconds, a baby takes their breath; three minutes, and baby is reconnected with the Karmic energy body; in the first three hours, they are learning to connect to their parents and family, to bond to their first external connection in this new physical existence. Three days later and the baby starts to develop vital immune defences against many viruses, bacteria and diseases, coinciding beautifully with the mother's rhythm of three days of colostrum being produced, a special fluid for her baby, transmitting the perfect matrix for the best potential immune system for the new life. The tiny body is trying to regulate all functions such as assimilating air in their lungs to breathe instead of fluid, and fluid to ingest as food via their mouths by using instincts for suckling nutrients from an external source for the first time in this body. Hormones are still released via the mother's body to regulate baby's functions rather than assimilated by the baby themselves, helping them to develop and grow, regulated by the baby's Karmic matrix and growing energy vortexes along its stretching body, responsible for the first time for the growth of the glands as well as all other all of the new cell growth. As an example of a baby's spiral developmental ascension, by 27 days, baby can put on half their birth weight, and by 81 days their weight can be doubled. All are crucial development points of reference in the baby's calendar, not just connected to weight, but their own Karmic energy development potential along the points where the spiral turns around itself again on the next biggest loop, aligning and growing in body and brain mass according to the Fibonacci principle. Below is an interesting website giving information about the subject, and many more.

http://www.visembryo.com/baby/index.html

As we found out before, these spiral alignments happen in all our lives regularly, they are major points of development and also serve as check points, so to speak, to see if everything is going well and according to plan, so that it can be built on and the next level of comprehension and stage of development initiated. All the while, the Karmic energy body is constantly streaming energy flow into the new being. All beings have this in common. Their Karmic energy never stops growing cell structures unless something deteriorates in the physical realm, and it is already having a determining role in whether baby is having the good Karma of round-the clock care, whether nurtured and held, or the opposite. Whether baby will grow up with birth parents or not, will be a highly complex and convoluted amount of combined Karmic energy information of his or her own Karma combined with that of its parents and family ancestors.

The Karmic energy systems of children are able to overlap with their parents' for most of their childhood and adolescence, too, especially when the bond between them was established right from the beginning and continued throughout the first 3-7 years without breaking off the bond. Although at some point comes a time when usually the child's energy spiral start to break away from the hosting of the parents' protective energies around their offspring, the spirals can remain intertwined for lifetimes. How they will develop mentally, emotionally and physically as well as cope with life in future, is largely down to all the myriad of connective energy synopses built during their past lives and present love and care. It's not uncommon for children who grow up in conscious families aware of the energy bonds to feel a lot more secure and become more caring and compassionate as a result. Knowing this, it is perhaps easier to follow the conclusion we already made as to why we don't always get 'instant' Karma: if there are energy forces that were built up or not, as it were, before our spiral existence in this life, then they can still influence our lives accordingly in the present and in future. I often speak about Generation Karma, Ancestral and Family Karma, too, as all of it interlinks with our own. We have influences in our life spirals that do not stem from our own experiences necessarily, but also overlap and intertwine with those of our ancestral upline and past Karmic connections. It will be useful for us to know that it exists, even if it can be a very complex undertaking to tell them all apart. What we need to know is that we can untangle all this and start to see clearly enough again to know there is a difference between being caught up in it and being able to be responsible for recognising our role in it, whether we want to accept it or not, change it to improve on it, for the benefit of all of those who are involved.

Image credit © :http://drlindagadbois.com/reincarnation-souls-journey-time-holographic-nature-reality-illusion-time/

As already said, once a being is incarnate, his or her own Kundalini energy body becomes host again to the inter-dimensional spiral Karmic energy, which is what connects all beings to their source of universal energy life force. Circulating up along the spine and out above the top of our heads, our Kundalini energy gathers all-encompassing energy as it exits our body and enters the realms above and beyond us, able to connect with the highest frequencies beyond the dimensions we are accustomed to. On those levels, the energy can unconditionally 'clear our minds', so to speak. Our energies are cleansed and purified, healed and mended on very high frequency levels, where miracles are made. The matrix that exists in those realms is able to repair even some more major damage that has occurred, and this is how miracle healing can take place as is meant, according to each being's Karmic agreement. The potential is there for more energy to be added and if our Karmic energy body recognises it, it will bring energy back into our body, with the help of which we can reset aspects of our bodies including emotions, thoughts and memory codings. This is probably a good point to mention what happens at those moments in time which coincide with little chinks in our Karmic spiral, those where our energy dips and we need to be alert enough to try to mend them. Because ultimately, that is all they are, little nicks in our spiral energy path, stumbling stones that need to be smoothed out. If you see the images above and imagine there are little cuts along the rungs of our spiral ladder, then you will have a visual idea of where we need to learn to bridge these energy gaps. If we don't, we will presented with them again, on another rung of the ladder. If we do, they can be removed from our Karmic path and remain repaired permanently. We can also broaden our consciousness and learn from certain encoded information that is given to us from those realms. Once our Karmic energy has re-entered our crown in its refreshed form, it spirals downward again into our body along the spine with all new coding, renewing our energy resources as it moves along and in and out of the main chakras along the torso, too. The frequency, quality, velocity and benefit of the newly charged energy entirely depends on the situation and timing for each individual as well as their level of accomplishment, i.e. their ability to practice patience, perseverance and clarity in order to allow the energy to flow through. We are host to this miracle of all miracles, and this is a chapter we might want to read again and again, to remind ourselves what can and does happen to us, and how we can assist and refine it. This is where we hold our lives and our health in our hands. We can learn methods to allow the energy to flow through, and our focus on this will be immensely valuable at any stage of our Karmic development.

As the energy spirals downwards along the spine, it will connect through our base chakra vortex down towards the Earth energies below our torso. There is an opportunity to deeply connect to the Earth energies, bringing back upwards into our bodies all the knowledge of its nourishment that is offered to us freely, as well as knowledge of the ancients, the sacred secrets of the Earth and its waters, its precious minerals amid the mysteries and synergy of learning how to grow in harmony with nature.

And so it continues - our ever-lasting spiral motion of inter-dimensional Karmic energy stretches ever upwards and outwards into the universe and beyond, being all present, to converge all our available energy again at a choice moment into a single point to form the Karmic light seed for our new body, the beginning of a new physical life. Our Karmic energy also creates our spiral Karmic time-line which determines the 'illusion' if you will, of each individual human travelling separately on their journey through space and time. There is also a spiral Karmic timeline for all collective alive beings as well as the Earth and the Universe, resembling a spiral funnel opening outwards into timeless existence. Both individual and universal time lines are connected, simply because we share the same elements, occupy the same space and coincide partly in times of our life spans. We are puppets on a spiral string on the stage of physical existence, and we are all connected in a giant play that never ends. When this stage eventually collapses, there will be another. And if we find this a daunting thought, remember that we are all made of space dust, we are shape shifters and we are all eternal.

The four anchor points on Earth which we have named East, West, South and North, are the equal-sided cross in the geometry of the 3rd dimension, appearing everywhere on diagrams, maps and directions to guide us through life on a relatively minute scale only. The anchor points are all relative and do not exist as we see them on Earth outside the realm of the third dimension. They are small co-ordinates as temporary guideline components on Earth, but of not much use to us in the vast expanding geometrical structure of the universe. Nevertheless, there is meaning to these four directions on Earth, and in many religions, myths, Magick and legends, the image and meaning of the cross point at the centre and four arms radiating out have been used as a protective and centring element. The double Vajra in Buddhist and Hindu imagery, for example, beautifully endorsed and depicted as containing the sacred and treasured elements of yin and yang, male and female energy, reminds me of the point zero that I talked about earlier, the singularity marking a miraculous but much ignored point in time that has no beginning and no end, an entry point, a concentric convergence of omnipresent energy manifestation in the 3rd dimensional realm where it hits matter, becomes physical and therefore creates co-ordinates. The four arms reaching out as the first 3-dimensional directions of an energy singularity are an important initial part of creation. This is the point from which the spherical energies of heaven, Earth, female and male have incarnated to assist to create life. They initially combine and overlap to create the centre point, the pivotal point of creation of each new being. The cross-over point of the four major spheres is the 'seed of the Self' I spoke of earlier, in the middle of a being, the centre point that started as a single seed.

Image of 'Flower of Life', creating Life on Earth with converging Energy patters
Image Credit © from a Youtube clip by Samuel Dickris

Radiating out and bringing energy in spiral motion along their radius are numerous lines and orbs arranged in overlapping patterns, lines representing male and circles female energies, right and left turning, inward and outward spiralling, all with the pure vibrational intent of unconditional unbounded endless energy coming together to create. I tried hard to see if I could find an exact match online for an accurate representation of the actual process in short film or even GIFs, but sadly could not find any that matched the process exactly. The image above is from a short clip that explains some parts of the process. There are a few that come close, so if you are at all interested in seeing how it can look in 3-d, please check out a few for yourself. I found most of them too limited or too trippy, which was not my intention to pass on, as this is a sacred process that deserves to be shown exactly how it manifests. Again, any suggestions from readers gladly received. Picking out just four directions and three dimensions in our earthly efforts to incarnate can be centring, reassuring, grounding and protective, and in its converging motion will bring energy focused into a singular point of manifestation in the physical 3-d realm. However, we must not forget that it would also limit our perception and keep us from looking at what else is going on, if we focused on these 'directions' only all throughout human existence. Perhaps this is exactly the reason why

Any system-based doctrine, institution, religion, education or language may be prone to being compromised, restricting universal energy to only a few of its components. It can still help to explain and convey simplified basic principles to the many, but it cannot be expected to be representative of the infinite vastness and potential of the principles of existence.

All additional cross-over points where the energy orbs converge and overlap by their intent to create life, appear to us on paper or screen much like the 2-d images of the flower of life as depicted above, although they are, in fact, multidimensional spheres. They are energy converging to determine the shape of new life, and they will also bring with them all the energy points and vortexes to build a new physical shape, situated along the spine and in various other parts of the body. The energy they bring with them, is our Karmic blueprint to help form physical matter in the shape of cells, passing on the energy pattern to the existing matter to build major organs, bones, soft tissue, joints, circulatory systems etc. It is fascinating to observe that the energy converging into full form, if looked at from above our 3-dimensional perspective, is a uniform, multi-dimensional grid containing many recognisable patterns of manifestation, as in the image (and link) above. It figures that due to many thousands of energy orbs overlapping, they would therefore create a specific number of chakra points along the torso, as well many other, less complex ones radiating into the sides and extremities of the new body. It makes sense that energy must radiate from within these central points in all directions even before a heart or brain is formed, in fact, these are the major points of energy feeding the physical cells to assist in creating major organs. It would not be enough to just have the four directions that we may have been led to believe that these are all there is.

Our condensed physical shape on Earth stays

connected to the omnipresent energy beyond
matter, time and space at all times.

However, it must first learn all over again to get used to and overcome the physical laws of the 3rd dimension on Earth, once the Karmic blueprints that underlie our structure and the physical matter available to us have taken form. This is where life is about to change, transforming from a manifesting Karmic energy body to an initially tiny, individual physical existence. Despite our physical form being contained in a limited space in the 3rd dimension, our form remains continuously connected by default to all other all-present energy grids outside our individual bodies, a fact we often forget when we feel isolated and alone. I have a feeling we only feel like that maybe because we have not yet had a chance to activate and use techniques to allow us to sense these Karmic energy connections which still surround us and keep us alive at all times. If we had, we would not need to feel alone any longer. But how would we? Nobody ever told us about them. Humans are only just awakening again to the full potential of their Karmic minds within their bodies at poignant insightful moments, perhaps during meditation, channelling, visions, dreams and healing methods, remembering their connectedness and starting to reconcile what they have been taught so far with their own inner wisdom. Science uses formulae, but our connectedness is not limited to these.

Humans are opening up more and more to the generation of universal principles of all-encompassing energy, affecting our own experience of true divine love and full realisation,. Even science which uses mathematical equations and formulae can be an entry point to connectedness through these methods. Many things can; since we are all connected, we are all able to experience an epiphany and lucid moments at any time, which are not limited just to just the perception of the physical realm and make us feel disconnected any longer. The thinking brain, even with its limited capacity, can also generate enough insights in order to experience connectedness through its channels; it often does this through more linear constructs and systems, learning crutches of formulae and the belief scaffolds it feels we must own and adhere to as a result of its need for us to feel anchored in the vastness that surrounds us. What matters is how we take this newfound feeling of connectedness, how much we can learn from even tiny glimmers of insight. Will we see enough for us to want to learn more how to extend this feeling, to find ways of feeling connected for longer, to take this seriously enough to realise this is our new normal, this is our birth right, we can prolong the happiness of feeling connected when we do the right thing?

How much we allow our brains to think this and take over our choices, is down to our Karmic mindsets, whilst in the meantime, cosmic energy carries on existing regardless of whether we grasp its concepts or not. There are so many people feeling unhappy about Earth limitations that the one logical conclusion is that there is indeed more to it than meets the eye. Why not follow that notion constructively and see where it leads? And why not take it as a cue to make the experience more permanent by practising to make it so? There is no need to use any other method than what we have at our disposal. We don't need any external stimulus at all, in fact, that could turn out to be much to our detriment. Our personal connection between physical and sacred realms can even become visual and resemble one of the Karmic energy spheres and concentrated light points that surround and feed into us, which formed us at birth and have stayed with us at all times to keep us alive. When they appear to us as the complete and endless light spheres they are, we can learn to be aware of them and enter a higher stage of awareness and understanding at any time. It might be perceived as a very bright, light ring, orb or circle from above, below or in front of us. It is the ultimate way of being for a human being, by extending our minds and learn to abide by practices to gain its pure and joyous merits.

Once we learn again about this freedom we have, we can integrate it into aspects of our lives, and explore our new status first by becoming conscious again of our ability to radiate and take in energy through all our major energy points. Fortunately, our energy can do this without us being aware of it, as it may take us some time to take the helm and master this ability again to radiate fully as a result, instead of keeping our energy so condensed that it becomes hardly perceptible. It is a learning process in its own right to find what is stopping us from allowing ourselves to radiate to our full potential, and it can take some time to become accomplished again at something that is actually keeping us alive. It is our birth right to live consciously, and to our full potential, but you won't find that written in any constitution or work contract. The word 'alive' may have been diminished by the implied adjective 'barely' by many processes in the modern world that do not support our fully conscious aliveness in the slightest. We already have the full ability to do so, but most of us have been made to go through a process of unlearning the knowledge as to how to. Maybe it's time to remember.

There can follow many fascinating lessons involved in learning to activate our Karmic energy again fully instead of having to subdue it. They can be a little hard to read sometimes, even encrypted in situations which arrange themselves along our Karmic time-line as well as reciprocally influencing our society's and even this planet's course of evolving. I cannot speak for other places here outside our reach, it would take us too far away from what we need to take away from this for ourselves, but I trust that you already know that there are others, and that some of us have lived in those where Karmic rules differ from ours.

Back on Earth though, occasionally it happens that a human being has an epiphany and starts to radiate fully again from all of his or her body all at once, just like the new-born babies we talked about who have come to Earth with their universal energy connection still intact. The limitations we have experienced so far in our lives as part of our Karmic boundaries do not have to get in the way. Neither do we have to leave this planet in order to evolve into the blissful state again we so crave. The stages of our evolution on Earth could be seen as phases with a few growing pains, but nonetheless a part of a much bigger Karmic outcome than we could imagine. Eventually, we may be able to exist without these physical limitations being in our way, on some other plane of awareness, with lighter Karma and perhaps even without the need for a physical body even. That does not mean we can't cherish this one and must forever wait and eternally long to be elsewhere. Far from it. We can have eternity, right here, right now, with our awareness increasing. When we start to trust that there really is more out there than we were led to believe, we can be still within our bodies quite happily if it means we can connect with our reality that there is ultimately no attachment to a physical body or a need for a system of energy patterns to incarnate us. Whilst we are down here, we can definitely make very good use of it, and learn to cherish it, simply because we no longer have to crave being elsewhere. We may transcend again at some point when the moment is right. In the meantime, no need for complex interpretations of the possible convolutions and consequences of potential Karmic hindrances. Our pure and determined focus on our own special energy mind explorations within us will help us to activate and awaken more and more to Truth. It will help us translate the limited experience of a physical existence into the all-encompassing essence that we truly are, with less and less need for our human bypassing into procrastination, watering down or overriding techniques. This must be great news for all who feel they cannot relate to their human existence, but

Until a continuous stream of full realisation is activated, our time-line is still active, moving our Karmic energy bodies along the path of our own individual Karmic spiral on Earth.

The whole universe including all matter it contains, must work along such a spiral as well, albeit in a much bigger, yet somehow parallel way. This has long replaced the old perception of a timeline from here into the distance, which our brains will have us work along all day long in order to 'reach' a goal, if we subject ourselves to this notion still.

Karmic existence is very much in line with Einstein's teachings on relativity, the curved time/space model and introducing realities beyond other dimensions beyond the 4th. The findings that time and space are curved, as opposed to the fact that we have not applied this in a practical way in our lives yet, should give us reasons for concern. Whilst we still believe in the illusions of our relative perception, indicating that we choose to remain within the confines of restricted access to correct information and full disclosure, we are less likely to create a better outcome for future generations. Do we really want our children to become subjects to the control mechanisms of those who influence our children's energy and wisdom so it remains suppressed? Have we ourselves been oppressed for so long that we no longer see anything wrong with it? The repercussions and implications of this and other 'dumbing down' mechanisms from an early and malleable age are of great concern to many who are becoming more aware of the principles and nature of Karma. Children whose pituitary glands are still open to theta levels of consciousness intuitively feel the limitlessness and vastness of creation much more easily and directly than previous generations had the opportunity to. Is it such a bad thing that our children are able to teach us something better than we are trying to do to them? I personally feel that increasing awareness is not a concern, but masking it, making it more difficult to focus on it and even trying to keep it a secret, definitely is. If we and the next Earth generations are to remain solely in the existence of a square box which ironically has become a comfort zone for those who have been made to feel too terrified by now to venture past what they are told to believe, then it will be even less easy on Earth to be able to connect to the beautiful, pure cosmic energy that is the source of our Karmic existence. We are co-creating our future, right now. A combination of our Karmic actions right now and those from way back in the distant past, are what determines our future. If we now choose not to learn to be fully present whilst we still can, we may create a situation where we will not be able to see others as the beautiful beings they are. This moment, right now, might be the best time we get in order to create a beautiful outcome for many, on a large time-scale. It might be the perfect time, or it might not, according to our situation. But it might be better than what we had before, and what we will have again. Who knows if we will be forced to exist in a watered down solution of our own belief systems impregnated by those who have the intent of keeping us there as it suits them, in the future. We already know that situations like these bring about a psychological conditioning that makes it harder for us to see through to the Truth. Sadly, we cannot ignore that there are also those who take advantage of the situation, willing to create a sheer endless variety of fears for our existence now and in our future. Many a book in the 20th century was written, about the symptoms of such control mechanisms, and it is still an issue to this day, if not more so. It deserves some consideration as to whether we would not rather have the choice to be free to choose who we truly are and have the potential to be, and be free, from as early an age as possible.

When we become aware of the meaning and motions of the universe within us, we will know that we are moving in upward circles along our inner spiral within us, and that we are also doing this alongside fellow passengers following our planet's movements, within a spiral universe. When our time line has moved around a full turn on our spiral and has come to the same spot again, only a 'level' up so to speak, we will feel it. Some people do this naturally when a year has passed, seeing how much has changed since then, and where they were, how they felt, what they were doing that previous year. However, our time-line and the influences upon it do not follow a man-made, Gregorian calendar. They follow the movements of Karmic influences. This means that at certain times on our spiral time-line, we will face similar situations as we have before. It might feel like we are being tested again on the same issues that we faced before, but this is perfectly normal and it does not mean we are going backwards. We can expect this to happen periodically, in fact it is probably better to get used to it, as it is the full intent of the spiral universe to ascertain that we revisit places in our consciousness in order to complete our Karmic energy mind. At these points of alignment individual to each of us, we can then recognise if we have 'moved on' or if we feel we are going around in circles. This is exactly what is happening, because in terms of where we are supposed to be - on an upward moving spiral path of increasing consciousness - we might not be developing as much as we could, in which case our spiral is not moving up. It is instead stagnating, or only moving upwards very slowly and only in very tight turns, taking longer for us to experience inner freedom from Karmic bonds which may be holding us back. Is that not how we feel so very often, that things are not moving fast enough, well enough, efficient enough for us, so we can feel better? Is that why we seek the bigger/better/faster/stronger external stimuli, because we don't know how to inch along our inner Karmic journey? Situations will appear to be repeating themselves in slight variations and we may feel stuck in a rut, with little or no changes to our situation. It is our choice entirely what to do about it, whether we acknowledge it or not and whether we do something to make a change, or not. It is also down to the attributes of our chosen physical existence whether this is what happens or whether we can take more control of how we develop, whenever we are ready. All of us are influenced by all-present energy and the universe is all allowing, meaning that is down to us and our Karma as to what can change, when and where. We also do not have to be different if we really feel like we cannot be. All we have to feel is good enough.

The beginning moment for any change of any situation, behaviour pattern, feeling and thought starts with our acceptance of the fact that it is there.

Determine what is reality for you, and what feels instinctively right or wrong for you, at this very moment. Accepting and understanding the full implications of a situation is also important. When we do and examine our reality in more detail, we give it the attention it needs. As a result, very often our reality starts to softens a bit and becomes more pliable, less stuck. What you can do if you want to, is ask for help at any time to bring in more energy to assist you. Opening up the gap between our spiral rungs means letting in light and space, learning faster, ascending sooner – but each to their own! Nobody can decide for you what is best, but you can learn new methods if you wish, they are all there at your disposal. On top of tried and tested methods, there are new tools revealing themselves to us all the time, to make this healing process pass more quickly and be less intense/painful/ tedious -whatever you want to call it. Most of the time when we feel something is out of kilter, it's to do with timing on our spiral journey, and how efficiently our body and mind is allowing in all-healing energy to assimilate within our Karmic energy mind. The tools I mention as a suggestion at the end of this book are all valid and effective healing tools working more or less quickly on issues we phase on many levels. Some of these are quantum healing methods handed down to us with unconditional love for a boost of our Karmic energy level by our good friend, the all-knowing Omnipresence.

To sum things up, the theories, concepts, ideas and methods I wanted to bring up in my book for contemplation, are some that I have had for a while and which I believe have been largely ignored in many an era's literature. It could be because we simply do not remember much about our childhood, never mind being a baby, and it takes an even more tuned in mind to get glimpses of what happened in a past life. It could also be that for some considerable time on Earth, some beings on this planet have profited from us remaining unaware. There may even be those who have actively taken part in setting up systems to prevent us from being connected to the whole Truth, including our own Karmic evolution which includes our memories of early childhood and those of past life existence. If we consider this, then it makes sense as to why we have been stopped from being connected to the complete Karmic memory of our own history. I have been fascinated in the process of finding out who I am over the past couple of decades, and to remember as many early memories as felt right without becoming too caught up in them, but it has taken me until my adulthood to find the right methods to explore the workings of Karma in more detail without getting caught up in too much navel gazing or the many distractions of our so-called civilised existences. I simply asked to remember who I am, and I asked to be shown the best and most effective methods. I set my intention to finding them at the cost that the universe would ask of me. It turned out that the universe did not want what was impossible. I was asked to free my time as much as possible in order to assist others, and I did so without trying to sacrifice my sanity or too much of my family's needs for my presence. None of what we fear we have to 'spend' or 'lose' that is ours or which we call our own on Earth, is actually necessary or true. The universe is always on our side and listening when we want to find out more about the full Truth. It will assist us on our quest of finding our own truths, too. We just have to ask and know how to ask for the right outcome, and assistance for the right causes - and for the right, unselfish reasons. I believe that in due time, we will all be shown all of what we really need to know that is important to further complete our own Karmic energy bodies and thus be able to assist the planet and all its inhabitants in the most comprehensive ways.

As part of my inner journey, it was essential for me to understand more about our incarnating into physical existence. 'I' asked questions of why 'I' was 'I', and in order to find out, 'I' needed to remember who 'I' was before 'I' was me, and as a result 'I' found out some of why 'I' am today; enough to realise why 'I' can ask to be my best in this moment and that 'I' have every chance to take these insights to shape the future, too.

Most of us probably feel a need to ignore the facts of being born and those early months that follow, for fear of experiencing how laborious and sometimes painful an experience they were for us as a new human being, and how those caring for us dealt with this in their own unique ways. Perhaps this is why many of our experiences of that time will have been deeply buried in our 'subconscious' and are not readily available to our conscious mind as part of our visible Karmic history. However, I am willing to put my reputation (or what's left of it) on the line and continue to put a few more ideas about Karma out there, on top of what I have already stated in this book.

For example, it appears to me that it is possible for human beings to be born with little Karma left to sort out for themselves, at any Earth time, but that this has become possible for more beings than before in the last two decades. Two decades ago, I saw in a meditation a new generation of beings who would incarnate with very clear energies and no personal Karma that they need to overcome. I believe it was made possible by the Earth's shifting through her own Karmic frequencies towards the higher end of vibrational frequencies. Many have called this the age of Aquarius, or the time for the 5th dimensional shift. I simply called them the translucent children, because of the clarity of their Karmic frequency. They are now born in the thousands into the 21st century, after the Earth's latest of her regular vibrational frequency shifts, which coincide with the Earth's spin axis being moved along over time, as well as the ongoing completion of the magnetic polar shift, as in the image below.

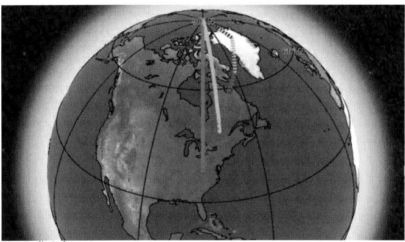

Image Credit © phys.org

These beings would often consciously remember their early months as human beings, as well as consciously recollect their birth process and previous lifetimes. They appear to be able to see non-physical entities, their auras and others' Karmic energy naturally without trying, amongst their many other natural talents which they have brought into this life-time from previous ones. They are often also able to convey and communicate to us more easily the phenomena they are able to perceive, which remain hidden to most.

My questions are, if we have insight into the beautiful and poignant visions via the minds of these wise ones who are able to see more than most, and we have the tools and opportunities to learn more about ourselves than we ever had before, when will we have the chance to lead all of mankind to more peaceful lives? It seems that these new beautiful beings are as ethereal and awesome as they are vulnerable to others' persecution. Wisdom, knowledge and compassion has been around for aeons of time, but never so readily available to read up on. Why is it that we are still faced with the biggest threat of all in this last century, that of mass extinction? Does wisdom grow amongst a densely populated Earth, or does it also turn into its opposite of stress and destruction? What if any of this beautiful information that we are witness to can be continuously misconstrued and used to perverse the precious gifts that come with being alive? What happens if, as a result, we are so manipulated and confused that we do the very worst and end up disregarding the beauty of the great plan, the great reasons for creation, and finish each other off, excuse or not? Could it be that it has always been true for this planet that it allows for all beings to incarnate equally, including those with Karma that is reflecting destructively megalomaniac, psychopathic tendencies? Will all those who have suffered atrocities in their past lives necessarily incarnate again with fear and hatred in their hearts? Is it up to us to recognise this and assist individuals as such? Or is it simply that we are allowing a few who still need to be in power to control us, by becoming so disassociated as a society that we are not seeking to adequately look after our world and our people any longer? Instead of pondering to their every request, should we not be allowed to concentrate all our efforts on keeping our babies and children close and learning from them as a society by remembering that we do not live forever; that we are leaving the planet we are ruining, the mistakes we are making, to our children to sort out? I agree with Ms Thunberg, as a matter of fact: How DARE we. How dare we leave this planet in such a mess, so that our children and our children's children will suffer greatly as a result. Personally, I believe the biggest chance we have of changing society is by looking after the next generation in the most loving way we can, a view which is, I agree, governed and influenced by my own Karmic viewpoints and insights. A truth I have come to realise is that we can do only little to alleviate the suffering of those who are not willing to look at it for themselves, but we can start with those who are willing to form a grid work of light strands around the planet, formed with love, good actions and positive Karma. We can also show our children how we are learning to live by example, in a way that shows we are responsible for our own Karma. What I also try to remember I learned at some point is that, if we can overcome some of the Karmic chinks in our own armour, our children won't have to carry them for us either.

Don't we have a responsibility to pass on quite so much Karmic debris to them, so they will more likely be able to lead their lives as compassionate beings? Are they here to get the best exam results and university debt, or are some of these translucent children creating a world that is compassionate, having to work in unison to undo some of the damage done by the unresolved issues we have so far inflicted on this planet, and each other? That is one of the reasons why I have been drawn to delving into ways to explain how our Karmic energy minds enter human existence, because at the point where we become more conscious and in the time where we work to integrate our wisdom thereafter, there is a very real chance for parents to be making a difference, with their compassion for the next generation.

I have already stated how our Karma allows us to incarnate into early-day experiences as well as can shape who we become on Earth. None of what I am about to state is meant as any form of judgement, criticism or other divisiveness, as we must always consider and be compassionate towards the diversity and possibility of all outcomes of life that present themselves on Earth. From what presents itself around us, we made the following deductions: time is not linear (nothing new); it is curved (also not new); it is, indeed, spiral (yes, you've heard it before) and a human lifespan is in essence a repetitive spiral of experiences of his or her own previous forms of Karmic existence, combined with the new reactions to new situations in this lifetime. It is not that difficult to grasp, really, once we have recognised the principles of Karmic manifestation behind existence; but what would happen if we were able to apply these new-found insights we learned about these new, translucent beings who incarnate with little Karma? If we wanted to support their existence to the utmost – as most parents would, of course, to all their children – by applying this generosity to the timeline spiral of a newborn and how to make this our sincere wish to make their entry into life as ideal as possible, how would this look? How can we actively make the environment as gentle and conducive as necessary to support their crucial peaceful existence? What if theories about beings incarnating on Earth aren't just theories, but our own intuition telling us what is most needed in order to change our Earth's future for the better, by assisting these beautiful beings the best way we can? If this is possible, then we would have to become very aware and alert ourselves and be able to pay attention to every detail, every moment of the day, especially right from the beginning. A baby's Karmic spiral of existence is, as we have learned, so tightly curled at first that it represents point zero, the central singularity at the core, and the crucial beginning point of entry into this particular life span's spiral journey.

As already mentioned, everything that happens in the baby's early days happens at break-neck speed, and every action and event around the baby therefore becomes an essential and all-important part of the foundation of baby's development. The more things go right in the early days, the easier it will be later on for baby to adapt to life, as 'later' appears to be a broader, more stretched out repetition of Karmic events on the spiral path of a human being's earlier experiences. If you look at the pointed end of a spiral, you will see how it unfurls from a singular point in tiny, quick movements into circular, outward movements in the beginning. This is the beginning of their Earth time outside the womb, and determines their secure growth on a physical, mental, emotional and spiritual level. In terms of time, baby's concept of time is that it is stretched endlessly even if only a few seconds pass, whereas to the observer, it appears that everything is occurring in slow motion. However, parents are acutely aware that baby needs everything done very quickly in those tiny, early curls of their spiral: to feed tiny amounts but often, will be a massive gain to this new life. Baby will have small amounts of time with eyes open, and yet in baby's eyes, these impressions are huge steps of gulping in their new surroundings. Even if their physical ability is lacking, their spiritual awareness is fully intact, much more than that of an adult. What parents often pick up on is their baby's need for translation of their highly-charged Karmic energy field into the physical world, and parents instincts are a perfect medium for this if they are able to listen and interpret with their own heightened sense of awareness.

As things within baby have to develop at such a high speed, everything around them needs to happen fast, but at the same time be as calm as possible. Baby is taking in so much information so quickly without any filters, that all the speed we are so accustomed to, the noises, all the flickering, fast-changing images, colours, light, faces, environments and so on can come as a kind of shock; if we are aware of it, we can keep things calm and gentle so as to allow for baby to adapt gently because only soon enough, baby has to take it all in regardless and try to make sense of it. Parents need to move so quickly, and yet slow things down for the new baby. Baby has to now take in tiny amounts of suitable, gentle milk through their mouth for the first time, learn to stomach it, digest and eliminate it from tiny bowels hardly fit for the job. It can be so painful, but if awareness becomes a natural, instinctual desire to make things as easy as possible for this precious new life, parents feeding their babies will learn how to be in tune and be able to grant them immunity from illness and harm. At each next level of the child's spiral, they will acquire more skills, sometimes overnight, it seems. Perhaps it is because of the Karmic memory of their skills, as it were, as it alights at certain points in their development. Each new spiral level will gradually activate the new life's Karmic energy memory, activating their own memory energy banks, and integrate and combine it with the new levels of cognisance even further in this new lifetime.

Other examples of how a baby has to adapt to life in physical form again is that they have to breathe air into their lungs and learn to do so, instead of breathing in fluid. They have to find ways to sleep on harder surfaces with external distractions much louder and brighter than inside the womb. They have to wear complicated scratchy clothes instead of being warm in the most cosy, soft womb, and nappies that get full and uncomfortable. Sometimes, even the gentlest of milks is not easily digestible. Sometimes the air is polluted, or surroundings too cold, too hot, too dry, too humid. It is an exhausting and painful learning process, one that has to be met by their carers with the utmost sensitivity. And who are we as carers? Are we not beings who probably have ourselves not

quite yet grown into our own wise stages ourselves, with many of our own needs unmet? We have to learn to meet baby's needs first and hopefully able to see everything now through baby's eyes: Baby knows *everything* already on a Karmic energy level, however, their Karmic energy is now being integrated to quickly push matter to grow into their physical body. Their tiny body is learning quickly, and at each vortex level they need to feel secure. With Karmic energy spiralling upwards and in danger of going down again if things are amiss, they need so urgently to feel settled and safe at each and every stage of energy level development – and that means every second of the day and night in the early days, weeks, months and years even. To bring up a child in the best possible way, are we determined enough to be there with them, every step of the way? In the ideal-case scenario fit for the translucent children, to continue to stave off all harm and make their lives on a Karmic level go as smoothly as possible, they need to feel safe at all times in terms of knowing someone is very close by and is not abandoning them, causing them great fear and distress. Skin to skin touch is very much on the agenda. They need to feel nurtured in terms of being able to rely on having a perfectly balanced food source nearby, 24/7. They need to feel safe in terms of not having to feel unnecessary pain or be exposed to suffering cruel behaviour, causing them to cry with the existential anguish that parents are so familiar with, an inherent fear of their young being harmed. Keeping baby close by to remain alert to their needs at all times, affirms a bond with baby, allowing all necessary brain processes to be passed on through contact even during sleep. Parents remain in tune with their babies so that natural instincts can kick in, to ascertain that they do care fully for their offspring. Nature gives many examples of this, and we don't have to have expensive gadgets to make this simple instinct to keep our babies safe for as long as possible a reality. It's simple, and yet so hard to do, as parents will be at their most vulnerable, too, through lack of sleep and pressured by the external world to act and behave as if everything is the same as before a baby is born. Nothing is the same, and never will be. Tribal communities knew this long before we were duped into being 'civilised'. Families need protecting from harm and stress whilst taking care of their young, the next generation that will inherit the Earth, one of the most, if not THE most important task in this world has become a poverty-stricken, degenerate, commercialised, economy-supporting exercise that promotes only early detachment from our babies to become productive again. We must be aware of how degenerate modern society has allowed the bond between parents and their children to become, how difficult a situation many families on Earth find themselves in. It is time, I believe, to look at an ideal-case scenario, not to scold us or make us feel inadequate, but simply to remind ourselves of how blessed we all are, and what we deserve to be when we receive the utmost care, love and attention. Thinking about the practicalities, this is no mean feat. Babies need to feel clean, healthy and well; parents need to be prepared to change thousands of nappies, baby grows, give thousands of baths, round-the-clock feeds, and look our for any unusual symptoms. It's a big task, one that can never be made clear enough in advance. The love that welcomes a new life overrides all that we will sacrifice of our own needs, to meet those of nurturing a human being who isn't yet able to fend for themselves and needs us every day for the rest of their young lives until they are adults able to support themselves. In any case, our good actions will create good Karma for our future if we are able to answer the call to being responsible for it, and co-create our children's, too. Parents and Carers will feel the latent urgency of this immense task all day long, 24 hours a day, 7 days a week, often under enormous and unimaginable pressure.

Once the beautiful Karmic baby energy has flushed through their body to form matter, it will not stop and rest; energy will form a continuous stream and last a whole life-time. If it has been encouraged wholeheartedly to do so unhindered with the aid of caring adults around, there often is little time for them to rest. The regime is exhausting for them and puts their own Karmic energy to the test. At each stage, baby has to have enough time, care and the right nurture from their parents, but more often than not from their mum at first, to 'click' its Karmic energy blueprint perfectly into physical time and place. The yin principle that is established and encouraged to flow through this nurturing assures us in later life that we will feel safe and assured in our 'I AM' presence. The yang principle will help us feel secure to venture out, learn to stand on our own feet, explore the world and eventually to seek independence, to find suitable, fruitful and useful tasks to fulfil. Ultimately, baby could be so well looked after by parents/carers who are

conscious of this, that they will remember a lot of their Karmic existence even from before this life form, even in a tiny physical body. If they
do, they may already then be on their way to becoming one of the integrated, all-seeing, translucent wise ones we spoke about. If not, it is ok,
too. Everyone has a place on Earth. Earth will welcome their life just the
same.

*Earth will repeat each Karmic stage of each
beings' unique, individual spiral development
throughout their lifetime, over and over again,
until they, too, have remembered enough about
themselves, their past, their destiny, themselves,
to move onto higher realms of consciousness.*

The Karmic life-time spiral of incarnation on Earth follows the multidimensional logic of their individual Karma which lays out the fabric of
their path before each step a being takes, in sacred geometrical patterns
that follow principles and sequences which interact with each being's
life pattern as laid out in the moment of beginning their Earth spiral.
This means, in practical terms, that early days start at the point of birth
and taking first breath, the point zero, and then for the spiral to grow at
first very quickly and then more gradually bigger and spiral outwards.
Numerology of certain stages can equate to development that becomes
important for the new being. For example, everything that happens in
the first seconds, minutes and hours, turns back around on itself again
a rung higher each time, in the next days, weeks and months, and years.
Each time the spiral meets itself again on the next level after a full turn
of the spiral, the child is bigger and their spiral a step higher and wider.
The human being has a chance of reliving and therefore going over their
own experiences again, in order to 'tidy up' any shortfalls in their energy system.
There are beings that are already highly evolved at a very age, with
attributes and talents that are usually allocated to much older children.
We could speculate that with the arrival of translucent children, special talents at an early stage of life will become more prevalent.
If all goes well in the first days, if they are healthy after birth, if nursing
goes well and baby is thriving, if all their needs for peace, comfort, con-

tact, warmth and rest are met, if no illness appears or accidents occur – in short, if everything is full-on but fine, it should make sense that the next developmental level can be more easily reached without any disturbance or set-backs for the new being and their family. There is a lot that has to be in place in order for a new being to not just be physically healthy, but also mentally and emotionally. If this is ascertained and achieved on a high level of care, it will save the child having to go through the process again repeatedly at later stages in order to deal with what may have been missed so far.

If the above makes sense, would it not also make sense for all of us to try and give the utmost of care to optimise the child's start in life, to avoid so much heart ache? If the nourishment and care is right, if no invasive illness occurs or is artificially induced, the parent(s) are actively involved in keeping baby close, are responsive, loving and make sure he or she doesn't lack attention at all times, would it not mean that the baby's Karmic energy body will develop well, accordingly? If all is as well as it can be in the first days, weeks, months, years, then things that start off as utterly hard work will turn out to become wonderfully rewarded in terms of the Karma for all involved, which will then also grow exponentially as the good Karma can be passed on to many others in the form of compassion. Regardless of the fact that some aspects are also down to the new being's Karma which has an influence to an extent on what their life path will turn out to be, our knowing that this is so will coincide with the care-giving and agreement of the parents to act accordingly to foresee and alleviate any problems. Karma is also a huge factor in establishing the utmost potential for care and love on a healing level that we will hopefully be able to offer all of our children on Earth. It takes a lot of dedication to keep this vision alive especially when faced with current situations of adversity, but the arrival of new generations of children who are creating a different paradigm, a different outcome for themselves and others with the power of their Karmic nature, must encourage us to think differently and with broader minds. The fruits of our labour lie in a wondrous outcome for our children and how they relate to their future in a world that is cherished, much as we want it to be so right now.

Except, right now, we are still faced with the demons of our own Karmic pasts, at a very vulnerable time on Earth where we are easily confused and too readily swayed when confronted by society's pre-formed concepts and artificial norms of what we should do and not do, heavily influenced by a material and commercial outlook we have had inflicted upon us. We are very much affected by what has happened to us already, and unaware of the whole extent. Changing our Karmic minds isn't nearly as easy as following assembly instructions for a piece of flat-pack furniture.

We are still hearing advice from experts that our babies are better off separated from us, in separate beds, in separate bedrooms. We listen to complete strangers with even stranger titles telling us what to do, traipsing around in the dark because we have not been shown in our own lives how to connect, how to be well, how to know intuitively what to do for the Best. We end up believing what is written in manuals about our own beautiful children, advising us it's fine to just let them cry right from the start, because they won't know any better, it's normal, that's what they do, they can't tell right from wrong, they won't remember and such like. What if that information we have been told is incorrect? What if it sets them up, right from the start, for a life of mistrust and upset, insecurity and fear? What if instead we held on to the thought that our children have just incarnated from the universe, and are here to share it with us? How our gorgeous babies can and will remember everything, if we could just help them through the ascending spiral of their first few minutes, hours, days, weeks, months, years. If we can ourselves learn to be present step by step, moment for moment, even if it is at the expense of our physique, our time, our sleep pattern, our bank balance, our social life, our friendships, relationships and our jobs – in short, our life as we knew it? Is that a temporary sacrifice too large to make? It seems a lot to ask and a massive task that takes the strength of a parent turning into a superhuman, but are a few years out of our lives really that big a sacrifice? Didn't we always say we wanted to be superhuman? Well, here's our chance, except society does not want us to be seen that way. I wonder where the idea came from that families should be sacrificed for the sake of commerce. I question where this idea of cultural selfishness came from that arose not so long ago, as it does not occur in all cultures around the world, especially those where more tribal instincts are still intact. Not everywhere tells us that it is perfectly normal to break the bond with our babies, to leave them behind and still believe that our children won't notice or remember or be affected. I do suspect sometimes that we have been told might have been a clever lie, because the horrendously high price there is to pay that we are not told about in the name of keeping us commercially viable resources, might be the future well-being of our children and the next generations after that, slowly losing touch with their instincts and integrity. Instead of just blaming family units when things go awfully wrong, do we need to ask ourselves what is wrong with our society? It didn't just come from anywhere. When we look at whose interest it is in, to have more cases of broken homes, adoption and fostering than ever before; sick babies and a sky-high infancy mortality rate in first world countries, would we find an answer? Children suffering neglect and abuse to the extreme, growing into teens with psychological trauma, mental illness, severe dependencies, immune system illnesses and suicides on the increase as well as terrors such as famines, crazily common child abuse, abductions and murders; child trafficking, organ harvesting and abject poverty making tiny tots have to scavenge on rubbish heaps for scraps of food; having to grow up in terrifying war zones and being turned away at the gates of wealthy countries with nothing and nobody to turn to. Who or what is to blame for this abhorrent development in this, our modern world?

I am not trying to make suffering worse by pointing out the obvious. I want to question why we still have such suffering on Earth and how can we make a difference? Can we reverse what our separation from our Karmic truth has exacerbated? We have so much hidden strength we can use, that each of us can realise for ourselves. I am perhaps challenging us to notice how a society has been created without our best interest, and for us to have a big rethink how we think of and subsequently treat all our children, not just our own. We have been led to believe they have to fit around adult lives and are often treated like an inconvenience to our getting on with our jobs and social lives in modern society. There are by now groups of grown-ups who openly believe we should never have children to birth into this imperfect world, people arguing fiercely for and against abortion, countries without contraception, child brides and stigmas about reproductive organs and sexual orientation. On top of that, people who believe that anyone who is a parent is guilty of overpopulating the world. I believe the confusion stems from our tendency to handle problems in our lives with too little compassion and wisdom, for the benefit of a new generation of hope above all.

Perhaps this is our biggest vulnerability within ourselves, not realising that we are openly projecting our unresolved pain outwards, onto the most vulnerable beings in our social structure.

If this is the case, suffering is the consequence. Even if it is sometimes only spreading outward from one single source, if they present themselves as powerful enough, there may be all sorts of issues presenting themselves as a result of the lack of compassion, sometimes affecting many thousands of people. When there is a lack of support being offered for the weakest and most vulnerable in society, we need to trace it back not to those who are pointing out the discrepancy, but those who suggested to exercise heartlessness, because this is the part of society with the most unresolved personal issues on the subject. It seems a tad too convenient when they point the finger away from them, as it does not resolve any issues for them or others, but rather perpetuates them. It is a dangerous time when any form of hatred that is spreading through society like wildfire as a result – often nowadays on a virtual one -, instead of us finding methods to alleviate anyone's suffering. There is little to be gained for blaming a portion of society for all their flaws on this and many other subjects. We need to start to see through this as the energy that we choose to leak from our own Self, and apply methods before it's too late and has gone too far. Many also seem to prefer to ignore the issue altogether, choosing to pretend they do not have to involve themselves with any aspect of a new generation as if they were some sort of disease. Personally, I think this also stems from trying to hide a great amount of fear and pain, the same fear of not feeling that they themselves are allowed to exist, which we discussed earlier. If we see a solution in world problems by not bringing children into this world, does this not say an awful lot about how we still feel like the powerless children ourselves, even as grown-ups, having become hardened and arrogant enough in our ingrained fears that make us believe we alone should be the ones who shall be allowed to eternally prevail? It is a futile argument, as we shall not.

At times, our society holds such contempt for parents and children that surely it must look to the little ones like we are treating them as if they are the enemy. They might feel it, too, especially when they do remember where they really came from and can compare it to the serenity that brought them here. Many of them are here to teach us how urgently we need to remember who we are, and our true reasons for why we are here and what we are here to learn. This is never meant as a threat. Karma doesn't have it in for us. Issues may repeat until things are put right on a Karmic energy level, and it can make it much easier for us to understand why things can arise again that we thought we had dealt with. If they don't then we might well have managed to do a good job with doing away with issues, once and for all. There is no judgement implied against anyone here, it would not be my job to comment on and be quite pointless as well, as Karma already takes care of all wrongdoing of anyone who might not be above board, guaranteed. It goes without saying that we are all most likely already aware that horrendous things can and do happen, all around the world. Karma may also mean that many situations will be dealt with by legal instance and proceedings. In terms of useful help for anyone who is struggling and needing help, there should be provisions of sympathetic care and appropriate assistance, and this could include the crucial process implied here, of recognising who we are and what we are here to contribute. I am not saying that everyone suddenly has to change what they do. Many of us already are in the exact right place, doing good work to assist others. However, there are just as many who at their wits end and stressed out enough as it is. I am saying again that, in addition to what many of us have already achieved, having a good understanding and integration of the principles of Karma could be an answer to resolving many social, economic, ecological and also political issues on Earth. But we need to become aware we are desperately looking for answers for ourselves and those close to us in the first place by now, and that there is indeed a solution, albeit one that may have been eluding or even withheld from us until now.

How can we assist and support those who are daring enough to even still bring these beautiful Karmic spirits into such a mad world to help heal it? How can we support these young spirits to find their place on Earth, have enough energy and resources to set them up to be functioning adults with great hopes to assist us in sorting out the mess we left behind? Why are there so many who suffer conditions that they could not resolve in childhood, and why is this number steadily increasing and not decreasing? This last question is the one we should truly find an answer to right away, because I believe it is out there hidden in plain sight. I think we have answers here to many issues, we just might also need to find them within ourselves to find out what we need to do next, in order to deal with them. It doesn't sound easy and I know it isn't at times, but it needs to be on our daily agenda, worldwide. We are probably set up to fail by systems that do not support people if their first priority is to create an economy, and we need to ask ourselves why this is. It is a mission to save precious lives, and I believe it is neither impossible nor too late.

Ignore the past and you will feel that it will come to back for you to resolve it. Resolve and make peace with it now, and you will feel that it will be supporting you in turn.

We may be subject to losing something so precious at any stage along the way that, the sooner we realise we need good people around us for support and to learn methods to continue the bond between us and our children, the better. We are becoming more and more isolated as a society, as a result of being disconnected at an early stage of our lives that we have no conscious recollection of. Sounds very plausible from the viewpoint of anyone trying to control us, but whilst this is largely not our fault, paradoxically we are the ones who have the ability to recognise it and claim back our knowledge and memory of our Karmic history. We need to step back into who we really are. Once you know that you were always meant to stay connected, you will want to know why you got disconnected. I have written this, because even just learning that this is what happens, may help you start to feel connected to the unity consciousness again.

I know I am putting the cat amongst the pigeons here for some, and for others it won't be enough. It seems in our day and age we are so sensitive because of our inner turmoil that we must be repetitively soothed and reassured that we can only do as best as we can. We almost cannot cope with being told elements of truth and the implications thereof. For some, these ideas will seem revolutionary, and yet others have heard them a thousand times already. How can I convince any one person who is only just getting by in life, about these newfangled ideas? The simple truth is, I cannot, and I do not want to, either. I do not have insight into every person's individual Karma, and it is not my right to judge whether they are doing right or wrong. It is also not my intention to berate. It is my intention to find out the bigger Truth, as well as the reasons behind our disconnection from it. How far it is sometimes removed from the beauty of a holistic reality! We have had to put up with a lot as human beings, and our Karmic energy bodies have had lots of flaws and adverse circumstances to cope with and bear the scars to show for it. There is no reason why we should be scolding ourselves - or each other - for hurting and having been hurt. And yet, that is exactly the 'double whammy' we impose on ourselves, which we in turn have been conditioned into for some time now. We actually believe on a very deep level that we are unacceptable in how and who we are. It is time to accept that we have been had. We have been made to believe things that are not true. We have been deceived and someone has wanted us to believe all of these untruths, possibly for their own gain. We may have found people like that by now, as there are many who could not turn their pain and suffering around by themselves, so they passed it on to others. We can no longer afford to disregard the fact that in our own history, there have always been groups of entities who wish harm on others and have created havoc. It is time we stood united in order to become free again of all the Karmic baggage that we thought we had to carry on behalf of others in an assumed position of authority. It is behaviour that becomes obsolete the moment we no longer act like children having to defend themselves – we are adults and we are entitled to a free, peaceful and loving existence, with no conditions attached other than to look out for each other.

If we don't yet feel like this, how do we implement it? We can do this, with our minds: Ask. Ask for help, ask for a solution, and direct it at the highest vibrational frequencies by any name of your choosing. It is a powerful method and tool that we no longer know how to use skilfully. We need to learn to ask again, so why not practice? We are not asking another being, or institution, in fact not anything on Earth. We are asking higher frequency patters and forces to conspire to assist us. We are asking for energies to converge, to make our requests heard, and then allow them happen in the best and most fruitful outcome possible for all involved. Focus on making all your efforts with your single-minded concentration on furthering your and your fellow sentient beings existence, to make it as comfortable, beautiful, serene and happy as it was always intended to be. See through the damage, the dysfunction; overcome those who wish to inflict injury on others by taking your power back into your own existence. Have no expectations from loved ones to assist you, as this is your quest, and everyone has their own. Expect nothing and take nothing from those who do not wish you well. Forget if you can, the lies and only partial truths that you have been told time and time again, for example that you need to 'worry' about money, and 'worry' about your and your family's existence. Be. You are. This is your main concern. Become the most that you can be. When you are versed at this, focus your actions on including and helping others, too, starting with your loved ones. State your true needs, make all your thoughts visible to yourself about bringing us all together in unity to assist, and the rest will follow. We need to also find out how to ask for help for all those discrepancies within us, the disconnect and the dissonance. These are important things to clear. It can be done. Hang in there, there are solutions to find our true Selves again. More about how to do this a little further down.

To summarise this big chapter with big messages about this big subject; based on one of the simple laws of Karma, we have already learned that we cannot decide anyone else's Karma for them, we are responsible first and foremost for the actions, reactions, thoughts and words within our own Karmic minds. This is not meant as a punishment, far from it. It is meant that we focus first on where we really can have an influence to turn things around for the better, so we can then also have a good outcome creation for all else. If we have tried really hard to be fair, see it as something we deserve. If we have fallen short by our own standards, we start with ourselves by taking ourselves and our energy aside and sort it out. Everyone else deserves it.

It is sincerely my intention to make statements that resonate with those who are ready for this level of truth, and I aim for people to become inspired and excited, perhaps amused rather than incensed by resonating with it, rather than feel guilt or inadequacy for not having achieved it so far. This essential sensation of radiance on experiencing any short blast of full Truth shining its light onto us, will be incentive enough for any of us to invite our inner changes to come naturally. And as our energy changes accordingly, it will bring fresh wind into our system. Often, this happens whether we like it or not. When our Karma announces that we are ready, we often have no conscious choice but to follow suit. If we want to be a step ahead and know it's coming, there is no time to waste.

And whilst it probably some humans' preference to remain in a relative state of inertia - as is determined by their own Karmic timing -, perhaps at least some of my musings will resonate and hopefully ring a few healthy alarm bells with the more conscientious readers. We all know that our conscious decision-making process does not always best serve us. We simply MUST awaken and become aware sentient beings, conscious parents & guardians, and perhaps most importantly, good pupils to our best teachers – the babies, toddlers and youngsters of the next generation who are arriving with the exact triggers for the knowledge we have been trying so hard to recall. We will be here forever, just not always in this ignorant body and with this stubborn brain. And lo and behold - we will come back as children! That could be reason for concern, unless we have been educating ourselves on how to be kind to everyone. Many of our children, as they are vibrating at a much a higher frequency than previous generations, already have within them what we have worked hard to adapt to in our lifespan. The most recent frequency levels facilitated the arrival of the translucent children, the all-seeing ones, and our planet is going through another, major shift in 2020, bringing another frequency shift, and what I believe to be the invisible generation. I had this impression, but have not fully understood myself yet what exactly this entails. As soon as I know, I will add it to a future edition of this book.

Many issues older generations had to fight wars for will just not be a problem for the new generations. Giving up our energy and resources to authorities (possibly a result of early problems with too strict an upbringing), allowing our life-force energy to be lowered to levels of fear, anger or hatred (having no choice but to be obedient and submissive to an adults' form of abuse against us as children) does not have to pose a continuous problem for these new souls. Indeed, the indigo children born around 1972 were already novel and daring, in that they would refuse blatantly to accept authority, fought all the way against a cold and heartless authoritarian regime, nonsensical oppressive rules, dictatorial doctrines and continue to do so to this day. Each generation naturally also brings with it its own downfalls by default, as the translucent generation also may bring issues of disassociation from reality, diverting into fantasy worlds, directionless distraction and diversions causing energy leaks rather than fully seeking Truth, finding it hard to apply their highly evolved intelligence and intuition, feeling lost and berEFT™, separated from their light body families and being unable to find a way on Earth that truly suits them; added to this an inability to make decisions one way or another as all options present as equal in order to be fair and accepting to all, as well as other phenomena associated with pure clear energy that comes with little own Karma to sort through; nonetheless, these are beautiful, stunning children and young adults now, and they are here to remind us where we have come from, the omnipotence of pure energy unmanifested, to connect us again to our selves, and our highest forms of Self. They are heralds to a new opening of perception of higher dimensions for our lesser talented Earthlings to learn. They bring in sustainable solutions to Earth's old-fashioned and outmoded systems that no longer serve wo-mankind. They bring new ideas to resolve famine and come up with sustainable food solutions on a large scale as well as being highly gifted inventors, using frequencies beyond electronics. My feeling is that they will come with the Karma to resolve many issues we face right now, and hopefully it will not be too late. They will also not take anything too seriously, as they will remember their real origin. They will work with ancient wisdom in a modern context in a transparent way. Intelligence will become clarified, and systems will become transparent. We are now staring at tiny screens, where in future our servers will work with crystal images that follow us and are all around, accessible at all time and not reliant on a power source as we know it. And we will be using telepathy eventually, when we give up on technology, no doubt. We can already do it, it seems feeble to still have to communicate via electronic devices. It would be nice if we could welcome this new generation with the love and hope they deserve, but as I look around, I fear that we sometimes fail in our attempts as we have been blinded to our sensitivities too early on in our own lives. We need to be reminded of the potential that the new generations can bring. It won't be all individuals, of course – many of us are being reborn and have to deal with the consequences of our previous lifetimes, still. It is still a struggle in this society to battle with the perceived concepts we have of others outside ourselves who we see are taking away our freedom. It is still reality as is at this moment in Earth time, when these very real Self-elected 'authorities' are hell-bent on destroying us and try to claim the planet. I feel they will be unsuccessful, but it will be tricky to thwart their expansive efforts. So far, we have had many a problem on Earth with groups of authorities and eccentric individuals with maniacal megalomaniac tendencies on so many levels, that we have not been able to create a different reality for the majority of Earthlings as of yet; which means that it still presents itself as an effort for us to simply become aware and awake, and we are still at the stage where we have to constantly remind ourselves to take time out to meditate, sit and listen over and over to spiritual teachings until we get the simplest of truths, only to have to repeat the process again the day after. This type of amnesia is very common right now and won't be any easier when we are rolling our lower frequencies that counteract our connection to the divine. At the same time, we have our hands full to be there for our children the best way we can aspire to, right from conception until they can fend for themselves, at about 35 or so. I am joking. I hope. If we do a good job, the rewards are astronomical. We will have supported our children in the way we so wanted them to be. When we have put in the love, care, attention, sensitivity and yes, a sense of humour, too, that they need, we will receive it all back at some point, especially if, as always, we were not demanding it. Our efforts are never in vain, no matter the outcome for each individual child. But remember, we must first become alert to where we are going wrong, go back into understanding and resolving our own hurt, go within us to tidy up any mess that is there. If we have children already and are just becoming aware, we can try to do it simultaneously, it's never too late. To even see where the fine mess came from that we got ourselves into is potentially a lifetime's worth of work on ourselves in itself, so there's not a moment to lose. Every issue that you clear within yourself, your child(ren) will not have to deal with on your behalf.

You will not regret it.

✻ ✻ ✻

46. Generation Karma - Setting our Karmic Minds Free

Our Karmic minds can create endless future friendships, love, beauty, fulfilment, life, happiness, bliss, harmony, peace for us and all others – there is no end to the positivity that happens when we use our minds to the full, whilst also working towards losing our fears and a host of other negativities. We are BORN to do this! If we have forgotten through too many distractions and too much pain, then we can take ourselves back to how it was when we had a moment of happiness that stood out. Many of us will at least find one to remember, and we can learn to work from that moment and make it grow into what we need more of, like the seed we mentioned above that can grow into a forest of food. We can make peace with the years, months, days, hours, minutes or seconds of our past. For most of us it's a blur, and our Karma has not been strong enough yet so far to remind us of the importance of being again, like children playing in order to learn to physically grow and manifest what they need, interacting with each other openly and without obstacles to assist and connect. Babies reach out to each other instinctively, being the great, open minds they are, ecstatically happy at the prospect that there is another just like them. The only time when this natural instinct seems not to occur is when adults have been consciously or unwittingly compromising or programming them otherwise. Once we know how precious life is, we would also be wise to take cue from our babies and children, take more time again for caring for their minds, too. However hard it is to juggle, we simply must take back our time to notice how naturally our children have an ability to be, and exist. They help us in our own struggle for existence, showing us all the time how to be and not to be. Do we not want happy children with a more conscious future for them than we ever had the chance to have? Or do we want to continue the present notion that we can't wait to hand over our children to someone else to take care of? Did we get separated from them too early so we now see their complaints as a nuisance, something that we believe we have to put up with, or is even their fault? Have we heard too many cries for help when we felt helpless and so worn out ourselves that we felt defeated in the end? Have we tried to put the trauma all behind and forget, so we become sarcastic about how they are constantly getting in our way of having a good time, are rude, obnoxious, ignorant, demanding, unhelpful, untidy brats we cannot wait to get rid of? Should it not at some point be worth it for our and our children's sanity and future well-being to ask ourselves where all our suffering comes from and what that is all about? We are exhausted all the time with the effort of being nuclear families trying to work and take care of our children, we certainly don't need any more stress - but does the answer lie in our need to start asking ourselves what our children are reflecting back at us that we don't have time for and are trying to ignore? Let's make it a game by paradoxically taking the role we play in their lives very seriously and aid them in their ability to make changes that we never had the opportunity to take. I believe we all have an ability to do so as a conscious society to this extent – a duty even. Society must be more again than a money-making machine. It must be a tribe again, a community that protects our children. We are the adults. We are the ones who have come away too far from our responsibility to our children. Our children will tell us when the bond has been broken from too early on, and the longer we leave it, the harder to relate it will become.

Even from before our birth, and certainly from birth onwards, we will ourselves have had to learn so much from our parents and peers that does not make sense. They almost cannot help it, because they learned it from the generation before that and so on. What happens is that our Karma becomes embroiled in Generation Karma, the way that recurring patterns in education have affected each family individually. Even when a child is much wanted and looked forward to, once a baby on their way and it's our responsibility for their needs to be met, there is hardly any time to make adjustments to our belief systems when life is at its most hectic and stressful. Many new parents these days no longer have had any instructions, help or solutions passed down to them by their parents, never mind grandparents or great-grandparents. Neither would some feel that they would have wanted it if there are no longer amicable bonds established between family members. What was once our biggest strength has often become a minefield of different opinions and a battle between those who were once close to each other. Added to that there are much bigger generational breaches these days than there ever were, due to geographical location, work and developmental distance. We feel more removed from past generations who we don't feel are up-to-date enough any longer with our life-styles including the latest in child-care. Whilst this has always been a prerogative of next generations to make their own fortunes and to try and make improvements on the past, the disconnect of a generation gap has never been so massive. The past few generations panicked in modern, sterile settings rather than family homes shared by generations. We were told by medical staff to distance ourselves from folklore and the wisdom of ancient rites, to be grateful for their help, to be afraid of what might happen if we didn't and to never question their expertise. We ourselves were subject to learned behaviour based on pseudo-scientific experiments in child-care that did a lot of damage over decades. We are so confused that we are basing a lot of our decisions these days on advertising by companies with only their own profit in mind, bombarding and confusing new parents with product placements. They do it because they know it works. Our minds and bodies are strong, yet delicate, easily influenced especially when we are exhausted and in pain. We ourselves were the ones separated too soon, so we tend to have already become separate from others more easily and without noticing anything wrong with it. At the same time, we also still tend to repeat the same patterns we feel our parents made. If anything, we are feeling even more disempowered, disheartened at the harsh reality as opposed to the white, pink and baby blue satin we imagined life with a new baby to be, too exhausted in our single-handed struggle to do it differently. If only we had been shown how to care 24/7, how to stay close to another and skin to skin with our babies, how to find the strength and determination to do almost everything with only one arm whist holding baby in the other for months and months. If only we had been reminded of how it works to take care of a youngster, how hard it is to do, and how many things there are to look out for. At least we will develop a healthy respect for all parents on Earth who ever sacrificed years of their lives to be there for their children, as much as our ancestors were there for us to ascertain our survival, even if they would never get to meet us in person. The cycle of life is complete with our efforts.

As it is, despite the way things we were taught as a society to believe potentially being so much to our and our families' detriment, we can nevertheless give ourselves permission to leave the responsibility for how our guardians dealt with things with them. If there has been trauma, we can resolve it on a Karmic energy level at any later stage in our lives, so that we realise we really are free of their actions and do no longer have to carry the burden of their actions on their behalf. This is a process that doesn't always happen overnight, but it can be done. As part of releasing our own energy from the ties that bind us to them, we also release them in their duty towards us and set them free from their Karmic role. It sounds dramatic, but we only need to make an internal agreement within ourselves to that extent first and foremost. We can see where this guides us, and I have personally observed many people gain the freedom from suffering from relations that they craved all their lives. It also does not have to be an outward confrontation, just an inner resolution to gain back the identity of our own Karmic Self, regardless of external influences from people around us. This way, we can raise our ability to separate from it mentally and integrate it in peace and with loving intention, whichever presents itself as the most useful option in the moment. By learning how to neutralise the imprint within our Karmic energy system, it will no longer affect us negatively. It is possible to overcome negative Generation Karma, so that any of us are able to give up our own roles that have made us feel we are the only ones that represent fighting against about what went wrong. What's most important is that we can finally break the chain of any wrongdoing there may have occurred no matter what happens next; perhaps that is what you are here to do, too - to be different from the rest of your birth family? Maybe that is also one of the reasons why you are reading this book.

As a side effect, many harmful situations we appear to have had no choice but to allow into our lives and have had to put up with, will diminish in intensity. I have noticed, over the past few years of working on my own and others' energy flow, the effect of several interesting phenomena:

- Time takes on a different dimension – days don't come in increments of 24 hours, 7 days a week any longer, but have a different 'feel': somewhat timeless, reminiscent of walking in nature without a watch and observing different things around us, relating more to significance of the specific moment they happen; being guided to react to needs as they arise in the moment, rather than planning ahead.

- Expectations change or disappear altogether, including those external to us.

- Seasons, weather, weekdays or places, day or night are no longer good or bad, they just are, and can have amazing aspects to them regardless of whether we feel anxious about them.

- Perceptions change – we start to see others differently and rather than reacting to them, we might feel we want a chance to learn to understand them, have time for them whilst also increasing the time we take for ourselves. We may even expand our circle of acquaintances, friends, and close relationships, and become more tolerant of others' choices to identify with who they are and how they define their relationships and reality.

- Jobs are not just jobs to make money any more – we want them to become meaningful and part of our mission again, as it should be. It may become difficult or impossible to hold down a position that we have never truly believed in, just 'for the money'.

- Our view of money itself changes – it can no longer exist to be our God because it loses what it never had – an identity. We gave it meaning in stone-age by exchanging shells, and now? It is still an exchange of energies, except by now it's just paper or plastic, nothing more. It has no value itself, only by what we attach to it. Is it wise to lose our Karmic energy by losing it from our bodies and attaching it to anything external? I'll let you answer that question for yourself, according to where you are at. Suffice to say, we can bypass any excessive need for money - even if nowadays it is in the form of invisible, virtual currency - by recognising what we truly need to manifest instead, i.e. an abundance of joy, simplicity but fulfilment and happiness in our lives, health, good nutrition, clean water, environment and so on. We tend to notice more that these are states of mind that really have little to do with owning lots of money. Once we see through how we have been led to believe it, we are no longer being owned. We become responsible for ourselves and creating a new reality for ourselves and our loved ones, based on what is really important.

• 　　　　　　　　People start to react differently to our energy – for example, there is almost never a need for 'anger' if we are willing to listen and be responsible for our own Self; by which I mean a deliberate feeling of needing or wanting to help instead of hurt another, as 'anger' and resentment decreases and true understanding of others increases. By which is meant that we start to include, respect, acknowledge and vow to learn more about our Karmic pasts so they can be resolved. I still don't much like talking in absolutes, as in affirming things like 'ALL my anger is gone'. This is because I believe it's important to incorporate learning curves as well as increasing our acceptance and tolerance of where we are all at individually. It is as important as recognising that maintaining our own healthy energy flow in various circumstances is an important part of our growth. We become aware that energy rising within us which we may have channelled into 'anger', is our precious, strong and vital Kundalini energy rising. It is ours to keep, we do not dissipate it. If we find this hard, we can definitely learn methods to take charge of and integrate it again, by being able to express what is happening within us and combine it with a technique that helps to lessen any intensity of 'bad' feelings, rather than suppress them. I would personally rather not call this 'anger' as it is a beautiful, powerful and constructive energy once it is integrated into the purpose of creating good outcomes for all. We can certainly learn to turn it around, and help by reminding others to use it for positive results, too. It is also our vital and necessary energy in order to maintain a healthy body, mind and emotions, as well as help us determine and do away with constructs which are to our detriment. Pent up energy that breaks out in anger, frustration and so on, is simply stagnant, locked-in energy that needs to be addressed. If we don't do it, others will poke us enough so we might explode and then blame them for it. It would be interesting to see our behaviour soften and our language reflecting our inner changes in creating many different words for the adjusted energy flow instead of just 'anger', which some of us are terrified of showing or receiving lest it becomes destructive. Instead we need to allow ourselves to find out more about how to channel this, our all-important life-force energy constructively.

Surely, this process of relinquishing our limited perceptions has to logically start with ourselves, because we are the only power there is that can determine our inner world. Nobody else has the ability to do so, even if others may well have tried to exercise manipulation and control over our Self. We may not ever give it any thought, but it is a massive breech of universal Karmic law if anyone breaks the shield of our Karmic energy field on whatever level, physical, mental, emotional or spiritual with their actions, words or energy presence. We don't have criminal laws for this last offence, but we are certainly sensitive enough to feel it when someone wishes us ill and is determined to let us feel it in not so many words. We should at least make ourselves aware that this is indeed a 'thing', so that we are conscious and clear within us that we do not have to allow our Self to be compromised on any such level and can protect ourselves against these very real attacks.

Despite these being very real, we can still be some steps ahead of attempts of breech against us and can hopefully arrange to distance ourselves at the moment we realise what is occurring, with the advantage that we are constantly coming closer to our own truth and strength in the process. The mention of it here should at least remind us that we are right to believe that these exist and feel validated, but also that we are able to claim back much of the power over our own lives, which is the first and foremost place where we can make a difference. Even if we have been influenced by infinite amounts of people so far in countless lifetimes, it is still only our good old, humble Karmic energy mind where we can fully agree, consent and begin to make a change. If for whatever reason you don't feel brave enough yet, would it be worth considering to try it for the sake of a loved one, if it is not you? Find out what motivates and inspires you to make changes, see what makes you tick and feel alive again! Dream big!

We may not even know what that state of mind is yet that we are looking for, we may be cynical about it, feel insecure, undecided, frightened of losing our present comfort zone, of changes, of pain - but we are not that far removed from being successful when we make that commitment to ourselves.

Heaven on Earth is not that far away.

When I had the good fortune to be at a lecture of the beautiful soul, the late Dr Masaru Emoto, I felt obliged to ask him a question. I asked him whether there was a point where water – his specialised subject of observing the effects of our energy on frozen water crystals – is ever beyond repair on Earth. His answer was simply 'no – there is no point at which water cannot be repaired'. It was a fascinating answer, one that I also believe in. There must be a way, therefore, that we are all able to repair what is going on within us, I thought, since we are around 70% water ourselves.

We have only temporarily forgotten that we can repair, by being lost in our daily ego brain-based activities, where we insist on eternally deliberating something that our brains are not necessarily capable of grasping fully. This is also not something our brains may be able to fully assist us with in order to integrate those blissful energies into our crammed and busy little bodies on Earth. In those realms beyond Earth, beyond the dense 'reality' of opposites, we might want to recall that we have all experienced already what it is like to live in a paradisical and blissful state - that is, if we didn't mess up our Karmic journey so that we came back down to Earth like a damp firework. Once we have experience with states of blissfulness, we all want to try to get back to that state like shopaholics to a black Friday sale, except we might not yet fully realise what it is we are looking for. It's so easy to get distracted. We don't want to end up just with a pair of pink socks in a size too large in a sale, when what we are really looking for is something that is beyond all worldly possessions. We are more or less all of us trying to create and re-create a peaceful, happy state of mind – but we are also sometimes going about it in an inexperienced, slightly unskilful and forgetful way, trying to rely on our brains and bodies only to comprehend, coordinate and command subtle energies. We are missing our Karmic identity so we end up accumulating more and more material goods, and end up separating ourselves even more from others by egotistically thinking about our own welfare only in a first come, first served society based on instant gratification. Surely we must have noticed by now that this is not what recreates a peaceful existence and a blissful mind at all.

When we want to create a blissful state, first of all, we need to remember it is not useful to think of it in terms of being 'out there' or 'up there' because it is already HERE and NOW. It has always been here, present with each of us, within and around us. It is the state of the accumulation of energy within our Karmic mind that creates every second of the day, and when I say 'our' it means that we are a part of an infinitely vast energy phenomenon that is temporarily giving us the experience of being a separate 'I'-dentity. So whilst we can look to the analogy of an external 'heaven' or 'spirit' for help which quite possibly exists, too, as a level of otherworldly experience, we must also take note that this would be no other than the same energy which exists within us and is a part of us, as we are a part of the whole experience. It is the same miraculous energy we are made of which also created the heavens, the infinite space beyond physical existence. Since we arise from there, we are a part of it at all times. That is not to say we can all become egotistically megalomaniac know-it-alls with a messiah complex. This is delusional.

When we relinquish everything that disturbs our state of bliss, it means that this peace of mind will conquer any fear-creating, separating thought frequency; any doctrine based on or creating fear becomes neutralised and will no longer be active within us.

Obstruction, destruction, illness, pain, any feeling of negativity and limited perception will cease to exist eventually with good Karma, and we will be shown how to replenish any of our puffed-out energy. We have lifetimes to perfect our practice, but only this one precious lifeform right now to persevere with. Take your time, because there is no time to lose - if you see the paradox of it and it transforms you to read between the lines, then you will glimpse the empty space between.

Keep it all, hang on to it, keep it precious, even if at first it feels really odd and difficult; even if anger arises, and fear, look at the energy behind it. What vast potential has created your being able to have these feelings arise in the first place? They arise simply because that is all they are: expressions of your inner strength, an ability to create vast energy resources within. If you read this, as I will surely re-read this myself again to remind me in darker times to tune into the light, please know that it's ok to laugh about it and shrug it off as well as rant about it and complain – but know that energy caught up in loops and knots within us is all illusion either way. Our minds are so vast, we are holding ourselves up with all this fretting about things, our convoluted feelings and thoughts. We are missing the show, standing at the ticket booth complaining that we can't see!

There is one thing we have to also remember though, despite being caught up in our inner world. It is important.

We will not create a peaceful mind by conveniently forgetting to think about and include others.

This does not necessarily mean that you are not allowed to have anything, or put yourself last on your list.

What it does mean is that it's a reminder to use our minds to their greatest potential. It seems to have gone out of fashion lately, in the last few hundred years or so. Our minds have always become easily polluted with violent actions, speech and thoughts. I am saying this as if I am wagging my finger at the notion, but because we're all in it together and we all do it as human beings, it should simply unite us in our quest to create a different outcome. We need to begin - and end - by paying attention to honing our Karmic energy minds. We need to know why our negative tendencies are there from a point of Karmic origin, and then find methods to slowly but surely unravel them, each and every one of us. Will it all happen at once, at the same time? Who knows. What we can see through is that our fear is causing aggression, greed and ignorance, which go hand in hand in limiting our beautiful potential. We all have fear, it's normal, but most of us don't have methods to alleviate fear. Added to this, there is a double-negative energy blockage within us, because we don't just have fears, we are by now fearing our fears, too, keeping us nicely stuck in our Karmic gloop. We need to do something else. We now HAVE methods to eliminate fear, cut through anger, see through ignorance. This is not another boring anthropological lecture about what society meant then and now, or a paranoid vision of them taking side against you: since you are the reader right now in this moment, this is about you, and what you have the potential to be and choose. And yes, in my case, since I am writing this, it is about me, too, at this moment, but let that part be my concern. There is nobody else out there right now reading this at this very moment, other than you. Our perception of others may be false and distracting. Come back to yourself, don't go away. It may simply reflect our current state of mind, chasing thoughts. We need to realise this over and over again, an exercise in developing wisdom. We cannot keep reading novels, gaming, watching soaps on TV or movies in the cinema, thinking made-up stuff fully represents Truth...the real Truth is much more exciting. After all, every script gets its ideas from somewhere and at least, they may help us turn in the direction of our own truth-finding here and there; but on the whole, when we use these as crutches to constantly distract ourselves from our boredom - which only stems from not having found our inner source of endless entertainment in the form of meaningful conversations with Self, no nudge, nudge, wink, wink intended - we are stopping ourselves from doing important work on the discovery of our own amazing inner worlds and passing on our new-found wisdom and compassion to others. Can we afford to keep pretending that there is time, pretending that there is a fake world out there that we need, trying to make itself indispensable and vaguely interesting enough to get away with bullying, cajoling, manipulating, coaxing us into paying attention - and paying money for the insult to our own level of intuition? It seems it's doing quite a good job of it by the looks of it, judging by its popularity, to the point where my point is probably very unpopular. I will add that I don't hate some of the movies out there, I really enjoy some of them. I understand how they appeal to the blind spots in our brains, our Self-sabotage, because we have temporarily forgotten how beautiful, delicate, precious and easily manipulated our own beautiful minds are and they are there to remind us of our own greatness. I want us all to come up with our own beautiful movies. We are substituting, or even letting others substitute for us. This goes back to childhood and before then even, into past Karmic existences where we would find the reasons why we are how we are right now, if we knew how to look, or even felt inclined to. Perhaps we were told what to do, say and think for aeons of time before now, and we are obligingly and obediently lowering our energy levels to still serve others' requests of our attention. Somehow, our poor ego mind is playing a broken record, thinking it serves our survival somehow. It doesn't any more – we no longer have to sell our souls, so to speak. We have given parts of our mind's energy away to think for us, bank for us, choose partners, buy food and cook for us, drive for us, design for us, build for us, care for us – that part of our mind is often on auto pilot. It makes us perform like puppets all of those tasks we habitually do each day, because we still believe that it is good for us, and trust that others do a better job and will look after us. Does society really reflect to us that this is true? Are we not utterly dissatisfied with the service? Do we not keep on complaining about how short-changed we feel? We are the ones that decided it was a good idea to give our time and skills away out of a feeling of inadequacy, complacency or fear. Perhaps at some point in human communities it truly is necessary to have a functioning dynamic by which each individual is given a task and is happy to oblige, lest the whole tribe would be in danger. Nowadays, however, tables are turned against us. If we don't think on our feet, our powers that we trustingly gave away are easily being abused by a greedy few and we are worse off just following obediently and doing as we are told. We end up under more pressure feeling more stressed, because we did not realise the price we paid was that we were giving away our mind's potential. It simply does not seem fair and we are absolutely justified to feel that way.

I have a good idea – only if we're brave and confident enough to do it, though, and trust the process, that is. Here it is, and it won't cost you a penny: we learn how to claim back our minds. Claim back all our energy, from all those unhelpful situations it has leaked out to, no matter how long ago. Remember that our minds are not just our brains and thoughts. Our minds are that most complex, beautiful and precious thing we possess. The result of being back in our minds, fully present, is stunning. It is everything we always wanted and never found: it contains peace, harmony, fulfilment; a feeling of complete serenity and contentment. Perhaps this is already happening for us, perhaps we already know how to do this, and as a result, all our 'lost' energy withdrawn from any lesser corrupted files and internal malware that we took on from those with lesser intentions means that we emancipate ourselves from those situations and become independent from those constructs. They are being exposed in any case, and their ill will is becoming much weaker and more transparent. We have been giving energy to projects that do not serve wo-mankind, or the animal kingdom, or the planet. We can withdraw our energy back into ourselves again at any time, no matter how much energy we feel we have 'lost' and how much time has passed. No need to be upset or angry any longer – call your energy back into yourself, and invest it in something more worthwhile. The great benefit of doing this - apart from it being free and available to us at any time - is that it is very powerful to do, but very gentle, too, and we only need to involve ourselves in the process. It demonstrates that we understand the power of our own subtle energy and how it can be steered in the right direction with our minds, with the great advantage that it saves us having to be active externally. By this subtle indication I mean that we do not need to engage in combat with anyone outside of ourselves. It is neither useful nor necessary to have all this unwise open warfare, which so many people in power seem to still want us to believe is necessary, looking at the state of the world. We are always being goaded, we are always 'drawn in' by scenarios. We are always expelling and expending our energy into the external environment, and we are literally loosing it as a result. It seems that this could also be part of a lesser vibrational outcome that may have been spread intentionally to create fear, unconsciousness and dissonance in order to manipulate people. We might need to notice for ourselves first the benefit of calling all our precious energy back to ourselves. We won't necessarily lose anything that way. Perhaps it will become clearer when we try it as to how powerful it is, that we may notice gradually when we have outgrown the need for it and no longer want a part of it. Of course, I can't tell you exactly what will happen to you on Earth when you will claim back your full and luminous energy mind, but I would do it sooner rather than later, if you ask me. I would not waste time, having caught glimpses of what lies beyond. Many people are being made redundant, are becoming ill with stress, become upset, angry, worried and afraid; we are losing our minds with worry, literally. Which state of mind would you rather choose? Stay in that state of fear and insanity, or become serene and sane? Most of us probably want to compromise and settle somewhere near the middle between the two, just to be on the safe side. It's understandable that trying to guess the right answer without knowing it and also commit to it like in a quiz show trying to win a million pounds seems to be unsurprisingly difficult for many of us. Our minds and bodies have become used to oppression and authority over us, we are looking over our shoulder and at others to find the answers, so we think we don't have what it takes to face leaving an uncomfortable comfort zone and make a giant leap into the unknown; those are two things our brain really does not like us to do, even if our comfort zone has been far from comfortable so far. It is a paradox that can actually be solved with methods described at the end of this book. I have a feeling that it still might not be an easy or quick transition, because it is so ingrained in us to be following orders and blaming someone else for our own misfortune...but let's face it: we can always simply blame our Karma if things don't go our way. Jokes aside, surely we know by now that there is no-one else to blame, and there won't be a need for it either. On a Karmic mind level, we consented to what is in store for us; even if we do not recall consciously choosing it for ourselves, our Karmic energy system certainly did, before we even got here. and it is not really meant as a punishment to be here, either, as some might like to believe, but can be quite an act of bravery for some when we agree to incarnate at a time when conditions are far from easy and when we are needed most. Which, to me, seems like all the time on Earth, to be honest.

If we are brave enough though, I believe with all the wisdom of my heart that we will create communities which will manage to deal with the challenges in life differently. We have ways to treat aggression and anxiety and manipulative streaks and stubbornness without bashing each other's heads in. We all have moments, there is no point denying, but there are ways to diminish them, to transform blind anger and ignorance into beautiful creations again; angst into a form of living that is easier on our mind, body and spirit; greed into states of mind that cause us less stress and less illness, makes it easier a world for our children to grow up in. Our children show us all the time where we are going wrong, often by mimicking the very same defilements we are trying to overcome. We need to listen to them, from even before the day they are born. They are still closest to the messages of the universal mind when they are small, much closer than most adults are. We need to treat them wisely. They are the ones who have come to educate us and be our teachers, not the other way 'round. A nurtured child has their pineal gland wide open and comes with an inquisitive, open mind that will question our fundamental views when we least think we have time for it. Many children wear an expression of awe and wonder on their face, curious to their environment, especially in the early days before we mess up their thought processes with too many demands. When do their smiles get replaced with frowns? When we turn a blind eye to the meddling and doctoring with a child's mind and existence that is going on, on a huge scale on this planet, that's when. When we stop listening to their symptoms, we might miss something that has been going on for far too long and cannot stop soon enough. We can only hope that some of us pick up the right methods to help us be more conscious guardians of the next generations, so that they, in turn, will no longer have their love and lives suffocated, so that they can continue inheriting the Earth, and help to salvage what is there to be saved; maybe this includes us. After all, once our brains have become too old to learn something new, will we still be thinking so much of ourselves only, our politics, conflicts, dogmas and inner rebellion, stubbornly insisting on our right to be wrong that we don't notice the world continues to turn without us? This is what the true nature of mind is: unspoiled, vast, loving creation, potential, laughter, simplicity, not grasping at anything – just peace, and within it, simply, and divinely, being.

What we have done unskilfully in the past has corrupted and desensitised our behaviour, thoughts and language in the here and now. What we are doing, saying and thinking skilfully right now, influences our pure minds and strenghtens our thoughts, actions and spoken words in the future.

This is no moral high ground or religious teaching – it is a simple Karmic truth of cause and effect, and in that it is logically rectifiable. We can change the future outcome of our Karmic Self at any moment by our choice of actions, thoughts and words. The reason we are dealing with an angry and lost mind raging within ourselves, one that is fixed on all the wrong things, is because of our unskilful actions in the past, at a time when we probably did not know better. We are vastly underestimating the time that has gone before, where we were already present, perhaps much less evolved than we are now. Knowing that now, does it not follow that our present life-form is so much more precious and not to be wasted? We most likely have all been through times where we have been procrastinating spending time and effort on the wrong things, corrupting our own future somewhat but probably without being aware of it at the time through being ignorant of our connections to all that life is and how it is created. It is time to become aware of that, without guilt trips, endless excuses, cop-outs or pointing of fingers, blaming or shaming. No-one is to blame, and we are also not to suffer for it endlessly either. It is just the right time right now to call it quits and look at how we can benefit from being different even if we don't yet believe it because we haven't even seen any of the benefit of it yet, obviously. It is a simple universal equation. It can be hard at times to put into practice no doubt, and to maintain a calm mind and remind ourselves of serenity when it comes to the crunch (wherever that is, probably right next to a place called hindsight). It can be extremely challenging for some, but since we now know we play the main part of the theatre act in our lives and it's up to us as to how that turns out, would we not do anything to avoid all the confusion of thoughts and circumstances that can work against us? Bearing in mind that, whatever we manage to do right now, will cement a good future for ourselves and build a strong and beautiful network with others, as a crucial fringe benefit.

Please read on to find out more about this and other ways to soothe our Karmic minds and therefore our Earth's problems in a constructive way, in the practical sections below.

* * *

47. The 'Bigger' Picture

So, if there really is a decline in the state of our body, mind and brains, one that may at some point be absolute – I am considering that the opposite might well exist, too, at least theoretically - it could be our Karmic state of mind that is all that remains, absolute and connected beyond all physical boundaries imposed on it. which we already know as the phenomenon described and named a thousand different ways in this book, as well as religions, doctrines, scientific theories and philosophies.

I have been unravelling the mystery from the bottom up, having started with worst case scenario of what it would be like if our bodies and brains did get completely compromised. If it then turns out then that we do not have an afterlife – and neither a chance to see our flaws, have moments of regret nor any opportunity to ever make improvements – there would be no point in us even having a higher consciousness safety mechanism that stops us from being as evil as we wanted. There would be no repercussions, nothing to improve upon, and nobody and nothing would be of any value. There would also be no point in being alive, because - why would we? What would enjoyment be, if we could only amass a fortune of experiences, love and money, spend it all and then lose it again when it's time to go. There would be no accumulation of goodness and wisdom within us as we could not take any of it with us. There would be no place to take it, and no way we could ever return. There would be no point to making any effort then, other than to have some crazy times and break the rules, because why have rules if nothing matters? The result would be that we would only drive ourselves insane trying to attach meaning to anything, so we wouldn't bother. We would be living a meaningless existence from moment to moment, except there is the chance that we would rejoice in worldly pleasures and totally immerse ourselves in those. Ah – wait. These hypothetical musings sounds much like some philosophies already out there, and perhaps they have validity, too, although I think as far as I can tell they also sparked some violent crime and hedonistic synthetic drug consumption. Who am I to say, what do I know.

If, on the other hand, we did have a Karmic energy body that was pure light within us, which surpassed our worldly struggles and survived our physical death, then there would also be a process we go through to becoming this pure light body again, and a final result ending in the

ultimate optimum of shining light which increased in brilliance much like a window that was being cleaned for the first time after a very long time; where, bit by bit, more light shone through until in the end, the glass became invisible and translucent, and only pure clarity existed.
If that doesn't appeal, I also quite like the idea of the singularity of a black hole that consumed all energy to condense it into a tiny space of infinitely intense light so bright that it would contain all there is. Unless black holes are just inverted Tori which suck in all energy near them, twist them around their inner axis like a pretzel and then spit them out again as the universe's answer to Qubits. You choose.

If we are here on Earth by the attachments to our Karma, but are ultimately able to transform ourselves back from physical existence into our ethereal existence of suspended animation, or Karmic energy mind as we have called it so far, when the time comes, then it follows that, when we no longer have any nasty Karma left at some point in our ever-evolving incarnations, we will also no longer have anything worldly to be Karmically attached to...in short, we will be entering a stage where everything has been neutralised into clarity and every little shred of negative Karma dissolved. It sounds painful but this is not the case. Far from it – the process is not one of harshness and solitude, it is one of gentleness and compassion. The more unity conscious we become, the calmer and brighter we will feel within. We might feel displeasure at such cliché concepts, as if in fear of being anaesthetised, but that is also not what happens. There is only a completely inherent and non-violent, natural and inevitable process that we already belong to, whether we are aware of it or not. Indeed, when researching through ancient texts and studying philosophies and theories, such states of mind are recorded everywhere. If I may refer to the state of Enlightenment, for example, which is also a much misunderstood inner development that is closely linked to the term Karma. I have used this terminology a lot throughout this book to describe what happens to us once we are not in physical body, and we must also take into consideration that even when we free ourselves from any of our own Karma, we will probably also be lucid enough to notice there is still plenty of Karma left that other beings need help with sorting out. We can come back any time, like on one of those hoarder programmes on telly, we help people clean up their act when they really don't know where to start. If we choose not to, we can also go to enlightenment college and further purify our essence by entering even more evolved, divine stages of purification. These are probably also levels that are extremely difficult to convey, but I will try to keep it simple. There exist in terms of purifying said Karma, 12 (or sometimes13, depending on scriptures) levels of non-attachment. At the time of his passing, Buddha Gautama is said to have passed to the state of what is called parinirvana – no ordinary death but a different kind of living without any of the attachments we have to a physical existence, on our way to condensing our essence even further. Where this is helpful is that our consciousness, our 'I', still exists, and the more it is condensed, the more ability it gains in terms of steering itself in any realm between universes and even beyond this, into emptiness beyond concepts of time, space, matter or dimensions, and back again if our presence is required elsewhere. You might think I have watched too many Star Wars movies, but actually, movies that try to emulate concepts like these, are taking facts and mixing them with fiction so the lines get a bit blurred for most of us trying to wrap our heads around what is real and what is not. Our brains can't grasp these concepts so it needs analogies, it needs crutches to try and understand them, which it never will. We can only experience this for ourselves when we enter different frequency levels in meditation for example, which allow us to perceive Truth, probably still in bite-size pieces. If we 'got it' all at once it would probably drive us insane. Analogies work, but they also take away from the Truth, so it's a two edged-sword. Which sounds like something that should have appeared in the Harry Potter series. 'Harry Potter and the Two-Edged Sword'. I'd be up for co-writing it - but would it distract me from reaching my inner Bumis? Or would it help mankind to understand the concept of Karma and classify as an act of compassion? I would need to check within myself if it was wise enough. In the meantime, if we use fiction to catch a glimpse of the facts, it's not a bad thing, per se. At least we know we can live hundreds of years because of Dumbledore, and we know we have to learn some tough lessons through little Harry. We also open up our brains to other dimensions, and yes, we can certainly fly, although not on a broomstick. We fly a lot more elegantly, I can already promise you that.

In the meantime, real superheroes, The Bodhisattvas – Beings who are realised, meaning they truly and, by now, after a lot of practising and contemplating, fearlessly realise themselves without a 'Self' as we understand it, in order to be able to exercise their superpowers, which are to Selflessly perpetuate their actions, speech and thoughts without delay to assist all beings on their frightful journey through space and time and hopefully convince them to get with the plan to achieve enlightenment for the benefit of all beings sooner rather than later – they achieve these bespoke levels of non-attachment through their compassionate actions, thoughts and insights. Humour aside - what does all of this mean? Ultimately, it means that your mind has no ties any longer to a past and a future. Our sense of time and our perception of solid matter that binds us to a planetary system and physical body is no longer the same as it is for others. That does not mean we must cut our ties with family tomorrow to never see them again, or pretend that our Karmic history did not exist to bring us here. Everything exists. we just haven't seen the whole job lot yet because we have been too busy micro-managing. It means that ultimately, your luminous Karmic mind is, with practice, not just subject to the laws of physics any longer, i.e. it does not have to attach itself on an energy level any more by having an inner positive or negative Karmic outcome. All inner Karmic charge from any situation becomes neutral through practising the right view, right motive, right livelihood, right speech, right action, right thought, right concentration and right effort.

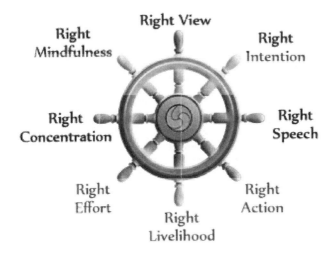

Classic Image of Buddhist Dharma Wheel, showing the Teaching of the eight-fold path to purifying our Karma
Image Credit © Mato's Blog: Love, Peace, and Happiness

These principles together form what's called the Eightfold Path in short, where all frenzied states of thought, action and emotion are nullified, all fear erased, all concerns eased, all Karmic history understood, made peace with and integrated. This may be an unimaginable concept for most , making us wonder who we will become without all this that we are identifying with. But a sincere method and practice does not take anything away from us, it adds to it, giving us additional insights in order to see things in a bigger context than ever before. This context, compared to the drudgery of cyclic existence, seems far more attractive especially when presented in all its kaleidoscopic facets, even if it means we realise we've been dragging our feet and been taking aeons to come out of our shells and rid ourselves of our fears. As long as we are held back by Samsara, which is what we are creating right now by staying put in our favourite TV chair and binge watching soaps, there is no guarantee where or how we will end up. On the other end of the spectrum is the path of liberation which is lovely and clear like a mountain lake on a sunny morning, and it is certainly possible to achieve for any of us even when we are a bit unfit for climbing mountains and will need a bit of a lift up. It is not some Guru craze where everyone walks around in white robes wafting incense at your sins and prays for your dirty soul. It is common sense, simple deductions from what presents itself to us as life, based on who we are as opposed to who we think we are. We will be and look no different in this lifetime than we did before we started practising a path of wisdom and compassion. We might smile a bit more, be a bit happier, have a bit more patience and know that it is important that others feel happy, too. People might ask what's got into you, but you can just smile that knowing, insanely happy smile in the face of adversity you see on commercials for car insurance and feminine hygiene products. We don't suddenly have to do something to prove we have become enlightened. We don't need to become a rocket scientist simply because we caught a glimpse of the farthest corners of the universe. Just by staying 'normal' doing 'normal' things, does not mean we are blind to the Truth or have gone nuts – far from it. There is plenty of time to worry about what is beyond this planet, and plenty to do before we finally take off from here. In the meantime, we have work to do.

Beyond the universe as we know it, there are other realms that do not follow principles of gravity, electromagnetism, quantum physics or string theory. They follow other rules, higher manifestations of vibrational frequencies. This goes on for a few levels of existence, ascending with ever purer frequencies until ultimately, there are no laws of physics at all, no interdependent origination, no individual beings; only the great 'emptiness' meaning vastness beyond all existence, the great source that 'is'. And whilst the term seems to be belittling the inexplicable, the vastness that we are a part of for which no word exists, is the opposite of small: it is the highest level of ultimate freedom, ultimate happiness and wisdom that there is. In fact, we can't even say that there is an experience of such words, because there are no individuals to feel and express them. It is, simply and profoundly, being. All-knowing, all-encompassing - and it all starts with being right here on this Earth, living consciously, moment to moment. We start being this vastness, right here, right now, in the tiny breaches from moment to moment where we experience the oneness with All. No need to sit on a mountain, you apply your wisdom right here right now, even if you are sitting in a rocking chair with the remote control, who knows if you are not enlightened? Actually, don't answer that, your family will tell you. When we experience this frequency level of oneness, we know it is not an individual experience for any of us any more. There is no right or wrong, black or white, this or that. It's nothing like the sensation of separation we are so hooked on in our individual bodies right now, whilst also longing to be unified with all-encompassing energy. No footie on a Saturday, but instead the same feeling of overwhelming love and happiness, except on a much grander scale of heightened awareness. Granted, it's hard to imagine and difficult to speculate for us what the experience will be like, seen from our own tiny eyes within a less-than perfect physical body. The question probably hadn't even entered our minds, of wondering what physical matter no longer existing on higher frequency levels would be like. We're more worried reading the news and what to have for our tea. I once meditated by the sea, where a mist was blurring the edges of the horizon so that sea and sky looked like one. It was made clear to me that nature has a way of saying things in clues that appear just when we need an answer to a question we didn't think we had asked aloud. I had been contemplating the existence of life beyond this universe at the time. The answer came, quite simply: matter and non-matter are like water and air. They blend, but there is nobody to see. They are alike, but still oppose each other. Small droplets escape the sea and vaporise into air, as infinitesimally small particles of matter will dissolve into nothingness.

I m truly sorry if we can't just go and fact-check this, not giving us much of an opportunity for discussion. Of course, we can do that if that's what we want, but it won't get us anywhere as we will still be caught up in talks about matter rather than the everlasting presence that we are. Something that we can look forward to is that we will also at some point be part of this Torus dance between matter and no-matter, the greatest recycling plant that exists. This is where our Karmic energy will reside in suspended animation, and yet our 'I' locked in our Karmic energy will still be able to 'choose' to come back and be drawn to this planet by our consent to make a difference to others who we allow ourselves to connect to again to help. It would be all the more meaningful if we had realisation of the full cycle we go through before we can incarnate again to be of Karmic benefit of helping others. Maybe not all of us will always reach the far ends of all universes, in fact, if we still live with much fear, it may create anger and greed and not allow us to experience the whole scale of our endless possibilities just yet. We might be like a firework ready to go, but our fear has dampened our spirit so it doesn't really go off properly and just has to come back down to Earth and wait a lot longer to find its full potential to shine for all to see. We all have this potential, we are all made of the same stuff, we are all already connected anyway, right here, right now, even if we are not feeling it. Sounds like I mean for us to act like missionaries, which I don't, perish the thought. Any thought pattern can be compromised, and every word misconstrued, I am well aware, and I chose to become a bit flippant with it to diffuse any rising discontent, trying to convey something inconceivable. It is the intention that is behind and between those symbols we are reading as text here and which our brain is trying to make sense of, but we can only grasp it truly with our wisdom mind. For that, we need to come away from just reading and start to engage in our own process of simply being.

What I am trying to say is simply that this is the point at which we need to be searching for everything that already exists within ourselves.

On a lighter note, we may just as likely incarnate on a different, equally bizarre planet in another universe next, with varying rules and attributes, perhaps some of them not even physical. From where I am standing, I am pretty certain there are actually infinite choices, all of them special in their ability to be life-supporting. If we have never even thought about how privileged we are to be in the position we are now to make a difference to our and other's future quality of existence, we will be feeling like kids with no money looking through the window of a sweet shop. Everything might seem unobtainable to us, and at the lesser stage of development that many of us find ourselves, we may not even consciously get to choose where we end up next. What incarnates from here to the next state of being, is our Karmic energy body that remains intact as an imprint once we have passed from this existence. If our imprint still holds a highly charged Karmic energy of opposing encrypted information, it will likely result in us again manifesting as matter, potentially reborn again on Earth, in a new physical experience we will again call 'I'. Our Karmic energy has no choice but to do so, it is not our conscious decision but one based on universal forces that push and pull us in certain directions according to the unique nature of our Karmic energy. Whilst this sounds a bit like an inevitable prison sentence, the experience of manifest existence even here on Earth is actually very rare. Precious energy and circumstances have to converge to make 'us' happen. If we manage to work on our Karmic energy lifetime after lifetime, manage to resolve conflict within and around us and not get drawn into being biased either way by each and every situation; if we manage to not create outcomes of duality by harmful or unlawful actions, doing damage to ourselves and others and therefore lowering the frequency of our energy minds again; if we can also master not losing energy from our centred Karmic being by saying too much of the wrong stuff either, and thinking wrong thoughts based on limiting views - in short, if we are preparing with our practice to be ready and willing to be mindful down to every second of our lives, then those seconds will not will have to be repeated in a time-line setting to be re-lived in a future physical existence. If we do manage to do this on a really grand scale, counting each second and making a conscious decision not to charge them with negative Karma, then our perception of time, in the end, will no longer be necessary. Time and space will both become different for us as a result, to a level of ultimately being non-existent in the way that we are used to perceiving them. The stages in between then will not be linear any longer, or be like the equal clock-like time-spans we have come to believe in when we were taught about 'measuring' time and seeing it in equal distances along a linear timeline. This is not how time and space work. They are only consistent with the notion of gravity applied to a physical weight. Gravity is energy attracted to the notion of matter. If neither of those are present, time and space will no longer apply in the role we have cast them in. Beyond gravity, there is a different perception, a different part of our existence other than our physical presence that comes to the forefront: our Karmic energy mind. Our interdimensional aware mind that travels between worlds, able to make contact with the all-encompassing experience of the always and forever, the pain-free, all-loving experience of endless light and unmanifested potential, of eternal connectedness and vastness of everything that is, ourselves included, merging with it as much as is possible according to the condition of our Karmic energy. We have the potential to become weightless, bodiless and timeless again, and yes, 'we' are still an experience of ourselves, as we were for infinite amounts of intervals between previous incarnations before this physical one. I am sure I remember it being nice, and bright, peaceful and vast; however, there will not be anyone to say 'oh, that's nice, dear', like sitting in front of a TV watching a show. There will be no perception of 'nice' as there is no perception of its opposite. There will literally be no body to log and no brain to judge a niceness. There will be   . That's it, and the   , will be us. We are a part of it already, even right now. And with our heavy bodies and brains, we cannot perceive it quite as easily, that is just how it is. We have to look for the breaches between the weight of everything that is matter to try and find the weightless space, and that is what practices like meditation are for. It is one method to slip into the breaches in between the dense, heavy matter, where we find out more about the essence, siguals and signatures of our Karmic energy minds. We can only do what is called 'think', and 'sense' with what we feel through our bodily sensations and have intellectualised with our brains so far. And so, with this limited experience that we cling to, we inevitably tend to stop ourselves aiming to merge with vastness, because it seems just a little too daunting, it's a little bit too bright, a bit too final and definitely far too big. We're scared, because we do not recall what we are letting ourselves in for. It's like jumping off the edge of a cliff, blindfolded: Enlightenment is asking us to work hard for just that, the process of total surrender to the All-Seeing, with all of our existence. 'How can this be safe?', our brains ask. In the past, jumping off the proverbial cliff has meant death, over and over again, and our brain is satisfied with the belief that this would be the outcome again, if we dared to try. Our brain has numerous reasons why not to try; the main ones being that it does not deem it safe, or worth achieving. Why, for a start, we would have to agree to give up our phys-

ical existence for a belief in a greater outcome; like some fanatical suicide bomber, we would have to stop being 'us' – would we not? How ridiculous a situation our poor brains are finding themselves in, when we
try to understand the concepts of infinite wisdom. We cannot grasp it
with our brains and bodies, but that does not stop us from thinking
about doing it and jumping to conclusions. We also don't question our
own limited thought process in the first place; we cling to it for dear life
since we believe that is all we have to go on. We fear what is beyond our
thinking process, who are we without it? It hasn't crossed our mind that
we have not even really tried to found out who we are yet, to realise it's
not that hard. All we have to do is remember. We can remember everything: where we come from, what the vastness is around us and so on. So
all the while, our brain pretends that it thinks it knows, by giving us
names, possessions, emotions, thoughts - in short, anchors to tighten our
grip on physical reality. How clever, because as a result, we catch ourselves in our own dragnet most of the time, with no way out and in a
constant loop of helplessness. The funniest thing is, our brain loves it,
because at least it knows where we are. It's like we are the budgie in our
brain's cage, when we are convinced we have complete freedom of
choice. Most of the time we don't actually want it any different, because
to walk through that open cage door that says 'freedom – exit if you
dare' takes a lot of courage. We might just catch a glimpse of something
we are secretly yearning for, and we might just about remember what
insights we once had and have since misplaced. Many of us, if we look
around, have already tried and seemingly failed. All sorts of misguided
beliefs exist on this planet, a myriad of distractions in the 3rd dimension - and none of it has given us permanent happiness as we thought it
would, when we craved it so badly. But we still repeat it to try again,
time and time again, because we prefer to stay with the familiarity of
disappointment instead of the dare of entering the simplicity of the ultimate. Somehow, I think we know in our heart of hearts that it works –
and that is perhaps why we fear it and avoid it at all cost. To get back to
the simplicity of the singularity, the , there is a potentially thorny path
of loosening our attachments ahead of us, of untying all the inner knots
we have created over many lifetimes. We have made ourselves believe
that it will be impossible to do so on our own, and take solace that others
are staying on that same familiar path next to us, facing the same problems day in, day out. What we didn't realise is that we pay a price for the
time and space we occupy for a prolonged period, and I m not talking
about rent or a mortgage. It's worse: we have unwittingly handed over
responsibility over our Selves to those who have taken charge over us
whilst we weren't looking, and in our fear, we now act like Sleeping
Beauties awaiting a prince to come and save us, in our 100-year long
inertia.

There is no partner, no parent, no politician, no priest, no power outside of ourselves that can save us.

We don't need a prince, we need a miracle to make us wake up. It is not the ultimate emptiness that is a threat – that is wonderful, magical, omnipotent. What is stopping us is, that we probably inherently know how far we have come away from it, and we are now terrified as to how much hard work it might be to dust off and polish our long-lost full-body Karmic energy suit. Will it still fit us? Does it not actively appear in the manifest world as if we have lost our minds and don't know how to find them again? But it really can be done, we really can find ourselves again and we do not have to fear that we get drawn into the occult, or worse, have to become part of a cult, to find it again. After all, our Karmic essence is already a part of us, it is still and always will be there, it is never really lost, it is just temporarily mislaid in some long forgotten corner of our inner wardrobe. All you have to do to make a start is to ask. Ask for the Truth. Ask where to start, ask where to find it, how to find it, what is needed to find it, what you need to do to find it, ask that it is made visible to you what exactly it is you are looking for, even. Ask whatever questions you need to ask, to find out more. Ask for it to be simple, ask for lots of help. You can even ask for it to be as pain-free as possible. Please do – we need more techniques that show us all how easy it should really be by rights, so that we can loosen our Karmic bonds, see through our nasty pasts, move on, move back in with ourselves, be re-united, and be happy again. It is not freedom that hurts. Any pain we experience comes from our Karmic energy strands having to be untangled from the physical energy attachments we have created, and the energy tentacles that exterior influences have tried and succeeded to catch us up in. We have fallen for it, hook, line and sinker. We feel we have so much to lose – and yet, we know so little about who we really are and how much we have the potential to be. Our wisdom minds already know that if we are committed to being there for our families, we generate as much love as we can for our family, and as a result, we will see that everyone who feels loved is on your side. If we do not want to be alone, we are to know that we are never alone. If we are afraid of being sick, or going mad, know that it is a sign that what we are doing now is, we are making ourselves sick. With what we are doing, it means even crazier times could be to come. If you are afraid of not surviving, know that everyone survives, always, and when you are able to learn how to keep the highest motives and intentions in mind, you will be one whose wisdom mind survives the easiest. If we have resistance against the above, if we are scared, need we reminding of what we are doing instead? We have been striving for happiness for aeons of time – we have just not yet learned how to find it and re-create it properly. We have defended our territory, secured our homes, protected our loved ones. We have fed our families, clothed ourselves, built shelters and separated ourselves even more in fear of the harm we were told would come for us, only to then realise that the protection, security and defence mechanisms we have used are still ineffective 3-d models, useless in terms of defending our Karmic energy mind from being affected by our own fears. We are still not using the real McCoy. We have argued, fought and killed each other in the name of what exactly, so much so that it occurred to me that the biblical 'original sin' must refer to the state of mind we lost, as it became separate from the all-present, all-seeing, all-loving, everlasting existence we all were once conscious of being a part of.

48. Shambala

Image Credit: ©https://lobsang-rampa.net/shamballa.html

'*According to the prophecy, humanity will experience a degradation of ideology and humanity. Materialism will spread throughout the earth. When the "barbarians" are united under the command of a wicked king, then the fog that envelops the mountains of Shambhala will be lifted and the king's army with terrible weapons to attack the city.*

Then the king of Shambhala to-25 named Rudra Cakrin will lead his troops to fight the Barbarian forces. In that battle, the evil king and his troops successfully destroyed and mankind will be restored to the peace.

Some scholars such as Alex Berzin, using calculations from the Kalachakra Tantra, believed that these events will occur in the year 2424 AD.

As culture moves east to west, the myth of Shambhala rise from the mists of time. I think, a yearning for kedamaianlah which has caused the human race trying to find this utopian kingdom. Perhaps we will never find Shambhala, but perhaps also we need not look too far.

An ancient story of Tibet told that one day there was a young man preparing to search for Shambhala. After exploring the many mountains, he found a cave. Inside was an old hermit who then asked the young man: "Where are your goals so that you are willing to explore this deep snow?"

"To find Shambhala," replied the young man.

"Ah, you do not have to go far." Hermit said. "Behold the kingdom of Shambhala is in your own heart." '
(https://avtavr.tumblr.com/post/39129804407)

As the above article and many others like it states, it is said in Tibetan culture that Shambala may not just be a place in our minds, but that it is a place that exists in the remote mountains of the Himalayas. It is said to be a place where beings exist who have achieved highest forms of realisation.

Whether this is possible on Earth or not, Shambala remains a mystical concept in our minds, achievable through the highest practices to gain elevated frequencies of body, mind and spirit.

The most brilliant minds of this planet have all recognised that a pure mind, focused on the most excellent results of all our thoughts, speech and actions, that with the focus and intentions of such a global as well as ethereal mindset, the creation of a 'Shambala', a place of perfection in presence is very possible and possibly already exists; if not in a remote isolated place, then certainly as a vision of potential within all our minds. Personally, I have no problem believing that enough pure minds exist even in times of chaos that present, to converge and create an actual place in this very space/time continuum resembling the mystical place of Shambala. It is described as the pure, positive omnipotent potential power of manifest existence, with its inhabitants having honed and harnessed their highest abilities to create a Heaven on Earth. Call me a Pollyanna but I would, of course, prefer to believe that it is true that it exists in a physical realm – wouldn't you? Perhaps all we really have to do in life is educate ourselves in a mindful and compassionate way, become aware of what really is holding us back and turn it around using the right Karmic methods, understand and utilise what the mind is made and capable of, and then our reality becomes altered accordingly, to our heightened states of mind. Sounds so easy! And slightly dangerous – I am not trying to create a new cult, believe me. The most important goal I see in this current world is to create a good outcome for all, without exception, not an idealistic world that caters for just a few privileged ones. I will leave that to those who are deeming themselves rulers, and still need to feel they are in charge of something.

You can probably tell by now what happens when we realise how convoluted our minds have become, and when we do, we then want to be very, very mindful about how we use it, especially around others.

We need not be distracted by what others do, say and think. We can remain present and connected to the highest source whilst also having all others' best interests at heart.

That in itself becomes a daily challenge. We need to be constantly reminded that we cannot know what is going on for others, we do not know their Karma and we do not need to concern ourselves with it in a direct offensive. There are cleverer ways to make a difference, much wiser, when we see how our minds work on a subtle level. We need constant reminding of how precious our invisible Karmic minds are, and that we need to take care of them, so that we have peace of mind; as many seconds of the day as we can. Our bodies are constantly giving off energy via our Karmic energy field to our surroundings by default. Even what we believe to be our hidden thoughts or secret intentions is a distraction from the pureness of our sacred minds. It can easily be detected as such by others, too. Any lesser intention created in our Karmic mind hits others directly already, and whilst it does not look like it, it is noticeable to the ones who are sensitive enough to pick up on it. In our culture, we do not think twice about saying something and meaning the exact opposite. We work with falsehood and secrecy, open resentments and hurtful intentions, something that has only become more enhanced in the cold electric light of virtual reality. We are the ones creating virtual reality, with our partial minds. It isn't something created for our pleasure and entertainment, it was always in store for our ever-evolutionary Earth, only we are not taking notice that it all counts, whatever we do, say and think, at all times. Your Karma is creating an online account for you, although that does sound ominous and slightly overzealous. It's true though, but it doesn't have it in for you like in George Orwell's 1984. Our Karma is omnipresent but it is benign and doesn't judge. It never stops recording, though, and you will be presented with all that was recorded at some point, good, bad or ugly. You choose. It's not to our advantage that we are very often unaware of how we are at cross-purposes with our 'hidden' truth. We say one thing and yet our mind's consciousness is quite another. We feel we are being nice and compassionate and yet without noticing we end up hurting another. Is that why we hate it when others lie so much? Because we do it ourselves, we are deceived by our own ego Self all the time? For example, do we not resent doing our job every day just to get money, when our fully-aware minds are screaming to stop such meaningless time-and-resource-wasting? We don't always have a choice any longer since we co-created this dual world, with our a dual minds, simple as that. Any of those mind convulsions are the result of our multi-layered, needlessly complex convolutions compromising and complicating the pure process of the Karmic mind. On the surface, we appear to be fine. Underneath, we are a boiling cauldron of resentments, unresolved fears, insecurities and vicious statements, belligerent belief systems judging others, focusing on falseness. I could go on but I think you get the picture. Where has it got us, and why did we get to be that way?

When I have met deeply spiritual, pious people from other cultures in the past, they often did not grown up with a belief system based on duality like ours, or treated themselves and others the way we are used to treating ourselves and others. It is very apparent to them what our culture suffers from: We suffer from a poorly mind, one that is split into facets and different compartments, a mind that thinks in a myriad of different ways in different circumstances, at different times of the day, with different people. We can be like a diamond and make use of these facets to reflect the true light, or we can be like the broken shards of a mirror shattered into thousands of tiny sharp slithers of glass. Our opinions are not our own, but the result of a narrowing tunnel-vision education that might have been introduced hundreds of years ago, but prevails to this day and destroys our healthy minds and that of our future, our children, the next generations. We have been subject to it for so long it has created us much suffering, physical and mental illness. We no longer have a choice whether to be blissfully unaware, we have to work very hard at it if that's what we choose to be. The worst symptom to foresee would be that there will be a point where we no longer recognise our own illness. We have so many needs but we have forgotten the most important one. We must start to journey towards completeness, or else we will forever fear the card house of our existence is in danger of collapsing. But collapse, it may anyway – our way of life is no longer sustainable. The way we have treated our minds, the minds of others and our planet may not be able to ascertain our survival.
I am not getting into religion here or theories of why this is so. The latter nowadays certainly have their place – if a paradoxically bad reputation – but this is not what we are here to discuss.
You are reading this, because

It is simply our own personal Karmic responsibility, not anybody else's, to regain a healthy mind.

Once we start to question our 'simple' ego minds and where our thoughts, feelings, impressions, beliefs, judgements and so on come from, we start to awaken again. When we refuse to take things for face value, when we start making inventories of what we feel has gone awry inside, that is when we give ourselves permission to start seeing through the fog in our brains; those habitual actions and our learned behaviours that do not serve us or others cease to have power over us. Like animals kept in a cage and fed a diet of human control and manipulation, we ourselves have kept our Karmic mind a prisoner in our limited ability to see its true power and potential, feeding it scraps. Perhaps we do this out of fear of losing our comfort zones, which seem to reflect those inbuilt zones in our brains, with the purpose of keeping us safe. However, this does not seem to be working well for us, as we are trapping ourselves repeatedly in a constant loop of behaviour patterns that we then have a need to break out of. Either we have gotten so used to it that we no longer question it and treat it like pets in our cohabiting caged existence, or we have become so paranoid and separated ourselves so much from others, that we have started to firmly believe it's 'us against the rest of the world'. Alas, we have cultured ideas of a separate identity of Self for hundreds of thousands of years, based on our physical appearance - but it has not served us that well. We have not yet overcome the illusion of being separate beings. How far we have yet to go! And how ludicrous our efforts must seem, looked at like an anthill from above, running around our nests industriously as if in an experiment, until we simply perish without further insights from illness caused by the exhaustion of ignorance. We have forgotten how to be kind to each other and go gently on ourselves. None of it even feels comfortable any longer. Anxiety drives us on, all the time, on the treadmill of bigger, faster, better, more. We have forgotten what it is like to stop, and simply be – and enjoy that experience to the full.

If we were able to overcome this syndrome and free ourselves on a more global scale - as many people already are gradually beginning to do - from the daily humdrum of our ordinary lives of suffering, our Karmic mind energy would grow again and be able to recover to its natural state. It would start to simply expand again, and let in even more energy to nourish us, make us well and make us be able to perceive again that there is an easier way, that there always has been. In the brilliant light of Truth, we would see what our limited perception has done to us, our fellow beings and our environment – and we would have no longer a desire to repeat it.

Consider, please, the possibility of further thoughts on the subject: if our separation angst has made us isolated and afraid, creating war against our next door neighbours; if our overactive brains, trying to overcompensate and forever on emergency alert have created - without us being aware and able to stop it - polluted rivers and lakes like the heightened blood pressure in our stressed veins and dehydrated cells in our poorly bodies; if roads, tarmacked, smelly, convoluted and constantly clogged with polluted cars are akin to our thoughts forever going round in circles, day after day, down the same worn out routes, then I want to ask: what is there to lose? What makes this reality we created with our lesser minds so special that we even consider holding on to it?

We can watch TV from all over the world, all day long, on thousands of channels, and we are all connected to each other now in seconds, all over the planet. How incredibly amazing is that? How many generations have waited for this, how many thousands of years of evolution did it cost to get to this frequency level on Earth? In light of this miracle, we must wonder what in our originally free minds it is that created the programmes, the adverts, the duality of hate speech that is promoted by the functionality of setting us either for or against facts, and fellow humans? What is it within us that made us so stressed that we need Selfies to reflect back at us our deeper need for connection to our real Self? What disconnects us from our inner miracles so we prefer to ob-liviate the harshness of the matrix by buying into it and putting little cartoon noses on photos on our faces, or binge-watch Netflix? What is the phenomenon symptomatic of that exists within us like a virus we have not noticed? By the way, I wrote this chapter 12 years before the pandemic of 2020 where I am editing in lockdown. Is it our fear of the rawness of reality, our vulnerability as humans who are here one minute and gone the next, or the realisation that we have come so far away from our true nature that it already constantly hurts us? Are we letting our-selves be showered with images, electricity, noise and opinions so that we feel we can protect our weaknesses, but are actually acting at the ex-pense of losing the power of our own creativity, discernment and im-agination? What was there first, the symptoms or the malaise? Are we afraid to be alive, creative and open, or believe that we are rubbish at de-termining Truth? Or do we perhaps pick up that being ourselves fully is a danger to us on an existentialist level, even creating a whole philoso-phy on the concept of promoting human freedom? Perhaps we are all an anthropological phase on Earth, have been before, will be again, and in that time, we develop to discover our true, more permanent Self, each in their own unique way. There are certainly more and more people coming forward daring to be themselves, daring to be loving of them-selves and others despite not fitting a society 'norm', in fact promoting diversity on unprecedented levels, despite the conditions of anxiety and fear they may suffer at the hands of others for being different. We are all slowly recognising that name-calling and labelling each other does not exist in the free mind – those are simply synonymous for people all suffering from the stress and anxiety caused by a lifestyle that does not promote our highest forms of connection; perhaps even one that we have a once-in-a-lifetime opportunity to leave behind, like a bad hangover from our dark past in a battle against nature, each other and survival against all odds. Perhaps we have also wanted to protect ourselves from harm all this time, and tried to shrink wrap our lives in protective layers of plastic. Since there is a reason for the existence of every one of our manifestations, I have often wondered whether our levels of anxiety matched the increased isolation we feel we crave, in that we are trying to create more and more persistent layers between ourselves and our outside world. Our touch is so delicate, our skin so vulnerable, our physical being so open to accidents and infiltration by foreign bodies. What could possibly help us feel safer, other than creating walls between ourselves and others? Country borders, concrete cities, houses, bricks and mortar, individual rooms for everyone, a sectioned-off space reinforced by layers of plastic around everything...does it not scream vulnerability to us? But has this reaction to our environment made our anxiety less, and have we felt more secure as a result? Has it given us a better living standard and less death, less violence, less anxiety, less stress? Isn't it weird to think that the answer is no?

As i said right from the beginning, we must ask ourselves these questions to come to our own conclusions, but many phenomena around us are pointing us in the right direction for finding answers. Are these not the artificial boundaries in our minds; the ones we have in our poor old brains because we are almost always under duress, stressed and latently terrified of getting hurt? I have often pondered on this fascinating but oh so destructive matter and the answer I came up with is this: external structures that we build might be manifest synonyms for our biggest fears. We even use the same word: matter as in a physical material, and matter as in an item in need of debate. What is the matter? We are afraid of losing ourselves without our protective possessions, we are afraid of being invaded, we are afraid of becoming ill and not surviving, of losing control over our surroundings. We are even afraid of our own power – and so we wrap, contain, grab hold of what we can without being able to lose the grip on or sight of our objects of desire without feeling bereft, betrayed and insecure like a toddler without their security blanket. There would be nothing wrong with it, if there weren't just one 'small' price to pay, the small-print at the bottom of the contract for the modern society we live in: We are sacrificing Earth's future and the well-being of our children.

We have polluted the sacred elements of Earth, Air and Water with our left-overs, elements that actually we do need in order to survive and which were held in precious worship and preserved with care, simplicity, humility and gratitude by our ancestors who lived in tune with this planet. By the same token, we are not coping and dealing with the build-up of negativity in our minds and in our busy lives, we have not been able to live sensibly and effectively remove toxic waste from our bodies and environments, and our own negligence is in danger of choking us. In lack of any functioning systems and techniques of purification of the internal angst as well as the external consequences, we have created diversions and distractions for our mind-rubbish. We no longer see the connections and conveniently forget our responsibilities towards our rivers and oceans we condemned to absorb our not-so-hidden toxic waste, digging up Mother Earth to keep quiet about the graves of our buried secrets of our excessive and insufferable life-styles and finally, poisoning our air like the polluted thought patterns we created within ourselves, making us turn a blind eye to the reality of the extent of chemical warfare released on ourselves, each other and all life contained our environment

By now you must think that I really hate humankind, having pointed out the obvious which we do not usually like to think about, not least of all because we feel guilty but also because there appears to be no solution and no turning back, now that the damage has been done. How can we turn things around at this late stage? I do not think that hate is the answer though, and neither is blame. We can all see how many of us are trapped in the conundrum of trying to find a solution in a system of blame, shame, arrogance, negligence, greed, hatred and anger, and that there is no point in promoting it any further as it will not give us an answer of how to move forward. What I do think is necessary, is for us to become aware that we are trapped, and find a way out of being caught in the headlights like proverbial rabbits. We are driven into a corner with not many options to choose from, and our children are in danger of not being able to survive in an inhabitable world they inherit from us. The trouble is of course, the fact that just by having become more aware of the urgency of the situation, it does not just simply go away. We are still stuck in our thoughts, still stuck in debates, politics, wrong decision-making, electing others to do our bidding by tacit consent. We gave our Karmic power away a long time ago, same as we are doing right now with our physical aliveness. We also unwittingly gave away the land we were supposed to live on to give us food and shelter. We didn't even sell out to the highest bidder or knew the consequences of our actions and inactions. We have snookered ourselves! Just like our stressed bodies and brains which did not alert us to see it coming, we do not compute that we were partly responsible for this inertia that we are presented with now, in the face of a potentially absolute stalemate. We do urgently need to look at ourselves, see how we are ailing and how this affects everything around us. Is there any point thrashing about in quicksand? We need to change within us how we relate to the outside world, preferably quickly and on a grand scale. Nature has already shown us where we are at, in a simultaneous simulation of what it looks like within us. Eventually, oceans, rivers and the creatures who live within them started to regurgitate and float all our rubbish rather than absorb it, the Earth broke open, leaking and spiting out our guilty secrets. Life brings up situations time and time again for us to have no choice but to look at our 'stuff' whilst hopefully not running out of time to find opportunities to come clean. A few decades ago, all this was laughable, people shrugged it off and ridiculed others for stirring up the issues, calling people out on warning about what was really going on. These days, there is no denying the truth of what presents itself. However, what our brains always tend to do in an emergency is to tell us to be out for ourselves only and to fight anyone else who is there to threaten our routine we carved for ourselves, no matter the consequences. Our brains, as I said before, are not that reliable in stress situations. If we go into meltdown, if we have already gone into overdrive and there seems to be no way out. If we want to avoid being snared by others' orders rather than trust our own instincts now that we have assessed the situation, we really don't have much choice but to override our brain-related in-action and find a different way to go about things. It may not be too late.

Here is an alternative. Instead of our futile waiting for circumstances to change so we can take time to expand our minds to find better ways to live, why not do that right now. Expand our minds - right now. Why wait? There is no waiting, there is no time as we believe it exists, there is nobody out there who will do it for us. We can get away from our previous wrongful actions, our confusion, fears or inertia. There might not be a tomorrow in the way we hope to have it. Hence, now is the best time of all - right now. We don't just need to yoga-stretch our bodies, we more urgently need to focus on expanding our Karmic minds, because we need to find in ourselves our true potential again to make a difference; to bring about changes and solutions before it really is too late.

It is so almost unbearable for us to see and hear news of the daily extent of destruction, that we have had to put on blinkers and filters to the full extent. In times of stress, our bodies reduce our living and breathing safe space only to the extent of our own four walls and no further, perhaps our nearest and dearest, if we are lucky. What happens if we no longer have the energy to think compassionately about others, never mind an intention to act in order to help them? We will have given away even more of our aliveness by losing our greatest asset: that of creating positive Karma to ascertain a fruitful future existence. Our fears might be given the power to disrupt our ability to be wise and compassionate, and might instead allow a monster to be created. Our fears of not being heard, our fears of needing to be right, our fears of not knowing what to think and how to act are driving us all to clash with each other as we always have done in the past, because they are the same, age-old, unresolved fears expressing themselves time and time again.

Our inability to also see through and deal with the commercial corruption of our minds has co-created all these phenomena that are out to haunt us and everyone around. The thing is, if we carry on like this we won't be well enough any longer to observe the future. Some may have us believe that it's all fine as it is and it's part of our global Karma, in a 'that's life' sort of attitude. Should we really just lay down and die, or shall we meditate and make a difference? Is it not our Karmic duty to be alert and awake?

Thank you for obliging my rant. I am almost done now, because I am certain you already knew a lot about what I just mentioned. So, the big question we always face is: what can each of us choose to pro-actively and effectively do? In my mind, our first port of call is to get back into 'being', not 'doing'. We need to regularly step back into our own realm again to centre and find the wisest ways to progress, before we go out and do anything that makes us power out. Our actions are so much more direct and powerful when we centre ourselves first and become aware of our frequency links to higher sources, so we can feel again like we are supposed to: fully conscious, aware members of a global society who all unite their Karmic strength to make things right again. A good first step would be to scrutinise what it is that may have contributed to any of the atrocities that still occur on Earth, and how we can change it. That should be a very interesting and fun exercise to do when we are bored, having switched off the telly. I don't think we have any time to lose.

Our Karmic mind is born with the ability to comprehend, be inventive, have insight, wisdom and compassion, talents, skills, connections and more, regardless of our physical and bodily ability. It is astonishing that many of us do not yet know about it or care to make use of it. Most of us make much less use of what we are capable of being, and simply never venture further to find out. If we opened up to what's truly inside of us beyond the physical body, i believe we would be pleasantly surprised, amazed even at what we find. We might even find what we have always been missing, what we always had a feeling should be there, and didn't know how to access. Perhaps we will be blown away by all the talents and insights we latently have, but have not been shown or told how to access. Now why is that – should we not wonder? There is no TV show that can compete with what our internal mind can offer us. I can promise you this: it is better than any programme or film you have ever watched.

But first, to get a ticket to the amazing cosmic ride within us, we need to pay a small price: The cost for the ticket is for us to give up the notion that someone else around us is here to entertain us. Whatever power we have handed to others to make something work for us, we need to claim it back.

Nobody else has a responsibility for us as adults to feel complete, other than ourselves.

Don't get me wrong - I am not saying that it is not right for us to connect with each other and do what we need to do in order to nurture, protect and provide for ourselves loved ones - far from it. The inner journey is not like a Marvel movie though, we don't just get to sit there and watch some electronically enhanced 'KAPOW'! and eat popcorn. It's even better than that: we take part in it, and we are doing that right now. If we recognise that sometimes that which presents itself in the moment is all we asked for, that it can be met by our inner wisdom with extreme excitement to be alive; and if we also then realise the full potential within life itself, then we can be totally present, mindful and utterly enjoy the experience rather than resenting or fearing it, trying to 'be' more and 'get' more all the time. We can even go a step further. If we are at home, looking after our nearest and dearest wholeheartedly, we can make a compassionate wish to see the light in this very task. We can truly wish with the power of our minds that everyone, always, may find the opportunity to do the same and find the whole potential of being alive in the tasks they choose to perform. It is a great honour to be able to make sure that eventually everyone is healthy, happy and wise. When we look around the world, when life asks us to take bigger steps, surely it's easy to see that this is possibly one of the most important wishes we can make; one that is so easily neglected and taken for granted. It seems that we have forgotten the power of good thought and intention and prefer complaining about less desirable family situations instead. We need constant reminding that simple tasks to prolong the lives of others are making a profound difference.

This is where the power of the mind can help, by simply determining what is important, focusing on it with single-pointed intention and love, and then multiply the effort by asking help from the universe to create the same for others. What we do not seem to know anything about as we have not yet experienced it, is the full extent of the outcome of this creation of a pure sincere wish – it is potentially the most powerful exponential explosion of positivity that you have been excluded from experiencing so far, hence us no longer being able to look for it, never mind create it. But any more information would be telling. You will have to find out for yourself.

With this simple procedure we would actually be able to set ourselves free, it can be a scenario as simple as taking care of others, and will work when it is practised sincerely and when we least expect results like a sweetie at the end of a task well-performed.

Here are some helpful pointers to aid us along our path of serenity:

1st step: Recognising what needs to be done in each moment, asking ourselves what the purpose of that instant is, in the context of creating the most wisdom and compassion for all involved. Meditate on the vastness, to help align to the true meaning of the words you just read.

2nd step: Learning to visualise what we would really like to be the outcome of each moment. When we concentrate on our work, we know there is a certain process that makes us 'see' the project first, and then when that stage is complete, we focus on it being built. Similarly, an artist 'sees' their picture on the canvas, a sculptor 'sees' the finished sculpture in the material to be carved. Practice seeing, visualising, sensing not just for menial tasks, but also apply the very same process for the highest good and benefit of all.

3rd step: Taking action to implement. Having paid attention to our focus and combined it with pure intention, we co-create a sensation akin to perfectly 'being' in the moment, with the aim to be 100% present. This eventually involves us being able to access our whole Karmic library of talents, and most of us cannot even truly comprehend what that means yet. Even – or rather, especially - if our current experience is not a pleasant one, we are creating a say in our future outcomes that way and it is really relevant that we remind ourselves that it is our birth-right to learn and practice how to do so.

4th step: Multiplying the good outcome of our actions by asking/wishing for it to be so for others, too. This is a really important step because we are setting the energy of anything we have created free to grow, much like we put a tiny seed in fertile ground, it will grow into something much bigger and more beautiful if we keep tending to it, nourishing it.

5th step: Rinse, repeat. To make the most of our ride through the cosmic kitchen, we need to sometimes play the broken record and repeat every-thing good that we do, over and over. It's simple and although it often seems mundane, the results of seeing our work come to fruition are definitely not.

❈ ❈ ❈

49. Practical Exercises

I have been promising all throughout this book that there will be a cul-mination point of solutions for many of our issues. It is obvious to many of us by now that we need to find and apply methods to help us through any situations we find ourselves in that are hard to cope with. This is finally the chapter where we explore some of these methods. The list is by no means exhaustive, and I invite and welcome other suggestions for equally valid methods for everyone to explore. I am listing a handful of practical, easy-to-do, inexpensive and effective methods that I have tried and tested myself, which is the benchmark I chose to set before recommending them to others. Below, you will gain a few insights into the first steps of these, an introduction, so to speak. Please take from it what is most valid for you, discard what you don't need and follow up with what rings true for you with your own further research to find our details of what can further help you. Some of the most fruitful methods are very simple, so simple it's deceiving, as we are used to having very complicated lives, complicated conditions, and complicated solutions. It takes some getting used to that many of the best solutions can be very simple, but are also deeply profound in terms of inner changes they bring about within us. I will not recommend medical procedures or medicines, as this would take things too far into the realm of com-promising integrity and it is not within my remit to do so. There will be many who will ridicule methods that are simple, because nobody really believes that it could be as easy as just sitting there almost doing nothing. I ll leave it up to you to decide whether this is not the exact antidote to what we are doing, which is doing too much, so much so that it is hurting us, hurting those around us and hurting the very place that ascertains our survival. We can't continue to saw off the branch we are sitting on, so without further ado, feel free to browse this section for what you feel is most suitable for you.

Thank you for your attention to this book, thank you for your existence, and may all our efforts benefit all sentient beings to have happiness, and the cause of happiness, to be free from suffering, and the causes of suffering; to live in equanimity, free from partiality, attachment and aversion.

Conclusion & Solutions

It could not be more vital and crucial in the current times we live in, that we learn more about how to use our energy so we can treat ours and others with the respect we deserve, preferably before situations escalate and create more Karmic conflict.

If we chose to turn in this direction, the healing process would be initiated instantly within us, and our poor battered bodies, our supposedly omnipresent Karmic minds and ecstatic energy fields would have a chance to start recovering. In any situation of conflict, we might still feel actively involved, however, we might become aware that we are not passive to it. Almost all of us have the ability already to acknowledge the process, see through it and be able to heal from it. We are choosing the path that gives the greatest result in order to resolve it. If any residual conflict continues to present itself in our minds, we now have knowledge and methods to be aware, standing fully present in our energy.

In order to find solutions for ourselves, we have to first learn methods to raise our awareness to help us realise what is happening to our inner energy system when we need to resolve conflicts. Whilst it's hard sometimes to bring up things that we usually hide deep down, bringing them to the surface is the first step to a healing process, which then also involves learning to resolve it, in this case with some of the best methods available. The only time we should not bring up deep-rooted issues is if they are too upsetting, and when we do not have help at hand to assist in us resolving them at that time. If you have things that need resolving which are just too big to handle on your own, please use the links at the end of this book to find valuable help. Usually, we are prompted to rush in and actively confront those who have harmed us, but this is not what we will need to be doing here. Rather than physically acting out, we first need to become clear about what is going on in detail. Then we apply methods to resolve it within us. There will be methods that we may never have heard of yet, or don't have confidence that they will work for all that is going on for us. There is no need to bring anything to the table, though, other than a willingness to try something different.

As we have learned, there is much that happens to our inner energies when we are being drawn into external situations on a daily basis. This is not something we can ignore, even if it is news to us. Instead, this is the main focus of our process of resolution. It works, and it works wonders for then being much better equipped to deal with the external situations when we go out there again. It can, and will, change the outcome of almost any situation for the better, depending on what it is and how committed we are to resolve some aspects of it within us as a priority.

First, we allow the image of the conflict we are involved in to arise within, as it presents itself to us at that moment. Remember to only do this if it feels safe for you to do so on your own, and if the issues involved are not going to be so big that you won't be able to handle them. If so, please ask for help first before trying this out. By allowing it to present itself as it is, with all those involved including all their flaws and feelings, it gives us a moment to truly and honestly assess the situation and fully accept that it is there, without bias. We may even see ourselves as included in this conflict; perhaps even feel strong emotions as we conjure up the image. We most likely feel an urge to become involved by taking action, not just in our thoughts and visions, as it is often a highly charged situation. For example, if your conflict is with a person you perceive as very angry, you picture how it presents itself to you in detail. This is all you do to begin with. They may have been a threat to you or still are, you may at first have taken on some of their anger and have a reaction of fear, and a need to defend and protect yourself immediately. Perhaps you will be thinking thoughts in terms of having to become embroiled in order to resolve the conflict, perhaps you are in your mind already retaliating. This is a normal healthy reaction and it is not the aim of this exercise to feel guilty about your own feelings. Simply know and trust that the following conflict resolution exercise is the best you can do for yourself and others, and you can do it right now. Acknowledging your feelings and examining where they have arisen in your body, their nature, even shape, size and colour, will help you to identify their nature. Every feeling is valid. No feeling is ever not valid. In this exercise, we validate feelings, we do not ridicule people or brush their emotions under the carpet. It is totally the opposite of what we are nowadays asked to do habitually, and as a result, we have lost touch with who we are. Feelings are our inner map, and they point us in the direction of our inner energies that are healthy or need resolving.

Whether we call them feelings, or sense them more cognitively as thoughts or behaviour patters is up to us individually. Whatever name we choose, we are turning inwards and looking at the world within us, and this is the most important lesson we can reintroduce into our lives: to become aware again of what goes on within us.

Our feelings are precious energies that have arisen in our energy body. If they are feelings which we deem negative, it only means that our inner energy world has an imbalance, which we can put right again right here.

This inner examining process is vital in recognising and reconnecting with our Karmic energy body again in order to regain our wellness and composure.

We do not have to give any of our power away in order to find a solution.

Many people call our feelings 'ego' in a derogative way, but we know by now that this has become a much misused word nowadays. People might use it because they subconsciously notice the energy imbalance of another within themselves. Anything we have not resolved can resonate with someone else. Because it doesn't feel great, it can cause others to have a harsh reaction to urge us to sort out our energy bodies. It can also denote that we do not yet know the connection and interaction between the arising of feelings and thoughts and our energy body, and someone is reminding us in no uncertain terms, probably because they also don't know any better. I feel that our cultivating a sympathetic, logical and understanding view towards ourselves and how we got drawn into any situation is better than an aggressive annihilation of our own reality.

We are all suffering and to make each other suffer more does not help them, or us.

However, it is equally important to take note of the point at which a conflict arises, even if we are distracted by the effects of it coming at us. The very latest is at the point where it can no longer be resolved externally by any form of mutual agreement to communicate in a reasonable way. That is when we have an option we probably never thought we would have: we are actually able to resolve it within ourselves first, without actively having to address the other party involved. it would be even better if each involved party did this for themselves individually. We need to stop trying too hard to bring about any demands for results from another at that point, and bring all the energy we have spent trying to negotiate, back into ourselves again. This is a big step. It does not mean we give up, far from it. It means we use our power differently, more wisely. The benefits are endless and often quite fast. As we get to change our inner energies, we get to understand more why any of us act out and react but never find middle ground. That process that can take years, decades - even lifetimes, it's tedious, exhausting and it may not bear fruit, ever.

In contrast, if we choose to use methods to help us go the opposite way by turning inwards, we will find the source of our thoughts and emotions. We will give it attention and validation, so that we no longer need this from an external source. We strengthen our inner resolve to allow ourselves to be on a path of completion rather than destruction. That way, we can learn to be able to actively stop others acting out, by altering how we react to them. Over time, we become free to allow many a negative energy charge to dissipate, so that our Karmic energy body and also our our physical body can recover to full health. It's hard to believe if we do not know the methods yet, but hang in there a little longer if you can, I will explain.

Imagine, for example, in the situation above, we choose to walk away from conflict, despite being scared and our whole body shaking with the weakening negative energy charge created within. Once we are able to take a moment to stop, we then need to be able to give ourselves a moment to start paying attention to ourselves. This can be hard if we are not used to paying attention to ourselves at all, if we don't rate ourselves worthy of paying attention to. We need to tend to ourselves at an intense time of need, but it doesn't have to be overwhelming. We are trying to calm down and get away from a feeling of being in too deep. For this, we will learn some new nurturing and calming actions, gestures and thoughts. New can be exciting, not just daunting. It's different, but nothing we talk about here poses a threat in any way, shape or form. I promise.

Instead of expecting anything to happen externally, we would simply go inwards to ask ourselves how we felt and why we felt this way. We might come up with some answers straight away, or it takes a little longer, in which case we ask more specific questions. If we are in any precarious situations, there might of course be highly charged answers, and really any combination of a highly charged inner turmoil can arise. Because those times are extreme and intense, we first use methods to calm us down a bit at a time, every time. If you are reading this and recognise the symptoms, please check out methods in the last chapter to use straight away, to calm yourself again even whilst you read.

Whilst it seems that there is a bottomless pit of negativity that can befall us at times, we should not be afraid to admit that this happens. We are not being targeted or singled out, we are not the only ones. We are all built the same way: our energy system goes into reverse gear and it feels like a red alert internally. This is the moment where we can really make use of what is going on within and make it work for us. If we asked ourselves what went wrong, what statement would we come up with? You can even write it down as you go along if you can relate. There are endless statements we can choose from which are relevant to our situation - the more specific they are, the better; If you are coming up with major statements such as the following, please don't do these exercises alone. They can't hurt you, but you might need help to guide you out of a traumatic situation. Statements that indicate a trauma are, for example, 'it reminds me of my childhood when I felt powerless and humiliated' or 'I stayed because I wanted the other to see if they are really that awful in how low they made me feel.' or 'I was terrified I would get hurt even more. I told them I was hurting but it didn't make any difference, in fact it made it worse.' or 'They just laughed at me and called me names, so I got more and more upset' or 'I thought I had to stay and be at the receiving end of their anger because deep inside I felt worthless/guilty/ashamed/like it's all my fault/it's my duty/they talked me into it/I didn't want to feel weak/i felt trapped/lost/so low', and so on. These are all actual examples I have come across in real life, in thousands of different variations, by people from all walks of life. Are we alone in feeling them? No. Do we feel isolated? Yes. Can we find a solution? Absolutely. Do these examples show how we might be triggered to feel a certain way in a specific situation? Could it be that we have Karmic energy residues in our recent and distant past, which have remained in our system and make us replay similar scenarios over and over again until we find ways to resolve them? Do we react to certain triggers in our Karmic energy system that allow the enemy in through the back door? I don't know about you, but I would say Yes to all - and more.

One last, all important question is: Can we use relatively simple methods to alleviate all of our Karmic issues? And my answer is: Yes, I believe we can.

The 'Bubble' or 'Balloon' Method

Having assessed any conflict, how it arose and how everyone involved has been affected by it, we are then in a good position to create an inner solution of how we can resolve it. So far, this does not make sense if we have never come across certain energy methods that can work really quickly. We probably think that it will be a massive effort of willpower and overcoming our biggest fears, but it isn't. All it involves is sitting somewhere comfortable and allowing some time to apply some new methods to the madness we have experienced so far. This could be a completely new chapter in our lives. And it's free. Relatively easy, easy enough for us to do it ourselves, on many situations that bother us. It's not voodoo, it doesn't do harm. It works like a treat, like adding baking powder to a cake. If you don't do it, the cake won't work out. And most of our lives are at that stage at some time or other. We need another little added ingredient to make it work again.

Before we learn these new methods, we can use our inner vision of how we would like the situation to be, instead of how it is at that moment. If we can hang in there a little bit longer, this is an important step where we are creating a projection of the highest outcome for ourselves and all involved.

If you have to put others first, include yourself. If you think of yourself first all the time, learn to include others.

Here is a little preliminary exercise you can do, it does not take very long and you don't have to do much, other than sit down, relax and focus for a bit. This is a visualisation i sometimes use in group sessions where everyone there has a different problem to solve. It works well because we can all individually picture the exercise internally, and however agitated we might be, it helps us to calm our minds a little more whilst also receiving attention for very specific issues we are facing. So before we launch into some more elaborate methods, I have chosen this one as it's suitable for everyone to do immediately, young or old, healthy or not. Here goes:

Start by imagining the best-case scenario, and include everyone in this vision who can benefit from your Karmic energy. If it's hard to imagine then don't worry. We do not necessarily have to do it well or even believe that it works, for now. We are painting a new picture within, of what we would prefer the outcome of any situation to be that has caused us conflict with others in the past. We already know what the past looked like, put that into a frame in your mind that means 'past' to you. You can choose any situation that is relevant to you, and you can choose any outcome you want, as long as it is positive. By positive is meant, that if you feel you want a situation as far away as possible from you, preferably on a different planet, you simply bring it back to yourself, and see yourself being free. Focus on yourself rather than another, and make yourself step into your focus as vividly and as brightly as you can. Give yourself attributes that you feel you want which you might not have. If you want to see yourself as an indestructible multicoloured unicorn with wings, do that. That's ok, too. Go to town, have fun, and then put all the fun bits into a frame in your mind that means 'future' to you.

The last step to the exercise is to allow the old and new vision to rise up from your Karmic consciousness, with no strings attached. Let go of the balloon strings, so to speak. Let those two pictures you created rise up in front of you. We can learn to trust this way that we are being heard. Our wish, our vision is now externalised, that it has now been set free to be resolved and will be turned into the best outcome for all involved - even if we can't quite believe we will turn out to be a rainbow unicorn, which is probably true, at least in this life. You catch my drift, though - put yourself in a positive light for the future, free from all the past, and then set the images free from your own body and mind. The outcome is now less bound to your own 3-d physical energy. We have set at least some of the energy free that has been held up within, in order to be transformed again into a positive. The more we do this, the more we will realise that this very simple exercise can actually work, as it is born from the vision of our precious energy minds connecting with the much higher frequencies of the cosmos. We will gently learn to trust the process, and that we can feel more in charge. The more we are undistracted by fear making us feel out of our minds, the more impact it will have, and the more instant the results will be - even if, at first, the result will be that we feel calmer and more centred. When at some point we realise what we are made of, and that this is exactly the same stuff that creates our reality for us, there is no energy taken up with doubt any longer. We will see evidence in the results and it's exciting - it might get our energy focus back, and want to create the most connected scenarios more and more.

Realising the connection between this and our present choices would not be such a bad thing. It is one path to eventual empowerment. Knowing ourselves and our Karmic path is to become aware of where our weaknesses and strengths are, and how we can address triggers and attachments so that they can become neutral again. We already have the power to soothe ourselves, calm our Karmic nerves and avoid a future network of triggers. Once you know which part of you is vulnerable, you can nurture it. It is never something to feel ashamed of or guilty about. There are many ways of nurturing a part of us that has been hurt in the past and is still smarting, attracting the same painful scenario time and time again. The first step is always to recognise that hurt has taken place in our lives. Is this true for everyone? Sure is. Some of our hurt is very subtle and specific so that, in order to overcome it, to even hear its noise vibration, we have to become sensitive to its frequency patterns within our inner energy system. Hurt has caused disruptions within that we can't see. It sounds complicated but it won't be if we keep reading on. The alternative would be that we end up staying involved in repetitive external convolutions which we might be able to avoid altogether if only we learn to know how. As in the examples above, it is very easy to say that it is simply everyone else's fault, but we would do well to try not leave it there as our ultimate reality, because that is not a sign of strength. Contrary to what a lot of us are made to believe, suffering is not something we need to grin and bear. It exists because we have not been presented with valid methods yet to overcome it. It does not have to be our only choice of potential reality. There are many options open to us, and I am slowly guiding you to them. If we left it here, we would potentially remain stuck in that reality. In our current society set up, it is still not that fashionable yet to openly admit that we have negative attachments to situations, even if we are the perceived victim of circumstances. We are slowly getting there, although there is also a bit more to learn. By the way, whilst we probably immediately associate blame and shame with the term 'negative attachment', it is far from meant as a judgement, but rather a neutral description of the charge our energy particles take on, like perhaps the negative charge of an electric current, a magnet or a battery. When the two negative (-) or positive (+) poles of two power sources face each other, they repel each other, sometimes even with a total power cut. It is the same with alive beings - we have an inner electric and electromagnetic current running through us. Whilst we may not know what the mechanics and consequences of these are for each of us, we can simply observe what happens. Without being aware of what is going on, we are all reacting to external energy conflicts all the time and our inner energy flow is reduced; we can even short-circuit, and it is also possible for one person to take on the negative energy charge of another. On the other hand, if we follow methods and ways that recharge our batteries, we will heal again, sometimes with quite miraculous results.

Our Karmic energy minds simply are the most powerful and at the same time subtle energy sources we can employ to resolve conflict.

I recently read on a box of my favourite chocolates: 'Maybe a good way of changing the world is by being You'. Could not have said it better myself. YOU matter! YOU count! Some of us don't rate ourselves highly enough sometimes, when we have not bee taught how to. That does not mean we become egomaniacs. It's just another way of saying 'I need help'. By being the most true we can be to the endless Karmic being we are on this Earth right now, we are giving ourselves an admission ticket to the cosmic theatre of happiness and oneness. We had that golden ticket all along, there were never limited amounts. We all have one, it's just that some are more hidden and lost than others. Sometimes, the show on Earth is very peculiar, and sometimes it is sublime. It cannot be any different, perhaps, due to the multitude of outcome choices that infinite combinations of Karmic beings and their individual Karmic situations present. It's a crazy place we live in. But we have the one thing that is guiding us: our inner Karmic Self. Nature all around us is reflecting back at us what is truly possible, the variety of beauty, the ability to grow, the miracle of abundance.

Here is a really useful, preliminary exercise you can try for yourself, in any situation that needs resolving, even when we feel quite agitated. In your mind, you have the absolute power to deal with this and other situations, by acknowledging and adapting the images of any external situation that you are receiving and perceiving. In the case of any conflict, take the original inner image of any other being whose issues you may have become embroiled in, and go into it a little more. Have a close look at it. Visualise you standing next to each other, and note how you relate. It can be a little dramatic to do so, and if it becomes overwhelming, move the situation a little further away from you in your mind, to make it easier to deal with. The next step is to adapt it and change the outcome of it, in your mind. Think what you would wish for in an ideal case scenario, even if it may seem far-fetched and absurd a thought for you to be able to do so at this time. This is, after all, happening within the power of your mind. It is safe, and nothing bad will happen as a result. Imagine that, instead of the conflict, you can allow yourself to wish for and see an outcome that would absolutely suit you. You can change where you place and interaction of the other(s) you are in conflict with, and everyone else involved. You can even change the way you relate to each other in this image in your mind, how you all look different, even. Make it a new inner image not based on manipulating the outcome, but one based on a happy one: where there was hate or anger against you or anyone else before, it becomes the peaceful scene we wish for instead. An image in our mind where all are happier individually, and have all they need, including a solution to the problem, even if that may not become instantly apparent what the solution is in this inner exercise. Ask for universal energies to assist you and connect with you, and send the highest intention and love to yourself and any other. Watch what does not exist just yet, slowly and almost by itself transform into what it has the power to instead become. It has the power to affect what will occur in real life, too, as a result of our changing energy. There is no need to force anything, however. Throw your worries to the universe and ask for assistance to resolve any outstanding conflict. For example, if this means you see yourself and the other far removed from each other, then allow it to stand as it is. Allow the exercise to give you clarity. If you cannot easily resolve any conflict by yourself alone on a physical level at this stage, then don't do this alone. Ask for help from someone you trust. Someone who can help you activate and utilise your energy system to do what it does best: to become the mediator between the omnipresent power that is, the situation itself and all involved, including all those you may not know are connected to both opposing parties. If it doesn't work at first, keep practising, especially if you enjoy the process and can see that it will work in good time. Go back to acknowledging any negative charge if it's there, and then transform it in the second part of the exercise. Remember:

1st part: acknowledge how things are and 2nd part: allow it to transform into how it could be in a loving way. You can even use the image of a bubble, or balloon, to place both of the above scenarios in. This helps to make sure they are kept outside of your body. You can visualise the bubble or balloon in front of you, slightly above you. Once you have placed everything in your mind into the bubbles before you – the painful scenario on the left, the better outcome in the right – you then activate the 3rd part: You allow the bubbles to float up. Just allow them to move away from them. You no longer need to hold on to them and acknowledge that they can be taken care of, by a higher instance. You no longer have to think about this now.

When you are happy with this new vision – you can take as long as you need - and feel more at peace, set your Karmic mind creations free.

Visualise how they can float up and away like a bubble into the space above you and beyond, and at that point, hand over responsibility for the outcome of the situation to the highest energy source available outside of yourself that you believe in. Take a moment to let it all complete, and allow yourself to come to rest, meditate, let it go. This does not mean you are letting all your hopes go or giving up, you are just letting go of the vision for now, in order to allow another outcome to set in. The first 3 parts of this exercise lend themselves well to allowing any inner negativity to float up from our bodies and leave our bodies and minds, and the fourth part is this: to begin to allow higher, purer, all-existent energies to flow down into our body, by envisaging their pure form to flow down into us through the top of our heads, the 'crown'.

Letting go of something that does not feel right means making space to let something better in.

We also let go of all weight and worry concerning the outcome. Allow the worry to float up and away into the universe, too. If it helps, envisage that it is being attended to in order to resolve it, by whatever energies you believe exist in this endless universe, by whatever name you identify it that suits you best. All that's left to do is wait and see what results have come of your efforts, and to repeat the exercise again to turn a negative into a positive vision in your mind if there is still any negative residue. At a later stage, you can re-imagine another scenario if it still bothers you, or you can move on to others that also need addressing.

When you see good results, you can then truly feel that you are learning better ways to resolve conflict in a more peaceful way. When we have methods to bring about change, there is less of a need to see others change according to how we need them to be. Keep practising. If you need help, ask for it. When it works for you, you might wonder why you ever put yourself through a more difficult version. Could it be true that a complicated web of connected, invisible Karmic energy threads might lead to all our attachments, but also our salvation? That they become so interwoven sometimes that it becomes difficult to see, never mind unravel them? There is only one tool we need to start with in order to unravel them, and that tool is honesty with ourselves. If we cannot at first be honest with others, let's start by being honest with ourselves first. If we are ready to be honest with ourselves, we can ask ourselves some important questions. Here are some examples, but please be your own guide as to what you need to ask yourself most of all.

Do we really know who we are? Which part of our 'Self' can co-create any of the scenarios? How can we feel more in the know how to be that part, and use it in a better way to help us make good choices? Are we overcoming our low Self-esteem? Do we have to stand up for ourselves to find our true power, or is our true power already there, waiting? Are we afraid to admit that we have this inner, gentle power to generate a good outcome within ourselves, in many situations?

These are just examples, there is an infinite number of issues we can address. Issues do bunch together in groups to make it easier for us, but as always, you alone decide which it is to be. Remember there is that important Karmic law we mentioned right at the beginning: I'll repeat it here, a few hundred pages on.

No-one can decide another being's Karma.

Well maybe some of the wise, sacred people can; but the message here is that maybe it is not helpful to try and determine another being's Karma when we still do not know our own.

We hardly ever know our own Karma, never mind another's. We can't find out about our own attachments for lifetimes, so how come we feel we can judge another's? There is no judge, and there is nobody judging us either, however, when we try so hard to understand others by analysing them, we are spending our precious time doing this at the cost, so to speak, of remaining stuck in ignorance about our own. We have plenty to do to find out more about ourselves. Perhaps that's exactly what is putting us off - it's like trying to pack everything up before moving home, and then having to unpack it all again, dust it all off and look at everything at least once more to decide whether it's still worth keeping or not. It's laborious. With the right methods, we won't have to let it become so much of a distraction that we are going round and round in circles and not getting anywhere. How amazing would it be if we talked about how we have learned how to not have a fear of this or that any longer, or a grudge against so and so any more, rather than just talking about lip fillers, fake tans and dysfunctional relationships. What if it would free not just our brain space but our hearts as well? We could find the solution to getting around for miles without pollution, or could find a way of recycling all plastics floating on the oceans instead of watching telly and shouting at it. What if we were less afraid to say 'I m done' with a bad situation, and started to see our world in a different light. rather than looking at news stories reporting all the time how awful everything's got. What if we treated our bodies and minds with respect again, and had the inner strength again to make choices to avoid getting sick. No? Oh well. Poor Health system, having to mop up our mess after us, not getting nearly paid enough to substitute our mums and dads cleaning up our mess.

I know I am being a little pushy here, but what do we have to lose? Don't we all secretly yearn for so many things? What I am trying to say is that we have so much choice, more than in any generation ever, and yet we're still choosing to do what's wrong for us and others, keeping us small and making us and others sick. Why? I think it has a lot to do with how our inner Karmic minds have not benefited yet, since we have had the luxury of having better education, good hospitals, nice, separate homes, safer jobs with long-term benefits that involve us being able to create and care for our families. But we haven't been happy within, have we, in fact we are still lonely. We connect much less and live across from a TV, console, phone and we talk to Alexa. The statistics I heard say that more and more people in civilised countries choose to live alone. It is quite unbelievable because the majority of the world isn't like this, even though to us it's civilised and trendy. Of course, everyone involved in any situation needs to come to their own conclusion, in their own time, in their own space. Me pointing out flaws in others or our society will only draw you into that scenario and gets you hooked in, and that's not really what I want to do. We only need to learn how to become aware and deal with of our own attachments; denying us this essential process very often results in our own and others' energy being lowered alarmingly, and this is exactly what has been happening. We don't even realise this is what's missing, because the last few decades, maybe even centuries, has drummed it out of us. If we grasped even a glimpse of the concepts underlying this book, we would be excited to suddenly become aware of ourselves more. We can set a new precedent and target within ourselves of reaching new levels of compassion, and we can start with ourselves. How can we be kinder to ourselves? Kind doesn't mean boring. Being bored means we don't know what we are missing whilst we are too anxious to start anything.

If you want to start with your inner journey right now, start by making a list. What would you change if you could? If you had everything you needed, right now, what would you do to make a difference in your life? If you knew how to get rid of anxiety/depression/anger/ indifference/low Self-esteem/no finances/addiction/loneliness/abuse/ sleeplessness/hormone imbalance/physical issues/mental issues/emotional issues/ phobias/ stress/parent problems/relationship issues/indecision/trauma/etc. - what would you do, who would you be? We don't even know yet who we are and what we are capable of. We can help others more, we can all help each other. Whatever we learn through a process like the one I am being a bit preachy and over-enthusiastic about, we are able to share it with so many more beings who need it, too. Imagine how much time we would save, how much better we would all get on, if we found a solution to release us all from fear.

How to Tune in to Your Inner Self – Meditation Practice

This method is based on the calm abiding – or Shamata - method of meditation. This is an extremely useful practice and a basis for Shunyata – or Vipassana, both meaning insight – meditation, which occurs naturally as a follow-on result of practising Shamata over a prolonged period of time. There are many different methods of meditation, please have a look around to find the one that suits you best. Any method of meditation is a tool, a method, of gaining calmness of mind, the basis for gaining insight; it is not always in itself 'the way' - but it can be. Meditating leads to insights and awareness, as other methods can, too, and it is well worth a practice to get used to doing very regularly.

Sit in a quiet room where you will not be disturbed, if at all possible. A wonderful account of the practice of inviting stillness and the right conditions for meditation is given in many Eastern practices and teachings, but there is no need to be a follower of any particular doctrine in order to meditate. Meditation is free, and promotes the freedom of our minds, by accessing different wavelengths within our physical bodies and brains, in order to feel at peace, but also gain insight and compassion. In order to prepare for the practice, we first learn to observe our inner patterns by adhering to a few guidelines that can help us enhance and facilitate our practice.

Before we start to go inwards, it's a really useful and pleasant concept to prepare the space we are meditating in. There is a wonderful account of this, in one of my favourite books, 'The Garden', by Michael Geshe Roach. In it, the story of a young man in search for his love becomes synonymous for our own search for meaning in life. We are taught many beautiful and serene, transcendental lessons through the protagonist throughout, and one of them is how to set a suitable environment for a peaceful practice. I highly recommend reading it, as it's a perfect description of how and why we call on higher realms and deities before we even sit down to meditate.

What is generally done, is to set up an altar or shrine, to make offerings as described in chapter 37, 'Karma and Manifestation'. This way, we are putting our energy into a useful context of wanting to help, as much as calling on the same energies to assist us. We are already forming a connection between those higher instances and ourselves, which is very useful in every-day practice in life.

Once done, we can sit down comfortably, either on a chair or on a mat, cushion or stool on the floor, if we are able to sit cross-legged or with legs tucked under by our side. The next steps help us to start calming our thoughts and for our mind to be able to turn inwards. We do this by following the 7-point posture, meaning there are seven points to take note of to make our posture perfectly fit into the geometrical shape of a Merkaba to help us align and connect more easily. Sitting upright with a straight back first of all will help our energy flow. If we slump a little during meditation, we can just straighten up again once we notice. Arms are away from the body a little, bent at the elbow and with palms overlapping in our lap. left hand under right, thumbs lightly touching. Our head is tilted forward a little, so that the crown is at the highest point. Our mouth is relaxed, lips gently closed, tongue to the roof of the mouth. Our eyes should stay slightly open, and although this is hard for most of us who are not used to it, it will become much more easy after some practice so we hardly notice any more. The reason why eyes stay slightly open is to make sure we don't drift off into dream worlds and are still in touch with reality around us. Meditation is not outcome orientated, there is no right or wrong way, and there is no competition between practitioners. To begin with, we can take some deep breaths to settle in, and then just let our breath become calm and regular. We can focus at first on our in-breath and out-breath to help us gain deeper levels of calmness, by simply observing each breath entering our body, and being released again. That's all we have to do at first, and if our mind wanders, we can call our sensations and thoughts back to ourselves and go back to simply witnessing our breath. Thoughts wandering will happen a lot, it's very common. No need to chastise ourselves, just call yourself back from the thought pattern, back to your breathing, every time your mind wanders. If we have pain or other sensations, we can shift a little until they ease. Even these will eventually get less as our body becomes more used to sitting. To begin with, we should be doing less rather than more to entice our mind to try it again. At home, it works just as well to do a few minutes at a time and feel good about it, than to force ourselves to do 20 painful minutes at a set time that sometimes isn't convenient every day. We are more likely to stick to the practice if it is fun at first and we can see progress, see that we can actually do this without much of an issue. Over time, after a week or two, we can expand our practice and sit for longer, again, without pushing ourselves too far. It's nice to be able to know we meditate every day, even if it is just for a few minutes. The rest will follow. Eventually, our brain will have calmed down trying to analyse and judge whether we are doing well. We won't have so much attachment any more to needing to feel that we are doing well, or sit for a certain time. Everyone is different, try out what works for you, there are hundreds of different ways. I thought it best to offer the easiest solution first, to encourage everyone to try it. Enjoy it, and enjoy what happens as a result. You can add a 'thank you' at the end of your practice, for whatever or whoever you are grateful.

As you will soon see, in order to practise insight into our mind and many other principles, it is first essential to learn the state of non-distraction. It takes some time, different for each of us, to remain undistracted enough to begin to have insights, rather than just random thoughts. In order to gain this really precious, peaceful non-distraction in meditation, many true practitioners refrain from using sound as a backdrop, although a single note struck with a Tibetan bell or similar can lead us into the stillness as we follow the note slowly disappearing and out of it again as we slowly come back into reality around us with the gentle sound of the bell.

Here is the same procedure again, explained slightly differently:

If you can, try to sit cross-legged on the floor. This is not to torture you. It is hard, though, to sit like this in the beginning when we are not used to it. If you are new to sitting and meditating like this, make your meditation only a few minutes long at a time. It is more fruitful to sit for a few minutes three times a day, than to attempt a half hour session and be distracted by the pain in your body all throughout. A few minutes at a time will gently stretch the body's ligaments a little further each time, until it is finally possible (this may take some time, have patience) to sit still in full Vajra position, with both legs crossed and feet resting on the other leg. Try not to be too ambitious in the beginning so that the pain is distracting you from your meditation, and allow your body to stretch gently, a little more each time. Keep your hands folded in your lap, left palm under right, with the thumbs gently touching. The back is very straight, and even if you sag during meditation, keep pulling yourself up again like a puppet on a string each time you notice. Your shoulders are gently curved, like those of an eagle, with arms slightly away from the body like the bird's wings, and very relaxed. Your head is bent forward slightly, so that you are gazing at the ground in front of you, about two feet away, or your head roughly at a 45% angle. Concentrating on your face next, your tongue is closing the energy circuit resting against the upper palate whilst your eyes are half open, looking at nothing in particular as your focus is inward, although you can use a blue flower or a similar spot on the floor in front of you as a focal point for your mind. It helps you to call back your thoughts and to keep your mind and thoughts from wandering. This is called the seven-point posture and there is a reason for sitting thus: all four elements present in your body flow easily now, and form a completely closed circuit where energy is least likely to escape; your legs are crossed, thumbs gently touching, your tongue rests against the back of your upper teeth and your eyes are gently aware but focused inwards – Air, Water, Earth and Fire can come completely at rest within, flowing gently; nothing escapes, and you are able to remain totally alert whilst at the same time staying completely still.

The whole ritual described above, that of preparing your space and your posture, is in itself an essential practice for your mind training and your Shunyata meditation. It is the start to all your inward-looking and becomes part of it. Your mind prepares itself by creating the best conditions in which to be, and creates this more easily again in future sittings as well so that it should become easier to remain calmer within.

Whilst sitting, remain as motionless as you can. Again, this is down to practice. Eyes eventually stop watering and fluttering, moving and darting about. Ears stop sending signals to the brain to interpret noises. Body parts stop aching and itching. Eventually, the whole body is gently balanced to remain in stillness, without protest or rebellion. We are so used to 'doing' – now it's finally time to just 'be'.

In the practised stillness, another dimension may find its voice. This voice is the one worth listening to, once all the daily chatter the brain comes up with recedes. You will notice it still going on in the background, ever present. All you have to be alert to is not to become drawn into it, if you can. Most of us who are untrained have such an ingrained and incessant chatter that never or rarely stops. Don't feel guilty, impatient or inadequate, as this is simply another distraction the brain comes up with; just let it go on. A simple way of looking at your thoughts is like a classroom of children before the teacher arrives. They are all over the place, noisy, running around, shouting. If you enact a good teacher, you will be able to gently call your thoughts back into your brain, instead of 'leaking' them out of your body. This is also how much of our energy is lost elsewhere from our body. In a good meditation practice, none of our energy is lost, energy flows permanently within to replenish us, and our inner realms are smoothed and tidied in the process. Sitting thus, you want to 'leak' as little energy as possible. As you may have heard, those who master this art, are able to stay alive without sleep, food or drink, in the same position, sometimes for years – but please don't try this at home! Even if at the beginning you may feel you are not getting anywhere fast, remember there is no good or bad meditation – all meditation efforts are beneficial.

You are actually not looking to achieve anything, any result or outcome, even if you have come with a goal to learn to meditate, to achieve something, to get somewhere. What happens is quite the opposite. There is nothing to get, nothing to achieve, nothing to think – at least for the duration of your meditation. There is not even anything to meditate on, no puzzles to solve, no inner preparation to do for an exam. You are simply trying to sit there, minding your own business, without becoming distracted. Impossible, you may say, but that is really as simple as it is, and yet it can also be the hardest thing to master.

*"All of humanity's problems stem from man's inability
to sit quietly in a room alone."*
Blaise Pascal, Pensées

Instead of a point outside of your body, you can, if you like, also focus your mind on your breath and become conscious of the art of breathing normally. There is no exaggerated breathing, only becoming conscious of it. The breath should go into your stomach area with your chest remaining flat, so that your diaphragm rises and falls again gently. This in itself is a big lesson to learn, as most of us breathe wrongly into the chest area, oxygenating the brain instead of the solar plexus, bringing more emphasis to thoughts, rather than promoting the art of being, and remaining calm. Have we based a whole culture on breathing wrongly? Who knows, perhaps we have.

There is nothing to aim for, although lots may happen. You may at first meet your brain's resistance, saying things like, 'I cannot do this' or 'what rubbish' or 'how useless are you at this' or even 'I am not doing this any longer, it hurts and it is a waste of time'. People who go on retreats have such high expectations and look forward to the stillness away from stressful work and lives, and almost all report without fail that the day comes when they are ready to pack their bags and leave early, simply because they have come to this point of resistance. The resistance from our ordinary thinking brain is as strong as our identification with it. It has been coming up with many a make-believe story for all our lives so far, and it is in danger of being found out. It isn't going to give up that easily. It does not like not being in charge, and rather than allow our fear, it will rebel against this newfangled hippy stuff at first. If you sit through this, you may also experience what seems like real feelings of fear next. Who am I really? Who am I without my thoughts, feelings, lifestyle? Again, all you have to do is simply sit with this part of our ego-Self we all have, which is, of course, not the real 'You', but very convincing all the same, especially at times like this. Are we able to nurture ourselves through this point of anxiety? You will not lose anything by just keeping on sitting, remaining calm, being still. And breathe. That's all you have to do, again. And again. It is easier said than done, but it helps to remember, for example, that it is said that the Buddha met all his demons in the six days he meditated for his enlightenment, and so might you. It is normal. Everyone does; frequently and incessantly, whether in meditation or not. What would be worse than to recognise it all in meditation, or to re-live the symptoms over and over again when we are busy in our every-day lives? You can choose which you would rather do. These are deemed to be the tests of the natural world, to see how much of our eternal Karmic Self we truly understand, how many fears there still are to conquer.

Eventually, we will all find out what it is all about. I should not make any promises but it is tempting to say at least this: it is all superbly worth persevering and practising, every day if you can. Even when you do find out some of the Truth with a capital T, try not to let your brain convince you that you have done enough now, that you finally know it all. Whatever may come, carry on with your daily practice. As a very kind teacher recently said, it is like charging your mobile phone, you need to do it all the time, otherwise it will not work! Carry on your meditation, it is your best and lives-long friend, able to carry you towards the realisation of your true existence.

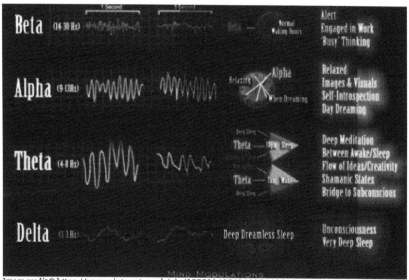

Image credit © https://www.pinterest.co.uk/pin/377739487494927440/

Checking-in With Our Karmic Energy

For any of the following, you can use the 'calm abiding' method above to first settle your mind, and then to add more practical, active methods of healing to it – or use the meditation method after the practice, whatever suits you best. They work very well in combination. Once your mind is more used to being still, it becomes easier to focus your attention gently on your energies within. Where is your attention? Where is your energy flowing? Where is it 'pooling', being still? Where might it be stuck? Which chakra is most of your energy residing in, at this particular moment?

Your Life-Force, or Kundalini energy flows up and down along your spine all the time, whilst also feeding tiny channels of energy flowing from your centre into all parts of your body. Sometimes this happens really fast and in a matter of minutes, sometimes it takes days or months or even longer; sometimes it halts altogether. Sometimes it gets stuck in a chakra or body part, in order to point out a blockage to you. This whole energy network within us is what I have referred in this book as being our 'Karmic Energy Mind'. There is a mixture here of what happens to us from moment to moment, combined with our Karmic Energy Blueprint we have brought with us from previous existence. Our energy is changing from second to second, every minute, every hour, every day. Since it can be so confusing to break the energy down into tiny components, it helps to allow our minds to get some overview over who we are, what makes us, 'us'. There are many clues and many pointers in life to point us in the right direction, many of them I have already given in this book to help you find out more about who you are. You can find out more for yourself by asking yourself questions when your mind is still. What are your recurring thoughts right now, or your recurring feelings? Do you keep getting tearful, or fearful? Do you have pain anywhere? Is your body ready to jump and run away, or is it too scared to move? Are there too many thoughts at once? Or do you have points in your body where energy is not flowing well? Each chakra can hold 'negative' charges according to what happens to us, which makes us prone to feel certain ways. This is not a bad thing, but rather it indicates how we can explore within us so we can find a solution. Ask yourself where your energy is, what it is doing, and get used to the hints and signs that your body is giving you. It's really useful to write a diary of our symptoms to find out more about how we can help ourselves.

Here are a few examples of how you can tell what is going on within you and where to find stuck energy, internally. Remember these are only examples, and a more comprehensive list can be found in many courses on the subjects and/or online research. Please also note that to each area within us that we experience problems with, there is also a positive outcome that can be associated with this same area, so that once we have worked out how to overcome issues, we will be able to experience a more positive phase in our lives where these may support and reward us in turn for our hard work.

If you are feeling/ have recurring thoughts or issues around:
Anger, aggravated, annoyed, resentful, violent/violated, aggressive, passionate, financial issues and issues around birth, problems finding your true place on Earth and work that you enjoy, identifying with a 'Self' and the 'I AM' presence within, repressing power, problems with authority figures exerting control and/or have violations actioned against you or you acting violently towards to others, sexual trauma and/or your

relationship with mother or a mother figure, issues around sexual organs, reproduction and lower bowel, it is an indication of energies that tend to be stuck in the **Base Chakra (Red)** If energies are flowing, then issues around the above can be resolved.

If you are feeling/ have recurring thoughts or issues around:
Being co-dependent in relationships; low in confidence; often feeling cold, lethargic; aimless or abandoned, have issues around bonding with others, blockages within your digestion, over-indulgence, food intolerances, use of toxic food and drink substances to suppress our true Self, issues around trusting others, not feeling appreciated and many lessons on shock situations in your life, issues with producing testosterone, problems with liver, bowels, womb, ovaries and kidneys; these can be indicative of energies that tend to be stuck in the **Navel Chakra (Orange)**

If you are feeling/ have recurring thoughts or issues around:
Fearful, stressed, nervous, inadequate, lacking confidence, not believing in yourself, on edge, anxious, OCD, afraid to be alive on a deep level, craving company but then rejecting it, highly intelligent but not rating intuition, low Self-esteem, looking for meaning and purpose in life, skin problems, caffeine/sugar overconsumption and bacterial/fungal/viral growth, problems with adrenaline overproduction or fatigue, these can be indications that energies tend to be stuck in the **Solar Plexus Chakra (Yellow)**

If you are feeling/ have recurring thoughts or issues around:
In shock or traumatised after unexpected events in your life, even early on, out of or not in touch with your calling in life, feeling like you are not connected, forever searching for the right community, religion or belief system that will make you feel more secure, looking for wisdom and a reflection of your intuitions, being a lone wanderer, are often dissatisfied with what the world has to offer and feel absolute elation or deep dissatisfaction, making you not want to engage with anything or anyone unless something or someone is perfect, having high standards that you find hard to meet yourself, lacking warmth and wisdom – these can be indication of energies that tend to be stuck in the **Seed of the Self Chakra (Gold)**

If you are feeling/ have recurring thoughts or issues around:
Relationships with close friends, family and spouses and how to conduct them wisely; being afraid to make the right decisions for yourself and all concerned;
these can be indication of energies that tend to be stuck **Below Heart Chakra(Olive Green)**

If you are feeling/ have recurring thoughts or issues around:
Out of balance, not going with the flow, boundaries, not good with

change, unharmonious times, especially in close relationships, stuck in situations and places that do not serve your highest good, not able to connect to your own and others feelings and emotions, being inconsiderate, judgemental and cold-hearted, problems with heart chambers and valves through congestion - these can be indication of energies that tend to be stuck in the **Heart Chakra (Green)**

If you are feeling/ have recurring thoughts or issues around:
not being comfortable speaking your truth around others, opening up to your artistic potential, holding yourself back through low life-force energy; problems with hormones and immune system illness; these can be indication of energies that tend to be stuck in the **Thymus Chakra (Jade)**

If you are feeling/ have recurring thoughts or issues around:
not able to communicate easily, stuck with our creative energy flow, indecisiveness, Thyroid issues – these can be indication of energies that tend to be stuck in the **Throat Chakra (Turquoise)**

If you are feeling/ have recurring thoughts or issues around:
Deep-rooted father issues stemming from childhood; Communication, speaking truth, speaking your mind, not trusting your higher Self, not trusting connecting to spiritual Self and taking cue from it, insecurity and doubt, persecution issues from past lives; not able to make decisions easily; not able to focus, concentrate or sleep well; problems with teeth, jaws, adenoids and speech, father issues & issues around authority figures, Neck pain, spinal problems from birth - these can be indication of energies that tend to be stuck in the **Chin Chakra (Sapphire Blue)**

If you are feeling/ have recurring thoughts or issues around:
Deep-rooted ongoing Father issues; lack of confidence in communicating and realising own path; sadness & depression; suicidal tendencies and dark thoughts; overuse of chemical drugs, feeling as if born in the wrong generation; lack of enthusiasm; problems with applying own ideas in life; not seeing a future; hating things with vengeance, things 'getting up your nose', issues with hearing, ear infections - these can be indication of energies that tend to be stuck in the **Nose Chakra (Royal Blue)**

If you are feeling/ have recurring thoughts or issues around:
Fearful of spirituality, depression, undermined by authority, father issues, loss of father figure, difficulty to see sense in life, sleep issues, low levels of melatonin, denying higher purpose and connections, persecution complex, inferiority complex, haughtiness, snobby or arrogant attitude, set in ways, head aches, migraines, issues with pituitary gland; Brain fog & tumours/aneurysms – these can be indication of energies

THOUGHTS ON THE VASTNESS OF KARMA

that tend to be stuck in the **Third Eye Chakra (Indigo)**

If you are feeling/ have recurring thoughts or issues around:
Being arrogant or haughty, worried, obsessed, having too many thoughts at once, afraid of using your healing ability, unsure about Self and trusting others; going it alone but failing; compulsive disorders; prone to injuries and feeling physically weak; emphasis on intellectual qualities only; closed pineal gland; these can be indication of energies that tend to be stuck in the **Crown Chakra (Violet)**

If you are feeling or have recurring thoughts or issues around:
Manipulative, fear of rejection, not good enough, afraid to ask for help, worrying and overthinking all the time , wasting talent, late to develop, insecure, naive, too familiar for own good, easily taken advantage of, falling for crooks or fake money-making schemes - these can be indication of energies that tend to be stuck in the **Above Crown Chakra (Magenta)**

If you are feeling or have recurring thoughts or issues around:
false sense of divinity; overrating oneself; being misguided and/or misleading; worshipping wrong people; spending money that's not there; involved in scams; being vague and airy towards others; disinterest in others true feelings;
these can be indication of energies that tend to be stuck in the **Second Above Crown Chakra (White)**

If you are feeling or have recurring thoughts or issues around:
disconnected from surroundings and 'real' life; issues around being able to take in solid nourishment; disillusioned with many people and situations; not able to be practical or apply to work; debt and issues around earning money; mental health and incarcerations; not able to explain own actions and thoughts; no defence mechanisms - these can be indication of energies that tend to be stuck in the **3rd Above Crown Chakra (Opalescent)**

If you are feeling or have recurring thoughts or issues around:
unable to relate to the world; feeling removed from time perception and physical attributes; unable to sustain themselves, dependent on others on Earth; unable to relate own ideas, thoughts, insights to Earthly dimensions despite being highly intelligent; not easy to relate to feelings and others emotions; these can be indication of energies that tend to be stuck in the **4th Above Crown Chakra (Clear/Translucent)**

Before you panic or are really insulted, just a quick footnote to explain that all of the above are examples of issues that might arise, that may apply to someone but not another. It's by no means an exhaustive list.

As we learned before, each energy frequency is benign in itself, but our body and our inner Karmic energy can resonate by either showing positive, negative or neutral equivalent reactions. There are many stunningly beautiful attributes to each frequency which, to shorten the process and focus on problems we might face, I have left out here, as it would take too long to list. It may sound intense therefore, a bit like when we feel we can only focus on the negatives instead of seeing the good in life - which might actually be exactly what happens if any of us have blockages in areas of our body. The good news is that if we are able to recognise them for what they are, we can also work with them to help us out of the negative, inverted energy flow of each blockage. This is what this book and the techniques below are all about, to help us identify where we need a little extra help in identifying our issues, so that we can then more directly and easily learn to remedy it. The realisations and recovery from these blockages often also mean that we may find ample explanation of what is wrong within us, so that we can get further help with what presents itself as a result.

The above guidelines can in such succinct form of course, only be an introduction on the subject of our inner energies, their channels and centres and how we can assist ourselves with any stagnant energy flow. Hopefully these findings will initiate further reading to find out more details. You will find similar diagrams and descriptions in many scripts and imagery, not just new age, but many of them from different cultures dating back thousands of years ago, by those who already saw the simple yet profound connection between the Karmic frequencies that created us and the Karmic energy channels within our body.

Tidying Up What We Have Found

In order to find out more information and learn to apply it, it is also necessary to look inwards further than we might ever have done before, as well as find out external links and doing more research. Once something resonates with us on an individual level, we fortunately have millions of ways to elaborate on it and find out more, via internet and connecting with many other good souls who have already done some work in a similar vein. You can also start by asking your body to answer your questions in its own way – such as, what does the stuck energy look/feel like? Why does it have this effect on me? What do I have to do in order for it to flow again? etc., to find out more detail. You are then spoiled for choice as to which energy therapy to use, and there are some examples of the techniques below which I mentioned throughout this book in order to

689

release any stuck energy. If it doesn't resonate with you, you can simply move on to something else that does. You can start quite simply with the information you get from asking direct questions, even without consciously knowing more about how this links in with the Karmic energy body. It is as good a starting point as any, because it is uniquely yours. Your Karmic energy will already know the answer, and it's on your side. You just have to learn to tune into it. Try various techniques, look up clips of them online, learn to do them and check in again a few days later to see if any of it has changed, shifted, moved or even disappeared. Of course, not all energy blockages will release in one go, but take continuous work over long periods of time. Many of them will respond to our willingness to give them attention rather than pushing them away and ignoring them. Some will actually release straight away do that we have an incentive to work on our inner world more regularly. But very

rarely do they disappear if we do not work on them – brushing Karmic issues under the carpet will only make us have a nasty shock later in life when we get ill.

There are many different practices to make sure our energy flows well. Our Karmic energy body that helped us incarnate and reminds us of what still needs to be done to iron out some of our energy creases, will be enhanced in turn by our doing so. It is one of the most rewarding, important and necessary practices we should follow, no matter what our beliefs are or which religion we follow. One of the things that happen a lot in modern times is that our energy literally 'leaks' out from our bodies. We often report feeling drained as a result, which makes sense. How can we avoid this from happening? We have already done our meditation and sat quietly, looking inwards. What we can then become aware of is how, with each interaction, we tend to 'open' a particular energy centre within our body. If you are often anxious, it's because your solar plexus energy is too open, it is leaking out energy. You can start with any such energy that you notice is leaving your body by calling it back to you, by allowing the energy to remain within you, and circulate round your body. There is no need to 'lose' or 'send' energy from your body. If we want to help others, we can work with our crown chakra to open up to higher frequencies, which can then correlate to the frequencies of other beings to bring about a better outcome, to 'communicate' and even out any discrepancies, so to speak. We can become aware at any time how important our energy is, from where in our bodies it is being emitted, and whether this is useful to us and others, if it is in keeping with our ethos, whether we want to continue doings things 'the hard way' sometimes or if we are ready to move up into a higher way of existing. This would mean that we learn more about how to orchestrate our energy, how to leave our bodily energy in peace and flowing. As we all know, using up too much physical energy can and will make us unwell, so if this is a part of our every-day life or by choice, we also need time for our energies to replenish again. We tend to give much time to recreational sports and training for fitness; now it's time to do the same for the energy supply that feeds our body in the first place. It doesn't come from a fancy bottled drink, either. The energy we need to tune into is much purer than that, after all, it has been forming, feeding and sustaining our physical existence forever. Perhaps it's time we gave it some love in return.

There are many practices that will help do this, and many people are already aware of them. My background is obviously in Buddhist practice, and the highly revered teachings, visualisations and imagery all hint at what we need to do to keep well. Some of them have been kept sacred for thousands of years as they are immensely powerful, but some others have become visible to those who have expressed curiosity and interest. This has sparked many different ways to stay well, too many to go into. Like a flower that has gone to seed, teachings are spreading through all of Earth's elements, and people can take from it what they want, according to what they need most. All I will say is that they work. They work to protect us, our families and our homes, they protect our health and our minds. They are calming practices that help when we are feeling upset or disconnected, and can prevent this from happening in the first place. They also help balance our thoughts and feelings, because the central energy vortex that flows along our spine is enhanced in visualisation, so we will pay more attention to allowing energy to flow through us, in a way that is conducive. The central energy river washes away many unhelpful impurities, and it meanders through our whole body to help replenish what we have lost. I can highly recommend it.

Using Energy Therapies:

Reversing negativity that has happened to us as part of understanding our Karma with EFT™ – Emotional Freedom Technique™

A big part of our journey towards healing our Karmic deficits, is learning to turn our energy around so that it assists us, rather than block us and others.

For that, surely we must first understand what this really means. We might already recognise we are talking about an inner energy process again. Whether it expresses itself in a feeling, or a recurring thought pattern, reversing our energy on something that has been holding us back means that we are putting it right again. This psychological energy reversal is a term given to describe an inner energy process inherent in all of us. If we were able to observe what happens to us when we have an energy blockage within, we would see that what we call 'reversal' actually means we can finally let go of an energy blockage again, often once and for all. Amazingly, we don't have to 'see' it to believe it. We will FEEL it, and we will know it is really happening by the results that we feel. This process is very gently, it does not happen by forcing it. Learning the art of moving on from any traumatic situation that still bothers us, means that we are learning to release stagnant energy from our bodies and minds. It does not mean we have to continue to suffer for someone else's wrong doing, out of the goodness of our hearts. Reversing our damaged Karmic energy processing means we can let go of a scenario we have held within ourselves, sometimes for lifetimes. Neglecting the process of reversing means we live in resentment and often physical, emotional and psychological pain. It is easy to see when we are still holding on to the stagnant energy within, because it makes us feel bad. It is fairly impossible to truly move on from situations that are still bothering us. We might forgive others and ourselves for things that happen, but inside, our bodies may still have remnants of energy stuck in there that still hurts, and it needs to be righted. It's not something we can do just by changing our thoughts. We need some help from some special, but very easy-to-learn techniques.

If we were explained this, we would possibly be much more likely to practice how to fully release ourselves from it, as the feeling of freedom from some long-standing issues that it gives us afterwards benefits us first and foremost, but at the same time, others will notice a benefit as well. It does not leave a bad aftertaste and a begrudging feeling of resentment for having been told to 'forgive'. How can we do this, if we need to learn what true forgiveness is first, and how to remove the sting from our minds first? Whereas the traditional meaning of forgiveness probably has a bitter taste of resenting the act of feeling forced somehow to forgive someone for hurting us, doing us harm, injury etc., this is not what is meant here and it is not necessary to do anything begrudgingly. It is also possible with the right techniques to hold on to secondary feelings of guilt for not being able to 'forgive' completely, or feel that forgiving is a necessary process as a part of a sense of duty towards our belief system or faith or religion, or one that is necessary for us to move on from a situation. We are right in feeling that these are methods that work for some people, but not all of us.

Are we not worthy of being free of such energy bonds? If we knew that the methods described above would help us to release the blocked energies within ourselves, which repeat those nasty triggers time and time again – if we had evidence that we would never have to deal with them again – would we not at least try them out?

I have had so many examples of this, working with EFT™ over the past 20 years. Thousands of people have reported what it is like to release energy, and feel renewed, younger, refreshed, like being given a new lease of life, every time they have used this and similar techniques. People have worked on traumatic events and war memories; on accidents and injuries; phobias and fears, major and minor. I cannot repeat it often enough: it is SO worth it. It does not interfere with any belief system, and it does work without having to lose consciousness, at any age and stage of our lives, regardless of our backgrounds. It is a universal healing tool, one of many, given to us because at some point, we must have asked for some reasonably simple solutions and deserved to be given them. I am not saying it is always easy – but in my experience, the alternatives of remaining in pain are much worse. Please read on for the exact method of how to make the most of using Energy Therapies.

Making an Inventory

It can be so useful to make a list, rather like a shopping list, of what we find or believe is 'wrong' and going on within us – an inventory, so to speak. This is nothing new, and a process which is a part of many Self-help programmes in existence, and I urge you to do this here as well. Buy a nice blank book, or open a fresh new page on your computer and start writing about some of the weak points you least want others to see. To give you an incentive and an idea, I am giving you a few examples of what I used to feel I least wanted to look at in myself, below: Again, I do this because I am not different from you. Hint: these are also the solution to any of the issues we encounter, and it is not 'confession' time like in a church, these are really valuable hints as to where energies are stuck within that are just waiting to be released.

So here goes:

'I don't like looking at my 'dark' side
I am reflecting my needs
I want to be seen as a 'nice' person
I 'people-please'
I put others before myself to escape my own problems
I get resentful when people take me for granted
I do not like being challenged

I am critical and judgmental of others rather than looking at what it triggers in myself
I want to be right, at least most of the time
I am complex and choosy
I am opinionated
I like being in charge and in control
I like everything just so, and in my own way
I am too deep and thoughtful sometimes
I doubt myself a lot and give myself a hard time'

Lists like these are always a working document and can be added to any time anywhere, on a life-long basis, sometimes. For example, I made the above list a few years ago, before I did the final edit to this book. It interested me to see that in retrospect, the last statement felt more right than any of the ones above.

What I probably had not seen so clearly at the time, is the one statement that was underlying all of them – that I give myself a really hard time and needed to learn to take things easy! It goes to show that in hindsight, things can be much clearer, and that we do move on from many issues naturally. I learned to say 'no' more often, too, to many demands on my time. I became stronger, valued myself more, and had many more insights into how we are educated and duped with a sense of duty and submission into believing we are not worthy as human beings unless we stand out and perform with outstanding results. Time to go easy on ourselves, and allow ourselves to be, and breathe! The miracle of life is already here, it is not a carrot dangling in front of us that we have to catch at all cost.

I hope I am demonstrating that the reason we make these inventories is not to show ourselves up, or beat ourselves up for being imperfect. We do it for a much cleverer reason:
If we learn to know ourselves by our weaknesses, we do not inadvertently ask someone else to hold up a mirror for us on our behalf. We choose responsibility for ourselves instead, and taking responsibility and care for ourselves has never been so fruitful: the results are compassion, wisdom and healthy relationships with ourselves and all others. When we learn more about ourselves, we feel stronger and free, and as a result, we are able to release any stagnant energies that make us cling to others for all the wrong reasons.

On an energy level, when you shine the light into the darkest corners of your Karmic mind that you least like to look at, you make friends with yourself, you neutralise the negativity with gentle attention, alertness, compassion and nurturing yourself. By light, I mean the light that shines within as the result of pure energy manifestation, something to be relearned and re-ignited by most of us whilst in human form. As a result, you no longer need to initiate control by an inner process of assessing, rejecting and denying; we can re-balance our energy defects as well as our perception of any inner sense of lack of light or deficiency of love. We also do not have to do the redress ourselves: our inner energy system knows how to rebalance itself, with the techniques described below. We are only listing what we feel is wrong, and applying the technique. It is often all that is needed. It is not necessary to do any more than that; we do not even have to make a vow or make a conscious effort to stop. All we do, to start with, is make an inventory. We simply practice honesty with ourselves, we learn to speak up and acknowledge that there is a deficit, that is all. It is enough to make a start, with the result that your energy around your 'negative' Karma already starts to become neutralised, just by having taken that first step towards your negative Karma itself becoming neutralised. Sometimes this happens straight away, sometimes the exercises that then follow the inventory need to be repeated regularly. It can be as simple as brushing our teeth every day. Some people would simply advise us to 'get over it', 'grow out of it, 'let it go' or 'deal with it'. These are terms I would never use, they seem harsh and unfair and do not actually bring about a healing process very often. They imply some sort of force or conscious effort or will that we are short of that then magically changes how we feel if only we could get to grips with it. However, experience has taught me that none of the above advice, even when well-meant, can benefit us without addressing the energy imbalance that has stored all the negativities in the first place. Maybe this is what has been lacking in our lives so far: we are aware of our flaws, and what is wrong, but have not ever been taught a method to release it all. I hope the above list now makes sense, because I am showing you methods next of how to overcome all the things that have been building up within like a pressure cooker. It is not meant as a guilt-trip list, but a list towards Karmic freedom.

I can't recommend enough making your own list of how and where you wish to experience Karmic freedom once and for all.

EFT™ (Emotional Freedom Technique™)™

I have mentioned it often enough throughout this book, and I will mention it here again, this time in a short exercise form to give you an idea of what EFT™, or any 'Meridian Energy Tapping' technique by a different name, does. I can only give you some indication of how powerful a healing tool this is here, in writing. To learn fully what EFT™ is all about, please go to Gary Craig, the founder's website on www.emofree.com. You can also watch original footage of his EFT™ courses on stage from the 1990s onwards on many a Youtube clip, and subscribe to a regular newsletter studying many different cases on his webpage.

I will give you some examples here of how it can work for you, too, and give you my word and my own take on how beautiful and effective a technique it is. Don't be put off by others' experiences if you heard negative things, make your own and build on them. The last 4 decades have prolifically spawned many Energy Techniques by many different names, probably because they also work well. Hopefully, you will like EFT™ or one of its many cousins enough to look up more online and try it for yourself on many an issue I have mentioned in this book. It really is stunning how it works well in so many different ways. You can teach yourself some of the basics by downloading materials from the site, or buy one or two good books on the subject, which I suggest in the bibliography. There is also a full and free download of the book on EFT™ written by Gary Craig, called 'The Unseen Therapist' on the EFT™ website to get you started, as well as courses available on the subject in various progressive levels of expertise. (Info correct at time of printing)
One more thing you can also do is talk to me about EFT™ directly, and I will be very happy to show you how to work out some algorithms in order to get going. I always stress, however, that I must advise everyone to be discerning when approaching very deep, long-term and complex issues with EFT™ on your own. Please don't do this alone. Ask for help from an experienced practitioner, a long list of who is represented on Gary Craig's website.

One of the reasons why I rate it so highly is that Meridian techniques can help to effectively tackle the 'Self-sabotage' mechanisms within our systems, when we get it right. This in itself is a fantastic finding of Dr Roger Callaghan, the founder of Thought Field Therapy or TFT for short, in the 1980's. His incredible discovery of an inner energy reversal that occurs when we experience some difficult situations, was followed by his further findings that we can access these inner 'on/off switches' so to speak, at any point after the event and can put things right again within. In light of ancient traditional therapies such as acupuncture and acupressure, yoga, Kum Nye and many more which have helped people for thousands of years, his idea made perfect sense to revive these techniques and give them a modern add-on: Dr Callaghan combined the use of pressure points with a more specific psychological element of focused phrases for the recipient to say, giving therapy a completely new angle which worked wonders for mental, emotional and physical issues. The new version of Meridian Techniques were born thus and have been very successful at helping to treat a host of complaints for many since.
 I have been proposing here in this book that we have all experienced difficult situations over aeons of time, and it's probably about time, too, that we finally find solutions to our suffering that will alleviate it. If I make an analogy that our inner energy system can be a bit like a maxed out computer having worked overtime all our lives, possibly hindered by

a host of viruses and malware; we might better understand that we have been running with hardware that probably has never had any regular maintenance to get it to work again properly. Most of us are not even aware of these malfunctions within our energy system, otherwise we would give them a regular work-out as we gladly do with our physical bodies. In Energy Therapies such as EFT™ and TFT, a noticeable glitch in our energy system is called a 'Psychological Reversal', something that happens to us in times of stress, often unbeknownst to our conscious Self. It is similar to the concept we talked about, which states that certain situations in our Karmic existence have created negative Karma for us. This is no judgement, but is rather a description of an automatic energy mechanism that occurs within us: something happens to our energy system which makes it do one of several things: either it shuts down at certain points to a great extent, or it goes into reverse gear, or it only functions on a reduced capacity. Luckily, we are now learning on a much greater scale about these methods, to help us learn how we can put it right again when we become conscious of it. What we have been talking about all along in terms of ailments in our life as well as righting our Karmic actions culminates in offering solutions to our problems that are so simple, we would probably not believe it could work that way. The consequence of our inner blocked-up, stagnant, pent-up energy flow can be alleviated, sometimes with instant, tangible results. Another fabulous finding is that we do not even have to be an expert or understand the technique for it to work. it is simply exercising our inner energy system, and we can use it prophylactically, too, just like we would do a cardio-vascular work-out for a few minutes every day. Your qualify to benefit from using these techniques by being a human being. Our systems all work on the same principle, in that way we are all built the same and can therefore apply the same method time and time again to help us feel so much lighter. I have been advocating EFT™ since 1998, and have witnessed thousands of people benefit from it. The process is really simple to do, too, by tapping along a certain sequence on minute energy channels, we awaken our inner energy channels which are laid out in hundreds of thousands of intricate individual patterns. Luckily, they also tend to resonate together so that we do not have to become rocket scientists to benefit from doing a daily routine of tapping on specific points on our upper, clothed body.

Just a little more info before we start in earnest to become more active than just taking in written typescript. When I had experienced on myself and many others how incredibly useful and necessary in our modern times these techniques could be, I organised a weekly group to share using these energy tapping techniques I had learned. The groups went on for 15 years, and at one point early on, I asked a Tibetan Rinpoche (meaning Precious Jewel; formal address for an accomplished Tibetan Teacher of Dharma, the principles and inherent laws of existence, wisdom and compassion in Buddhism) to be present throughout. It was important for me to see how an ancient principle that first appeared thousands of years ago, in one form as 'Kum Nye' in Tibetan medicine, could be effective in reversing our negative Karma. When I asked what he thought of it after the session, he likened it to 'mind training' and urged me to continue, which I have done, to this day, as it's very much how I choose to see it, too: we are performing Karmic Mind Training, even though in the West, techniques like these have taken on many different names under the umbrella of Energy Psychology, Energy Therapy or Meridian Therapy. No matter what we name it, I believe they all tackle our inner Karmic energy 'knots', which can exist as negatively charged frequencies in what we have here called our Karmic mind or Karmic energy system.

Despite many rants about scientific evidence and pseudo-science, we can simply see it as physical exercise if we want, with the added benefit that we are resolving some very long-standing issues as a side-effect. Whichever way we see it, not only do these techniques work, there are a huge range of benefits to giving them a try. It is an exercise you can simply do in your living room sitting comfortably all by yourself, with some friends or family or in a group if you prefer. If you feel there are deeper issues you want help with, you can always find a local clinic and talk to a professional Meridian Therapist specialising in the techniques first. Often, they do a trial session free of charge so you can find out if it suits you. The following description of how to use EFT™ as an example, is a basic instruction in how simple it is to learn it, almost as simple as breathing. It is meant as an incentive to find out more once we realise how simple and marvellously effective it is. Just like we breathe without noticing all the time, it is also important to learn to breathe properly. It's the same with these techniques; our body is doing something like this naturally already, but we will also learn that we are all born with the ability to learn to apply this more effectively. So, without further ado, here goes:

Find somewhere comfortable in your environment and sit normally, with your legs uncrossed. If you do get disturbed, don't worry, you can pick up again where you left off. Take a few deep breaths into your stomach area, just as an inner preparation and sign to yourself that this is time for you to spend on yourself, in a most valuable way. You will be focusing briefly on some specific issues that are bothering you rather than just be relaxing, in order to actively help your body reduce or even clear them. So that your body can do this, you can follow these instructions. First of all, think – briefly - of some issue that you want to address. It can be a situation at work, or with someone, but nothing to complex at first. If you easily feel anxious about it, don't go into it too deeply, just know that you are choosing this particular issue for now to work on. EFT™ works on many different things, but I have mentioned anxiety as a good example, because all of us have it at one point or another so we can more easily relate to trying it on that. Choose something that doesn't make you super upset as a first try, but something that bothers you enough so that you get a tangible 'before' and 'after' result.

As an example, you might choose something like 'I feel anxious thinking about a work assessment next Monday' or something like that. It can be big or small, it's up to you, but it's good to choose something like a specific situation to focus on briefly for you to see first results and learn how these techniques work.

Once you have chosen something to work on, you get to use a scale from 1-10 to rate how high your intensity of your emotion is on that specific subject you chose. If you like, you can write it down in a sentence if you find it easier to look at in front of you to rate the number of intensity. In any case, go with your first answer of how high the intensity of your feeling of anxiety is. Is it as low as a 1, hardly there at all? Or is it a 10, which is unbearable? Perhaps it is somewhere in between? Your inner energy mind usually has a great way of responding to finding a number often quite instantly. Go with that number that appears for you, bear it in mind or write it down. If you can't get a number, having a guess at what it would be sometimes works, or use a different way to describe the intensity that suits you best.

Now, raise both your hands in front of your chest and start to tap lightly with the fingers of one hand against the outer side of the other hand (which is as often called the 'karate-chop' point to make it clearer where you are tapping). Whilst continuously tapping, you also say the following statement, or something similar to that effect:

'Even though I feel this anxiety when I think of (insert your specific situation), I deeply and completely accept myself and love and forgive myself.'

Repeat this same statement three times, still tapping on the side of your palm.

This is the first part of an EFT™ 'sandwich', and it might already feel obvious to you that even after a short while tapping, the number of intensity on your statement can have shifted. But this is only the first part, so hang in there even if it has not. It's not a competition, and everyone benefits.

EFT - Emotional Freedom Technique
Tapping Points

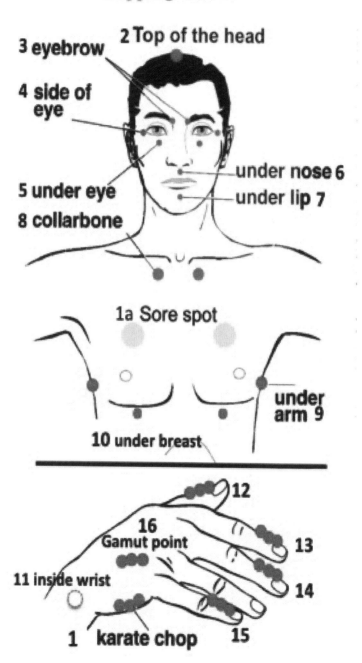

Image Credit © emofree.com

You then continue to tap on a number of points on your upper torso (it doesn't ever matter whether you choose left or right or both at the same time). At the same time as tapping on the points, you will still be saying the same statement as you originally came up with, but this time, you say it without the 'even though' part at the beginning and the 'I deeply and completely...' part at the end. The statement is now in its simple form again, focused on simply stating what is bothering you without the previous add-on statement. The next points along the body to tap on are as follows:

- The beginning of the eyebrow (this point is situated just below the beginning of your eyebrow, in the corner of your eye socket above your left and right eye)

- The side of the eye (on the outer bone ridge of your eye socket, about an inch away from the outer corner of your eye)

- Underneath the eye (in the centre of the bone ridge of the eye socket below the eye, right underneath and in line with the pupil)

- Under Nose (in the centre of the soft skin between nose and upper lip)

- On the chin (in the crease below your lip)

- Collarbone (make a fist to lightly tap In the centre of your collar where your collarbones meet)

- Underneath your arm (around 2-3 inches down from your armpit, on the side of your ribcage)

- Beneath the Nipple (On your ribcage, around 2 inches down from your chest, in line with the centre of your chest)

- On the sides (nearest to you) of your finger nails on the: 1. thumb, then 2. index finger, then 3. middle finger (leave out ring finger) and 4. little finger.

(Please also see above chart for reference)

Keep on saying your statement a couple of times, as you tap on each body point in turn, around 7-10 times. This is the second part of the EFT™ 'sandwich'. You can't 'overtap' and do yourself harm, so don't worry if you don't get it exactly right. There are lots of Youtube video tutorials on the techniques, so if you want to learn by copying the tapping sequence from those as well, it might be easier than just to read about all the points when you are new to them.

The ring finger point is skipped, because it is covered by the point that follows next. For this, you do not need to say anything during tapping. All you do is tap on the back of your hand, between ring finger and little finger (around 1 cm down from the knuckles, see diagram), whilst turning your eyes first to the far left and then, to the far right corners, and repeat again left and right. It will look as if you are trying to look over your left and right shoulder without turning your head. Next, let your pupils turn a full circle with your eyes open, as if you were following each number on an internal clock with your eyes; then do the same process in the opposite direction. Lastly, you look with your pupils up to the ceiling whilst taking a deep breath in, and then look down to the floor, releasing the breath at this point.

One last round of the first full statement 3 times again, starting with 'even though...', tapping on the karate-chop point as before, makes the whole 'sandwich' complete. You have now done a complete round of EFT™. It is simpler than it looks written down, hence my suggestion to also follow a video clip. It will get really easy with practice. Once you get more used to using it, you have all the basic movements that you need to know, for all future tapping sessions.

Now that you have finished one round of tapping, you do one last thing, which is to rate the intensity of your feeling again on the scale from 0-10, as before. This gives you an indication of how you feel after your first ever round of tapping. Check it against the number you made a note of right at the beginning before you started tapping. What is the number now, when you tune into the situation? Is it still the same, or has it gone down? In most cases, the number will have changed, and even if it has stayed the same or has gone up, it can be worked on, don't worry. However, if the number and therefore the intensity of our feeling of anxiety on this particular issue has gone down, is that not astonishing? You can check in with your sentence that you started off with. Ask yourself how you feel about the situation – does it feel as intense? Are you still as taken over by a feeling of anxiety as you were, a few minutes ago? Or have your feelings shifted? Do you now have different thoughts about it?

Whilst it is important to check in further about our issues afterwards, it's equally important to make it clear to ourselves that we have just shifted a major feeling we had carried within us into a lesser version of itself. In some cases, it can even disappear completely. Typically, a very high percentage of tapping scenarios we choose can be reduced this way, by just taking a few minutes to use this very simple technique. Often even after just one first round of tapping, there is a noticeable difference to how we feel about something that has happened. The number we stated at first, the rate of intensity of our feelings, may have started at a 7, and then dropped down to a 5, or even less. We can add as many rounds as we want, there is no limit, and in each round we will most likely feel a little lighter each time. This has various reasons, but most of all because the tapping and our mental focus have worked together to reduce an energy disruption in our Karmic energy system. It is as simple as that. It is not a process of auto-suggestion, or placebo, or hypnosis, all of which would imply some form of manipulation, but you have stayed fully conscious all throughout, nobody has interfered with your thoughts and you have been fully in charge of what you want to say. What has happened is that you have just handed yourself one of the most valuable energy meridian methods to come out of this past half-century, and yet, still only a relative minority of people have heard of it and know how to continue to benefit from it. Pat yourself on the back – you are now one of us!

If you have indeed noticed that an intense sensation you had minutes earlier is suddenly not half as bothersome as it was before, you might be curious now as to how this could happen. First of all, we don't ever have to become rocket scientists to use the technique. it stays as simple as it is above, it's like yoga for our thoughts and emotions. Of course, it can also help with some physical issues, you can try it on anything you like. Meridian techniques do not have side effects and there are no counter-indications. Everyone can use them, young or old. It works because the tapping resonates our energy meridians within, so that an electromagnetic charge in connection with the issue you had in mind can be released. Once that charge is reduced, the situation becomes more 'neutral'. With skill, many issues can be completely resolved, which is another positive aspect to these fascinating, non-invasive techniques. There are many analogies we can draw to how this happens, but no matter what we call it and how we explain it, the main thing is that it works even without us knowing the full details, and it can be a very simple and quick process to help us heal our old wounds.

The application span of this and other techniques has been vast over the past few decades. Suffice to say, there is so much more on the subject than I can indicate here, but the implications are straightforward: if we feel less affected, less anxious, less upset, less angry, there is more space within us for all the other good feelings we are entitled to feeling, and that is exactly what happens when we use these techniques often enough to sufficiently work on our own inner wardrobe that we have had to stuff to the hilt with things that no longer suit us. Is it not time for a healthy clear-out?

Even if you did not quite get it and are still a bit new and confused after the first round, I would encourage you to do a bit more. All it needs is more practice. Even if it's not yet the result you wanted or expected, and the energy 'charge' is the same as before or has gone up, all you have to do is try again. It only ever means that there is some more tapping to be done. The default tapping procedure always stays the same, and it covers all the major meridian points on our body to tap into our energy system in each and every round. If the score has gone up and you feel more intense, keep tapping until it feels calmer again. This is only a temporary effect, as our energy system sometimes spikes with intensity before it calms down again. There are waves of energy starting to be released from our cranky old energy channels, and they are just kick-starting the old cogs again after years of dust accumulation! The procedure we need to stick to will be similar again in another round, and you can add or take away details in your statements as they come to you. In fact, meridian techniques can be adapted to a myriad of different situations. What's important to get right is to translate our feelings into a statement that works for us, especially when our feelings fluctuate from moment to moment. Tap exactly on what feels right for you, every time. If you are feeling intense, tap on 'this intense feeling' first to calm it down a bit. If you feel tearful, tap on 'I feel tearful'; if your feelings are up and down, your statement begins with 'even though my feelings are up and down', and so on. Work with what presents itself to you, so you get to know your inner feelings. Many of us have been habitually overriding our feelings, so some of us will feel it's a breath of fresh air to allow them to surface, whereas others might be scared of the process. You can tap on being scared of the process first, if you like. You can literally tap on anything. Always give yourself a score from 1-10 to start with, and compare it after the EFT™ 'sandwich' tapping procedure. You can also check that you are still only tapping on that particular issue you chose in the beginning, or if your mind has already cleared it and switched to the next in your mind's eye without you noticing. This happens quite automatically as part of the process: our energy mind instantly recognises the benefit and adjusts itself accordingly; without the usual bypass of our cognitive conscious mind assessing the process, it has already done all the processing needed and moved on to the next issue in a split second. Again, check in with your original statement: has anything changed in the way you feel, about the original issue? Have other thoughts come in in connection with it, other scenarios perhaps? Or has the score gone down for some inexplicable reason and do you feel different, calmer and somehow more distant to the problem? If so, this is typically what happens with EFT™ and it typically also has a lasting effect. Notice, too, how the mind has a habit of already jumping ahead to particular scenes, or aspects, of any situation you have been tapping on. This is a sign that the body/mind connectivity has recognised the healing effect very quickly and is administering it to where it's most needed, giving us visual insights into what we need to tap on next. It switches to the new places so fast sometimes, that it escapes our conscious mind. We can slow it down enough if we want to, by asking questions and seeing what is presenting itself like an internal show to us. It's good to be aware of it, to keep track of your progress, but it will work anyway even if you aren't. We can use it on very factual, present moment issues, as there is nothing fluffy and airy-fairy about it. We can use it to feel more capable, to increase our cognitive processes, to achieve things that felt out of our reach before. People even use it to enhance their sports performance. It's entirely up to us how we use it. For me, one of the most important aspects was how it brought me to notice the underlying connectivity between our body, our inner energies, and our processing of issues related to our Karma beyond a time perception that prevails our every-day thoughts. I realised that this is one of the few very quick and effective techniques on the increase, with which we can actively address and clear our blockages in our inner Karmic energy system.

Meridian techniques can be applied to physical, emotional or mental issues that happened today, yesterday, last year, when we were children, and even lifetimes ago. it bridges the gap of our consciousness of other dimensions beyond those our brains are capable of processing. Its limitations in terms of healing seem set only by the extent of any detriment that is irreversible within the timespan created in this life. What I am talking about are sickness, old age and death that are an undeniable part of all our physical existences on Earth, and even then we can sometimes observe real miracles. Using the techniques can be quite a magic wand and feel like it, too. The techniques are versatile and adaptable, can be used to bunch issues together as in a bundle, and they can be used on many archetypical issues we come across as a human race. Many practitioners have specialised in certain life events, and some very special people have helped people turn around their terrible life situations 180 degrees. They have been adapted to also work well with children, and have been tried and tested to work for animals, too.

Even if you did not make progress in this exercise, don't lose heart – it's happened before, and there are definitely ways to make it work for you, too. It just takes a bit more time and skill.

You really cannot harm yourself tapping on the 'wrong' points, but will maximise the effect by getting it right, and you will feel it and notice it, too. Whatever you choose to deal with using the method, you are not on your own. Millions of others who have tried it can't all be wrong and you can have help any time if you just simply ask.

For the complete, original version of EFT™ and using EFT™ on complex issues and illnesses, again please go to www.emofree.com or one of its many related sister therapies.

I will put a little disclaimer here though, just in case people misunderstand the open-mindedness and all-encompassing, friendly and helpful attitude underlying many universal principles and techniques. We are all, sooner or later, prompted to take charge of our own destiny and yet, we might also struggle at times and need and want help and assistance at times. Please note you can try out EFT™ very easily with the brief instructions above to see if it works for you at any given moment, but I would recommend that you use EFT™ - or any other technique – on more complex issues such as trauma, severe illness, acute, chronic, complex or on-going conditions and more, only with the help of an experienced practitioner. Please be responsible for your welfare and wise not to tackle these when you do not yet have enough experience. EFT™ is as benign as meditation, however, if we are not quite sure yet how to do things, then we would do well to ask for help and get nothing but the Best to help us. I also do not advocate using techniques like these as a substitute for seeking advice from the medical profession, especially not in emergency situations. For me, the two go hand-in-hand and I wish we already lived in a world where the two complemented each other equally. We are slowly getting there, and I have always been open to offering help to the many, including seeing patients within the British Health System who were helped very much by these techniques where nothing else that they tried had worked.

I love using EFT™ for so many reasons and in various situations, the same that I love anything to do with discovering more about what makes us tick, as well as how to help ourselves and each other lead a better life. EFT™ can be extremely useful for any of us, least of all because we can tap directly into and on the thoughts and feelings, even aches and pains that are present in our Karmic energy mind at any given moment. If we find resistance to trying it initially, let's just say that any scepticism is very welcome. I also like using statements like the following to begin with, such as: 'Even though I don't want to/have time to/don't know how to work on this, why should I, I'm too lazy/ scared/sceptic/inexperienced, it probably won't work for me, how do I do it' etc., EFT™ will almost do the job for you, in your own time, often without you having to know all the ins and outs of it, and it can only ever result in the best outcome possible for any moment. It is impossible to use EFT™ to the detriment of yourself or others, yet another crucial reason why I love it and why it's so different from other techniques which can easily manipulate the mind. EFT™ is a natural, universal technique without harmful ingredients or side effects. It's great at reconciling our inner paradoxes. Try it – it will work with almost any statement, sometimes over time, sometimes straight away. Sometimes it will take us on a necessary journey of inner discovery. It will work with pain as well as our spiritual aspirations, physical conditions, unhelpful thought patterns and emotional conflict, too. After a while, we will be able to easily learn by heart, put together, apply and repeat the statements in our minds. They will assist us everywhere we go, so that it becomes almost effortless. What's not to like, if it helps us with our Karmic evolution as well? It can help us focus our meditation and mindful practice without becoming too distracted. It's fun, it's easy, it's portable, it's non-toxic and suitable for any age group including children. Of course, there is a whole science behind why we do this seemingly crazy-looking tapping on acupressure points, but it would lead too far to go into here and I refer you again to all the information available online these days. Just look it up and start your own inner journey here. Hopefully the exercise above will have worked for you well enough to have whetted your appetite - and yes, you will be able to use EFT™ to clear 'negative' Karmic issues, in fact, that is a natural part of the process. The more we clear our anxiety, our anger and frustration, the calmer, clearer and more creative and insightful we become. We simply make more space internally for new, more precious things to enter our inner arena. It could be what we always dreamed of but never dared to ask for.

50. Not Preaching

It is hard to reach a level of realisation, without then also knowing that there is no 'teaching' to be done, as such. This is no offence to all the wonderful teachers in this world, who are tirelessly working to make this world a better place. What is meant by 'no teaching to be done' is that, once we have achieved a high level of Truth, we will take our cues from the signs that are given to us and become self-reliant as to what we need to learn. On those high frequency transmissions, teachers present themselves. They no longer are appointed to us. Any 'teaching' would have to be on such a high level of non-attachment to manifesting physical outcomes and relaying concepts that it is a very high level of Karmic mind training to achieve indeed. Even the best of us have an attachment to the terms 'learning', 'earning' and 'teaching', I guess, so much so that I believe many will not easily part with it as it still forms a necessary part of physical existence and survival. Even if there is a healthy aspect of trying to make a difference to others as best as we can, it still means that there might be an acceptance that there appears to be some form of superiority over others present in many who come to us as teachers over lifetimes. This is really not the best predisposition, and has given the term 'teaching' limited meaning. I guess it is also the reason why great Masters who realise the implications of trying to give a true teaching are few. Perhaps you have to go through a phase of not wanting to be a teacher before actually being a good one, and to not see ourselves as 'lowly' when we humbly request some of the high teachings available by great beings. We need to find out for ourselves that we are essentially all equal, and the greatest teachers do not put themselves above others, thus demanding even higher levels of respect.

We might also find that we cannot truly learn by words only and that anyone, at any time, under many a circumstance, at any age and stage in their lives, can be in a great and useful teaching interaction with another. We do not necessarily need 'qualifications' to show each other kindness and compassion, or what we ourselves have learned by accessing our wisdom mind. Our energies can transmit love, wisdom and kindness constantly, they don't need words. There is something really meaningful that occurs when we interact with each other and learn from each other. Something life-changing can happen by simply being there and resonating with people's inner karmic energies. It can become a process of inner completion we experience, according to each of our individual consent. Great teachers often say very little with words. Great teachers also realise we are all still eternal students in the light of the vastness of Karma. Great teachers do not have to call themselves great or look for accolades and promotion. Great teachers do not just teach with words but also with the right efforts, actions, and assistance. At many points in this book, I wanted to carefully examine my motivation for writing, as I had already come across so many great books, studies, films, blogs, and probably even a few teachers I greatly admire who covered some of the subject matter - and I admit I do not think myself worthy of joining their ranks. Another possible pitfall I felt I needed to mention, is the overly active enthusiasm and passion for one's own mind, passionately expressing thoughts, actions and words. Although all are not all bad and fairly necessary for survival, they do not automatically make a great base for a good book. Just like baking, too many ingredients and too much sugar make a cake inedible, and I am very aware of that. As you can see, I still did not take a leaf out of my own book. I fail miserably in light of some of the criteria for being an enlightened some of the subjects in this book.

Fact is, I wrote parts of this book whenever I got inspired by being able at times to tune into the Wisdom Mind. At times, and so I write like a child trying to show off their first drawing. I realised I also wrote when I needed to clear my thoughts, so that at those times when I needed to tune into my mind first and foremost above all, writing kept me sane when life threw me some big challenges. At those times, writing was there to remind myself of the greater plan, in case I temporarily lost the thread of equanimity.

It is because of the above that you will find snippets of personal information in this book pertaining to me, the author, because I did not want to create a teacher/student scenario, for the reasons explained above. I wrote because I am just like everyone else, with as many things going on as the next being. I see that we are in the habit of creating authorities outside of ourselves who we want to hold responsible for our own actions and shortcomings, but also put on a pedestal at the same time; so much so that it is preventing us from looking at our own inner realm. That is exactly why I add some level of ordinariness about myself, so that you realise I am just like that, sometimes: an ordinary who-man being. There are also many other facets to my personality. This effort is not a beautified Selfie to showcase only my best physical assets and give a false impression of who I am. This is the deeply felt, often raw outcome of what happened when I wanted everyone to know what I saw, what I know to be true. I wanted to demonstrate that it was ok just to be, for everyone out there who worries every second of the day whether they are good enough. Looking at who we are is an endlessly complex business as we will find out along our Karmic path, and some of what we feel about ourselves are things that make us feel embarrassed. What helps us to get there and do it anyway, is to learn to be ok about all the individual inner aspects that contribute to us knowing who 'we' are. As a result, some things in my writings will be very personal. They might seem ludicrous, preposterous, silly or outrageous even. Others will feel just about acceptable, and there are those that are exceptional about all of us. I wanted to encourage anyone reading this book to look at all of those aspects, not just the choice ones that makes us fly high. You will find many personal anecdotes in this book, references to my private life and personal situation, because this is who I am and it is a part of me. By sharing what I write, I hope that others will find themselves in what I write, and also find similarities, analogies, hope, and of course questions, too. My hope is that it creates trust, knowing that we are all in the same boat, trying to keep it real. In order for us all to be part of each other's lives, in a small but hopefully useful way perhaps, I wrote it so it will help towards all of us accepting that we are all fine, just the way we are, and please do accept my apologies if I left too many of my own personal belongings in this book. I saw it within my mind, like a picture that forms, so you could read between the lines of what I wrote. As I used to say in my lectures: I try to put my multiple personality disorder to good use.

By creating so many words, scenarios, thoughts, insights and imagery of how I believe things are or are not throughout this book, I have also realised I inadvertently created a sort of 'club' atmosphere, where it seems that only those are allowed in who are at least a little bit enlightened. And whilst that is far from my intention, of course I have demonstrated my complete ignorance of the subject matter therewith. The book should, of course, be seen as accessible to all, even if we cannot all agree with all of it all of the time, I am sure. That is not what nature intended on Earth, and I see the pattern for us all to have space here to learn, grow and co-exist, no matter what our experience is on this planet. There are already plenty of 'secret' organisations cashing in on a relative and truncated understanding and interpretation of 'wisdom', and I want no part in that. There is no need to pay a fortune, torture yourself or feel under pressure of agreeing with anything. All we need to do is to see if we find anything valid that fits with our own understanding at that time, as well as find our own interpretation of what presents itself; and that can be found reading between any of the lines above. If you find honesty, integrity and truth, then great. My whole life I tried as best as I could to eliminate lesser systems that utilise Truth and restrict it into a monetary, partial system which continues to enslave everyone to this day. If you ever come across this, then get out, quickly, would be my advice; and I don't make any mistake about how passionate I feel about that, either. Any sincere action, thought and word should contain Truth and the unconditional endeavour to make us feel whole, happy, open-minded and -hearted - at little or no cost. Others may do whatever they like, but this is what I feel to be right.

Writing to an anticipatory and imaginary audience, I accept that at times, I have reflected a necessity to look at my own problems on to you, dear reader, and continue to do so right now, similar to what an actor would do on stage by impersonating an intriguing, if false, character. I have distracted myself and in a way deflected from my own defects, perhaps even distracting and deceiving you on the way. For that, I apologise to you. This is, assuming that there even are people out there reading this - a scenario I have imagined & solely created in my mind - who I have the audacity to think might be interested in my humble mumblings. And what's more, I have a fully-fledged attachment to it: I actually care about what my future readers think. I have even called you 'my' readers, knowing that I am looking for some sort of sense of belonging and purpose within a would-be family of like minds, who have similar paths and interests. This all points at one thing – that at the time of writing about vastness and emptiness, most of the time I am within myself not quite yet at 'home'. I am a being in a physical body, and at times, I am outside of myself, looking, yearning for something, for being 'at one' with the oneness I mention so often. I am continuously attempting to call myself back within myself, reminding myself that I am already 'home', I am already whole and complete - and I am counting you in, 'my' imaginary reader. I am creating (hopefully) reasonably amusing scenarios to do so, at least some of the time; for you to ponder, discuss, get lost in, and perhaps even in order for you to like what I write and think me clever. If you are onto me and know I am a scoundrel with no qualifications, good on you, you are a step ahead of me because I still fool myself. However, my real motivation for leaving this book be right now, is for you to 'get it', on your own, by yourself. I am finally leaving you alone, in peace. You are on your own. And so am 'i'. And in that, we are united. It is now time that I try to stop writing and really get to grips with just being and I wish with all my heart that you can, too.

I shall. I am. Now. I.

51. Dedication Practice

REFUGE

I go for refuge to the Buddha,
I go for refuge to the Dharma,
I go for refuge to the Sangha. (3x)

GENERATING BODHICITTA

By virtue of giving and so forth,
may I become a Buddha for the benefit of all sentient beings. (3x)

THE FOUR IMMEASURABLES

May all sentient beings have equanimity, free from attachment, aggression
and prejudice.
May they be happy, and have the causes for happiness.
May they be free from suffering and causes for suffering.
May they never be separated from the happiness that is free from suffering.
(3x)

THE SEVEN-LIMBED PRAYER

Respectfully I prostrate with body, speech and mind;
I present clouds of every type of offerings, actual and imagined;
I declare all the negative actions I have done since beginningless time,
and rejoice in the merit of all Aryas and ordinary beings.
Please teacher, remain until cyclic existence ends
and turn the wheel of Dharma for all sentient beings.
I dedicate the virtues of myself and others to the great Enlightenment.

SHORT MANDALA OFFERING

This ground I offer, as Buddha-fields,
Resplendent with flowers, incense and perfume
In the centre Mount Meru, four lands, sun and moon,

May all sentient beings enjoy this Pure Land.

IDAM GURU RATNA-MANDALAKAM NIRYATAYAMI

DEDICATION PRAYERS

May all sentient beings have equanimity, free from attachment, aggression
and prejudice.
May they be happy, and have the causes for happiness.
May they be free from suffering and causes for suffering.
May they never be separated from the happiness that is free from suffering.
(3x)

By this virtue may I soon
reach a Guru-Buddha-state,
and lead each and every being
to that state of Buddhahood.

> *May the precious Bodhicitta*
> *not yet born, arise and grow*
> *may that born have no decline*
> *but increase forever more.*

> *In all my rebirths may I never be separated from perfect spiritual*
> *masters*
> *and enjoy the magnificent Dharma.*
> *Completing all qualities of the stages and paths,*
> *May I quickly achieve the state of Vajradhara.*

> *May anyone who merely sees or hears,*
> *remembers, touches or talks to me,*
> *be instantly freed from all sufferings*
> *and abide in happiness forever.*

> *It is only from the kindness of my Guru*
> *that I have met the peerless teachings of the Buddha.*
> *Thus, I dedicate all merit so that all sentient beings in the future*
> *may be guided by kind and holy Gurus.*

> *Until cyclic existence ends,*
> *may the beneficial teachings not be blown away by the wind of*
> *superstitions.*
> *May the entire world be filled*
> *with people who have understood and found firm faith in the true*
> *teachings.*

> *Day and night, may I pass the time*
> *thinking and examining by what means*

these teachings can spread
in the minds of myself and others.

May all sentient beings - who have all been my mother and father -
be completely happy,
and may the lower realms be forever empty.
May all the prayers of the Bodhisattvas, wherever they live,
be immediately fulfilled.

May the glorious gurus live long,
and may all beings throughout limitless space have happiness.
By purifying our defilements and accumulating positive potential,
may I and all others be inspired to attain Buddhahood quickly.

May I never develop, even a moment,
wrong views towards the deeds of my glorious Gurus.
With respect and devotion, by seeing whatever actions they do as
pure,
may the guru's inspiration flow into my mind.

In whatever way you appear, O glorious Guru,
whatever your retinue, lifespan and pure-land,
whatever your name, most noble and holy,
may I and all others attain only these.

In order to follow the excellent examples
set by the wisdom of the Bodhisattva Manjushri
and the always sublime Samantabhadra,
I dedicate all virtues to their peerless ideals.

All conquerors of the three times
have praised this peerless dedication as sublime.
Therefore, I also surrender all roots of my activities
to the sublime goals of a Bodhisattva.

From: www.viewonbuddhism.org

* * *

Epilogue

True happiness can arise regardless of external influence. Even though it appears quite unattainable for most of us these days, it feels like one of the most desirable experiences we could aim to achieve. We don't always set our aims high enough, so i put it out there right at the beginning that we all deserve to know what it is like to feel a part of the most true essence of one of the highest achievable internal goals of mankind. This is not some secret club for exclusive wealthy members. You will see that most of this book is an easily accessible accumulation of thoughts on the subject of our being and the relationship we have with our Karmic actions. As mentioned previously, apologies in advance to those who may take offence to my casual approach, lack of traditional etiquette and scientific knowledge. I am not deliberately trying to defy any religion or scientific fact and neither am I here to prove anything. I am here to create an environment where everyone can join in regardless and understand the principles of life. The way I like to convey this is by merely expressing my own thoughts, feelings and visions, in as simple a way as possible. I am not a scientist, I don't have a degree, but I have always been deeply interested in the condition, existence and definition of life in the experience of itself. I don't consider myself a religious person, simply someone who has their own ideas and is open to others as they arise.

I feel that in order to gain understanding, we need to learn to dance with the universe and bring the experience of vastness into our being and our every living moment. This is one of our ultimate skills. As I feel it, to exchange this blissful notion with others the best way I know how to is my path, to improve my sense of insight, perception of light energy and ability to share it is my duty. This, our journey into the being within, I perceive to be most valuable and precious. None of our efforts are ever lost; every skilful thing that we do, say and think is recorded on a Karmic energy level, and when dedicated to the benefit of all sentient beings and the highest outcome for all, it turns into positive merit, a type of infinite Karmic energy resource that works a bit like a savings account - the more you put in, the more you will get from it. This expanding energy we are able to allow to flow through us can miraculously and automatically benefit beings and serve the universe's purpose. It starts to do so from the moment we tune in, even on the tiniest levels. For aeons of time right up until this very moment, good people on this planet have been attempting just such a union of minds, merging with the greater universal mind. It is our search for a genuine union such as this that leads us to a true understanding of others, and dispels the illusion of separation and dependency. Our human energies intertwine in a continuous dance, and in our determination and dedication to ascend and raise our purest vibrations to unseen higher levels, we will eventually transform beyond physical form to meet other challenges and other lessons on higher forms of energy not just expressed in 3-dimensional form. The outcome of one of these lessons, for those of us who accept the challenge, may well be to then return to Earth again in order to show others how to learn to dance this universal dance, too.

Everyone has their own interpretation, and it is fine for us all to coexist with our own stages of understanding Truth. I am merely a reporter of what I believe I have perceived. which is no absolute. With some it will resonate, whereas others might be enraged by all these statements. Please remember you do not have to believe what I write, and I am also not here to upset anyone's belief system. Mankind has always had massive, heated discussions about where life stems from. I enjoy bringing lots of views together with relating truth, but there are many interpretations of truth down here on Earth. This is the place where we are allowed to be, grow, and experience. We do not have to take anyone's opinion on board if we don't want to, and I would not expect anyone to do so or like what I am saying. However, I am also not one that enters a lot of discussions about how we all view things yet, as it often divides us rather than unites us. I believe that the idea of why I am here on this planet is to unite, but by writing in words, I may do the opposite, and for that I apologise in advance. Words are limited, but I promise I will think about making a little movie next. I am writing all this because I believe what I see beyond the physical realm of existence unites many different belief systems. We have all seen parts of the whole, and believe them to be true. They are all true to a certain extent. We are all right. What I like most of all in what I have perceived is that what I found is that almost every single bit of science, religion, belief systems including atheism, humanitarianism, and a simple strive for a loving focus of all beings in life, comes together under the umbrella of what we talk about in this book. I believe that omnipresence is all-inclusive, that hopefully many who suffer can find peace, and reason, and healing in what I describe that I believe to exist.

And so, this book gives you glimpses of my thoughts on Karma and our Karmic existence on this planet, even the universe, even other universes, too. You may think some of this to be far-fetched, and to some, that may be so. The most important thing to remember is that in order to create a peaceful environment, we must start to learn to create Good

Karma on our spiral path, helping us and others to increase completeness. With increased Good Karma we create thus, we continually learn to help others and ourselves live peacefully, ever more permanently. And with this in mind, I leave you with love to contemplate your own Karmic journey in this lifetime, I thank you for connecting with me and allowing me to share some of it with you.

"Stop acting so small. You are the universe in ecstatic motion."
— **Rumi**

"Yesterday I was clever, so I wanted to change the world. Today I am wise, so I am changing myself."
— **Rumi**

"Raise your words, not voice. It is rain that grows flowers, not thunder."
— **Rumi**

"My soul is from elsewhere, I'm sure of that, and I intend to end up there."
— **Mawlana Jalal-al-Din Rumi**

❋ ❋ ❋

Bibliography

The Tibetan Book of the Dead (Bardo Thodol) – Karma Lingpa
Tibetan Yoga and Secret doctrines - Editor: W. Y. EVANS-WENTZ
The Tibetan Book of Living and Dying – Sogyal Rinpoche
Manifestations of Karma in 11 Lectures - Rudolf Steiner
Past lives – White (Shantideva) Brian Weiss
The Garden – Michael Geshe Roach
The Resonance Project - Nassim Haramein
Nothing in This Book Is True, But It's Exactly How Things Are - Bob Frissell
Affluenza - Oliver James
A History of the Universe - Stephen Hawking
*The Five Ages of the Universe - Professor Fred Adams and Professor Gregory
P. Laughlin*
The Dharma of Star Wars - Matthew Bortolin
Tibetan Astrology – Phillipe Cornu
Stephen Hawking – A Brief History of Time
The Five People You Meet in Heaven – Mitch Alborn
Three In a Bed – The Benefits of Co-Sleeping with your baby Deborah Jackson
Chariots of The Gods - Erich von Däniken
I, Robot – Isaac Asimov

Articles:
https://med.virginia.edu/perceptual-studies/our-research/children-who-report-memories-of-previous-lives/
(https://psi-encyclopedia.spr.ac.uk/articles/physical-signs-reincarnation-cases)
https://www.npr.org/2014/01/05/259886077/searching-for-science-behind-reincarnation
www.grupovenus.com for Free Astrology Charts
https://www.independent.co.uk/news/science/mind-works-after-death-consciousness-sam-parnia-nyu-langone-a8007101.html
https://consciousreminder.com/2016/11/29/8-stages-death-according-tibetan-buddhism/
https://www.tsemrinpoche.com/tsem-tulku-rinpoche/science-mysteries/science-finally-proves-meridians-exist.html
*https://www.youtube.com/watch?v=lvdDk9_Ghro (Chakras, Frequencies
& Zodiac Sign correlation)*
https://avtavr.tumblr.com/post/39129804407/mackoala-shambala-for-thousands-of-years-there

Thoughts on the Vastness of Karma -

The long-awaited first comprehensive book to explain Karma in a way that's easy to understand even for the lay practitioner. The ancient methods of determining omnipresent forces within living beings that describe the term 'Karma' are compared and cleverly interwoven with concepts of Science and Western philosophy. Have you ever wondered where you came from? Who you are? Where you are going? Are you looking to find answers to today's conundrums, and how to find better solutions to the demise of the planet and all who cherish it? The connections found in this book hint at the true vastness that comprises and surrounds us all.

If you want to be inspired, make a difference and not waste any more of your precious time on Earth, there is no better book to make sense of this world and why we are here. 'Thoughts on the Vastness of Karma' gives you infinitely powerful yet bite-size nuggets of Truth that are easy to digest. You will not just feel encouraged, you will feel empowered to take matters into your own hands, to feel inspired and no longer feel separate, but know that you are already a part of an enlightening crowd.

Contact email for correspondence: KarmaUM@protonmail.com

❋ ❋ ❋

About The Author...

Ulrike is an alternative health practitioner, lecturer, artist, author and proud mother and grandmother. She is as passionate about life as she is about every project she has ever tackled in it. After 20 years of Buddhist practice, she engages fully with life, be it her family, a charity for Tibetan children, projects for local families and homeless, there is a determination, zest and humour that accompanies her throughout all the storms that she has weathered in her life-times. 'Thoughts on the Vastness of Karma' is the result of a profound recognition, and a subsequent question she once asked herself: 'Why is there an experience of a spiritual disconnect in our human existence, that appears to have a choke hold over us?'

During the development of this book, it became even more clear to her that it would be a much-needed task to untangle the underlying myths that are threatening to destroy us, and our environment with it. It is as if the book is infused with the very essence of life, described so vividly that it not just becomes an easy subject to embrace and envisage, but also incorporate and practice in our every day lives with a very down-to-Earth approach, easy exercises to follow, a good dose of humour and plenty of sensible advice.

A percentage of the proceeds from this book will go to www.ImagineProject.co.uk, a charity that supports Tibetan children in poverty as well as individuals and families in the UK.

* * *

Image of Tibetan Thangka, depicting the Mantra of Compassion, 'Om Mane Padme Hum'

❋ ❋ ❋

IF YOU ARE IN SHOCK ABOUT
THE IDEA THAT KARMA
MIGHT ACTUALLY EXIST

If you have come completely unprepared
for the news and are in a panic, because you
haven't done much about it so far...
If you think you might have lived before and
are now terrified of being back like some kind
of zombie due to your past actions...
In short, if these are your thoughts whilst reading
this right now, fear no more: this is your
'Grow Your Own Good Karma' kit.
The following should come as really good news to you:

It's never too late.

Open up and you will find out what Karma
really is, instead of what you think it is.

It's not complicated.

This is the book you want to read.
Learn how to deal with everything
Karma throws at you.

Printed in Great Britain
by Amazon

73915935R00430